Boko Haram and International Law

John-Mark Iyi • Hennie Strydom
Editors

Boko Haram and International Law

Springer

Editors
John-Mark Iyi
School of Law
University of Venda
Thohoyandou, South Africa

Hennie Strydom
Faculty of Law
University of Johannesburg
Johannesburg, South Africa

ISBN 978-3-030-09112-5 ISBN 978-3-319-74957-0 (eBook)
https://doi.org/10.1007/978-3-319-74957-0

Printed on acid-free paper

This Springer imprint is published by the registered company Springer International Publishing AG part of Springer Nature.
The registered company address is: Gewerbestrasse 11, 6330 Cham, Switzerland

To all the victims of the Boko Haram conflict

Preface

There has been a resurgence in terrorism in the last few decades, and Africa is increasingly becoming a fertile ground for different Jihadi groups, including one of the deadliest of such groups, *Jama'atu Ahlus-Sunnah Lidda'Awati Wal Jihad*, otherwise known as Boko Haram. Boko Haram is a terrorist organisation like no other. The group began as a religious sect with extremist views, but as its extremism grew, it came in direct confrontation with the State. Boko Haram's resort to violent strategies initially placed it in the sphere of violent disturbance and sporadic attacks, but this soon changed dramatically as the group became more ferocious in its attacks both in intensity and in geographical spread. Since launching its current insurgency in 2009, Boko Haram has deployed terror as an instrument of war committing mass atrocities in violation of human rights and international humanitarian law. At all material time in the conflict, there has been scant regard for the rights of civilians and other protected persons caught in the conflict.

The Boko Haram conflict raises questions not only about the new threats posed by the growing spectre of terrorism in sub-Saharan Africa but also about the preparedness of relevant authorities at the national, regional and international levels to respond through appropriate international legal framework and mechanisms to combat terrorism and also hold perpetrators of mass atrocities in the guise of religious terrorism to account in order to end impunity. Some of the challenges have been attributed to the inability of contemporary international law to deal with new forms of threats posed by terrorist groups like Boko Haram. Connected to the above is the fact that the activities of Boko Haram quickly assumed cross-border character as the group launched attacks in neighbouring countries of Nigeria: Chad, Cameroon and Niger. Furthermore, the activities of Boko Haram have implications for the regional security and stability of the Lake Chad Basin States as the conflict has displaced millions of people within the affected countries and also resulted in the influx of refugees across the Lake Chad Basin countries.

This book was informed by the fact that the burning issue of terrorism in Africa is yet to receive adequate consideration from scholars, particularly from an international law perspective. Particular effort was made to bring contributors from diverse backgrounds in the hope that the insights that their contributions provide will deepen our understanding of the causes, motivations, ideology and modus operandi of terrorist groups like Boko Haram. Thus, in addition to furthering the debate on the subject of Africa and the growing threat of terrorism, it is hoped that this volume will also contribute to the creative thinking needed to develop appropriate responses to combat terrorism in Africa.

Thohoyandou, South Africa — John-Mark Iyi
Johannesburg, South Africa — Hennie Strydom
November 2017

Acknowledgements

This book is the outcome of an international conference hosted by the National Research Foundation South African Research Chair in International Law (SARCIL), University of Johannesburg, from 25–26 February 2015. Other papers presented at the conference appeared in the South African Yearbook of International Law (2016) under 'Conference on Boko Haram and International Law'. A project of this nature would normally require the assistance of many people in order to bring it to completion. We would like to thank the Vice Chancellor and Principal of the University of Johannesburg, Professor Ihron Rensburg, for finding time to attend and support the conference that culminated in this book. We are grateful to the following people at SARCIL, Freddie Mudzokeri, Margaret Thogho, Jentley Lenong, Marieke Roose, Musa Shongwe Njabulo, John Kandala, Ncube Swikani, and the undergraduate students at the School of African Diplomacy who actively participated and worked with us during the conference to address the pressing issues that form the theme of this book. We are extremely grateful to all the participants at the conference, as well as all the contributors to this volume for their commitment. All the chapters in this volume were subjected to peer review. We are indebted to all the anonymous reviewers for the time and efforts they put into the peer review process of all the chapters in this volume. We thank our respective families for their patience, support and understanding in the course of this project.

Contents

About the Editors and Contributors

Mariam Adepeju Abdulraheem-Mustapha is a lecturer in the Faculty of Law, University of Ilorin, Nigeria. She is a PhD candidate, an awardee of the American Council of Learned Society and All African Universities. She is a member of the American Law Society Association and a member of many local and national professional associations in Nigeria. She attended many international and national workshops, among which is a five-day Advanced Human Rights Course on the Role of Men and Boys in Achieving Gender Equality organised by Sonke Gender Justice Network held at Centre for Human Rights, University of Pretoria, South Africa, in 2014. She is currently a fellow at the Rhodes University, Grahamstown, South Africa.

James E. Achibong holds a PhD in international humanitarian law and teaches international law, international humanitarian law and jurisprudence at undergraduate and postgraduate levels at the University of Calabar, Rivers State, Nigeria. His primary research interest is in international law and international humanitarian law, and he has also presented papers and published in these areas.

Oludamilola A. Adejumo is the legal officer at the University of Medical Sciences, Ondo City, Nigeria. She obtained her LLB from the Obafemi Awolowo University and was called to the Nigerian Bar as a barrister and solicitor of the Supreme Court of Nigeria. Oludamilola holds a LLM from the University of Benin and is currently a doctoral candidate at the University of Benin. She has very keen research interest in human rights and humanitarian law, with a bias for women and children's rights. She has delivered papers at conferences within and outside Nigeria and has published research articles on key human rights and humanitarian law issues. She is an associate of the Chartered Institute of Arbitrators (UK) and the Women's Health and Action Research Centre (WHARC).

Romola Adeola is a Steinberg Fellow in International Migration Law and Policy, Centre for Human Rights and Legal Pluralism, Faculty of Law, McGill University, in Montreal, Canada. She has worked as an expert on issues of international migration law, human rights and legal pluralism with African governments and international organisations, including the UNHCR and the African Union. She was formerly a legal researcher at the Centre for Human Rights, Faculty of Law, University of Pretoria, in South Africa, where her areas of expertise were law and policy aspects of forced migration, refugee protection and international development law. She holds a doctorate and masters in law (cum laude) from the University of Pretoria.

Muyiwa Adigun holds an LLB (First Class Honours) and an LLM (Distinction) both from the University of Ibadan, Nigeria, in 2006 and 2010 respectively. Between 2008 and 2009, he was MacArthur Graduate Research Fellow at the Faculty of Law, University of Ibadan, Nigeria, and his LLM thesis was nominated by the African Studies Centre, University of Leiden, as one of the top nine theses in Africa. Muyiwa Adigun received his PhD from the University of the Witwatersrand, Johannesburg, in 2015. His research interest is international criminal law. Between 2008 and 2015, Adigun was in private legal practice, and he is currently a lecturer at the Faculty of Law, University of Ibadan, Nigeria.

Avitus Agbor is a Research Associate Professor at the School of Postgraduate Studies and Research, Faculty of Law, North-West University. His research interests are in the fields of international human rights law, (international) criminal law and public international law. He is also a general reader of public law and has several publications in this field.

Akinola Akintayo holds a doctorate degree in law from the Department of Public Law, Faculty of Law, University of Pretoria, South Africa. He is a constitutional law, human rights and democracy expert and a law teacher, researcher and consultant at the Department of Public Law, Faculty of Law, University of Lagos, Lagos-Nigeria. He is a qualified legal practitioner and a member of the African Association of International Law (AAIL), Law and Society Association (LSA), Nigerian Association of Law Teachers (NALT) and Nigerian Bar Association (NBA). Akintayo has researched into and published on a wide range of topics. These include the criminal justice system and politically exposed persons in Nigeria, socio-economic rights, development and democracy, and violent conflicts and democracy in Africa, among others.

Godwin O. Anyalemechi is Brigadier-General and is presently Commandant, Nigerian Army School of Legal Services, Zaria. Previously, he was Deputy Director, Legal Services, Defence Headquarters, Abuja, and Colonel, Military Justice Headquarters, Q Directorate of Legal Services (Nigerian Army). He was the Assistant Director (Legal Services) at the Defence Headquarters Nigeria. He received his LLM from the University of Jos, Nigeria, and he is also a solicitor and advocate of the Supreme Court of Nigeria. Colonel Anyalemechi joined the Nigerian Army in 1983 and has attended several courses on military criminal jurisprudence, including those on *Legal Aspects of Counter-terrorism*, *International Human Rights*

Law, Military Justice Administration, Military Justice and Civilian Protection in Armed Conflict, all at the Nigerian Institute of Advanced Legal Studies. He is a member of the US-African Military Law Forum, as well as the International Association of Military Jurists, and actively participates in the activities of the African Military Law Forum, Stuttgart, Germany.

Ahmed Garba received his LLB and LLM from the University of Jos in Nigeria and was called to the Nigerian Bar in 2005. He has been in active legal practice ever since serving as head of chamber of ABC Attorneys, Jos, Nigeria. In 2011, he joined the Faculty of Law of the Bauchi State University, Gadau, and is currently the Deputy Dean and Head of the Department of Private and Business Law. Ahmed Garba is also completing his PhD at Bayero University Kano, where his thesis focuses on the regulation of religious preaching in some states of Northern Nigeria. Mr Ahmed was at various times visiting scholar at the University of Iowa College of Law, and he has presented papers at several local and international conferences.

Michael Ibanga is a Reader in Law at the University of Calabar, Nigeria. He served as the managing editor of the Calabar Law Journal for many years. His interests lie primarily in jurisprudence and legal theory and international law, and he has published extensively in the area of international humanitarian law. He is the author of *Legal Theory and Legal Method* (1996) and *International Humanitarian Law* (2003).

John-Mark Iyi is an Associate Professor of Law in the School of Law, University of Venda. He holds a PhD in law from the University of the Witwatersrand. Between 2014 and 2016, he was a Post-Doctoral Research Fellow at the South African Research Chair in International Law, University of Johannesburg, during which he initiated the publication of this volume. He researches in public international law, jurisprudence, and international peace and security. He is the author of *Humanitarian Intervention and the AU-ECOWAS Intervention Treaties Under International Law: Towards a Theory of Regional Responsibility to Protect* (Springer 2016) and co-editor of *Developments in International Criminal Law and International Criminal Justice: Perspectives from the Global South* (Routledge, forthcoming 2018).

Dan Kuwali is an Extraordinary Professor at the Centre for Human Rights at the University of Pretoria, South Africa; Distinguished Professor of Law at the University of Lilongwe, Malawi; Chief of Legal Services in the Malawi Defence Force; fellow at the Harvard Kennedy School of Government, USA; and senior fellow at the Canadian Centre for the Responsibility to Protect. Previously, he worked as a research fellow at the Danish Institute of International Legal Studies; Marie Curie Researcher at the Grotius Centre at Leiden University in the Netherlands; guest researcher at the Nordic Africa Institute in Uppsala, Sweden; senior researcher at the Centre for Conflict Resolution in Cape Town; and Division Legal Advisor at the United Nations Organisation Mission in the Democratic Republic of the Congo (MONUC). Professor Kuwali is the author of numerous publications, including

Responsibility to Protect: Implementation of Article 4(h) Intervention (Brill 2011). He is the co-editor of *Africa and the Responsibility to Protect* (Routledge 2014) and *By All Means Necessary: Protecting Civilians and Preventing Mass Atrocities in Africa* (Pretoria University Law Press 2017).

Ngoie Ngalingi Ngoto is an Associate Professor of Law at the University of Kisangani, Democratic Republic of the Congo.

Adedokun Ogunfolu is a senior lecturer at the Faculty of Law, Obafemi Awolowo University, Ile-Ife, Nigeria. He has taught tax law, the law of business associations, intellectual property law, human rights law and international humanitarian law over the years at both undergraduate and postgraduate levels. He has presented papers on international economic law, human rights law and international humanitarian law at conferences within and outside Nigeria. His present research interests cover accountability in public governance, socio-economic rights, foreign policy and human rights, as well as international humanitarian law and targeted killings by drones. He was a postdoctoral fellow at Cornell University Law School, Ithaca, New York, from 2013 to 2014. He is also a solicitor and advocate of the Supreme Court of Nigeria. He enjoys reviewing articles for peer-reviewed journals.

Elijah Oluwatoyin Okebukola is the Head of Department, Public and International Law, at the Faculty of Law, Nasarawa State University, Keffi. He is also the programme manager of the University's Refugee and International Humanitarian Law Programme. He is an alumnus of The Hague Academy of International Law, a barrister and a solicitor of the Supreme Court of Nigeria, as well as a non-practising solicitor of the Supreme Court of England and Wales.

Dejo Olowu Oladejo Justus Olowu (known in his writings as Dejo Olowu) holds the degrees of LLB (Hons.) and LLM, Obafemi Awolowo University, Ile-Ife, Nigeria (1991 and 1998 respectively); LLM in Human Rights and Democratisation in Africa, University of Pretoria, Pretoria, South Africa (2001); Graduate Diploma in International Human Rights, Åbo Akademi University, Turku, Finland (2003); and JSD *cum laude*, University of Notre Dame, Notre Dame, Indiana, USA (2004). Dejo Olowu was admitted to the Nigerian Bar in 1992, practised law until 1997, when he joined academia. His main research interests include public international law, legal theory, human rights and comparative constitutionalism. Dejo Olowu has taught at several universities in Nigeria, Fiji Islands, Vanuatu and South Africa. He was formerly Research Professor of Law and director of the School of Postgraduate Studies at the North-West University, Mafikeng, South Africa, and was a ministerial adviser to the South African Law Reform Commission. As a researcher, he has been rated by the South African National Research Foundation. Dejo Olowu is currently the Dean of Law at the American University of Nigeria, Yola, Nigeria.

Azubike Onuora-Oguno A.C., LLB (Nig), BL (Nig) LLM (Pretoria), LLD (Pretoria). He is a researcher with the Centre for Human Rights, University of

Pretoria. Onuora-Oguno's area of research interest includes the right to education, children's rights and international human rights law. He teaches at the Faculty of Law, University of Ilorin, Nigeria.

Udoka Ndidiamaka Owie is a senior lecturer in law at Baze University, Abuja, Nigeria, and the Arthurs Visiting Fellow at Osgoode Hall Law School, York University, Canada. She holds an LLB from the University of Nigeria, and she is a barrister and solicitor of the Supreme Court of Nigeria. She obtained her LLM and PhD, both in International Law, from the London School of Economics and Political Science. Her scholarly interests lie in the areas of public international law, international humanitarian law, international criminal law, international human rights, and the law and practice of international organisations.

Hennie Strydom is Professor in International Law and holds the National Research Foundation Chair in International Law at the University of Johannesburg, South Africa. He is also the president of the South African Branch of the International Law Association, and his research focus includes United Nations law, African Union law, international humanitarian law, international criminal law, international human rights law and international environmental law.

Maria Assim Usang is a senior researcher at the Dullah Omar Institute for Constitutional Law, Governance and Human Rights, Faculty of Law, University of the Western Cape, South Africa. She also teaches undergraduate and postgraduate courses, and she has published on various aspects of human and children's rights, the right to alternative care, child justice and socio-economic rights. Maria Assim Usang holds a LLB from the Obafemi Awolowo University, Nigeria, and has been admitted to the Nigerian Bar as a barrister and solicitor of the Supreme Court of Nigeria. She obtained her LLM and LLD from the University of Pretoria and the University of the Western Cape respectively.

Marek Jan Wasiński PhD, LLM (University of Lodz, Poland), Assistant Professor, Faculty of Law and Administration, University of Lodz, Poland. Upon completing a traineeship at the Polish Ministry of Foreign Affairs in 1996, Wasiński graduated from the University of Łódź in 1997 and joined the Department of Public International Law and International Relations as a PhD candidate. His doctoral thesis, completed in 2002, examined problems of state jurisdiction and the act of state doctrine, the latter as developed in USA jurisprudence. While working for *Grzejszczak and Skrzydlo Legal Practitioners* as a legal assistant (2000–2005), he was involved in counseling individual applicants before the European Court of Human Rights in Strasburg. In 2013, Wasiński completed the advanced course on African human rights system in comparative perspectives organised by the Centre for Human Rights, University of Pretoria. He works in the field of jurisdiction of states, human rights, diplomatic and consular law, indigenous peoples, as well as transitional justice. He is the author of numerous publications in Polish and English, and he also coaches student groups participating in various international moot court competitions.

Part I
Violence and Statehood: International Law and New Insurgencies in Africa

Chapter 1
On the Brink? The Nigerian State and the Making of Boko Haram

John-Mark Iyi

1.1 Introduction

Terrorism as a phenomenon has been around for a long time, but its definition as a concept has always been controversial.[1] This is because what is described as 'terrorism' is relative and has varied from time to time in history in its manifestations, thus making an acceptable definition difficult.[2] It has controversially been used interchangeably with insurgency, guerrilla warfare and militancy.[3] The indiscriminate use of violence against civilian populations with the object of causing fear and terror is accepted as a defining characteristic of the phenomenon.[4] Besides the increase in the incidence of terrorist activities in the last few decades, terrorism is increasingly taking more diverse forms ranging from hijacking of airplanes[5] to bombing of passenger trains[6] and buses[7]; hotels,[8] airports,[9] government buildings[10] and

[1] There is an enormous wealth of literature on the subject of terrorism. For a comprehensive account of the history of terrorism, see for example, the collection of essays in Chaliand and Blin (2007). The question of who is a terrorist is almost always evident in every literature on the subject. Depending on the persuasions of the observer, this view is also reflected in our conception of the subject and its history. See for example, Burleigh (2010), Harper Collings.

[2] For a detailed account of the ancient history of terrorism, see Laqueur (2001), pp. 3–20; Begorre-Bret (2006), p. 1990.

[3] Laqueur (2001), p. viii.

[4] Gasser (2002), p. 556.

[5] For example, the hijacking of Al Israeli aircraft, the September 11 attacks in the USA, are just a few.

[6] See Sciolino (2004).

[7] Cowell (2005).

[8] Bonner and Perlez (2005), Hana et al. (2015) and Bluy et al. (2015).

[9] BBC News (2016a).

[10] BBC News (2016b).

J.-M. Iyi (✉)
Department of Jurisprudence, School of Law, University of Venda, Thohoyandou, South Africa

J.-M. Iyi, H. Strydom (eds.), *Boko Haram and International Law*,
https://doi.org/10.1007/978-3-319-74957-0_1

industrial facilities have also been targeted.[11] Terrorist attacks have also expanded to targeting sporting and recreation centres like stadiums,[12] museums,[13] restaurants, clubs[14] and beaches.[15] Media houses[16] and schools have not been spared as we have witnessed the mass murder of students in Kenya[17] and Nigeria.[18] Clearly, there is a resurgence in terrorism and a proliferation of terrorist groups, some operating on a localised scale, others on regional and international levels, but often with criss-crossing links and overlapping networks of relationships.[19] Whether operating at a local, regional or international level, there is an increasing tendency to forge different types of alliances amongst different terrorist organisations sometimes across sectarian, ideological and geographical divides and for different strategic and operational purposes and benefits.[20] We have now seen the franchising of terrorist groups' brand names as a strategy of expanding their global reach capability and extending their influence, attracting a wider following, as well as recruitment opportunities. Groups like Al Qaeda and (more recently) the Islamic State (IS) have come to dominate the contemporary literature on terrorism. This is partly explained by the commitment of these two groups to the establishment of a global Islamic caliphate. It is within this international context that the Boko Haram conflict in Nigeria should be understood. However, as the collection of papers in this volume will reveal, the interaction of factors in the local context more than any external element or influence precipitated the rise of Boko Haram. Some of the contributors to this volume already dedicated significant space to analysing the remote and immediate causes of the rise of the Boko Haram insurgency, and I will not dwell on it here save to say that this convergence of local, regional and international dynamics has produced a group that not only poses existential threat but in fact puts the Nigerian state on the brink.

---

[11] Ahmed (2013).

[12] Robinson and Landauro (2015).

[13] BBC News (2015b).

[14] BBC News (2016c).

[15] BBC News (2016d).

[16] BBC News (2012, 2015a).

[17] BBC News (2015c).

[18] Human Rights Watch (2016).

[19] Some groups like Abu Sayyaf in the Philippines, Al Shabab in Somalia, Boko Haram and Al Nusra all start off as domestic terrorist groups with local grievances and largely limiting their operations to their host-states bases. But they subsequently link up with more established and better resourced groups like Al Qaeda and IS with global expansionist agendas and thereupon begin to project regional expansionist tendencies. See generally, Ranstorp (2009), pp. 209–219.

[20] See for example, Zelin (2014), p. 1.

1.2 Terrorism and International Law at a Glance

For a long time, the international community has grappled with the challenge of combating terrorism, an effort that has been largely hampered by the inability of the international community to craft a generally accepted legal definition of terrorism as a first step to forging appropriate community normative and legal response.[21] At the heart of the controversy is the political element of what constitutes terrorism. In much of the twenty-first century, there was a raging debate on an appropriate definition of terrorism. Part of the disagreement centred on the insistence by the developing world that a comprehensive definition of terrorism should exclude 'freedom-fighters' or 'national liberation movements' struggling against colonial domination.[22] While generally opposed to this idea, many states in the West rejected any definition of terrorism that could introduce any form of what was termed 'state terrorism'.[23] This disagreement mirrored the ideological divide at the time and can be found reflected in the definitions adopted in the anti-terrorism treaties of some regional organisations such as the League of Arab States,[24] the Organisation of Islamic Conference,[25] the Organisation of African Unity[26] and the European Council.[27] Although this divide has narrowed in recent years, the definitional question has remained largely unanswered and has hampered the emergence of a comprehensive treaty on terrorism.[28] At the domestic level, different states have enacted anti-terrorism legislation in which they have provided different definitions of terrorism based on their own domestic circumstances and foreign policy calculus.[29]

[21] Higgins (1997), pp. 14–15.

[22] See the contribution by Udoka Owie in this volume.

[23] See Higgins (1997), p. 16.

[24] See Article 1(2) of the Arab Convention for the Suppression of Terrorism, adopted by the League of Arab States on 22 April 1998 at Cairo. (Translated from Arabic by the United Nations English translation service (Unofficial translation) 29 May 2000).

[25] See 1(2) of the Convention of the Organisation of the Islamic Conference on Combating International Terrorism, Annex to Resolution No: 59/26-P, adopted at the Twenty-Sixth Session of the Islamic Conference of Foreign Ministers, Ouagadougou, Burkina Faso, 1 July 1999.

[26] See Article 3(a) of the Organisation of African Unity Convention on the Prevention and Combating of Terrorism, adopted at Algiers on 14 July 1999.

[27] See Council of Europe Convention on the Prevention of Terrorism adopted at Warsaw on 16 May 2005. Article 1 of the Convention defines terrorism by reference to the definitions adopted in eleven other instruments on terrorism listed in the Appendix to the Convention.

[28] According to Ben Saul, acts labelled terrorism are as significant as those not labelled terrorism and given the varied occasions and circumstances in which the term has been used, it would be 'fallacious to assert pragmatically that terrorism is recognizable without difficulty, or to claim intuitively that "what looks, smells and kills like terrorism is terrorism". Disagreement about terrorism runs much deeper than technical disputes about drafting; it reflects doctrinal, ideological, and jurisprudential arguments about who is entitled to exercise violence, against whom, and for what purposes.' See Saul (2008), p. 4. (Footnotes omitted).

[29] Cassese (2006), p. 934.

Notwithstanding these conceptual differences, the transnational character of the activities of terrorists and terrorist groups has made cooperation amongst states to combat terrorism inevitable. A single terrorist act could implicate the interests of scores of states—an attack at an airport, for example, might kill dozens of nationals from different countries; the airplane might belong to a carrier from one country insured by an insurance company from another country; and so on. All of these have made it clear that terrorism is a common problem and has persuaded states to fashion a way of addressing the problem regardless of the lack of consensus on a commonly accepted definition. This led to the adoption of several specific international conventions addressing different manifestations of terrorism and building international cooperation by obliging states to arrest, prosecute and punish or extradite terrorists.[30]

The events of 11 September 2001 attacks on the United States, coupled with the thaw in East-West tensions, and the transformation of most national liberation movements into political parties and national governments following the success of the decolonisation decades contributed in no small measure to bringing about the change in the attitudes of states towards combating terrorism, and leading to a never-before-seen momentum and international cooperation to combat international terrorism.[31] Even though this has not necessarily produced a comprehensive treaty on terrorism as of yet, it has led to the adoption of a series of international legal instruments and mechanisms aimed at suppressing terrorism, particularly since 9/11.[32] It has also produced a shift in legal opinion amongst scholars on, first, whether a legal definition of terrorism should be considered a prerequisite for appropriate legal response to terrorism[33] and, second, whether a definition of terrorism does in fact already exist in general international law and rules of customary international law[34] and, according to a third view, whether the absence of a legal definition is necessarily fatal to effective international legal response to terrorism.[35]

Then there is the view, albeit controversial, that the events of 9/11 were so fundamental that they ushered in a new era of threats and challenges of a different character and proportions.[36] These new threats and challenges are underscored by the activities of terrorist organisations with transnational reach and of ever-increasing capabilities. According to this argument, these new threats are so grave that they cannot be addressed within the existing international legal frameworks.[37]

---

[30] Greenwood (2003), p. 506. See also, Luck (2004), pp. 86–88.

[31] Dupuy (2004), pp. 4–6, discussing the shifts in the attitudes of States towards combating terrorism in the absence of a generally accepted definition.

[32] Saul (2008), p. 5.

[33] Flory (1997), p. 35. See also, Duffy (2005), pp. 2–3. See Saul (2008), p. 5.

[34] See Cassese (2006), p. 935. See Saul (2008), p. 4.

[35] Duffy (2005), pp. 43–45.

[36] See for example, Slaughter and Burke (2002), p. 2 arguing that new rules are required to deal with the new kinds of threats the war on terrorism poses in the twenty-first century.

[37] Slaughter and Burke (2002), pp. 1–21; Franck (2004), pp. 686–688; Heinz (2009), pp. 87–105; French (2003), pp. 31–46. For an earlier expression of this view prior to the events of 9/11, see

One legal consequence of these new threats and challenges is that they transformed the existing international legal order in ways not contemplated when the post-1945 international legal order was established. Hence, it calls for a new legal approach that would remove the restraints imposed on states by the 'old international legal order' so that states are able to respond to these new threats posed by international terrorism.[38]

There are arguments whether the 'new' threats posed by international terrorism and other forms of transnational threats are in fact new in such significant ways as to necessitate a change in the existing law.[39] Opponents of this view caution against an 'emotional push' to abolish the restraints imposed on states by the post-1945 international legal order in their conduct of international relations because it implicates a wide range of elements that have served as safeguards for the maintenance of international peace and security and underpinned important community values on the use of force, human rights, humanitarian law, state responsibility, international criminal law and so on, for over half a century.[40] For its part, the UN Security Council has responded to cases of terrorism by adopting resolutions that seek to impose obligations on states to cooperate in combating international terrorism, and it has done so without proffering a definition of terrorism, so the legal debate continues.

Those who argue that there are grey areas requiring further development and clarifications insist that the existing international legal framework nevertheless provides sufficient basis for states to respond to the threat of international terrorism without necessarily compromising legal safeguards established to protect shared universal values.[41] According to Duffy, it is safe to say that there is as yet no agreed definition of terrorism in international law and a person cannot be prosecuted for an act that did not constitute a crime when it was committed. However, this is not to say that terrorists cannot be prosecuted; the contentious part is the legal criteria for determining who is a 'terrorist' for purposes of establishing who could legally be the author of terrorism. Thus, though there is no generic definition of terrorism, a conduct may still be prosecuted under the existing conventions dealing with different aspects of terrorism such as hostage-taking, attacking protected persons, crimes aboard aircraft and so on.[42] The only difficulty is that since these conventions are treaties and not customary law rules, they are only binding on states signatory to them.

The necessity of an international legal framework lies in the need to, firstly, impose an international obligation on states to enact domestic legislation criminalising terrorism and, secondly, ensure that states cooperate to suppress terrorism by

Blum (1986), pp. 133–138.

[38] Slaughter and Burke (2002), p. 2. This new development in international law, it is argued permits countries like the US and its allies to respond to terrorist attacks. See Byers (2002), pp. 409–410.

[39] See Okafor (2005), pp. 171–191 disputing this claim of newness and fundamental change brought about in international law by terrorism; Abi-Saab (2004), pp. xiii–xxii.

[40] See Abi-Saab (2004), pp. xiii–xxii.

[41] Duffy (2005), pp. 2–3.

[42] Cassese (2006), p. 942.

either prosecuting or extraditing terrorists for prosecution.[43] While admitting the complexity of the legal conundrums that different scenarios of terrorism could give rise to, Cassese nevertheless makes a strong case that contemporary international law is indeed capable of addressing international terrorism.[44] Space will not allow a deeper interrogation of the divergent views on the subject save to say that to the extent that the conceptual controversy surrounding terrorism at the international level has serious implications for how states treat cases of domestic terrorism, whether in terms of policy and legal responses or in terms of their preparedness to observe their international law obligations in their treatment of persons alleged to be engaged in 'terrorist' activities. The latitude states have to respond to terrorism both at the domestic and international levels, and this has expanded in the last few decades because of the upsurge in terrorist activities across the world. It is, however, an irony that rather than suppressing the scourge of terrorism, research shows that incidents of international terrorism and terrorist attacks have not waned within this period, notwithstanding the international mobilisation and legal instruments and mechanisms aimed at combating terrorism.[45] This argument is underscored by the rise of the *Jama'atu Ahlus-Sunnah Lidda'Awati Wal Jihad*, otherwise known as Boko Haram, in Nigeria, to which we now turn. However, before examining the rise of Boko Haram, it is imperative to sketch a socio-economic and political overview of the Nigerian state in order to better appreciate the context in which Boko Haram emerged.

1.3 Nigeria and Its Socio-Economic and Political Fault Lines

One thesis used to explain the rise of Boko Haram in Nigeria is what has been described as the 'wobble economy' effect.[46] By this, it is meant that the dwindling fortunes of the Nigerian economy and the crushing poverty in the country have had a debilitating effect on Nigerians, which has forced some to resort to violence. However, there are a few questions to be asked: first, why did poverty not produce this type of violence prior? Second, though there is a link between violence and poverty, it is not clear what the nature of that link is,[47] and the poverty-terrorism nexus cannot simply be used to explain the emergence of Boko Haram. The nature of conflict in Nigeria is more complex and structured around a dangerous mix of ethno-religious and political bases. As a commentator puts it:

> set against the inability of the government to provide basic infrastructure and basic services for its populace, new conflicts have emerged through politicized agents who have used the conditions of the poor to address the responses or non-responses of the state to the lawful yearning of the citizens. This has led some groups to engage in and try to influence the

[43] Duffy (2005), pp. 43–48.

[44] See generally, Cassese (2006), pp. 933–958.

[45] See Institute for Economics and Peace (2016).

[46] See Okpaga et al. (2012), p. 79.

[47] Imre (2008), p. 10.

> political process themselves. These conflicts in Nigeria are purposeful in intent and directed at key targets, whether economic or political. Armed violence is about more than oil, ethnicity, or politics. In essence, such actions [*sic*] is about access to resources, whether through committing crimes, playing communal tension, stealing oil or winning elections.[48]

It is the view in some quarters that Boko Haram was created by northern politicians as a bargaining chip designed to wrestle political power from the Jonathan administration for breaking the North-South/Christian-Muslim rotational presidency arrangement.[49] For example, it is alleged that governors of Kano, Borno and Bauchi states who needed the support of Boko Haram to win state elections and political bargain at the national level were at some point known to have put the group on payroll in their respective states.[50] Unfortunately, the group grew beyond what was anticipated and what it was designed for. Whatever is the extent of complicity, what is beyond doubt is that the poverty-terrorism nexus is inadequate to explain the rise of Boko Haram in Nigeria.

1.4 The Rise of Boko Haram Terrorism and the Collections in This Volume

Terrorism has been around for a long time manifesting itself in different forms in different ages. Hence, there is a wealth of literature on the subject. In recent times, particularly since the 9/11 attacks in the United States, there has been increasing research on the different aspects of terrorism. However, with respect to the Boko Haram terrorist group, much of the research that has been done has focused on political, economic and social analyses. Very little exists in terms of legal research on Boko Haram. There is a dearth of literature on the legal implications of the Boko Haram insurgency, whether from a purely municipal law perspective or from an international law perspective. This volume is a modest effort intended as a contribution to bridging the gap in the legal scholarship on Boko Haram.

Chapter 1 sets the context for the book by providing a general background on terrorism and the general political, social and religious landscape in Nigeria. Iyi begins by setting the tone through a general discussion of the theme of terrorism. He outlines the general legal debates surrounding terrorism, particularly the question of a generally accepted definition and how this initially hampered the international response and coordinated efforts to tackle the Boko Haram threats, especially on the part of the United States, which initially refused to designate Boko Haram as a ter-

[48] Okpaga et al. (2012), p. 85.

[49] Walker (2012), p. 13.

[50] Agbiboa and Maiangwa (2014), p. 74. Senator Ndume was once arrested and charged with financing Boko Haram; recently, a Local Council boss was also arrested for links with Boko Haram. Several security personnel within the armed forces and the police, sometimes at very senior levels have been implicated for either being members, funders, or sympathisers of Boko Haram. See for example, Onuoha (2010), p. 56; Walker (2012), p. 3.

rorist organisation. The chapter provides a sketch of the domestic sociopolitical and economic context within the Nigerian state in which Boko Haram emerged. To understand or explain the origin of Boko Haram—its motivations, objectives, ideology, tactics and funding and the response of the Nigerian state and different stakeholders—one must take into account these local dynamics of Nigerian society.

The chapters in Part I of the book provide a background and set the context in which the subject of Boko Haram and violent extremism in Nigeria is examined—the idea of the nation state as the principal subject of international law in this regard, a fundamental principle underpinning the international legal order is examined—sovereignty—and the rise of insurgencies and self-determination movements as a manifestation of an increasing contestation of this exclusive right of state. This is the subject of Dejo Olowu's contribution in Chap. 2. In Chap. 3, Akintayo draws on Frantz Fanon's theory of violence to explain the evolution of political violence and insecurity in Nigeria. He contends that the Boko Haram insurgency reflects the embedded long history of material, physical, psychological and structural violence to which Nigerians have been subjected for decades first by the colonial masters, then by a series of military regimes and currently by a ruthless and ethically bankrupt political class. This history of violence constantly reproduces itself, reinforced by old and new centrifugal forces that dominate the miserable life in the post-colony; each new case of re-enactment of violence tends to be more vicious and brutal than the preceding ones.

This theme of violence is taken up by Jose Ngoto in Chap. 4 on 'Responding to Foreign Insurgencies in the East Democratic Republic of the Congo', where he sheds light on how contending domestic centrifugal forces reproduce and perpetuate the cycle of violence that engulfed the DRC and defied every known peace effort to date. There is, however, a marked difference in the nature of the insurgencies in the DRC and the Boko Haram conflict in Nigeria. Whereas the former is primarily driven by political objectives, Boko Haram is mainly driven by religious extremism. Yet the two insurgencies share some characteristics in terms of, firstly, the scale of atrocities committed particularly against women and, secondly, the preponderance of the insurgent groups to launch cross-border attacks in neighbouring countries.

Boko Haram is a terrorist organisation like no other. It grew as a religious sect with extremist views, and as it grew in extremism, it came in confrontation with the state. Its resort to violent strategies in its confrontation with the state initially placed it in the sphere of violent disturbance with its sporadic attacks. However, this changed, and its attacks grew in intensity and geographical spread. It also continued to deploy terror as an instrument of war as it intensified its attacks against the state. Furthermore, even when the conflict reached the threshold of non-international armed conflict, Boko Haram continued to deploy terror during the war. At the same time, the activities of Boko Haram quickly assumed transnational character as the group launched attacks in neighbouring countries: Chad, Cameroon and Niger. Besides, the activities of Boko Haram had regional consequences as it led to an influx of refugees fleeing Northeast Nigeria into neigbouring countries such as Cameroon, Chad and Niger. These raised several legal issues, which have yet to receive adequate consideration from scholars and are thus tackled in Part II of this book.

Part II of the book consists of Chaps. 5–8 and examines Boko Haram as a terrorist group, the nature of the armed conflict and its characterisation and implications under international law. In Chap. 5, Udoka Owie grapples with the age-old problem of defining terrorism. After tracing the debate around the definition of terrorism in international law or lack thereof, she examines how this lack of a universally acceptable definition of terrorism underscores the inadequacy of contemporary international law, which in turn undermines the ability of international law to effectively respond to the new threats posed by terrorism in general and Boko Haram in particular. She calls for a counterterrorism approach that includes international cooperation, such as multifaceted programmes between public and private sectors, local and international civil organisations and NGOs. For its part, Nigeria should develop a coherent and cohesive domestic counterterrorism strategy, coupled with an overhaul of critical state institutions, including the police, the judiciary, security, the prisons, amongst others.

As Boko Haram grew in strength and the conflict intensified, the group expanded its operations, launching attacks in neighbouring Chad, Cameroon and Niger. At its height, Boko Haram controlled territories it called its Caliphate in Northeast Nigeria, where it collected taxes, carried out other administrative functions and enforced its strict version of Shar'ia law by public beheadings and amputations of offenders in transboundary attacks. In Chap. 6 entitled 'Terrorism and Cross-Border Insurgencies as New Threats and Challenges to Peace and Security in Africa: The Boko Haram Insurgency', Godwin Anyalemechi takes up the transboundary nature of the Boko Haram insurgency. His contribution offers a more practical exposé on the Boko Haram conflict and the response of the Nigerian state. Anyalemechi explores how cross-border insurgencies evolve and their operational modalities. He examines the drivers of these insurgencies, the response of state authorities and the expectations and limitations of the strategies of states in their response to insurgencies, and he suggests how state response to these new threats to peace and security in Africa could be ratchetted up for more effectiveness. This includes working with local, regional and international partners within the framework of international law and international cooperation and coordination of efforts both at bilateral and multilateral levels to combat not only Boko Haram but also other incidence of terrorism and cross-border insurgencies as new threats to peace and stability in Africa.

Michael Ibanga and James Achibong's chapter on 'The Boko Haram Insurgency: Characterisation and Implications Under Municipal and International Laws' continues with the international law perspective of the Boko Haram conflict, focusing on the import of the designation of Boko Haram as a terrorist group under both municipal and international laws. The significance of the classification of Boko Haram is important as this was crucial in determining the initial response of the Nigerian state, as well as the international community. This theme is then taken forward by Elijah Okebukola in Chap. 8, where he examines the legal obligations of the different parties to the Boko Haram conflict under international humanitarian law and international human rights law.

Part III of the book consists of Chaps. 9, 10 and 11. In Chap. 9, Ogunfolu et al. adopt a comparative approach to underscore the similarities between the descent of

Nigeria and Algeria into anarchy. The authors argue that there are certain factors that underlie and precede the emergence of radicalisation and violent extremism in Algeria from which Nigeria could have drawn a lesson to prevent the rise of Boko Haram. In Chap. 10, Adigun undertakes an in-depth analysis of the ideology of Boko Haram both at doctrinal and practical levels. He then tests Boko Haram's radical ideology and practices against Islamic jurisprudence and international law and concludes that Boko Haram's ideology is inconsistent with the Koran and, more so, the interpretations of the Koran according to the Sunni Muslims, which Boko Haram claims to belong. In Chap. 11, Ahmed Garba takes up the often neglected subject of the constitutional protection of the religious rights of minority groups. He contends that the use of regulatory authority and institutions by state officials to promote certain religious sects over others in some states in Northern Nigeria has promoted sectarian resentment and violence amongst the Muslim community and perhaps contributed to the rise of Boko Haram.

Part IV of the book consists of Chaps. 12, 13 and 14, all of which focus on the plight of victims of the Boko Haram conflict, particularly women and girls, and the response of international law. In Chap. 12, Iyi examines the systematic use of women by Boko Haram as instruments of warfare. He analyses the various ways in which women have come to contribute to the war effort of Boko Haram and the unspeakable violence and abuses they have suffered. He argues that notwithstanding the protections offered to women under international humanitarian law, international human rights law and international criminal law, victims of Boko Haram atrocities particularly women and girls are unlikely to get justice in Nigeria and proposes an ad hoc regional or international criminal tribunal to prosecute the perpetrators. In Chap. 13, Adeola examines the plight of internally displaced persons and the obligations of the Nigerian state under the Kampala Convention to protect these people affected by the Boko Haram conflict. She underscores the failure of the Nigerian state to discharge its international law obligations in this regard as underscored by the continued abuses that IDPs suffer in camps at the hands of Boko Haram operatives and state officials alike. In Chap. 14, Agbor takes a critical look at the infamous abduction of 276 school girls by Boko Haram in the town of Chibok, Borno State. Agbor challenges how the debate has been framed, particularly the use of the term 'gender-based crimes', which he describes as a legal misnomer, contending that the use of this terminology, which has become dominant in the literature, cannot be traced to any legal instrument in international criminal law.

Part V of the book consists of Chaps. 15, 16, 17 and 18 and focuses on how to respond to Boko Haram and terrorism through legal and socio-legal means. In Chap. 15, Kuwali proposes what he calls the '10 Cs', by which he means the formulation of a holistic approach that goes beyond mere legal response to combating radicalisation and violent extremism such as the Boko Haram terrorist group. This theme is taken further in Chap. 16, where Onuora-Oguno and Abdulraheem-Mustapha argue that the protection and promotion of the right of the Nigerian child by the state can actually be a more effective way of preventing radicalisation and violent extremism. The authors argue that although Nigeria has ratified the Convention on the Right of the Child, Nigeria has consistently failed to uphold its obligations under the treaty, and this has contributed to producing and reproducing vulnerabilities to radicalisation and violent extremism particularly in Northern Nigeria, where the right of the child to education is arguably one of the most violated. In Chap. 17, Wasinski examines the international responsibility of states for human rights violations committed by non-state actors such as Boko Haram. He adopts a comparative methodological approach to examine the degree of state responsibility attributable to the Nigerian state for the atrocities committed by Boko Haram and whether international human rights law offers any remedies. He underscores the different levels of obligation owed by the territorial state in respect of violations of international human rights by non-state actors operating within the state's territory. In the concluding chapter, Iyi takes up the question of 'domestic terrorism' and 'international terrorism' in the context of the Boko Haram insurgency and whether Boko Haram is a domestic terrorist group or an international terrorist group. He argues that, regardless of its origin and the geographical spread of its operations, based on accepted legal criteria, Boko Haram qualifies as an international terrorist group and the group should be treated as such.

References

Abi-Saab G (2004) The proper role of international law in combating terrorism. In: Bianchi (ed) Enforcing international law norms against terrorism. Hart Publishing, Oxford, pp xiii–xxii

Agbiboa DE, Maiangwa B (2014) Nigeria united in grief: divided in response: religious terrorism, Boko Haram and the dynamics of state response. Afr J Confl Resolut 14(1):63–97

Ahmed A (2013) At least 37 hostages killed in Algeria gas plant standoff, says Prime Minister. CNN, 23 January 2013. Available at http://edition.cnn.com/2013/01/21/world/africa/algeria-hostage-crisis/. Accessed 12 May 2016

BBC News (2012) Nigeria's ThisDay Newspaper hit by Abuja and Kaduna blasts. BBC News, 25 April 2012. Available at http://www.bbc.com/news/world-africa-17856362. Accessed 24 Sept 2016

BBC News (2015a) Charlie Hebdo: gun attack on French magazine kill 12. BBC News, 7 January 2015. Available at http://www.bbc.com/news/world-europe-30710883. Accessed 20 Sept 2016

BBC News (2015b) Tunis attack: gunmen kill tourists in museum rampage. BBC News, 18 March 2015. Available at www.bbc/news/world-africa-31941672. Accessed 10 Feb 2016

BBC News (2015c) Kenya attack: 147 dead in Garissa University assault. BBC News, 3 August 2015. Available at http://www.bbc.com/news/world-africa-32169080. Accessed 14 Jan 2017

BBC News (2016a) Brussels attacks: Zaventem and Maelbeek boobs kill many. BBC News, 22 March 2016. Available at http://www.bbc.com/news/world-europe-35869254. Accessed 6 Jan 2017

BBC News (2016b) Somalia Parliament attacked by al-Shabab in Mogadishu. BBC News, 24 May 2016. Available at http://www.bbc.com/news/world-africa-27554498. Accessed 21 Jan 2017

BBC News (2016c) Orlando nightclub shooting: how the attack unfolded. BBC News, 15 June 2016. Available at http://www.bbc.com/news/world-us-canada-36511778. Accessed 18 Jan 2017

BBC News (2016d) Ivory Coast: 16 dead in Grand Bassam attack. BBC News, 14 March 2016. Available at http://www.bbc.com/news/world-africa-35798502. Accessed 18 Jan 2017

Begorre-Bret C (2006) The definition of terrorism and the challenge of relativism. Cardozo Law Rev 27:1987

Blum YZ (1986) The legality of state response to acts of terrorism. In: Netanyahu B (ed) Terrorism: how the West can win. Farrar, Straus & Giroux, New York, pp 133–138
Bluy T, Searcey D, Callimachi R (2015) At least 20 killed in siege by militants in Burkina Faso. The New York Times, 15 January 2016. Available at https://www.nytimes.com/2016/01/16/world/africa/gunmen-attack-hotel-in-burkina-fasos-capital.html. Accessed 19 Feb 2017
Bonner R, Perlez J (2005) Bali bombing kill at least 25 in tourist spots. The New York Times, 2 October 2005. Available at http://www.nytimes.com/2005/10/02/world/asia/bali-bombings-kill-at-least-25-in-tourist-spots.html. Accessed 4 Jan 2017
Burleigh M (2010) Blood and rage: a cultural history of terrorism. Harper Collings, New York
Byers M (2002) Terrorism, the use of force and international law. Int Comp Law Q 51(1):401–414
Cassese A (2006) The multifaceted criminal notion of terrorism in international law. J Int Crim Justice 4:933–958 at 934, 942
Chaliand G, Blin A (eds) (2007) The history of terrorism: from antiquity to Al Qaeda. University of California Press, Berkeley. (Trans: Schneider E, Pulver K and Browner J)
Council of Europe Convention on the Prevention of Terrorism adopted at Warsaw on 16 May 2005. Available at https://www.coe.int/en/web/conventions/full-list/-/conventions/treaty/196. Accessed 23 Aug 2016
Cowell A (2005) Subway and bus blasts in London kill at least 37. The New York Times, 8 July 2005. Available at http://www.nytimes.com/2005/07/08/world/europe/subway-and-bus-blasts-in-london-kill-at-least-37.html. Accessed 28 Jan 2017
Duffy H (2005) The 'war on terror' and the framework of international law. Cambridge University Press, Cambridge
Dupuy P-M (2004) State sponsors of terrorism: issues of international responsibility. In: Bianchi A (ed) Enforcing international law norms against terrorists. Hart Publishing, Portland, pp 3–16
Flory M (1997) International law: an instrument to combat terrorism. In: Higgins R, Flory M (eds) Terrorism and international law. Routledge, London, pp 30–39
Franck TM (2004) Criminals, combatants, or what? An examination of the role of law in responding to the threat of terror. Am J Int Law 98:686–688
French SE (2003) Murderers not warriors: the moral distinction between terrorists and legitimate fighters in asymmetric conflicts. In: James Sterba P (ed) Terrorism and international justice. Oxford University Press, New York, pp 31–46
Gasser H-P (2002) Acts of terror "Terrorism" and international humanitarian law. Int Rev Red Cross 84(847):547
Greenwood C (2003) War, terrorism and international law. Curr Leg Probl 56(1):505–530
Hana J, Payne E, Almasy S (2015) Deadly Mali hotel attack: 'They were shooting at anything that moved'. Available at http://edition.cnn.com/2015/11/20/africa/mali-shooting. Accessed 18 Jan 2017
Heinz EA (2009) Non-state actors in the international legal order: the Israeli-Hezbollah conflict and the law of self-defense. Glob Gov 15(1):87–105
Higgins R (1997) The general international law of terrorism. In: Higgins R, Flory M (eds) Terrorism and international law. Routledge, London, pp 13–29
Human Rights Watch (2016) They set the classrooms on fire: attacks on education in Northeast Nigeria. 11 April 2016. Available at https://www.hrw.org/sites/default/files/report_pdf/nigeria0416web.pdf. Accessed 23 Aug 2016
Imre R (2008) Terrorism: causes and curses: the socio-politics of terror, poverty, evil statecraft and modernity. In: Imre R, Mooney B, Clarke B (eds) Responding to terrorism: political, philosophical and legal perspectives. Ashgate Publishing, Aldershot, pp 7–18
Institute for Economics and Peace (2016) Global terrorism index 2016. Available at https://reliefweb.int/sites/reliefweb.int/files/resources/Global%20Terrorism%20Index%202016_0.pdf. Accessed 20 Dec 2016
Laqueur W (2001) A history of terrorism. Transaction Publishers, Piscataway
Luck EC (2004) Tackling terrorism. In: Malone DM (ed) The UN Security Council: from the Cold War to the 21st Century. Lynne Rienner, London, pp 85–100

Okafor OC (2005) Newness, imperialism and international legal reform in our time: a TWAIL perspective. Osgood Hall Law J 43(1&1):171–191

Okpaga A, Uwgu SC, Eme OI (2012) Activities of Boko Haram and insecurity question in Nigeria. Arab J Bus Manag Rev (OMAN Chapter) 1(9):77

Onuoha FC (2010) The Islamist challenge: Nigeria's Boko Haram crisis explained. Afr Secur Rev 19(2):54–67

Ranstorp M (2009) Terrorism in the name of religion. In: Howard RD, Sawyer RL, Bajema NE (eds) Terrorism and counterterrorism: understanding the new security environment, 3rd edn. McGraw-Hill, New York, pp 209–219

Robinson J, Landauro N (2015) Paris attacks: suicide bomber was blocked from entering Stade de France. Wall Street Journal, 15 November 2015. Available at http://www.wsj.com/articles/attacker-tried-to-enter-paris-stadium-but-was-turned-away-1447520571. Accessed 2 Apr 2016

Saul B (2008) Defining terrorism in international law. Oxford University Press, Oxford

Sciolino E (2004) Bombings in Madrid: the attacks, 10 bombs shatter trains in Madrid killing 192. The New York Times, 12 March 2004. Available at http://www.nytimes.com/2004/03/12/world/bombings-in-madrid-the-attack-10-bombs-shatter-trains-in-madrid-killing-192.html?_r=0. Accessed 13 Mar 2017

Slaughter A-M, Burke W (2002) An important constitutional moment. Harv Int Law J 43(1):1–21

The Arab Convention for the Suppression of Terrorism, adopted by the League of Arab States on 22 April 1998 at Cairo. (Translated from Arabic by the United Nations English translation service (Unofficial translation) 29 May 2000). Available at http://www.refworld.org/pdfid/3de5e4984.pdf. Accessed 12 Jan 2016

The Convention defines terrorism by reference to the definitions adopted in eleven other instruments on terrorism listed in the Appendix to the Convention

The Convention of the Organisation of the Islamic Conference on Combating International Terrorism, Annex to Resolution No: 59/26-P, adopted at the Twenty-Sixth Session of the Islamic Conference of Foreign Ministers, Ouagadougou, Burkina Faso, 1 July 1999. Available at http://www.refworld.org/docid/3de5e6646.html. Accessed 23 Aug 2016

The Organisation of African Unity Convention on the Prevention and Combating of Terrorism, adopted at Algiers on 14 July 1999. Available at https://au.int/sites/default/files/treaties/7779-treaty-0020_-_oau_convention_on_the_prevention_and_combating_of_terrorism_e.pdf. Accessed 23 Aug 2016

Walker A (2012) What is Boko Haram? Special Report 308. United States Institute of Peace, Washington, DC, pp 1–16

Zelin AY (2014) The war between ISIS and al-Qaeda for supremacy of the Global Jihadist Movement. The Washington Institute for Near East Policy No. 20, p 1. Available at http://www.washingtoninstitute.org/uploads/Documents/pubs/ResearchNote_20_Zelin.pdf. Accessed 24 Oct 2016

Chapter 2
Dialectics of Sovereignty, Self-Determination and Violent Strategy in Africa

Dejo Olowu

2.1 Introduction

Any quick survey of Western media reports will suggest that the African landscape is perpetually punctuated with wars, conflicts and violent upheavals. Understandably, this is the backdrop against which Africa's most pronounced violent conflicts—such as the genocide in Rwanda; the civil wars in the Democratic Republic of Congo (DRC), Liberia, Sierra Leone, Sudan; the recent religious upheavals in the Central African Republic (CAR); the disturbances in Mali and South Sudan; and, of course, the Niger-Delta tensions and Boko Haram insurgency in Nigeria, among others—are viewed not only in Western media but also among scholarly commentators. In the perception of the supposed experts on Africa and African affairs, therefore, the continent is nothing more than one irredeemably locked down in savagery, barbarity and unending conflicts. Such perceptions about Africa, however, lend themselves to oversimplification and obfuscation of the delicate web of the factors underlying Africa's seemingly intractable conflicts.

Comprehending the nature and origins of African conflicts and building institutional mechanisms designed to manage conflict have engaged researchers and regional organisations in Africa for almost half a century. Regional bodies, including the African Union (AU) and the Economic Community of West African States (ECOWAS), have established security frameworks that include early-warning capability, conflict resolution mechanisms and peace-keeping and peace-building institutions. Without doubt, some success stories in conflict management have been recorded across the continent, particularly in Angola, Lesotho, Liberia, Mali, Sierra Leone, Rwanda and the DRC, albeit with some degree of external assistance in certain cases. Nevertheless, other seemingly intractable conflicts remain, for example, in Burundi, Central African Republic, Somalia and Sudan. Although there is a

D. Olowu (✉)
School of Law, American University of Nigeria, Yola, Adamawa, Nigeria

J.-M. Iyi, H. Strydom (eds.), *Boko Haram and International Law*,
https://doi.org/10.1007/978-3-319-74957-0_2

surfeit of analyses on the sources of African conflicts and suggested pathways to their resolution, many gaps remain in much of the contemporary analyses and recommendations. Critical questions engendered by any objective analysis of Africa's myriad violent conflicts must include the following: to what extent are post-colonial politics in Africa shaped by the legacy of the colonial state? Why are state structures weaker in Africa than elsewhere? What accounts for Africa's slow pace towards consolidation and stability?

This chapter attempts to deconstruct the notion of self-determination as it relates to the contestations around such concepts as sovereignty and statehood in Africa. This deconstruction is imperative for a proper understanding of the complex web and foundations of Africa's past, present and ongoing tensions and conflicts.

2.2 Self-Determination and Conceptual Quandaries: Some Critical Questions

The modern expression right to self-determination is traceable to the theories articulated by Woodrow Wilson at the Versailles Peace Conference, in 1917, where he posited:

> No peace can last, or ought to last, which does not recognize and accept the principle that governments derive all their powers from the consent of the governed, and that no right anywhere exists to hand people about from sovereignty to sovereignty as if they were property.[1]

Before the Second World War (WWII), therefore, international law did not recognise the right to self-determination. At the time that the 50 founding UN member nations gathered in San Francisco in 1945, in their ranks were states with unenviable human rights records, such as Saudi Arabia, Spain, Turkey, the United States, apartheid South Africa, among others.

It was the nationalistic fervour that swept through the colonised world, particularly in the so-called Third World countries, which led to a gale of demand for independence for colonised peoples. The Western powers could not resist the pro-independence movements around the world, and so, in 1960, the UN General Assembly adopted the Declaration on the Granting of Independence to Colonised Territories and Peoples, UN GA Resolution 1514 (XV), 14 December 1960.[2] Article 2 of that Declaration proclaims: 'All peoples have the right to self-determination; by that right they freely determine their political status and freely pursue their economic, social and cultural development.'

Today, there are other instruments giving explicit recognition to the right to self-determination in international law. Among these are the UN Programme of Action for the Full Implementation of the Declaration, 1970, and the UN Declaration on

[1] Wilson (1917).

[2] Connolly (2013), p. 68.

Principles of International Law Concerning Friendly Relations and Cooperation Among States in Accordance with the Charter of the United Nations, 1970 (UN Declaration on Friendly Relations), both of which reaffirm the 1960 Declaration.[3]

The right to self-determination was also recognised in the UN Charter way back in 1945—Article 1(2) UN Charter—wherein the purposes of the UN are stated as including as follows: to 'develop friendly relations among nations based on respect for the principle of equal rights and self-determination of peoples'. Articles 55 and 56 of the UN Charter also allude to this right. The right is reaffirmed in Article 1 common to both the International Covenant on Economic, Social and Cultural Rights (ICESCR) and the International Covenant on Civil and Political Rights (ICCPR), both of 1966.

In pertinent regional context, Article 20 of the African Charter on Human and Peoples' Rights, 1981, recognises the right to self-determination in these terms:

1. All peoples shall have the right to existence. They shall have the unquestionable and inalienable right to self-determination. They shall freely determine their political status and shall pursue their economic and social development according to the policy they have freely chosen.
2. Colonized or oppressed peoples shall have the right to free themselves from the bonds of domination by resorting to any means recognized by the international community.
3. All peoples shall have the right to the assistance of the State Parties to the present Charter in their liberation struggle against foreign domination, be it political, economic or cultural.

Despite the various normative frameworks for securing the right to self-determination, there remain numerous problems. For instance, what is the scope and content of this right? How far can it go?

Within the context of decolonisation, little controversy arises. This is because resolutions of the UN General Assembly unambiguously recognised this right for colonised peoples. The UN General Assembly has recognised this right for the peoples of South Africa (1965), East Timor (1975), the Western Sahara (1975) and Palestine (1987). It is because of this recognition that Palestine sits in the UN General Assembly in an observer status.[4]

Apart from these resolutions, there have been significant judicial pronouncements by the International Court of Justice (ICJ).[5] Indeed, in the 1995 decision in the *East Timor Case*,[6] the ICJ pronounced that the right to self-determination has acquired a special status as 'one of the essential principles of contemporary

[3] Connolly (2013), p. 72; Saul (2011), pp. 613–614.

[4] Spector (2011), pp. 129–131.

[5] See the *Legal Consequences for States of the Continued Presence of South Africa in Namibia (South West Africa) notwithstanding Security Council Resolution 276 (1970)*, Advisory Opinion, 1971 ICJ 16 at 31, and the *Western Sahara Case, Advisory Opinion,* (1975) ICJ Reports 12, 31–33.

[6] *Case Concerning East Timor (Portugal v. Australia)*, Judgment, 1995 ICJ 90.

international law…[that] enjoys an *erga omnes* character'.[7] This pronouncement was significant in the final push towards the attainment of independence for East Timor in 2002.

The notion of self-determination refers to the right of a people living in a territory to determine the political and legal status of that territory. As the ICJ noted in the *Western Sahara Case*, the methods of achieving self-determination include the creation of an independent state, free association or integration with another state and the choice of any other political status freely accepted by people. The UN General Assembly Resolution 1541 of December 1960 recognised that while self-determination normally leads to independence, the people of a non-self-governing territory might choose integration with an independent state or free association with an independent state as an alternative to independence. The exercise of self-determination may therefore not necessarily lead to statehood.

The UN continues to actively support colonial peoples seeking self-determination by allowing their representatives the right to participate at UN platforms, conducting plebiscites (as in the case of East Timor, Samoa and South Sudan), providing technical training to exercise self-government and imposing sanctions on states refusing to allow peoples the right to self-determination (e.g., apartheid South Africa and Namibia).

Despite resounding recognition of the right to self-determination by the global community as represented by the UN, all efforts to make the right to self-determination translate into tangible entitlement have not created sufficient counterbalance to prevent the political and legal framework around the just struggle for liberation—from colonialism and neocolonialism—from becoming a post-colonial myth. Controversy therefore abounds when the right to self-determination is discussed beyond the context of decolonisation. Why is this so?

When one examines the idea of self-determination itself, one finds something of a conceptual jumble. In order to get a grip on the various meanings of this term, therefore, one must, first, pay attention to its fundamental evolution in international law, precisely with respect to the meaning of what constitutes 'peoples' (under the notion of self-determination). Its meaning has progressed from being a problem of the political independence of ethnic or national communities—the status that it had in the Wilsonian era—to the post-WWII meaning of 'peoples' as multifaceted, emerging from colonial rule. In this second connotation, it has been taken as the right of the majority within an accepted political unit to demand and exercise political power.[8] In these numerous usages, self-determination has often been discussed in terms of the issue of the legitimacy of secession in international law.

Among the many prisms through which the concept of self-determination is perceived and discussed are the following:(1) the established right to be free from colonial domination, with plenty of well-known examples in Africa, Asia and the Caribbean; (2) the opposite of that—a right to remain dependent, if it represents the will of the dependent people who occupy a defined territory, as in the case of the

[7] At p. 102.

[8] Gould (2006), p. 47; Saul (2011), p. 615.

Island of Mayotte in the Comoros or Puerto Rico; (3) the right to dissolve a state, at least if done peacefully, and to form new states on the territory of the former one, as in the former Soviet Union and Czechoslovakia. The breakup of the former Yugoslavia, except for Serbia and Montenegro, might even be considered an example of this, after the initial skirmish in Slovenia ended and the Yugoslav federal forces ceased operating as such in Croatia and Bosnia-Hercegovina. The later fighting in Croatia and Bosnia-Hercegovina could be seen as efforts not so much to hold the old state of Yugoslavia together as to define the territories and ethnic composition of the new states, including possible new states within Bosnia-Hercegovina; (4) the disputed right to secede, as in the case of Bangladesh and Eritrea; (5) the right of divided states to reunite, as in Germany; (6) the right of limited autonomy, short of secession, for groups defined territorially or by common ethnic, religious and linguistic bonds—as in autonomous areas within confederations; (7) rights of minority groups within a larger political entity, as recognised in Article 27 of the ICCPR and in the General Assembly's 1992 Declaration on the Rights of Persons Belonging to National or Ethnic, Religious and Linguistic Minorities; and (8) the internal self-determination freedom to choose one's own form of government or, even more sharply, the right to a democratic form of government, as in Haiti.[9]

In the years following WWII, as colonised nations increasingly agitated and secured independence from their colonial masters, international lawyers began to grasp the inevitability of recognising the right of colonised peoples to exercise their right to self-determination and to secure their independence. However, in the 'second wave' of agitation, following the era of independence struggles, the protagonists of the right to self-determination were now mainly minority groups and other ethnic nationalities within post-colonial entities.[10] The question that has continually pestered international lawyers is: does the right to self-determination guarantee a right to any minority group to break away from an independent nation? This is where the quandary lies.

The fundamental questions relating to self-determination that are yet to be resolved have not changed. They remain: does the right of self-determination confer the right of seceding from an independent State? Who constitutes the 'self', that is, the 'peoples' who must determine their own future? How is self-determination to occur and how are the identified peoples to exercise this right? What is the nature and scope of the 'self', or the 'peoples' determination? What form will it assume for its expression? What issues will it cover: economic, social, political, security or what?

The international community is presently involved in resolving the demand for the right to self-determination by the Basque ETA group in Spain, the Irish Republican Army in the United Kingdom, the West Papuans' in Indonesia, and the Bougainville Republican Army in Papua New Guinea. In Africa, secessionist threats remain in Casamance (Senegal), Cabinda (Angola), Zanzibar (Tanzania), Somaliland (Somalia) and Western Sahara (the disputed territory bordering Morocco).

---

[9] Brilmayer (1991), pp. 284–285; Kirgis Jr (1994), p. 307; Titanji (2009), pp. 58–63.

[10] Titanji (2009), p. 63.

There has been no consensus among states, international law scholars and jurists, and a consensus may not be forthcoming in the nearest future. In general, minorities do not have a right to secession and are restricted to some form of autonomy within a state. However, Article 39 of the Constitution of the Federal Democratic Republic of Ethiopia, 1995, provides: ‘Every nation, nationality or people in Ethiopia shall have the unrestricted right to self-determination up to secession.’ This is constitutional leeway to secession that has not been replicated anywhere else.

It would therefore appear, from the attitude of the UN, major political actors and some eminent jurists, that the right to self-determination is not meant to lead to secession from an independent state.[11] In 1961, for instance, the UN General Assembly denied recognition to the people of the Katanga region of Zaire (now Democratic Republic of Congo or DRC). Their rebellion was quashed. Furthermore, in 1967, the south-eastern region of Nigeria declared itself the Republic of Biafra. Because of the identification of some foreign nations that were backing the Biafran secessionist bid, the UN adopted the Declaration on Principles of International Law Concerning Friendly Relations and Co-operation Among States in Accordance with the Charter of the United Nations. This Declaration sought to promote friendly relations among independent states and ensure that states do not support any secessionist movement within an independent State—Part 1 of the Declaration.[12]

Again, in 1998, the Supreme Court of Canada, in *Re Secession of Quebec*,[13] unequivocally declared that the right to self-determination relates only to its internal exercise and has no external component.

As hinted earlier, another controversy encountered in defining the scope and content of the right to self-determination is the question of its beneficiaries. Who are ‘peoples’? This question defies easy solution, and international law is yet to come up with a clear definition of ‘peoples’, except in isolated juridical interpretations such as the view of the African Commission on Human and Peoples’ Rights in *Minority Rights Group v Kenya* (the *Endorois Case*), a decision that lacks efficacy in states’ compliance, going by the antecedents of the African Commission.[14] The beneficiaries of this right, therefore, remain indefinite and vague.[15] To resolve some of the problems surrounding the meaning of the right to self-determination, therefore, one must have recourse to some of the dynamic events of the past few decades that have implications for the right to self-determination.

In 1971, Bangladesh successfully seceded from Pakistan, and today, Bangladesh is a UN member state. In 1991, Yugoslavia dissolved into several nations—Bosnia-Herzegovina, Croatia, Macedonia and Slovenia—not by consensus but more through secession. Except for the Former Yugoslav Republic of Macedonia, which had a diplomatic row with Greece over its originally chosen name, all these states are now UN members and are widely recognised. In 1993, Eritrea seceded from

[11] Kapitan (2006), p. 360.

[12] Okoronkwo (2002), pp. 87–88.

[13] *Re Secession of Quebec*, (1998) 37 ILM 1340.

[14] Wachira (2008), pp. 10–12.

[15] Pavkovic and Radan (2003), pp. 10–11.

Ethiopia, and both are separate entities that are widely recognised. The same scenario recently played out in the excision of South Sudan from Sudan in 2011.[16]

Based on these contradictory events, where exactly do the borders of the right to self-determination lie? We are left with no other choice but to conclude that where a secessionist bid succeeds, the international community may have no option but to accept and recognise that emergent state, particularly where the emergent State has strong political clout. As Malanczuk puts it, 'there is no rule of international law which forbids secession from an existing State; nor is there any rule which forbids the mother State from crushing the secessionary movement, if it can'.[17]

2.3 Problematics of Statehood, Sovereignty and Self-Determination in Africa

To commence the excursion into 'statehood' in the African context, there is a need to place the state in proper perspective and to appraise its varied interpretations after decolonisation. Although statehood in the African context has always been elusive, it has nonetheless remained an authoritative actor in the last five decades. The impulsive metamorphosis of the colonial state to the post-colonial state prevented African nations from steadily consolidating the essential workings of performing developmental state roles. The incapacity of these countries to master their developmental functions forced many to morph into a one-party state, a military state or a crossbreed state of sorts.[18]

More than a half-century ago, increasing demands among erstwhile colonial entities for independence forced European powers to grant sovereignty to African states. The stepping up of the pace of decolonisation can be attributed to two trajectories: one, the amazing pace with which promising nationalist leaders organised rustic populations that had seemed passive, contributing to the popular belief that decolonisation was inescapable and, two, the gargantuan cost of containing armed challenges, or even waves of violent protest, and the escalating fatalities on both sides. Whether the new states were ready for the tasks ahead was immaterial. Clapham had captured the interrelated awkwardness of statehood and sovereignty in post-colonial African states, which gave rise to what he termed 'quasi-statehood' in Africa in the following words:

> As African regimes lost the popular support which they had generally enjoyed at independence, and refused to renew it at the price of risking their own incumbency, so the moral justification for quasi-statehood – that the states which it protected represented their own populations – was lost. In the process, quasi-statehood was converted into a mechanism by which those who controlled governments, regardless of the means by which they had attained power or by which they exercised it, claimed the right to external support with

[16] Vidmar (2013), pp. 63, 66.

[17] Malanczuk (1997), p. 78.

[18] Clapham (1998), pp. 143–144; Forje (2003), pp. 59–60.

> which to repress their own populations. For the outside states which provided this support, whether these were superpowers or former colonial rulers, sustaining African regimes became an internationalized equivalent of colonial indirect rule: indigenous rulers remained in power, as part of a pact which served the interests alike of themselves and of their external protectors. This formula could only be maintained, however, for as long as the domestic regimes within quasi-states were able to supply benefits to their protectors at a price which these were prepared to pay.[19]

That the historical asymmetries of African states contribute in large measures to the perennial post-colonial crises on the continent is not in doubt. Indeed, the post-colonial crises of legitimacy across much of Africa are evident in the high number of sovereign states whose births were disconnected from the organic evolution of the peoples they incorporated within their boundaries. As a pointer, except for very few instances, African independence did not mark the return to pre-colonial institutional forms of sovereignty. Thus, the newly independent states suffered from a deficit of 'vertical legitimacy', ensconced in the disconnection between society and governmental institutions.[20] The consequence was that post-independent rulers had to devise zero-sum strategies for their very survival alongside the tasks of nation-building.

Kissinger described the stark realities of post-colonial Africa as follows:

> In Africa, borders not only follow the demarcations between the spheres of influence of the European powers, as in Asia; they also reflect the administrative subdivisions within each colonial area. In East and West Africa, Britain and France governed colonies with long coastlines. Hence it proved efficient to divide these colonies into a multiplicity of administrative units, each with its own outlet to the sea, which later became independent states. On the other hand, in Central Africa, tiny Belgium governed a region nearly as large as the British and French possessions without, however, any significant coastline. Possessing only a very short outlet to the sea at the mouth of the Congo River, this vast territory was ruled by Belgium as a single unit, which later emerged as a single state with an explosive ethnic mixture. Most importantly, the administrative borders in each colony were drawn without regard to ethnic or tribal identities; indeed, the colonial powers often found it useful to divide up ethnic or tribal groups in order to complicate the emergence of a unified opposition to imperial rule.[21]

The weakness of the state, seen in much of Africa, is fundamentally an expression of institutional weakness, compounded by other common sources of state vulnerability endemic to post-colonial Africa. The absence of unbiased bureaucratic systems necessary to enforce obligatory organisation and to efficiently administer the state reduced the capacity for policies attempting to provide public goods and services to be coordinated and implemented effectively. As a consequence, citizens turn to parochial and ethnic loyalties that are their main recourse in time of insecurity and their main default source of economic opportunity to compensate for the failure of the state to provide adequately for its population. This resulted in social fragmentation and the delegitimisation of the state as state institutions became

[19] Clapham (1998), pp. 1998: 147.

[20] Holsti (1996), p. 97.

[21] Kissinger (2001), pp. 201–203.

increasingly regarded as corrupt, illegal, or ineffective and incapable of maintaining satisfactory levels of civic welfare.[22]

Orthodox bureaucratic systems configured by rational, objective rules and standards that ensure that impartial policies prevail in decision-making—neutralising personal or sectional considerations from public administration—are also lacking as institutions vital in curbing 'privatisation of state power'[23] and nepotistic tendencies either are non-existent, are partisan or have insignificant effect in constraining entrepreneurial actors. Evidence of this is noticeable in the rise of neo-patrimonial systems in post-colonial Africa that are a consequence of the absence of autonomous self-reinforcing institutions capable of curbing prebendal politics, the 'privatisation of the state' and cronyism.

The fact that this scenario continues under numerous African leaders who base their support on clan/tribal patronage further typifies the pervasive lack of institutional constraints in the region. Thus, the lack of effective institutional framework demarcating clear separation of powers, rule of law and accountable governance and capable of counterbalancing excessive concentrations of political influence has also contributed to weak statehood in Africa.

Furthermore, the artificial nature of the inherited colonial boundaries that (deliberately or otherwise) cut across prior ethnic, social, economic and political communities also leads to promote frictions and cracks, which Holsti termed one of 'horizontal legitimacy': a lack of agreement on the principles for membership in the statist society due to the absence of a link between the population and the territory of the state.[24] In sociological terms, in the illegitimate state, there is agreement neither on the contents of the social contract nor on the identity of those entitled to negotiate the contract itself.[25]

In this perspective, legitimacy is understood not as a normative conclusion about juridical right or moral quality but in the socio-political sense of whether or not the structures of a given polity have evolved in an autochthonous from within society itself and whether its institutions can claim some historical endurance.[26]

The challenge for African states since independence has thus been how to orientate the imposed polity into an organisation that is not only steady but will also be accepted by its citizens as legitimate, as well as adequately capable of performing the basic functions of statehood, namely, control over national territory, management of natural resources, real and balanced collection of revenue, maintenance of adequate national infrastructure and capacity to govern and maintain law and order, including respect for human rights and the rule of law.[27]

The post-colonial African state, as the centre of power, coercion and control, did not leave much room for citizens' participation in the political process. This, in

[22] Wunsch and Olowu (1995), p. 95.

[23] Clapham (1998), p. 154.

[24] Holsti (1996), p. 97.

[25] Zeleza and McConnaughay (2004), pp. 6–8.

[26] Englebert (2000), p. 57.

[27] Badie (2000), p. 28; Osaghae (2006), pp. 4–7.

modest estimation, is a core issue in discourse about Africa's recurrent crises of insurgency and collapse. Contemporary African politics indicates the continued and growing relevance of various insurgent or armed groups taking charge of vast portions of settled national territories and at times seriously questioning where exactly actual sovereignty lies in several African countries. Readily coming to mind were the Eritrean People's Liberation Front (EPLF), which controlled a considerable portion of the territory of Eritrea, steadily limiting the Ethiopian government forces to Asmara precincts and ruling a vast portion of the total populace, just in like manner as UNITA in Angola, the National Patriotic Front of Liberia (NPFL); the Revolutionary United Front (RUF) in Sierra Leone; the Lord's Resistance Army (LRA) in Uganda; the Movement for the Emancipation of the Niger-Delta (MEND) in Nigeria; the Seleka Coalition in the Central African Republic; and, to an extent, the Jama'atu Ahl as-Sunnah li-Da'awati wal-Jihad (otherwise known as 'Boko Haram') in northern Nigeria. If Jackson and Rosberg's conception of the state as a 'human association that successfully claims the monopoly of legitimate use of physical force within a given territory'[28] were to be applied in interpreting several armed struggles against juridical sovereignty in Africa, empirical statehood may be said to exist only to the extent to which a government is able to enforce compliance with the laws, regulations and institutions that it has created. The practical curtailment of the duly constituted government of Somalia to Mogadishu since the 1991 upheaval is a veritable pointer.

It stands to reason that where people are subject to exploitation, marginalisation, exclusion and deprivation by others, resistance is bound to happen. And when that resistance happens—by whatever means—the organised patterns of resistance often rely on the unanimity of coercion, clandestineness and restraint to prevail against the established order. When such organised resistance struggles become successful—to any extent—the purveyors of the resistance become *de jure* or at least de facto sovereigns, with all the temptation to ensure untrammelled authority over the area under their suzerainty.[29] This explains the new ruling class that emerged from Ghaddafi's putsch in Libya (1969), Eyadema's takeover in Togo (1966), Rawlings regime in Ghana (1979), Taylor's crushing of the Doe oligarchy in Liberia (1997), Kabila's ouster of Mobutu in the DRC (1997) and several other scenarios like that in Africa.

The restiveness of contenders who seize the opportunity of the illegitimacy, weakness or failure of the real state to acquire de facto sovereignty over the territory of the state, in whole or in part, explains the vicious cycle of armed struggles and insurgency against the African state. Even though not all African intra-state armed struggle can be classified as targeting the creation of a separate state within the complex connotations of 'self-determination', there is no denying that every armed struggle and insurgency in Africa seeks directly to challenge the *status quo*, the ordinary arrangement of sovereignty and the legitimacy of those who wield the authority of the state.

---

[28] Jackson and Rosberg (1982), p. 2.

[29] Pavkovic and Radan (2003), p. 76.

2.4 Web of Violence and the Future of Intra-Boundary Contestations in Africa

In his foreword to the landmark publication by the UN-affiliated University of Peace (UPEACE) and SaferAfrica, in 2006, titled *Compendium of Key Documents Relating to Peace and Security in Africa*, Ambassador Djinnit, Commissioner for Peace and Security at the AU Commission, posited:

> Very few areas in the world have witnessed the diversity and intensity of conflicts that Africa has undergone in recent years. Africa has suffered both interstate wars (Ethiopia-Eritrea) and intrastate conflicts (e.g., Central Africa's Great Lakes Region and the 'conflict-domino-effect' throughout West Africa). Many of the most commonly recognised sources of violent engagements are present in Africa: underdevelopment, extreme poverty, human rights violations, bad governance, identity-based divisions and small arms proliferation, to mention but a few.[30]

There is no gainsaying the fact that Africa is beleaguered by the crisis of underdevelopment, and most of its constituent states are under the threat of insurgency, reinforced largely by the coalescence of identity conflicts and the struggle for distribution—identity: the mobilisation of people in communal groups based on race, religion, ethnicity, culture, language and the like and strengthened by the ideology of distribution: the means of sharing the economic, social and political resources within a society—and resulting in a range of socio-political challenges.[31] Although, superficially, Africa is becoming more peaceful, recent events across the continent depict a tale of a continent crumpling into disorder. This is aggravating the conditions of a continent whose states have failed to utilise their vast economic resources for the public good. With some 20 secessionist efforts in Africa,[32] there seems to be no end in sight to a half-century of near-incessant warfare and sporadic conflicts with staggering levels of human suffering.

Osaghae captured the stark realities of the post-colonial African state and the persistent questioning of its legitimacy this way:

> in addition to global changes, there are local factors within Africa itself that support a de-privileging of the state and the growth of alternative forms and sites for reconstructing the social order, of which ethnicity is certainly one. These include the chronic ineffectiveness (read as non-legitimacy) and failure of the centralized state, which have led significant segments of the citizenry to exit into parallel and largely self-propelling organizations…the reinvigoration of civil society and voluntary ethnic associations…and the drive for self-sustaining and autonomous centers of power and administration, as well as mobilization of local resources to complement or substitute for the dwindling resources of the weak and incapacitated state.[33]

That the colonial enterprise and the contrived emergence of neo-colonialism foisted incongruities of awkward territorial maps, systemic incompetence and weak

[30] UPEACE (2006), p. vii.

[31] Clapham (1998), pp. 150–153.

[32] Seymour (2013), p. 6.

[33] Osaghae (2006), p. 13.

policy-making on post-independence African states is no longer disputed.[34] The inevitable consequences of the coalescence of the flawed premises that marked the foundations of the post-colonial African state were ethnic loyalties and mistrust, lack of social integration and cohesion, irredentism and separatist conflicts,[35] often dressed in the garb of self-determination.

While the continuity of colonial boundaries across Africa (except for Eritrea's agreed exit from Ethiopia in 1993, South Sudan's supervised independence from Sudan in 2011 and the settlement of the Bakassi peninsula in favour of Cameroon against Nigeria by the ICJ pursuant to the 2002 decision in *The Land and Maritime Boundary Between Cameroon and Nigeria (Cameroon v. Nigeria: Equatorial Guinea intervening)*)[36] may suggest the inviolability of territorial sovereignty of African states, particularly with the crushing of earlier secessionist bid in the Katanga region of Zaire (DRC) and the failed Biafran attempt in Nigeria. These do not diminish ongoing low-tempo secessionist conflicts in the Casamance region of Senegal and in the Cabinda region of Angola and the secessionist activities in the Caprivi Strip of Namibia, among others.

Furthermore, Africa's numerous intra-boundary conflicts present the amazing interrelatedness of statehood, sovereignty, legitimacy and self-determination, all converging in the perennial conflict over the control of power.[37] Despite all the tensions and disagreements within African post-colonial territories, the colonial territories have largely remained because, according to Herbst, 'The boundaries have been singularly successful in their primary function: preserving the territorial integrity of the state by preventing significant territorial competition and delegitimating the norm of self-determination'.[38] Despite all its flaws and frailties, the colonial boundaries retained the pathways to international recognition, foreign aid and preservation against external aggression. Of course, from time to time, repression and marginalisation by the ruling elites are met with sustained struggles on the part of the subordinate classes. This has been the reality of the vicious cycle of African numerous demands around access to the control of state power, often witnessing insurgency, armed conflict and such other violent expressions.[39]

The admixture of self-determination's original characterisation and subsequent understandings has inevitably triggered significant misinterpretations, not only in Africa but also throughout the world. From the Middle East to Eastern Europe and Asia, the end of the Cold War and the collapse of communism have ushered in critical questioning of the colonial state, an experience that by itself is resisted through the adherence of ruling elites to the doctrine of *uti possidetis juris* (Latin for 'as you

[34] Mutua (1995), p. 1117.
[35] Bates (1974), p. 461.
[36] ICJ Reports 2002, p. 303.
[37] Seymour (2013), p. 18.
[38] Herbst (2000), p. 253.
[39] Blanton et al. (2001), pp. 481–483.

possess'), which desperately seeks to exclude any debate on the basis of the legitimacy of the state and its inherited boundaries.[40]

Today, the goal of states should be, first, to identify and explicitly define self-determination and the criteria that determine which entities are entitled to exercise the right. Contemporary political movements in Africa that demand the right to secede have frequently resorted to violence precisely because of the confusion and uncertainty surrounding their proclaimed goal of self-determination, and both international law and formal Western responses have done little to clarify the situation. Second, the global community should develop some strictures that define precisely what the right to self-determination encompasses. For instance, some people or groups may be entitled to invoke and exercise this right, but it should be confirmed that this does not necessarily include the right to independent statehood within an existing sovereign arrangement.

One aspect of the longstanding approach of the global community to armed struggles pertaining to self-determination claims is the hurried arrangement of organising elections in establishing a 'democratic order' in countries just emerging out of wanton conflict. From East Timor, Afghanistan, Iraq and Cambodia to Angola, Somalia and South Sudan, the idea of holding 'democratic elections' in order to establish orderly states, ruled by law and respect for human rights, has rigorously been applied without any conscientious effort at resolving the inherent foundations of the armed conflict in the first place.[41] A situation in which elections only end up installing warlords and potential war criminals—where rebel movements simply transform into political parties, as was the case in Liberia, Sierra Leone, South Sudan and so on—serves as counterproductive to genuine democratisation of a fractured state and grants licence for other warlords and militias elsewhere to embark on a gale of impunity knowing fully well that they would be pacified with political offices in the long run.

The international community must pay greater attention to the internal aspects of self determination. Claims to self-determination become violent, leading to civil wars, and are at times likely to spread regionally (such as evident in the Ethiopia/Eritrean conflicts of the 1990s) when there are no diplomatic mechanisms for pursuing these claims and settling competing ones through the process of conciliation. The role of preventive diplomacy, early-warning systems and peaceful settlement of disputes through arbitration, mediation, conciliation and negotiations needs to be explored.

Africa's march towards political stability, economic transformation and cohesion will be futile unless past failures and present weaknesses are acknowledged and addressed headlong. In other words, colonial histories, imposed economic orientations, ethnic alliances and geopolitical tensions cannot be swept under the carpet. Furthermore, the pathway to future national stability and development where the state is not only dutiful to its citizens' basic freedoms and rights but also capable of providing them not only security against internal and external threats but also

[40] Hasani (2003), pp. 7–15.

[41] Jaye (2003), p. 115.

minimal economic and social assurances that will guarantee its acceptance as legitimate abides in revisiting the dynamics of the past, including revisiting the very foundations of contrived statehood. While this pathway is fraught with risks and dangers, it is worthwhile to pursue that pathway than to embark on the sustenance of the current illegitimate colonial arrangements at all costs. If nothing more, granting the space for discourses on the 'national question' no matter how painful, brutal and harsh it may be for the continuity of age-long coexistence, the justice in giving opportunity to vent concerns about the terms of coexistence cannot be overemphasised.

In addition to the highlighted political solutions, it is equally imperative for African states to embark on the establishment and consolidation of effective state institutions. The ethno-religious multiplicity that is a frequently mentioned as the root of state frailty can only evolve into weak statehood when there are no effective institutions capable of averting and extenuating it from growing into intra-state armed conflict or insurgency. After all, effective institutions, and particularly impartial and proficient judiciaries, are necessary for controlling and resolving conflicts. Absence of credible home-grown institutions acting as mediators is what has prompted alternative violent, sporadic and extra-constitutional methods to express dissatisfaction and pursue amends as we have seen in Mali, Sierra Leone, South Sudan and lately Northern Nigeria.

2.5 Conclusions

The underpinning premise of this chapter is that conflicts cannot be interpreted independently of their historical contexts. The history of the people who are participants in a conflict, of the systems in which the conflict is occurring and of the issues themselves has a powerful influence on the course of the conflict.[42] History thus provides the momentum for the development and resolution of conflict. Quite frequently, we attempt to comprehend a conflict in seclusion from its historical roots and as a result are confounded by the rigidity of the role actors. The lengthy history of the conflicts in Somalia, the Niger-Delta or Cabinda, for example, does not mean that current conflicts in these regions will never be resolved. To assume that sort of historical determinism is precarious and distorted. Yet such conflicts cannot be solved without an appreciation of the intricate systems of interaction that have evolved over time and the extent to which the conflict itself has become part of the parties' identities. An attempt has been made to analyse the conflicting demands of statehood, sovereignty, legitimacy and self-determination in the ever-evolving power contestations in Africa, with an unmistakable advocacy for commitment, openness, dialogue, tolerance and political will as antidotes.

The preponderance of the challenges highlighted and the solutions explored in this piece is a direct summons to the AU to shake off its habitual practice of waiting

[42] Mayer (2000), p. 5.

for Western nations to wade in first before it reacts—as we saw in the cases of Ivory Coast and Mali—to provide the needed leadership for continental stability. Far from being an *ex-cathedra* pronouncement on all the dynamics that should inform the future resolution of intra-country self-determination conflicts and other threats of instability in Africa, this piece would have achieved its purpose if it stimulates further intellectual inquiry.

References

Badie B (2000) (C Royal, Trans.) The imported state: the westernization of the political order. Stanford University Press, Stanford

Bates R (1974) Ethnic competition and modernization in contemporary Africa. Comp Pol Stud 6(4):457–484

Blanton R, Mason TD, Brian A (2001) Colonial style and post-colonial ethnic conflict in Africa. J Peace Res 38(4):473–491

Brilmayer L (1991) Secession and self-determination: a territorial interpretation. Yale J Int Law 16:177–202

Clapham C (1998) Degrees of statehood. Rev Int Stud 24:143–157

Connolly CK (2013) Independence in Europe: secession, sovereignty, and the European Union. Duke J Comp Int Law 24:51–105

Englebert P (2000) State legitimacy and development in Africa. Lynne Rienner Publishers, Boulder

Forje JW (2003) Self-determination, nationalism, development and pan-Africanism stuck on the runway: are intellectuals to be blamed? Afr J Int Aff 6(1&2):54–86

Gould CC (2006) Self-determination beyond sovereignty: relating transnational democracy to local autonomy. J Soc Philos 37(1):44–60

Hasani E (2003) Uti possidetis juris: from Rome to Kosovo. Fletcher Forum World Aff 27(2):85–98

Herbst J (2000) States and power in Africa: comparative lessons in authority and control. Princeton University Press, Princeton

Holsti KJ (1996) The state, war, and the state of war. Cambridge University Press, Cambridge

Jackson RH, Rosberg CG (1982) Why Africa's weak states persist: the empirical and the juridical in statehood. World Polit 35(1):1–24

Jaye T (2003) Issues of sovereignty, strategy and security in the Economic Community of West African States (ECOWAS): intervention in the Liberian civil war. Edwin Mellen Press, Lewiston

Kapitan T (2006) Self-determination and international order. Monist 89(2):356–370

Kirgis FL Jr (1994) The degrees of self-determination in the United Nations era. Am J Int Law 88(2):304–310

Kissinger H (2001) Does America need a foreign policy? Toward a diplomacy for the 21st century. Simon & Schuster, New York

Malanczuk P (1997) Akehurst's modern introduction to international law, 7th edn. Routledge, London

Mayer B (2000) The dynamics of conflict resolution. Jossey-Bass, San Francisco

Mutua M (1995) Why redraw the map of Africa: a moral and legal inquiry. Mich J Int Law 16:1113–1176

Okoronkwo PL (2002) Self-determination and the legality of Biafra's secession under international law. Loyola Los Angeles Int Comp Law Rev 25:63–114

Osaghae EE (2006) Ethnicity and the state in Africa. Working paper series no. 7. Afrasian Centre for Peace and Development Studies, Kyoto

Pavkovic A, Radan P (2003) In pursuit of sovereignty and self-determination: peoples, states and secession in the international order. Macquarie Law J 3:1–12
Saul M (2011) The normative status of self-determination in international law: a formula for uncertainty in the scope and content of the right? Hum Rights Law Rev 11(4):609–644
Seymour LJM (2013) Sovereignty, territory and authority: boundary maintenance in contemporary Africa. Crit Afr Stud 5(1):17–31
Spector SJ (2011) Negotiating free association between Western Sahara and Morocco: a comparative legal analysis of formulas for self-determination. Int Negot 16:109–135
Titanji ED (2009) The right of indigenous peoples to self-determination versus secession: one coin, two faces? Afr Hum Rights Law J 9:52–75
UPEACE, SaferAfrica (2006) Compendium of key documents relating to peace and security in Africa. Pretoria University Law Press, Pretoria
Vidmar J (2013) Democratic statehood in international law. Hart Publishing, Oxford
Wachira GM (2008) African court on human and peoples' rights: ten years on and still no justice. Minority Rights Group International, London
Wilson W (1917) Address to senate, 64 congressional records 1741–1742 (1917)
Wunsch JS, Olowu D (eds) (1995) The failure of the centralized state. ICS Press, San Francisco
Zeleza PT, McConnaughay PJ (eds) (2004) Human rights, the rule of law, and development in Africa. University of Pennsylvania Press, Philadelphia

Chapter 3
Vipers Are Offsprings of Dragons: A Fanonian Analysis of Violent Conflicts in Africa with Specific Reference to the Boko Haram Insurgency in Nigeria

Akinola E. Akintayo

3.1 Introduction

There are a number of theories to explain conflicts and violence. While some of these theories are relevant and useful in explaining and understanding the phenomenon of violence, I suggest in this chapter that with reference to Africa and with particular reference to the Boko Haram insurgency in Northeast Nigeria, a Fanonian/violence analysis of the insurgency appears to offer a better explanation and understanding of the conflict. Thus, my main argument in this paper is that just like colonialism being a violent phenomenon in Africa precipitated and provoked force and violence in native Africans during colonial times, strong evidence suggests that post-colonial African states and politics characterised by force and violence as it were may be responsible for the present multiplication and spread of violent conflicts on the continent of Africa. This argument I try to validate through the examination of force and violence of the Nigerian state and its politics and how these appeared to have precipitated and fostered the Boko Haram insurgency in Nigeria.

In order to establish the arguments above, I briefly examine some theories of violence vis-à-vis Fanon's analysis of violence in Africa. And to validate Fanon's thesis about the force and violence of colonialism precipitating and fostering force and violence in Africa, I thereafter examine evidence validating Fanon's thesis about colonialism as a violent phenomenon in Africa. After this, I examine the violent nature and character of the Nigerian state and politics. I thereafter discuss how the violent character of the Nigerian state and politics may have provoked and fostered the insurgency, after which I seek to explain the insurgency in terms of Fanon's theory of violence and thereafter conclude the chapter.

A. E. Akintayo (✉)
Department of Public Law, Faculty of Law, University of Lagos, Akoka, Lagos State, Nigeria

J.-M. Iyi, H. Strydom (eds.), *Boko Haram and International Law*,
https://doi.org/10.1007/978-3-319-74957-0_3

3.2 Some Theories of Violence and Fanon's Thesis

Before I proceed to the discussion of some theories of violence, I think it is desirable that I set out my conception of 'violence'. Like all other terms, violence has no generally accepted definition or meaning. However, it appears that most conceptions of violence make a distinction between force and violence. While force is often conceived as a legal and legitimate use of violence by governments to safeguard the state, violence on the other hand is conceived as an illegitimate and illegal use of force by non-governmental actors and persons. In Leys' view, for instance, use of physical aggression and force by person(s) whose aims are not regarded as legitimate and within the purview of the state is categorised as violence, while use of violence by the coercive institutions of the state like the police and security forces to maintain law and order is regarded as legitimate and is therefore called force.[1] Violence thus conceived serves as 'a catch all for every variety of protest, militancy, coercion, destruction or muscle flexing which a given observer happens to fear or condemn'.[2]

While the distinction between force and violence and legitimate and illegitimate use of force is viewed as justified by some scholars,[3] the distinction will, however, appear to me to be misconceived for at least three reasons. First, there is robust literature pointing out that conflict and violence are inherent in and constitutive of politics[4]; thus, even Arendt, who argues that power is the essence of all governments, is constrained to concede that violence and power although distinct phenomena appear together in politics.[5] Some scholars have consequently noted that violence is in fact a form of political action or an instrument of politics through which the levers of power in a society are arranged, rearranged and maintained, which when used for selfish ends by the political class can only breed further violence.[6] Second, a conception of violence that makes a distinction between legitimate and illegitimate use of force introduces into the debate the question of who is to decide what is legitimate and what is illegitimate in the use of force. Third, as rightly argued by Anifowose, such a conception of violence also assumes that governments will always use force in the interest of the public at large or that the citizens will regard governmental use of force as legitimate all the time.[7] Consequently, Anifowose proffered a definition of violence as.

> …the use or threat of physical act carried out by an individual or individuals within a political system against another individual or individuals, and/or property, with the intent to cause injury or death to persons and/or damage or destruction to property; and whose

[1] Leys (1965).

[2] Anifowose (2011), pp. 3–4.

[3] Leys (1965).

[4] Mouffe (2005), pp. 64–88; Fraser (1989); Botha (2009), p. 11; Zolberg (1968), pp. 80–85.

[5] Arendt (2015).

[6] Dudley (1965), pp. 21–22. See also Zolberg (1968), pp. 80–85.

[7] Anifowose (2011), pp. 3–4.

> objective, choice of targets or victims, surrounding circumstances, implementation, and effects have political significance, that is, tend to modify the behaviour of others in the existing arrangement of power structure that has some consequences for the political system.[8]

The above definition of violence aptly captures my conception of political violence as a form of political action and conflicts and insurgency in Africa as political acts executed to further political purposes. Having dispensed with the discussion of my conception of violence in this paper, I now turn to the discussion of some existing theories of violence.

There are three main theories of violence articulated by scholars. The relative deprivation, rising expectation/frustration—aggression theory; the systemic theory; and the group conflict theory.[9] These theories are now examined in turn.

The relative deprivation, rising expectation/frustration—aggression theory is a psychological explanation of violence. This theory has two strands. The first strand of the theory is the frustration/aggression theory. This strand of the theory postulates that violence/aggression is the end result of the frustration of citizens' expectations. According to theorists in this school of thought, when the expectations of citizens are not met, this results in anger, which in turn leads to aggression and violence. Thus, aggression always presupposes frustration.[10] The reverse is, however, not always the case.[11] The second strand in the theory is the idea of relative deprivation. This is described by some theorists in this school of thought as the gap between the value expectations and value capabilities of individuals.[12] Theorists in this school regard relative deprivation as the basic precondition of civil strife.[13]

The systemic theory/explanation of violence ties conflict and violence to the social context within which they occur.[14] Some variant of this theory therefore ties violence to the structure and developmental stage(s) of a society.[15] In this theory, society is categorised into three different types: traditional, modern and modernising societies.[16] According to this theory, conflict is most noticeable and predominant in modernising societies.[17] The reasons for this are, among other things, the clash of tradition and modernity and the fact that modernisation produces an undue amount of expectations in the citizens, and when these expectations are not satisfied, this produces frustration and transferred aggression and violence to perceived sources of

[8] Anifowose (2011), p. 4.

[9] Anifowose (2011), pp. 5–16.

[10] See for instance, Davies (1962).

[11] Miller (1941).

[12] See for instance, Gurr (1968).

[13] Gurr (1968). See also Agbiboa (2013).

[14] Anifowose (2011), p. 9.

[15] See for instance, Olson (1963).

[16] Anifowose (2011), p. 10.

[17] See for instance, Olson (1963), pp. 532–547.

frustration and intensification of conflicts between different groups in society over the distribution of scarce resources in and among the groups.[18]

The group conflict theory/explanation of violence is to the effect that conflict and violence is the inevitable result of groups' struggle for power and resources in a body politics.[19] According to the theorists in this school of thought, there cannot but be conflict between different groups in a society that on grounds of cultural, religious or ethnic differences struggle among each other for power, resources and dominance in the society, a point buttressed by Feit in his analysis of military coups and political development in Ghana and Nigeria.[20] According to Feit, post-colonial Ghanaian and Nigerian political parties were personal-tribal machines built upon and motivated by a tribal desire to capture political power and control at the expense of the other tribes.[21] Feit argued that this desire brought about the demise of the early post-colonial governments in both Ghana and Nigeria and produced the early military coups in both countries.[22] More recent literature on political developments in Africa continues to confirm the ethnic underpinnings and struggle for power on African political terrain.[23]

As Anifowose rightly points out, these various explanations of violence are useful in analysing conflicts and violence in Nigeria.[24] For instance, elements of the three theories discussed above can indeed be deduced from the Boko Haram insurgency. As regards relative deprivation, rising expectation/frustration—aggression theory, for instance, there is some evidence that acute poverty, illiteracy and general underdevelopment in Northeastern Nigeria are contributory factors in the blossoming and sustenance of the insurgency. This is because the socio-economic dissatisfaction and frustration of the citizens in that area of the country provided fertile grounds for easy recruitments of foot soldiers and suicide bombers for the insurgents. This appears to support the argument of relative deprivation, rising expectation/frustration—aggression theorists. There is also some evidence that there is a clash between the old and the new, a clash between modernity and tradition in the insurgency. This is, for instance, noticeable in the insurgents' aversion to and loathing for western civilisation and form of government. In fact, the name Boko Haram means 'western civilisation is forbidden'. This also appears to support the systemic theorists of violence. Finally, there is also some evidence that the conflict has religious and ethnic undertones, which therefore supports the group conflict theory of violence.[25]

---

[18] Olson (1963), pp. 532–547.

[19] Anifowose (2011), pp. 11–14.

[20] Feit (1968).

[21] Feit (1968), pp. 184–192.

[22] Feit (1968), pp. 184–192.

[23] See for instance, Van de Wall (2003), Bogaards (2003) and Lewis (2003).

[24] Anifowose (2011), pp. 11–14. Agbiboa has in fact used the relative deprivation theory to specifically explain the Boko Haram insurgency: Agbiboa (2013).

[25] See for instance, Adesoji (2010) and Muzan (2014).

However, notwithstanding the usefulness of some of these theories in analysing the insurgency, as pointed out above, my argument in this chapter is that an analysis of the Boko Haram insurgency using these theories may in fact be incomplete and remain inadequate in explaining the crisis or providing clarity on the subject. Hence, I argue that a Fanonian/violence analysis of the insurgency could arguably shed more light on the precipitation and blossoming of the insurgency. This is because the violent character of the Nigerian state and its politics as provoking counter-violence from the citizens appear from evidence to be a predominant factor in the insurgency. I now turn to the examination of Fanon's thesis.

As far as Fanon is concerned, the native African is a violent being who was conceived, was born, was nurtured and died in colonial violence.[26] Fanon therefore states, for instance, that the African native is an oppressed person whose permanent desire is to supplant the settlers who are the oppressors.[27] According to Fanon, the settlers' symbol of social order—the police, the bugle calls, military parades, among others—inhibits and stimulates the native one at the same time because these symbols put the native in perpetual motion and edge ready to attack and ready to test the mettle of the colonial system or take the place of the persecutor.[28] Furthermore, the Africans' violent constitution, according to Fanon, will appear to be not something that is natural to the Africans but something that was foisted on them by the forceful and violent character of colonialism.[29] To Fanon, it was colonialism that brought violence into the minds and homes of Africans.[30] Fanon therefore sees colonialism as a violent phenomenon in Africa that sowed and nurtured the seeds of violence in Africans.

Fanon goes further to state that whatever natural or cultural inhibition Africans might have had against violence was removed by the violence and oppression of colonialism. According to Fanon, the native's fancies and natural inhibitions were violently removed from him or her by the heavy hands of the persecutors, and the native will consequently no longer have resort to his or her fancies and inhibitions during the struggle for freedom after centuries under the heavy yoke and violence of the colonists.[31]

Furthermore, Fanon opines that colonialism changed the course, channels or outlets of violence in Africans. According to him, violence was originally channelled and discharged through the 'emotional outlets of dance and spirit possession', but subsequent to colonialism, violence was exhausted through 'fratricidal combats' in Africans.[32] That is, the seeds of violence sown by colonialism in the minds and homes of Africans when matured were regularly let out and/or relieved through

[26] Fanon (1963), pp. 35–95.
[27] Fanon (1963), p. 53.
[28] Fanon (1963), p. 53.
[29] Fanon (1963), pp. 38–40.
[30] Fanon (1963), p. 38.
[31] Fanon (1963), p. 58.
[32] Fanon (1963), p. 58.

tribal warfare and feuds, violent and bloodthirsty quarrels between individuals and collective auto-destruction. Fanon put this point graphically thus:

> The settler keeps alive in the native an anger which he deprives of outlet; the native is trapped in the tight links of the chains of colonialism. But we have seen that inwardly the settler can only achieve a pseudo petrification. The native's muscular tension finds outlet regularly in bloodthirsty explosions—in tribal warfare, in feuds between septs, and in quarrels between individuals. Where individuals are concerned, a positive negation of common sense is evident. While the settler or the policeman has the right the livelong day to strike the native, to insult him and to make him crawl to them, you will see the native reaching for his knife at the slightest hostile or aggressive glance cast on him by another native; for the last resort of the native is to defend his personality vis-a-vis his brother. Tribal feuds only serve to perpetuate old grudges buried deep in the memory. By throwing himself with all his force into the vendetta, the native tries to persuade himself that colonialism does not exist, that everything is going on as before, that history continues. Here on the level of communal organizations we clearly discern the well-known behavior patterns of avoidance. It is as if plunging into a fraternal bloodbath allowed them to ignore the obstacle, and to put off till later the choice, nevertheless inevitable, which opens up the question of armed resistance to colonialism. Thus collective autodestruction in a very concrete form is one of the ways in which the native's muscular tension is set free.[33]

In summary, Fanon thinks Africans have a violent constitution brought about by the violent phenomenon of colonialism and that when the seed of violence sown in the minds and homes of Africans by colonialism matures, it is regularly let out by Africans against their neighbour, whom they have easier access to rather than the oppressive force and authority, which is far away from them. Thus, while the African will tolerate insults and provocation from violent and oppressive forces that are greater than him or her, he or she will not countenance even the slightest hostile or aggressive glance from his or her neighbour. He or she is therefore quick to explode in a destructive force against his or her neighbour or anybody that appears to wield a lesser force or violence than himself or herself, in tribal warfare and feuds and in bloodthirsty and violent quarrels between individuals. And since this phenomenon applies to every native African, force and violence are thereby multiplied as Africans engage in what Fanon called collective auto-destruction. This violent response of the African against his or her neighbour Fanon attribute to the behavioural pattern of avoidance, which tends to put off the inevitable violent confrontation between the oppressor and the oppressed till later.

The gravamen of Fanon's thesis, as can be gathered from the foregoing, is therefore that Africans as victims of violence with no channels or outlets for their frustration, grievances and anger will find outlets for their frustration and anger through destructive violence against less powerful or less violent neighbours, in tribal warfare, in bloodthirsty and violent feuds and quarrels between individuals and, I dare add, also through religious extremism at the slightest provocation or excuse and thereby perpetuate violence in what Fanon called collective auto-destruction.[34]

[33] Fanon (1963), p. 54.

[34] Westley's study appears to later confirm Fanon's theory of violence: Westley (1966).

Of course, Fanon and his thesis about Africans and violence have been variously criticised by scholars. While some criticised him for methodological delinquencies, others cited his lack of sociological rigour and contradictions in his concept of African peasantry.[35] Perinbam has, however, opined that criticisms of Fanon's concept of African peasantry will appear not to be made out because available evidence suggests that Fanon is right on this score.[36] Perinbam is also of the view that had Fanon waited for an appropriate methodology or availability of empirical data to make his arguments, his voice may never have been heard.[37] Fanon's thesis about colonialism as a violent phenomenon that provoked and fostered violence in Africa is, however, in my view correct, as I show in the next section below.

3.3 Colonialism and the Seed of Violence in Africa

There is robust literature confirming colonialism as a violent phenomenon in Africa. According to Ake, for instance, because the colonial economy was based on exploitation and pillage of the colonised, the ideology of the colonisers had to be and was force.[38] Force was used in the allocation of roles, it was used to ensure regular supply of labour and it was also used to distribute surplus capital.[39] The colonial state was thus synonymous with force and violence. It had to be that way because the system was all encompassing and all powerful.[40] It needed to be all powerful to maintain its hold on power and to carry into effect the economic objectives of colonialism. Ake notes that the colonial state involved itself in practically every sphere of the colonised economic life.[41] The state allocated land and decided who was to produce, what and how.[42] The state ensures steady flow of labour and saw to the disposal of the produce.[43] The state also provided the necessary infrastructural and human resource support for the colonial economy, determined and facilitated the kind of education for the natives that will complement and support the colonial economy, among many other things. The power of the colonial state had to be, and it was, absolute.

In addition to being absolute, the power of the colonial state was also arbitrary. It was exercised mainly to fit the exigencies of colonialism and its exploitative economy. Ake notes that these two features of absolutism and arbitrariness framed

---

35 Perinbam (1973).

36 Perinbam (1973), pp. 427–432.

37 Perinbam (1973), pp. 427–432.

38 Ake (1976), pp. 228–230.

39 Ake (1996), p. 2.

40 Ake (1996), pp. 2–3.

41 Ake (1996), pp. 2–3.

42 Ake (1996), p. 2.

43 Ake (1996), p. 2.

colonial politics.[44] In the context of the present analysis, however, it should be noted that these features of absolutism and arbitrariness exacted and prompted similar responses from colonial subjects who at any rate regarded the colonial state as illegitimate.[45] The subjects also, consequently, paid no regard to the norms of legitimacy or legality in the struggle to advance their interests either. According to Ake, colonial politics was consequently reduced to crude mechanics of power and violence.[46] This view of colonialism as a violent phenomenon in Africa has been confirmed by other scholars.[47]

In addition to this, there is ample evidence that colonial Africa carried over the violence of the colonial state and politics into post-colonial Africa. Thus, what changed in the politics of post-colonial African states was not the nature and character of the colonial state but its composition. Thus, the unbridled power politics and violence of colonial politics is still evident in post-colonial African states and politics. This is because the new African political elites came to see political power as an end in itself and were prepared to do anything and everything to capture it. This stems from the fact that political power came to mean not only power and prestige but also a source and guarantor of material wealth both for the elites in power and the elites out of power. For those in power, political power ensured access to the state treasury. For those out of power, political power ensures that they get to keep what they have fraudulently acquired through abuse of office without harassment and persecution from the opposition. In this kind of political climate, pursuit of political power became a zero-sum game, a do-or-die affair. The nature and character of African post-independence politics are aptly summarised by Ake thus:

> To recapitulate, at independence the form and function of the state in Africa did not change much for most countries in Africa. State power remained essentially the same: immense, arbitrary, often violent, always threatening. Except for a few countries such as Botswana, politics remains a zero-sum game; powers was sought by all means and maintained by all means. Colonial rule left most of Africa a legacy of intense and lawless political competition amidst an ideological void and a rising tide of disenchantment with the expectation of a better life.[48]

The above view of Ake confirmed Fanon's thesis of colonialism as the sower of violence in post-colonial African states and politics.[49] Ake and Fanon are, however, not the only scholars establishing a link between colonialism and the force and violence of post-colonial African politics. Jackson and Rosberg, for instance, made a clear link between tyranny, coercion and force in Africa's post-colonial politics and colonialism.[50] Howard also thinks that there is a link between the tyranny and

---

[44] Ake (1996), p. 3.

[45] Ake (1996), p. 3.

[46] Ake (1996), p. 3.

[47] See for instance, Howard (1980), p. 728 who refers to colonialism as a benevolent dictatorship. See also Rodney (1973), pp. 37–57.

[48] Ake (1996), p. 6.

[49] Fanon (1963), pp. 181–183.

[50] Jackson and Rosberg (1986).

undemocratic posture of African political leaders and what she called benevolent dictatorship of colonialism.[51] Mamdani's view is also to the same effect.[52] He pertinently notes that post-colonial African politics is marked by self-interest of the political class, the tendency of regimes to monopolise power, the exploitation of the peasantry and repression.

The violent nature of African post-colonial politics and its effects in precipitating and fostering force and violence in the body politic has also been described by Zolberg, who correctly notes that post-colonial African states and politics have shifted from power to force.[53] According to Zolberg, although African political elites continue to pay lip service to democracy, evidence of use of force and violence by African rulers to maintain themselves in power abound in the post-colony.[54] These evidence ranges from intimidation and detention of political opponents to assassinations, from fraudulent electoral arrangements to the use of political thugs to bulldoze opponents, among many others.[55]

As regards the deleterious effects of this shift from power to force of African states and politics on the political life of the society, Zolberg pertinently notes that the shift from power to force as a technique of government oftentimes serves as the prelude to more violence in the form of anti-government coups and revolutions.[56] Zolberg posits that this can occur in four different ways.[57] First, state/government that relies on force/violence as instrument of governance tends to quickly use up its stock or capital of force because such a state/government tends to apply excessive force against small irritations to the detriment of more serious threats and consequently become more vulnerable to more serious threats when they occur. The second is that the shift from power to force vastly increases the influence and importance of the coercive structures and machineries of such a state to the detriment of democratic structures and institutions. Third, although resort to force is meant to overcome the legitimacy and inadequate power crisis of a state, it paradoxically achieves the opposite result because it operates to weaken the legitimacy and highlight the inadequate power problem of a state. Last, a shift from power to force by a state makes violent dissent and demands the preferred mode of expression for individuals and groups that are denied the right and opportunity to dissent and make their demands in a peaceful manner and that quickly discovered that government's stock or capital of violence is in fact limited.

In addition to the foregoing, more recent literature continues to confirm the violent nature and character of the post-colonial African states and politics. According to Mbembe, for instance, the notion of the post-colony in fact identifies specifically '…societies recently emerging from the experience of colonisation and the violence

[51] Howard (1980), p. 728.

[52] Mamdani (1990).

[53] Zolberg (1968).

[54] Zolberg (1968), pp. 76–77.

[55] Zolberg (1968), pp. 76–77.

[56] Zolberg (1968), p. 77.

[57] Zolberg (1968), p. 77.

which the colonial relationship, *par excellence,* involves'.[58] Mbembe opines that the post-colony is a distinctive regime of violence and excesses, a regime of obscene and grotesque display of power.[59] Mbembe goes further to show that the dominated in the post-colony, at least in some parts of French West Africa (Cameroon and Togo), use humour and comedy (not violence) to cope with and domesticate the violence and domination of the post-colony.[60] Mbembe's thesis will, however, appear not to be generally applicable to all African post-colony, as analysis in this chapter shows.

Furthermore, Mehler in his study of some post-colonial African states' electoral systems also shows that violence not only continued to be used as instruments of politics by African political elites and parties; it may have in fact become an established mode of competition.[61] Mehler identified some of the different ways in which violence is employed by African political parties as follows[62]: first is employment of violence to profit from 'historical opportunities'. This occurs when political parties resorted to violence to protect historic victory at the polls against a repressive incumbent who was bent on scuttling the will of the electorate. Second is the employment of violence by African political parties to express grievances. This occurs when political parties resort to violence to protest election manipulations. Third is the use of violence as instrument of domination by the state and government parties. Mehler notes in this regard that African ruling parties frequently use the coercive forces of state, party thugs and militias to terrorise and intimidate leaders and members of opposition parties.[63] Mehler further notes that the use of violence by ruling parties creates a dilemma for opposition parties, which are caught between resorting to violence with the risk of stigmatisation and playing by the rules with the risk of losing adherents to more radical forces.[64] Fourth is the use of violence by former ruling parties that are sometimes able to exploit long-standing relations between the elites of the party and security forces to foment trouble in the forms of coups and mutinies.[65] Fifth is provoking violence to discredit the opposition. This occurs when opposition parties provoke violence in order to erode and wither away the local and international prestige and democratic credentials of ruling parties. Ruling parties may also provoke violence in order to label the opposition as terrorists.[66] Sixth, political entrepreneurs may also resort to violence to acquire political rents in the form of co-option into government or securing other material benefits for refraining from or suspending the use of violence.[67] In the light of all

[58] Mbembe (1992).
[59] Mbembe (1992).
[60] Mbembe (1992), pp. 5–29.
[61] Mehler (2007).
[62] Mehler (2007), pp. 201–208.
[63] Mehler (2007), pp. 204–206.
[64] Mehler (2007), p. 206.
[65] Mehler (2007), pp. 206–207.
[66] Mehler (2007), p. 207.
[67] Mehler (2007), pp. 207–208.

these, Mehler concludes that violence may in fact be a mode of political competition more common than consensus and co-operation in post-colonial Africa than in more advanced democracies.[68]

The above literature, among many others, appears to confirm Fanon's thesis about colonialism as a violent phenomenon in Africa that fostered a violent constitution in native Africans during the colonial period. The literature also shows that colonialism socialised African political elites into violence and thus promoted force and violence in post-colonial African states and politics.[69] Having established the foregoing, I now turn to examine the violent nature and character of the Nigerian state and politics, as can be gathered from available evidence in the section below. Thereafter, I specifically examine how these violent nature and character of the state and politics may have provoked and fostered the Boko Haram insurgency, after which I explain the insurgency in the light of Fanon's theory of violence.

3.4 The Violent Nature and Character of the Nigerian State and Politics

While there is no agreement among theorists regarding the precise meaning or constitutive elements of democracy, there appears to be a consensus in the literature that substantive democracy goes beyond periodic elections.[70] Legal and political theorists and scholars alike agree that democracy that is worth its name must allow ample space for the participation and involvement of the citizens in public decision-making processes.[71] Pateman opines, for instance, that participation is at the core of classical theories of democracy, which should also underlie the practice of contemporary democracy.[72] A functioning democracy must also provide room for the robust deliberation and engagement of the citizens with government and authorities in public decision-making processes.[73] Thus, Manin et al., for instance, have correctly argued that deliberation is an essential and necessary precondition for the legitimacy of public decision-making processes and the practice of majoritarian

[68] Mehler (2007), p. 209.

[69] The above point is succinctly explained by Ake thus: 'Colonial politics was power politics in the most literal sense of the phrase. Those in power used their power with little or no restraint to maintain their privileges, and to repress those out of power who wanted to replace them. Those who were not in power sought power with the same indifference to restraints, and with the same indifference to the 'rules of the game'. The colonial political culture to which the nationalist leaders were socialised was one characterised by a lack of public-spirited restraint in the quest for, and the exercise of, power.' Ake (1973), p. 358.

[70] See for instance, Kolakowski (1990), Giddens (1994), Bader (1995), Zurn (2002), Uprimmy and Garcia–Villegas (2005) and Roux (2006); among many others.

[71] Pateman (1970), Dzur (2012) and Sheth (2005).

[72] Pateman (1970), pp. 105–111.

[73] Habermas (1996); Warren (2002), p. 182; Benhabib (1996).

democracy.[74] Substantive democracy, as opposed to formal democracy, ought to also give ample room and robust space for some kind of consensus and dissent in a substantive, as opposed to formal, practice of democracy.[75] Thus, Mouffe notes, for instance, that conflict is at the heart of politics and democracy.[76] According to her, '[m]odern democracy's specificity lies in the recognition and legitimation of conflict and the refusal to suppress it by imposing an authoritarian order'.[77] In Mouffe's view, therefore, the non-acknowledgement of conflict and antagonism as constitutive of politics and absence of political channels to ventilate grievances will ensure the failure of democratic experiments.[78]

By the provisions of section 14 (1) and (2) of the Constitution of the Federal Republic of Nigeria, 1999 (the Nigerian Constitution), Nigeria is constitutionally prescribed to be a democratic state. Section 14 (1) of the Nigerian Constitution provides that '[t]he Federal Republic of Nigeria shall be a State based on the principles of democracy and social justice'. Governance in the country is therefore constitutionally required to be in accordance with democratic norms and practice. It is important to note that the provisions of section 14 (1) and (2) of the present Nigerian Constitution are conspicuously absent from both the 1960 and 1963 Constitutions of the Federal Republic Nigeria. The provisions made their debut in section 14 (1) and (2) of the Constitution of the Federal Republic of Nigeria 1979, from where they were imported verbatim into identical section of the present Nigerian Constitution. Nevertheless, it is beyond doubt that the form of government that the British bequeathed to Nigeria in 1960 is the liberal democracy of the Westminster type. A cursory examination also revealed that the general text, tenor, form and structure of these earlier constitutions also generally accords with the Westminster type and practice of democracy. Thus, except for the periods of military interregnum into politics when the constitution was usually suspended by the military,[79] Nigeria, whether in the early days of formal independence or today, has always been a democratic state (at least on paper) whose form and practice of government ought to accord with the norms and practice of democracy. There is, however, robust evidence that the Nigerian state is a violent state that relies mainly on force and violence as tools and instruments of governance contrary to accepted democratic norms and practice. There is also ample evidence that politics in Nigeria is characterised

[74] Manin et al. (1987), p. 360.

[75] Wiredu (2013); Louw (2013); Van der Walt (2008), p. 82; Botha (2000).

[76] Mouffe (2005).

[77] Mouffe (2005), p. 30.

[78] Mouffe (2005), pp. 64–88.

[79] Nigeria has spent 29 out of 54 years of its existence to date under military rule: from 1966 when the first military government took over the reins of government to 1979; again from 1984 until May 29, 1999 save for a brief spell of military imposed Interim National Government which ran for only 82 days from 26 August 1993 to 17 November 1993. The constitution was usually suspended during these periods of military interregnum and there is robust literature which confirmed that despite their pretenses to the contrary, the nature and character of military regimes during these periods of time in Nigeria was the very anti-thesis of the tenets of democracy. See, for instance, Olukoshi (2000), pp. 21–23; Olowu (2013), pp. 322–331; Jegede (2013), pp. 339–345.

and conducted in an atmosphere of violence contrary to accepted democratic norms and practice. The illustration of these facts from available evidence is the focus of this part of the essay.

3.4.1 Violent Nature and Character of the Nigerian State

Regarding the violent character and nature of the Nigerian state, available evidence appears to support the view that undue reliance is placed on force and violence as instruments of governance to the detriment of democratic frameworks and institutions. This is evident from at least two instances: the use of the coercive machineries of state by ruling parties to suppress opposition and maintain themselves in office and the violent response of the state to citizens' dissent, demands and expectations. These instances are illustrated here from the Tiv riots of 1960 and 1964 and their aftermaths, the Niger Delta of Nigeria militancy and its aftermaths and the more recent violent suppression of the mass protests against the removal of fuel subsidy in January of 2012.

3.4.1.1 The Tiv Riots of 1960 and 1964 and Their Aftermaths[80]

The Tivs are a tribe in Nigeria's middle belt area. They are stocky in stature, and their major occupation is farming. They inhabit the land area that lies along the banks of River Katsina Ala and the south of the Benue River. Tiv land was, during the period under study, an administrative unit in the then Northern Region of Nigeria, which was then controlled at the regional level by the Hausa-Fulani-dominated political party, the Northern People's Congress (NPC), while in the Tiv Division, the Tiv-dominated United Middle Belt Congress and Action Group (UMBC/AG) coalition enjoyed overwhelming support and held sway. However, because Tiv land was only a division in the structure of the then Northern Regional government of Nigeria's First Republic, effective political and administrative power of the division was in the hands of the Hausa-Fulani-dominated NPC, while the UMBC/AG was only the opposition political party with insignificant representation and voice in the Northern Region's legislature. However, because Nigeria was at this time operating the Westminster model of democracy with its dominant and overbearing influence of the legislature in the structure of government, the UMBC/AG had very little say in what went on both at the regional and at the divisional levels in spite of the overwhelming support that the party enjoyed in the division.

As Anifowose has rightly noted, the opportunities and space within which opposition parties may operate in a democratic political environment depends largely on the rules and rule-enforcing agencies of democratic politics in a society.[81] Thus,

[80] See Anifowose (2011), pp. 73–141 for a more detailed discussion of the riots.

[81] Anifowose (2011), p. 92.

while particular rules of engagement may not be overtly discriminatory or restrictive, the rule-enforcing agencies, if beholden to the ruling party, may apply the rules discriminatorily and restrictively to prejudice opposition parties and favour the party in government. Anifowose, in his analysis of the Tiv riots, points out that the Northern Region ruling party, the NPC, subjected the opposition, the UMBC/AG, to severest pressure and turned the Region into a de facto one-party region using the coercive powers of the state through the discriminatory and restrictive application of rules in spite of the robust support enjoyed by the UMBC/AG in the Tiv Division.[82]

Anifowose catalogues the different instruments of coercion employed by the ruling NPC to frustrate the opposition UMBC/AG out of existence in the Tiv Division as follows[83]: first, the extensive regulatory powers of native authority system that were used against the opposition. Permits for the holding of public meetings where issues of common interest could be discussed by the Tivs were denied the UMBC/AG and its members, while the same was granted the ruling party and its supporters.[84] UMBC/AG members who dared to defy this quasi-official ban on politics were arrested and jailed.[85] Second, the native courts were another veritable weapon of coercion deployed by the ruling party against the opposition. The courts were extensively used by the ruling party as a forum to display party allegiance and to victimise and frame opposition party members, especially during periods of elections.[86] Third, the native authority police was another coercive institution of the state that was robustly utilised by the ruling party to harass, detain and pressure opposition party members while maintaining the ruling party in power. Fourth, economic pressures and violence were also brought to bear upon opposition party members. This was done through the withholding of due economic benefits, sack of opposition party members from their jobs, non-promotion of opposition party members, refusal of trading permits for specific goods and services for opposition party members, among others.[87]

The foregoing coercive measures of the ruling party were gradually met by resistance and open defiance by the Tivs. The defiance and resistance grew into a full-scale and widespread violence accompanied by some deaths and unprecedented burning and looting of the houses and properties of NPC members and presumed oppressors of the people in August of 1960 in the Tiv Division. Although only about 16 lives were reported to have been lost in the riots, properties lost were put at over a million naira.[88] After the riots, some palliative measures to pacify the Tivs were put in place by the Northern Region government. These measures will, however, appear to have been cosmetic only and did not address the root causes of the violence. This, in addition to the forceful imposition of N5.10 tax on every adult Tiv to

[82] Anifowose (2011), p. 92.

[83] Anifowose (2011), p. 92.

[84] Anifowose (2011), p. 94.

[85] Anifowose (2011), p. 95.

[86] Anifowose (2011), pp. 95–97.

[87] Anifowose (2011), pp. 99–100.

[88] Anifowose (2011), p. 124.

pay for the damages caused by the 1960 riots, led to a more violent and widespread outbreak of violence in the Tiv Division in 1964.[89]

Like the 1960 riot, the 1964 riot was precipitated by oppressive use of coercive instruments of the state by the ruling NPC. As reported by Anifowose, the 1964 violence started when opposition party members summoned to court for displaying opposition party logo in their houses refused to answer the summons.[90] Attempts by the police to arrest the accused persons were resisted by force of arms of their colleagues who drove the police away with poisoned bows and arrows.[91] This was followed by the murder of an NPC supporter who was alleged to have had a private cell in his house where he arbitrarily detained opposition party members in February of 1964.[92] The killing of the NPC supporter was followed by a free-for-all fight between his supporters (NPC members) and the opposition members (UMBC/AG members). The situation quickly degenerated, and the violence spread throughout Tiv Division with intensity far greater than that of the 1960 riots. As reported by Anifowose, official estimates put the casualty figure of the 1964 riots at 12 policemen and about 47 civilians, while unofficial estimates of fatalities were put at between 2000 and 4000 people as against 16 lives that were reportedly lost in the 1960 riots.[93]

3.4.1.2 The Niger Delta Militancy and Its Aftermath

The Niger Delta of Nigeria is that geographical area of Nigeria that cut across eight states of the Federation, viz. Delta, Edo, Bayelsa, Rivers, Cross River, Abia, Ondo, Imo and Akwa-Ibom states.[94] The people of the Niger Delta are mainly farmers and fishermen who rely on the land and water bodies being despoiled by oil spillage and gas flaring resulting from the oil exploration activities of oil companies for their livelihood. The Niger Delta militancy started in the late 1980s, when different communities in the Ogoni part of the Niger Delta started peaceful protests against the degradation of their environment by oil prospecting and exploration activities of the Royal-Dutch Shell Company.[95] Violent suppression of these peaceful protests has been a recurring feature of the Nigerian government's response to the agitation of the Niger Delta people. This point of view is buttressed by Owolabi and Okwechime, who opine that Nigeria is a country with repressive state institutions with the Niger Delta the theatre where these repressive state institutions inflict obscene brutalities at the behest of multinational oil corporations.[96]

[89] Anifowose (2011), p. 128.
[90] Anifowose (2011), pp. 130–131.
[91] Anifowose (2011), p. 131.
[92] Anifowose (2011), p. 131.
[93] Anifowose (2011), p. 132.
[94] Frederick et al. (2013), p. 123.
[95] 'The life and death of Ken Saro-Wiwa (2015).
[96] Owolabi and Okwechime (2007), p. 4.

Further evidence of the repressive strategy of the Nigerian state in the Niger Delta abounds.[97] For instance, it has been reported that during one of the peaceful protests by Iko community, the Mobile Unit of the Nigerian Police Force was called in, and they violently put down the protests, at the end of which 40 houses were destroyed and 350 people were rendered homeless.[98] Another peaceful protest by the Etche community at Umuechem was also reported to have been violently put down by the Mobile Unit of the Nigerian Police Force resulting in 80 fatalities and the destruction of nearly 500 homes.[99]

In 1990, the Movement for the Survival of the Ogoni People (MOSOP), a non-violent action group under the leadership of Ken Saro Wiwa, was formed to carry on the peaceful protests of the Ogonis against the environmental degradation of Ogoniland and the destruction of the sources of the livelihood of the Ogoni people by the activities of Royal-Dutch Shell Company. The formation of MOSOP constituted a watershed in the efforts of the Niger Delta people to protest the destruction of their homes and sources of livelihood by oil companies. This is because MOSOP largely succeeded in calling attention to the plight of the Ogonis not only locally but internationally as well. However, true to its nature and character, the Nigerian state continued to engage MOSOP violently through coercive mechanisms of the state. Thus, after subjecting Ken Saro Wiwa, the MOSOP leader, to serial arrests, he was finally arrested alongside eight other members of MOSOP and allegedly framed for the murders of some conservative Ogoni leaders in January 1995. Saro Wiwa and his eight colleagues, popularly referred to as the Ogoni Nine, were tried by a military tribunal, convicted and sentenced to death for the murders of the conservative Ogoni leaders. The Ogoni Nine were subsequently executed, in defiance of local and international appeals for leniency, on 10 November 1995.[100]

It does appear from subsequent events that the execution of the Ogoni Nine effectively brought the non-violent posture and approach of the Niger Delta agitators to an end. Soon after their execution, militant groups from other Niger Delta ethnic groupings that did not buy into the non-violent agitation of Ken Saro Wiwa and Ogoni's MOSOP proliferated in the Niger Delta.[101] The Ijaw Youth Council, the Niger Delta Vigilante Group, the Niger Delta People's Volunteer Force (NDPVF) of Alhaji Mujahid Dokubo-Asari (an Ijaw, Niger Delta's largest ethnic group) and the Movement for the Emancipation of the Niger Delta (MEND), among many others, emerged to take up arms against the Nigerian state.[102] These militant groups engaged in kidnappings, abductions, extortion, pipeline and oil facilities sabotage and armed

[97] See Owolabi and Okwechime (2007), pp. 5–10 for a catalogue of some of the violence and repression the Nigerian state meted out to the Niger Delta agitators.

[98] See for instance, 'The life and death of Ken Saro-Wiwa (2015).

[99] Owolabi and Okwechime (2007), p. 5.

[100] 'The life and death of Ken Saro-Wiwa (2015).

[101] See for instance, Council on Foreign Relations (2015).

[102] Council on Foreign Relations (2015). See also Etemike (2009), pp. 153–161 for a more detailed discussion of the different militants groups that proliferated in the Niger Delta before the grant of amnesty in the region in 2009.

confrontations with the Nigerian state to press home their demands. The militancy and the resulting violence were so acute that Nigeria's oil business was almost crippled.[103] The government of former President Shehu Yar'Adua was therefore compelled to grant amnesty to all who have been directly or indirectly involved in the Niger Delta militancy on 25 June 2009.[104] It was after the government granted the militants amnesty that relative peace returned to the Niger Delta. The amnesty is set to expire this year (2015).

3.4.1.3 The Violent Suppression of the Mass Protests Against the Removal of Fuel Subsidy of January 2012

The importance of oil to Nigeria's socio-economic well-being cannot be gainsaid. This is underlined by the fact that oil resources contribute about 88% of government revenues and continue to constitute the mainstay of the Nigerian economy.[105] It has in fact been pointed out that '[n]ational and personal dreams, hope and aspiration are built around oil'.[106] As a result of this centrality of petroleum products, especially Premium Motor Spirit (PMS) (otherwise known as petrol), to personal and national sociopolitical life in Nigeria, the pricing of petroleum products has always been a very thorny issue. While governments have always tried to maximise revenue through increases in the price of petroleum products, individuals and civil-society groups have always resisted this because of the deleterious impact of the increases on the majority of the people who are poor. Thus, since 1978, when the first removal of the fuel subsidy took place in Nigeria, prices of PMS have been increased a record 16 times.[107] Most of these increases have been accompanied by widespread resistance, protests and, most times, even nationwide strikes.[108]

---

103 Aghedo (2012), pp. 270–271.

104 Aghedo (2012), pp. 270–271. See also Egwemi (2010).

105 See for instance, Frederick et al. (2013).

106 Ering and Akpan (2012).

107 Prices of PMS was increased from 8.4 kobo to 15.37 kobo per litre in 1978; from 15:37 kobo to 20 kobo per litre in January 1982; from 20 kobo to 39.50 kobo per litre in March 1986; from 39:50 kobo to 42 kobo per litre in April 1988; from 42 kobo to 60 kobo per litre for private cars in January, 1989; from 60 kobo to 70 kobo per litre in March 1991; from 70 kobo to N5.00 per litre in November 1993 but reduced to N3.25 kobo per litre after nation-wide protests; from N3.25 kobo to N15.00 per litre in October 1994 but reduced to N11.00 per litre 2 days later after widespread protests; from N11.00 to N25.00 per litre in December 1998, later reduced to N20.00 per litre after much protests by Nigerians; from N20.00 to N30.00 per litre in June 2000 only to be reduced to N22.00 per litre after massive protests and strikes by organised labour and civil society organisations; from N22.00 to N26.00 per litre in January, 2002; from N26.00 to N40.00 per litre in June 2003; from N40.00 to N70.00 per litre in 2007 but later reduced to N65.00 per litre; from N65.00 it was increased to N141.00 per litre in January of 2012 pursuant to a policy of total deregulation of the downstream of Nigerian oil sector but was later reduced to N97.00 per litre after weeks of massive and widespread protests by organised labour and civil society organisations.

108 See Lasisi and Augoye (2012) for more detail.

Although strikes and mass protests by organised labour and civil society groups were a feature of earlier struggles against the removal of fuel subsidy in Nigeria, they became a much more important and potent tool of the struggle from 1999 onwards. The struggle of the populace against fuel price increases in Nigeria came to a head on 1 January 2012, when the Federal Government of Nigeria (FGN) pursuant to a policy of total deregulation of the downstream sector of Nigeria increased the price of petrol from N65.00 to N141.00 per litre.[109] The FGN had towards the end of 2011 been consulting and interacting with relevant stakeholders and civil society groups to apprise the populace of the deregulation policy of the government.[110] Before the conclusion of consultations, however, the government suddenly aborted the consultation processes, implemented the policy and hiked the price of petrol from N65.00 to N141.00 per litre.[111] This unilateral and rather arbitrary action of the FGN prompted mass protests and strikes reminiscent of the Arab Spring, the like of which has not hitherto been seen in Nigeria.[112] The mass protests, which lasted for about 15 days, took place in most major cities across the length and breadth of Nigeria and grounded all economic and social activities throughout the period of the protests.[113] The strike and protests were finally called off by Nigerian Labour leaders on the 16th of January 2012 after the government deployed security forces on major streets of Lagos and other parts of the country to break up the protests and after labour leaders were allegedly coerced into accepting a price reduction instead of the total reversal of the price.[114] That is, rather than follow the democratic line of dialogue and consensus, the government forcefully broke up the mass protests. In the process of breaking up the strike and mass protests, however, there is evidence that Nigerian security forces committed serious atrocity against the people. There were several reports of police brutality and even extrajudicial killing of protesters during the mass protest.[115]

The above illustrations show clearly that the Nigerian state defines its relationship with the citizens as a violent one and therefore relies on violence and repression as primary instruments of governance to the detriment of democratic mechanisms. The illustrations also show that, in majority of the cases, the force and violence of the state precipitate and provoke a more serious violence from the people, who quickly learn that the government does not have a monopoly of violence and that violence may be a much more effective way to air their grievances and make their demands.

---

[109] *Vanguard* (2012).

[110] See *This Day Live* (2011) for a detailed discussion of the position of the different stakeholders on the removal of fuel subsidy at different fora.

[111] Sahara Reporters (2015a, b).

[112] See also National Mirror (2014) where the mass protest was described as unprecedented.

[113] National Mirror (2014).

[114] Sahara Reporters (2015a, b).

[115] See for instance, Channels Television (2014a).

3.4.2 The Violent Nature and Character of Nigerian Politics

There are many dimensions to violent politics in Nigeria. These include assassination of political opponents, coercion and inducement of voters, violent electioneering campaigns, election rigging, ballot box snatching, post-election violence and politics-related terrorism, among others.[116] I focus on violent electioneering and other election-related violence in this chapter because of the importance of election to bourgeois liberal democracy, which Nigeria practices. The importance of election to bourgeois liberal democracy has been stressed by quite a number of legal and political theorists and scholars. For instance, elections and the concomitant right to vote have rightly been said to lie at the very core of liberal-legal theory of democracy.[117] According to Ugochukwu, elections and the concomitant right to vote are liberal democracy's life-sustaining oxygen without which the practice may not survive.[118] The right to vote and be voted for has also been referred to as one that is preservative of civil and political rights.[119] It is the means through which political elites get to power or renew themselves in power. As a result of this importance of elections to Nigeria's type of democracy, as identified above, Nigerian politicians have been noted to be prepared to do just about anything to contest and win elections. I therefore submit that the investigation of election-related violence is a good place to gauge the nature and character of violent politics in Nigeria.

The meaning of electoral violence and what it entails have helpfully been analysed by Laakso.[120] According to Laakso, electoral violence should be seen as an activity informed by the desire to influence the results of elections either through the manipulation of electoral procedures or the contestation of its legitimacy.[121] Laakso also rightly notes that electoral-violence-related activity might involve intimidation and harassment of electoral candidates and voters, killings, attack and damage of opposition property, unlawful detentions, rioting and violent displacement of would-be voters, among others.[122] As the author rightly points out, both ruling and opposition parties may use violence as election strategies. While ruling parties and their supporters may use violence strategy to keep their hold on power, opposition parties and their supporters may use it to gain access to power.[123] Laakso also notes that electoral violence in Africa is actually exacerbated by the African economic

[116] Recent reports indicate that Nigerian politicians may be buying into the suicide bombing *modus operandi* of Boko Haram to deal with political opponents. See for instance, Channels Television (2015c) which reports that a suicide bomber went to the house of a politician where a political meeting was being held and blew himself up killing six people.

[117] Ugochukwu (2012), pp. 543–544.

[118] Ugochukwu (2012), pp. 543–544. See also Azinge (1994) where the author also makes the point that the right to vote is intertwined with the concept of representative democracy.

[119] See for instance, *Harper v Virginia State Board of Elections* 383 US 663 at 667 (1966).

[120] Laakso (2007).

[121] Laakso (2007), pp. 227–228.

[122] Laakso (2007), pp. 227–228.

[123] Laakso (2007), p. 228.

context. In the scholar's view, while poverty may not be a sufficient cause for violence, the endemic poverty in Africa appears to have made the desperate populace, who faces ever-dwindling economic fortunes, much more easily roused to violent actions because they often have very little to lose.[124]

As regards Nigeria, there is robust literature detailing the violent nature of politics and elections in the country.[125] According to Dudley, for instance, thuggery, which he called 'naked violence', is a generally accepted political practice of Nigeria's political elites of the 1960s.[126] In Dudley's view, the reason for the prevalence of violence in Nigeria's politics is because politics in Nigeria is an open avenue and doorway to government patronage, lucre, prestige and power, which Nigeria's political elites are prepared to use violence to access and retain.[127] Dudley, however, observed that the Nigerian political class by using violence to get to and maintain themselves in power may have created a condition that makes resort to violence inevitable in changing the structure of political power in the country.[128] This view of Dudley has more recently been confirmed by Onebamhoi, who opines that electoral violence with its concomitant effect has been the bane of democratic transition in Nigeria.[129]

In Ologbenla's view also, the myriad of problems bedevilling Nigeria today is traceable to the flawed electoral system and the attitudes and activities of Nigeria's political class, which see power as an avenue to fulfil private selfish interests and amass illegitimate wealth.[130] In his opinion, the violent and fraudulent activities of Nigeria's political class, which engaged in all manner of election malpractices, have made it impossible to conduct a free and fair election in Nigeria since independence.[131] In addition, Ologbenla correctly notes the critical role of Nigerian youths in electoral violence in Nigeria.[132] According to him, Nigerian youths of today are a critical factor in the destabilisation of the country's democratic process.[133] He notes that unscrupulous politicians oftentimes exploit the criminal and violent tendencies of jobless and idle Nigerian youths by employing them (the youths) as hitmen and assassins, bodyguards and militias for political parties, among others.[134]

Ologbenla also rightly observes that high-ranking politicians and public office holders in Nigeria retain criminally minded youths as salaried personnel who later turn around to commit all sorts of atrocities with impunity as political thugs with the

[124] Laakso (2007), pp. 228–230.

[125] See for instance, Human Rights Watch (2014).

[126] Dudley (1965), p. 22.

[127] Dudley (1965), p. 23.

[128] Dudley (1965), p. 23.

[129] Onebamhoi (2015).

[130] Ologbenla (2003).

[131] Ologbenla (2003), p. 70.

[132] Ologbenla (2011).

[133] Ologbenla (2011), pp. 20–22.

[134] Ologbenla (2011), p. 20.

full backing and support of their politician employers.[135] In addition to Ologbenla's assertion, it should also be stated that besides placing these political thugs on salaries, the politicians also procure arms and ammunition for them, with which these political thugs wreak havoc on political opponents. And after election periods, these youths, now idle with nothing to do, more often than not, turn these weapons and aggression against hapless and innocent citizens.

Finally, Fagbule has also correctly opined that vote buying and violence are epiphenomenal features of Nigeria's electoral system.[136] According to him, there is simultaneous operation of the carrot of vote buying and the stick of political violence in Nigeria's elections. The scholar surmises that a strong incumbent will buy votes and a weak opposition resorts to violence, while a strong opposition will buy votes and a weak incumbent will more likely resort to violence.[137] The above opinion of Fagbule regarding the simultaneous operation of vote buying and violence in Nigeria's elections is buttressed by Bratton.[138]

The above review of the literature shows that Nigeria's electoral system is in fact characterised by both physical and economic violence induced by Nigeria's political elites for their selfish ends and purposes. The review also shows the critical role that the youths play in electoral violence in Nigeria and how it is that during post-election periods when the youths are idle with no positive outlet for their energies and aggression they turn the weapons distributed to them by their politician godfathers during election periods upon the general populace with the result that electoral violence is exacerbated even beyond election periods. The foregoing analysis also shows that by using violence to capture and maintain themselves in power, the Nigerian political class may have created a condition that makes resort to violence imminent in changing the levers of political power in the country. Nigeria is in another election year, and as if to confirm the above analysis, there are already very worrying signs and reports of a violent electioneering—from youths attacking the campaign train of the incumbent President across the northern part of the country,[139] gun and bomb attacks against the opposition party's secretariats in some states of the Federation,[140] disruption of the opposition party's campaign rally by gunmen[141] and violent clashes between supporters of opposing political parties[142] to threats of violence and war by kinsmen of the incumbent President if he does not win the election.[143] The evidence and the signs are foreboding indeed. It therefore does

[135] Ologbenla (2011), p. 21.

[136] Fagbule (2014).

[137] Fagbule (2014).

[138] Bratton (2008).

[139] Yahoo News (2015) and Channels Television (2015a, b).

[140] The Punch (2015b, c).

[141] Channels Television (2015e).

[142] Channels Television (2015d).

[143] See for instance, News24 Nigeria (2015).

appear that Nigeria is probably set for a more turbulent politics and elections in 2015 than previously.[144]

Having established the violent nature and character of the Nigerian state and its politics above, I now turn to examine how these characteristics may have specifically provoked and exacerbated the Boko Haram insurgency in the Northeast of Nigeria.

3.5 The Nexus Between the Violent Character of the Nigerian State and Politics and the Boko Haram Insurgency

Historical and other accounts and examination of the Boko Haram group and the insurgency and the heart-numbing atrocities that the group has so far committed are not in short supply.[145] I focus on observed interactions between the Boko Haram insurgency and the Nigerian state and politics, which may have provoked or fostered the violence.

While there are different historical accounts about the evolution of Boko Haram in Nigeria, the different accounts appear to largely coincide on one point: that the Boko Haram group did not start off as a violent or a terrorist group. According to one account, Boko Haram metamorphosed from a non-violent movement, the *Ahlulsunna wal'jama'ah hijra* sect formed by one Abubakar Lawan at the University of Maiduguri, Borno State, in 1995.[146] This account of Boko Haram's evolution goes further to state that when Lawan proceeded to Saudi Arabia for further studies, the movement metamorphosed through different names before transmuting into Boko Haram and came under the leadership of Mohammed Yusuf in 2002. This non-violent account of Boko Haram's evolution is supported by a United States Institute of Peace Special Report (USIP).[147] As rightly pointed out by USIP, the formation of the group is a reaction against the corruption and lawlessness of Northern Nigeria's political elites and the extreme poverty, injustice and other societal ills perceived by the group as un-Islamic.[148]

---

[144] This prediction was in fact only averted through the unprecedented concession of defeat by the incumbent President, former President Goodluck Jonathan on the night of 31st March 2015 when from all indication it appeared that the incumbent had lost the election. This unprecedented concession of defeat by an incumbent in Nigeria is generally acknowledged by all and sundry as what averted impending political crisis and violence in the election. See for instance, This Day Live (2015) and The Punch (2015d).

[145] See for instance, Aghedo and Osumah (2012), Cook (2015), Agbiboa (2014) and Amnesty International (2014a, 2015); among others.

[146] Onuoha (2015).

[147] USIP (2015).

[148] USIP (2015), p. 2.

While there is also controversy as regards the group or institution that started the violence, some put the blame at the door of Boko Haram, others identify the Nigerian state as the culprit; there, however, appears to be a consensus that the violent crackdown of the state upon the group and the extrajudicial execution of its leader, Mohammed Yusuf, in July 2009 exacerbated the insurgency.[149] Some of the events that led to the July 2009 violent crackdown on the group by the state are as follows.

The confrontation was allegedly started when members of the group got into an altercation with security personnel when travelling *en masse* to a funeral of one of their members (apparently in a convoy of motorcycles) and they resisted attempts by security operatives to enforce the rule requiring them to wear helmets on motorcycles, this being against the dictates of their religion.[150] An argument thereafter ensued between the members of the group and security operatives. What transpired after this was not clear. While some accounts of the event alleged that a member of the group fired on and wounded a number of the security operatives,[151] other accounts alleged that security operatives killed 17 members of the group at the scene of the confrontation.[152] Whatever may have been the case, however, what appears not to be in dispute is that this event, among others, precipitated a very violent crackdown on the Boko Haram group resulting in the death of about 1000 persons, most of them members of the group.[153] Mohammed Yusuf, the leader of the group, was also arrested and extrajudicially executed by men of the Nigerian Police Force.[154] Properties of suspected members of the group who could not be found were also reportedly confiscated by the state and parcelled out to Imams and traditional leaders who co-operated with the security operatives.[155]

As pointed out above, there appears to be a consensus inside and outside Nigeria that this brutal crackdown and extrajudicial execution of Mohammed Yusuf and about 1000 members of the group by the state exacerbated the insurgency. After the crackdown and repression of July 2009, the group went underground for about a year and re-emerged with a vengeful reign of terror against politicians, the police and Islamic authorities in Northeastern Nigeria, apparently to avenge the brutal crackdown and slaughter of its members in July 2009.[156] Boko Haram appeared to have extended its tentacles, objectives and targets only when it had become stronger and bolder as a result of its several successes. The conclusion is thus that the extreme violence with which the Nigerian state responded to the unorthodox ideology, views

[149] Aghedo and Osumah (2012); Cook (2015), pp. 12–21; Agbiboa (2014), p. 56; among others.

[150] See for instance, Onuoha (2015), p. 2. The group has other unorthodox believe like believing that the Earth is flat, that rain is not a result of evaporation and wearing of shoes inside a mosque, among others. See USIP (2015), p. 7.

[151] USIP (2015), p. 4.

[152] Last (2008–2009).

[153] Agbiboa (2014), p. 56.

[154] Cook (2015), pp. 10–12.

[155] USIP (2015), p. 4.

[156] USIP (2015), p. 2.

and relatively smaller threats (at the time) of the Boko Haram group exacerbated the insurgency on a large scale to what it is now. This view is confirmed by the USIP thus: 'Tactics employed by government security agencies against Boko Haram have been consistently brutal and counterproductive. Their reliance on extrajudicial execution as a tactic in "dealing" with any problem in Nigeria not only created Boko Haram as it is known today, but also sustains it and gives it fuel to expand.'[157] Thus, the extremely violent response of the Nigerian state to the Boko Haram dissent will appear to be responsible for its becoming the monster that it is today.

The handling of the insurgency by the Nigerian security forces after it metamorphosed into a monster is also a factor that has been implicated in the festering and escalation of the insurgency. There are reports of equally, if not more, horrific atrocities by Nigerian security forces in the course of conducting operations against the insurgents.[158] There are evidence and reports of brutality and high handedness by the Nigerian security forces in conducting operations against the insurgents.[159] The Nigerian military has been implicated in the arrests, intimidation, extortion and extrajudicial executions of innocent civilians and the commission of other war crimes.[160] This approach has naturally alienated the civilian population and denied the security forces the much-needed support of the civilian population, which is said to fear the security forces more than the Boko Haram group.[161] The brutality, high handedness and wanton killing and destruction of the properties of the innocent civilian population by the security forces are also said to be compelling some aggrieved members of the society who would like to avenge the injustices meted out to them to join Boko Haram, thus swelling the ranks of the insurgents.[162] This violent and repressive approach of Nigerian security forces has been rightly noted by Solomon to be escalating the insurgency.[163] Thus, the brutal and repressive handling of the insurgency by the state through its security forces has continued to escalate the insurgency through the loss of the support of the civilian population and the consequent swelling of the ranks of the insurgents by aggrieved members of the society.

Another factor in the nature and character of the Nigerian state that appear to be responsible for the festering insurgency is the refusal of the Nigerian state to dialogue with the insurgents. This of course is consistent with the reliance of the state on force and repression as primary instruments of governance at the expense of democratic mechanisms, including dialogue. It is on record that the Nigerian state has consistently refused to dialogue with the insurgents, preferring a military solution to the insurgency instead.[164] And when the government finally decided to

[157] USIP (2015), p. 12.

[158] Amnesty International (2014b), pp. 11–23; Yahoo News (2014).

[159] The Punch (2015a).

[160] See for instance, Amnesty International (2014a).

[161] Yahoo News (2014).

[162] Solomon (2012).

[163] Solomon (2012), p. 9.

[164] See for instance, Pointblanknews.com (2015).

dialogue, it appeared to have done so in a half-hearted and insincere manner so much so that the insurgents and the negotiator called off the talks citing the insincerity of the government.[165] It is also on record that the insurgents had since then repudiated any desire or commitment to dialogue or negotiate with the Nigerian state, preferring instead to continue with the insurgency and violence.[166] This, in my opinion, was a missed opportunity to end the five-year-long insurgency relatively quickly and without further violence, as was done with regard to the Niger Delta militancy.

Lastly, another factor that may have contributed to the escalation of violence of the insurgency is the violent nature and character of Nigerian politics and the readiness and preparedness of Nigerian politicians to exploit situations, peoples and events in the society for their personal and selfish political purposes and gains. This view is confirmed by the USIP Special Report thus: 'A weakness in the institutions of politics and the security services has created a political situation where such threats to stability are not dealt with until violence is a certainty. Only when a politician in control of a state is convinced that such a threat cannot be bent to his advantage will he order any action be taken against it.'[167]

In support of the foregoing view, there is some evidence that the Boko Haram group may be an offshoot of private militia set-up, armed and used by politicians as political thugs in the run-up to the 2003 general elections in Nigeria.[168] A Presidential Panel Report is, for instance, said to have traced the origin of private militias in Borno State (of which the Boko Haram group is said to be an offshoot), to the creation and arming of political thugs by politicians in the run-up to the 2003 general elections.[169] Having achieved their political objectives, the politicians were reported to have left these private militias to their fate, who with no visible means of sustenance and with the arms and ammunition provided them by politicians gravitated towards religious extremism.[170] The Presidential Report obviously supports my argument regarding the nexus between violent politics and the insurgency and violence in Nigeria.

There is further evidence also that the Boko Haram group enjoyed government patronage and funding from some state governments and politicians in the northern part of the country in the early stages of the group's evolution, apparently in order to obtain illicit advantage over political opponents.[171] It has been alleged, for instance, that the Boko Haram group received support and funding from the Borno State government, either directly or indirectly.[172] Buji Foi, a former Commissioner for Religious Duties in Borno State, was, for instance, reported to have been funding

---

[165] 247 UReports (2015).

[166] See for instance, Al Jazeera (2015).

[167] USIP (2015), p. 2.

[168] Channels Television (2014b).

[169] Channels Television (2014b).

[170] Channels Television (2014b).

[171] Baca (2015).

[172] Baca (2015).

the group.[173] Foi was executed by policemen alongside other members of the group during the July 2009 crackdown on the group by security forces. It has also been reported that a spokesman for the group confessed that the governors of Kano and Bauchi States placed members of the group on monthly salary.[174] Patronages and the support received by the Boko Haram group from politicians during these early days will appear to have enabled the group to provide goods and services, which endeared it to the people at the grassroots and dramatically expanded its membership base, as well as provided money for terrorist training abroad.[175] Furthermore, there continue to be serious allegations and reports of government officials and politicians in and out of government who are alleged to still be funding the Boko Haram group for one selfish reason or another.[176] Obviously, these covert and overt supports and funding of the group by unscrupulous politicians can only continue to fuel the insurgency and multiply the violence.

Having examined the connections between the Boko Haram insurgency and the violent character of the Nigerian state and its politics above, I proceed to explain the insurgency in terms of Fanon's thesis in the section below.

3.6 Fanon's Theory of Violence and the Boko Haram Insurgency

Fanon's theory of violence has been broken down into three parts by Mamdani: the first is as a description of the violence of the colonial system, the second is as a claim that anti-colonial violence is not an irrational manifestation but a script of modernity and progress and the third is as a prophecy of the fact that victims of violence will eventually turn killers both in order to exterminate the humanity of others as their own humanity (the victims' humanity) have been exterminated and to defend their humanity.[177] According to Mamdani, the main thesis of Fanon's argument is that African violence was the violence of yesterday's victims who put aside their victim status to become masters of their own destiny.[178]

With regard to Fanon's thesis and the insurgency, I make three principal arguments in this chapter. The first is that colonialism was a violent phenomenon in Africa. Second, I argue that the violent nature and character of colonialism sowed the seed of violence in African states, a phenomenon that was carried over into the post-colony and is responsible for the violent nature of African states and politics. Third, I argue that Nigerian post-colonial state, while pretending on democratic

[173] See for instance, Last (2008–2009), p. 8.

[174] Agbiboa (2014), p. 57.

[175] USIP (2015), pp. 3–4.

[176] See for instance, This Day Live (2014) and Sahara Reporters (2014).

[177] Mamdani (2002), p. 5.

[178] Mamdani (2002), p. 5.

credentials, not only maintained but also expanded the use of state apparatus of coercion to spread violence and also to capture and retain political power. The consequences of this are widespread disenchantment, frustrations in the face of socioeconomic deprivations, absence of legitimate avenues for dissent and expression of frustration and, ultimately, resort to violence, such as the Boko Haram insurgency. Thus, proceeding from Fanon's thesis, my argument is that the Boko Haram insurgency is the violence of yesterday's victims of the violence of the Nigerian state and its politics, who with no legitimate channels or outlets for their frustration, grievances and anger find outlets in bloodthirsty violence against less powerful or less violent neighbours at the slightest provocation or excuse under the guise of Islamic revivalism and thereby perpetuate violence in what Fanon referred to as collective auto-destruction. This counter-violence against neighbours and the vulnerable Fanon attributes to a behavioural pattern of avoidance, which puts off the inevitable face-off between the oppressor and the oppressed until later when the latter may have become stronger or have their backs against the wall. This explanation, I suggest, is consistent with evidence thrown up by facts and the surrounding circumstances of the insurgency as follows: firstly, available evidence, as can be gathered from the analysis in this chapter, suggests that the insurgency is a creation of the violence of the Nigerian state, which defines its relationship with the citizens as a violent one through the non-toleration of dissent and undue reliance on violence and repression as a preferred mechanism of governance as opposed to democratic mechanisms consistent with the violent nature of the post-colony. Thus, although there were isolated incidents of violence by the group prior to the violent and ruthless crackdown on the group by the Nigerian state in July 2009, available evidence suggests that the violent crackdown and the extrajudicial execution of the leader of the group, Mohammed Yusuf, and about 1000 members of the group precipitated vengeful reprisals by the group and exacerbated the insurgency to what it is today. This seems to confirm Fanon's prediction of victims of violence becoming killers in order not only to exterminate the humanity of others but to defend their own (victims') humanity as well.

Secondly, evidence, as can be gathered from this chapter, also suggests that consistent with the inherited violent nature of the politics of the post-colony, Nigerian politicians resort to violent means to actualise their political goals and objectives. These means, as I point out earlier in this chapter, include creating, arming and funding political thugs and militias who after elections were abandoned by their politician godfathers and who gravitate towards religious extremism. I point out earlier that there is some evidence that Boko Haram may have been an offshoot of these political thugs and militias created and armed by politicians during the run-up to the 2003 general elections who after the elections were abandoned by the politician and who with nothing to engage their energies and aggressiveness gravitated towards religious extremism.

Additionally, there is also some evidence that the group received funding from a number of northern state governors and politicians during the early days of the group apparently in furtherance of these politicians' do-or-die kind of politics. I point out earlier that the funding received by the group in the early days may have helped enlarge its membership base by enabling it to provide services that endeared it to the grassroots. I also point out that this funding may also have provided resources for terrorist training abroad. As I further point out earlier in this chapter, there are also allegations of continued funding of the group by some unscrupulous politicians after the violence worsened, probably in order to perpetuate the state of insecurity in that part of the country and violently displace large numbers of would-be voters for undoubtedly selfish political reasons and objectives. The evidence, among others, presented in this chapter will appear to confirm the thesis that the inherited violent nature of the post-colony helped in creating and sustaining the insurgency.

Thirdly, there is also some evidence, as I state earlier in the chapter, that the Nigerian state privileges violent and repressive tactics over more democratic approaches in dealing with the insurgency consistent with the violent nature and character of the post-colony. There is therefore evidence of as serious, if not more serious, violence and atrocities by the Nigerian security forces against civilian population in terms of unlawful arrest, detentions and extrajudicial executions of innocent members of the public, which appeared to have operated to swell the ranks of the insurgents by disenchanted and aggrieved members of the public and their kith and kins who have been unjustly treated and who desire to have their own pound of flesh from the state. Furthermore, there is also evidence of the refusal and insincere desire on the part of the Nigerian state to dialogue with the group consistent with the inherited repressive and violent nature of the state. This appears to have had the effect of prolonging the violence and bloodshed.

Finally, it would appear that all of the above evidence and circumstances of violence and repression created victims of violence in the members of the group who with no outlet to vent their anger and frustration against the state exploded with destructive violence against near neighbours, who they had easier access to and upon whom they can conveniently vent their pent-up anger and violence until the group became stronger and more embolden by its successes whereupon they took up arms against the Nigerian state in a bid to carve out an Islamic state. We therefore initially see the group's bloodthirsty and violent explosions against less powerful opponents: Christian neighbours, Muslims who do not share the groups' ideology, vulnerable politicians, lower cadre members of the Nigerian security forces, women and children, among others. The group later changed tactics to directly challenge the state only after its string of successes. From the foregoing analysis, it appears that Fanon's explanation of violence is more consistent with the facts and circumstances surrounding the insurgency and appears to be a more suitable and fuller explanation of the insurgency because of the particular and predominant features of violence and counter-violence inherent in the creation and sustenance of the insurgency, as explained in this chapter.

3.7 Conclusion

My main thesis in this chapter is that Fanon's theory of violence, which sees violence in Africa as the violence of yesterday's victims of violent colonialism and the resulting violent post-colony and who lacking the requisite outlets for their frustration and anger explode in bloodthirsty counter-violence and thereby perpetuate violence is a more suitable and adequate explanation of the Boko Haram insurgency. This is because available evidence suggests that violence of the Nigerian state and its politics and the counter-violence of the Boko Haram group are predominant factors in the creation and blossoming of the insurgency.

The above thesis I tried to substantiate in this chapter through the examination of how colonialism, a violent phenomenon in Africa, sowed the seed of violence in the minds and homes of Africans. I also examined how African post-colonial states carried the violent nature and character of colonialism into the post-colony and accounted for the violent nature and character of African states and their politics. Furthermore, I examine how consistent with the nature of African post-colony, the Nigerian state relies on coercive mechanisms of the state and violence as primary instruments of governance and politics. I illustrated how these violent features of the Nigerian state and its politics may have given birth to and nurtured the insurgency. I suggest that available evidence appears to show that the Boko Haram group is yesterday's victims of the violence of the Nigerian state and its politics, who with no legitimate channels to vent their frustration and anger on the state resorted to destructive violence against their less able neighbours under the guise of Islamic revivalism and only directly confronted the Nigerian state after having been embolden by its string of successes consistent with Fanon's theory of violence. I therefore conclude that, in the light of the foregoing, Fanon's theory of violence appears to be a more adequate explanation of the insurgency.

References

247UReports, "'Boko Haram accepts dialogue only if' – Sanusi'. http://247ureports.com/boko-haram-accepts-dialogue-only-if-sanusi/. Accessed 16 May 2015

Adesoji A (2010) The Boko Haram uprising and Islamic revivalism in Nigeria. Afr Spectr 45(2):95–108

Agbiboa DE (2013) Why Boko Haram exists: the relative deprivation perspective. Afr Conflict Peacebuilding Rev 3(1):144–157

Agbiboa DE (2014) Peace at daggers drawn? Boko Haram and the state of emergency in Nigeria. Stud Conflict Terrorism 37(1):41–67

Aghedo I (2012) Winning the war, losing the peace: amnesty and the challenges of post- conflict peace-building in the Niger Delta, Nigeria. J Asian Afr Stud 48(3):267–280

Aghedo I, Osumah O (2012) The Boko Haram uprising: how should Nigeria respond? Third World Q 33(5):853–869

Ake C (1973) Explaining political instability in new states. J Mod Afr Stud 11:347–359

Ake C (1976) The congruence of political economies and ideologies in Africa. In: Gutkind PCW, Wallerstein I (eds) The political economy of contemporary Africa. Sage Publications, Beverly Hills, pp 228–242

Ake C (1996) Democracy and development in Africa. Brookings Institution, Washington

Al Jazeera, Nigeria's 'fake' ceasefire with Boko Haram. http://www.aljazeera.com/indepth/opinion/2014/11/nigeria-fake-ceasefire-with-b-20141111103442243308.html. Accessed 08 Feb 2015

Amnesty International (2014a) Nigeria: gruesome footage implicates military in war crimes. http://www.amnesty.org/en/for-media/press-releases/nigeria-gruesome-footage-implicates-military-war-crimes-2014-08-04. Accessed 18 Oct 2014

Amnesty International (2014b) Nigeria: more than 1,500 killed in armed conflict in North-Eastern Nigeria in early 2014. http://amnesty.org/en/library/asset/AFR44/004/2014/en/543f7ac9-6889-4f02-bf5a-d73832e04229/afr440042014en.pdf. Accessed 19 Oct 2014

Amnesty International, Nigeria: massacre possibly deadliest in Boko Haram's history. http://www.amnestyusa.org/news/press-releases/nigeria-massacre-possibly-deadliest-in-boko-haram-s-history. Accessed 09 Jan 2015

Anifowose R (2011) Violence and politics in Nigeria: the Tiv, Yoruba and Niger Delta experience, 3rd edn. Sam Iroanusi Publications, Lagos

Arendt H 'From on violence'. http://warhistorian.org/mershon/arendt-on-violence.pdf. Accessed 06 May 2015

Azinge E (1994) The right to vote in Nigeria: a critical commentary on the open ballot system. J Afr Law 38:173–180

Baca M. Boko Haram and the Kanuri factor – By Michael Baca. http://africanarguments.org/2015/02/16/boko-haram-and-the-kanuri-factor-by-michael-baca/. Accessed on 16 Feb 2015

Bader V (1995) Citizenship and exclusion: radical democracy, community, and justice. Or, what is wrong with communitarianism? Polit Theory 23(2):211–246

Benhabib S (1996) Towards a deliberative model of democratic legitimacy. In: Benhabib S (ed) Democracy and difference: contesting the boundaries of the political. Princeton University Press, Princeton, pp 67–94

Bogaards M (2003) Electoral choices for divided societies: multi-ethnic parties and constituency pooling in Africa. Commonw Comp Polit 41(3):59–80

Botha H (2000) Democracy and rights: constitutional interpretation in a postrealist world. J Contemp Roman-Dutch Law 63:561–581

Botha H (2009) Equality, plurality and structural power. S Afr J Hum Rights 25:1–37

Bratton M (2008) Vote buying and violence in Nigerian election campaign. Elect Stud 27:621–632

Channels Television (2014a) Fuel subsidy protest: court awards N4 million compensation to victims of police shooting. http://www.channelstv.com/home/2013/06/14/fuel-subsidy-protest-court-awards-n4million-compensation-to-victims-of-police-shooting/. Accessed 20 June 2014

Channels Television (2014b) How Ali Modu Sheriff Sponsored Boko Haram- Femi Falana. http://www.channelstv.com/2014/09/04/ali-modu-sheriff-sponsored-boko-haram-femi-falana/. Accessed 04 Sept 2014

Channels Television (2015a) APC condemns attack on Jonathan's convoy in Katsina. http://www.channelstv.com/2015/01/22/apc-condemns-attack-jonathans-convoy-katsina/. Accessed 23 Jan 2015

Channels Television (2015b) Hostile youths attack Presidential convoy in Bauchi. http://www.channelstv.com/2015/01/22/hostile-youths-attack-presidential-convoy-in-bauchi/. Accessed 22 Jan 2015

Channels Television (2015c) Suicide bomber targets politician, kills 6 In Yobe. http://www.channelstv.com/2015/02/01/suicide-bomber-targets-politician-kills-6-in-yobe/. Accessed 01 Feb 2015

Channels Television (2015d) Suspected APC thugs attack PDP supporters in Kaduna. http://www.channelstv.com/2015/02/03/suspected-apc-thugs-attack-pdp-supporters-in-kaduna/. Accessed 03 Feb 2015

Channels Television (2015e) Violence mars political campaign in Rivers Okrika. http://www.channelstv.com/2015/01/24/violence-mars-political-campaign-in-rivers-okrika/. Accessed 24 Jan 2015

Cook D, Boko Haram: a prognosis. http://bakerinstitute.org/media/files/news/c90b9ac8/REL-pub-CookBokoHaram-121611.pdf. Accessed 04 Jan 2015

Council on Foreign Relations Mend: the Niger Delta's umbrella militant group. http://www.cfr.org/nigeria/mend-niger-deltas-umbrella-militant-group/p12920. Accessed 31 Jan 2015

Davies JC (1962) Towards a theory of revolution. Am Sociol Rev 27:5–19

Dudley B (1965) Violence in Nigerian politics. Transition 21:21–23

Dzur AW (2012) Four theses of participatory democracy. Constellations 19(2):305–324

Egwemi V (2010) From militancy to amnesty: some thoughts on President Yar'adua's approach to the Niger Delta crisis. Curr Res J Econ Theory 2(3):136–141

Ering SO, Akpan FU (2012) The politics of fuel subsidy, populist resistance and its socio-economic implications for Nigeria. Glob J Hum Soc Sci 12(7):13–20

Etemike L (2009) The struggle against exploitation and marginalization: a historical survey of and implications of the uprisings and protests in Nigeria's Niger Delta. In: Ojakorotu V (ed) Contending issues in the Niger Delta crisis of Nigeria. JAPSS Press, Inc., Florida, pp 151–164

Fagbule T, Rice, votes and violence: democracy in Nigeria. In: Business Day (29 July 2014). http://businessdayonline.com/2014/07/rice-votes-and-violence-democracy-in-nigeria/#.VJ2hJD10NjE. Accessed 26 Dec 2014

Fanon F (1963) The wretched of the Earth (trans: Farrington C). Grove Press, New York

Feit E (1968) Military coups and political development: some lessons from Ghana and Nigeria. World Polit 20(2):179–193

Fraser N (1989) Talking about needs: interpretive contests as political conflicts in welfare-state societies. Ethics 99:291–313

Frederick OO, Asmuni A, Idris K, Othman J (2013) The causes, effects and potential solutions to the deep-rooted Niger Delta oil crisis. Int J Soc Behav Sci 1(6):122–129

Giddens A (1994) Beyond left and right: the future of radical politics. Polity Press, Cambridge

Gurr T (1968) A causal model of civil strife: a comparative model using new indices. Am Polit Sci Rev 62:1104–1124

Habermas J (1996) Three normative models of democracy. In: Benhabib S (ed) Democracy and difference: contesting the boundaries of the political. Princeton University Press, Princeton, pp 21–30

Howard R (1980) The dilemma of human rights in Sub-Saharan Africa. Int J 35:724–747

Human Rights Watch, Political violence. http://www.hrw.org/reports/2007/nigeria1007/4.htm. Accessed 26 Dec 2014

Jackson H, Rosberg CG (1986) Sovereignty and underdevelopment: juridical statehood in the African crisis. J Mod Afr Stud 24(1):1–31

Jegede AO (2013) From military rule to constitutional government: the case of Nigeria. In: Mbondenyi MK, Ojienda T (eds) Constitutionalism and democratic governance in Africa: contemporary perspectives from Sub-Saharan Africa. Pretoria University Law Press, Pretoria, pp 337–354

Kolakowski L (1990) Uncertainties of a democratic age. J Democr 1(1):47–50

Laakso L (2007) Insights into electoral violence in Africa. In: Basedau M, Erdmann G, Mehler A (eds) Votes, money and violence: political parties and elections in Sub-Saharan Africa. University of KwaZulu-Natal Press, Pietermaritzburg, pp 224–252

Lasisi A, Augoye J, A history of protests against subsidy removal. http://www.punchng.com/news/a-history-of-protests-against-subsidy-removal/. Accessed 10 Sept 2012

Last M (2008–2009) The pattern of dissent: *Boko Haram* in Nigeria 2009. Annu Rev Islam Afr 10:7–11

Lewis P (2003) Nigeria: elections in a fragile regime. J Democr 14(3):131–144
Leys C (1965) Violence in Africa. Transition 21:17–20
Louw DJ, Ubuntu: an African assessment of the religious order. http://www.bu.edu/wcp/Papers/Afri/AfriLouw.htm. Accessed 13 July 2013
Mamdani M (1990) The social basis of constitutionalism in Africa. J Mod Afr Stud 28:359–374
Mamdani M (2002) Making sense of political violence in postcolonial Africa. Identity Cult Polit 3(2):1–24
Manin B, Stein E, Mansbridge J (1987) On legitimacy and political deliberation. Polit Theory 15:338–368
Mbembe A (1992) Provisional notes on the postcolony. Africa 62(1):3–37
Mehler A (2007) Political parties and violence in Africa: systematic reflections against empirical backgrounds. In: Basedau M, Erdmann G, Mehler A (eds) Votes, money and violence: political parties and elections in Sub-Saharan Africa. University of KwaZulu-Natal Press, Pietermaritzburg, pp 194–223
Miller NE (1941) The frustration – aggression hypothesis. Psychol Rev 48:337–342
Mouffe C (2005) On the political: thinking in action. Routledge, New York
Muzan AO (2014) Insurgency in Nigeria: addressing the causes as part of the solution. Afr Hum Rights Law J 14:217–243
National Mirror, One year after Occupy Nigeria protests. http://nationalmirroronline.net/new/one-year-after-occupy-nigeria-protests/. Accessed 18 Jan 2014
News24 Nigeria, Niger Delta militants threaten war if Jonathan loses election. http://www.news24.com.ng/Elections/News/Niger-Delta-militants-threaten-war-if-Jonathan-loses-election-20150125. Accessed 05 Feb 2015
Ologbenla D (2003) Political instability, conflict and the 2003 general elections. In: Anifowose R, Babawale T (eds) General elections and democratic consolidation in Nigeria. Friedrich Ebert Stiftung, Abuja, pp 69–102
Ologbenla D (2011) Evaluation of election violence in Nigeria: the involvement of the youth. Commun Rev 5(2):1–25
Olowu D (2013) Constitutional governance, democratisation and military legacies in post-independence Nigeria. In: Mbondenyi MK, Ojienda T (eds) Constitutionalism and democratic governance in Africa: contemporary perspectives from Sub-Saharan Africa. Pretoria University Law Press, Pretoria, pp 315–336
Olson M (1963) Rapid growth as a destabilising force. J Econ Hist 23(4):529–552
Olukoshi AO (2000) Economy and politics in the Nigerian transition. Afr J Polit Sci 5:5–29
Onebamhoi ON, Curbing electoral violence in Nigeria: the imperative of political education. http://www.ajol.info/index.php/afrrev/article/view/72297/61230 Accessed 02 Feb 2015
Onuoha FC, Boko Haram: Nigeria's extremists Islamic sect. http://studies.aljazeera.net/ResourceGallery/media/Documents/2012/2/29/2012229113341793734BOKO%20HARAM%20NIGERIAS%20EXTREMIST%20ISLAMIC%20SECT.pdf. Accessed 04 Jan 2015
Owolabi O, Okwechime I (2007) Oil and security in Nigeria: the Niger Delta crisis. Afr Dev 32(1):1–40
Pateman C (1970) Participation and democratic theory. Cambridge University Press, New York
Perinbam BM (1973) Fanon and the revolutionary peasantry – the Algerian case. J Mod Afr Stud 11:427–445
Pointblanknews.com, Nigeria will not negotiate with Boko Haram – Mark. http://pointblanknews.com/pbn/press-releases/nigeria-will-not-negotiate-with-boko-haram-mark/. Accessed 08 Feb 2015
Rodney W (1973) How Europe under-developed Africa. Tanzanian Publishing House, Dar –Es – Salaam
Roux T (2006) Democracy. In: Woolman S, Bishop M (eds) Constitutional law of South Africa, 2nd edn. Juta and Co, Calremont, pp 10-1–10-77

Sahara Reporters, Australian negotiator insists Modu Sheriff, Ihejirika sponsor Boko Haram, exonerates Buhari, El-Rufai. http://saharareporters.com/2014/08/31/australian-negotiator-insists-modu-sheriff-ihejirika-sponsor-boko-haram-exonerates-buhari. Accessed 01 Sept 2014
Sahara Reporters (2015a) Full text of the press release from the PPPRA announcing removal of fuel subsidy. http://saharareporters.com/2012/01/01/full-text-press-release-pppra-announcing-removal-fuel-subsidy. Accessed 13 May 2015
Sahara Reporters (2015b) NLC did not consult us before calling off strike action-Civil Society Groups. http://saharareporters.com/2012/01/16/nlc-did-not-consult-us-calling-strike-action-civil-society-groups. Accessed 13 May 2015
Sheth DL (2005) Micro-movements in India: towards a new politics of participatory democracy. In: De Sousa SB (ed) Democratising democracy: beyond the liberal democratic cannon. Verso, New York, pp 3–37
Solomon H (2012) Counter-terrorism in Nigeria. RUSI J 157(4):6–11
'The life and death of Ken Saro-Wiwa: a history of the struggle for justice in the Niger Delta. http://remembersarowiwa.com/wp-content/uploads/life_death_ksw.pdf. Accessed 31 Jan 2015
The Punch (03 March 2015a) Boko Haram: is the military protecting civilians? http://www.punchng.com/opinion/boko-haram-is-the-military-protecting-civilians/. Accessed 16 May 2015
The Punch (17 January 2015b) APC secretariat bombed again in Rivers. http://www.punchng.com/news/apc-secretariat-bombed-again-in-rivers/. Accessed 22 Jan 2015
The Punch (22 January 2015c) Gunmen attack Ekiti APC secretariat. http://www.punchng.com/news/gunmen-attack-ekiti-apc-secretariat/. Accessed 22 Jan 2015
The Punch (21 May 2015d) I conceded defeat to prevent crisis – Jonathan. http://www.punchng.com/news/i-conceded-defeat-to-prevent-crisis-jonathan/. Accessed 09 June 2015
This Day Live (08 November 2011) Fuel subsidy: stakeholders' quest for vital policy framework blueprint. http://www.thisdaylive.com/articles/fuel-subsidy-stakeholders-quest-for-vital-policy-framework-blueprint/102287/. Accessed 13 May 2015
This Day Live (29 August 2014) Australian negotiator names Ihejirika, Sheriff as sponsors of Boko Haram. http://www.thisdaylive.com/articles/australian-negotiator-names-ihejirika-sheriff-as-sponsors-of-boko-haram/187635/. Accessed 30 Aug 2014
This Day Live (22 May 2015) Nigeria would have been in crisis if Jonathan did not concede defeat, says Buhari. http://www.thisdaylive.com/articles/nigeria-would-have-been-in-crisis-if-jonathan-did-not-concede-defeat-says-buhari/209978/. Accessed 09 June 2015
Top of FormUgochukwu B (2012) Ballot or bullet: protecting the right to vote in Nigeria. Afr Hum Rights Law J 12:539–563
Uprimmy R, Garcia–Villegas M (2005) The constitutional court and social emancipation in Colombia. In: De Sousa SB (ed) Democratising democracy: beyond the liberal democratic cannon. Verso, New York, pp 66–100
USIP, What is Boko Haram? http://www-dev.usip.org/sites/default/files/SR308.pdf. Accessed 04 Jan 2015
Van de Wall N (2003) Presidentialism and clientelism in Africa's emerging party systems. J Mod Afr Stud 41(2):297–321
Van der Walt AJ (2008) Normative pluralism and anarchy: reflection on 2007 term. Const Court Rev 1:77–128
Vanguard (09 January 2012) Fuel subsidy removal: a Nigerian dilemma. http://www.vanguardngr.com/2012/01/fuel-subsidy-removal-a-nigerian-dilemma/. Accessed 13 May 2015
Warren M (2002) Deliberative democracy. In: Carrter A, Stokes G (eds) Democratic theory today: challenges for the 21st century polity. Polity Press, Cambridge, pp 173–202
Westley WA (1966) The escalation of violence through legitimation. Ann Am Acad Polit Soc Sci 364:120–126
Wiredu K, Democracy and consensus in African traditional politics: a plea for a non-party polity. http://them.polylog.org/2/fwk-en.htm. Accessed 14 July 2013

Yahoo News, Once a force for good, Nigeria's military, through militias, crosses border into darkness. https://za.news.yahoo.com/once-force-for-good--nigeria-s-military--through-militias--crosses-border-into-darkness-161348616.html. Accessed 11 Sept 2014

Yahoo News, Angry youths stone Nigerian leader's convoy; police fire gas. http://news.yahoo.com/angry-youths-stone-nigerian-leaders-convoy-police-fire-140709557.html. Accessed 30 Jan 2015

Zolberg AR (1968) The structure of political conflict in the new states of tropical Africa. Am Polit Sci Rev 62:70–87

Zurn CF (2002) Deliberative democracy and constitutional review. Law Philos 21:467–542

Chapter 4
Responding to Foreign Insurgencies in the Eastern DRC

Ngoie Ngalingi Ngoto

4.1 Overview of Foreign Insurgencies Acting in the Eastern DRC

Four foreign rebel movements have been particularly active in the eastern DRC, including Allied Democratic Forces-National Army for the Liberation of Uganda (ADF/NALU), Forces Démocratiques pour la Libération du Rwanda[1] (FDLR), FLN and Lord's Resistance Army (LRA).

4.1.1 ADF/NALU

4.1.1.1 Background

The ADF/NALU is a joint venture of two Ugandan rebel movements. Each of them had their own history until their destinies crossed and merged into a single one. The NALU finds its historical roots in the first Rwenzururu independence movement, formed in the ethnic crucible of the Bakonzo community, a minority tribe in western Uganda. Between 1967 and 1982, the Rwenzururu movement conducted a low-intensity guerrilla war in an attempt to gain the Ugandan government's recognition of the Kingdom of Rwenzururu. Milton Obote appointed a member of the community in his cabinet and granted autonomy to the Kingdom of Rwenzururu rather than independence. He managed to end the struggle. In 1986, Yoweri Museveni overthrew Milton Obote's government. Then deposed regime's head of intelligence

[1] The English translation for this is Democratic Forces for the Liberation of Rwanda.

N. N. Ngoto (✉)
Faculty of Law, University of Kisangani, Kisangani, Democratic Republic of the Congo
University of Pretoria, Pretoria, South Africa
e-mail: jose.ngoto@unikis.ac.cd

J.-M. Iyi, H. Strydom (eds.), *Boko Haram and International Law*,
https://doi.org/10.1007/978-3-319-74957-0_4

services, Amon Bazira, created the NALU. This movement brought together supporters of former Ugandan presidents Milton Obote and Idi Amin Dada. In 1988, the Ugandan army chassed the NALU from Uganda. The group established itself in the Congolese territories of Beni and Lubero.[2]

The Muslim movements of Uganda suffered oppression from the Milton Obote and Yoweri Museveni governments. They sought and obtained financial support from the Sudanese government to recruit Ugandan youth and became a major player in the local Muslim community. On 22 March 1991, a violent confrontation between Tabligh members and members of the Ugandan Muslim Supreme Council (UMSC) in Kampala caused five dead, including four police officers. This violence justified the arrest of Tabligh leaders, including Jamil Mukulu, between 1991 and 1993. After their release, the group's members, led by Sheikh Sulaiman Kakeeto, established themselves in Hoima, western Uganda. In 1994, they created the Movement of Ugandan Combatants for Freedom, which immediately received support from Khartoum. Kampala destroyed the movement's training camp in 1995. The UFFM combatants took refuge in the Congolese town of Bunia, whereas the leaders of the Tabligh movement in Uganda, including Sheikh Sulaiman Kakeeto and Jamil Mukulu, fled to Kenya and Tanzania.[3]

In September 1995, a NALU leader and Yusuf Kabanda, a comrade of Jamil Mukulu, formed an alliance between their two movements. They named the newly born movement the Allied Democratic Forces-National Army for the Liberation of Uganda (ADF/NALU). The Muslim combatants stationed in Bunia fled to Beni, where they joined the NALU personnel. Congolese officers received and trained ADF/NALU militiamen. The ADF/NALU openly recruited with the support of the Congolese government, mainly among the Muslim community in Beni.[4]

4.1.1.2 Aims and Objectives

The ADF/NALU claims to pursue the overthrow of the government of President Yoweri Museveni. However, it is difficult to verify this stated objective. This is why many observers describe the ADF/NALU as rebellion without a cause.[5]

4.1.1.3 Leadership and Networks

Between 1995 and 2005, the ADF/NALU alliance had consisted of a political branch, the Allied Democratic Movement (ADM), and a military branch, the Allied Democratic Forces (ADF). The military branch reported to the political branch made up of joint ADF/NALU leadership. Jamil Makulu is believed to be the top

[2] International Crisis Group (2012), pp. 2–3.

[3] International Crisis Group (2012), p. 4.

[4] International Crisis Group (2012), p. 4.

[5] Conflict & Transitions Consultancies (2007), p. 83.

political leader of the ADM.[6] Jamil Mukulu was born in 1961. Initially a catholic and critical of Islam, he converted to Islam after following Tabliq Jamaat teachings. He reportedly lived in Khartoum (Sudan) early 1990s and allegedly became close to Osama Bin Laden, the founder of al-Qaeda.[7]

In its beginnings, the ADF/NALU benefited from the support of Congolese and Sudanese governments. The government of Sudan offered intelligence support, weapons and coordination, as well as access to training facilities in Juba (southern Sudan).[8] The Congolese regime offered military basis, financial support and military training. The main rationale for this support of the ADF/NALU alliance was the destabilisation of President Museveni.[9] The government of Sudan decided to destabilise President Museveni to prevent him from supporting the armed struggle of the Sudan People's Liberation Army (SPLA).[10] The Mobutu regime also aided this movement that it believed to be a counter-force to the growing Uganda-Rwandan collaboration against Hutu militias in eastern Zaïre.

After the collapse of the Mobutu regime in 1997, the ADF/NALU was forced to rely on the support of the local population for its survival. The ADF/NALU excelled in the harvesting and commercialisation of timber and coffee, often illegally exported to Uganda through local commercial networks. The ADF/NALU is still heavily involved in the exploitation and trafficking of diamonds and minerals, mainly gold and coltan.[11] The group reportedly maintains a network of cars and motorcycle taxis operating between the DRC towns of Beni, Butembo and Oicha, which generates some income.[12] The group reportedly receives financial support through money transfers from London, Kenya and Uganda, which are directed to the group's intermediaries in Beni and Butembo.

There are allegations of financial support to the ADF/NALU from al-Qaeda groups, as well as from al-Shabaab.[13] The Group of Experts on the Democratic Republic of the Congo followed up those allegations but found no evidence to support such a connection. High-level officials of the Democratic Republic of the Congo and Uganda informed the group that there was no evidence linking the ADF to those groups.

4.1.1.4 Operations

Since 1996, the ADF/NALU has killed more than 2000 people and has forced the displacement of more than half a million people. Local farmers suffer continuous insecurity and the threat of landmines or being abducted or killed by ADF/NALU

[6] Conflict & Transitions Consultancies (2007), p. 84.

[7] Sunguta West (2015), p. 6.

[8] See Conflict & Transitions Consultancies (2007), p. 81.

[9] Conflict & Transitions Consultancies (2007), p. 81.

[10] Conflict & Transitions Consultancies (2007), p. 81.

[11] Sunguta West (2015).

[12] Sunguta West (2015).

[13] See S/2015/797 para. 21.

rebels. In addition to small-scale raids on individual farmers or small groups of civilians, the ADF/NALU, like BOKO HARAM, also targeted schools. In February 1998, they abducted 30 students. In June 1998, they burnt to death at least 50 students, and they abducted more than 200 others. Between 2014 and 2016, they killed at least 500 people in the eastern DRC.[14]

4.1.2 FDLR

4.1.2.1 Background

In the immediate aftermath of the Rwandan genocide in 1994, the majority of Hutu Rwandan refugees fled to the DRC (Zaïre). The cohort encompassed ordinary civilians led by former government officials, former army officials and a large number of the Interahamwe militia. The fugitives of the Habyarimana regime and the political actors that played a key role in the genocide created a Rwandan government in exile in the eastern DRC refugee camps. Fearing prosecutions, the majority of the wealthier refugees personally incriminated in the genocide fled onwards to destinations like France, Belgium, Canada or francophone African countries that offered them security and a comfortable life in exile. Those who remained created the Rassemblement pour le retour des Réfugiés Rwandais (RDR).[15]

With the support of the Mobutu regime, the RDR recruited and trained refugees and launched military operations in Rwanda. The militia grew as large as 70,000 men. Given the diverse background of the militia, they called themselves Interahamwe.[16] In 1996, the government of Rwanda prompted and backed the rebellion of the Alliance des Forces pour la Libération du Congo[17] (AFDL) with Laurent Désiré Kabila. The RDR could not resist the attacks from AFDL backed by the Rwandan Patriotic Army (RPA). The militia collapsed, and around one million refugees returned to Rwanda. A number of 30,000 militiamen reportedly settled back in Rwanda on the same occasion.

Those who remained in the Congo reorganised progressively and created the Armée pour la Libération du Rwanda[18] (ALIR). They even fought in the ranks of General Sassou Nguesso against then President Pascal Lissouba. The ALIR failed to maintain unity and discipline. In 1998, Laurent Desiré Kabila strongly disagreed with his Rwandan and Ugandan allies. Uganda prompted a rebellion in the western part of the Congo under the leadership of Jean Pierre Bemba.[19] Rwanda

---

[14] Conflict & Transitions Consultancies (2007), p. 81.

[15] This means: Assembly for the return of Rwandese Refugees.

[16] This means: those who combat together.

[17] This means: Alliance of Forces for the Liberation of Congo.

[18] This means: Army for the Liberation of Rwanda.

[19] Human Rights Watch (March 2001), p. 16.

prompted a rebellion in northern and southern Kivu.[20] The government of the Congo decided to cooperate with the Rwandan militiamen disseminated in the eastern part of the DRC. This is how the FDLR came into existence in May 2000 in the town of Lubumbashi. In the beginning, the FDLR tried to distance itself from the genocidaires. But progressively they occupied key positions in its hierarchy.[21]

4.1.2.2 Aims and Objectives

One can classify FDLR's objectives as official and hidden. Officially, the FDLR pursues peace and reconciliation in Rwanda and the Great Lakes region in general. Off the records, in their communications with combatants and the refugees, FDLR leaders affirm that their real objectives are to overthrow the current government of Rwanda, pardon those who played a role in the genocide and establish a majority Hutu government.[22]

4.1.2.3 Leadership, Strength and Networks

The FDLR has a political wing and a military one. The latter is called the Forces Combattantes[23] Abacunguzi (FOCA). Murwanashyaka conducts the political wing, while General Mudacumura commands the FOCA. The relationship between the two wings is undisclosed. But one can mention the cleavages between those supporting Murwanashyaka and the ones supporting Mudacumura. The former claims that Murwanashyaka is the soul of the FDLR because he provides the means of the fight, while the latter accuses him of spending a lavish life in Europe while Mudacumura is battling on the field.

Conflict & Transition Consultancies believes that the FDLR currently has a military strength (including military police) of approximately 7000 combatants. The FDLR was significantly stronger a few years ago, with an estimated 15,000–20,000 armed combatants as recently as 2003. The strength has waned as a result of failed military operations, casualties, disease, defections, repatriation and retirements.[24] The FDLR has also armed many Rwandese civilian refugees. Consequently, the Congolese, as well as foreigners, fail to distinguish between armed Rwandese civilians and combatants. It is even more difficult to estimate the number of civilians associated with the FDLR.[25] The FDLR has cells or satellites in numerous countries: Republic of the Congo, Tanzania, Sudan, Zambia,

[20] Human Rights Watch (March 2001), p. 10.

[21] Conflict & Transitions Consultancies (2007), p. 11. See also SSRC (March 2014), p. 2.

[22] Conflict & Transitions Consultancies (2007), p. 45.

[23] Combatant Forces.

[24] Conflict & Transitions Consultancies (2007), p. 47.

[25] Conflict & Transitions Consultancies (2007), p. 48.

Cameroon, Uganda, Zimbabwe, Mozambique, South Africa, Germany, Belgium, France, Norway, the Netherlands, Austria, Switzerland, Sweden, Denmark, Canada and the USA.[26]

4.1.2.4 Key Operations

The first key operation of the FDLR in connection with its stated objective was baptised 'Opération Amizero'. The aim of Amizero included forced recruitment in primary and secondary schools in Rwanda, political propaganda (instilling a political ideology among women and youth to 'love their country'), identification of markets to purchase arms, training of combatants, identification of targets for sabotage and distributing arms. FDLR deserters warned the government of Rwanda. This explained in part the failure of Amizero. Another explanation came from the lack of means to implement the operation. The FDLR continues to plan attacks against Rwanda in order to overthrow the sitting government. The real goal of the threat of overthrowing the government seems to be forcing the government to accept a dialogue or a power-sharing agreement. The FDLR has set its basis in the DRC while maintaining intelligence network in Rwanda.

In the DRC, the two sides to the conflicts, including the Congolese army and the FDLR, have perpetrated mass atrocities. The civilian population paid for its alleged support to the opposite camp: the FDLR punished the population for the Congolese army's choice to breach the alliance with them, whereas the Congolese army punished civilians for their alleged support to the FDLR.[27] Human Rights Watch reported the killing of more than 1400 civilians between January and September 2009. It documented over 7500 cases of sexual violence against women and girls over the first nine months of 2009. It reported that, in addition to killings and rapes, thousands of civilians have been abducted and used as forced labour to carry weapons, ammunition or other baggage by government forces and FDLR militia as they deploy from place to place. These forces killed civilians who refused. Other civilians died due to the overload of the baggage. The military operations forced almost a million of civilians to flee from their homes.[28] According to HRW, between January and September 2009, the FDLR deliberately killed at least 701 civilians in North and South Kivu. They killed them by different means, including chopping to death by machete or hoe, shooting and burning to death in their homes.[29]

---

[26] Conflict & Transitions Consultancies (2007), p. 49.

[27] This reality on the ground has prompted Human Right Watch to entitle its report (cited above) 'You will be punished'.

[28] Conflict & Transitions Consultancies (2007), p. 10.

[29] Conflict & Transitions Consultancies (2007), pp. 12, 51–70.

4.1.3 FNL[30]

In 1972, the Micombero[31] regime committed acts of genocide against Hutus. The Hutus resisted in many ways until they decided to create the PALIPEHUTU (*Parti pour la Libération du Peuple Hutu*).[32] This party used to have a military wing called FNL (*Forces Nationales de Libération*). The political objective of the FNL is to institutionalise a Burundian state that is ruled by the ethnic majority in a proportion that reflects the actual ethnic demographics of the Burundian population. The FNL seeks 85% of positions in the government, army and the judiciary for the Hutu ethnic group.[33] Although the FNL acknowledges that there are also poor Tutsis, the party insists that the Hutus are poorer (as a result of repression and discrimination).[34] It is of the view that a new government needs to help them escape the poverty trap.[35]

Between 1991 and 1993, the FNL benefited from increased support of the government of Rwanda. The Habyarimana regime considered the FNL to be an ally against the insurgency of the Rwanda Patriotic Front (RPF) in Rwanda.[36] The FNL reportedly receives some material from the FDLR as the FNL continues to facilitate the infiltration of the FDLR into southern Rwanda via Burundi.[37] The FNL has concentrated its forces in the eastern DRC in a single camp in the vicinity of Sake, not far from Uvira town.[38] However, the FNL has never played a major role in the DRC civil war.

4.1.4 LRA

4.1.4.1 Background

Apollo Milton Obote has ruled Uganda twice, including from 1966 to 1972 and from 1980 to 1985. He came from the Lango ethnic group, one of minorities in Uganda. During his tenures, the army was Acholi dominated. At the downfall of his first tenure in 1972, President Idi Amin Dada ordered that all the Acholi soldiers return to barracks, where they underwent an ethnic cleansing.[39] In 1986, when President Museveni came to power, fearing a repetition of the 1972 cleansing, they

[30] Conflict & Transitions Consultancies (2007), pp. 11–12.

[31] Michel MICOMBERO ruled Burundi between 1966 and 1976.

[32] Conflict & Transitions Consultancies (2007), p. 69.

[33] Conflict & Transitions Consultancies (2007), p. 71.

[34] Conflict & Transitions Consultancies (2007), p. 71.

[35] Conflict & Transitions Consultancies (2007), p. 71.

[36] Conflict & Transitions Consultancies (2007), p. 70.

[37] Conflict & Transitions Consultancies (2007), p. 74.

[38] Conflict & Transitions Consultancies (2007), p. 75.

[39] Van Acker (2004), p. 340.

refused to report to barracks. Acholi political and military leaders failed to protect Acholi interests. In that vacuum, two young Acholi in their twenties (Alice Lakwena and Joseph Kony) suggested a holistic solution based on healing and cleansing. Alice Lakwena created the Holy Spirit Mobile Forces (HSMF), which included former soldiers, students and other civilians.[40] They believed to fight under the inspiration and the protection of the Holy Spirit. Joseph Kony served as an altar boy in the HSMF.[41] But the latter did not last long. 'Prophet' Joseph Kony created the Lord's Resistance Army (LRA) in 1988.

4.1.4.2 Aims and Objectives

The media present the LRA as a religiously motivated terrorist group without political agenda, whereas the LRA displays itself as a political group driven by a desire for a rule of law based on the Ten Commandments.[42] The LRA has published manifestos over the years calling for the restoration of multiparty politics and the introduction of constitutional federalism.[43] It also called for support for human rights, the development of a nationwide socio-economic balance, the promotion of peace and security and ending corruption. It has seriously questioned the concentration of military, legislative and executive powers in the hands of President Museveni.

4.1.4.3 Leadership, Networks and Strength

Joseph Kony is the chairman of the LRA. Vincent Otti has seconded him for a long time. Commanders Dominic Ongwen and Okot Odhiambo[44] have played major roles in the LRA's fight. In 2014, Joseph Kony appointed his son Salim Saleh, aged 22, as his deputy in the LRA command. LRA has benefited from the support of the Acholi community in Uganda, as well as in exile.[45] It has also received an open and remarkable support from the government of Khartoum in order to destabilise the government of Kampala, which was supporting the struggle for independence of South Sudan.[46] The LRA established political alliance with Colonel Kizza Besigye, the famous opponent of President Museveni. The government of Uganda once accused Rwanda of supporting this alliance through its proxies in the DRC.[47] The LRA has taken

---

[40] Van Acker (2004), p. 347.

[41] Van Acker (2004), p. 347.

[42] Small Arms Survey HSBA Working Paper 8, p. 15.

[43] Small Arms Survey HSBA Working Paper 8, p. 15.

[44] He died in 2015.

[45] Van Acker (2004), p. 352.

[46] Small Arms Survey HSBA Working Paper 8, p. 24.

[47] Van Acker, Idem, p. 353.

advantage of the proliferation of small arms due to conflicts in the DRC and South Sudan. It has also built a partnership with the nomad pastor Mbororos in the DRC and CAR.[48]

There is no precision on the organisation and size of LRA's military wing. In essence, the LRA once reached a pick of several thousands of fighters in 2003, and it dwindled to roughly 200–400 fighters in 2011.[49]

4.1.4.4 Key Operations

The LRA has been responsible for numerous atrocities, including massacres, summary executions, torture, rape, pillage and forced labour. It is also known for its massive abduction of children and their use in combat operations.[50] When the LRA moved to the DRC, in 2006, it did not target the Congolese people. It only started violence on Congolese civilians in September 2008.[51] Its first wave of attacks apparently aimed at punishing local communities that helped the defectors to escape.

For instance, between 14 and 17 December 2009, the LRA carried out a horrific attack in Makombo, a remote area in the Haut-Uele district in Orientale province of the DRC.[52] During this carefully planned operation, the LRA killed more than 321 civilians and abducted more than 250 others, including around 80 children.[53] The majority of those killed were adult men. The LRA combatants first tied them up and then either hacked them up to death with machetes or crushed their skulls with axes or heavy wooden sticks.[54] They killed the abductees who walked too slowly, who refused or were unable to carry the heavy loads or who tried to escape. During their captivity, the abducted children were taught to kill. The LRA forces them to undergo a so-called military training, and at the end of which 9- to 15-year-old boys and girls are able to kill without hesitation.[55] Thereafter, they follow a ritual to consecrate their affiliation with the LRA and make them 'invulnerable' to bullets. Most of the abducted girls were subjected to sexual slavery. They were assigned as wives to LRA commanders, who usually tortured them.[56] Women underwent the same treatment, and along with men, they were used as porters.[57] The LRA atrocity in the DRC clearly amounts to war crimes and crimes against humanity under the ICC Rome Statute.

[48] The Enough Project (November 2010), p. 15.

[49] Kisiangani (2011), p. 5.

[50] See Human Rights Watch (March 2010), p. 13.

[51] See Human Rights Watch (February 2009), p. 20.

[52] See Human Rights Watch (March 2010), p. 18.

[53] Human Rights Watch (March 2010), p. 18.

[54] Human Rights Watch (March 2010), p. 18.

[55] Human Rights Watch (March 2010), p. 39.

[56] Human Rights Watch (March 2010), p. 40.

[57] Human Rights Watch (March 2010), p. 41.

Between 2012 and 2015, the LRA has reportedly perpetrated 44 attacks, three murders and 85 abductions. As of 2015, over 162,000 people remain displaced in the Bas-Uélé and Haut-Uélé provinces, which host an estimated 9243 CAR refugees.[58]

4.2 Responses to Foreign Insurgencies in the DRC

National governments bear the legal responsibility to protect civilians living on their territories. The responsibility to protect entails the responsibility to prevent, to react and to rebuild.[59] The effective prevention requires knowledge of the fragility of the situation and the risk associated with it (so-called early warning). It also requires the understanding and availability of measures aiming at addressing the roots of serious conflicts.[60] As for the responsibility to react, it requires that appropriate responses be given to situations where human rights are at risk. These measures may include peaceful or coercive measures. The collection of evidence and information requires greater use of impartial non-governmental sources for accurate, reliable reports and greater use of independent fact-finding missions by the Security Council or the Secretary General.[61]

The responsibility to rebuild entails principally security concern. After mass atrocity, the state or the international community should grant a minimum of security and protection to the entire population, without discrimination based on ethnic origin or relation to the previous regime. To this end, they should work at disarmament, demobilisation and reintegration of armed groups and at the rebuilding of new national armed forces and police, with the integration, as far as possible, of elements of formerly competing armed factions.[62] In 2005, heads of state convened a World Summit in order to formalise the responsibility to protect. They unanimously affirmed states' responsibility to protect their populations from international crimes.[63] They agreed on the assistance of the international community to states in the exercise of the responsibility to protect and in building their capacities. They also agreed on the necessity of UN's timely and decisive action in case of a state's failure to fulfil its responsibility to protect.[64]

The UN Secretary General suggests a three-pillar approach for the implementation of the responsibility to protect, including the following:

---

[58] OCHA (April–June 2015).

[59] See WFM-IGP (2001), p. 4.

[60] See S/RES/1533 (2004) as example for arm embargo.

[61] See WFM-IGP (2001), p. 6.

[62] See WFM-IGP (2001), p. 6.

[63] See A/RES/60/1 para 138.

[64] See Id para 139.

- pillar one: state's responsibility to protect its population from international crimes and their incitement;
- pillar two: the readiness of the international community to assist states in meeting their obligations related to the RtoP;
- pillar three: the international community's responsibility to respond in a timely and decisive manner when a state is either unable or unwilling to fulfil its RtoP.[65]

It is appropriate to assess different responses to foreign insurgencies in the DRC with regard to the three pillars of the responsibility to protect.

4.3 Responses from the DRC

The government of the DRC has shown a commitment to end foreign insurgencies in its territory. However, it faces serious difficulties. On the one hand, it has no enough military forces to handle all insurgencies: apart from foreign insurgencies, the DRC also faces numerous internal rebellions. On the other hand, in most cases, foreign rebels are mixed with the Congolese population, they live together and they have married Congolese wives, and they do not control any part of the territory. So it is quite difficult to launch military operations against them. Notwithstanding those difficulties, the DRC has launched operation Sukola[66] II against the FDLR. This military operation has remarkably reduced the strength of the FDLR.[67]

The Congolese judiciary has prosecuted foreign insurgents. In its judgment of 11 August 2011, the military tribunal of Bukavu[68] convicted Maniraguha Jean Bosco alias Kazungu and Sibomana Kabanda alias Tuzargwana, both FDLR militiamen and Rwandese. The latter was serving as bodyguard of the former. Maniraguha Jean Bosco alias Kazungu faced charges related to crimes against humanity through murder and rape. The indictment states that he had, between June and July 2006 and January 2007, caused the death of Mister Mbimbi, burned 56 houses in the Rwamikundu village and caused the death of 52 other people.[69] The two accused (Maniraguha and Sibomana) faced charges of crimes against humanity through imprisonment as a way of deprivation of physical liberty, torture, rape of several women in inhumane conditions.[70] A total of 400 victims participated in the proceedings of their civil claims. The tribunal sentenced the accused to 30 years of imprisonment.[71] As for the civil claim, the tribunal ordered the Congolese government to pay reparation to victims due to its failure to fulfil its responsibility to protect, as

[65] See ICRtoP (2011), p. 1.

[66] Sukola means Clean.

[67] S/2015/797, para. 26–29.

[68] Bukavu is a town in the South Kivu province.

[69] See Tribunal Militaire de Garnison de Bukavu, RP 275/09 et 521/10.

[70] They raped women after having attached them and (or) while they menstruated.

[71] See Tribunal Militaire de Garnison de Bukavu, idem.

prescribed by article 52 of the Congolese constitution.[72] One should mention the proceedings of the International Criminal Court against foreign militiamen for their activity in the DRC. The ICC is complementary to Congolese jurisdiction.[73] Therefore, it acts whenever Congolese jurisdictions are either unable or unwilling to prosecute international crimes.

The ICC indicted Callixte Mbarushimana for international crimes committed during widespread and systematic attacks launched by the FDLR against the civilian population in the North Kivu province during 2009.[74] French authorities arrested him on 11 October 2010 and transferred him to The Hague on 25 January 2011. On 16 December 2011, the Pre-Trial Chamber declined to confirm the charges against him,[75] and he was released from the ICC's custody on 23 December 2011. The ICC's Prosecutor applied and obtained an arrest warrant for Mr Mudacumura, the commander of FDLR's military wing. The prosecution believes that he is criminally responsible for committing nine counts of war crimes, from 20 January 2009 to the end of September 2010, in the context of the conflict in the North and South Kivu provinces of the DRC.[76] This includes attacking civilians, murder, mutilation, cruel treatment, rape, torture, destruction of property, pillaging and outrages against personal dignity. Mudacumura is still at large. The ICC has also indicted Joseph Kony and Dominic Ongwen for their activities in Uganda.

4.4 Responses from the International Community

Responses come from national governments and regional organisations.

4.4.1 National Governments

The governments of the Great Lakes region are fully conscious of the incapacity of the Congolese government to achieve the dismantling of foreign rebellions alone. They have conducted joint military operation with the Congolese army, and those operations have sensibly reduced the strength of the ADF and FDLR. However, the history of violence in the Great Lakes leaves small room for trustworthiness between governments of the region. The DRC has supported the ADF/NALU against Uganda and the FDLR against RWANDA.[77] Uganda has prompted the MLC of Jean Pierre

[72] Tribunal Militaire de Garnison de Bukavu, RP 275/09 et 521/10.

[73] ICC Statute, article 17.

[74] See Warrant of Arrest for Callixte Mbarushimana, No.: ICC-01/04-01/10.

[75] See decision No ICC-01/04-01/10, para 134.

[76] Situation in the Democratic Republic of The Congo, case N° ICC-01/04-01/10.

[77] Conflict & Transitions Consultancies (2007), p. 45.

Bemba against the DRC.[78] Rwanda has reportedly prompted RCD against the DRC.[79] Notwithstanding this lack of trustworthiness, the governments of Uganda and Rwanda have provided their support to the government of the DRC in order to dismantle the LRA,[80] ADF/NALU and FDLR.[81]

The US Army has provided remarkable support to Congolese forces in terms of training and operations aimed at tracking the LRA in the eastern DRC. Starting in October 2011, the USA has deployed approximately 100 U.S. military advisors to Uganda and to LRA-affected areas of CAR, South Sudan and the DRC to assist the Ugandan military in conducting counter-LRA operations.[82] The U.S. advisors have also trained small teams of DRC and South Sudanese forces engaged in counter-LRA operations. One should note that the Congolese government has strictly prohibited Ugandan troops from conducting counter-LRA operations within the DRC since 2011 due to political sensitivities, as well as allegations of Ugandan military involvement in resource smuggling. The Africa Command (AFRICOM) has sensibly decreased the strength of LRA and continues to support the regional force.[83]

4.4.2 Regional Organisations

In 2012, the African Union deployed a Regional Task Force (RTF) to tackle LRA in CAR, the DRC and South Sudan.[84] The RTF has remarkably contributed to the protection of civilians.[85] The presence of the RTF contingents has deterred LRA attacks; they have facilitated the defection and return of LRA combatants and abductees.

4.5 Responses from the United Nations

The UN has sent its most imposing peacekeeping mission to the DRC. The MONUC (MONUSCO) has conducted the DDRRR (disarmament, demobilisation, repatriation, reintegration and resettlement) of foreign rebels in the DRC. The DDRRR and the MONUC managed to repatriate approximately 13,000 Rwandan combatants and dependents. The majority of these belonged to the FDLR. To achieve this, MONUC conducted numerous missions into the forests of eastern Congo in order to seek out

[78] See Human Rights Watch (March 2001), p. 5.
[79] Human Rights Watch (March 2001), p. 5.
[80] US Congressional Research Service (2015), p. 10.
[81] See Human Rights Watch (December 2009), p. 85.
[82] US Congressional Research Service (2015), p. 10; Human Rights Watch (December 2009), p. 85.
[83] US Congressional Research Service (2015), p. 10.
[84] Conciliation Resources (May 2015), p. 8.
[85] Conciliation Resources (May 2015), p. 8.

the foreign combatants and encourage them to join the voluntary DDRRR process.[86] Furthermore, with the support of DFID, USAID and the World Bank, it developed and distributed public information tools, such as a Kinyarwanda radio programme, as well as pamphlets, videos and comics on the DDRRR process.[87] MONUC deployed serious efforts to convince the FDLR leadership to comply with its 2005 declaration after the Rome agreement and enter the DDRRR. This diplomacy caused the FDLR split.[88] Some of the FDLR junior commanders disobeyed the movement's leadership and went back to Rwanda.

Besides the DDRRR, the MONUC conducted fact-finding missions. It has investigated over the allegations of human rights violations committed by foreign-armed groups, as well as by the Congolese militia and Congolese army.[89] Between May 2008 and June 2009, the UN sent teams of officers from the United Nations Joint Human Rights Office (UNJHRO) in the DRC, on human rights violations committed by the LRA, under the command of Joseph Kony and other senior officers wanted by the ICC. The UNJHRO conducted a total of 14 missions, and during which it held dozens of meetings, conducted site visits and collected hundreds of testimonies from victims and witnesses.[90]

It is appropriate to mention that the Sukola II military operation was initially a joint operation between MONUSCO and the Congolese army.[91] But MONUSCO suspended its collaboration following the appointment of two generals (Brigadier General Bruno Mandevu to head the Sukola II operations and Brigadier General Fall Sikabwe to command the 34th Military Region of North Kivu), both of whom MONUSCO had criticised as having poor human rights records.

4.6 Conclusion

Foreign-armed groups have been active in the eastern DRC for the past two decades. Enjoying the sponsorship of some governments of the region, they have caused serious damages to local communities, including deaths, forced displacement, abduction, rape, pillaging. With the support of the international community, the Congolese army has managed to reduce their strength. The United Nations has offered to combatants a credible alternative to armed activity under the DDRRR programme.

The case of foreign insurgents in the DRC has some common grounds with the Boko Haram, including their international activities, their modus operandi (killings and abductions). No single country can manage to stop Boko Haram. Affected countries should seek the support of the United Nations, as well as the African

---

[86] See MONUC Bulletin, nº 208, p. 13.

[87] Echos de la MONUSCO (janvier 2015), p. 5.

[88] Echos de la MONUSCO (janvier 2015), p. 5.

[89] See http://monusco.unmissions.org. See also S/RES/1756 (2007) and S/RES/1794 (2007).

[90] MONUC/OHCHR (December 2009), p. 4.

[91] S/2015/797, para. 26.

Union. Furthermore, the International Criminal Court should open a case against Boko Haram leaders. Like in the DRC, the combination of national efforts, international community support and UN intervention will reduce the effects of Boko Haram and contribute to the fulfilment of the responsibility to protect.

References

Conciliation Resources (2015) In New Light: protection of civilians, the Lord's Resistance Army and the African Union Regional Task Force

Conflict & Transitions Consultancies (2007) Opportunities and constraints for disarmament & repatriation of foreign armed groups in the DRC: the cases of the FDLR, FNL and ADF/ NALU, June 2007

Decision No ICC -01/04-01/10

Echos de la MONUSCO, vol VII, N° 41, janvier 2015

http://monusco.unmissions.org. Accessed 30 Apr 2016

Human Rights Watch (March 2001) Uganda in EASTERN DRC: fuelling political and ethnic strife. vol 13, no 2(A)

Human Rights Watch (13 Dec 2009) "You Will Be Punished": Attacks on civilians in Eastern Congo

Human Rights Watch (28 March 2010) Trail of Death: LRA Atrocities in Northeaster Congo

ICC -01/04-01/10 Warrant of Arrest for Callixte Mbarushimana issued under seal on 28 September 2010

International Coalition for the Responsibility to Protect (ICRtoP), Clarifying the Third Pillar of the Responsibility to Protect: Timely and Decisive Response, 2011

International Crisis Group (19 Dec 2012) Eastern Congo: the ADF-NALU's lost rebellion

Kisiangani E (Dec 2011) Comparing Somalia's al Shabaab and Uganda's Lord's Resistance Army. ISS Paper 229

MONUC Bulletin, n° 208

MONUC/OHCHR (Dec 2009). Special Report: summary of fact-finding missions on alleged human rights violations committed by the Lord's Resistance Army (LRA) in the districts of Haut-Uélé and Bas-Uélé in Orientale province of the Democratic Republic of Congo

Office of the CHA (Apr–Jun 2015) LRA regional update, Central African Republic, DR Congo and South Sudan. Available at http://ea.humanitarianresponse.info. Accessed 30 Apr 2016

Rome Statute of the International Criminal Court ICC

S/2015/797 (16 Oct 2015) Midterm report of the Group of Experts on the Democratic Republic of the Congo

S/RES/1533 (2004) Resolution establishing a Sanctions Committee to oversee the arms embargo imposed by resolution 1493 (2003) and a group of experts to gather and analyse all relevant information in the Democratic Republic of the Congo, adopted by the Security Council on 12 March 2004

S/RES/1756 (2007) adopted by the Security Council at its 5674th meeting, on 15 May 2007

S/RES/1794 (2007) adopted by the Security Council at its 5814th meeting, on 21 December 2007

Small Arms Survey HSBA Working Paper 8, September 2007

The Enough Project, The Lord's Resistance Army of Today

Tribunal Militaire de Garnison de Bukavu, *affaire Kazungu et consort, jugement du 16 Aout 2011*, RP 275/09 et 521/10

United Nations (2005) World Summit Outcome, Resolution adopted by the General Assembly on 24 October 2005, A/RES/60/1, 2005

US Congressional Research Service, The Lord's Resistance Army: The U.S. Response

Van Acker F (2004) Uganda and the lord's resistance army: the new order no one ordered. African Affairs 103/412. Available at http://afraf.oxfordjournals.org/. Accessed 30 Apr 2016

West S (9 Jan 2015) The rise of ADF-NALU in Central Africa and its connections with al-Shabaab in Terrorism Monitor, vol XIII, issue 1, January 9, 2015

WFM-IGP (2001) Available at http://responsibilitytoprotect.org/R2PSummary.pdf. Accessed 30 Apr 2016

Part II
Terrorism, Boko Haram and the Classification of Armed Conflicts in International Law

Chapter 5
International Law Response to Terrorism: Boko Haram in Perspective

Udoka Ndidiamaka Owie

5.1 Introduction

A radical Islam and extremist jihadist group known as *Jama'atul Alhul Sunnah Lidda' Wati wal Jihad* (People Committed to the Propagation of the Prophet's Teachings and Jihad) has been involved in an escalating campaign of terror against the government and people of the Federal Republic of Nigeria, at least since July 2009, in assertion not of a claim of a right of self-determination but of a claim to establish an Islamic State.[1]

The *Jama'atul Alhul Sunnah Lidda' Wati wal Jihad* group is more commonly known as *Boko Haram* due to its rejection of Western education and culture.[2] *Boko Haram* has carried out and claimed responsibility for numerous armed attacks and bombings against the government and the civilian population of Nigeria resulting in considerable carnage. More specifically, the group has targeted police stations, the Police Force Headquarters, military and defence facilities, the United Nations building in the Federal Capital Territory, churches, schools, markets, newspaper offices, recreational places and motor transport garages. It has carried out and taken responsibility for assassinations of politicians and civilians, including non-radical and moderate Muslim clerics, as well as traditional leaders who the group allege to be saboteurs.

The group's increasing threat to the power of the Federal Government has manifested in its ability to take control of areas under local government authority and

[1] See Comolli (2015), pp. 45–49 for various accounts of the rise of the group. However it was not until 2009 that the extremist and radical form of the group manifested.

[2] The term 'Boko Haram' means 'Book is a sin' which is reflective of the group's abhorrence for Western education. See Comolli (2015), p. 49.

U. N. Owie (✉)
Osgoode Hall Law School, York University, Toronto, ON, Canada

Baze University, Abuja, Nigeria
e-mail: uowie@yorku.ca

J.-M. Iyi, H. Strydom (eds.), *Boko Haram and International Law*,
https://doi.org/10.1007/978-3-319-74957-0_5

control in the northern part of Borno State, expulsion of local government officials and taking over government structures. In furtherance of its extremist agenda, the group has attacked schools, slaughtered teachers and students, as well as engaged in the abductions of female students whom they have gang raped and threatened to sell as slaves.[3] Male school children have not been spared from the campaign of terror by the group as barely 3 weeks after the Federal Government announced a ceasefire agreement reached between the government and the group, the group attacked a government science secondary school for boys in the Nigerian northeastern town of Potiskum during assembly, killing 46 children and wounding over 79 boys.[4]

The Federal Government, successively, is complicit in the current invective of terror by Boko Haram by its indecisive and ineffective action until February 2015 and by underestimating the group's capacity for terrorist activities, its terrorist affiliations and funding.[5] Hindsight, whether as a benefit or curse in this case, shows that the government should have foreseen that entrenching a culture of corruption, the establishment of sharia by northern States in violation of the Constitution,[6] the underdevelopment of the masses and entrenchment of a culture of 'almajiri',[7] which furthers the socio-economic and political gap between individuals and regions in the country, the instability of neighbouring States like Niger, Chad and Mali, together with Nigeria's porous borders, the fallout of the Libyan crisis, the proliferation of arms and weapons in the sub-Saharan region of the continent fuelled by the deplorable socio-economic conditions in the country (especially in the North), made Boko Haram a time bomb waiting to explode and launch the country into the security black hole that it currently finds itself.

Despite the prior attacks and killings of innocent civilians by Boko Haram, the abduction of over 200 (two hundred) female students from a school in Chibok, Borno State, in April 2014 precipitated national, regional and international action forcing the Federal Government of Nigeria and the international community to rise from the inertia that had characterised their response to devastating activities of the group. Despite the wave of bombings and armed attacks resulting in deaths of civilians and military personnel, the government has been unable to contain the Boko Haram and its audacious activities so as to secure the lives and property of the

[3] BBC News (29 June 2015).

[4] BBC News (10 Nov 2014).

[5] Until recently, the Government, politicians and traditional rulers have politicized this security challenge by electioneering through their calculations and permutations.

[6] Section 10 of the Constitution of the Federal Republic of Nigeria 1999, Laws of the Federation of Nigeria, forbids the Government of the Federation or of a State from adopting a State religion. The religious extremism and intolerance in the country, the rise of the Boko Haram and its ideology as well as its objective to establish Nigeria as a Sharia State goes beyond mere coincidence with the establishment of Sharia systems in the Northern part of Nigeria. On Sharia and its nexus to radicalization in Northern Nigeria, see Ray (2016), pp. 1–20.

[7] Means 'immigrant' and was a term which was used to refer to students under qu'ranic system of education who were sent to live with teachers and had to resort to begging to cater for themselves as the teachers could not afford to do so; but now used to refer to children beggars.

people of Nigeria. This situation has resulted in the internal displacement of over one million civilians with many seeking refuge in Cameroon, Chad and Niger.[8]

Against the backdrop of the foregoing, this paper seeks to appraise the international legal landscape with respect to terrorism. Terrorism is an often-bandied word, but the paper will consider the scope of terrorism in international law. The paper will ask and address the questions of what is terrorism? How has international law responded to terrorism? Can international law provide an effective and adequate legal framework for terrorism? The paper will also consider the existence of terrorism as a distinct crime in international law and the necessity, or otherwise, of a definition of terrorism in the global efforts at combating and suppressing terrorism. In addition, the activities of regional organisations would be considered, as well as the domestic efforts of the Federal Government of Nigeria. Lastly, in its concluding remarks, the paper will set out prospects of international law in global counterterrorism.

5.2 In Search of a Meaning

5.2.1 Origins of the Term 'Terrorism'

Terrorism is not a new phenomenon. However, globalisation and development of technology evident in modern weaponry, information and communications networks; radicalisation of political thought; and religious extremism have contributed to terrorism being at the fore of issues threatening international peace and security.

The term 'terrorism' came to light during the French Revolution when 'La Grande Terror'[9] was proclaimed in 1793. With the proclamation, the Committee of Public Safety established under the authority of Maximillian Robespierre employed mass executions involving the public execution of tens of thousands of people as a means to suppress external invasion and internal unrest by instilling fear in the population.[10] Following the Thermidorian Reaction in 1794, a *coup d'état* against the Jacobin Party, Robespierre was overthrown, accused of 'terrorism' and executed.[11]

By the late nineteenth century, the term 'terrorism' turned from its earlier association with the activities of the State against its population and was used with reference to the activities of the nihilists in Russia and the anarchists in Europe that were directed against the State.[12] In contemporary times, terrorism is used with reference

[8] According to the National Emergency Management Agency of Nigeria (NEMA), the number of internally displaced persons due to the Boko Haram crisis stands at almost 1.4 million as at July 2015. See NEMA (5 July 2015).

[9] The Great Terror.

[10] Guillaume (2004), p. 537. See also Acharya (2009), p. 654.

[11] Responsibility for the proclamation of 'la Grande Terreur' being on the National Convention, a faction of which subsequently overthrew Robespierre, he could not be accused of having caused the state of terror so was accused of 'terrorism', see Guillaume (2004), pp. 537–538.

[12] Guillaume (2004), pp. 537–538.

to the activities of individuals and groups,[13] usually fuelled by political or religious extremism, that are targeted at destroying modern society and modern living. Irrespective of the form that terrorism may take, whether by the State or against the State, its defining feature remains its potential for creating fear among people by targeting civilian populations and bringing about destruction of lives and property.

5.2.2 *Towards a Definition of 'Terrorism'*

Over time, international law has been pitted against ideologies with terrorism presenting a profound ideological conflict. Despite having 'vexed' international law for a long time and in grave measure, a universally acceptable definition of terrorism has eluded international law.[14] International law has struggled to respond to a concept that it has been unable to define. According to Guillaume:

> It was somewhat paradoxical – at least at first glance – that the international community was seeking to suppress terrorism but couldn't really pinpoint its meaning.[15]

At the heart of international efforts and international legal discourse on terrorism is the issue of the definition of the term 'terrorism'. On the one hand, there is the school of thought that considers the definition imperative for effectively tackling terrorism.[16] On the other, it is thought that the nebulous nature of terrorism and the prodigious problems of defining the concept make the necessity of a definition of the concept irrelevant.[17]

The first school of thought reflects the view of many legal scholars, a fact that is partly attributable to the preference of lawyers to approach issues from a conceptual and definitional perspective. Words, being the tools of trade of lawyers, make language and communication imperative to law. According to Cooper:

> We undertake the task of definition in order to give meaning or significance to an idea or some aspect of reality. Clearly, the object of such an exercise can exist or manifest itself without any such attentions on our part. The business of definitions only takes on importance when we find it necessary to relate ourselves and others to some abstraction or reality; it is thus a necessary part of meaningful communication.[18]

---

[13] United Nations, 'Measures to Prevent International Terrorism Which Endangers Or Takes Innocent Human Lives Or Jeopardizes Fundamental Freedoms, And Study Of The Underlying Causes of Those Forms of Terrorism and Acts of Violence Which Lie in Misery, Frustration, Grievances and Despair and Which Cause Some People to Sacrifice Human Lives, Including Their Own, in an Attempt to Effect Radical Change' (Study Prepared by the Secretariat for the Sixth Committee), UN Doc.A/C.6/418 (1972), 6.

[14] Scharf (2004), p. 359.

[15] Guillaume (2004), p. 539.

[16] Saul (2006), p. 5.

[17] Baxter (1974), p. 380.

[18] Cooper (1978), p. 106.

On the other hand, there are the views of Richard Baxter and Rosalyn Higgins, who happen to have been judges of the International Court of Justice. Baxter argues that 'The term [terrorism] is imprecise; it is ambiguous; and above all, it serves no operative legal purpose'.[19] On her part, Higgins contends:

> Terrorism is a term without any legal significance. It is merely a convenient way of alluding to activities, whether of States or of individuals, widely disapproved of and in which either the methods used are unlawful, or the targets protected, or both.[20]

For Higgins, '... it is more sensible to proceed pragmatically in the absence of a definition...' as international law has done in other areas and that '... the pragmatic response was the only possible one, because there simply was not the consensus to identify what acts did or did not constitute terrorism'.[21]

However, there is a need for international law to define terrorism, to set out the parameters of conduct that could be characterised as terrorism. This is especially so in view of the legal consequences of such a characterisation and the obligations of States in global counterterrorism, as will be seen later in the paper. In addition, the effective implementation of counterterrorism measures and the necessary multifaceted cooperation among entities in this regard will be better achieved with a global definition of terrorism. A definition will give clarity to the concept and avoid abuse, either by way of expansion or reduction of its meaning and scope, i.e. it will avoid the situation of exaggerating ordinary criminal acts as terrorist acts and underplaying terrorist acts as ordinary criminal acts. The regulation of counterterrorism measures also stands to benefit from a universal definition of terrorism by curtailing excesses through the unilateral and subjective determination of terrorism.[22] Ben Saul articulates the benefits of a global definition of terrorism thus:

> Defining terrorism as a discrete crime normatively recognizes and protects vital international community values and interests, symbolically expresses community condemnation, and stigmatizes offenders. The overreach inherent in sectoral treaties would be clarified by a more calibrated response which differentiates political from private violence.[23]

One of the earliest calls for a regulatory framework for terrorism came in 1926, when Romania requested the League of Nations to consider drafting a convention that would make terrorism universally punishable, but this request was not accepted.[24] However, it was not until a series of conferences held in Europe, in the 1920s and 1930s, on the Unification of Penal Law under the auspices of the International Association of Penal Law that efforts at defining terrorism were first considered.[25] It was proposed at the Third Conference, held in Brussels in 1930, that

---

[19] Baxter (1974), p. 380.

[20] Higgins (1997), p. 28.

[21] Higgins (1997), p. 14.

[22] Saul (2006), p. 5.

[23] Saul (2006), p. 7.

[24] League of Nations, Committee of Experts for the Codification of International Criminal Law, Replies of Governments 1927, LoN Doc C.196.M.70.1927.V.221.

[25] Nawaz and Singh (1977), p. 66.

> The intentional use of means capable of producing a common danger that represents an act of terrorism on the part of anyone making use of crimes against life, liberty or physical integrity of persons or directed against private or State property with the purpose of expressing or executing political or social ideas will be punished.[26]

At the Fourth Conference, held in Paris in 1931, a proposal was made to the effect that

> Whoever, for the purpose of terrorizing the population, uses against persons or property bombs, mines, incendiary or explosive devices or products, fire arms or other deadly or deleterious devices, or who provokes or attempts to provoke, spreads or attempts to spread an epidemy, a contagious disease or other disaster, or who interrupts or attempts to interrupt a public service or public utility will be punished...[27]

The proposal at the Fourth Conference was not well received, but the Conference approved a recommendation for the conclusion of an international convention to 'assure the universal repression of terrorist attempts'. The Fifth Conference, held in Madrid in 1934, commenced efforts to define terrorism, and the proposal of the Committee that adopted a bifurcated approach to the definition of terrorism was approved by the Sixth Conference, held in Copenhagen in 1935. The proposal defined terrorism as 'the deliberate use of means capable of producing a common danger to commit an act imperilling life, physical integrity or human health or threatening to destroy substantial property'.[28] It also defined a terrorist thus:

> Any person who, by wilful acts directed against the life, physical integrity, health or freedom of a Head of State or his or her spouse, a person exercising the prerogatives of the Head of State, Crown Princes, members of a Government, persons possessing diplomatic immunity, or members of constitutional, legislative or judiciary bodies, has endangered the community or created a state of terror calculated to cause a change in or impediment to the operation of the public authorities or to disturb international relations.[29]

The proposal then went on to enumerate a list of specific terrorist acts to include impeding railways, maritime, river or air communications; using explosives; poisoning drinking water; destroying public buildings; etc.[30]

In October 1934, following the violent assassination of King Alexander I of Yugoslavia and the French Foreign Minister in Marseilles by Croatian separatists, France petitioned the League of Nations to conclude a convention on terrorism.[31] In December 1934, the Committee for the International Repression of Terrorism was established by the Council of the League of Nations to draft a preliminary conven-

---

[26] Quoted in Zlataric (1975), p. 478; Saul (2005), p. 59.

[27] Zlataric (1975), p. 480.

[28] UN Secretariat Study 1972, see note 12; Kolb (2004), p. 237.

[29] See Romaniuk (2010), p. 27; Zlataric (1975), pp. 480–482.

[30] Zlataric (1975), pp. 480–482.

[31] Walters (1969), p. 599. See also Proceedings of the International Conference on the Repression of Terrorism, League of Nations Doc. C.94.M.47.1938.V (1938.V.3), pp. 49–50.

tion 'to assure the repression of conspiracies or crimes committed with a political and terrorist purpose'.[32] In 1937, a conference was convened to consider a convention on the prevention and punishment of terrorism and another convention on the creation of an international criminal court to try terrorism offences.[33] The Convention for the Prevention and Punishment of Terrorism 1937 defined acts of terrorism as '...criminal acts directed against a State and intended or calculated to create a state of terror in the minds of particular persons, or a group of persons, or in the public'.[34] The Convention reaffirmed the duty of States to 'refrain from any act designed to encourage terrorist activities directed against another State and to prevent acts in which such activities take shape'.[35] Though signed by 24 States, it was ratified by only India and so never entered into force.[36]

With the dissolution of the League of Nations and the establishment of the United Nations in 1945, the United Nations, at first, was more concerned with war trials in Germany and Japan, as well as the reconstruction of Europe, which had been ravaged by the Second World War. Charged with the primary responsibility for the maintenance of international peace and security,[37] the Security Council of the United Nations first referred to terrorism in 1948 in a Resolution condemning the assassination of the United Nations mediator in Palestine by Jewish extremists.[38] Reference to terrorism was made in the International Law Commission (ILC) Draft Code of Offences Against the Peace and Security of Mankind 1954, wherein the Code adopted the definition of terrorism as contained in the 1937 Convention. Further references were made to terrorism in other international legal instruments, including the Definition of Aggression and the Friendly Relations Declaration, albeit without a definition of the concept.[39] The onset of the Cold War soon after the establishment of the United Nations, resulting in the deadlock within the Security Council, limited the action of the Council with regard to an international response to terrorism.

It was not until 1972, following the attack on the Munich Olympic Games, that the United Nations revisited the issue of terrorism and its definitional challenges.[40] The General Assembly on the recommendation of the Sixth Committee decided to

[32] League of Nations, Committee for the International Repression of Terrorism, Geneva, 10 April 1935, LoN Doc CRT 1.

[33] Romaniuk (2010), pp. 28–29.

[34] League of Nations Doc. C.546(I0.M.383(I) (1937). It opened up for signature on 16 November 1937, but never entered into force. See Lillich (1982), p. 175, Appendix I.

[35] League of Nations Doc. (1937), Article 1.

[36] The Convention was ratified by India on 1 January 1941.

[37] Charter of the United Nations, 59 Stat. 1031, 1 UNTS XVI, Article 2(4). Reprinted in (1945) American Journal of International Law 39 (Supp. 190), Article 24.

[38] S/RES/57 (1948).

[39] UN General Assembly, Definition of Aggression, 14 December 1974, A/RES/3314, Articles 3(g) and 4; UN General Assembly, Declaration on Principles of International Law concerning Friendly Relations and Cooperation among States in Accordance with the Charter of the United Nations, 24 October 1970, A/RES/2625 (XXV), Article 1.

[40] Richards (2015), p. 41.

establish an Ad Hoc Committee on Terrorism.[41] An *Ad Hoc* Committee on International Terrorism was established with a subcommittee given responsibility for the definition of terrorism.[42] A definitional consensus eluded the subcommittee because of the political element in terrorism with the so-called Third World States and Non-Aligned States from Africa, Asia, Europe and the Middle East insisting that the inalienable right of people subjected to colonial and racist regimes must be excluded from the definition of terrorism, while State terrorism (i.e., governmental acts) being 'the most dangerous brand of violence' should be included.[43]

Political motivation dominated negotiations with Western States insisting that State terrorism should not be included in the definition since international law already prohibits use of force by States and that any definition should not take cognizance of political motivation whether in furtherance of national liberation or self-determination.[44] Thus, in its Report to the General Assembly in 1979, the Ad Hoc Committee did not include a definition of terrorism.[45] In 1987, the General Assembly requested the UN Secretary General to report on the possibility of convening an international conference to define terrorism and distinguish it from national liberation struggles.[46] The Secretary General noted in his Report that the definitional challenge was still persistent.[47]

Following the thawing of relations between the East and the West (Cold War) by the end of 1989, the General Assembly adopted without vote Resolution 44/29, wherein the Assembly condemned, unequivocally, 'all acts, methods, practices of terrorism wherever and by whomever committed' as criminal and unjustifiable.[48] In 1994, the General Assembly reaffirmed the 'unequivocal condemnation of all acts, methods and practices of terrorism, as criminal and unjustifiable, wherever and by whomever committed' and declared the obligation of States to take effective measures in accordance with international law to combat terrorism.[49] The General Assembly has avoided including a political element in dealing with terrorism, instead describing it as 'criminal acts intended or calculated to provoke a state of terror in the general public, a group of persons or particular persons for political purposes'.[50]

---

[41] UN Doc.A/8969 (1972).

[42] A/RES/3034 (XXVII), 27 UN GAOR Supp., Paragraph 9 (1972).

[43] Observation to the ad Hoc Committee on International Terrorism submitted by the Syrian Republic, UN Doc.A/AAC.160/1 (1973), 6. See also Franck and Lockwood (1974), p. 73; Schmid (2004), p. 386.

[44] Franck and Lockwood (1974), p. 74.

[45] UN Doc. A/34/37 (1979), GAOR, 34th Session, Supp. No. 37.

[46] A/RES/42/159 (1987).

[47] UN Doc. A/44/456/Add.1, 10 October 1989.

[48] A/RES/44/29 (1989), para 1.

[49] See the Declaration on Measures to Eliminate International Terrorism, A/RES/49/60 (1994), Annex. See also the Declaration to Supplement the 1994 Declaration on Measures to Eliminate international Terrorism, A/RES/51/210 (1996), Annex.

[50] A/RES/49/60 (1994); A/RES/51/210 (1996).

The United Nations Draft Comprehensive Convention on Terrorism has been in the pipelines since 2000.[51] The Ad Hoc Committee established, in 1996, by the General Assembly pursuant to Resolution 51/210 was tasked with the responsibility of developing the comprehensive legal framework to combat international terrorism.[52] According to the Draft Convention:

> Any person commits an offence within the meaning of this Convention if that person, by any means, unlawfully and intentionally, causes:
>
> a) Death or serious bodily injury to any person; or
>
> b) Serious damage to public or private property, including a place of public use, a State or government facility, a public transportation system, an infrastructure facility or the environment; or
>
> c) Damage to property, places, facilities, or systems referred to in paragraph 1(b) of this article, resulting or likely to result in major economic loss, when the purpose of the conduct, by its nature or context, is to intimidate a population, or to compel a Government or an international organisation to do or abstain from doing any act.[53]

The Convention is yet to be finalised 'due to the lack of unanimity on key issues'· particularly as concerns the scope of the crime and as such is yet to come into the framework of international law.[54]

Ideological relativism has contributed to the nebulous nature of terrorism and the definitional challenges experienced. The common saying that 'one man's terrorist is another's freedom fighter' highlights the problem of drawing a line between 'the quest for nationalist identity and an act of terrorism, between legitimate political demands and suppression of those who make the demands'.[55] The relativism has been centred on the actors whose activities would amount to terrorism; i.e., are the activities of States included or just the activities of non-State actors or groups? Also, which activities qualify for categorisation as terrorism? Thus, a group may not be a terrorist group but may employ terrorist means to achieve its political objectives, and on the other hand, a terrorist group may employ legitimate means to achieve its political objectives; thus, is categorisation as a terrorist a lifetime label (i.e., once a terrorist, always a terrorist)?[56] It is not so much as the group in question rather the activities that are of concern to international law as labels should not be a substitute for analysis.

---

[51] India had proposed a comprehensive convention against terrorism and in the wake of the terrorist attacks of 11 September 2001, the United Nations Secretary General submitted a Report to the General Assembly on a comprehensive convention on terrorism, United Nations Secretary General's Report to the General Assembly, 56th General Assembly Meeting, GA/9914 (24 September 2001).

[52] A/RES/51/210 (1996), para 9.

[53] Annex I of Report of the Working Group on Measures to Eliminate International Terrorism, UN Doc. A/C.6/65/L.10 (3 November 2010), Article 2.

[54] Conte (2010), p. 47; Abi-Saab (2004) p. xiii, xx.

[55] Acharya (2009), p. 656.

[56] Acharya (2009), p. 657.

5.3 International Law Response to Terrorism

5.3.1 A Sectoral Approach

In the absence of an agreement on the definition of terrorism and whether terrorism includes politically motivated violence, international law devised a response to the acts, albeit on an *ad hoc* basis.[57] This piecemeal or sectoral approach resulted in thirteen (13) international conventions and protocols addressing various manifestations of terrorism.

In response to the spate of hijackings and offences against aircraft, a series of multilateral agreements were prompted with a view to combating acts of terrorism as applicable to the civil aviation sector. In 1963, the Convention on Offences and Certain Other Acts Committed Aboard Aircrafts (Tokyo Convention) was concluded to enable States exercise jurisdiction over offences committed on planes that were above the high seas.[58] Unlike some later conventions, the Tokyo Convention was not so much about the suppression of terrorist acts; rather, its main objective was to enable the exercise of jurisdiction over offences coming within the ambit of the Convention. The Convention applies to offences against penal laws and acts that jeopardise the safety of aircraft or persons and property on board or that jeopardise good order and discipline on board an aircraft while in flight.[59]

In 1970, the Convention for the Suppression of Unlawful Seizure of Aircraft (Hague Convention) was concluded.[60] The Convention obliges States parties to impose 'severe penalties' for unlawful seizure of aircraft and requires States, including landing States, to take measures to exercise jurisdiction against hijackers.[61]

The Hague Convention is limited to aircraft that is 'in flight'.[62] Thus, in 1971, the Convention for the Suppression of Unlawful Acts Against the Safety of Civil Aviation (Montreal Convention) was reached to cover incidents against civil aviation going beyond unlawful seizures of aircraft in flight.[63] It also prohibits acts that are likely to endanger the safety of an aircraft even while in service.[64] A subsequent Protocol to the Montreal Convention (Montreal Protocol) was reached in 1988 to encompass terrorist acts at airports serving international civil aviation, necessitated by the attacks on international airports in Rome and Vienna in 1985.[65]

Next, the protection of diplomatic officials and State officials, including heads of State, heads of government and other senior State officials, from terrorist attacks

---

[57] Romaniuk (2010), p. 33.

[58] 704 UNTS 219. It entered into force on 4 December 1969.

[59] 704 UNTS 219, Article 1.

[60] 860 UNTS 105. It entered into force on 14 October 1971.

[61] 860 UNTS 105, Articles 2–4.

[62] 860 UNTS 105, Article 1.

[63] 974 UNTS 177. It entered into force on 26 January 1973.

[64] 974 UNTS 177, Article 1.

[65] 1589 UNTS 473. It entered into force on 06 August 1989.

came within the optic of international law. Replicating regional efforts within the Organisation of American States, the Convention on the Prevention and Punishment of Crimes Against Internationally Protected Persons, Including Diplomatic Agents, was concluded in 1973 (New York Convention).[66]

Following the German Embassy siege in Sweden in 1975, the hostage crisis that occurred in Entebbe in 1976 and the hostage situation at the Embassy of the United States in Tehran in 1979, the International Convention Against the Taking of Hostages was concluded in 1979.[67] The Convention defines hostage-taking as where a person 'seizes or detains and threatens to kill, or to injure or to continue to detain another person (hostage) in order to compel a third party, namely, a State, an international intergovernmental organization, a natural or juridical person, or a group of persons, to do or abstain from doing any act as an explicit or implicit condition for the release of the hostage'.[68] States parties are obliged to punish acts of hostage taking, including attempts.[69]

The Convention on the Physical Protection of Nuclear Material was reached in 1980.[70] The Convention sets out the standard for the protection of nuclear material and requires States parties to punish by 'appropriate penalties' offences including the use or threat of use of nuclear material to compel a natural or legal person, international organisation or State to do or refrain from doing any act.[71]

Following the attack on the *Achille Lauro* in 1985, the Convention for the Suppression of Unlawful Acts Against the Safety of Maritime Navigation was concluded in 1988 (Rome Convention).[72] The Convention proscribes, *inter alia*, taking control of a ship by force (actual or threatened) or intimidation, performing of acts of violence against persons on board or destruction of a ship, causing damage to a ship or its cargo or being involved in placing on a ship a device or substance likely to destroy the ship.[73] States parties to the Convention are required to take appropriate measures to prevent and punish the commission of the offences within the ambit of the Convention.[74] A Protocol for the Suppression of Unlawful Acts Against the Safety of Fixed Platforms Located on the Continental Shelf was concluded in 1988 (Rome Protocol).[75] It extends the applicability of the Rome Convention on Safety of Maritime Navigation 1988 to fixed platforms, including those engaged in offshore exploitation of oil and gas, within the continental shelf of States.

---

[66] 1035 UNTS 167. It entered into force on 20 February 1977. See OAS Convention to Prevent and Punish Acts of Terrorism taking the Form of Crimes against Persons and Related Extortion that are of International Significance 1971, OAS Treaty Series No. 37, entered into force 16 October 1973.

[67] A/RES/34/146 (XXXIV), 34 UN GAOR Supp. (No.46) at 245, (1979); 1316 UNTS 205.

[68] 1316 UNTS 205, Article 1.

[69] 1316 UNTS 205, Articles 1–2.

[70] 1456 UNTS 101. It entered into force on 08 February 1978.

[71] 1456 UNTS 101, Article 7.

[72] 1678 UNTS 221. It entered into force on 01 March 1992. See Plant (1997), p. 69.

[73] Rome Convention (1988), Article 3.

[74] Rome Convention (1988), Article 5.

[75] 1678 UNTS 304. It entered into force on 01 March 1992.

As a result of the bombing of Pan Am Flight 103 in 1988, the Convention on the Marking of Plastic Explosives for the Purpose of Detection was concluded in 1991.[76] States parties are required to take measures to prevent and punish the manufacture, as well as movement within their territories, of unmarked and undetectable plastic explosives.[77] Also, States are to exercise strict and effective control over the possession and transfer of possession of unmarked explosive manufactures within their territory prior to the entry into force of the Convention.[78]

The International Convention for the Suppression of Terrorist Bombings was concluded in 1997[79] in response to 'bombings against US interests in Saudi Arabia in 1996, gas attacks in Tokyo, and bombings in Sri Lanka, Israel, and Manchester in the UK'.[80] The Convention 'creates a regime of expanded jurisdiction over the unlawful and intentional use of explosives and other lethal devices in, into or against various defined public places with intent to kill or cause serious bodily injury or with intent to cause extensive destruction of the public place'.[81]

With a view to hitting at the core of terrorism, the International Convention for the Suppression of the Financing of Terrorism was concluded in 1999.[82] Unlike other conventions dealing with particular terrorist acts like taking of hostages, the Convention Against Terrorist Financing deals with the financing of any terrorist activity within the scope of the conventions listed in the annex.[83] The Convention criminalises the intentional use of funds,[84] by any means, to carry out the following:

---

[76] Convention on the Marking of Plastic Explosives for the Purposes of Detection. 30 ILM 721. It entered into force on 21 June 1998.

[77] See Articles 2–3 of the Convention on the Marking of Plastic Explosives for the Purposes of Detection (1991).

[78] See the Convention on the Marking of Plastic Explosives for the Purposes of Detection (1991), Article 4.

[79] UN Doc. A/RES/52/164; 2149 UNTS 284. It entered into force on 23 May 2001.

[80] Saul (2006), p. 131.

[81] United Nations Office on Drug and Crime (2009), p. 13. See generally, Convention on Terrorist Bombings (1997), Articles 2–6.

[82] UN Doc. A/RES/54/109; 39 ILM 390. It entered into force on 10 April 2002.

[83] Includes the Convention for the Suppression of Unlawful Seizure of Aircraft 1970, Convention for the Suppression of Unlawful Acts against the Safety of Civil Aviation 1971, Convention on the Prevention and Punishment of Crimes against Internationally Protected Persons including Diplomatic Agents 1973, International Convention against the Taking of Hostages 1979, Convention on the Physical Protection of Nuclear Material 1980, Protocol for the Suppression of Unlawful Acts of Violence at Airports Serving International Civil Aviation 1988, Convention for the Suppression of Unlawful Acts against the Safety of Maritime Navigation 1988, Protocol for the Suppression of Unlawful Acts against the Safety of Fixed Platforms Located in the Continental Shelf 1988 and the International Convention for the Suppression of Terrorist Bombings 1997.

[84] The term 'funds' means "assets of every kind, whether tangible or intangible, movable or immovable, however acquired, and legal documents or instruments in any form, including electronic or digital, evidencing title to, or interest in, such assets, including, but not limited to, bank credits, travellers cheques, bank cheques, money orders, shares, securities, bonds, drafts, letters of credit." See Terrorism Financing Convention (1999), Article 1(1).

(a) An act which constitutes an offence within the scope of and as defined in one of the treaties listed in the annex; or

(b) Any other act intended to cause death or serious bodily injury to a civilian, or to any other person not taking an active part in the hostilities in a situation of armed conflict, when the purpose of such act, by its nature or context, is to intimidate a population, or to compel a government or an international organisation to do or to abstain from doing any act.[85]

The Convention obliges States parties to establish criminal offences under their domestic laws and even to take measures to ensure criminal civil or administrative liability for persons managing or controlling legal entities.[86] It provides expansive jurisdiction for States parties, as well as obliges States to freeze or seize funds implicated in offences under the Convention, including proceeds therefrom.[87]

The next focus of international law was nuclear terrorism, and this led to the adoption of the International Convention for the Suppression of Acts of Nuclear Terrorism in 2005.[88] The Convention makes the unlawful possession, and use, of radioactive material, nuclear facility or device with intent to cause death, serious bodily injury and substantial damage to property or to the environment.[89] The Convention excludes from its ambit the activities of armed forces during an armed conflict.[90] It also obligates States to ensure mutual judicial cooperation and assistance in investigative and criminal proceedings with respect to nuclear terrorism.[91]

In the absence of a general consensus as to concept and scope of terrorism, this sectoral approach was imperative to bridge the normative gaps in the regulation of activities transcending the territorial jurisdiction of States. Most of the treaties proscribe certain conduct and require States to proscribe and punish similar conduct in their national laws. Importantly, the treaties also provide for extraterritorial assertion of jurisdiction, i.e. *aut dedere, aut judicare*, obligating States parties on whose territories persons alleged to have committed the offences subject of the treaties to either prosecute or extradite them. The treaties adopted a problem-oriented approach to terrorist activities and avoided the political and definitional challenges, thus enabling the international community to respond to a myriad of manifestations of terrorist activities, albeit without referring to the term 'terrorism' in their substantive provisions.[92]

---

[85] See Article 2(1) of Terrorism Financing Convention (1999).

[86] Terrorism Financing Convention (1999), Articles 4–5.

[87] Terrorism Financing Convention (1999), Articles 7–8.

[88] International Convention for the Suppression of Acts of Nuclear Terrorism 2005, UN Doc.A/RES/59/290. It is yet to enter into force.

[89] See Article 2, International Convention for the Suppression of Acts of Nuclear Terrorism 2005.

[90] Article 4(2) of the International Convention for the Suppression of Acts of Nuclear Terrorism 2005. These activities are governed by international humanitarian law as well as under general international law.

[91] See Article 14 of the International Convention for the Suppression of Acts of Nuclear Terrorism 2005.

[92] Saul (2006), pp. 131–132.

All the international treaties on terrorism, except the Tokyo Convention (1963), require States to criminalise the acts subject of the treaties and to punish the acts accordingly, to establish jurisdiction over the offences, as well as to take the offenders into custody and to either prosecute or extradite them. They also require that States involved in the actions taken are notified and obligate States parties to render assistance and cooperation in the prosecution of terrorism.

5.3.2 *An Institutional Approach*

5.3.2.1 The United Nations and Counterterrorism

The 13 treaties addressing specific aspects and activities of terrorism are only part of the international legal architecture with respect to terrorism. There have been counterterrorist measures implemented at various levels of the international society and various arms of international organisations. Charged with the primary responsibility for the maintenance of international peace and security,[93] and a limited responsibility with regard to international peace and security subject to Articles 9–12 of the Charter of the United Nations, the Security Council and the General Assembly, respectively, have been at the forefront of the global response to terrorism. In addition, the Secretariat of the United Nations has also been actively involved in the implementation of counterterrorism efforts.

There is a paradigmatic shift in the way the Security Council has carried out its primary responsibility for the maintenance of international peace and security under the Charter of the United Nations.[94] It used to be the practice that only the actions of States were considered to be threats to international peace and security. However, the Council has broken out of the mold and characterised the actions of terrorists as threats to international peace and security.[95] The Security Council has also actively responded to terrorism through its counterterrorism programme, including the establishment of several subsidiary bodies. The Council has sanctioned States that have been implicated in acts of terrorism, for instance Libya[96] and Sudan[97]; terrorist groups, including

[93] See Article 24 of the Charter of the United Nations.

[94] Article 24 of the Charter of the United Nations.

[95] See S/RES/748 (1992), S/RES/883 (1993), S/RES/1044 (1996), S/RES/1189 (1998), S/RES/1267 (1999), S/RES/1269 (1999), s/RES/1368 (2001) regarding the 11 September 2001 bombing of the United States, S/RES/1373 (2001), S/RES/1438 (2002), S/RES/1440 (2002), S/RES/1450 (2002), S/RES 1465 (2003) with regard to the bomb attack in Bogota, S/RES/1516 (2003) regarding the bombing in Istanbul, S/RES/1530 (2004) regarding the bombing in Madrid, S/RES/1611 (2005) regarding the bombing in London, S/RES/1618 (2005), S/RES/2133 (2014), S/RES/2178 (2014) and S/RES/2249 (2015). The Council in S/RES/1624 (2005), S/RES/2170 (2014) and S/RES/2253 (2015) went further and considered acts of terrorism as one of the most serious threats to peace and security.

[96] S/RES/748 (1992).

[97] S/RES/1054 (1996).

Taliban[98] and Al-Qaida[99]; as well as individuals.[100] The Council has called upon all States to fully implement the international treaties concerning terrorism to which they are parties, to adhere to those that they are not parties and to speedily adopt pending treaties on the subject matter.[101] It has been unequivocal in its condemnation of 'all acts, methods and practices of terrorism as criminal and unjustifiable, regardless of their motivation, in all their forms and manifestations wherever and by whomever committed, in particular those which could threaten international peace and security'.[102]

The Security Council established a committee pursuant to Resolution 1267 to monitor sanctions against the Taliban and, subsequently, Al-Qaida.[103] It has also urged States to take action against groups and organisations that were not subject to the review of the 1267 Committee, including Boko Haram.[104] Following the terrorist attack of 9/11 on the United States, the Council has intensified its involvement in counterterrorism and in the wake of the attack passed Resolution 1373, which obliged Member States to take measures to prevent and suppress the financing of terrorist acts, criminalise various forms of terrorist actions and take measures to assist and promote cooperation in the implementation of international conventions with respect to terrorism, albeit without a definition of terrorism in international law.[105] Pursuant to Resolution 1373, the Council set up a Counter-Terrorism Committee and mandated States to report regularly to the Committee on the measures they have taken to implement Resolution 1373.[106]

The Council set up a Counter-Terrorism Committee Executive Directorate to monitor the implementation of Resolution 1373 and to facilitate the provision of technical assistance, through capacity building, to Member States.[107] In addition, the Security Council has also established a counterterrorism-related body (1540 Committee) to monitor the compliance of Member States with Resolution 1540, which calls on States to prevent non-State actors (including terrorist groups) from developing, acquiring, manufacturing, possessing, transporting, transferring or the use of nuclear, chemical or biological weapons and their means of delivery.[108]

Acting pursuant to Resolution 1566, the Security Council established a working group to recommend practical measures against individuals, groups or entities involved in terrorism, as well as to explore the possibility of establishing an

---

98 S/RES/1267 (1999).

99 S/RES/1333 (2000).

100 S/RES/1390 (2002), S/RES/1989 (2011), S/RES/2161 (2014).

101 S/RES/1269 (1999), Operative Paragraph 2.

102 S/RES/1269 (1999), Operative Paragraph 1; see also preamble of S/RES/1390 (2002), S/RES/1989 (2011), S/RES/2083 (2012), S/RES/2161 (2014).

103 S/RES/1267 (1999).

104 S/RES/2253 (2015).

105 S/RES/1373 (2001).

106 S/RES/1373 (2001), Operative Paragraph 6.

107 S/RES/1535 (2004), Operative Paragraph 2.

108 S/RES/1540 (2004), Operative Paragraph 1.

international fund for the compensation of victims of terrorism and their families.[109] The Council has also urged upon Member States to take measures against incitement to terrorism and to deny 'safe haven' to persons reasonably considered to be guilty of such conduct, as well as to strengthen the security of international borders.[110]

The General Assembly has been actively involved in efforts at combating terrorism since 1972. It has responded to terrorism through a myriad of resolutions and by its involvement in treaty making, i.e. adoption of terrorism-related treaties and elaboration of international instruments on terrorism through its *Ad Hoc* Committee on Terrorism, as well as the Working Group of the Sixth Committee. The important role of the General Assembly in the analysis of international law and its response to terrorism are evident in the adoption of two important resolutions, *viz* the Definition of Aggression and the Friendly Relations Declarations.[111] While these two documents neither define terrorism nor even expressly mention 'terrorism', they are an integral part of the international legal framework on the prohibition on the use of force, as will be seen later in the paper.

The General Assembly, in 2006, adopted a Global Counter-Terrorism Strategy and Plan of Action to address the conditions conducive to the spread of terrorism, to prevent and combat terrorism, to take measures to build State capacity to fight terrorism, to strengthen the role of the United Nations in combating terrorism and to ensure the respect of human rights while countering terrorism.[112] Importantly, the Global Counter-Terrorism Strategy is anchored on the elimination of prolonged unresolved conflicts, the absence of rule of law, human rights violations, discrimination, political exclusion and anomie, socio-economic marginalisation and the lack of good governance. This Global Strategy has been affirmed in Member States in biennial reviews.[113]

The United Nations Secretary General established a Counter-Terrorism Implementation Task Force in 2005.[114] The Task-Force has the responsibility of ensuring coordination and coherence in counterterrorism within the United Nations system, as well as to catalyse and coordinate initiatives for the implementation of the Global Counter-Terrorism Strategy. The Task Force has working groups that undertake specific initiatives and thematic aspects of the Global Counter-Terrorism Strategy and Action Plan.

---

[109] S/RES/1566 (2004), Operative Paragraphs 9–10.

[110] S/RES/1624 (2005), Operative Paragraphs 1–2.

[111] See the UN General Assembly, Definition of Aggression, 14 December 1974, A/RES/3314, Articles 3(g) and 4; UN General Assembly, Declaration on Principles of International Law concerning Friendly Relations and Cooperation among States in Accordance with the Charter of the United Nations, 24 October 1970, A/RES/2625 (XXV).

[112] A/RES/60/288, 20 September 2006.

[113] A/RES/62/272 (2008), A/RES/64/297 (2010), A/RES/66/282 (2012) and A/RES/68/276 (2014).

[114] The Counter-Terrorism Implementation Task Force was endorsed by the General Assembly through the Global Counter-Terrorism Strategy.

In addition to the efforts of the Security Council, the General Assembly and the Secretariat, a number of programmes, offices and agencies within the framework of the United Nations, e.g. INTERPOL, International Atomic Energy Agency, United Nations Office on Drugs and Crime, have also been engaged in the response to terrorism, especially with regard to technical assistance and capacity building with a view to ensuring the effective implementation of international counterterrorism measures.

5.3.2.2 Regional Organisations and Counterterrorism

In addition to the efforts of the United Nations, there have been regional responses to terrorism. As far back as 1971, the Organisation of American States, in responding to the growth of terrorist activities, concluded the Convention to Prevent and Punish Acts of Terrorism Taking the Form of Crimes Against Persons and Related Extortion That Are of International Significance.[115] In 2002, the Inter-American Convention Against Terrorism was concluded, and it primarily seeks to encourage Member States to become parties to, as well as implement, the various sectoral conventions on terrorism and to domestically institute a legal and regulatory framework for the suppression of the financing of terrorism.[116]

At the European level, the European Convention on the Suppression of Terrorism (European Convention) was adopted in 1977.[117] The Convention excludes terrorist offences from political offences for the purpose of extradition and obligates States parties to take measures to prosecute terrorists found within their territory in the absence of an extradition request.[118] In 2002, the EU adopted the Framework Decision on Combating Terrorism, which was amended in 2008 and seeks to introduce new terrorist offences like public provocation to commit terrorism, recruitment for terrorism and training for terrorism.[119] Following the terrorist attack of 9/11, a protocol was adopted, in 2003, to strengthen international obligations under the existing international convention.[120] In 2005, the Council of Europe adopted the Convention on the Prevention of Terrorism, which provided for new criminal offences, including the public provocation to commit a terrorist offence, recruitment for terrorism and training for terrorism.[121]

[115] See OAS Convention to Prevent and Punish Acts of Terrorism taking the Form of Crimes against Persons and Related Extortion that are of International Significance 1971, OAS Treaty Series No. 37, entered into force 16 October 1973.

[116] OAS Treaty A-66, 42 ILM 19, Articles 3–4.

[117] ETS No. 90 (1977); 1137 UNTS 93.

[118] European Convention (1977), Articles 1, 2 and 6.

[119] Council of the European Union, 'Framework Decision of 13 June 2002 on Combating Terrorism', 2002/475/JHA; Council of the European Union, 'Framework Decision of 28 November 2008, amending Framework Decision 2002/475/JHA on Combating Terrorism', 2008/919/JHA.

[120] ETS 190 (2003); the Protocol is not yet in force; Saul (2006), p. 148.

[121] ETS No. 196, Articles 5, 6 and 7 (Not yet in force).

In 1987, the South Asian Association for Regional Cooperation (SAARC) concluded the SAARC Regional Convention on Suppression of Terrorism.[122] An Additional Protocol to the Convention was adopted in 2004 for the purpose of implementing the Convention on the Suppression of Terrorist Financing 1999 and the counterterrorism obligations of States pursuant to Resolution 1373.[123]

There is also the Arab Convention on the Suppression of Terrorism adopted by the League of Arab States in 1998.[124] The Convention defines terrorism as follows:

> Any act or threat of violence, whatever its motives or purposes, that occurs in the advancement of an individual or collective criminal agenda and seeking to sow panic among people, causing fear by harming them, or placing their lives, liberty or security in danger, or seeking to cause damage to the environment or to public or private installations or property or to occupying or seizing them, or seeking to jeopardise a national resource.[125]

Despite the broadly worded provision, the Convention provides:

> All cases of struggle by whatever means, including armed struggle, against foreign occupation and aggression for liberation and self-determination, in accordance with the principles of international law, shall not be regarded as an offence. This provision shall not apply to any act prejudicing the territorial integrity of any Arab State.[126]

This Convention has proven controversial because of the explicit justification of terrorist acts pursued in the exercise of a right of self-determination against non-Arab States but not Arab States.

The Organisation of the Islamic Conference (OIC) also adopted the Convention on Combating International Terrorism in 1999, along the lines of the 1998 Convention of the Arab League.[127] While the OIC Convention excludes a 'peoples' struggle, including armed struggle against foreign occupation, aggression, colonialism and hegemony aimed at liberation and self-determination',[128] it does not contain a proviso to the applicability of the exclusion.

Joining the regional efforts in responding to terrorism, the emerged States following the break-up of the Soviet Union, in 1999, adopted the Treaty on Cooperation Among the States Members of the Commonwealth of Independent States in Combating Terrorism.[129]

---

[122] UN GAOR, 44th Sess., UN Doc.A/51/136 (1989); South Asian Association for Regional Cooperation (SAARC) Regional Convention on Suppression of Terrorism, South Asian Association for Regional Cooperation (SAARC), 4 November 1987. Saul (2006), p. 153.

[123] South Asian Association for Regional Cooperation (SAARC), Addition Protocol to the SAARC Regional Convention on Suppression of Terrorism, 6 January 2004.

[124] See League of Arab States (April 1998), The Arab Convention on the Suppression of Terrorism 1998. Entered into force 07 May 1999.

[125] See Article 1(2) of the Arab Convention on the Suppression of Terrorism 1998.

[126] See Article 2(a) of the Arab Convention on the Suppression of Terrorism 1998.

[127] See Convention of the Organisation of Islamic Conference on Combating International Terrorism, 1 July 1999, annexed to Resolution 59/26-P (Not yet in force).

[128] See Article 2(a) of Convention of the Organisation of Islamic Conference on Combating International Terrorism 1999.

[129] Treaty on Cooperation among the States Members of the Commonwealth of Independent States in Combating Terrorism, 4 June 1999.

Following the establishment of the Shanghai Cooperation Organisation in 2001, a regional body comprised of Kazakhstan, China, Kyrgyzstan, Russia, Tajikistan and Uzbekistan, the Shanghai Cooperation Organisation Convention on Combating Terrorism, Separatism and Extremism was adopted.[130] By the Convention, the parties undertake to cooperate in the prevention, identification and suppression of terrorism, separatism and extremism, as defined in Article 1.

At its 30th Ordinary Session in June 1994, the Assembly of Heads of State and Government of the Organisation of African Unity adopted a Declaration on the Code of Conduct for Inter-African Relations unequivocally condemning all forms of terrorism and extremism.[131] The Organisation for African Unity adopted the Convention on the Prevention and Combating of Terrorism in 1999.[132] By this Convention, States parties are to criminalise terrorist acts that comprise the following:

> a) Any act which is a violation of the criminal laws of a State party and which may endanger the life, physical integrity or freedom of, or cause serious injury or death to, any person, any number or group of persons or causes or may cause damage to public or private property, natural resources, environmental or cultural heritage and is calculated or intended to:
>
> (i) Intimidate, put in fear, force, coerce or induce any government, body, institution, the general public or any segment thereof, to do or abstain from doing any act, or to adopt or abandon a particular standpoint; or to act according to certain principles; or
>
> (ii) Disrupt any public service, the delivery of any essential service to the public or to create a public emergency; or
>
> (iii) Create general insurrection in a State.
>
> b) Any promotion, sponsoring, contribution to, command, aid, incitement, encouragement, attempt, threat, conspiracy, organizing, or procurement of any person, with the intent to commit any act referred to in paragraph (a)(i) to (iii).[133]

Struggles for liberation or self-determination are excluded from the Convention.[134] However and somewhat ironically, the Convention provides that 'political, philosophical, ideological, racial, ethnic, religious or other motives shall not be a justifiable defence against a terrorist act'.[135] In 2004, the Assembly of the African Union (formerly the OAU) adopted a Protocol to the Convention on the Prevention and

[130] See Organisation of African Unity (1994) Declaration on a Code of Conduct for Inter-African Relations, Assembly of Heads of State and Government, Thirtieth Ordinary Session, Tunis, 13–15 June 1994. See also Saul (2006), p. 160.

[131] AHG/Decl.2 (XXX); see also Report of the Chairperson of the Commission on Terrorism and Violent Extremism in Africa, Peace and Security Council 455th Meeting at the Level of Heads of State and Government, Nairobi, 2 September 2014, PSC/AHG/2 (CDLV), Paragraph 30.

[132] OAU Doc. AHG/Dec.132 (XXXV) 1999, adopted by the 35th OAU Summit in Algiers, 14 July 1999. Entered into force 6 December 2003.

[133] Organisation of African Unity (1999), Article 1.

[134] Organisation of African Unity (1999), Article 3(1).

[135] Organisation of African Unity (1999), Article 3(2).

Punishment of Terrorism 1999.[136] The Protocol was adopted to ensure the effective implementation of the Convention and other relevant international instruments and, importantly, to give effect to the provision relating to the establishment of the Peace and Security Council of the African Union in the coordination of efforts within the continent aimed at the countering terrorism.[137]

The Peace and Security Council of the African Union established a subcommittee on counterterrorism to ensure the implementation of the international instruments, as well as instruments of the African Union on terrorism.[138] The African Centre for the Study and Research on Terrorism was established in 2004 as a structure of the African Union Commission and the Peace and Security Council, pursuant to the Plan of Action of the African Union High Level Inter-Governmental Meeting on the Prevention and Combating of Terrorism in 2002.[139] The Centre was established to study and analyse terrorism, build capacity and develop training programmes for Member States that would facilitate counterterrorism in Africa, as well as globally. Under the Commission, a process was initiated (Nouakchott Process) in 2013 involving Algeria, Burkina Faso, Chad, Côte d'Ivoire, Guinea, Libya, Mali, Mauritania, Niger, Nigeria and Senegal to increase security cooperation and address security challenges, including terrorism, transnational crime and the proliferation of weapons in the regions of the Sahel and Sahara.[140]

5.4 Terrorism and the Use of Force

Since terrorism necessarily involves violence, whether as a means or in the results or both, the use of force in international law, especially as it pertains to a response to terrorism, is implicated in this enquiry. To begin with, an analysis of the place of the use of force is imperative, and this will be examined under the extant and preceding legal orders.

The Covenant of the League of Nations 1919 did not prohibit the use of force among States.[141] Rather, the Covenant sought to restrict instances that a State may

[136] African Union (8 July 2004) Protocol to the Convention on the Prevention of and Punishment of Terrorism adopted by the 3rd Ordinary Session of the Assembly of the African Union in Addis Ababa, 8 July 2004. (The treaty is not yet in force).

[137] African Union (8 July 2004), Article 2.

[138] PSC/PR/COMM.(CCXLVIX).

[139] African Union High Level Inter-Governmental Meeting on the Prevention and Combating of Terror, Algiers, Algeria, 11–14 September 2002, Mtg/HLIG/Conv.Terror/Plan (I).

[140] African Union, (17 Mar 2013) Ministerial Meeting on The Enhancement of Security Cooperation and the Operationalization of the African Peace and Security Architecture (APSA) in the Sahelo-Saharan Region, Nouakchott.

[141] 225 Parry 195; 1 Hudson 1; [1919] UKTS 4 (Cmd. 153). Reprinted in (1919) American Journal of International Law 13 (Supp. 128).

resort to the use of force.[142] It was not until 1928 that the General Treaty for the Renunciation of War as an Instrument of National Policy (Kellogg-Briand Pact) sought to outlaw the resort to war.[143] While the Treaty is of customary international law status, it is narrower than the regime under the Charter of the United Nations 1945, which provides the current legal framework on the use of force in international law. The Charter prohibits the threat or actual use of force against the territorial integrity or political independence of States or in any manner that is inconsistent with the purposes of the United Nations.[144]

5.5 The Right of Self-Defence Against Terrorist Attacks

The Charter is explicit on the right of States to use force in self-defence as an exception to the prohibition on the use of force contained in Article 2(4). Article 51 of the Charter recognises the 'inherent right of individual or collective self-defence if an armed attack occurs against a member of the United Nations'.[145]

As stated earlier, in contemporary times, terrorist acts have been perpetrated by non-State actors, i.e. armed groups. This seems to present a problem under the Charter framework and is highlighted by international legal discourse following the terrorist attacks of 9/11 on the United States, wherein it was argued in some quarters that the terrorist attacks fell outside the existing framework of international law.[146]

Thus, States involved in terrorism are in violation of their obligations under general international law, and such involvement would engage their State responsibility, as well as the right of self-defence of an affected State. The more difficult issue is where it is non-State actors that are engaging in terrorist activities and in which case certain pertinent questions arise. Firstly, what does the right of self-defence involve? Secondly, does it include a right of States to defend themselves against terrorist attacks?

In the *Case Concerning Military and Paramilitary Activities in and Against Nicaragua (Nicaragua v. United States of America)*, the International Court of Justice imported into its decision the question of imputability by holding that the action of irregulars could constitute an armed attack if they were sent by or acting on behalf of a State and if the scale and effects of the acts were of sufficient gravity as to have been classified as an armed attack had it been perpetrated by regular

[142] Members are obligated to settle their disputes through arbitration or judicial settlement or enquiry by the Council and are not to resort to force until 3 months after the arbitral award or judicial decision or report as the case may be. See, Article 12.

[143] 93 LNTS 343.

[144] See Charter of the United Nations, 59 Stat. 1031, 1 UNTS XVI, Article 2(4). Reprinted in (1945) American Journal of International Law 39 (Supp. 190), Article 24.

[145] United Nations (1945) Article 51.

[146] See Greenwood (2002), p. 301, on the controversial views adopted in the wake of 9/11; however, he argues that the Charter of the United Nations adequately covers the response to the 9/11 attacks.

armed forces.[147] In its Advisory Opinion on the *Legal Consequences of the Construction of a Wall in the Occupied Palestinian Territory*, the Court also sought to import the idea that an armed attack by terrorists can only justify the exercise of the right of self-defence under the Charter if such attacks can be imputed to a State. The International Court of Justice, rather dismissively, held:

> Article 51 of the Charter thus recognizes the existence of an inherent right of self-defence in the case of armed attack by one State against another State. However, Israel does not claim that the attacks against it are imputable to a foreign State.[148]

The decision of the Court flies in the face of the express provisions of the Charter of the United Nations and customary international law. The view of the Court has been strongly criticised from within the Court, as well as outside.[149] While it used to be more likely the case that the concept of an 'armed attack' would be more applicable to the action of the regular forces of States, the reality of international law is that the concept also applies to the action of irregular forces. In a later decision, in *Armed Activities on the Territory of the Congo (Democratic Republic of Congo v. Uganda)*, the International Court of Justice left open the issue of whether States can defend themselves from the activities of non-State actors.[150] As rightly argued by Greenwood:

> It would be a strange formalism that regarded the right to take military action against those who caused or threatened such actions as dependent upon whether or not their acts could be imputed to a State. There is, however, no reason to think that international law adopts such a formalistic approach.[151]

The United Nations General Assembly, in its Definition of Aggression and Declaration on Friendly Relations, envisaged certain types of terrorist acts.[152] In response to the 9/11 attack, the United States invoked its right of self-defence, a right that was recognised by the Security Council in Resolution 1386[153] and reaffirmed in Resolution 1373.[154] The North Atlantic Treaty Organisation, for the first time, invoked its right of collective self-defence under Article 5 of the Washington

[147] *Nicaragua Case* (1986) ICJ Reports 14, at 103, Paragraph 195.

[148] International Court of Justice (2004) ICJ Reports 136, Paragraph 139.

[149] See *Legal Consequences of the Construction of a Wall in the Occupied Palestinian Territory*, Separate Opinion of Judge Higgins, Paragraph 33; Wedgwood (2005), pp. 57–59; Murphy (2005), pp. 62–70; Kretzmer (2013), p. 246. See also Greenwood (2003), pp. 16–18; Greenwood (2002), p. 307; Franck (2001), pp. 839–840; Paust (2002), p. 533.

[150] See *Armed Activities on the Territory of the Congo* (*The Democratic Republic of the Congo v Uganda*) (2005) ICJ Reports 168, Paragraph 147.

[151] Greenwood (2003), p. 17. For a contrary view, see Fassbender (2010), pp. 86–92; and Dupuy (2010), pp. 12–14.

[152] See UN General Assembly, Definition of Aggression, 14 December 1974, A/RES/3314, Articles 3(g) and 4; UN General Assembly, Declaration on Principles of International Law concerning Friendly Relations and Cooperation among States in Accordance with the Charter of the United Nations, 24 October 1970, A/RES/2625 (XXV), Article 1.

[153] S/RES/1368 (2001)

[154] S/RES/1373 (2001)

Treaty following the terrorist attack on the United States, a member of the North Atlantic Treaty Organisation.[155]

The applicability of the right to self-defence against terrorist attacks from non-State actors is within the ambit of the Charter of the United Nations. Firstly, the Charter is unequivocal in the phrase 'if an armed attack occurs against a member of the United Nations'. It does not limit the right of self-defence to only where an attack is by a State against a member of the United Nations. Likewise, the Charter recognises the inherent right of self-defence as existing under customary international law. The right of self-defence under the Charter regime does not extinguish the right under customary international law as both coexist, as was held in the *Nicaragua Case*.[156] In fact, customary international law on the right of self-defence recognises action against non-State actors, as evident in the classical *Caroline Case*.[157]

The problematic issue in responding to terrorist attacks by exercising the right of self-defence is whether a State may lawfully rely on the right of self-defence in the absence of an 'armed attack', a view that the United States in responding to the 9/11 terrorist attacks canvassed in its National Security Strategy Document in 2002.[158] The Charter of the United Nations is explicit that States have a right of self-defence when 'an armed attack occurs'; however, with advancement in technology and modern weaponry, as well as the capacity of nuclear weapons to annihilate States and citizens, the issue of a State having to wait until the occurrence of an armed attack before lawfully exercising its right of self-defence leaves a lot to be desired. Two competing views exist. On the one hand, there is the view that a right of self-defence may only be lawfully exercised upon an armed attack based on the express provisions of the Charter.[159] On the other hand, there is the view that a State need not wait till an armed attack occurs before defending itself.[160]

The right of self-defence predates 1945, and as such the right existed prior to the Charter of the United Nations, which recognises the right in Article 51. Christopher Greenwood contends that 'the right of self-defence is not created by the Charter – it is a customary law right of some antiquity and is said to be inherent in the concept of Statehood'.[161] Thus, the question of whether a State may lawfully exercise its right of self-defence even in the absence of an armed attack is one that cannot be answered only within the framework of the Charter of the United Nations.

Under customary international law, a State possesses a limited right of anticipatory self-defence in the absence of an armed attack. In the *Caroline Case*, the right of anticipatory self-defence was acknowledged where there existed a threatened

[155] NATO Press Release 124, 12 September 2001.

[156] See *Nicaragua Case* Paragraphs 178 and 188.

[157] Jennings (1938), p. 82.

[158] United States Government (Sept 2002), The National Security Strategy of the United States of America, September 2002.

[159] *Nicaragua Case*, note 147; Gray (2013), pp. 251–252.

[160] Greenwood (2003), pp. 16–18.

[161] Greenwood (2003), p. 11.

armed attack provided that the 'necessity of that self-defence is instant, overwhelming, leaving no choice of means and no moment for deliberation'.[162] In the wake of the Second World War, the International Military Tribunals at Nuremberg and Tokyo also acknowledged the criteria established in the *Caroline Case*.[163] According to the International Military Tribunal at Nuremberg:

> It must be remembered that preventive action in foreign territory is justified only in case of an instant and overwhelming necessity for self-defence, leaving no choice of means, and no moment for deliberation.[164]

The view that a State need not wait till an armed attack occurs before defending itself is one that is supported by State practice, 'though not always unequivocal, by any means', as evident in Israel's use of force against Egypt in 1967 during the six-day war, as well as the fact that the international condemnation of Israel's attack on Iraq's nuclear reactor in 1981 was justified not on the non-existence of a right to anticipatory self-defence in international law but rather on the fact that the requirement of imminence of the threat was not satisfied.[165] The preponderance of international legal opinion supports the existence of a right of anticipatory self-defence for imminent threats, and this right is limited by the necessity for action and must be proportionate to the threat presented.[166] As aptly stated:

> In a nuclear age, common sense cannot require one to interpret an ambiguous provision in a text in a way that requires a State passively to accept its fate before it can defend itself. And, even in the face of conventional warfare, this would also seem the only realistic interpretation of the contemporary right of self-defence. It is the potentially devastating consequences of prohibiting self-defence unless an armed attack has occurred that leads one to prefer this interpretation....[167]

5.6 Enforcement Action

At the core of the collective security mechanism obtainable under the Charter of the United Nations, the Security Council is empowered to act with respect to threats to the peace, breaches of the peace and acts of aggression. Upon a determination of the existence of a threat to the peace or breach of the peace or act of aggression, the

---

[162] Letter from Daniel Webster to Henry S. Fox (24 April 1841), 29 British and Foreign State Papers 1129, 1138 (1857). In: Damrosch et al. (2001), pp. 922, 923.

[163] Greenwood (2003), p. 13. See also Rothwell (2005), p. 339.

[164] International Military Tribunal (Nuremberg), Judgment and Sentences, 1 October 1946 (1947) American Journal of International Law 41: 172, p. 205.

[165] Greenwood (2003), p. 14.

[166] Greenwood (2003), pp. 12–16 citing Sir Arthur Watts, Sir Robert Jennings, Sir Humphrey Waldock, Sir Gerald Fitzmaurice, Judge Stephen Schwebel, and D.W Bowett as proponents of the view supporting a right of anticipatory self-defence; Franck (2002), pp. 103–107; Kretzmer (2013), pp. 264–266; Sofaer (2003), pp. 225–226; Daudet (1997), p. 204.

[167] Higgins (1994), p. 242.

Council may take a range of measures, including the imposition of sanctions, as well as military enforcement action.[168] The Council has severally made determinations that acts of terrorism are threats to the peace. Pursuant to the determinations, the Council has also imposed sanctions on States like Libya and Sudan for their involvement in terrorism and also imposed sanctions on Al-Qaida and groups, as well as individuals, connected to it, including Boko Haram.[169]

5.7 Terrorism and International Criminal Law

5.7.1 Towards Terrorism as a Distinct Offence in International Law

Efforts towards the establishment of a distinct international crime of terrorism can be seen as far back as 1954 in the works of the International Law Commission (ILC) during the drafting of the 1954 Draft Code of Offences Against the Peace and Security of Mankind, wherein attempts were made to codify terrorism.[170] The Draft Code, while noting that offences against peace and security of mankind are offences in international law, included as part of such offences 'the undertaking or encouragement by the authorities of a State of terrorist activities in another State, or the toleration by the authorities of a State of organised activities calculated to carry out terrorist acts in another State'.[171] The international crime of terrorism envisaged under the Draft Code was one that had a nexus with the State, i.e. it only applied to the activities of those acting on behalf of the State.[172] It was also envisaged that the acts in question would be directed against a State. Thus, 'private terrorism with international effects' was excluded from the ambit of the Code.[173]

Jurists have questioned the inclusion of terrorism in the Draft Code 1954. Higgins is of the opinion that the inclusion was merely politically convenient seeing as international law on the use of force and the law of State responsibility exist with regard to terrorist acts, as envisaged by Article 2(6) of the Draft Code 1954.[174] This is especially in view of the fact that the Code is explicit on its applicability only with

[168] Charter of the United Nations, see note 37, Articles 39, 41 and 42.

[169] S/RES/748 (1992), S/RES/1054 (1996), S/RES/1333 (2000), S/RES/1390 (2002), S/RES/1989 (2011), S/RES/2083 (2012), S/RES/2161 (2014).

[170] International Law Commission (1954) ILC Draft Code of Offences against the Peace and Security of Mankind (Part I), in ILC 6th Sess. Report (3 June-28 July 1954), UN Doc A/2693, as requested by UN General Assembly Resolution 177(II), 21 November 1947; (1951) Volume II Yearbook of the ILC 134. See also Saul (2006), p. 176.

[171] International Law Commission (1954), Article 2(6).

[172] Saul (2006), p. 176.

[173] Saul (2006), p. 176.

[174] Higgins (1997), pp. 26–27; Saul (2006), p. 177.

regard to individual criminal responsibility,[175] more so that the ILC was already working on the separate issue of State responsibility.

Owing to a lack of consensus on the concept of aggression, the work of the ILC on the Draft Code was interrupted, and even the subsequent Definition of Aggression did not expressly include a distinct offence of terrorism.[176] With the resumption of efforts on the Draft Code, the ILC adopted a first reading of the Draft Code in 1991.[177] The 1991 Draft Code included within its ambit the international crime of terrorism, i.e. when

> An individual who as agent or representative of a State commits or orders the commission of any of the following acts: undertaking, organizing, assisting, financing, encouraging or tolerating acts against another State directed at persons or property and of such a nature as to create a state of terror in the minds of public figures, groups of persons or the general public.[178]

Like the 1954 Draft Code, the 1991 Draft Code excluded the acts of individuals acting in their private capacity, as well as required a nexus between the direction of the acts and a State. It went further than the earlier Draft by its specificity in the inclusion of acts of organisation, assistance and finance of terrorist acts, as well as being applicable to acts against property.[179] The adoption of the 1991 Draft Code was complicated by the work on the Statute for a permanent international criminal court, and so the Code was referred back to the drafting committee of the ILC.[180]

The Draft Code was finally adopted in 1996.[181] The 1996 Draft Code, unlike earlier drafts, did not include a distinct crime of international terrorism but rather subsumed the offence under war crimes by expressly including terrorism as 'acts committed in violation of international humanitarian law applicable to armed conflict not of an international character'.[182] Thus, 'there was no longer any broader offence of creating a state of terror outside armed conflict'.[183]

---

[175] International Law Commission (1954), Article 1.

[176] See General Assembly, Definition of Aggression, 14 December 1974, A/RES/3314, Articles 3(g) and 4; UN General Assembly, Declaration on Principles of International Law concerning Friendly Relations and Cooperation among States in Accordance with the Charter of the United Nations, 24 October 1970, A/RES/2625 (XXV), Article 1.

[177] (1991) Volume II Yearbook of the ILC, para 175; ILC (47th Sess.), 13th Report of the Special Rapporteur (1995), UN Doc. A/CN.4/466.

[178] (1991) Volume II Yearbook of the ILC, Article 24.

[179] Saul (2006), p. 179.

[180] Allain and Jones (1997), p. 100.

[181] ILC, Report on 48th Sess., 6 May – 26 July 1996, UN Doc. A/51/10; 51 UN GAOR Supp. (No. 10) p. a14.

[182] (1996) Volume II Yearbook of the ILC (Part II) 17, Article 20(f)(iv); see also Saul (2006), p. 180.

[183] Saul (2006), p. 180.

5.7.2 An International Court with Jurisdiction Over Terrorism?

The international prosecution of terrorist acts before international courts is limited. Firstly, the jurisdiction of the International Court of Justice is limited to States and does not include criminal prosecution. However, where a State is implicated in terrorist acts or is found wanting with regard to its international obligations under terrorism-related treaties, then its responsibility may become engaged, and the International Court of Justice may provide the forum for adjudication. The *ad hoc* international criminal tribunals established by the Security Council pursuant to Chapter VII of the UN Charter, i.e. the International Criminal Tribunals for Yugoslavia (ICTY) and Rwanda (ICTR), are already in the winding up process with their residual mechanisms having been established. Nevertheless, the jurisdiction of the tribunals is limited under their statutes, *ratione materiae* and *ratione temporis*. The jurisdiction of the ICTY is limited to serious violations of international humanitarian law committed in the territory of the former Yugoslavia since 1991 and is with respect to war crimes, violations of the laws and customs of war, genocide and crimes against humanity.[184] In *Prosecutor v. Stanislav Galić*, the ICTY held that it had jurisdiction over the acts of terror as a violation of the laws and customs of war, with which the accused was charged, because it was within the jurisdiction *ratione materiae* of the Tribunal under Article 3 of its constitutive Statute.[185] The jurisdiction of the ICTR is limited to serious violations of international humanitarian law committed in the territory of Rwanda and Rwandan citizens responsible for violations committed in the territory of neighbouring States between 1 January 1994 and 31 December 1994.[186] The jurisdiction of the ICTR is with respect to the crimes of genocide, crimes against humanity and war crimes.[187]

The United Nations General Assembly drew to the attention of States participating in the Preparatory Committee on the Establishment of the International Criminal Court (ICC) the relevance of the Draft Code to their work.[188] The relevance of the Draft Code to the establishment of the ICC was with regard to offences over which the ICC could exercise jurisdiction. The Draft Statute of the ICC included terrorism as a crime within the jurisdiction *ratione materiae* of the Court.[189] Some States were in favour of the inclusion of terrorism within the jurisdiction of the ICC, while

[184] Annexed to Security Council Resolution 827 (1993), UN SCOR 48th Sess., UN Doc. S/RES/827 (1993); 32 ILM 1159, Articles 1–5.

[185] Case No. IT-98-29-T (Trial Chamber Decision, 5 December 2003, Paragraphs 133 and 138.

[186] Annexed to Security Council Resolution 955 (1994), UN SCOR 49th Sess., UN Doc. S/RES/955 (1994); 33 ILM 1598, Article 1.

[187] See Articles 2–4 of the ICTR Statute.

[188] A/RES/51/160 (1996), Paragraph 2.

[189] Draft Statute of the ICC, Article 5, in Official Records of the UN Diplomatic Conference of Plenipotentiaries on an International Criminal Court, Rome, 15 June -17 July 1998, UN Doc. A/CONF.183/13, volume III, 21. See also Report of the Preparatory Committee, UN Doc A/Conf.183/2/Add.1 (14 April 1998) 2, GAOR 51st Sess., Suppl. No.22, Volume I.

others were not. Even among the States that supported the inclusion of terrorism, there was disagreement on the extent of such inclusion. According to Saul:

> Among States that supported the inclusion of terrorism, there was variation in the approach to definition and criminalization. Some States thought that terrorism should be included as a crime against humanity. Russia thought the offence should be limited to the most serious terrorist crimes; Turkey believed systematic and prolonged terrorism against a civilian population should be covered; and Albania argued that institutionalized State terrorism should be included. Though in favour of including terrorism, Egypt sought to exclude national liberation movements, while a number of Islamic States impliedly urged the same result by invoking the 1999 Arab League Convention as a model approach…[190]

Highlighting the ambivalence of the States at the preparation for the establishment of the ICC as to the crimes that should be subject to the jurisdiction of the ICC, Ortega states:

> Some delegations were in favour of a much more detailed definition of the crimes, some others would like new crimes to be included, and several representatives even proposed a review mechanism to enable States parties to add additional crimes to the Court's jurisdiction. In this sense, it was suggested that the general descriptions of the crimes of drug trafficking and terrorism should be included in the Draft Statute, as well as the crime against UN personnel. On the other hand, some delegations affirmed that the Draft Statute was not the right place to characterize the particular crimes… In an initial stage, only the most indisputable crimes should be under the jurisdiction of the Court. Moreover, crimes such as drug trafficking and terrorism were not of the same kind as the traditional crimes mentioned in Article 20(a) to (d) and could be dealt with much better at a national level.[191]

The Rome Statute of the ICC was adopted in 1998.[192] It does not include terrorism as a distinct crime of international law over which the Court could assert jurisdiction. Article 5(1) of the Rome Statute expressly provides:

> The jurisdiction of the Court shall be limited to the most serious crimes of concern to the international community as a whole. The Court has jurisdiction in accordance with this Statute with respect to the following crimes:
>
> a) The crime of genocide;
>
> b) Crimes against humanity;
>
> c) War crimes; and
>
> d) The crime of aggression.[193]

---

[190] Saul (2006), p. 181.

[191] Ortega (1997) The ILC Adopts the Draft Code of Crimes against the Peace and Security of mankind. Max Planck Yearbook of United Nations Law 1: 283, p. 304; Report of the Preparatory Committee for the Establishment of an International Criminal Court, GAOR 51st Sess., Suppl. No. 22, Volume I, paras 5–115.

[192] A./CONF.183/9 of 17 July 1998.

[193] 2187 UNTS 90. It entered into force on 1 July 2002.

It is inherent in the nature of the offences mentioned in Article 5 of the Rome Statute and the specificity of Articles 6–8 of the Statute that terrorism is excluded from the ambit of Article 5. It has been contended that 'the option of referring terrorism to the ICC was also intended to avoid jurisdictional disputes between States, and supply the Security Council with a means of referring terrorist threats for resolution'.[194] That terrorism falls outside the ambit, and jurisdiction, of the ICC is clearly manifest from the language of the Rome Statute, *expressio verbis*. While the Rome Statute envisages a situation whereby the Court may exercise jurisdiction when the Security Council refers a matter to it, this cannot include where acts of terrorism are involved. Firstly, while admittedly the Security Council can refer matters to the ICC, however when the Council makes such a referral, it must be within the framework of the Rome Statute. Secondly, Article 13 is explicit that a referral by the Council has to be with regard to where acts coming within the jurisdiction of the ICC are alleged to have been committed. The Rome Statute in Article 13 (b) explicitly provides thus:

> The Court may exercise its jurisdiction with respect to a crime referred to in Article 5 in accordance with the provisions of this Statute if a situation is one in which one or more of such crimes appears to have been committed is referred to the Prosecutor by the Security Council acting under Chapter VII of the Charter of the United Nations.[195]

The exclusion of terrorism from the Rome Statute is 'normatively significant',[196] especially in view of the fact that the jurisdiction of the ICC is 'limited to the most serious crimes of concern to the international community as a whole'.[197] The omission was occasioned by a myriad of factors, including the nebulous nature of terrorism and the lack of a generally accepted definition of the concept of terrorism in international law, as well as for the fact of its 'legal novelty and lack of prior definition; disagreement about national liberation violence; and a fear that it would politicise the ICC'.[198] In addition, it was felt in some quarters that national authorities were best suited to investigate and prosecute terrorist offences.[199] However, to the extent that terrorist acts amount to crimes against humanity as part of a widespread or systematic attack against any civilian population, in line with Article 7 of the Rome Statute of the ICC, then the perpetrators can be prosecuted for crimes against humanity before the ICC.[200]

As it currently stands, while it cannot be said that there is no international court with jurisdiction to try individuals for acts of terrorism, the extent to which this may be the case is very limited. The jurisdiction of the Special Court for Sierra Leone is with regard to serious violations of international humanitarian law and Sierra Leonean law committed in Sierra Leone since 30 November 1996 and extends only

[194] Saul (2006), p. 181.

[195] See 2187 UNTS 90. It entered into force on 1 July 2002.

[196] Saul (2006), pp. 182–183.

[197] Rome Statute of the ICC (1998), Article 5.

[198] Saul (2006), p. 182.

[199] Arsanjani (1999), p. 29.

[200] See also Saul (2006), p. 183 and Arsanjani (1999), p. 31.

to crimes against humanity, war crimes, violations of international humanitarian law and crimes under the domestic laws of Sierra Leone.[201] Terrorism is excluded from the jurisdiction of the Extraordinary Chambers in the Courts of Cambodia, which is only in relation to serious violations of Cambodian penal law, international humanitarian law and international law recognised by Cambodia between 17 April 1975 and 6 January 1979. While this seems wide enough to permit jurisdiction for crimes under international law, as contained in terrorism-related treaties, the law establishing the Court is explicit on its applicability only to violations of Cambodian penal laws, genocide, crimes against humanity and war crimes committed during the period of Democratic Kampuchea.[202]

Although the jurisdiction of the Special Tribunal for Lebanon extends to terrorism, it is very narrow and exclusively reliant on Lebanese domestic criminal law, i.e. 'to prosecute persons responsible for the attack of 14 February 2005 resulting in the death of former Lebanese Prime Minister Rafiq Hariri and in the death or injury of other persons'.[203] The jurisdiction of the recently established Extraordinary Chambers in the courts of Senegal extends to serious violations of international law, customary international law and international conventions ratified by Chad committed in the territory of Chad between 7 June 1982 and 1 December 1990. It exists with respect to genocide, crimes against humanity, war crimes and torture.[204] Interestingly, the Statute of the Extraordinary Chambers in Senegal includes, as part of war crimes within its jurisdiction, acts of terrorism.[205] However, the extent to which the Court has jurisdiction to try acts of terrorism is limited to the international conventions ratified by Chad and committed on the territory of Chad between 7 June 1982 and 1 December 1990.

5.8 International Law and Boko Haram

The Security Council's Al-Qaida Committee approved the inclusion of Boko Haram to the list of individuals and entities subject to the financial sanctions and arms embargo contained in Resolution 2083.[206] The Council acting under Chapter VII of the Charter of the United Nations obligated Member States to freeze the funds and

---

[201] UN Doc. S/2002/246, Appendix II, 2178 UNTS 138, (2003) American Journal of International Law 97: 295, Articles 1–5.

[202] Law on the Establishment of The Extraordinary Chambers in the Courts of Cambodia for the Prosecution of Crimes Committed During the Period of Democratic Kampuchea 2001, As Amended on 27 October 2004 (NS/RKM/1004/006).

[203] Annexed to SCR 1757 (2007), 5685th Meeting, U.N. Doc. S/RES/1757 (2007), Article 1(1).

[204] See Articles 3 and 4 of the Statute of the Extraordinary African Chambers within the Senegalese Judicial System for the Prosecution of International Crimes Committed on the Territory of the republic of Chad during the period from 7 June 1982 to 1 December 1990.

[205] See Article 7(2)(d) of the Statute of the Extraordinary African Chambers within the Senegalese Judicial System for the Prosecution of International Crimes Committed on the Territory of the republic of Chad during the period from 7 June 1982 to 1 December 1990.

[206] Security Council Press Release, SC/11410, 22 May 2014.

financial assets of the group, prevent travel into or through their territory of members of the group, prevent supply, sale or transfer of arms and related weapons, military equipment, including vehicles and technical assistance.[207]

The Council's Al-Qaida Sanctions Committee also approved the addition of Abubakar Mohammed Shekau, the current leader of Boko Haram, and Ansarul Muslimina Fi Biladis-Sudan, an armed splinter group of Boko Haram, to the list of individuals and entities subjected to the targeted financial sanctions and arms embargo contained in Resolution 2161.[208] By Resolution 2161, the Council obligated Member States to freeze the assets and funds of these entities, as well as prevent entry into, transit through and exit from their territories, as well as prevent the direct or indirect sale or supply of arms, military equipment and technical assistance.[209] The European Parliament has also passed several resolutions condemning the attacks by Boko Haram in Nigeria.[210] In addition, the European Union has included Boko Haram to its list of persons, groups and entities subject to an asset freeze.[211] Within the institutional framework of the African Union, there have been condemnations of the continued threat of terrorism in Africa, including the activities of Boko Haram, by the Peace and Security Council[212] and the Chairperson of the African Union Commission.[213]

With a view to meeting its international obligations, the Federal Government of Nigeria has considered, developed and implemented different domestic strategies to address the security crisis, including amnesties, negotiations, legislation, armed military response, ceasefire agreement, international diplomacy and international military alliances, as well as a declaration of a state of emergency in some States of Northern Nigeria. The Terrorism (Prevention) Act was passed in 2011 criminalising acts of terrorism, terrorist meetings, support for terrorism, harbouring of terrorism, provision of training for terrorism, obstruction of terrorism investigation, financing of terrorism and hostage-taking.[214] The Act defines terrorism as follows:

> [An] act which is deliberately done with malice aforethought and which may seriously harm of damage a country or an international organisation; is intended or can reasonably be regarded as having been intended to unduly compel a government or international organisation to perform or abstain from performing any act; seriously intimidate a population; seriously destabilise or destroy the fundamental political, constitutional, economic or social structures of a country or an international organisation; or otherwise influence such government or international organisation by intimidation or coercion.[215]

---

[207] S/RES/2083 (2012), Operative Paragraph 1.

[208] Security Council Press Release, SC/11455, 26 June 2014.

[209] S/RES/2161 (2014), Operative Paragraph 1.

[210] Resolution of 17 July 2014 (2014/2729 (RSP)); Resolution of 04 July 2013 (2013/2691 (RSP)); Resolution of 15 March 2012 (2012/2550 (RSP).

[211] Regulation No. 583/2014, Annex.

[212] Assembly/AU/Dec.536 (XXIII).

[213] Press Release of 12 January 2015; Press Release of 21 May 2014; Press Release of 02 May 2014.

[214] Act No. 10, 03 June 2011, Articles 1–13.

[215] See Section 1((2) of the Terrorism Prevention Act (2011), Laws of the Federation of Nigeria.

Following the inability of the government to rescue and bring back the abducted girls in the face of mounting national and international pressure, the President of Nigeria asked the United States and France for their assistance in bringing an end to Boko Haram's reign of terror.[216] The United States has chosen to offer assistance through advisory and intelligence support to the Federal Government rather than direct military action in Nigeria.[217] While the legal basis of such military action by the United States, outside the Security Council of the United Nations, would be dubious, the practical consequences, including funding, logistics and post-conflict reconstruction, especially in the wake of Iraq and Libya, are contributories to the decision of the United States to render assistance in capacity building.

Unfortunately, other than statements of the president of the Security Council, the United Nations Security Council is yet to adopt a resolution expressly condemning the activities of Boko Haram, unlike regional organisations like the African Union and the European Union. While a resolution expressly condemning the activities of Boko Harm is desirable from a moral and political perspective, as the Council has done with regard to the terrorist attacks against the US and the UK, the pervasive and escalating nature of terrorism calls for more concrete efforts than mere condemnation. Rising to its responsibility within the African region, which has become home to some terrorist networks, the African Union by January 2015 authorised a 7500 strong regional force comprised of military and other personnel, which was later increased to 10,000 men strong in March 2015 to combat Boko Haram.[218] The operationalisation of the African Union Force is dependent on funds, which the African Union lacks and shows the limitation of its efforts with regard to containing Boko Haram and terrorism not just in West Africa but also within the African continent.

The United Nations Security Council has the sole discretion to employ a range of measures, including military and non-military measures, against Boko Haram. The financial and weapon sanctions imposed by the United Nations on Boko Haram, as well as the travel ban on certain individuals associated with the group, while commendable, have not contained the group. It is in recognition of the fact that an effective response to terrorism must transcend military action that programmes by the UN Development Programme, the World Bank and international agencies like the United States Agency for International Development (USAID) and the Department for International Development (DFID) to address the political and socio-economic factors that contribute to terrorism, as contained in the Global Counter-Terrorism Strategy, are currently underway. At the same time, the United Nations has to recognise the importance of military action under its auspices to combat terrorism and to discourage the need for unilateralism. Thus, while it may be pragmatically difficult for the Security Council to launch enforcement action against Boko Haram, this makes it imperative for the Council to lend its support to the operationalisation of the Multinational Joint Task Force.

---

[216] Blanchard and Blanchard (2015).

[217] Blanchard and Blanchard (2015).

[218] See Communiqué of the Peace and Security Council of the African Union, 489th Meeting, 3 March 2015, Addis Ababa, Ethiopia, PSC/PR/Comm.CDLXXXIX) REV. 1. See also Blanchard and Blanchard (2015).

Despite the activities of Boko Haram having acquired an international dimension because of threats to the territorial integrity and political independence of neighbouring States like Cameroon and Chad, which could have engaged the right of self-defence of the affected States, a concerted response has been favoured. A Joint Task Force was established in 1994 as a national initiative to address criminal activities along its Northern border but was expanded into a Multinational Joint Task Force in 1998 between Nigeria, Chad, Niger, Cameroon and Benin to combat transnational crime in the Lake Chad region, and following the rise of Boko Haram, the objective of the Task Force became addressing the terrorist activities of the group. However, the Multinational Joint Task Force is yet to achieve this objective due to funding, personnel, technical and tactical challenges with its headquarters in Baga, Nigeria, being overrun by Boko Haram in January 2015. While the headquarters has now moved to N'djamena in Chad with commitments to improve logistic, personnel and tactical operations, the success of the Multinational Joint Task Force in bringing an end to Boko Haram remains to be seen.

There is a glaring lack of coordination in the efforts of the Nigerian Government, as well as in the concerted efforts of the Multinational Joint Task Force, which resulted not only in the abandonment of the headquarters of the Force by Cameroon and Chad prior to its being overrun by Boko Haram but also in the unilateral decision of Chad to enter into Nigerian territory, in February 2015, to launch a ground offensive against Boko Haram. While it is not argued in this paper that the entry of Chadian troops into Nigeria is a breach of the prohibition against the use of force, it is put forward as evidence of an incoherent and poorly coordinated response to terrorism by the States involved.

The state of the Nigerian criminal justice system compounded by the paucity of skill sets to investigate and prosecute terrorist offences, as well as the limited ability of security agencies to gather intelligence and undertake forensic investigation, considerably undermine counterterrorism measures. The idea of creating special courts to try terrorist offences has been bandied to obviate the problems of a notoriously slow judicial process in Nigeria.[219] However, even if these special courts are created, in the absence of skilled manpower to investigate and prosecute terrorist offences, as well as to administer these special courts, the problems will continue. On the other hand, there is the prospect of international criminal law. Although the Federal Government,[220] as well as the United Nations Security Council,[221] can refer the situation in the northeastern part of Nigeria to the International Criminal Court for investigation and prosecution for crimes against humanity,[222] an international or internationalised court can also be established with jurisdiction for terrorism as a response to Boko Haram either by the United Nations or the African Union or under a multilateral agreement between the affected States in the Lake Chad region.

[219] Oyebode (2012), p. 13.

[220] Rome Statute of the ICC (1998), Articles 13(a) and 14.

[221] Rome Statute of the ICC (1998), Article 13(b).

[222] Rome Statute of the ICC (1998), Articles 5 and 7.

5.9 Conclusion

This chapter set out to address, in the main, three issues—what terrorism is, how international law has responded to terrorism and whether international law provides an effective and adequate legal framework for the suppression of terrorism. The first two have been addressed in detail in the body of the chapter, and the last will be addressed in these concluding remarks.

The metastasising threat of terrorism has presented itself as a multifaceted and complex phenomenon, in response to which international law must adopt a comprehensive approach. International law has been extensively engaged in its response to terrorism, as evident in the chapter, from the definitional efforts, efforts at creating an international court with jurisdiction over terrorism to the law on the use of force. In addition, there are elaborate counterterrorism procedures and mechanisms established pursuant to Resolution 1373, but the effectiveness of these is dependent on the cooperation of States. Despite political challenges that have hindered a universally agreed definition of terrorism, the adoption of a sectoral approach through thirteen (13) wide-ranging multilateral instruments is pivotal in the suppression of terrorism. The adoption of a universal definition of terrorism, while ideal, its prospects remain uncertain, and the reality of international law is that it must continue to strive at efforts to combat terrorism. In the face of this uncertainty, States have had to adopt definitions that strike at the core of terrorism and that reflect the sectoral approach of international law to terrorism.

As Islamic militancy grows within the African continent, the Middle East and beyond, international law must go beyond condemnation and suppression of terrorism and ensure a more broad-spectrum approach to the scourge of terrorism, including addressing its root causes and contributory factors, the prevention of radicalisation and violent extremism through the implementation of programmes aimed at countering radicalisation and promoting de-radicalisation. It is imperative that programmes to rehabilitate and re-integrate terrorists must form part of any veritable action plan in the suppression of terrorism. Tackling the conditions conducive to terrorism, as identified under the Global Counter-Terrorism Strategy, is imperative and requires a multifaceted cooperation across the board between public and private sectors, civil society groups and non-governmental organisations.

On its own, Nigeria has a more fundamental role to play in combating Boko Haram. Despite the dominant role that Nigeria has played in regional peace and security, its inability to contain Boko Haram has been most telling about the malaise that has plagued the political and security agencies of the country. There is an urgent need for the overhaul of the criminal justice system, which would include the independence of the judiciary. As contributories to terrorism, unemployment, poverty, corruption, poor democratic governance, absence of rule of law and poor education demand the attention and mitigating action of the Federal Government. In the absence of a coherent and cohesive domestic counterterrorism strategy and mechanisms supported by effective processes and institutions, efforts to combat Boko Haram would remain ineffective.

References

Abi-Saab G (2004) The proper role of international law in combating terrorism. In: Bianchi A (ed) Enforcing international law norms against terrorism. Hart, Oxford, pp xiii–xxii

Acharya UD (2009) War on terror or terror wars: the problem in defining terrorism. Denver J Int Law Policy 37:653–679

Allain J, Jones JRWD (1997) A patchwork of norms: a commentary on the 1991 draft code of crimes against peace and security of mankind. Eur J Int Law 1:100–117

Arsanjani M (1999) The 1998 Rome statute of the international criminal court. Am J Int Law 93:22–43

Baxter RR (1974) A skeptical look at the concept of terrorism. Akron Law Rev 7:380–387

Blanchard LP, Blanchard CM (2015) Nigeria's Boko Haram and the Islamic State. Congressional Research Service Insights March 12, 2015 (IN10242)

Comolli V (2015) Boko Haram: Nigeria's Islamist insurgency. Oxford University Press, Oxford

Conte A (2010) Human rights in the prevention and punishment of terrorism. Springer, Dordrecht

Cooper HHA (1978) Terrorism: the problem of the problem of definition. Chitty's Law J 26:105–108

Damrosch L et al (eds) (2001) International law: cases and materials. West Group, St. Paul

Daudet Y (1997) International action against state terrorism. In: Higgins R, Flory M (eds) International law and terrorism. Routledge, London, pp 201–216

Dupuy P (2010) State sponsors of terrorism: issues of international responsibility. In: Bianchi A (ed) Enforcing international law norms against terrorism. Hart, Oxford, pp 3–16

Fassbender B (2010) The UN security council and international terrorism. In: Bianchi A (ed) Enforcing international law norms against terrorism. Hart, Oxford, pp 83–102

Franck TM (2001) Editorial comments: terrorism and the right of self-defence. Am J Int Law 95:839–842

Franck TM (2002) Recourse to force: state action against threats and armed attacks. Cambridge University Press, Cambridge

Franck TM, Lockwood BB Jr (1974) Preliminary thoughts towards an international convention on terrorism. Am J Int Law 68:69–90

Gray C (2013) The International Court of Justice and the use of force. In: Tams CJ, Sloan J (eds) The development of international law by the International Court of Justice. Oxford University Press, Oxford, pp 237–260

Greenwood C (2002) International law and the war against terrorism. Int Aff 78:301–317

Greenwood C (2003) International law and the pre-emptive use of force: Afghanistan, Al-Qaida, and Iraq. San Diego Int Law J 4:7–3

Guillaume G (2004) Terrorism and international law. Int Comp Law Q 53:537–548

Higgins R (1994) Problems and process: international law and how we use it. Oxford University Press, Oxford

Higgins R (1997) The general international law of terrorism. In: Higgins R, Flory M (eds) International law and terrorism. Routledge, London, pp 13–29

Jennings RY (1938) The Caroline and McLeod cases. Am J Int Law 32:82–99

Kolb R (2004) The exercise of criminal jurisdiction over international terrorists. In: Bianchi A (ed) Enforcing international law norms against terrorism. Hart, Oxford, pp 227–281

Kretzmer D (2013) The inherent right to self-defence and proportionality in Jus Ad Bellum. Eur J Int Law 24:235–282

Lillich RB (1982) Transnational terrorism: conventions and commentary. Michie Corporation, Charlottesville

Murphy SD (2005) Self-defence and the Israeli wall advisory opinion: an Ipse Dixit from the ICJ. Am J Int Law 99:62–76

Nawaz MK, Singh G (1977) Legal control of international terrorism. Indian J Int Law 17:66–82

Ortega MC (1997) The ILC adopts the draft code of crimes against the peace and security of mankind. Max Planck Yearb U N Law 1:283–326

Oyebode A (2012) Legal responses to the Boko Haram challenge: an assessment of Nigeria's terrorism (prevention) act 2011. Forum Publ Policy 1:1–13
Paust J (2002) Use of armed force against terrorists in Afghanistan, Iraq and Beyond. Cornell Int Law J 35:533–558
Plant G (1997) Legal aspects of terrorism at sea. In: Higgins R, Flory M (eds) International law and terrorism. Routledge, London, pp 68–96
Ray N (2016) Growing threat of terrorism in Africa: the case of Boko Haram. Indian Council of World Affairs Issue Brief, 20 February 2016
Richards A (2015) Conceptualizing terrorism. Oxford University Press, Oxford
Romaniuk P (2010) Multilateral counter-terrorism: the global politics of co-operation and contestation. Routledge, Oxford
Rothwell DR (2005) Anticipatory self-defence in the age of international terrorism. Univ Queensland Law J 24:337–353
Saul B (2005) Attempts to define 'terrorism' in international law. Neth Int Law Rev 52:57–83
Saul B (2006) Defining terrorism in international law. Oxford University Press, Oxford
Scharf MP (2004) Defining terrorism as the peacetime equivalent of war crimes: problems and prospects. Case West Reserve J Int Law 36:359–374
Schmid A (2004) Terrorism: the definitional problem. Case West Reserve J Int Law 36:375–419
Sofaer AD (2003) On the necessity of pre-emption. Eur J Int Law 14:209–226
United Nations Office on Drug and Crime (2009) Handbook on criminal justice responses to terrorism. United Nations, New York
Walters F (1969) A history of the league of nations. Oxford University Press, Oxford
Wedgwood R (2005) The ICJ advisory opinion on the Israeli security fence and the limits of self-defence. Am J Int Law 99:52–61
Zlataric B (1975) History of international terrorism and its legal control. In: Bassiouni MC (ed) International terrorism and political crimes. Charles C. Thomas, Springfield, pp 474–484

Chapter 6
Terrorism and Cross-Border Insurgency as New Threats and Challenges to Peace and Security in Africa: The Boko Haram Insurgency

Godwin O. Anyalemechi

6.1 Introduction

Insurgency and terrorism apparently lack acceptable all-encompassing single definition. Attempting a definition of insurgency creates the problem of dissociating in context, what is not and what is. Strictly speaking, insurgency is neither conventional warfare nor terrorism, for example, but it shares with both concepts the use of force to achieve a political end. The crucial difference is the scope and scale of violence.[1] On the other hand, terrorism rarely results in political change on its own insurgency attempts to bring about change through force of arms.[2] In an insurgency, the adversaries are asymmetric, weaker, and almost always a substate group attempting to bring about political change by administering and fighting more effectively than its state-based foe through the use of guerrilla tactics. These tactics are characterized by hit-and-run raids and ambushes against local security forces. Confusion often results from insurgent movement using terrorist tactics to achieve local results.

The threat of terrorism mounted by the Boko Haram insurgency in Nigeria and her interest is real. It appears that terrorism has become a persistent and permanent feature of our national security environment. It is now obvious that further terrorist attacks could occur at any time. Over the past 11 years, the world has seen a succession of terrorist campaigns, supporting various ideological or nationalist causes. Methods of attacks have evolved, and terrorists have proved to be innovative, adaptive, and ruthless in pursing their goals.

Prior to the rise of indigenous self-styled terrorism fostered by political, ethnic, and religious undertones, Nigeria was not a specific target. We are now. Between March 2011 and June 2012, more than 1000 Nigerians were killed in terrorist

[1] Lewis (2013).

[2] Lewis (2013).

G. O. Anyalemechi (✉)
Nigerian Army School of Legal Services, Zaria, Nigeria

J.-M. Iyi, H. Strydom (eds.), *Boko Haram and International Law*,
https://doi.org/10.1007/978-3-319-74957-0_6

attacks in the country. Numerous other attacks have been thwarted. But who are this group? A charismatic, educated, and westernized individual called Mohammed Yusuf rose up to share his own ideal of what he termed "The Evils of Western Education."[3] This he started in the Northern Nigerian City of Maiduguri and used the native Kanuri dialect to propagate his idea—"BOKO HARAM" (i.e, "western education is forbidden"). This organization is known as Jama'atu Ahlis Sunna Lidda' Awati Wal-Jihad (People Committed to the Prophet's Teaching for Propagation and Jihad).

These people follow a distorted and militant interpretation of self-help that calls for violence as the answer to perceived grievances. The broad movement comprises Al Qa'eda, groups allied or associated with it, and others inspired by extremist ethnic and environmental ideologies. Their constituency, while small in global terms, shows every sign of persisting war, even when and if their current senior leadership were killed or captured. It should be noted that in Nigeria, Boko Haram remains significant, but not the only threat. There are other extremist groups like MEND (Movement for the Emancipation of Niger-Delta) operating in various parts of the country. All of them advocate the use of violence to gain control over others. In doing so, they threaten our national life and psyche.

The nature of free and open societies enables terrorists' networks to take advantage of freedom of movement, communications, financial system, and logistical support. They influence their directions through both propaganda and actions. Their extremist ideologies, goals, and interpretations of world events allow local grievances to be worked into their vision. Their messages resonate around the world, with Jihadist terrorists attracting new adherents. Their activities challenge governments and communities locally and threaten prosperity and security in various parts of the country. They can operate and exploit seams between states, between military and police forces, and between international and local laws. Consequently, in their cross-border exploitation, Nigerian neighboring states (within the Lake Chad Basin) remain highly vulnerable to terrorist violence designed to undermine their national unity and cohesion and cause some dissentions among "nationalities" and "foreigners" alike mooting to "opt out."[4]

Violent extremist organizations (like Boko Haram) are transnational movement—cutting across national boundaries. In recent times, Boko Haram established bases along Nigeria-Cameroon border, Nigeria-Chad border, Nigeria-Niger border, Nigeria-Mali and Mauritania borders. Boko Haram has its affiliates in the Al Qa'eda in the Islamic Maghreb (AQIM). It is also affiliated with Al Shabaab in Somalia. Its fighters are now mostly mercenaries from M23 rebels from DR Congo and AQIM fighters from Algeria, Mali, and even Sudan. Many Chadian rebels also identify with Boko Haram. Intelligence sources have it that the Chadian leader, a rebel himself who brokered the failed cease-fire between the Nigerian Federal Government and Boko Haram sometime in November, has sympathies for the group.

---

[3] Nigerian Defence Headquarters (2014a), p. 28.

[4] Nigerian Defence Headquarters (Special Edition 2014b) p. 38, excerpts by Col Onyema Nwachukwu Assistant Director Defence Information.

The aim of this chapter is to examine the incidences of cross-border insurgencies as posing new threats and challenges to peace and security in Africa. The chapter will examine the following—armed conflicts under international humanitarian law (IHL) and their relevance to terrorism and transborder operations, means employed by the various groups to achieve their objectives, and the gap between what is expected of governments and what can be delivered. This is followed by concluding remarks.

6.2 A Brief Overview of Boko Haram and the Classification of Armed Conflicts Under International Humanitarian Law

Traditionally, armed conflict under IHL is the existence of either an international or a noninternational armed conflict. However, the concept of transnational armed conflict against nonstate actors underscores the legal as well as operational complexities of issues at stake. The importance of this classification in relation to insurgent groups like Boko Haram and other organized armed groups with links to terrorism and/or transborder operations cannot be underestimated. It is therefore necessary to define the status of insurgent groups across Africa to determine their obligations under IHL.

6.2.1 The Status of Boko Haram

Questions have been asked as to the status of Boko Haram within the context of IHL, whether Boko Haram is a terrorist group. It is arguable that there are incidences of terrorist acts of "political Boko Haram."[5] Nonetheless, terrorist act is not sufficient to label an organization as a terrorist group. The United States is the leading country monitoring terrorist organizations globally with a special yearly report known as Country Terrorism Report.[6] The Report for 2012 captured the incidence of the terrorist acts of Boko Haram. The US, after detailed representation, i.e. John Campbell, arrives at the conclusion that its diffused organizational structure and leadership style, coupled with its agenda, do not qualify Boko Haram as a foreign terrorist organization. Ambassador John Campbell posited:

> Boko Haram, an Islamic Sect terrorizing the Northern part of Nigeria, is different from foreign Terrorist Organization (FTOs). Boko Haram is different from other FTOs, such as Hezbollah, Hamas, or the Tamil Tigers, which had an organizational structure, a unified command and goal. Boko Haram is a highly diffused movement with little central organization

[5] See Aloziuwa (2012), pp. 3–4.

[6] See Alobo (2013).

Ambassador John Campbell, who was one of the 20 scholars who recently sent a letter to the Secretary of State Hilary Clinton to warn the United State against its moves to designate Boko Haram as a foreign terrorist group, pressed further that most observers agree that the violence in the northern part of Nigeria was perpetrated by myriad of actors, including former followers of the murdered preacher Mohammed Yusuf, as well as criminal and other elements.[7] Ambassador Jonnie Carson, the US Assistant Secretary of State on African Affairs, clarified the US position and stated that:

> "The US gave reason why it resisted pressure to label the Boko Haram sect as a terrorist organization. The US said it was because while the activities of the militant group are of concern to Nigeria's neighbors, its major aim is to discredit the Nigerian government and present it as one incapable of protecting its people. It, however, clarified that it decided to classify three (3) members of the group, Abubakar Shekau, Adam Kambar, and Khalid al Barnawi, as terrorists because of the discovery that they are involved with some terrorist groups and have intentions that go beyond discrediting the Nigerian government".[8] Mr Jeffery Hawkins, Consul General, US consulate, Lagos, stated thus:
>
> We do not see Boko Haram as a Unified Organization. However, we acknowledge the destruction and killing of innocent persons perpetrated by members of the group and we condemn in very strong terms this activity. Already the United States has identified three individuals as sponsors of Boko Haram and I believe this is part of the process[9]

There was wide condemnation by some Nigerians of the decision by the United States not to designate the *Jamaa tu Ahh'l Sunna Lidawati Wal Jihad* as a foreign terrorist organization (FTO) in spite of its global efforts on the campaign against terror. The designation of a body as an FTO has grave consequences. It is apposite to state that Nigeria opposed the US bid of attempting to designate Boko Haram as a foreign terrorist organization.[10] Nigerian Ambassador to the US Prof Ade Adefuye said that the government was opposed to such a designation because it might subject Nigerian travelers to the kind of intensive search and scrutiny around the world, especially in western capitals and cities, after the Farouk Abdulmutallab incident in December 2009.

Ambassador Adefuye, in his defence of the government's action, said that he feared the likelihood of Nigerians being opened to all kinds of harassment at international airports, including intensive and intrusive body searches once such a designation comes from the US. However, within the contemplation of the broad provisions of the Terrorism Prevention Act[5] 2011, it is safe to conclude that Boko Haram fits the national mould of a terrorist group. "Terrorism" is defined by the Act as follows:

An "Act of terrorism" means an act which is deliberately done with malice, aforethought and which:

---

[7] Alobo (2013).

[8] Alobo (2013).

[9] Alobo (2013).

[10] Alobo (2013).

(1) May seriously harm or damage a country or international organization.
(2) Is intended or can reasonably be regarded as having been intended to:

   i. Unduly compel a government or international organization to perform or abstain from performing any act.
   ii. Seriously intimidate a population.
   iii. Seriously destabilize or destroy the fundamental political, constitutional, economic or social structures of a country or internal organization; or
   iv. Otherwise influence such government or international organization by intimidation or coercion.

(3) Involves or causes, as the case may be:

   i. An attack upon a person's life which may cause serious bodily harm or death.
   ii. Kidnapping of a person.
   iii. Destruction to a government or public facility, transport system, an infrastructure facility, including an information system, a fixed platform located on the continental shelf, a public place or private property, likely to endanger human life or result in major economic loss.
   iv. The seizure of an aircraft, ship or other means of public or goods transport and diversion or the use of such means of transportation for any of the purposes in Paragraph (b) (iv) of this Subsection.
   v. The manufacture, possession, acquisition, transport, supply or use of weapons, explosive or of nuclear, biological or chemical weapons, as well as research into, and development of biological and chemical weapons without lawful authority.
   vi. The release of dangerous substance or causing of fire, explosions or foods, the effect of which is to endanger human life.
   vii. Interference with or disruption of the supply of water, power or any other fundamental natural resource, the effect of which is to endanger human life.

(4) An act or omission in or outside Nigeria which constitutes an offence within the scope of counter terrorism protocols and conventions duly ratified by Nigeria.
(5) An act which disrupts a service but is committed in pursuance of a protest. However, demonstration or stoppage of work is not a terrorist act within the meaning of this definition provided that the act is not intended to result in any harm referred to in subsection 6.

The nature of terrorism means that its implication may result in the crossing of jurisdictional boundaries. On the whole, the legal implications of this classification are as follows: first, as an insurgent group employing terrorist tactics in the achievements of its objectives in a noninternational armed conflict, the group is subject to the observance of international humanitarian law. Its leaders can be charged with crimes against humanity and genocide. In the same vein, the state party involved in the conflict (the Armed Forces of the Federal Republic of Nigeria, in collaboration with the self-styled Civilian Joint Task Force) is under obligation to play by the Rules of Engagement (ROE), which must meet international law and international best practices.

Any defaulting party can be brought for trial before a domestic criminal court. Where the domestic criminal jurisdiction is weak or the government shows a brazen ineptitude to discharge its responsibility, the Prosecutor of the International Criminal Court (ICC), while attending a seminar organized by the Nigerian government on the "need to observe International Humanitarian Law in internal security operations," observed that the ICC can, on its own, institute criminal proceedings against any defaulting party at The Hague.[11]

6.3 Terrorism and Trans-Boundary Operations

An in-depth look at the chronicle of terrorism in the past two decades, particularly with the demise of the Cold War, leaves an impression that it has become a phenomenon that not only has attained universality but has also come to coexist with mankind. The Taliban, for example, is based in Afghanistan but has its tentacles spread over Pakistan, Kashmir, and India. Modern terrorists exploit the primordial sentiments and disagreements in international relations between states to crave a thriving enclave from where they operate. This makes almost all of them "transnational" in outlook. It should be observed that the breeding of terrorism everywhere is almost always traceable to specific (real or perceived) conditions of injustice, inequity, or unjust socioeconomic or political relations.[12] A terrorist act is considered transnational if more than one territory can be identified with the planning, preparation, targeting, execution, and effects of the act. Scholars believe that most extremist groups are primarily organized around localized interests, although they might develop links with movements in other countries over time.[13]

Militant groups of every persuasion thrive in situations that provide convenient links to already existing conflicts; hence, virtually all terrorist groups are products of states or internal and or regional conflicts.[14] Many African states lack the administrative capacity and political will to drive through their own development agenda. They are often referred to as the "Soft State."[15] It is therefore difficult for African countries to cope with the challenges of domestic and international terrorism. Broad-based alliances are formed between former ethnic militia groups and clandestine organizations inside and outside the country. Conditions that can encourage domestic terrorists to assume a global posture include the rare opportu-

[11] ICC Prosecutor: Conference on Observance of IHL on Internal Security Operations in Nigeria 2012.

[12] See Nigerian Defence Headquarters (2014a), p. 37.

[13] Nigerian Defence Headquarters (2014a), p. 37.

[14] Nigerian Defence Headquarters (2014a), p. 37.

[15] Nigerian Defence Headquarters (2014a), p. 37.

nity to exploit natural resources, donations from diaspora, and training and financial assistance from hostile governments. In Nigeria, there is evidence that many of the groups canvassing for group rights have enjoyed tremendous support from their kin outside Nigeria.[16] In the case of the Maitasine riots of 1982 in Kano, in the North, Sudanese and Libyans contributed resources and trained many Nigerians in and outside the country prior to the mayhem, whereas Boko Haram recruited from countries bordering Nigeria. Many youths in the Niger Delta area of Nigeria were recruited for training in Cameroon, Equatorial Guinea, and so on. These levels of support come not only from diaspora but also from sympathetic groups and governments all over the world. The current domestic terrorism in Nigeria undoubtedly possesses the internal dynamics that enabled it to increase its terror potentials and enter the existing transnational terrorist network.

6.4 Means Employed by Various Groups Towards Achieving Their Objectives

"*Terrorist operations are typically prepared to minimize risk and achieve the highest probability of success. Terrorists avoid an adversary's strengths* and concentrate on adversary's weakness. Emphasis is on maximizing security and target effects".[17] This normally means the minimum number of attackers to successfully conduct an operation with the most effective weapons available. While some targets may be "Soft" enough for shorter periods of observations, the information gathering will still be intense. Operations planned or underway may be altered, delayed, or canceled due to changes in the targets or local conditions. Tactical missions combine to complement operational objectives and strategic goals. The psychological impact on the target population is the overreaching objective of any terrorist operation. On the whole, seven aspects frame the assessment of terrorism trends, which are more common among terrorist groups in Africa. These are discussed below.[18]

6.4.1 Intensified Ideological Extremism

An assessment of global terrorism states Al Qa'eda's strategic objective—reestablishing the Islamic caliphate, unified by a common ideology rooted in a violent rejection of apostasy and characterized by fervent opposition to western influence in

[16] Nigerian Defence Headquarters (2014a), p. 37.
[17] Olsen (2012), p. 210.
[18] Olsen (2012), p. 210.

traditionally Islamic countries. This propels Al Qa'eda commitment. Senior leaders of Boko Haram have repeatedly stated an aim of establishing Islamic states that would include the entire northern region of Nigeria. Other regions of the world have terrorist organizations with similar ideological aims such as the Armed Islamic Group (GIA) in Algeria and Al Shabaab in Somalia. Recently, Boko Haram announced that they were formally in alignment with Al Qa'eda.

6.4.2 Enhanced Operational Capabilities

Terrorists employ new electronic and cyber technologies and adapt existing ones to their uses. To exchange information, terrorists have exploited disposable cellular phones, over-the-counter long-distance calling cards, Internet cafes, and other means of relative anonymous communications. Embedding information in digital pictures and graphics and sending them over the Internet is another innovation employed to enable the clandestine global communication that modern terrorists require.

Terrorist groups and other illegal substate actors are rapidly becoming indistinguishable from each other. The increasing role of criminals in financing terrorism either in partnership or in competition with traditional criminal activities is making it difficult, if not impossible, to clearly determine the difference between the two. These enterprises include well-publicized activities such as bank robberies. They also include newer, less well-known illegal activities such as drug trafficking and smuggling. With governance challenges, the ruling elites sometimes use terrorists to hold on to what power or authority they can. This interpenetration of a criminal element into government while government officials are sweeping down to the terrorists' level is the result of governments feeling that legality in the international sense is luxury they cannot afford and perhaps do not need. Eventually, there is no distinction between the two as they effectively merge.

6.4.3 Flexible Organizational Network

Terrorists have shown the ability to adapt to the techniques and methods of counterterrorism agencies and intelligence organizations over the long term. The decentralization of the network firm of organization is an example.

Adopted to reduce the disruption caused by the loss of key links in a chain of command, a network organization also complicates the task of security forces and reduces predictability of operations. They improve upon their sophistication and abilities in virtually all aspects of their operations and support. The aggressive use of modern technology and information management communication and intelligence has increased the efficiency of their activities. Weapons technology has become more available, and the purchasing power of terrorist organizations is on the rise. The trained availability of both technology and trained personnel to operate it for any client with sufficient cash allows the well-funded terrorist to equal or exceed the sophistication of government countermeasures.

6.4.4 Increased Weapon System Lethality

On a practical level, it is already noted by all that terrorism will continue to increase in lethality. Terrorism involves the merging and combining of one state actor with various other state and substate actors, further blurring the difference between criminals, rogue governments, and terrorists. There are concerns regarding the impact and interaction of mass media, technological advances, urbanization, and illegal fund raising with regard to terrorism; while terrorists' attacks account for only a small fraction of insurgent violence, the high-profile nature of terrorist operations has a disproportionate impact. Recent improvised explosive device (IED) attacks in the northeast of Nigeria have caused considerable casualties.

6.4.5 Intended Mass Casualties: Mayhem

Ongoing conditions in the northeast provide an example of changing dynamics in conflict with growing casualties and a perception by portions of the civilian population that cochecked violence is creating an atmosphere of fear, hardening sectarianism, empowering militias and vigilante groups, hastening a middle-class exodus, and shaking confidence in government and security forces. Terrorism plays a key role in much of this physical and psychological violence. This is not just a function of efficiency and developing skills but a tendency of increasing the number of terrorists to view the ever-larger casualty lists as a measure of their influence and power.

6.4.6 Targeted Economic Disruption

Modern high-technology societies are susceptible to the concept of complex terrorism. Dependence on electronic networks, sometimes with minimal redundancy, and concentrating critical assets in small geographic locals can present lucrative targets for the terrorists. Ensuring that a redundant system exists, dispensing critical assets physically, and creating buffers, firewalls, or other types of safeguards can enhance defence and recovery from such complex terrorist attacks. The military will not be the only or necessarily the primary target of new strategies useful against leading-edge technologies and organizations. The dispersal of key civilian infrastructure nodes into locations remote from the urban complexes they serve increases their vulnerability, and the reliance on a computerized control system to monitor and control these nodes increases their exposure to cyberterrorism. Many of the emerging entities are rising to wield effective power in falling states, and states are only concerned with the immediate tactical effects of their actions. They therefore look at modern terrorism as an effective mode of conflict. They can point to the fact that Al Qa'eda invested only $500,000.00 in an attack that is estimated to eventually cost the US Government $135 billion in damages and recovery cost.

6.4.7 Exploited Mass Media Marketing

Exploiting media coverage is a norm for the terrorist. Effectiveness of information operations will be measured by ability to cause a dramatic impact of fear and uncertainty in a target population. Surprise and sustained violence will be normal against specified people representing elements of civil or military control and order or common citizens as prey for terrorists in a culture of violence. Damage or destruction of community, regional, or national infrastructure and governance will be used to gain attention, provoke excessive reaction by host nation or coalition military forces, and attempt to alienate general population support for government policies and programs. Likewise, due to the increase in information outlets and competition with increasing numbers of other messages, terrorism now requires a greatly increased amount of violence or novelty to attract the attention it requires. The tendency of major media to compete for ratings and the subsequent revenue realized from increases in their audience size and share produce pressures on terrorists to increase the impact and violence of their actions to take advantage of this sensationalism. A sinister yet simple aspect of media marketing is the indoctrination of children to hate and to promote violence and terror in distorted views of the world they live in. For example, wearing a robe or fragmentation jacket and speaking in Hausa will act as an incentive to the impressionist with no job. Such propaganda campaigns continue to recruit and expose listeners to ideological rationale for terrorism.[19]

6.5 Enablers of Terror

In our clime, many states are still not viable, and most of them have governance challenges. This is compounded by population pressure and lack of foresight, thereby encouraging rapid depletion of finite resources. Thus, the absence of a viable economic system to support a national government becomes impractical. Illegal activities replace a gap in regular market development and create a setting prime for links to terror. Tensions between religious, tribal, or ethnic factions or a minority group in one geopolitical region can be destabilizing. Nonstate and substate organizations and power blocs are assuming military roles and utilizing organized forces

[19] See Armed Forces of Nigeria counter Terrorism Strategy pp. 20–28.

in conflicts and terror tactics in social or political conflicts. Major corporations, private security companies, and well-funded transnational terror groups have all played significant roles in failed or dysfunctional states. These create enablers for the employment of all manners of unconventional threats; terrorism is a key component of this strategy. The AFN unit leader, operator, and planner must be prepared to act in a chaotic and unstructured contemporary operational environment. Terrorism, unfortunately, will be a constant in the conditions of the future.

6.5.1 The Gap Between What Is Expected of Government and What Can Be Delivered

Violent extremism, as exhibited by the Boko Haram/Anaru elements in Nigeria, has been identified as a major threat to national security. This has over the years affected the peaceful coexistence, socioeconomic development, law and order, among others, in the country. The emergence of these violent groups stems from radicalization of individuals. The persistence of radicalization has been adduced to several factors such as bad governance, poverty, corruption, mass unemployment, economic disparity, perceived injustice, external influence, and religious extremism, among others. It is widely believed that the fight against terrorism will not entirely be successful unless the drivers' radicalizations are prevented.

6.5.2 Governmental Responsibilities

Socioeconomic deprivations have been identified as major drivers to radicalization. The deprived individual thus becomes vulnerable to radicalization and violence to get back at the society. Therefore, good governance that would ensure equity and justice in all facets of human endeavor could be a panacea to radicalization.

Furthermore, respective levels of government could ensure that, first, there is provision of essentials and infrastructure such as electricity, water, health care, and agriculture support, among others; second, provision of social security system to give hope to the less privileged and to guarantee sustenance of life; third, provision of a sound and qualitative education, especially standardizing and streaming the Almajiri education system in the northern states of Nigeria; fourth, provision of effective information machinery to counter radicalism propaganda such as the use of jingles and psychological operations (PsyOps); fifth, strengthening the capability of security agencies through capability building, vetting/revetting, review of standard operating procedures (SOPs), and the provision of modern equipment; sixth, creation of employment opportunities and implementation of profitable skill acquisition programs; seventh, eradication of corruption and implantation of poverty alleviation programs; eighth, engagement of sincere religious scholars to discuss religious matters with youths; ninth, enactment of enabling laws to regulate radical preaching in the society and review/amendment of outdated laws to meet contemporary challenges; tenth, training and retraining of relevant stakeholders to counter radicalism; eleventh, aggressive civic education to instill moral and national values, as well as national pride in the youth; and, twelfth, closer monitoring of youths to check negative peer group effects and deviant tendencies.

6.5.3 Societal Responsibilities

The environment where an individual grows up could influence his/her perception, opinions, and way of life. The society can therefore play an important role in preventing individuals from joining radical groups through the following ways: firstly, creating awareness at community levels on the need for proactive reportage of unusual activities to relevant stakeholders; secondly, use of NGOs and CBOs to mobilize the youth against radical tendencies exhibited by Boko Haram/Ansaru elements; thirdly, engaging religious leaders to continuously condemn the activities of terror elements using relevant verses from the Holy Scriptures during their sermons; fourthly, mobilizing traditional leaders, communal leaders, and tribal groups to speak fervently against terrorist acts at their gatherings; fifthly, using the entertainment industry to win the hearts and minds of the youth; sixthly, use of jingles and media campaigns to preach against the activities of the Boko Haram/Ansaru sects; and, seventhly, effective community policing to detect, detain, punish, and deter radical elements.

6.5.4 Individual Responsibilities

The individual has a role to play to avoid being radicalized. To ensure this, the individual must have self-esteem, sense of belonging, and contentment. These virtues, in most cases, are a manifestation of family upbringing. Therefore, at the family level, the individual must imbibe these virtues in addition to humility, love, discipline, and respect for the sanctity of human life. Furthermore, the individual could ensure the following: firstly, close monitoring of the activities of children and their peer groups and, secondly, careful selection of the religious institutions/clerics that the child is sent to.

6.5.5 Security/Operational Responsibilities

The responsibilities of the security agencies could include but is not limited to the following: firstly, close monitoring of persons exhibiting radical tendencies akin to that of the Boko Haram/Ansaru elements with a view to unearthing the modus operandi and neutralizing them; secondly, arrest, detention, and prosecution of suspected Boko Haram/Ansaru elements; and, thirdly, punishment of convicted Boko Haram/Ansaru elements to serve as deterrence to others.

6.6 Proposals by Ministers of Foreign Affairs and Defence Towards Solving the Threats Posed by Boko Haram

The Ministers of Foreign Affairs and Defence of Benin, Cameroon, Equatorial Guinea, Chad, Niger, and Nigeria, as well as representatives of Canada, China, France, the United State of America (USA), Germany, the United Kingdom (UK), Spain, the United Nations (UN), the European Union (EU), the Economic Community of West African States (ECOWAS), the Organization of Islamic Cooperation (OIC), the African Union (AU), the Lake Chad Basin Commission (LCBC), and the Community of Sahelo-Saharan States (CENSAD), met in Niamey, Niger, in January 2015, under the chairmanship of Honorable Minister Mohammed Bazoum, Minister of State, Minister of Foreign Affairs, Cooperation, African Integration and Nigerians living abroad to consider the implementation of the decisions and commitments made at the Paris London and Abuja Conferences within the framework of the fight against Boko Haram.

6.6.1 At the Security Level

First is the enhancement of cooperation between the states bordering the Lake Chad Basin through the exchange of intelligence. This will include, in particular, the organization, as soon as possible, of a seminar of chiefs of defense forces/chiefs of staff of the countries of the region to prepare the Concept of Operations (CONOPS) of the Joint Multinational Task Force (JMNTF) and the finalization of the establishment of a headquarters. Second is the establishment of the headquarters of the MNJTF in N'Djamena Chad. Third is the establishment of a secure common radio communication network for the security forces operating in and around the Lake Chad Basin. Fourth is defining the modalities of a stronger commitment of strategic partners in the fight against Boko Haram. Fifth is urgent finalization of the Coordination and Liaison Cell, in Ndjamena, by the dispatch of officers from countries of the region and the P3 members. Sixth is the implementation of civil-military actions to enhance cooperation between the defence and security forces and the populations.

6.6.2 At the African and International Levels

First is requesting the AU Commission to submit a report on the regional and international effort being deployed in the fight against Boko Haram, particularly the conclusions of this meeting, for the PSC to authorize the deployment and mandate the MNJTF. Second is requesting the AU commission to organize, in cooperation with the LCBC, ECOWAS, Economic Community of Central African States (ECCAS), CENSAD, OIC, and international partners, a meeting of experts during the first week of February 2015 to finalize the Concept of Operations, the Concept of Logistical Support, the rules of engagement, and other relevant documents for the full operationalization of the MNJTF. Third, the Concept of Operation of the MNJTF should be flexible so as to facilitate the provision, within the framework of the MNJTF, of timely support to bilateral or tripartite arrangements such as the one between Chad and Cameroon. Fourth is transmission, by the Chairperson of the Commission, of the CONOPS and PSC Communiqué to the Security Council for the adoption of a resolution authorizing the MNJTF and the establishment of a trust fund. Fifth is the organization of a donors' conference to mobilize resources for the MNJTF. Sixth is the establishment of a support group around the Member States of the LCBC and an appeal to the strategy developed by the LCBC. Seventh is the strengthening of the international emergency humanitarian action for internally displaced persons in Nigeria and refugees in Niger, Cameroon, and Chad. Eighth is to request the International Criminal Court to expedite progress in the ongoing process relating to crimes against humanity committed by Boko Haram in Nigeria.

6.7 Conclusion

There is no doubt that the Boko Haram insurgency has posed new threats and challenges to the peace and security in Nigeria and Africa in general. While the Armed Forces of Nigeria have engaged this enemy in all fronts, the guerrilla tactics adopted by the insurgent group has made it difficult to effectively deal with them. Nonetheless, many factors have contributed to their apparent expansion and strength. The disenchanted large but poor population of some northeastern states, without good education, be it western or Islamic, coupled with the general absence of social amenities and unemployment, among others, has been the enablers of this malaise. Furthermore, primordial sentiments and ethnic chauvinism aggravated by religious bigotry among the elite class deepened the animosity that already existed among the populace. The people appear to be striving on the edge of a precipice. The insurgency has threatened the peace and security in Africa, and the end is far from sight except that the AU and the international community will expedite actions on their fronts to aid the subregion. This intervention call is urgent and necessary to save Africa's biggest and fastest-growing economy from disintegration.

References

Alobo J (2013) Boko Haram: threat to national security and right to life. Diamondreal Resources Consult, Law Publications Department, Abuja

Aloziuwa SHO (2012) Contending theories on Nigeria's security challenge in the era of Boko Haram insurgency. Peace Sec Rev 7(1):3–4

Armed Forces of Nigeria counter Terrorism Strategy

Armed Forces of Nigeria counter Terrorism Strategy (First Edition)

Lewis A (2013) 'Unpacking terrorism': revolution and insurgency in Yemen, real and imagined threats to regional security. Perspect Terrorism. 7:5. Available at http://www.terrorismanalysts.com/pt/index.php/pot/article/view/292/html. Accessed 20 Aug 2016

Nigerian Army (2014a) Nigerian Defence Magazine (A publication of the Defence Headquarters 2014) (On file with author)

Nigerian Army (2014b) Nigerian Defence Magazine (Special Edition 2014) excerpts by Col Onyema Nwachukwu Assistant Director Defence Information. (On file with author)

Office of the Prosecutor of the International Criminal Court (2012) Conference on observance of international humanitarian law in internal security operations in Nigeria

Olsen D (2012) Tactical counterterrorism: the law enforcement manual of terrorism prevention. Charles C Thomas Publishers Ltd, Springfield

Terrorism Prevention Act 2011, available at http://www.icnl.org/research/library/files/Nigeria/tpa2011.pdf. Accessed 20 Aug 2016

Chapter 7
The Boko Haram Insurgency: Characterisation and Implications Under Municipal and International Laws

Michael Ibanga and James Archibong

7.1 Introduction

Traditionally, armed conflicts are classified as international armed conflicts[1] and armed conflicts of non-international character.[2] Different rules apply to the two types of conflict.[3] Non-international armed conflicts are defined by the San Remo Manual on Non-international Armed Conflicts as 'confrontations occurring within the territory of a single state and in which the armed forces of no other state are engaged against the central government…'[4] Non-international armed conflict is governed by common Article 3 of the Geneva Convention of 1949 and Additional Protocol 11 of 1977. Common Article 3 provides that 'in the case of an armed conflict not of an international character occurring in the territory of one of the High Contracting Parties, each Party to the conflict shall be bound to apply' its provisions as a minimum standard. In the commentary on common Article 3, the ICRC states:

> Speaking generally, it must be recognized that the conflicts referred to in article 3 are armed conflicts, with armed forces on either side engaged in hostilities – conflicts, in short, which are in many respects similar to an international war, but take place within the confines of a single country. In many cases, each of the Parties is in possession of a portion of the national territory and there is often some sort of front.[5]

---

[1] The four 1949 Geneva Conventions (with the exception of common Article 3) and 1977 Additional Protocol I govern international armed conflicts.

[2] Non-international armed conflict is regulated by common Article 3 to the Geneva Conventions of 1949 and Additional Protocol II of 1977.

[3] Bartels (2009), p. 37.

[4] International Institute of Humanitarian (2006), p. 2.

[5] International Committee of the Red Cross (1949), p. 36.

M. Ibanga (✉) · J. Archibong
Faculty of Law, University of Calabar, Calabar, Cross River State, Nigeria

J.-M. Iyi, H. Strydom (eds.), *Boko Haram and International Law*,
https://doi.org/10.1007/978-3-319-74957-0_7

Control of a portion of territory by a non-state armed group is not required for the application of common Article 3.

7.2 Criteria for the Existence of Armed Conflict

In most cases of non-international armed conflicts, the hostilities started in the form of disturbances, riots, or isolated and sporadic acts of violence. Often the government describes such acts of dissent as banditry. But what started as mere banditry may develop into full-fledged armed conflict involving organised armed groups.[6] The Arab Spring, which culminated in brutal civil war in some countries, started as protests against authoritarian regimes. Sometimes a problem arises as to whether the violence has attained the level of intensity that would elevate the confrontation to the status of non-international armed conflict. It may be very difficult to ascertain when disturbances, tensions, riots and sporadic acts of violence crystallise into an armed conflict within the meaning of common Article 3. As noted by Gasser, 'The paramount question here is what level of violence the conflicts must reach before what began as an internal state problem becomes an issue of international law'.[7] In other words, at what point can the level of violence be said to have crossed the threshold to qualify as an armed conflict? Common Article 3 does not have the answer to the above question as it did not provide direct criteria for its application. Its advantage was its flexibility, especially in a volatile and politically charged environment.[8] Article 3 failed to define or lay down the criteria for determining an armed conflict not of an international character and how such conflict could be distinguished from other forms of public violence referred to as internal disturbances and tensions.[9] This vaguely defined condition for the application of Article 3 was clarified and the criteria well-articulated in Additional Protocol II of 1977. Article 1, paragraph 1, of Protocol II applies to all armed conflicts that are not covered by Article 1 of Protocol I and that take place in the territory of a High Contracting Party between its armed forces and dissident armed forces or other organised armed groups that, under responsible command, exercise such control over a part of its territory as to enable them to carry out sustained concerted military operations and to implement this protocol. Protocol II, however, excludes certain types of conflict. Article 1(2) provides that 'This protocol shall not apply to situations of internal disturbances and tensions, such as riots, isolated and sporadic acts of violence and other acts of a similar nature, as not being armed conflicts'.

---

[6] Examples of these could be found in the Liberia and Sierra Leone armed conflicts which started as cross border skirmishes.

[7] Gasser (1993), p. 70.

[8] Gasser (1993), p. 70.

[9] Abi-Saab (1988), p. 222.

7.3 The Perspective of Case Law

According to the International Criminal Tribunal for the Former Yugoslavia (ICTY), the question whether an insurgency has reached the threshold of a non-international armed conflict has to be handled on a case-by-case basis and involves certain factual evaluations:

(i) whether the parties have a sufficient level of organisation;
(ii) whether the hostilities are of a sufficient intensity.[10]

Regarding the two kinds of evaluation stated above, the ICTY in the *Boskoski* case[11] presented a number of 'indicative factors' that could serve as a 'useful practice guidance' to an assessment of whether a factual situation or armed hostilities can be classified as a non-international armed conflict. According to the Tribunal, in evaluating whether the hostilities are of a sufficient intensity to qualify as armed conflict, factors to consider include the following:

(i) whether the attacks can be said to be sufficiently serious;
(ii) where there has been an increase and spread of armed clashes over a territory and over a period of time.

And concerning an evaluation of the requisite level of organisation by an armed group, factors to consider include the following:

(i) the existence of a command structure;
(ii) the ability to carry out military operations in an organised fashion and control territory;
(iii) logistic and communication capabilities;
(iv) the level of discipline and the ability to implement common Article 3 of the Geneva Conventions 1949.

Based on the above guidelines, an insurgency will not be termed an armed conflict if those indicative factors are lacking, and international humanitarian law will not apply to it. Indeed, the Tribunal in an earlier case had stated that an insurgency that has not reached the threshold of 'protracted armed violence between governmental authorities and organized armed groups or between such groups within a state' is not an armed conflict and is not governed by international humanitarian law.[12] Such an insurgency is to be governed by municipal criminal law and applicable human rights norms.[13]

[10] *The Prosecutor v Tadic*, Case No. IT-94-1, Judgment (Trial Chamber) 7 May 1997, para 562.

[11] *The Prosecutor v Boskoski,* Case No. IT 04-82-T, Judgment (Trial Chamber II) 10 July 2008, para 193.

[12] *The Prosecutor v Tadic*, Case No. IT-94-1-AR72, Merits (Appeals Chamber), 2 October 1995, para 70.

[13] *The Prosecutor v Tadic* para 562.

It is important to properly categorise an armed confrontation as this will determine if the principles of international humanitarian law are applicable. In this regard, international tribunals have made landmark contributions in the bid to define and determine conflicts of non-international character. The International Criminal Tribunal for the Former Yugoslavia (ICTY) stated that non-international armed conflict exists whenever there is 'protracted armed violence between governmental authorities and organised armed groups or between such groups within a state'.[14] From this definition, there are two basic requirements for determining a conflict of non-international character, namely, that there must be protracted hostilities and the armed groups must be organised.[15]

There have been further clarifications since the *Tadic* case was decided. The term 'protracted' is used in relation to 'intensity' rather than duration.[16] The ICTY Trial Chamber in the *Haradinaj* case threw light on the meaning of armed conflict of non-international character, as expounded by the Tribunal in *Tadic*.[17] It was, however, in *Boskoski* that the Trial Chamber of ICTY articulated the basic elements, namely, 'intensity' and 'organisation of the armed group' as the prerequisites for a non-international armed conflict.[18]

7.4 Features of the Conflict in Northeast Nigeria

Campaign of Violence by the Group Jama'atu Ahlis Sunna Lidda Awati Wal Jihad (Boko Haram)

The group launched its military operation in July 2009 with attacks across four northern states. The attacks and shoot-out with the security forces resulted in at least 800 deaths. The sect leader, Mohammed Yusuf, was arrested and died in the custody of the police.[19] The group has also been referred to as 'Nigerian Taliban'.[20] Several prisons have been attacked by the insurgents. In September 2009, they attacked a prison in Bauchi and freed about 700 inmates.[21] Researchers and human rights organisations have chronicled a long list of attacks carried out by the insurgents and security forces.[22] There were coordinated bomb attacks in 2010. In September 2010,

---

[14] *The Prosecutor v Tadic* para 562.

[15] See also Prosecutor v Akayesu, Case No. ICTR-96-4.

[16] Prosecutor v Zenjnil Delalic, *Zdravko Mucic, Hazim Delalic, Zdravko Mucic, Hazim Delic and Esad Landzo* Case No. IT-96-21 (Celebici Case), para 184.

[17] Prosecutor v Ramush Haradinaj, *Idriz Balaj and Lahi Brahimaj* Judgment (Trial Chamber), Case No. IT-04-84-T, 3 April 2008.

[18] Prosecutor v Boskoski *and Tarculovski*, Judgment (Trial Chamber), Case No. IT-04-82-T, 10 July 2008, paras 175–206.

[19] Amnesty International (March 2014), p. 5.

[20] Walker (2012), p. 3.

[21] Okpaga et al. (2012), pp. 86–89; Zenn and Pearson (2014), p. 46.

[22] Okpaga et al. (2012), pp. 86–89.

the insurgents attacked a prison in Bauchi State and freed 150 of its members and several hundred other inmates.

Since June 2011, Boko Haram has attacked bars and beer parlours in northeastern Nigeria.[23] On 16 June 2011, the Nigeria Police Force Headquarters was bombed, resulting in the death of three people.[24] The United Nations building in Abuja was bombed on 28 August 2011 by Boko Haram, killing 24 people and injuring about 80.[25] In Damaturu, Yobe State, about 100 people were killed on 4 November 2011.[26]

The group carried out a spate of bombings in 2011 on Christmas day targeting churches. In four separate bombings, not less than 44 people were killed. There was an explosion at St. Theresa Catholic Church in Madalla, a town near Abuja, which left at least 25 people dead.[27] Seven people were killed in bomb blasts in Jos, Plateau State, and Damaturu, Yobe State.[28]

In continuation of its attack on Christians, Boko Haram killed 20 Christian students at Ado Bayero University, Kano, on 2 May 2012. It attacked a church service in Maiduguri, killing five worshippers, among them the priest. On 3 June 2012, the Harvest Field Church of Christ in Bauchi was attacked by a suicide bomber who drove a bomb laden car into the church premises.[29] The group has also targeted traditional rulers and Muslim clerics. On 13 July 2012, the insurgents tried without success to kill the Shehu of Borno and the deputy governor of the state after Friday prayer.

According to Amnesty International, within the first three months of 2014, more than 1500 people had been killed in Borno, Yobe and Adamawa states: about 43 people died and many others injured when a car bomb attributed to Boko Haram exploded in Maiduguri (14 January 2014); Boko Haram attacked Alau Ngawo Fatie village in Borno State and killed 18 people (19 January 2014); Boko Haram attacked Kawuri village, Borno State, and killed between 52 and 85 people. It also attacked a church in Waga Chakawa Village, Adamawa Siate, killing between 31 and 47 people (26 January 2014). More than 50 people were killed by Boko Haram in Konduga town, Borno State. Houses, shops and vehicles were burnt down (11 February 2014). Sixty-five people lost their lives during attacks on some villages in Adamawa State by Boko Haram (16 February 2014); the palace of a traditional leader and a school were attacked in Bama, Borno State, by Boko Haram, resulting in the death of between 60 and 90 people (19 February 2014). Between 43 and 59 people were killed by the insurgents in an attack on a school in Buni Yadi, Yobe State, resulting in the death of many school children (25 February 2014); Boko Haram fighters killed 37 people in attacks on Kirchinga, Michika and Shuwa villages in Adamawa State (26 February 2014); in an attack in Mainok village, Borno

[23] Amnesty International (2012), p. 257.

[24] Amnesty International (2012), p. 257.

[25] Amnesty International (2012), p. 257.

[26] Amnesty International (2012), p. 257.

[27] Walker (2012), p. 6.

[28] Amnesty International (2012), p. 257.

[29] Walker (2012), p. 6.

State, 39 people were killed by Boko Haram members. The group also exploded two bombs in Maiduguri, killing 52 people (1 March 2014); Boko Haram killed 29 people and destroyed several houses in Mafa village in Borno State (2 March 2014); Boko Haram killed between 40 and 48 civilians and destroyed shops and the police station in Konduga Local Government Area of Borno State (3 March 2014). Over 210 Boko Haram members were allegedly killed by the security forces in their camps in the Sambisa forest (9 March 2014).

Hundreds of escaped Boko Haram detainees were rounded up and shot in Maiduguri (14 March 2014); an improvised explosive devise killed at least 16 in a market in Ngurosoye village, and the military fought back by bombing Kayamla village, killing ten residents (20 March 2014); the Joint Task Force killed 18 suspected Boko Haram members (24 March 2014). On 14 April 2014, Boko Haram abducted more than 200 girls from a secondary school in Chibok, Borno State. This action caused global outrage, leading to the formation of the 'Bring Back Our Girls' movement.[30] The insurgents launched a devastating attack on Baga, a large commercial town in Borno State on 4 January 2015. They captured the town and the military formation located there. There were reports and accounts of widespread killings and destruction of property. Though the death toll is disputed, some estimates put it at around 2000. Satellite photographs released by Amnesty International showed that at least 3700 houses were destroyed.

7.5 Violent Response by Nigerian Security Forces

The Federal Government, in response, established the Joint Task Force (JTF), a special task force, in Maiduguri in June 2011 to fight Boko Haram. The JTF has been brutal in its confrontation with the insurgents. The Nigerian armed forces have carried out hundreds of summary executions of suspected members of Boko Haram.[31] They shot dead 25 people and burned downed several houses in Kaleri Ngomari Custain area on 9 July 2011.[32] More than 200 people were killed and others wounded by the JTF in Barga, Borno State, in April 2013.[33] The Nigerian government opted for a counterterror military strategy against Boko Haram.[34] The Nigerian security forces supported by civilian volunteers known as 'Civilian JTF' and local hunters have engaged the insurgents in fierce battles and have been accused of widespread violations of human rights and humanitarian law.

---

[30] Barna (2014), p. 16.

[31] Ojo (2010), pp. 45–62.

[32] Amnesty International (2012), p. 257.

[33] Pérouse de Montclos (2014), p. 15.

[34] Onapajo (2013), p. 54.

7.6 Responsibility to Respect International Humanitarian Law by Parties to a Conflict

The parties must be in a position to implement the principles of international humanitarian law embodied in Additional Protocol II. The Protocol provides that persons who do not take a direct part or have ceased to take part in hostilities shall in all circumstances be treated humanely. It prohibits violence to life, torture, taking of hostages, terrorism, slavery and outrages upon personal dignity, among others.[35] The Protocol also prohibits attacks against civilians.[36] However, in the conflict between the Nigerian security forces and Boko Haram, humanitarian law is observed more in its breach. Apart from the violence against civilians by both sides, thousands of victims have no access to medical assistance, food supplies and other basic needs. Women, children and the elderly have taken the brunt of the conflict. There have been many cases of enforced disappearances, torture and other forms of cruel, inhuman and degrading treatment.[37] Children have been widely used by the insurgents to carry out attacks. In January 2015, a ten-year-old girl carried an explosive device that detonated near the Maiduguri market, killing her and 18 others. Death in military custody is a common occurrence. The conflict is replete with thousands of unlawful killings, extrajudicial executions and deliberate attacks on civilians.[38] Some respite was provided for the victims of Boko Haram attacks when the Federal Government established the Victims Support Fund Committee in July 2014. There are thousands of internally displaced persons spread cross Nigeria.[39] The number is conflicting and has been rising rapidly. Nigeria also has thousands of refugees arising from the insurgency in Chad, Niger and Cameroon.

7.7 Determining the Character of the Armed Confrontation

It is important to determine the character of the armed confrontation between Boko Haram and Nigerian government security forces as this has implications under municipal and international laws. The issue under consideration is whether the armed confrontations between Boko Haram's militants and the Nigerian security forces have reached the minimum level of intensity to meet the threshold of an armed conflict.[40] If the confrontation is characterised as a non-international armed conflict, Nigeria is bound by certain obligations under municipal and international

[35] Article 4(2), Additional Protocol II.

[36] Article 13, Additional Protocol II.

[37] Amnesty International (2014), p. 5.

[38] Amnesty International (2014), p. 5.

[39] Barna (2014), p. 9.

[40] Office of the Prosecutor of the International Criminal Court (2013), pp. 21–29.

laws. The Nigerian security forces and Boko Haram would be bound by the rules of international humanitarian law and international human rights law.[41]

7.7.1 *Intensity of the Armed Confrontation*

At the inception of the rebellion, Boko Haram adopted the hit-and-run tactics. It mounted sporadic attacks using improvised explosives and suicide bombers. It was more of an asymmetric warfare. One of its traits was the use of gunmen on motorbikes to carry out attacks. Its targets were initially the police and later politicians, clergymen and those who criticised them. The group widened its attacks to include churches, mosques, schools, motor parks, markets, farmlands, communication installations, prisons, military barracks, police stations, governmental buildings and other symbols of state authority. Currently, Boko Haram has acquired the status of a conventional army. As a conventional fighting force, it has thousands of men under arms. There are also special units that train in bombings.[42]

7.7.2 *Ability to Mount Sustained and Concerted Military Operations*

Boko Haram militants now have in their arsenal armoured tanks, armoured personnel carriers, rocket launchers, anti-aircraft guns, anti-tank weapons, sub-machine guns and new AK riffles.[43] A day hardly passes without headline news of Boko Haram attacks and death toll, such as the following: 'Fire and Fury as Boko Haram Kills 43 Pupils'[44] and 'Boko Haram Batters Bama'.[45] The intensity and sustainability of the attacks by Boko Haram left the Nigerian defence and military formations in a dilemma on how to ensure effective response.[46] President Goodluck Jonathan declared a state of emergency in Adamawa, Borno and Yobe states in May 2013. The Nigerian security forces also responded with its full might using fighter jets to bomb Boko Haram targets.[47] The Nigerian Army suffered huge losses, and, out of frustration, the Nigerian House of Representatives wanted the Army Headquarters relocated to Maiduguri. In view of its inability to defeat the insurgents, the JTF was replaced by the 7th Division of the Nigerian Army in September 2013.

---

[41] Amnesty International (2014), p. 10.

[42] BBC (2014).

[43] Council on Foreign Relations Africa (2014).

[44] The Nation, Wednesday, February 26, 2014, Vol. 9, No. 2771, p. 1.

[45] The Nation, February 20, 2014, Vol. 9, No. 2765, p. 1.

[46] Oarhe (2013), p. 67.

[47] Pérouse de Montclos (2014), p. 15.

7.7.3 Boko Haram as an Organised Armed Group and Under a Responsible Command

To determine what constitutes non-international armed conflict, the ICTY Trial Chamber in *Boskoski* elucidated the element of 'organization' of an armed group.[48] Factors highlighted are the existence of military/operational capacity, logistical capacity, a command structure, the ability to speak with one voice, an internal disciplinary mechanism and the ability to implement IHL.[49] Boko Haram is an ideologically driven, well-organised armed group. It was originally a peaceful Islamic group under the leadership of Mohammed Yusuf, a cleric. The group has now acquired a franchise. According to Jean Herskovits, 'Boko Haram has evolved into franchise that includes criminal groups claiming its identity'.[50]

Boko Haram has also been designated internationally as a terrorist organisation.[51] The American government categorised it as a violent fundamentalist organisation having connections with al-Qaeda.[52] It was designated as a Foreign Terrorist Organization (FTO) and as a Specially Designated Global Terrorist under Executive Order (E.O.) 13324 on 14 November 2013.[53] The Boko Haram leader, Abubakar Shekau, Khalid al-Barnawi and Abubakar Adam Kambar were in June 2012 named as Specially Designated Global Terrorists under section 1(b) of E.O. 13224.[54] The British government also designated Boko Haram and Ansaru as terrorist organisations in 2013.[55] From a local breed that Boko Haram originally was, it now has fighters from other countries such as Benin, Chad, Mauritania, Niger, Somalia and Sudan.[56] An ICC *Report* stated that 'Boko Haram is an armed group which seems to meet a minimum level of organization'.[57]

The group has, since its arms struggle began in 2009, broken into four dissenting bodies, though with a common objective and ideology. One of the groups is Ansaru (Jama'atu Ansaru Muslimina Fi Biladis Sudan), which broke away from Boko Haram in January 2012 on ideological grounds.[58] The Ansaru militants kidnapped two Italian priests and a Canadian nun in Tchere, Cameroon, in April 2014, and

[48] Bartels (2009).

[49] *Boskoski,* (n 11) para 193.

[50] Herskovits, "How American experts allowed growth of Boko Haram" *Vanguard* at www.vanguardngr.com last visited 18/01/2015.

[51] Okemi (2013), pp. 1–9.

[52] Barna (2014), p. 21.

[53] Office of the Spokesperson US Department of State, "Boko Haram and US Counterterrorism Assistance to Nigeria" FACT SHEET May 14, 2014.

[54] Office of the Spokesperson US Department of State, "Boko Haram and US Counterterrorism Assistance to Nigeria" FACT SHEET May 14, 2014.

[55] Campbell (2014), p. 3.

[56] Siegle (2013), pp. 86–87.

[57] Office of the Prosecutor of the International Criminal Court (2013), p. 28.

[58] Barna (2014), p. 10.

brought them to the Nigerian border.[59] On 17 May 2014, the group also kidnapped ten Chinese engineers in Waza, Cameroon.[60]

In spite of the fact that Boko Haram is split into smaller units, the main faction, under Abubakar Shekau, is well equipped, well-armed, well-funded and well-motivated. During engagements, they often outnumber and outgun the Nigerian security forces.[61] Though there are splinter groups carrying out attacks under the flagship of Boko Haram, the group has an overall leader, Abubakar Shekau, whom the Nigerian Army claimed to have killed. According to an ICC Report, Boko Haram 'appears to be under a responsible command, namely the leadership exerted by Abubakar Shekau'.[62] The report states: 'Further, a consistent pattern of incidents suggests that the group actually possesses the means to carry out a widespread or systematic attack, and displays the degree of internal coordination and organizational control required to that end.'[63] The insurgents operate in battalion size units.

7.7.4 *Exercise of Control Over a Part of Territory*

For a conflict to be regarded as non-international under Additional Protocol II, the armed group must exercise control over a part of the territory. Boko Haram is in effective control of parts of the territory of Nigeria. From its stronghold in the Sambisa forest, Borno State, the group captured[64] and exercised control over several towns in northeast Nigeria. As of January 2015, Boko Haram was said to have controlled about 20,000 square miles, an area equivalent to the size of Belgium.[65] It is not, however, certain how much territory Boko Haram really controls. This has been attributed to government-controlled communication from the region.[66] The Catholic archbishop of Maiduguri, Oliver Dashe Doeme, in September 2014 put the number of towns under Boko Haram at 25.[67] As of January 2015, the group is said to be controlling 13 Local Government Areas across Borno, Yobe and Adamawa states.[68] In Borno State, the affected local governments are Gworza, Bama, Mafa, Dikwa, Kala-Balge, Ngala, Marte, Abadam and Mobbar. The others are Michika and Madagali in Adamawa State and Gujba and Gulani in Yobe State. They are in partial control of some local government areas such as Mungono, Kukawa, Guzamala, Gubio, Magumeri, Damboa, Konduga, Chibok, Askira Uba and Jere in Borno State.

[59] American Foreign Policy Council (2013), p. 8.

[60] American Foreign Policy Council (2013), p. 9.

[61] Barna (2014), p. 10.

[62] Office of the Prosecutor of the International Criminal Court (2013), p. 23.

[63] Office of the Prosecutor of the International Criminal Court (2013), p. 28.

[64] Boko Haram began capturing territories in August, 2014.

[65] Barna (2014), p. 8.

[66] Council on Foreign Relations Africa (2014).

[67] Council on Foreign Relations Africa (2014).

[68] Barna (2014), p. 9.

The group was defeated and driven out of some towns, namely Gombi, Hong, Maiha and Mubi.

Boko Haram declared an 'Islamic Caliphate' in the area under its control. Its leader, Abubakar Shekau, declared Gwoza town the headquarters of the caliphate on 23 August 2014 and hoisted a flag there. Also in the area under its control, Boko Haram has established a strong administration based on Islamic Law. During the duration of its occupation of Mubi town in Adamawa State, ten people were tried and convicted of looting and other offences and had their hands amputated.[69]

7.8 The Threshold of Non-international Armed Conflict with Reference to the Boko Haram Insurgency

In the light of the foregoing, is the Boko Haram insurgency an uprising or rebellion falling under disturbances, tensions, unrests and riots or a non-international armed conflict within the meaning and purview of Article 3 common to the Geneva Conventions of 1949 and Additional Protocol II of 1977? Put differently, at what point does an armed confrontation assume the status of armed conflict? There is no fixed rule to determine when such violence becomes an armed conflict. Situations are assessed on a case-by-case basis, using certain indicators. In terms of organisation, the group is well organised, with a command structure and distinct leadership. It has demonstrated the capacity to plan and carry out systematic and coordinated attacks, to communicate and enforce orders and to recruit, train and arm its fighters. Boko Haram has also been able to intensify and sustain the conflict since July 2009. The nature of weapons used by the group has also been upgraded from clubs, small arms and improvised explosives to rocket launchers, armoured personnel carriers and tanks. The confrontation has also witnessed the transformation of the tactics and size of Boko Haram from guerrilla warfare, involving a few hundred men, to a conventional force of over 6000 fighters who control territories. In some instances, they outgun and outnumber the Nigerian security forces, forcing many of them to abandon their positions and flee into neighbouring Cameroon.

There has been massive destruction of lives and property, as well as the displacement of over one million people. The group's allegiance and affiliation to international terror organisations have guaranteed its funding, supply of arms and sustainability of the conflict. The escalation of the conflict is also regarded as a threat to international peace and security. Thus, the United Nations Security Council imposed punitive sanctions on the group in May 2014.

In relation to the characterisation of armed confrontation, the criteria earlier on established for the existence of a non-international armed conflict may be reduced to two, namely, the level of organisation of the group and the degree of intensity of the violence. These criteria have been met in the armed confrontation under

[69] Sotubo (2014).

consideration. Netsanet Belay, Research and Advocacy Director for Africa at Amnesty International, said of the character of the Boko Haram/Federal Government of Nigeria conflict:

> The escalation of violence in north-eastern Nigeria in 2014 has developed into a situation of non-international armed conflict in which all parties are violating international humanitarian law. We urge the international community to ensure prompt, independent investigations into acts that may constitute war crimes and crimes against humanity.[70]

The International Criminal Court (ICC) led by its Prosecutor, Fatou Bensouda, took a trip to Abuja to examine the conflict in Nigeria in July 2012.[71] For the ICC to have jurisdiction, Article 8 of the Rome Statute requires the existence of an armed conflict.[72] The Prosecutor's Report stated:

> The required level of intensity and the level of organization of parties to the conflict necessary for the violence to be qualified as an armed conflict of non-international character appear to have been met. The Office has therefore determined that since at least May 2013 allegations of crimes occurring in the context of the armed violence between Boko Haram and Nigerian security forces should be considered within the scope of article 8 (2) (c) and (e) of the Statute.[73]

The Office of the Prosecutor concluded that Boko Haram has satisfied an ample amount of applicable benchmark to be regarded as organised non-state armed group with capacity to plan and execute military operations. In confirmation of the degree of intensity of the armed confrontations, the Prosecutor's Office has documented over 200 incidents that occurred between July 2009 and May 2013. The Report stated further:

> In particular, the Office has assessed the extent and sustained nature of such incidents, as well as their seriousness; the frequency and intensity of armed confrontation; their geographical and temporal spread; the number and composition of personnel involved on both sides; the mobilisation and the distribution of weapons; and the extent to which the situation has attracted the attention of the UN Security Council, said the Report.[74]

The ICC again in January 2015 vowed to prosecute international crimes committed in the conflict in Nigeria.[75] According to the Prosecutor, Fatou Bensouda, 'No one should doubt my resolve, if need be, to prosecute those individuals most responsible for war crimes and crimes against humanity'.[76] Another group, the Nigerian Coalition for the International Court (NCICC), believes that the conflict has reached the threshold of non-international armed conflict. As noted by the NCICC, 'The

[70] Amnesty International (2013).

[71] Office of the Prosecutor of the International Criminal Court (2013), p. 8.

[72] According to Trial Chamber 1 "an armed conflict exists whenever; see Situation in the Democratic Republic of the Congo, *The Prosecutor v Thomas Lubanga Dyilo*, Judgment pursuant to Article 74 of the Statute, ICC - 01/04-01/06 (14 March 2012), para 533.

[73] Office of the Prosecutor of the International Criminal Court (2013), p. 8.

[74] Office of the Prosecutor of the International Criminal Court (2013), p. 8.

[75] Daily Sun, Wednesday, Jan 21, 2015, Vol. 10, No. 3061, p. 16.

[76] Daily Sun, Wednesday, Jan 21, 2015, Vol. 10, No. 3061, p. 16.

conflict between Nigerian forces and Boko Haram insurgents is currently a non-international armed conflict and therefore the provisions of the Rome Statute cover the crimes committed during the conflict'.[77]

As it has been observed by Amnesty International, the fighting has met the required criteria for it to be considered as a non-international armed conflict. The human rights watchdog concludes that 'The fighting in north-eastern Nigeria has reached the threshold of a non-international armed conflict'.[78] It cited the International Criminal Court (ICC), which through the Office of the Prosecutor also determined in 2013 that the fighting in northeastern Nigeria is a non-international armed conflict.[79] Presently, the question as to whether an intra-state armed confrontation has attained the status of non-international armed conflict is left to scholars, humanitarian organisations and civil society groups to determine. Often the issue is contentious and marred by conflicting interests. In this regard, there is need to clarify, define and determine the parameters of non-international armed conflict to fill any lacunae and eliminate vagueness in the law. It took some time before the Nigerian government acknowledged the existence of an armed conflict on its territory, a reality it was unwilling to accept.

7.9 Implications Under Municipal and International Laws

The confrontation is without doubt a non-international armed conflict. This has a number of implications under Nigerian law, as well as international humanitarian law. Both parties are bound by common Article 3 of the Geneva Conventions of 1949 and Additional Protocol II of 1977.

7.9.1 Commitments Under Relevant Treaties

Nigeria has ratified the 1949 Geneva Conventions and the 1977 Additional Protocols. Nigerian authorities are bound by the instruments and must ensure compliance with international humanitarian law. Its obligations include training of members of the armed forces in the principles of the law, dissemination of the law, punishing of violations, humane treatment, and protection of the civilian population and provision of assistance to victims of the conflict. Humanitarian law also prohibits violence to life, torture, taking of hostages, terrorism, slavery and outrages upon personal dignity,[80] and attacks against the civilian population.[81]Apart from domesti-

[77]The Nigerian Coalition for the International Criminal Court (1 Aug. 2014).

[78]Amnesty International (March 2014), p. 10.

[79]Amnesty International (March 2014), p. 10.

[80]Article 4(2) of APII, 1977.

[81]Article 13, AP II, 1977.

cating some aspects of the Geneva Conventions,[82] Nigeria is also a party to major regional and international human rights treaties such as the African Charter on Human and Peoples' Rights, which Nigeria ratified in June 1983, the International Covenant on Civil and Political Rights (ICCPR), to which Nigeria acceded in October 1993.

In 2001, Nigeria ratified the Rome Statute of the International Criminal Court (ICC). To ensure that perpetrators of international crimes are criminally responsible for their actions, the Federal Government submitted to the National Assembly the 'Crimes against Humanity, War Crimes, Genocide and Related Offences Bill, 2012'[83] for the domestication of the Rome Statute of the ICC on 17 July 2012. When the Bill becomes law, it will ensure cooperation between Nigeria and the ICC in the prosecution of war criminals in Nigeria or The Hague.[84]

7.9.2 Individual Criminal Responsibility for Violations of Human Rights and Humanitarian Law

Persons who commit serious violations of international humanitarian law and human rights law can be held criminally responsible for their actions under international criminal law. The Nigerian government has an obligation to prosecute crimes that 'deeply shock the conscience of humanity'.[85] The government enacted the Terrorism (Prevention) Act 2011 to prevent, prohibit and fight terrorism. A few of the sect members have been prosecuted. An emerging trend in the trial of captured members of Boko Haram is the secrecy surrounding the hearing, conviction and sentencing of sect members. In October 2014, three Boko Haram members were convicted in a secret trial and sentenced to 25 years in prison each by a Federal High Court.[86] Safeguarding national security was adduced as the reason for the secret trial. Journalists and the public were prevented from witnessing proceedings, at the request of the Attorney General of Lagos State. The situation is, however, different in the trial of an alleged Boko Haram sponsor, Senator Mohammed Ali Ndume. The Federal High Court, Abuja Division, refused an application for the secret trial of Senator Ndume.[87] Some members of the Nigerian Army have also been put on trial for aiding Boko Haram, an offence punishable under the Armed Forces Act.[88] In Jos, 18 soldiers appeared before a General Court Martial.[89]

---

[82] The Geneva Conventions Act, Laws of the Federation 2004.

[83] Rome Statute Bill.

[84] The Nigerian Coalition for the International Criminal Court (1 Aug. 2014).

[85] Daily Sun, Wednesday, Jan 21, 2015, Vol. 10, No. 3061, p. 16.

[86] P. M. News Nigeria (2014).

[87] The Vanguard (2014).

[88] Cap A 20 Laws of the Federation of Nigeria.

[89] The Punch (2013).

7.10 Regional Security Implications

Boko Haram attacks and brutal killings have created a large number of refugees. It has contributed to the displacement of many people in the sub-region. The United Nations High Commission for Refugees (UNHCR) maintains that Boko Haram insurgency and other wars have rendered 750,000 people stateless.[90] The insurgents now carry out raids into neighbouring Cameroon Republic, kidnapping, killing people and destroying property. The escalation of such attacks has incurred the wrath of regional leaders. The heads of state of ECOWAS are contemplating the establishment of a joint military force to confront Boko Haram. To do this, ECOWAS has sought the support of the African Union.[91] The Boko Haram insurgency has developed beyond the ability of the Nigerian government to contain. The Republic of Chad, one of the neighbouring countries, has reportedly sent a contingent of troops to northeastern Cameroon to help the country fight Boko Haram at the Nigerian border.[92] The African Union is also seeking ways of combating the Boko Haram sect. The terror in Nigeria and Kenya is expected to dominate its agenda at its next summit.[93] The Paris Summit of May 2014 dwelt extensively on foreign support to Nigeria. Other international institutions such as the UN and EU have taken punitive actions against Boko Haram. In May 2014, the UN Security Council imposed sanctions on the insurgents listing them among sponsors of terrorism. This step was followed by the EU.

7.11 Conclusion

The armed confrontation between Boko Haram and the military forces of Nigeria has had devastating consequences for the victims caught in the middle. An important issue concerning this conflict is whether or not it has, over the period, assumed the status of a non-international armed conflict, thereby creating some implications under both municipal and international laws. In contemporary international law, the existence of a non-international armed conflict between the state and rebel forces is not based on declarations issued by the parties but is on the basis of objective criteria relating to intensity of the armed confrontation, command structure on the part of the insurgents and other factors. Assessed against the background of criteria necessary for the existence of an 'armed conflict' established by international tribunals, the conclusion is that Boko Haram and the Nigerian armed forces are engaged in a non-international armed in northeast Nigeria. Under Nigerian municipal criminal law, for levying war on the Nigerian state, Boko Haram leaders are involved in an

[90] Tribune (2014).

[91] The Punch (2015).

[92] Aljazeera (2015).

[93] News 24.com/Nigeria (2014).

act of treason for which they could be tried if arrested. International humanitarian law does not apply unless a violent situation qualifies as an armed conflict. In the instant situation, the law applies, with the implication that the parties to the conflict are bound to respect fundamental principles of the law applicable to non-international armed conflict. Thus, members of the opposing forces who have committed serious violations of international humanitarian law are criminally liable for their conducts and could be tried for such acts either in the domestic forum or at the international level.

References

Abi-Saab G (1988) Non-international armed conflicts. In: UNESCO international dimensions of humanitarian law. Henry Dunant Institute, Geneva, pp 217–243

Aljazeera (2015) "Chadian troops join war against Boko Haram" at m.aljazera.com/story last visited 20/1/2015

American Foreign Policy Council, "Boko Haram" World Almanac of Islamism, p 8

Amnesty International, "Nigeria: war crimes and crimes against humanity as violence escalates in north-east" *Annual Report* 2013 at www.amnesty.org/.../nigeria-war-crimes last visited 18/1/2015

Amnesty International, Nigeria: "more than 1,500 killed in armed conflict in north-eastern Nigeria in early 2014". Index: AFR 44/004/2014. Amnesty International, March 2014, p 10

Amnesty International, *Report* 2012. Index: POL 10/001/2012, p 257

Barna J (2014) Insecurity in context: the rise of Boko Haram in Nigeria. Directorate-General for External Policies, Policy Department, p 16

Bartels R (2009) Timelines, borderlines and conflicts. The historical evolution of the legal divide between international and non-international armed conflicts. Int Rev Red Cross 91(873)

BBC, "Who are Nigeria's Boko Haram Islamists?" at www.bbc.com/.../world-africa-13809501 last visited 23/3/2015

Campbell J (2014) Boko Haram: origins, challenges and responses. NOREF Norwegian Peacebuilding Resource Centre Policy Brief – October

Council on Foreign Relations Africa, "Boko Haram control in Northeast Nigeria" at blogs.cfr.org/.../boko-haram-control-in last visited 26/1/2015

Daily Independent, ".7m internally displaced persons in North East Nigeria – UNHCR" available at dailyindependentnig.co last visited 14/2/2015

Daily Sun, "Boko Haram: ICC vows to prosecute crimes in Nigeria" Wednesday, January 21, 2015, Vol. 10, No. 3061

Gasser H (1993) International humanitarian law – an introduction. Henry Dunant Institute, Haupt, p 70

Herskovits J, How American experts allowed growth of Boko Haram. *Vanguard* at www.vanguardngr.com last visited 18/01/2015

ICRC Commentary on the Four Geneva Conventions of 1949

International Institute of Humanitarian Law (2006) The manual on the law of non-international armed conflict. International Institute of Humanitarian Law, San Remo

News 24.com/Nigeria last visited 19/1/2015

Oarhe O (2013) Responses of the Nigerian defense and intelligence establishments to the challenge of Boko Haram. In: Mantzikos I (ed) Boko Haram anatomy of a crisis. e International Relations, Bristol, p 67

Office of the Prosecutor of the International Criminal Court (n 57)

Office of the Prosecutor of the International Criminal Court, "Situation in Nigeria," *Article 5 Report*, 5 August 2013, pp 21–29

Office of the Spokesperson US Department of State, "Boko Haram and US Counterterrorism Assistance to Nigeria" FACT SHEET May 14, 2014
Ojo EO (2010) Boko Haram: Nigeria's extra-judicial state. J Sustain Dev Afr 12(12):45–62
Okemi ME (2013) Boko Haram: a religious sect or terrorist organisation. Global J Polit Law Res 1(1):1–9
Okpaga A, Chijioke US, Innocent EO (2012) Activities of Boko Haram and insecurity question in Nigeria. Arab J Bus Manage Rev (OMAN Chapter) 1(9):86–89
Onapajo H (2013) Why Nigeria is not winning the Anti-Boko Haram War. In: Mantzikos I (ed) Boko Haram anatomy of a crisis. e International Relations, Bristol
P. M. News Nigeria, "3 Boko Haram members convicted of terror in secret trial" at www pmnews Nigeria
Pérouse de Montclos M-A (2014) Nigeria's interminable insurgency? Addressing the Boko Haram crisis. Chatham House. The Royal Institute of International Affairs, Africa Programme, September, p 15
Prosecutor v Akayesu, Case No. ICTR-96-4
Prosecutor v Boskoski and Tarculovski, Judgment (Trial Chamber), Case No. IT-04-82-T, 10 July 2008, paras 175–206
Prosecutor v Ramush Haradinaj, Idriz Balaj and Lahi Brahimaj Judgment (Trial Chamber), Case No. IT-04-84-T, 3 April 2008
Prosecutor v Zenjnil Delalic, Zdravko Mucic, Hazim Delalic, Zdravko Mucic, Hazim Delic and Esad Landzo Case No. IT-96-21
Rome Statute Bill
Siegle J (2013) Boko Haram and the isolation of Northern Nigeria: regional and international implications. In: Mantzikos I (ed) Boko Haram anatomy of a crisis. e International Relations, Bristol, pp 86–87
Sotubo J (2014) Terrorists Amputate 10 under Sharia Law in Mubi. Available at http://www.pulse.ng/news/boko haram. Accessed 19 Jan 2015
"Terrorists Amputate 10 under Sharia Law in Mubi" at Pulse.ng/news/boko haram last visited 19/1/2015
The Geneva Conventions Act, Laws of the Federation 2004
The Nation, February 20, 2014, Vol. 9, No. 2765, p 1
The Nation, Wednesday, February 26, 2014, Vol. 9, No. 2771, p 1
The Nigerian Coalition for the International Criminal Court, "NCICC calls on Nigeria to pass International Crimes Bill" NCICC Press Release Abuja 1 August 2014
The Prosecutor v Boskoski, Case No. IT 04-82-T, Judgment (Trial Chamber II) 10 July 2008, para 193
The Prosecutor v Tadic, Case No. IT-94-1, Judgment (Trial Chamber) 7 May 1997
The Prosecutor v Tadic, Case No. IT-94-1-AR72, Merits (Appeals Chamber), 2 October 1995, para 70
The Prosecutor v Thomas Lubanga Dyilo, Judgment pursuant to Article 74 of the Statute, ICC - 01/04-01/06 (14 March 2012)
The Punch, "18 Soldiers on trial for aiding Boko Haram" at www.punchng.com last visited 18/1/2015
The Punch, "Boko Haram: ECOWAS mulls regional force" at www.punchng.com/.../boko-haram-ecow last visited 20/1/2015
The Vanguard, "Boko Haram Sponsorship: No Secret Trial for Ndume" at www.vanguardngr.com last visited 19/1/2015
Tribune, "Boko Haram, other wars render 750,000 stateless in West Africa – UN agency" at tribune. Com.ng/.../book-haram/12855 last visited 18/1/2015
Walker A (2012) What is Boko Haram? United States Institute for Peace, SPECIAL REPORT 308, June
Zenn J, Pearson E (2014) Women, gender and the evolving tactics of Boko Haram. J Terrorism Res 5(1) (Special Issue)

Chapter 8
Calibrating the Legal Obligations in the Ongoing Non-international Armed Conflict in Nigeria

Elijah Oluwatoyin Okebukola

8.1 Introduction

The present Boko Haram conflict re-echoes some of the social and legal problems that arose during the Nigerian civil war of 1967–1970 (the Civil War). It would therefore appear that legal scholars, commentators and, above all, persons involved in the conflict can be guided by reference to legal documents and guidelines influenced by facts and actions from the Civil War.[1] In reality, however, the present conflict is different in certain factual particulars. These factual differences make it impossible to apply the legal conclusions from the Civil War to the Boko Haram conflict. Given that both sides to the conflict have been accused of violating their legal obligations,[2] it becomes imperative to ascertain what the law requires from the persons taking part in the conflict. In this regard, this paper does not seek to address all the principles of law relevant in a conflict of this nature. Rather, it seeks to identify responsibilities that arise from the peculiar facts of the Boko Haram conflict.

For this purpose, the paper first of all considers whether the Boko Haram conflict is an international armed conflict or a non-international armed conflict. This exercise is important because of the involvement of other States in the conflict and the extraterritorial activities of Boko Haram. Next, the paper considers some of the legal consequences of the facts that the Civilian Joint Task Force (CJTF) is involved in the Boko Haram conflict, bordering States are participating, the conflict is of an asymmetrical nature and it deeply involves non-military law enforcement authorities. These are radical factual differences between the Civil War and the Boko Haram conflict. The paper concludes that notwithstanding aspects of the law that require additional work and clarification, the multiple actors in the Boko Haram

[1] Such guidelines will include the National Defence Policy.

[2] An accusation the Government has denied but Boko Haram has embraced.

E. O. Okebukola (✉)
Public and International Law, Nasarawa State University, Keffi, Nigeria

J.-M. Iyi, H. Strydom (eds.), *Boko Haram and International Law*,
https://doi.org/10.1007/978-3-319-74957-0_8

conflict have roles, duties and rights in law. In all, the BH conflict is not a chaotic legal black hole where everything goes. All the parties involved are accountable in international law and domestic law.

8.2 Does the Boko Haram Situation Amount to a Non-international Armed Conflict?

8.2.1 Facts Relating to Armed Activities of Boko Haram

Boko Haram is a non-State armed group that considers Western education to be sinful and therefore seeks to displace the present governmental structures in Nigeria by replacing them with its own extreme interpretation of Islamic rule. Contrary to reports that BH became violent in 2009,[3] its earliest publicly known armed confrontation with the State was towards the end of 2003 and the first days of 2004.[4] Between December 2003 and January 4, there were armed clashes between BH and elements of Nigeria Army and Nigeria Police.[5] About 200 BH members and hundreds of Nigerian soldiers took direct part in the clashes.[6] The clashes were, however, not nationwide and were limited to three Yobe State towns (Kanamma, Geidam and Damaturu).[7] The clashes ended in what appeared to be a dispersal of BH from their known camps.[8]

Following the first Yobe State clashes, BH continued to asymmetrically strike at the State by means of unprovoked killings and kidnappings. For example, in October 2004 at Kala-Balge in Borno State,[9] it 'attacked a police convoy, killing three officers and abducting a dozen'.[10] BH intermittent attacks have continued unabated from 2004 but are sometimes difficult to distinguish from the activities of other armed groups that also engage in killings and kidnappings. For example, in April 2007 at

[3] See for example, Chothia, BBC News (4 May 2015), where it is suggested that the group 'Launched military operations in 2009'.

[4] Mbachu, Associated Press (4 Jan 2004).

[5] Harbom and Wallensteen (2005), p. 633.

[6] For the number of BH participants see, Frontier Star (January 4, 2004). For the number of Nigeria Army participants see, 'Nigerian 'Taleban' launches uprising; Group, which seeks to set up an Islamic state, storms police stations in some towns,burns buildings and steals large weapon caches' *The Straits Times (Singapore)* (9 Jan 2004).

[7] Yobe State is one of the 36 federating units of the Federal Republic of Nigeria. It is in the North-Eastern part of the country where the Boko Haram (BH) conflict is presently concentrated.

[8] It is instructive that BH has been known by various names in the past including Nigerian Taliban as the group was known at the time of the Yobe clashes of late 2003 and early 2004. See for example, 'NIGERIAN 'TALIBAN' STRIKE AGAIN' January 4, 2004).

[9] Borno State is also a federating unit in the Federal Republic of Nigeria and also in the North-Eastern part of the country.

[10] Edmonton Journal (Alberta) (10 Oct 2004).

Kano,[11] assailants 'estimated in the hundreds, first attacked a police station and then ambushed a group of officers who responded to assist'.[12] At least 12 police officers were killed, and the military was called in to repel the attack.[13] It is, however, not clear if the assailants in this attack were BH or some other group(s),[14] even though the incident bears the BH signature, including deliberate attacks on structures and persons with real or symbolic connection to governmental structures or facilities of the State.

It suffices to say that between the first publicly known concerted armed assault in 2003/2004 and 2015, BH has metamorphosed from a group attacking police stations to one that not only attacks military barracks but also holds territory with a view to setting up its own administrative and governmental structures.

It is important to determine if the BH conflict amounts to a non-international armed conflict (NIAC) or an international armed conflict (IAC) because the applicable laws differ in international and non-international armed conflicts.[15] These differences are becoming less marked,[16] and some scholars now call for the elimination of the distinction.[17] Nonetheless, it suffices for our present purposes to note that '[s]pecific distinctions between the two still remain'.[18]

As a background to determining if the BH conflict is a NIAC or an IAC, it is relevant to point out that there have been various situations of armed violence in the post-independence period of Nigeria.[19] The Civil War is a well-documented and largely conventional armed conflict. Between 1970 and 2015, there have been several confrontations between non-State groups *inter se*, as well as clashes between non-State groups and government forces. Most of these conflicts share certain elements. Many of these conflicts have resulted in loss of life and property, as well as displacement of persons. Most of the conflicts involve the use of small arms and light weapons by non-State actors. Most of the groups involved have identifiable hierarchical structures.

---

[11] Kano city is the capital of Kano State, which is also a federating unit in the Federal Republic of Nigeria. There have been intermittent BH attacks in the State but BH has not held on to the State's territory as it has done in the North-East.

[12] Timberg (The Washington Post 18 Apr 2007).

[13] Timberg (The Washington Post 18 Apr 2007).

[14] Dowden, The Independent London (19 Apr 2007).

[15] Byron (2001), p. 63.

[16] For example, under the Rome Statute of the ICC, most war crimes in international armed conflicts are also war crimes in non-international armed conflicts. See also, Zegveld (2002), p. 33.

[17] See for example, Crawford (2007), p. 441.

[18] Bartels (2009), p. 41.

[19] See for example, Adesoji (2010), pp. 96–97 who identifies the following religion-related violence among others: The Maitatsine uprisings of 1980 in Kano, 1982 in Kaduna and Bulumkutu, 1984 in Yola and 1985 in Bauchi; Kano riots of October 1982, Ilorin riot of March 1986, the Kafanchan/Kaduna/Zaria/Funtua religious riots of March 1987, the Bauchi/Katsina riots of March/April 1991, the Kano riot of October 1991, the Zangon-Kataf riot of May 1992, the Kano civil disturbance of December 1991, the ongoing Jos crisis.

However, with the exception of the Civil War, none of the other conflict situations has been as protracted, intense and costly as the ongoing BH conflict. Both the Civil War and the BH conflict involve concerted steps by anti-government military forces that do not only take over but also install their administration in large swathes of Nigerian territory.

The BH conflict differs from the Civil War in certain factual particulars. During the Civil War from 1966 to 1970, there were two identifiable sides, namely, the Federal Government of Nigeria on the one hand and Biafra on the other. The two sides battled for the control and sovereignty over territory. Both sides deployed conventional armed forces with traditional command and control structures. The Federal Government was led by General Yakubu Gowon, and the Biafran side was led by Colonel Odumegwu Ojukwu. In addition to deploying regular armies, both sides relied on traditional international law principles in justification of their participation in the armed conflict. The Biafran side relied on the right to self-determination, and the Nigerian side relied on the right of absolute sovereignty over national territory. The conflict terminated in a capitulation by the Biafran side by means of a formal declaration of surrender, which cumulated in the execution of articles of surrender on 14 January 1970.

Unlike the Civil War that had two clear conventional armed forces combatting against each other, the Boko Haram conflict involves asymmetrical armed conflict. On the one hand, there are the Boko Haram operatives, and on the other hand, there are the armed forces of Nigeria, Chad, Niger and Cameroon. The Nigerian governmental forces are complemented by non-military law enforcement agents, as well as civilians directly participating in hostilities. Some facts arising from the ongoing Boko Haram conflict are so different in character and scope from the Civil War that they raise legal questions that were never in contemplation during the Civil War.

For instance, during the civil war, the Nigerian government did not actively deploy civilians to engage in the fighting against the anti-government forces. However, the present fight against Boko Haram involves active combat roles for State-recognised civilian groups described as the 'Civilian JTF'. The involvement of the Civilian JTF raises the important legal question as to whether the operatives of the Civilian JTF are combatants. There is also the question as to who bears command responsibility for actions of the Civilian JTF.

Next, there were no foreign armed forces involved in the Civil War. On the contrary, governmental military forces from Chad, Cameroon and Niger are participating in the fight against Boko Haram. The participation of several States in the armed conflict raises the important question as to the nature of the armed conflict. Is the conflict an international armed conflict or a non-international armed conflict? In addition, there is at present no publicly available status of forces agreement delineating the rights, privileges and duration of stay of the foreign armed forces on Nigerian soil. This raises practical legal questions such as the point in time the foreign armed forces may be deemed to be violating the sovereignty of the host or even engaging in unlawful use of force against the territorial integrity or political independence of the host.

Another significant distinguishing fact between the Boko Haram conflict and the Civil War is the translation of the asymmetrical nature of the conflict into direct unconventional attacks on non-military locations outside the immediate areas of military confrontation. These non-military targets include schools,[20] police stations and customs locations.[21] BH also forcefully conscripts children for direct participation in fighting and frequently deploys them as child suicide bombers. This asymmetry is stretched further as Boko Haram operatives extend their unconventional attacks beyond the northeast (where the military confrontation is taking place) to the whole country. This raises the question as to the legal regime that will apply where Boko Haram members are caught or found outside northeastern Nigeria. Particularly, would the conduct of hostilities or law enforcement paradigms apply? This question is accentuated by non-military law enforcement authorities of the State such as the police, Directorate of State Security, Immigration Service, Customs and Civil Defence Corps who are directly involved in the conflict.

8.2.2 Legal Basis for Determining the Existence of a Non-international Armed Conflict

Certainly, not every situation of armed violence by a non-State actor amounts to armed conflict. Whether or not the above factual events relating to the BH conflict amount to an armed conflict is a question of law. To determine whether the BH conflict amounts to a NIAC recourse must be made to Article 3 common to the four Geneva conventions of 1949 (Common Article 3)[22] and Article 1 of Additional Protocol II to the Geneva Conventions. Prior to the codification of Common Article 3, where there were uprisings within a State, such will be a purely internal matter and not governed by international law. International law would only become relevant if the situation deteriorated from rebellion to insurgency to belligerency.[23] Characterisation of civil strife as rebellion, insurgency or belligerency was determined by the duration, extent, purpose and intensity of the conflict.

The expression 'rebellion' was used to describe situations of short-lived or sporadic challenge to the legitimacy of government.[24] Falk described rebellion as 'a sporadic challenge to the legitimate government'.[25] Provided the government was

[20] Moland (2015), p. 8.

[21] Aljazeera 27 July 2009.

[22] Geneva Convention I for the Amelioration of the Condition of Wounded and Sick in Armed Forces in the Field, 1949; Geneva Convention II for the Amelioration of the Condition of the Wounded, Sick and Shipwrecked members of Armed Forces at Sea, 1949; Geneva Convention III Relative to the Treatment of Prisoners of War, 1949; and Geneva Convention IV Relative to the Protection of Civilian Persons in Time of War, 1949.

[23] Bartels, 'Timeliness, Borderlines and Conflicts - The Historical Evolution of the Legal Distinction between International and Non-International Armed Conflicts' n 13, p. 48. See also, Paulus and Vashakmadze (2009), p. 99, where it is stated that the notion of recognition of belligerency is obsolete.

[24] Wilson (1988), p. 23.

[25] Falk (1964), p. 199.

able to speedily suppress the upheaval 'by normal procedures of internal security',[26] the situation would not be characterised as armed conflict.

The International Criminal Tribunal for the Former Yugoslavia (ICTY) in *Prosecutor* v. *Dusko Tadić* observed that 'states preferred to regard internal strife as rebellion, mutiny and treason coming within the purview of national criminal law and, by the same token, to exclude any possible intrusion by other States into their own domestic jurisdiction'.[27] As such, under traditional international law, 'a rebellion within the borders of a sovereign State is the exclusive concern of that state'.[28] The rebellion would not amount to an armed conflict; therefore, how the State dealt with the rebels was outside the scope of international humanitarian law.[29]

Where the government failed to effectively suppress the upheaval, it could change in status from rebellion to insurrection.[30] The change in status, however, occurred only if the legitimate government on its own accord decided to recognise the situation as an insurgency.[31] The recognition of insurgency did not, however, automatically create a situation of armed conflict requiring the introduction of the provisions of international humanitarian law. Rather, the provisions only applied if expressly conceded by the legitimate government.[32] The *de jure* government ordinarily would only recognise an insurgency where there was the necessity to establish formal relations with the insurgents so as to protect the interests of the government or those of a third State.[33]

If the insurgency was not suppressed, the 'the parent government or a third state could, by declaration, grant the insurgents recognition as a belligerent party'.[34] According to Lauterpacht, four criteria had to be met before insurgents became recognised as belligerents:

> [F]irst, there must exist within the state an armed conflict of a general (as distinguished from a purely local) character; secondly the insurgents must occupy and administer a substantial portion of national territory; thirdly, they must conduct hostilities in accordance with the rules of war and through organised armed forces acting under a responsible authority; fourthly, there must exist circumstances which make it necessary for outside States to define their attitude by means of recognition of belligerency.[35]

Following the recognition of belligerency, the principles of international humanitarian law became immediately applicable to the conflict. It is important to note that even before upheavals reached the stage where international humanitarian law

---

26 Falk (1964), pp. 198–199.

27 *Prosecutor* v. *Dusko Tadić*, (the *Tadić Decision*) 2 October 1995 ICTY, Case No. IT-94-1-AR72, para. 96 (Decision on the Defence Motion for Interlocutory Appeal on Jurisdiction).

28 Wilson (1988), p. 23.

29 Moir (2002), p. 4.

30 See generally, O'Brien (1978), p. 193.

31 See Higgins (1971), p. 88.

32 See Higgins (1971), p. 88.

33 Cullen (2005), pp. 66, 72.

34 Bartels (2009), p. 50.

35 Lauterpacht (1947), p. 176.

became applicable, municipal laws, including human rights obligations, remained in force.[36] Thus, under traditional international law, the BH situation would have reached the threshold of an armed conflict, triggering the operation of IHL, if the Nigerian government recognised the situation as one that has degenerated upheaval to insurgency to belligerency.

With the advent of the four Geneva Conventions of 1949, it no longer became necessary to formally recognise civil strife as insurgency or belligerency for international humanitarian law to come into operation between the parties. Common Article 3 to the Geneva Conventions commands the application of international humanitarian law to 'all armed conflict not of an international character'.[37] Thus, irrespective of whether the situation is described as a rebellion, an insurgency or belligerency, it may be viewed by Common Article 3 as an armed conflict to which international humanitarian law applies.

In effect, a situation of armed conflict can arise in law even if the parent State does not or refuses to recognise the events as reaching the threshold of an armed conflict. So under the regime of the 1949 Geneva Conventions, the characterisation of the BH situation as an armed conflict is not a matter left to the parent State. Rather, it is a matter of law. In an attempt to improve upon the provisions of the 1949 Geneva Conventions, two additional protocols, Additional Protocol I[38] and Additional Protocol II,[39] were adopted in 1977. Additional Protocol II 'develops and supplements Common Article 3 to the Geneva Conventions of 12 August 1949 without modifying its existing conditions of application'.[40] In particular, Article 1 (1) of Additional Protocol II defines non-international armed conflicts as those

> which take place in the territory of a High Contracting Party between its armed forces and dissident armed forces or other organized armed groups which, under responsible command, exercise such control over a part of its territory as to enable them to carry out sustained and concerted military operations and to implement this Protocol.[41]

In all, while Common Article 3 applies to all non-international armed conflicts, Additional Protocol II applies only to those that meet the objective criteria set out in its Article 1 (1). Thus, Additional Protocol II has a more restrictive threshold of application than Common Article 3.[42] Common Article 3, however, does not define what is meant by armed conflict. This leaves room for ambiguity and subjective interpretation by parties to an armed conflict. The situation has, however, been ameliorated since the ICTY in the *Tadić Decision* stated that an armed conflict exists

---

[36] Kalshoven (1983), p. 67.

[37] Article 3 common to the Geneva Conventions 1949.

[38] Protocol Additional to the Geneva Conventions of 12 August 1949, and relating to the Protection of Victims of International Armed Conflicts.

[39] Protocol Additional to the Geneva Conventions of 12 August 1949, and Relating to the Protection of Victims of Non-International Armed Conflicts, 1977 (Additional Protocol II).

[40] Article 1, Additional Protocol II.

[41] Article 1, Additional Protocol I.

[42] See Clapham (2006), pp. 491, 497.

> whenever there is a resort to armed force between States or protracted armed violence between governmental authorities and organized armed groups or between such groups within a State. International humanitarian law applies from the initiation of such armed conflicts and extends beyond the cessation of hostilities until a general conclusion of peace is reached; or, in the case of internal conflicts, a peaceful settlement is achieved. Until that moment, international humanitarian law continues to apply in the whole territory of the warring States or, in the case of internal conflicts, the whole territory under the control of a party, whether or not actual combat takes place there.[43]

It is instructive that Additional Protocol II expressly declares that 'internal disturbances and tensions, such as riots, isolated and sporadic acts of violence and other acts of a similar nature',[44] do not amount to armed conflicts. Thus, situations where individuals or groups of individuals openly express their opposition, their discontent or their demands to a government do not necessarily amount to armed conflict.[45] This remains the case even if the protests include isolated and sporadic acts of violence.[46] Human rights law apply to such internal disturbances, but the disturbances remain outside the purview of international humanitarian law whether

> State repression is involved or not, whether the disturbances are lasting, brief with durable effects, or intermittent, whether only a part or all of the national territory is affected or whether the disturbances are of religious, ethnic, political or any other origin.[47]

Thus, for the general application of international humanitarian law, including Common Article 3, a non-international armed conflict may be said to exist whenever there is a protracted armed violence between governmental authorities and organised armed groups or between such groups within a State. For the specific purposes of Additional Protocol II, a non-international armed conflict exists where (1) there is resort to armed force between a State and an armed dissident group or between armed groups and (2) the group(s) are under responsible command and (3) control a part of the State's territory such that they can mount sustained and concerted military operations and (4) they are capable of implementing the provisions of Additional Protocol II.

For armed violence between a State and a terrorist group to constitute a non-international armed conflict, that conflict must reach the 'prescribed degree of intensity and involve a military-like formation that possess a command structure enabling it to maintain internal discipline and respect international humanitarian law'.[48]

Given the involvement of several States in the armed conflict, it is important to point out why the BH conflict is not an IAC. The most direct approach for this clarification is to highlight the simplified definition of an IAC as one that is between

---

[43] The *Tadić Decision,* para 70.

[44] Article 1 (2) Additional Protocol II. For a discussion on available laws during disturbances, see Momtaz (1998).

[45] Harroff-Tavel (1993).

[46] Harroff-Tavel (1993).

[47] Harroff-Tavel (1993).

[48] Stewart (2007), pp. 26, 28.

two or more States.[49] Additional Protocol I to the Geneva Conventions extends the definition of IAC to include fighting against colonial domination, alien occupation or racist regimes.[50] The States involved in the BH conflict are on one side, while BH is on the other. It is therefore not a conflict between two or more States. Moreover, BH is not fighting for self-determination. Therefore, the conflict is certainly not an IAC.

Rather, the BH conflict involves resort to armed force between the State and the armed dissident group; BH has a command structure, including a leader or leaders who can be held responsible for the activities of the group; it, from time to time, controls part(s) of Nigerian territory from where it mounts concerted military operations, and it is capable of complying with the provisions of Additional Protocol II. The BH situation would therefore amount to an armed conflict of a non-international nature under the regime created by Additional Protocol II.

8.2.3 *Does IHL Exclude BH from the Application of Municipal Criminal and Other Laws?*

It is highly significant that international humanitarian law does not change the status of the parties to an armed conflict.[51] Thus, the claims of an illegitimate or unlawful contender to the control of the government or territory do not become validated by the application of international humanitarian law.[52] Indeed, the Geneva Conventions emphasise that application of their provisions 'shall not affect the legal status of the Parties to the conflict'.[53]

The irrelevance of international humanitarian law to the status of the parties to an armed conflict is momentous in a NIAC to the extent that the recognition of combatant status does not result in the suspension of domestic laws and regulations. Arrests, detention and internment are governed by national laws and legislation and not IHL.[54] Thus, although the Nigerian armed forces and BH combatants are equally obliged to comply with IHL principles in the ongoing armed conflict, nothing in IHL precludes the arrest and prosecution of BH members for offences including violations of the Criminal Code Act, Penal Code Laws and the Terrorism (Prevention) Act.[55]

[49] Schindler (1979), p. 158; See also Common Article 2 to the Geneva Conventions.

[50] Additional Protocol I, Article 1, paragraph 4 refers to 'armed conflicts in which peoples are fighting against colonial domination and alien occupation and against racist regimes in the exercise of their right of self-determination, as enshrined in the Charter of the United Nations and the Declaration on Principles of International Law concerning Friendly Relations and Co-operation among States in accordance with the Charter of the United Nations'.

[51] Okebukola (2012), p. 163.

[52] Okebukola (2012), p. 163.

[53] Geneva Conventions 1949, Common Article 3.

[54] Sassoli (2004), p. 105.

[55] However, the applicable national legislation must be in line with international human rights law.

8.2.4 Characterisation of Boko Haram

Governmental authorities and observers have been using various terms to describe the BH. These terms include insurgents, terrorists, militants, Islamists, criminals, etcetera. In the non-international context of the BH troubles, characterisation is important as it is a first step in determining governmental policy towards BH, as well as the general relationship between BH and domestic law. For example, if BH operatives are characterised as insurgents, government policy towards those captured in battle may be different from if the operatives are characterised as criminals or terrorists. In addition, characterisation of participants in a NIAC may be relevant in determining tortious liability or other civil claims in domestic courts.

The law of war applies four characteristics to differentiate non-State groups that are involved in NIAC from other categories of armed or violent actors.[56] First, the non-State participants in NIAC are commanded by a person responsible for his subordinates.[57] In effect, they must have a discernible command structure. Second, they have a fixed distinctive emblem recognizable at a distance.[58] Third, they carry arms openly,[59] and fourth, they conduct their operations in accordance with the laws and customs of war.[60]

Although the situation may be different in an IAC,[61] in a NIAC, such as the ongoing BH situation in Nigeria, a distinction can be made between (1) insurgent-combatants, (2) terrorist-combatants and (3) terrorists. While terrorist combatants may have a command structure, distinctive emblem and carry arms openly, a main distinction between insurgent-combatants and terrorist-combatants is the latter's manifest intention and deliberate constant practice of not adhering to the laws and customs of war. Terrorist groups simpliciter are distinguishable from terrorist-combatants and insurgent-combatants because the latter two operate in the context of an armed conflict. In making these characterisations, it is worth emphasising that whether or not an armed conflict exists in a given situation is not a question to be determined by the parties involved. It is a question of law.

In relation to BH, before the troubles degenerated into a non-international armed conflict, BH operations were such that they qualified the group as terrorists. However, since the troubles have reached the threshold of a NIAC and BH still maintains its terrorist doctrine and practices, BH operators as participants in the NIAC are terrorist-combatants. If BH drops its terrorist doctrines and practices while still continuing in armed conflict, it may from that point onwards be regarded as insurgents.

---

[56] Hague Regulations 1907, Article 1.

[57] Hague Regulations 1907, Article 1 item 1.

[58] Hague Regulations 1907, Article 1 item 2.

[59] Hague Regulations 1907, Article 1 item 3.

[60] Hague Regulations 1907, Article 1 item 4.

[61] See for example, Kretzmer (2005), p. 171.

If the government views and characterises BH as insurgents, then captured operatives may be treated as prisoners of war (POW). The sovereignty of the State is not extinguished by NIAC, and the parent government is at liberty to designate and treat captured insurgents as POW. There are many arguments against the conferment of prisoner of war status on guerrillas and insurgents.[62] The State may also implement a policy of granting amnesty to insurgents who have not violated international humanitarian law or international criminal law.[63] Characterisation is also important as regards third persons (natural or legal) or third States. Persons providing support or finance for insurgents may not be considered as financing terrorists.[64] Similarly, third States may recognise insurgents as belligerents under international law.[65]

On another note, if the State views BH as terrorists-insurgents, then captured operators may be detained and prosecuted as violators of extant criminal law provisions, especially the Terrorism Prevention Act. In this case, prisoners are not given the duties, rights and privileges of POW. Also, and probably more importantly, the State may not grant amnesty to terrorist-insurgents.[66] This is because there is a duty to prosecute or extradite violators of the law of war—*aut dedere aut judicare*.[67] In addition, third States may not recognise terrorists who are engaged in armed conflict in the same way as they would recognise bare insurgents. Moreover, individuals supporting such terrorist-insurgents may be aiding or financing terrorism. A good example is the Swiss Criminal Code, which does not extend the prohibition of financing of terrorism to acts that do not contradict the rules of international law pertaining to armed conflict.[68] Thus, financial support to terrorist-insurgents is prohibited as the terrorist-insurgents are avowed violators of international humanitarian law. Finally, characterising them as mere terrorists has even more far-reaching implications, which will be highlighted in part D below.

Regardless of whether these characterisations are accurate or not, all parties to NIAC are obliged to comply with the law of armed conflict. Just as *jus ad bellum* has no bearing on the obligation to adhere to *jus in bello* in international armed conflicts, the difference between insurgent-combatant and terrorist-combatant has no bearing on the requirement of the parties to a NIAC to adhere to applicable prin-

---

[62] Ruud (1985), p. 433.

[63] Where international crimes are committed, a domestic amnesty will not deprive other States of jurisdiction. See SCSL Lome Amnesty Decision Para 67.

[64] Pieth (2006), p. 1074.

[65] See for example, Lauterpacht (1947), p. 176, where it was stated that four criteria must be met before insurgents are recognised as belligerents: [F]irst, there must exist within the state an armed conflict of a general (as distinguished from a purely local) character; secondly the insurgents must occupy and administer a substantial portion of national territory; thirdly, they must conduct hostilities in accordance with the rules of war and through organised armed forces acting under a responsible authority; fourthly, there must exist circumstances which make it necessary for outside States to define their attitude by means of recognition of belligerency.

[66] See for example Williams (2005), p. 271 where it is suggested that the validity of an amnesty should be assessed on a case by case basis.

[67] See generally, Bassiouni and Wise (1995).

[68] Swiss Criminal Code, Article 260 quinquies, paragraph 4.

ciples of IHL, human rights and international criminal law. Thus, whether or not BH fighters are regarded as insurgents-combatants or terrorist-combatants, they are obliged to refrain from attacking civilians and civilian targets; be proportionate in attack; treat prisoners of war appropriately; not recruit, use or train children for armed conflict; not kidnap women as sex slaves; refrain from terrorising the civilian populace; etc. Terrorist-combatants cannot rely on their own unlawful conduct to claim a right of exemption from the laws and customs regulating armed conflict. This idea is similar to the *ex turpi causa non-oritur actio* principle in civil matters. A person cannot rely on his own wrongful conduct to confer a right on himself.

8.3 Legal Consequences of the Involvement of the Civilian Joint Task Force

8.3.1 Combatants or Not?

State-recognised civilian groups described as the 'Civilian JTF' are involved in direct participation in hostilities.

The term 'non-combatant' 'covers a broad range of people with very different characteristics'.[69] A definition that fairly covers the broad range of characteristics is in the US Naval *Commander's Handbook on the Law of Naval Operations*, which states:

> Noncombatants are those individuals who do not form a part of the armed forces and who otherwise refrain from the commission of hostile acts. Noncombatants also include those members of the armed forces who enjoy special protected status, such as medical personnel and chaplains, or who have been rendered incapable of combat by wounds, sickness, shipwreck, or capture.[70]

Civilians are ordinarily non-combatants as long as they do not form a part of the armed forces and refrain from the commission of hostile acts. Where civilians take part in hostilities, even though they may be regarded as military targets, they are entitled to IHL protections conferred on combatants. For example, when captured, they are entitled to POW treatment; when hors de combat, they cease to become lawful targets, and they are not legitimate targets if their role is limited to the performance of the functions of persons who enjoy special protected status such as medical personnel and chaplains.

Additional Protocol II imposes an obligation on the parties in a NIAC to ensure that the civilian populace and individual civilians enjoy general protection against the dangers arising from military operations.[71] In the fulfilment of this obligation, the parties shall not make civilians the object of attack. In addition, the parties may not

[69] Kalshoven (1991), p. 301.

[70] Kalshoven (1991), p. 301.

[71] Additional Protocol II, Article 13 paragraph 1.

engage in acts or threats of violence that are primarily aimed at spreading terror among the civilian population.[72] The protection afforded by these provisions of Additional Protocol II is, however, available to a civilian taking a direct part in hostilities.[73]

The CJTF is a fusion of civilian and military status. This sort of conflation is not a unique creation of the Nigerian military authorities. A similar concept is apparent in the Norwegian Military Penal Code, which recognises the status of persons assimilated to the military as 'civilian-military persons'.[74] The civilian-military status is one of three possible military-employee designations under the Norwegian Military Penal Code.[75] The other two are military persons and civilian personnel.[76]

The operational structure of the CJTF and its relationship with the formal military authorities are not yet fully documented. It would, however, appear that unlike the Norwegian civilian-military personnel, who may or may not be combatants,[77] Nigeria's CJTF are combatants. They do not function as persons following armed forces, nor are they civilian employees of the armed forces.[78] Rather, they directly participate in fighting BH.

8.3.2 Command Responsibility for the CJTF

One of the inevitable fallouts of armed conflict is the accusation that participants have violated the law of armed conflict. The question then arises as to who bears command responsibility in the inevitable event that the CJTF is accused of breaching international humanitarian law.

Essentially, command responsibility is the liability of a superior for actions of his subordinates. In the *Hadžihasanović and Others* case, the International Criminal Tribunal for the Former Yugoslavia (ICTY) held that the command responsibility is a principle of customary international law and is applicable in non-international armed conflicts.[79] The applicability of the principle in non-international armed conflicts has also been upheld by the International Criminal Tribunal for Rwanda (ICTR) in the *Akayesu* case and *Kayishema and Ruzindana* case.

---

[72] Additional Protocol II, Article 13 paragraph 2.

[73] Additional Protocol II, Article 13 paragraph 3.

[74] Military Penal Code, § 4. (Note that the text in this link is in Norwegian).

[75] Monsen (1971), p. 201.

[76] Monsen (1971), p. 201.

[77] Military Penal Code (Norway), § 4.

[78] Armed Forces Act (Nigeria), sections 146,223 and 272 recognises that civilians may be employed by the armed forces. Such civilians may be subject to military law in certain instances but they are not combatants.

[79] ICTY, *Hadžihasanović and Others*, Case No. IT-01-47-AR72, § 57 (Disposition on the first ground of appeal), 16 July 2003. Decision on Interlocutory Appeal Challenging Jurisdiction in Relation to Command Responsibility.

The principle is applicable to both military and civilian superiors.[80] The relationship between the commander and the subordinate(s) may be *de jure* or *de facto*.[81] The crucial criterion is that the de facto or de jure commander must have control over the actions of the subordinates in the sense that the commander has material ability to prevent and punish the violations of the law.[82] For the application of the principle, the commander, leader or superior must have actual or constructive knowledge of the violations perpetrated or about to be carried out by the subordinate(s). There is constructive knowledge where the commander 'had reason to know'[83] or '(owing to the circumstances at the time,) should have known'.[84] Finally, the superior must have failed to take necessary and reasonable measures to prevent the prohibited conduct of the subordinate(s) or punish the subordinate(s) for the conduct.[85]

The CJTF has its own organisational structure with leaders at different levels. It is, however, not an independent fighting force because it operates at the pleasure of the State. There is, however, no publicly available legal instrument that establishes a *de jure* relationship between the CJTF and the State or agents of the State. It is nevertheless apparent that the CJTF has internal leaders who command and control the members of the CJTF group(s). It is also apparent that the CJTF works under the *de facto* supervision of the armed forces. The 'civilian' leaders of the CJTF and supervisory military commanders would therefore have command responsibility for CJTF conduct where the criteria highlighted above are met. The logical end of the principle will mean that political or civil superiors who are in de jure control of the military may be held accountable for CJTF conduct for which military commanders bear responsibility. Apart from individual responsibility for actions of CJTF members, the CJTF leaders have command responsibility for their fighter's actions.

The authorities in charge of the CJTF must ensure that violations are not widespread and systemic. In this regard, incidents of violations must be promptly investigated. If investigations reveal a *prima facie* case, the alleged violators must be promptly brought to trial. An aspect of CJTF activities that requires close scrutiny by the military authorities is the recruitment, training and use of children for the armed conflict against BH.[86] Additional Protocol II provides that '[c]hildren who have not attained the age of fifteen years shall neither be recruited in the armed forces or groups nor allowed to take part in hostilities'.[87] This duty is not extinguished by the fact that BH itself may be violating the law by using children as fighters in the NIAC. A systemic pattern of violations, plus a failure to investigate

[80] See the *Akayesu case; Kayishema and Ruzindana case;* and the *Delalić case.*

[81] Aleksovski case, Blaškić case, Judgment, Kunarac case, Judgment and Kvočka case, Judgment 714).

[82] ICTY, *Delalić case*, Judgment; see also Article 28 of the Statute of the International Criminal Court.

[83] See for example ICTY Statute, Article 7(3); ICTR Statute, Article 6(3).

[84] ICC Statute, Article 28.

[85] Ambos (2007), pp. 159 at 161.

[86] See generally, Okebukola (2014), p. 588.

[87] Additional Protocol II, Article 4, paragraph 3 (c).

and bring alleged perpetrators to trial, may lead to 'command responsibility'. In this event, senior commanders, including the commander-in-chief, may be held accountable for the violations committed by the CJTF.[88]

8.4 Effect of the Participation of Bordering States

8.4.1 Does the Involvement of Multiple States Make the Conflict 'International'?

Ordinarily, when an event involves a plurality of States, it is taken to be international. The involvement of multiple States in the BH conflict may give it the colouration of an international armed conflict. This view is given some more weight by the BH activities that go beyond the territory of Nigeria into neighbouring States.

However, the status of a conflict as either IAC or NIAC is not determined by the number of Sates in which it is taking place. Rather, NIACs are distinguished from IACs 'by the parties involved rather than by the territorial scope of the conflict'.[89] In *Hamdan v. Rumsfeld*, the majority of the US Supreme Court found that non-international armed conflicts are not limited to internal conflicts but include any conflict that is not a conflict between States.[90]

Therefore, as the conflict is not between State(s) and BH is a non-State actor, it is a NIAC. Its status does not change to IAC, although BH elements operate across international borders of Nigeria, Chad, Niger and Cameroon. Furthermore, the involvement of all these States in the fight against BH does not make the conflict an IAC.

8.4.2 Warnings from the Armed Activities Case

On 19 December 2005, the International Court of Justice (ICJ) delivered judgment in the *Case Concerning Armed Activities on the Territory of the Congo* (Armed Activities case).[91] In that case, the Government of Democratic Republic of Congo (DRC) consented to the presence of Ugandan military forces in eastern DRC to prevent cross-border raids into Uganda by anti-Ugandan Congolese rebel forces. The DRC consent for Ugandan military activities was subsequently withdrawn. Rather than leave the DRC, Ugandan military forces launched operation 'Safe haven' and advanced further into DRC territory occupying several towns, airports

[88] See generally, Vetter (2000), p. 89; Arnold (2002), p. 191; Rowe (2008), p. 165; Bonafe (2007), p. 599.

[89] Zegveld (2002), p. 136.

[90] Hamdan v. Rumsfeld, 126 S.Ct. 2749 (2006), pp. 2794–2796.

[91] *Democratic Republic of the Congo v. Uganda.*

and a large portion of eastern DRC. The ICJ held that Uganda violated the sovereignty and territorial integrity of the DRC.

Just as in the *Armed Activities* case, military forces from neighbouring States are in northeastern Nigeria with the consent of the Nigerian government. At the moment, apart from crude oil, which is speculated to be in northeastern Nigeria, there is nothing to suggest a practical incentive for the neighbouring States to not leave when Nigeria withdraws its consent for their presence on Nigerian territory. Nevertheless, all States involved must learn from history and ensure that the roles, conditions participation and modalities of withdrawal from Nigerian territory are well defined.

8.5 Asymmetrical Nature of the Conflict and the Role of Non-military Law Enforcement Authorities

8.5.1 *Arrest or Kill?*

Two conflicting paradigms are relevant to the BH situation. The 'law enforcement paradigm' demands that fighters must be captured or arrested unless capturing them poses an imminent threat to life.[92] Conversely, the 'conduct of hostilities paradigm' allows the killing of the fighters without first attempting to arrest them.[93] Thus, if, for example, the Nigerian law enforcement agents run into a vehicle bearing BH fighters, the law enforcement paradigm requires that the first line of action would be to take reasonable measures to capture the BH fighters.[94] The conduct of hostilities paradigm, on the other hand, allows the law enforcement agents to open fire on the BH fighters without the necessity of attempting to arrest them.

The difference in approach between the two paradigms is better explained by reference to the legal theoretical basis of each. While the armed conflict paradigm is based on international humanitarian law, the law enforcement paradigm is based on human rights law. International humanitarian law allows parties to an armed conflict to use deadly force against military objectives and personnel. All that is required is that the rules regulating means and methods of warfare are followed.[95]

On the other hand, human rights law requires that lethal force must be used only as a last resort. This position is clarified by the guidance contained in the *UN Code of Conduct for Law Enforcement Officials* and the *UN Basic Principles on the Use of Force and Firearms by Law Enforcement Officials*. These instruments expect that

---

[92] Gaggioli (2013), p. 1.

[93] Gaggioli (2013), p. 1.

[94] Gaggioli (2013), p. 1.

[95] The parties are to apply the principle of distinction, avoid indiscriminate and disproportionate attacks, observe precautionary rules in attack, aimed at avoiding or minimizing incidental harm to civilians and civilian objects.

force may not exceed what is strictly or absolutely necessary to protect life. In effect, arrests must be by using non-lethal means.[96]

The designation of BH fighters as mere terrorists presupposes that the activities of the group(s) do not reach the threshold of a NIAC. For example, neither the British conflict with the IRA nor the Spanish campaigns against the ETA have been treated as an armed conflict.[97] The consequence of this designation is that the agents of the State would have to adopt the law enforcement paradigm in dealing with BH members.

The designation of BH as terrorist-combatants can be construed in two main ways. First, the terrorist-combatants are engaging in armed conflict wherever they may be found in Nigerian territory. Thus, the State does not have to try to capture them wherever they may be found. As long as they are not *hors de combat*, they can be attacked with deadly force. The consequence of this position would be that BH members, including those arrested in vehicles and houses outside the immediate battlefield, can be attacked even if no attempt has been made to capture them.

Second, the terrorist-combatants may be viewed as having the dual status of persons participating in armed conflict as well as criminals breaking anti-terrorism and other penal laws. Where BH operatives are found outside the conflict zone(s), their BH camps or BH-held territory and in a context where they do not pose any real threat, then the law enforcement paradigm would apply. Where, however, the reverse of the foregoing is the case, the conduct of hostilities paradigm would apply.

The second viewpoint appears to be the most legally prudent for States as it is the less likely to amount to a grave breach of international humanitarian law. Moreover, it aligns with the position of international human rights bodies. For example, in the context of the NIAC in Colombia, the UN Human Rights Committee decided, in the *Guerrero* case,[98] that the use of force against unarmed alleged *guerrilleros* by policemen who lay in wait for them at their house was disproportionate and violated the right to life. The Human Rights Committee condemned the facts that no warning was given, the *guerrilleros* were not given the opportunity to surrender and the use of force did not pursue a legitimate aim (self-defence, lawful arrest, preventing the escape of a person lawfully detained).[99]

This second viewpoint may not be expedient, but as pointed out by the Israeli Supreme Court,[100] 'a democracy fights with one hand tied behind her back: The ends do not justify the means … in a democracy, the fight against terror is subject to the rule of law'.[101] In another case, the same Court held:

[96] Gaggioli (2013), p. 7.

[97] McCoubrey and White (1992), p. 318.

[98] *husband of Maria Fanny Suarez de Guerrero v. Colombia*, Communication No. R.11/45, U.N. Doc. Supp. No. 40 (A/37/40) at 137 (1982).

[99] Gaggioli (2013), p. 14.

[100] *HCJ 769/02 The Public Committee against Torture in Israel v. The Government of Israel.*

[101] *HCJ 769/02 The Public Committee against Torture in Israel v. The Government of Israel* Summary Judgment p. 3.

> … That is the fate of democracy, in whose eyes not all means are permitted, and to whom not all the methods used by her enemies are open. At times democracy fights with one hand tied behind her back. Despite that, democracy has the upper hand, since preserving the rule of law and recognition of individual liberties constitute an important component of her security stance. At the end of the day, they strengthen her and her spirit, and allow her to overcome her difficulties.[102]

In the BH situation, the answer to the kill or capture question will then be kill when in battle, capture when it is practicable and no real immediate threat is posed. At any rate, in dealing with armed non-State actors in general and parties to NIACs in particular, States must be wary of the self-foisted conundrum that arose from the refusal of the USA to acknowledge the application of IHL to the conflict in Afghanistan and Iraq. Even if the participants are correctly classified as 'unlawful combatants', they will still be entitled to the IHL protection guaranteed by common Article 3 to the Geneva Convention of 1949.[103]

8.5.2 Direct Participation of Non-military Law Enforcement Authorities

One of the elements of a NIAC involving a State and a non-State group is the deployment of the State's armed forces as against regular or ordinary law enforcement agents.[104] In an IAC, the definition of combatants does not ordinarily include police and other regular law enforcement agents who are classified as civilians for the purpose of the armed conflict.[105] However, in an IAC, law enforcement agents may be incorporated into the armed forces and thereby lose their civilian status.[106]

The case is a little more complex in a NIAC because opposition fighters are in violation of domestic law by virtue of their armed activities, and law enforcement agencies are empowered by domestic law to deal with law breakers.[107] Additional Protocol II, which deals with NIACs, prohibits attacks on the civilian population, which invariably includes the civil law enforcement agents.[108] However, the protection from attack afforded to a civilian in a NIAC is lifted 'for such time as they take a direct part in hostilities'.[109]

---

[102] *HCJ 5100/94 The Public Committee against Torture in Israel v. The State of Israel* 53(4) PD 817, 845.

[103] Vierucci (2003), p. 284.

[104] Sassoli (2004), p. 100.

[105] See for example Aldrich (2002), p. 898 where it is opined that Al Qaeda was not capable of being a party to which Additional Protocol 1 would apply.

[106] Schmitt (2012), p. 125.

[107] Schmitt (2012), p. 125.

[108] Additional Protocol II, Articles 13, 14.

[109] Additional Protocol II, Article 13, paragraph 3.

The concept of direct participation is relevant to the principle of distinction between civilians and combatants.[110] The importance of this principle was underscored by the ICJ in the *Legality of the Threat or Use of Nuclear Weapons*, Advisory Opinion, where it was held that the principle is cardinal. So when can law enforcement agents be said to be taking direct part in hostilities?

According to the *travaux préparatoires* for Additional Protocol II, the armed forces in a NIAC include armed actors that do not necessarily qualify as armed forces under domestic law.[111] For example, law enforcement agents such as the National Guard, Customs, or the police qualify as armed forces in a NIAC where the law enforcement agents assume the function of armed forces.

Law enforcement agents do not, however, have to assume the function of armed forces before their actions can be contrary to the military objectives of the non-State parties to a NIAC. The question then arises as to whether law enforcement agents are combatants when they are performing their traditional functions distinct from the function of armed forces.

A possible answer lies in the ICRC Interpretive Guidance on direct participation. In defining direct participation in hostilities, the ICRC Interpretive Guidance proposes three cumulative criteria:

1. The act must be likely to adversely affect the military operations or military capacity of a party to an armed conflict or, alternatively, to inflict death, injury, or destruction on persons or objects protected against direct attack (threshold of harm), and
2. there must be a direct causal link between the act and the harm likely to result either from that act, or from a coordinated military operation of which that act constitutes an integral part (direct causation), and
3. the act must be specifically designed to directly cause the required threshold of harm in support of a party to the conflict and to the detriment of another (belligerent nexus).[112]

Going by the above cumulative criteria as formulated by the ICRC, it will appear that virtually every act of preventive law enforcement will amount to direct participation in armed conflict. For example, where the police raid the cell of BH operators who are planning an attack, such a raid would meet the three cumulative criteria. Similarly, where immigration officers at a border post forcefully prevent BH operatives from entering the country illegally, the acts of the officers would fall within the definition of direct participation.

The corollary of this position is that law enforcement agents going about their legitimate duties *ipso facto* become combatants in the NIAC. This position is untenable in logic and is unacceptable to States.[113] There is nevertheless need for a more

---

[110] Schmitt (2010), p. 700.

[111] Sandoz (1987), p. 4462.

[112] Melzer (2002/2009), p. 20.

[113] Given that the existence of a NIAC does not amount to a suspension of domestic laws.

detailed study, well beyond the space of this paper, to deliberate on the status of non-military law enforcement agents in NIACs.

8.6 Conclusion

The BH conflict is different in intensity and duration from other sporadic incidents of armed violence in Nigeria. In the light of the applicable law, the BH conflict has reached a status of a NIAC. This automatically imposes international humanitarian law obligations on all the parties to the NIAC. The application of international humanitarian law neither legitimises BH as a group, nor does it extricate the activities of BH from the penal and other relevant provisions of domestic law. The situation is, however, not a lineal conflict between BH and the Armed Forces of Nigeria; there are several other angles to the conflict. Rather, the situation is complicated by the participation of the CJTF, the armed activities of bordering States and the involvement of non-military law enforcement agents. Despite the multiplicity of actors, the roles, duties and rights of all parties are defined in law. There are nevertheless aspects of the law that require additional work and clarification. Chief among this is the law relating to the definition of direct participation of non-military law enforcement agents in armed conflict. It would seem that the ICRC Interpretative Guidance does not adequately cover this issue. In all, a NIAC such as the BH conflict is not a chaotic legal black hole where everything goes. All the parties involved in a NIAC are accountable in international law and domestic law.

References

Adesoji A (2010) The Boko Haram uprising and Islamic revivalism in Nigeria/Die Boko-Haram-Unruhen und die Wiederbelebung des Islam in Nigeria. Afr Spectr 45:95

Aldrich GH (2002) Taliban, AL Qaeda, and the determination of illegal combatants. Am J Int Law 96:891. Editorial comment

Ambos K (2007) Joint criminal enterprise and command responsibility. J Int Crim Just 5:159

Armed Forces Act (Nigeria), sections 146,223 and 272

Arnold R (2002) Command responsibility: a case study of alleged violations of the laws of war at Khiam Detention Centre. J Confl Secur Law 7:191

Bartels R (2009) Timeliness, borderlines and conflicts - The historical evolution of the legal distinction between international and non-international armed conflicts. Int Rev Red Cross 91:35

Bassiouni MC, Wise EM (1995) Aut Dedere Aut Judicare: the duty to extradite or prosecute in international law. Kluwer Academic Publishers

Bonafe BI (2007) Finding a proper role for command responsibility. J Int Crim Just 5:599

Byron C (2001) Armed conflicts: International or non-international? J Confl Secur Law 6:63

Chothia F (2015) Who are Nigeria's Boko Haram Islamists? (http://www.bbc.com/news/world-africa-13809501 4 May 2015)

Clapham A (2006) Human rights obligations of non-state actors in conflict situations. Int Rev Red Cross:491

Crawford E (2007) Unequal before the law: the case for the elimination of the distinction between international and non-international armed conflicts. Leiden J Int Law 20:441
Cullen A (2005) Key developments affecting the scope of internal armed conflict in international humanitarian law. Mil Law Rev 183:66
Declaration on Principles of International Law concerning Friendly Relations and Co-operation among States in accordance with the Charter of the United Nations
Democratic Republic of the Congo v. Uganda
Dowden R (2007) Army kills Islamists after assault on police station. The Independent (London)
Falk RA (1964) Janus tormented: the international law of internal war. In: Rosenau JN (ed) International aspects of civil strife. Princeton University Press, Princeton
Gaggioli G (2013) The use of force in armed conflicts interplay between the conduct of hostilities and the law enforcement paradigms
Geneva Convention I for the Amelioration of the Condition of Wounded and Sick in Armed Forces in the Field, 1949
Geneva Convention II for the Amelioration of the Condition of the Wounded, Sick and Shipwrecked members of Armed Forces at Sea, 1949
Geneva Convention III Relative to the Treatment of Prisoners of War, 1949; and Geneva Convention IV Relative to the Protection of Civilian Persons in Time of War, 1949
Hamdan v. Rumsfeld, 126 S.Ct. 2749 (2006) at 2794–2796
Harbom L, Wallensteen P (2005) Armed conflict and its international dimensions. 1946–2004. J Peace Res 42:623
Harroff-Tavel M (1993) Action taken by the International Committee of the Red Cross in situations of internal violence. Int Rev Red Cross, May–June
HCJ 5100/94 The Public Committee against Torture in Israel v. The State of Israel 53(4) PD 817, 845
HCJ 769/02 The Public Committee against Torture in Israel v. The Government of Israel
Higgins R (1971) Internal war and international law. In: Black CE, Falk RA (eds) The future of the international legal order. Princeton University Press, Princton
Husband of Maria Fanny Suarez de Guerrero v. Colombia, Communication No. R.11/45, U.N. Doc. Supp. No. 40 (A/37/40) at 137 (1982)
ICTY, *Hadžihasanović and Others*, Case No. IT-01-47-AR72, § 57 (Disposition on the first ground of appeal), 16 July 2003. Decision on Interlocutory Appeal Challenging Jurisdiction in Relation to Command Responsibility
ICTY, *Delalić case*, Judgment; see also Article 28 of the Statute of the International Criminal Court
ICTY Statute, Article 7(3); ICTR Statute, Article 6(3)
Kalshoven F (1983) Guerrilla and terrorism in internal armed conflict conference: The American Red Cross - Washington College of Law Conference: International humanitarian and human rights law in non-international armed conflicts. April 12–13, 1983. Am Univ L Rev 33:67
Kalshoven F (1991) Noncombatant persons - A comment to Chapter 11 of the Commander's Handbook on the Law of Naval Operations International Law Studies 1991: The Law of Naval Operations: Chapter X' (1991). Int Law Stud Ser US Naval War Coll 64:300
Kretzmer D (2005) Targeted killing of suspected terrorists: extra-judicial executions or legitimate means of defence? Eur J Int Law 16:171
Lauterpacht H (1947) Recognition in international law. Cambridge University Press, Cambridge
Mbachu D (2004) Nigeria's Army and Police Claim Victory over Armed Islamic sect eight killed in clashes the lasted five days. Associated Press, Saint Paul Pioneer Press, St. Paul
McCoubrey H, White ND (1992) International law and armed conflict. Dartmouth
Melzer N (2002) Interpretive guidance on the notion of direct participation in hostilities under international humanitarian law (ICRC, 2009)
Military Penal Code (Norway), § 4
Moir L (2002) The law of internal armed conflict. Cambridge University Press, Cambridge
Moland NA (2015) Featured article: can multiculturalism be exported? Dilemmas of diversity on Nigeria's sesame square. Comp Educ Rev 59:1

Momtaz D (1998) The minimum humanitarian rules applicable in periods of internal tension and strife. Int Rev Red Cross 324:445–453
Monsen A (1971) Concept of war and the concept of combatant in modern conflicts, The studies. Mil Law Law War Rev 10:197
O'Brien WV (1978) The Jus in Bello in revolutionary war and counter-insurgency. Va J Int Law 18:193
Okebukola EO (2012) Legal restraints in non-international armed conflicts. Just J 4:151
Okebukola EO (2014) Training children for armed conflict - where does the law stand? Int Crim Law Rev 14:588
Paulus A, Vashakmadze M (2009) Asymmetrical war and the notion of armed conflict – a tentative conceptualization. Int Rev Red Cross 91:95
Pieth M (2006) Criminalizing the financing of terrorism. J Int Crim Just 4:1074
Prosecutor v. *Dusko Tadić*, (the *Tadić Decision*) 2 October 1995 ICTY, Case No. IT-94-1-AR72, para. 96 (Decision on the Defence Motion for Interlocutory Appeal on Jurisdiction)
Protocol Additional to the Geneva Conventions of 12 August 1949, and relating to the Protection of Victims of International Armed Conflicts
Protocol Additional to the Geneva Conventions of 12 August 1949, and Relating to the Protection of Victims of Non-International Armed Conflicts, 1977 (Additional Protocol II)
Rowe P (2008) Military misconduct during international armed operations: 'Bad Apples' or systemic failure? J Confl Secur Law 13:165
Ruud M (1985) Term combatant an analysis, the studies. Mil Law Law War Rev 24:425
Sandoz Y et al (1987) Commentary on the additional protocols of 8 June 1977 to the Geneva conventions of 12 august 1949. ICRC, Geneva, p 4462
Sassoli M (2004) The status of persons held in Guantanamo under international humanitarian law. J Int Crim Just 2:96
Schindler D (1979) The different types of armed conflicts according to the geneva conventions and protocols. Recueil Des Cours 163(158):150–151
Schmitt MN (2010) Deconstructing direct participation in hostilities: the constitutive elements. Int law Polit 42:697
Schmitt MN (2012) The status of opposition fighters in a non-international armed conflict. In: Watkin K, Norris AJ (eds) Non-international armed conflict in the twenty-first century. Naval War College
Stewart JG (2007) The military commissions act's inconsistency with the Geneva Conventions: an overview. J Int Crim Just 5:26
Swiss Criminal Code, Article Art. 260 quinquies
Timberg C (2007) Nigerian fundamentalist group kills 12 police officers in North. The Washington Post
United Nations Charter, 1945
Vetter GR (2000) Command responsibility of non-military superiors in the International Criminal Court (ICC). Yale J Int Law 25:89
Vierucci L (2003) Prisoners of war or protected persons qua unlawful combatants? The judicial safeguards to which Guantanamo Bay detainees are entitled. J Int Crim Just 1:284
Williams S (2005) Amnesties in international law: the experience of the Special Court for Sierra Leone. Hum Rights Law Rev 5:271
Wilson HA (1988) International law and the use of force by liberation movements. Oxford University Press, Oxford
Zegveld L (2002) The accounatbility of armed opposition groups in international law. Cambridge University Press, Cambridge

Part III
Boko Haram and Radical Ideology in Islamic Jurisprudence and International Law

Chapter 9
Boko Haram: On the Road to Algiers?

Adedokun Ogunfolu, Usang Maria Assim, and Oludamilola Adejumo

9.1 Introduction

Boko Haram, from 3 January to 7 January 2015, decimated Doro Baga and Baga towns about 160 km from Maiduguri, the capital of Borno State, and according to the Nigerian army, only 150 civilians were slaughtered, but satellite images procured by Amnesty International and first-hand testimonies of survivors indicate around 2000 slaughtered victims.[1] Nigerian President Goodluck Jonathan immediately sent condolence messages to France over the 7 January 2015 terrorist attacks on a Jewish shop and French satirical newspaper that claimed 17 lives but failed to commiserate for over a week with residents of Doro Baga and Baga towns.[2] The authors' observation of northern Nigeria generally is that, most sections of the north seem caught up in a time warp of arrested socio-economic development and never-ceasing endemic poverty, while tiny elites continue to live off state revenues.[3]

[1] Amnesty International (2015).

[2] The Punch Editorial (2015), p. 28.

[3] One of the authors traversed several towns in 16 of the 19 northern Nigerian states between 1981 and 2007. Another studied for admission into the Nigerian Bar in Abuja and undertook her Court Attachment programme (a prerequisite for admission into the Nigerian Bar) in the central Nigerian city of Jos, Plateau State between 2006 and 2007. She made regular visits to family members living in parts of northern Nigeria, including Plateau and Jigawa states, between 2008 and 2010, and she lost a cousin to the Nyanya Abuja bomb blast by Boko Haram in April 2014. Another author in

A. Ogunfolu (✉)
Faculty of Law, Obafemi Awolowo University, Ile-Ife, Nigeria

U. M. Assim
Dullah Omar Institute for Constitutional Law, Governance and Human Rights, Faculty of Law, University of the Western Cape, Cape Town, South Africa
e-mail: uassim@uwc.ac.za

O. Adejumo
Legal Services Unit, University of Medical Sciences, Ondo City, Nigeria

J.-M. Iyi, H. Strydom (eds.), *Boko Haram and International Law*,
https://doi.org/10.1007/978-3-319-74957-0_9

The following paragraphs attempt to synthesise media coverage of Boko Haram atrocities from 2010 to 2015. Due to space constraints, the most horrendous atrocities are focused upon while not discountenancing the horror and unimaginable pains experienced by the victims and the survivors of more numerous but lower casualty rates of Boko Haram attacks. Section 9.2 of the article maps out the genesis of Boko Haram leading to a synthesis of mass atrocities perpetrated by the group and by Nigerian security troops in Sect. 9.3. Section 9.4 traces Boko Haram's association with countries north of Nigeria and the historical chilling parallels between Nigeria and Algeria. In Sect. 9.5, foreign response to Boko Haram is examined, while Sect. 9.6 focuses on the domestic response. Section 9.7 provides a brief overview of the Boko Haram insurgency through the lens of international humanitarian law and international criminal law. We reach our conclusions in Sect. 9.8.

9.2 The Emergence of the Boko Haram Insurgency in Nigeria

Reminiscent of the sequential genealogical debate about the chicken and the egg, is poverty the precursor of insecurity, or is insecurity the harbinger of poverty? Insecurity fostered by the misinterpretation of Islam and murder of both Christians and moderate Muslims is obliterating economic investment in northern Nigeria.[4] A lack of inclusiveness and alienation of the citizenry from governance rather than poor governance, corruption and the resultant impoverishment of the governed have been fingered in the emergence of the Boko Haram movement in northern Nigeria. This is because poor governance, corruption and albeit lower levels of poverty also exist in southern Nigeria.[5] However, the Niger Delta region of southern Nigeria has also experienced violent attacks by militant groups against oil installations and security forces and kidnapping of foreigners and personnel of oil companies for huge ransoms.[6] The most prominent militant group in the Niger Delta, the Movement for the Emancipation of the Niger Delta (MEND), set off a bomb on 1 October 2010, in Abuja, in the midst of Nigeria's 50th independence anniversary parades. Ten people were killed, and 30 sustained injuries.[7]

The traditional mode of education in the north was a well-organised and regulated Islamic educational system. But British colonial rule privileged the offspring of traditional rulers with western education under a feudal indirect rule system,

---

2009, commenced the mandatory 1 year national youth service, for fresh college graduates, in the central Nigerian city of Jos; the epicentre of bouts of horrendous violence and she had to be evacuated from Jos a few months later.

[4] Ishaku (2009), p. 170.

[5] Adibe (2012), pp. 60–66.

[6] Anozie (2012), pp. 206–225.

[7] Anozie (2012), p. 220.

which produced western-educated northern elites.[8] Thus, the proponents of the anti-western education agenda view the western educated northern elites as purveyors of mal-governance, corruption and poverty in society.[9] General Sani Abacha, who ruled Nigeria from 1993 to 1998, is a very good example. He hailed from Kano in northwest Nigeria and is reputed for stealing billions of dollars from Nigeria's oil revenues. Recently, Lichtenstein agreed to return 167 million euros ($227 million) Abacha loot to Nigeria.[10] Nigeria is one of the most unequal societies in the world, and that is a recruitment sales pitch for Boko Haram.[11] Young impressionable minds have been easily influenced and recruited by a set of Islamic preachers tagged Boko Haram, who preach for a violent overthrow of kleptomaniacs masquerading as political elites.[12] Mohammed Yusuf, a future leader of Boko Haram, was a secondary school dropout who acquired Islamic education in Nigeria's neighbouring Chad and Niger. Ironically, Mohammed Yusuf lived in luxury, while his followers lived an ascetic life mired in poverty.[13] An anonymous publication in the authoritative peer-reviewed *Journal of Religion in Africa* argues convincingly that acquisition of political power and wealth propelled Boko Haram under Mohammed Yusuf's leadership, rather than the combat of poverty and unemployment of his followers caused by bad governance.[14]

Ahlas-Sunnah wa al-Jama' ahala Minhaj as-Salaf (People of the Way of the Prophet Muhammed [peace be upon him] and the Community [of Muslims], in line with the earliest generation of Muslims) came to public knowledge in December 2003. This was under the leadership of Mohammed Yusuf, when the movement encamped at the Kanamma shore of Kamadugu-Yobe river in Yobe State and attacked the Kanamma police station. Members of the movement who had earlier gone to resolve a land dispute at the police station had been arrested. Locals termed the movement "Taliban" due to their avowed movement out of a society plagued with sin. Their conflict with the police led to the movement's relocation to nearby Geidam in Yobe State. At Geidam, the movement adopted the name Taliban and distributed leaflets that detailed its plans to create an Islamic Republic on Nigerian soil at the border with Niger Republic. They were routed out by the Nigerian military, which killed around 28 members. They resurfaced on 20 September 2004 in Bama and Gwoza towns of neighbouring Borno State, where they attacked police stations, but they were routed out again by the military, which killed 28 of them.[15]

---

[8] Usman (2008), pp. 67–68.

[9] Winters (1987), pp. 177–178.

[10] Somorin (2014).

[11] York (2014).

[12] Audu (2012), pp. 184–194.

[13] Onuoha (2012a, b), pp. 136–137, 159–163.

[14] Umar (2012), pp. 118–144; "In light of the continuing violence in Nigeria, it is imperative and prudent to publish this essay anonymously to avoid the very real threat of violence against the author or the author's colleagues and informants." Umar (2012), p. 142.

[15] Mohammed (2010), pp. 27–30.

As early as 2000, Mohammed Yusuf, an uncertified preacher in Maiduguri, Borno State, had broken ranks with his colleagues at the Imam Malik Islamic Centre and Indimi mosque in Maiduguri, Borno State, over his trenchant criticism of western education. The Chief Imam, Ibrahim Ahmed; Islamic scholars; and the Shehu (King) of Borno, Mustapha Umar El-Kanemi, met with Mohammed Yusuf, but they failed to change his views.[16] The unemployed, including university graduates and illiterates, heeded Mohammed's clarion call that Boko (western education) was Haram (forbidden) and was the cause of public corruption, unemployment, great disparity in wealth and poverty, presided over by decadent western-educated political elites.[17] The clashes between Boko Haram and security forces are reminiscent of the 1980s. The army had learnt lessons from its 1980 public display of the exhumed corpse of Muhammed Marwa, a Cameroonian citizen (who led the Maitatsine uprising in Kano that killed thousands), which created a martyr out of him and sparked further uprisings between 1982 and 1985 in northern Nigeria.[18] Perhaps this explains why law enforcement authorities in many countries now adopt a practice of censoring the pictures of dead leaders of terrorist organisations such as the United States of America's censorship of pictures of a dead Osama Bin Laden.

9.3 Atrocities of Boko Haram and the Nigerian Security Architecture

In July 2009, Boko Haram under Mohammed Yusuf launched series of attacks in Bauchi, Borno, Kano and Yobe states to avenge the killing of dozens of its members in July 2009 in Bauchi by security operatives.[19] Over 30 policemen were killed.[20] Close to midnight on 26 July 2009, Boko Haram launched coordinated attacks to take over Maiduguri, the capital of Borno State. Soldiers quelled the uprising and arrested Mohammed Yusuf, whom they handed over to the police on 30 July 2009, and minutes later the police executed him in public.[21] His 72-year-old father-in-law, who reported to the police on 31 July 2009, was also executed in public. Ironically, he had instructed his son to write and submit a letter to the Borno State governor to alert him about Mohammed Yusuf's planned attacks.[22] Soldiers on 31 July 2009 also arrested Buji Foi, a former Borno State commissioner, an alleged Boko Haram financier, and handed him to the police, who shot him a few minutes later.[23] The

[16] Mohammed (2010), pp. 42–43.

[17] Mohammed (2010), pp. 44–57, 86.

[18] Mohammed (2010), p. 176.

[19] Human Rights Watch (2012), pp. 32–34.

[20] Human Rights Watch (2012), p. 41.

[21] Human Rights Watch (2012), pp. 33–35.

[22] Human Rights Watch (2012), pp. 63–64.

[23] Human Rights Watch (2012), pp. 62–63.

police executed 24 men in public at their Maiduguri headquarters between 28 July and 1 August 2009.[24] Soldiers also engaged in extrajudicial killings in July 2009.[25] In the aftermath of a Boko Haram attack on 9 July 2009, against a military vehicle, soldiers executed 12 men in Kaleri, Maiduguri.[26]

The attitude of the Nigerian government to the extrajudicial killing of the Boko Haram leader, Mohammed Yusuf, drove the movement to greater extremities. Dora Akunyili, Nigeria's information minister in 2009, described the killing of Mohammed Yusuf as 'the best thing to have happened to Nigeria'.[27] However, his death provoked the most violent elements in Boko Haram to go underground and seek revenge for his death in the most murderous way. On 24 December 2010, Boko Haram detonated improvised explosive devices in a largely Christian-populated Jos, Plateau State, which killed several people and left a greater number severely wounded.[28] Boko-Haram-linked attacks claimed over 1000 lives, including hundreds of security operatives, between June 2010 and November 2012.[29]

In what may be described as revenge attacks, the police and military have engaged in numerous documented cases of extrajudicial killings and torture of innocent young men and even elderly men with no proven links to Boko Haram.[30] Nigerian security forces have also employed enforced disappearances as a tool of repression and intimidation of residents of areas that ironically suffered from Boko Haram attacks.[31] Another reprehensible practice by soldiers in Maiduguri is the looting and burning of houses with gasoline when residents are attacked by Boko Haram or when soldiers encounter Boko Haram attacks or during the arrest of suspected Boko Haram operatives.[32] Boko Haram members and their relatives are held indefinitely incommunicado in the most appalling and atrocious conditions of torture and starvation by Nigerian security operatives.[33]

The first recorded case of suicide bombing in Nigeria was launched on 16 June 2011 against the convoy of the Inspector General of police by a car laden with explosives that trailed him into the police headquarters at Abuja. The car was diverted to the car park, where it detonated and missed its target but killed two persons and wrecked most of the cars in the park. Boko Haram claimed that the attack was launched by one of its men trained by al-Shabaab, an al-Qaeda affiliate in Somalia.[34] Eighteen people were killed, and over a hundred were injured when a suicide bomber drove a car full of explosives into the UN building in Abuja at

[24] Human Rights Watch (2012), p. 61.

[25] Human Rights Watch (2012), p. 64.

[26] Human Rights Watch (2012), pp. 65–66.

[27] Human Rights Watch (2012), p. 36.

[28] Pham (2012), p. 4.

[29] Amnesty International (2012), p. 11.

[30] Amnesty International (2012), pp. 19–26.

[31] Amnesty International (2012), pp. 27–28.

[32] Amnesty International (2012), pp. 29–33.

[33] Amnesty International (2012), pp. 34–38, 39–43.

[34] Maiangwa et al. (2012), pp. 40–48.

10:26 a.m. local time on 26 August 2011, Friday.[35] Casualty figures were later confirmed at 19 by the National Emergency Management Agency.[36] The figure increased to 25 on 23 December 2011, when Fred Willis, a United Nations worker evacuated to South Africa on life support, passed on. Thirteen of the victims were UN workers.[37] Nigeria's State Security Service (SSS) revealed that Mamman Nur, a Somali-trained Boko Haram operative with al-Qaeda connections, masterminded the UN bombing with two other persons.[38] The SSS also disclosed that it was tipped off 8 days before the UN bombing.[39] President Jonathan on 2 September 2011, at the launch of a new computerised data-based scheme for capturing drivers and vehicle licence data in Abuja, assured Nigerians and the international community that the government had strong leads as to the identity of the terror/war mongers and that they would be fished out.[40] A few months after President Jonathan's promise, Boko Haram carried out its most monstrous suicide bomb attack on Christmas day of 2011, when a vehicle drove into worshippers coming out of the Saint Theresa Catholic Church at Madalla in Niger State, a short distance to Abuja. Thirty-five worshippers and pedestrians were all murdered by the bomb blasts, including a family of five.[41] Reverend Isaac Achi of Saint Theresa Catholic Church confirmed a death toll of 43 on 29 December 2011.[42]

In the midst of the tragedy and mayhem, the government proposed N4.14 billion (naira) for defence spending in 2012 and N11.25 billion (naira) for foreign trips by government officials.[43] N988 million (naira) was slated for feeding and kitchen expenses for the presidency in 2012, including N300 million (naira) on plates and cutleries.[44] David Blair notes:

> The danger is that Boko Haram will continue to draw strength from all the factors that combine to cripple Nigeria: astonishing levels of corruption, the constant misuse of the country's oil wealth and an ever-widening gap between a venal elite and the impoverished majority. Just as the largely Christian youth of southern Nigeria join militias who kidnap oil workers, supposedly to win a fairer share of their country's natural wealth, so northern Muslims will be tempted by an armed group that claims to be fighting a corrupt and predatory government. And in this interdependent world, Nigeria's domestic problem could soon be ours as well.[45]

[35] Alechenu (2011), pp. 1, 3–6.

[36] Iroegbu and Obi (2011), pp. 1, 8.

[37] Oloja et al. (2011), p. 63.

[38] Abonyi (2011), pp. 1, 7.

[39] Adepegba (2011), pp. 1–2.

[40] Onogu (2011), pp. 1, 3.

[41] Daily (2011), pp. 1, 4, 6–9.

[42] Ali et al. (2011), p. 1.

[43] Odebode et al. (2011), pp. 1–2.

[44] Akinmutimi and Adeyemi (2011), pp. 1, 5.

[45] Blair (2011).

On 14 January 2014, a suicide bomber killed 30 people in Maiduguri and wounded 50 others.[46] On 12 April 2014, Boko Haram killed 38 people in Ngoshe in Gwoza local government and Kaigamari in Konduga local government both in Borno State. Kaigamari is only 40 km from Maiduguri, the capital city, and not a single state security operative turned up during the several hours that Boko Haram operated.[47] In the early hours of 14 April 2014, Boko Haram set off bombs in a crowded Nyanya mass transit park, full of low-income workers shuttling to offices within Abuja, and over 70 people were killed, including women and children.[48] President Jonathan visited the gory scene and appeared in a trance in the pictures splashed on the front pages of the dailies.[49] He expressed his condolences and again reassured Nigerians that the situation is 'temporary' and that 'we will get over it'.[50]

Boko Haram abducted over a hundred girls during the night of 14 April 2014 from the Government Girls' Secondary School in Chibok, Borno State, a greater step-up in number compared to previous abduction cases largely ignored by the international media.[51] On 16 April 2014, the military claimed that it had rescued most of the girls except eight, and the school principal, joined by parents, swiftly rebutted the claim.[52] Major General Chris Olukolade, the Director of Defence Information subsequently retracted the military's claim thus: 'In the light of the denial by the Principal of the school, the Defence Headquarters wishes to defer to the school principal and the governor's statement on the missing children.'[53] President Goodluck Jonathan visited Borno State capital, Maiduguri, on 15 January 2015, 276 days after the Chibok girls were abducted, with presidential elections taking place on 14 February 2015.[54] What might be the first female suicide bomb attack in Nigeria occurred in Gombe on 8 June 2014 at the gate of a military barracks, and the bomber as well as a soldier were killed.[55]

While the terrorist activities of Boko Haram must continue to be condemned and tackled, the socio-economic issues that (partly) gave rise to and that continue to fuel the attacks need to be addressed urgently and decisively. The government has been taking some action against the militants, as will be discussed later in Sect. 9.6 of the paper. However, without a commitment to address the socio-economic imbalances, Boko Haram may continue to increase in popularity and following or, at the very least, gain more sympathisers within the region and country.

---

[46] Soriwei et al. (2014a, b), pp. 1–2.

[47] Sowerei et al. (2014a, b), p. 12.

[48] Jimoh et al. (2014), pp. 1–2; Soriwei et al. (2014a, b), pp. 1–2.

[49] Jimoh et al. (2014), pp. 1–2; Soriwei et al. (2014a, b), pp. 1–2.

[50] Ehikioya (2014a), p. 4.

[51] Ameh et al. (2014), p. 1: 1–2; The Nation (2014a, b), p. 1.

[52] Ameh and Owuamanam (2014), p. 2.

[53] Soriwei and Idowu (2014), p. 2.

[54] Adetayo et al. (2015), p. 2.

[55] Josiah and Adetayo (2011), p. 11.

9.4 Boko Haram Reaches Out North and the Algerian Connection

Nigeria confirmed in July 2012 that Boko Haram had procured military equipment from Libya.[56] Some weapons recovered from Boko Haram by the Nigerian army were obtained from Libya.[57] The alleged mastermind of the 14 April 2014 Nyanya, Abuja, motor park bombings was arrested in Sudan in May 2014. Seventy people were killed by the bombs.[58] In 2002, the al-Qaeda of Sudan gave the Nigerian Taliban $300,000 kept in a London bank for recruitment in Nigeria and training purposes in Mauritania. Furthermore, in October 2007, two Nigerian Taliban members were arrested in Kano for attending a training camp in Algeria, and this led to the arrest of nine others in November 2007 in Kano, Kaduna and Yobe states. They were all charged with undergoing training in Algeria organised by the Groupe Salafist pour la Prédication et la Combat (GSPC), which on 23 January 2007 changed its name to al-Qaeda in the Land of the Islamic Maghreb (AQLIM).[59] The fall of the Qaddafi regime in Libya in 2011 and its desperate act to survive had left its armouries open, creating strong suspicions that sophisticated Libyan weaponry had fallen into the hands of AQLIM and Boko Haram.[60]

Algeria, just like Nigeria, was ruled after independence by an indigenous military elite, and Algeria is still colonised by the military. The current Algerian ruler, Abdelaziz Bouteflika, was 'voted' into office on 14 April 1999 under a military-organised election, which led to the withdrawal of six opposition candidates amidst massive electoral rigging.[61] In 1991, Abassi Madani (who earned a PhD from the University of London) and a charismatic teacher, Ali Benhadji, guided the Front Islamique du Salut (FIS) to victory on a promise to replace a decadent, corrupt and autocratic military rule with a fair arrangement under Islamic law. The masses voted the FIS to victory, winning 188 out 231 seats in the first round of voting on 1 December 1999. But the army annulled the elections and retained power.[62] This led to a violent insurrection whose foot soldiers were the unemployed and those who felt a sense of hopelessness and exclusion under military rule.[63] The rebels and the Algerian security forces on both sides of the conflict, from 1992 to 1997, perpetrated mass atrocities that mimicked the Front de Liberation (FLN) war of independence against France's brutal scorched-earth policies from 1954 to 1962.[64] Algerian state security forces tried to outdo the rebels in the magnitude of atrocities carried

[56] Crowley and Wilkinson (2013), pp. 99–103.
[57] International Crisis Group (2014), p. 25.
[58] Soniyi (2014).
[59] Botha (2013), p. 92.
[60] Botha (2013), p. 105.
[61] Evans (2012), p. 365.
[62] Hussey (2014), pp. 225–229.
[63] Hussey (2014), p. 235.
[64] Fisk (2005), pp. 513–585.

out.[65] Algeria was clearly in breach of its international law obligations, expressed in various human rights instruments.

There are chilling parallels between Nigeria and Algeria. The military annulled elections in both countries in 1993 and 1992 respectively. They are both heavily dependent on hydrocarbon exports, which were fleeced by their military rulers for the most part of their independence. Nigeria is an ex-British colony, while France ruled Algeria. Algeria experienced one of the most brutal liberation wars for independence and an equally vicious civil war after the annulment of the 1992 elections by the military. Nigeria also experienced a horrendous civil war from 1967 to 1970 and is experiencing an ongoing insurgency from 2009 till date, orchestrated by Boko Haram in northern Nigeria. In the 1990s, one of the rebel groups in Algeria, the Groupe Islamic Armé (GIA), perpetrated mass murders of civilians, including families of military officers and the police. Girls of 15 years and above, as well as women, were abducted, raped and forcibly married off into the GIA.[66] Infighting within the Algerian military led to allegations of rogue units' attacks on civilians to discredit the ruling faction. A chilling side of this infighting manifested on 22/23 September 1997, when over 400 villagers, mostly women, children and babies, were slaughtered at Bentalha village, 12 miles from Algiers. Babies were thrown alive into ovens; Oum Saad lost all her eight children. The perpetrators numbered from 50 to a hundred, and half of them wore military uniforms.[67]

Western investments in hydrocarbons have enriched a tiny Algerian elite, while the masses wallow in poverty. 'Algerians feel angry and frustrated because the system offers no future.'[68] President Bouteflika in 1999 issued the Law on Civil Concord, which granted amnesty to all sides in the ongoing civil war to achieve a peaceful resolution.[69] Under Bouteflika's second term in office, the 1999 law was supplanted by the 2006 legislation on the 2005 Charter for Peace and National Reconciliation, which offered a blanket amnesty and immunity from prosecution.[70] In 2008, GSPC, a splinter group from the GIA (which had accused the GIA of being infiltrated by the military) announced a merger with al-Qaeda in Iraq. Its leader, Abdemalek Droukdal, disclosed to the New York Times in a 2008 interview that while the large proportion of the GSPC members (*mujahedeen*) comprised of Algerians, 'there is a considerable number of Mauritanians, Libyans, Moroccans, Tunisians, Malians, and Nigerian brothers'.[71] Droukdal had earlier on 24 January 2007 announced Osama Bin Laden's personal endorsement of the name change from GSPC to al-Qaeda au Maghreb Islamique (AQMI). Just like al-Qaeda attacked the United Nations Offices in August 2003 in Baghdad, on 11 December 2007,

[65] Fisk (2005), p. 572.

[66] Evans and Phillips (2007), p. 219.

[67] Evans and Phillips (2007), pp. 238–245.

[68] Evans and Phillips (2007), p. 297.

[69] Le Sueur (2010), p. 77.

[70] Le Sueur (2010), pp. 90–91.

[71] Le Sueur (2010), pp. 155–156. See also, an interview with Abdelmalek Droukdal – New York Times.com (2008).

AQMI suicide bombers killed 41 people at the United Nations Office in Algiers.[72] And in 2011, Boko Haram also orchestrated a bomb blast at the United Nations building in Abuja. Ambassador Herman Cohen, an official of the Reagan and Bush presidencies with African postings, compared Boko Haram to its Algerian counterpart thus:

> In late 2012, Boko Haram started to emulate the Algerian AQIM by moving into Christian villages in the dead of night and slitting the throats of every man, woman, and child. The group is now a major threat to Nigerian national cohesion.[73]

The parallels between Algeria and Nigeria reveal a sobering fact: long-ignored or long-established systems of socio-economic imbalances in the face of massive corruption and gross human rights abuses and violations provide fertile ground for terrorist groups and terrorist activities to blossom unabated. Military and political responses without a socio-economic component will only result in a never-ending siege on the nation(s) concerned, with the ordinary civilian population bearing the brunt of the attacks.

9.5 Foreign Response to Boko Haram

In December 2011, the subcommittee on counterterrorism and intelligence of the Committee on Homeland Security of the U.S. House of Representatives published a report of its findings titled 'Boko Haram: Emerging Threat to the U.S. Homeland'.[74] The report essentially focused on the nexus between Boko Haram, AQIM and al-Shabaab, which created fears that western interests in Nigeria could become targets of enhanced Boko Haram attacks, which ominously could later be launched within the United States. It recommended to the then Secretary of State, Hillary Clinton, to investigate whether Boko Haram should be designated as a foreign terrorist organisation (FTO). The subcommittee on 30 November 2011 had a follow-up hearing to the above report to garner testimony from American academics and researchers on Boko Haram. Their consensus was that American diplomatic presence was absent in northern Nigeria. American resources must be scaled up in the education and skills acquisition of the youth in northern Nigeria to address unemployment and poverty, which drive recruits into Boko Haram. The tension of premature designation of Boko Haram as an FTO was unresolved.[75] Mr. Meehan, the Chairman of the subcommittee, concluded:

[72] Le Sueur (2010), p. 166.

[73] Cohen (2013), pp. 63–68.

[74] Available at http://www.gpo.gov/fdsys/pkg/CPRT-112HPRT71725/pdf/CPRT-112HPRT71725.pdf. Accessed 20 Jun 2014.

[75] Available at http://www.gpo.gov/fdsys/pkg/CHRG-112hhrg74645/pdf/CHRG-112hhrg74645.pdf. Accessed 20 Jun 2014.

> There may be a difference between people acting out of poverty versus those like we see in the Middle East who are saying they don't want any American presence, they are trying to get rid of. But do we have to be concerned about the threat while we are trying to determine whether there is ways (sic) that we can help Nigeria develop itself into an economy and a government that can sustain itself on its own merits?[76]

The Committee on Foreign Affairs of the U.S. House of Representatives held a hearing on 25 April 2012 on the Lord's Resistance Army (LRA), Boko Haram and al-Shaabab.[77] Principal Deputy Assistant Secretary Don Yamamoto of the Bureau of African Affairs of the U.S. State Department testified:

> Boko Haram is not a monolithic group, although its various factions remain focused on discrediting the Nigerian government…It is vital to emphasize that religion is not the primary driver of extremist violence in Nigeria. While some seek to inflame Muslim-Christian tensions, Nigeria's religious and ethnic diversity is one of its greatest strengths.[78]

He stated that Africa must take responsibility for its own security and that America would avoid the trap of extremist groups provoking direct American security assistance to Americanise local conflicts.[79] He added:

> In Nigeria, the government must effectively engage communities vulnerable to extremist violence and promote respect for human rights by its security forces, whose heavy-handed tactics and extrajudicial killings reinforce northerners' concerns that the Nigerian government does not care about them. The appointment of a credible northerner to lead the government response to northern grievances would be an important step in that direction.[80]

On 21 June 2012, the American State Department, classified as Specially Designated Global Terrorists Boko Haram Commander Abubakar Shekau, together with Khalid al-Barnawi and Abubakar Adam Kambar, who both had ties with Boko Haram and al-Qaeda in the Islamic Maghreb, a designated FTO.[81] On 10 July 2012, the subcommittee on Africa, Global Health, and Human Rights and International Organizations of the Committee on Foreign Affairs of the U.S. House of Representatives held a hearing about American foreign policy on Nigeria.[82] During the first panel, Honourable Karen Bass in her questioning was concerned whether FTO designation of Boko Haram would embolden the group with an American recognition as opposed to solving the socio-economic conditions that birthed it.[83] Honourable Robert Turner wanted to know why the Department of State resisted the designation of Boko Haram as an FTO.[84] Assistant Secretary Bureau of African

[76] Available at http://www.gpo.gov/fdsys/pkg/CHRG-112hhrg74645/pdf/CHRG-112hhrg74645.pdf. Accessed 20 Jun 2014, at 41.

[77] Committee on Foreign Affairs House of Representatives Hearing (2012).

[78] Committee on Foreign Affairs House of Representatives Hearing (2012), p. 15.

[79] Committee on Foreign Affairs House of Representatives Hearing (2012), p. 16.

[80] Committee on Foreign Affairs House of Representatives Hearing (2012), p. 18.

[81] Office of the Spokesperson, U.S. Department of State (2012).

[82] U.S. Policy Toward Nigeria: West Africa's Troubled Titan (2012).

[83] U.S. Policy Toward Nigeria: West Africa's Troubled Titan (2012), p. 4.

[84] U.S. Policy Toward Nigeria: West Africa's Troubled Titan (2012), p. 5.

Affairs, U.S. Department of State, Johnnie Carson, explained that a tiny element in Boko Haram was responsible for violent acts against western and international targets and that the larger part of Boko Haram was focused on Nigerian targets,[85] hence America's designation of the three Boko Haram leaders, individuals with links to foreign insurgent movements, as Specially Designated Global Terrorists.[86] Chairman of the subcommittee Christopher H. Smith asked for further clarifications, and Ambassador Carson stated:

> But we have not designated the entire organization because we do not believe that Boko Haram is a homogenous organization. We believe that it is an organization of several parts. We believe that the individuals that we have designated represent a core group who lead a part of Boko Haram which is desirous of attacking not only Nigerian targets and interests but also Western and international targets and interests. We believe that the larger element of Boko Haram is not interested in doing anything but attempting to discredit, disgrace the Nigerian Government. Discredit, disgrace, and embarrass by carrying out attacks against Nigerian Government security and government officials and judges. But the bulk of the organization we believe to be mainly aimed at going after Nigerians.[87]

Ambassador Carson further attributed the root causes of Boko Haram to endemic poverty and appalling socio-economic indices in northeastern Nigeria, which ranked as the worst in Nigeria and Africa.[88] Chairman Smith in response stated:

> Ideology that is highly, highly radicalized may exploit poverty at times, but poor people don't necessarily become terrorists and killers. That is an insult, frankly, to poor people. I think we made the same mistake with all due respect, with South Sudan.[89]

During the second panel, the president of the Christian Association of Nigeria (CAN), Pastor Ayo Oritsejafor, stated in relation to the non-designation of Boko Haram as an FTO as follows:

> By refusing to designate Boko Haram as a foreign terrorist organization, the United States is sending a very clear message, not just to the Federal Government of Nigeria, but to the world that the murder of innocent Christians and Muslims who reject Islamism, and I make a clear distinction here between Islam and Islamism, are acceptable losses. It is hypocritical for the United States and the international community to say that they believe in freedom and equality when their actions do not support those who are being persecuted. A nondesignation (sic) for the group only serves to hamper the cause of justice and has emboldened Boko Haram to continue to strike at those who are denied equal protection under the law.[90]

America's State Department on 13 November 2013 designated Boko Haram and its splinter group Ansaru as FTOs.[91] Ambassador Linda Thomas-Greenfield, the newly appointed Assistant Secretary of State for African Affairs, disclosed this on the same day in her testimony to the joint sitting of the subcommittee on Africa, Global

---

[85] U.S. Policy Toward Nigeria: West Africa's Troubled Titan (2012), pp. 12–13.

[86] U.S. Policy Toward Nigeria: West Africa's Troubled Titan (2012), p. 14.

[87] U.S. Policy Toward Nigeria: West Africa's Troubled Titan (2012), p. 29.

[88] U.S. Policy Toward Nigeria: West Africa's Troubled Titan (2012), pp. 31–32.

[89] U.S. Policy Toward Nigeria: West Africa's Troubled Titan (2012), p. 32.

[90] U.S. Policy Toward Nigeria: West Africa's Troubled Titan (2012), p. 44.

[91] US State Department (2013).

Health, Human Rights, and International Organizations and subcommittee on Terrorism, Nonproliferation, and Trade of the House Foreign Affairs Committee. This was an application of section 219 of the Immigration and Nationality Act.[92] The International Religious Freedom Act of 1998 established the U.S. Commission on International Religious Freedom (USCIRF) to advise the American President on the status of observance by foreign countries of freedom of religious belief guaranteed by the 1948 Universal Declaration on Human Rights and relevant international treaties. USCIRF in 2013 observed that the Nigerian government had allowed a culture of communal and sectarian violence to thrive without making the architects of violence accountable. USCIRF concluded that the sole reliance on military force as a counterterrorist strategy to defeat Boko Haram was not effective. It then recommended a judicial approach with American capacity-building assistance, to bring to book the architects of communal, sectarian violence and Boko Haram, to guarantee enduring security and economic prosperity in a democratic setting.[93]

The Africa Programme Director of the International Crisis Group (ICG) claims that over 4000 lives were lost to the Boko Haram attacks between 2009 and 2014, while 2014 accounted for around 1500 victims. Amnesty International also indicated that 1500 people had been killed in the first 3 months of 2014 in northeastern Nigeria.[94] The ICG Africa Programme Director recognised that the group operates from Cameroon and Niger:

> However, while outsiders have a role, Nigeria remains the key. Abuja needs to address the underlying problems that led to Boko Haram's birth and sustain its fighters' grievances -systemic corruption, bad governance, decaying infrastructure and massive unemployment. Without a clear commitment to do that, international assistance will amount to little more than placebo.[95]

President Jonathan in May 2014 appointed an Australian cleric to negotiate with Boko Haram.[96] Julie Bishop, Australian foreign minister, on 3 June 2014 offered services of its Special Air Service (SAS) to procure the release of the abducted Chibok girls.[97] Eleven girls were again abducted on Sunday 5 May 2014. This was the beginning of the week that Nigeria hosted Africa's version of Davos, the World Economic Forum, to announce its ascension as Africa's biggest economy. But, alas, global media coverage focused on the unrelenting Boko Haram abduction of girls.[98] On 22 May 2014, the United Nations Security Council listed Boko Haram as being associated with al-Qaeda and AQIM.[99]

---

[92] US State Department (2013), p. 15.

[93] Available at http://www.uscirf.gov/sites/default/files/resources/Final%20Nigeria%20Factsheet%20%20August%2019,2013.pdf. Accessed 20 Jun 2014.

[94] Amnesty International (2014).

[95] Ero (2014), p. 9.

[96] The Nation (2014a, b).

[97] Soniyi et al. (2014), p. 4.

[98] Nossiter (2014), p. A1.

[99] The Al-Qaida Sanctions Committee, available at http://www.un.org/sc/committees/1267/NSQE13814E.shtml. Accessed 20 Jun 2014.

On 5 June 2014, Boko Haram abducted 20 nomadic Fulani women close to Chibok.[100] President Obama on 5 May 2014 promised to send a team of American hostage negotiators and police and military personnel to assist in the search for the girls abducted by Boko Haram. America's Secretary of State, Joe Kerry, had a conversation with President Jonathan on 6 May 2014 about Obama's offer of assistance to find the abducted girls. According to White House Press Secretary Joe Carney, 'What I can tell you is that it is certainly Nigeria's responsibility to maintain the safety and security of its citizens'.[101] President Obama admitted as much while stating that America would assist Nigeria in its efforts to rescue the missing girls and to put an end to the scourge of terrorism generally.[102] Nevertheless, America, during the second week of May 2014, deployed surveillance drones to track the whereabouts of the abducted Chibok girls and hesitatingly shared satellite imageries with Nigerian forces due to their poor human rights records in battling Boko Haram.[103] It also provided $6 million to fund Arewa24 satellite television channel to cover northern Nigeria with programmes to counter Boko Haram propaganda as done in Pakistan and Afghanistan to counter al-Qaeda broadcast.[104] In 2010, the US had earlier provided Nigeria with $614 million for security reform, healthcare, education, economic reform, democratic governance, and $8 million was provided for the formation of an infantry counterterrorism unit.[105]

France hosted African leaders for a security summit during the weekend of 16 May 2014 and a follow-up security summit was slated for the last weekend of May 2014 in South Africa. President Paul Kagame of Rwanda admonished African leaders to accept their failures and team up to solve them. He stated:

> I find that our leaders, who should have been working together all along to address these problems that only affect their countries, wait until they are invited to Europe. Why does anybody wait for that? What image does it even give about Africa?[106]

Nigerians have also expressed mixed feelings about the acceptance of foreign military assistance as it is an unusual and unfamiliar development.[107] This notwithstanding, all foreign responses or attempts to assist in the war against Boko Haram have rightly placed primary responsibility for dealing with the insurgency in the hands of the Nigerian government. The Nigerian government must display a commitment to address the problem in a holistic manner and take concrete steps that demonstrate its willingness and ability to secure the lives and properties of its citizenry. All forms of foreign assistance should be complementary to the government's efforts.

---

[100] BBC News (2014a, b, c, d).

[101] Miller (2014).

[102] BBC News (2014a, b, c, d).

[103] The Nation (2014a, b).

[104] Nixon (2014).

[105] Forest (2012), p. 105.

[106] BBC News (2014a, b, c, d).

[107] Nwaubani (2014).

9.6 National Response to Boko Haram

The Police in January 2012 arrested Kabiru Sokoto, the alleged mastermind of the Saint Theresa Catholic Church bombing, but he escaped from custody on 15 January 2012, and the Inspector General of Police was sacked. Sokoto was rearrested by the State Security Service (SSS) on 10 February 2012.[108] He was successfully prosecuted and sentenced to life imprisonment on 20 December 2013.[109] President Jonathan on 31 December 2011, acting under section 305(1) of the 1999 Constitution, declared a state of emergency in five local governments each in Borno and Yobe, four in Plateau and one in Niger states and shut the international borders contiguous to the affected areas in Yobe and Borno states.[110] Almost 3 weeks later, on 20 January 2012, Boko Haram detonated several bombs in Kano, the largest city in northern Nigeria, and murdered scores of people.[111] A number of 162 people were killed by the explosions and several more wounded.[112] The attacks triggered a mass exodus of southerners who had spent a lifetime in Kano.[113] Uzairu Abba Abdullahi, a textile merchant, a 2002 Mass Communication graduate of the Bayero University Kano and an alleged Boko Haram leader, was gunned down with his pregnant wife in Hotoro, Kano, by soldiers and policemen on 24 January 2012.[114]

President Jonathan declared a state of emergency in Adamawa, Borno and Yobe states on 14 May 2013, which was renewed in November 2013.[115] It was extended by another 6 months in May 2014. However, a year after the declaration of a state of emergency, 'it seems to have had little effect in curbing the Islamist insurgency'.[116] More women and children are being abducted on a daily basis.[117] On 24 June 2014, a bomb went off in a busy EMAB shopping plaza in Abuja and killed 22 people.[118] The International Covenant on Civil and Political Rights and regional human rights treaties recognise derogation from human rights obligations during times of armed conflict or public emergency that threatens the survival of a country.[119] But such derogation clauses exclude certain fundamental human rights guarantees, which include the rights to life, freedom from retroactive criminal law, freedom from torture and slavery.[120] The African (Banjul) Charter, however, does not provide for

[108] Adepegba and Soriwei (2012), p. 6.

[109] Ikhiale (2014).

[110] Josiah and Adetayo (2011), pp. 1, 11.

[111] Balogun et al. (2012), pp. 1, 7.

[112] Okpi (2012), p. 3.

[113] The Guardian (2014), pp. 1–2.

[114] Salihu (2012), p. 8.

[115] Soriwei and Adetayo (2014), p. 2.

[116] BBC News—Walker (2014).

[117] BBC News (2014a, b, c, d).

[118] THISDAY LIVE—Iroegbu (2014); Hinshaw (2014), pp. A1, A8.

[119] Shelton and Carozza (2013), pp. 647–649.

[120] Oraá (1992), pp. 96–97. See also Articles 27, American Convention on Human Rights and 15

non-derogation.[121] Rather, it contains a plethora of clawback provisions that subject the enumerated rights to national legislation. The African Commission on Human and Peoples' Rights has ruled that clawback provisions must conform to international human rights standards.[122]

The government of Nigeria has also enacted laws against terrorism. In 2011, the Prevention of Terrorism Act was enacted.[123] It was substantially amended by the Terrorism Prevention (Amendment) Act 2013.[124] The Office of the National Security Adviser is responsible for coordinating all security and enforcement agencies listed under the Act, while the Attorney General shall ensure Nigeria's conformity with international standards, including the United Nations Conventions on Terrorism, as well as maintaining international cooperation and the effective prosecution of terrorist cases.[125] On 24 May 2013, Boko Haram was proscribed by the Terrorism (Prevention) (Proscription Order) Notice 2013.[126] On 24 September 2013, Nigeria assented to the International Convention for the Suppression of Terrorist Bombing, which was adopted in 1997 and came into force on 23 May 2001.[127] Earlier in 2003, Nigeria ratified the International Convention for the Suppression of the Financing of Terrorism.[128]

In 2011, the Money Laundering (Prohibition) Act was enacted; it repealed the Money Laundering Act of 2004 and mandates financial and non-financial institutions to place under special surveillance suspicious financial transactions involving the financing of terrorism.[129] Such transactions must be documented and reported within 7 days to the Economic and Financial Crimes Commission (EFCC).[130] The Commission or the Central Bank of Nigeria can issue a stop order of 72-h duration to freeze the funds until their true nature becomes verified.[131] The stop order can be extended by an order of the Federal High Court to complete financial forensic investigation.[132] Financial and non-financial institutions that fail to comply with the

European Convention on Human Rights.

[121] Oraá (1992), pp. 209–210.

[122] Heyns (2003–2004), pp. 679–689.

[123] Available at http://www.nassnig.org/nass/acts.php?pageNum_bill=1&totalRows_bill=214. Accessed 20 Jun 2014.

[124] Available at http://www.sec.gov.ng/files/TERRORISM%20PREVENTION%20AMENDMENT%20ACT%202013.pdf. Accessed 20 Jun 2014; http://www.nassnig.org/nass/acts.php. Accessed 20 Jun 2014.

[125] §1(4)(1)(a) Terrorism Prevention (Amendment) Act (2013).

[126] Terrorism (Prevention) (Proscription Order) Notice (2013), available at http://www.cenbank.org/Out/2013/FPRD/TERRORISM%20(PREVENTION)%20(PROSCRIPTION%20ORDER)%20NOTICE,%202013.pdf. Accessed 20 Jun 2014.

[127] Available at https://treaties.un.org/doc/Treaties/1997/12/19971215%2007-07%20AM/ch_XVIII_9p.pdf. Accessed 20 Jun 2014.

[128] It was adopted in 1999 and entered into force in 2002, in compliance with its Article 26.

[129] S.6(1)(d), Money Laundering (Prohibition) Act (2011).

[130] S.6(1)(d), Money Laundering (Prohibition) Act (2011). §6(2).

[131] S.6(1)(d), Money Laundering (Prohibition) Act (2011). §6(5)(b).

[132] S.6(1)(d), Money Laundering (Prohibition) Act (2011). §6(7)(8).

above procedures, if convicted, face a daily fine of one million naira for the duration of non-compliance.[133]

In addition to the legislation enumerated above, the government has also adopted a 'Soft Approach to Countering Terrorism'. It was unveiled by the National Security Adviser, Mohammed Sambo Dasuki, on 18 March 2014.[134] Components of the strategy include the establishment of three new units, the Counter Terrorism Centre (CTC), the Joint Terrorism Analysis Branch (JTAB) and the Behavioural Analysis and Strategic Communication Unit (BASCU). Dasuki stated that their goal was to ensure cooperation and information sharing among agencies in order to disrupt numerous terrorist cells and abort attacks throughout Nigeria. In addition, another CTC, in conjunction with international partners, non-state actors and outstanding academics, formulated a NACTEST strategy to research into the factors that push the youth into joining Boko Haram; they identified identity crisis as one of the factors. NACTEST's goal is to prevent youths reaching a stage of identity crisis that would propel them towards Boko Haram or similar groups. Dasuki had in 2012 directed officials of the BASC Unit to develop the prevention and counterterrorism strategy of NACTEST and learn from the counterterrorism experiences of other countries by visiting Algeria, Australia, Indonesia, Saudi Arabia and Singapore. In addition, they had conversations with American, British and European Union officials, as well as with academics and civil society groups within and outside Nigeria. He also directed the Economic Intelligence Unit in his office to learn the poverty alleviation, job creation and economic development approaches that other countries experiencing terrorism have successfully used, to be applied in Adamawa, Borno and Yobe states under emergency rule.[135]

Also developed under the 'soft approach' is a Countering Violent Extremist (CVE) programme with four components: the de-radicalisation of repentant convicts and suspects awaiting trial,[136] capacity-building support in CVE of Nigerian NGOs through the United Nations,[137] strategic communication as part of the curriculum of the Nigerian Defence Academy to ensure clear communication through proper channels[138] and economic revitalisation of the six northeastern States impacted by terrorism, all revitalisation efforts supported by the federal government.[139] In addition to all these, President Jonathan on 29 May 2014 offered amnesty to Boko Haram members who renounce violence.[140]

---

[133] S.6(1)(d), Money Laundering (Prohibition) Act (2011). §6(9).

[134] Dasuki (2014).

[135] Dasuki (2014).

[136] Dasuki (2014).

[137] Dasuki (2014).

[138] Dasuki (2014).

[139] Dasuki (2014).

[140] The Nation—Ehikioya (2014b).

9.7 Boko Haram Insurgency Under International Humanitarian Law and International Criminal Law

International crimes have been committed both by Boko Haram and the Nigerian troops fighting the insurgents. This section briefly examines the Boko Haram insurgency under the general principles of both international humanitarian law and international criminal law.

9.7.1 International Humanitarian Law

According to the International Criminal Tribunal for the Former Yugoslavia jurisdiction decision of 2 October 1995 in the *Tadic* case[141]:

> An armed conflict exists whenever there is a resort to armed force between states or protracted armed violence between governmental authorities and organized armed groups or between such groups within a state. International humanitarian law applies ….[142]

International humanitarian law (IHL) (or the 'law of war' or the 'law of armed conflict') is a special branch of law governing situations of armed conflict or war. IHL seeks to mitigate the effects of war by, first, limiting the choice of means and methods of conducting military operations and, second, obliging the belligerents to spare persons who do not or no longer participate in hostile actions.[143] These two are known as the principles of proportionality and distinction respectively. Soldiers are licensed to kill enemy combatants, but 'proportionality' only permits collateral damage of the most minimal incident of civilian death in the conduct of hostilities.[144] 'Distinction' enjoins combatants to distinguish between military objectives and civilian objects, as well as combatants from civilians.[145]

The situation in Nigeria with respect to Boko Haram can be classified as an armed conflict of a non-international nature as it is occurring between governmental armed forces and Boko Haram as an organised armed group within the Nigerian territory.[146] Nigeria is a party to the Geneva Conventions, and the government has repeatedly declared that it is at war with Boko Haram.[147] Article 3 common to the Four Geneva Conventions of 1949 protects persons not taking an active part in a non-international armed conflict (NIAC) and prohibits extrajudicial killings, taking

[141] Available at http://www.icty.org/x/cases/tadic/acdec/en/51002.htm. Accessed 20 Jun 2014.

[142] Id at 70; *The Prosecutor v. Tadic* Case No. 160 ICTY (1995), reproduced in Sassoli and Bouvier (1999), p. 1169.

[143] Haug (1993), p. 491.

[144] Article 43 Additional Protocol I (of 8 June 1977) to the Geneva Conventions of 1949.

[145] Dinstein (2013), pp. 72–85. See also Article 57 of Additional Protocol I (of 8 June 1977) to the Geneva Conventions of 1949.

[146] International Committee of the Red Cross Opinion Paper (2008), p. 1.

[147] BBC News Africa (2014).

of hostages, torture and cruel treatment, among others. Although Article 3 is quite clear on the fact that the legal status of the warring parties is not affected by its application, states are generally reluctant to recognise situations of internal armed conflict (involving non-state actors) as armed conflict or civil war situations since such admission suggests a State's inability to prevent internal wars or crises.[148] This notwithstanding, in the case of Nigeria, so far, there have been several breaches of Article 3 by both the Nigerian Army and Boko Haram insurgents against a significant proportion of the civilian population.[149] Among others, Boko Haram has serially murdered children, women and the elderly, as well as unarmed men between 2009 and 2015.

The Second Protocol additional to the Geneva Conventions (AP II) covers more specifically the protection of civilian populations in the context of NIAC and provides a narrow scope of requirements for the classification of groups involved in armed conflicts. It obliges combatants (whether militias, other groups or state armed forces) to respect the principles of 'humane treatment' in the course of armed conflict. Article 1 of AP II provides a minimum threshold for non-state entities to meet in order to be classified as engaging in a NIAC: 'have a responsible command, exercise sufficient control over territory to enable them to carry out sustained and concerted military operations and possess the ability to implement the Protocol'.[150] However, these are stringent requirements that make AP II rarely applicable to armed conflicts of an internal nature. From the discussions in earlier parts of this paper, it can be argued that Boko Haram clearly has a command structure and has control over parts of the Nigerian territory (the government's justification for the postponement of general elections in 2015 by 6 weeks was the control of about 14 local government areas by Boko Haram). With the targeted and systematic modus operandi of Boko Haram, it would be hard to argue that the group is unable to implement the Protocol. In any case, the requirements of the *Tadic* definition of armed conflict generally lower 'the threshold for the application of the threshold for the existence of an armed conflict as compared with Article 1(1) of Protocol II'.[151] Although not without criticisms from some scholars, the test provided by this definition has been subsequently endorsed by the International Committee of the Red Cross and the Rome Statute of the International Criminal Court.[152]

Article 4 of AP II guarantees the protection of '[a]ll persons who do not take a direct part or who have ceased to take part in hostilities…They shall in all circumstances be treated humanely, without any adverse distinction. It is prohibited to

---

[148] Paulus and Vashakmadze (2009), p. 98.

[149] It is striking to note that, Osama Bin Laden's declassified letters retrieved by American soldiers who killed him on 2 May 2011, in Abbot Tad, Pakistan, expressed strong disagreement with al-Qaeda affiliated insurgent groups who killed non-combatants. See Lahoud et al. (2012), p. 14.

[150] Paulus and Vashakmadze (2009), p. 104.

[151] Paulus and Vashakmadze (2009), p. 104.

[152] Paulus and Vashakmadze (2009), p. 99. See also International Committee of the Red Cross (ICRC) Opinion Paper (2008); See also Article 8(2)(f) of the Rome Statute of the International Criminal Court (1998).

order that there shall be no survivors.'[153] Acts that are specifically prohibited but which that been carried out by both the Boko Haram insurgents and the Nigerian Army include violence to life and general well-being, collective punishments, taking of hostages, acts of terrorism and threats to commit any such act.[154] Children are provided with special protection under AP II to secure, among others, their education, family environment and non-involvement in hostilities (for children below 15 years of age).[155] Children have, however, been clear and direct targets in the course of the Boko Haram insurgency.

9.7.2 International Criminal Law

On 13 December 2011, the office of the prosecutor (OTP) of the International Criminal Court (ICC) released a preliminary report of investigations, which commenced in November 2010 and covered the period from 2002 to 2011 in Nigeria.[156] In November 2012, the OPT released its preliminary examination reports on Boko Haram and stated:

> The Office considers that there is a reasonable basis to believe that since July 2009, Boko Haram has committed the following acts constituting crimes against humanity: (i) murder under article 7(1)(a) and (ii) persecution under article 7(1)(h) of the Statute. In particular, the information available provides a reasonable basis to believe that since July 2009 Boko Haram has launched a widespread and systematic attack that has resulted in the killing of more than 1,200 Christian and Muslims civilians in different locations throughout Nigeria, including Borno, Yobe, Katsina, Kaduna, Bauchi, Gombe and Kano States in the North as well as Abuja, Kaduna and Plateau States in Central Nigeria. The consistent pattern of such incidents indicates that the group possesses the means to carry out a widespread and/or systematic attack, and displays internal coordination and organizational control required to that end. The attacks have been committed pursuant to the policy defined at the leadership level of Boko Haram, which aims at imposing an exclusive Islamic system of government in northern Nigeria at the expense of Christians specifically. Opponents to this goal have been targeted as well. Boko Haram leaders or spokesmen have issued public statements evincing the intention to attack civilians in furtherance of this policy, including a January 2012 ultimatum urging Christians to leave Northern Nigeria. The targeting of an identifiable group or collectivity on political, racial, national, ethnic, cultural, religious, gender or other ground is a constitutive element of the crime of persecution under article 7(1).[157]

Surprisingly, however, the OPT concluded that the conflict did not reach the threshold for qualification as a non-international armed conflict (NIAC).[158] On 5 August 2013, the OPT 'decided to move the situation in Nigeria to phase 3 of the preliminary examination with a view to assessing whether the Nigerian authorities are

[153] Article 4(1) Additional Protocol II (of 12 August 1949) to the Geneva Conventions of 1949.

[154] Article 4(2) Additional Protocol II (of 12 August 1949) to the Geneva Conventions of 1949.

[155] Article 4(3) AP II to the Geneva Conventions.

[156] OTP Report on Preliminary Examinations (2011), pp. 12–13.

[157] OTP Report on Preliminary Examinations (2012), p. 89.

[158] OTP Report on Preliminary Examinations (2012), p. 90.

conducting genuine proceedings in relation to the crimes committed by Boko Haram'.[159] In November 2013, the OPT concluded that the situation in Nigeria amounted to a NIAC.[160] The OPT was swayed by the series of declarations of emergency by the Nigerian government, heightened security operations and renewal of armed conflict, as well as display of organisational command by Boko Haram.[161]

The statute creating the ICC gives primary jurisdiction to states to prosecute (international) crimes that have occurred on the states' territory that are within the jurisdiction of the Court. Such crimes include terrorism, genocide, war crimes and crimes against humanity.[162] However, the ICC can go ahead and try such crimes where the state concerned is either unwilling or unable to carry out the investigations and prosecutions of the crimes.[163] While there have been various reports about proceedings by the Nigerian government against members (and sponsors) of Boko Haram for their crimes within the territory, actual prosecutions remain to be seen. It may, however, be premature at this stage to conclude that there is unwillingness or inability on the part of the Nigerian government. With the recent classification of the insurgency as a NIAC, the ICC's OTP is continuing a jurisdictional assessment of the crimes committed (pending a determination on admissibility), and it remains to be seen what the outcome of this process will be.

9.8 Conclusion

John Paden, an American professor who has done fieldwork and taught in northern Nigeria periodically for almost five decades, has advised:

> The key to stability is not to overreact to the threats of religious extremists in the north by using disproportionate military power. The militarization of the response to Boko Haram may well provoke further violence. Boko Haram has taken responsibility for the killings of key officials in Borno and also for bombings in Abuja, including the suicide bombing of the national police force headquarters. It has threatened to bring violence to Jos, Lagos, and even the presidential mansion ('Aso Rock'). What has been the police response? Inspector General of Police Alhaji Hafiz Ringim promised to deal quickly and harshly with Boko Haram. In turn, the group declared him a legitimate target for assassination. The fact that Boko Haram would make such a threat even though Ringim is a northerner underscores the reality that the police are the enemy of Boko Haram, regardless of their origins.[164]

In effect, the government must promote respect for its local populations by its security forces while taking concrete measures to address the underlying political and

[159] SAS - NGA - Public version Article 5 Report (2013), p. 131.

[160] OTP Report on Preliminary Examination Activities (2013), p. 18.

[161] OTP Report on Preliminary Examination Activities (2013), pp. 214–219.

[162] See generally, Articles 5–9 of the Rome Statute of the International Criminal Court. See also Maiese (2003).

[163] See generally, Articles 11–14 of the Rome Statute of the International Criminal Court.

[164] Paden (2012), pp. 64–65.

socio-economic problems in the north and in Nigeria as a whole 'in order to effectively deal with the Boko Haram security issues'.[165] As aptly put by Gurr, the 'disposition to collective violence depends on how badly societies violate socially derived expectations about the means and ends of human action'.[166]

In this article, we have tried to map out the origins of Boko Haram and its evolution into a full-blown terrorist organisation within Nigeria and other parts of West Arica. Some of factors providing the context for the group and its activities to thrive have also been highlighted. While terrorism is a global phenomenon requiring the assistance of the international community at various levels and stages, it usually begins as a localised situation allowed to fester for too long. As such, in the case of Nigeria (the focus of this article), accountable and inclusive democratic political leadership, with a clear strategy for addressing socio-economic imbalances, is the long-lasting proactive panacea to Boko Haram's murderous terrorist attacks. Most of the strategies adopted by the government have so far been largely political and military in nature, which only seem to add more fuel to the fire, given the realities of poverty, among other socio-economic conditions, corruption and human rights abuses.

References

A Closer Look at Nigeria: Security, Governance, and Trade, 29 March 2012. Available at http://www.gpo.gov/fdsys/pkg/CHRG-112shrg77372/pdf/CHRG-112shrg77372.pdf. Accessed 20 Jun 2014

Abonyi I (2011) Boko Haram trained in Algeria, Afghanistan: SSS unveils suspects, confirms Al Qaeda link. Thisday 16(5974):1, 7

Adepegba A (2011) SSS unmasks alleged UN bombing masterminds: we got a tip eight days before bombing-security agents. The Punch 17(20,958):1–2

Adepegba A, Soriwei F (2012) SSS re-arrests Kabiru Sokoto inside Wardrobe: how he influenced late Yusuf's visit to Sokoto in 2009. The Punch 7110(1660):6

Adetayo O et al (2015) 276 days after Chibok girls abduction, President visits Borno. The Punch 39(20,838):2

Adibe J (2012) Nigeria without Nigerians? Boko Haram and the crisis in Nigeria's nation-building project. Adonis & Abbey Publishers Ltd, Abuja

Akinmutimi T, Adeyemi D (2011) Jonathan to Spend N300m on Dinner Sets…higher than ICPC capital vote, fuelling vehicles, generators, cooking gas to gulp N168.72m. National Mirror 1(263):1, 5

Alechenu J (2011) 18 killed in Abuja UN Bombing. Saturday Punch 7086(1576):1–6; UN, U.S. Join in fight against Boko Haram: AFRICOM commander reportedly warned Nigeria ahead of attack. The Guardian 29(11,932):1, 3–6

Ali Y et al (2011) Xmas day bombings: church death toll hits 43. The Nation 7(1990):1

Ameh J, Owuamanam J (2014) Military lied about schoolchildren recue-principal, parents. The Punch 38(20,643):2

[165] A Closer Look at Nigeria: Security, Governance, and Trade (2012) available at http://www.gpo.gov/fdsys/pkg/CHRG-112shrg77372/pdf/CHRG-112shrg77372.pdf. Accessed 20 Jun 2014. See also Habermas (1975).

[166] Gurr (1970), p. 317.

Ameh J et al (2014) B'Haram abducts 100 schoolgirls in Borno. The Punch 38(20,641):1–2; Parents join soldiers in bush search for 99 girls. The Nation 9(2822):1

Amnesty International (2012) Nigeria: trapped in the cycle of violence, (London) 11. Available at http://www.amnesty.org/en/library/asset/AFR44/043/2012/en/04ab8b67-8969-4c86-bdea-0f82059dff28/afr440432012en.pdf. Accessed 20 Jun 2014

Amnesty International (2014) Nigeria: more than 1,500 killed in armed conflict in North-Eastern Nigeria in Early 2014. Available at http://www.amnesty.org/en/library/asset/AFR44/004/2014/en/543f7ac9-6889-4f02-bf5a-d73832e04229/afr440042014en.pdf. Accessed 20 Jun 2014

Amnesty International (2015) Nigeria satellite images show horrific scale of Boko Haram attack on Baga. http://www.amnesty.org/en/news/nigeria-satellite-images-show-horrific-scale-boko-haram-attack-baga-2015-01-15. Accessed 22 Jan 2015

An Interview with Abdelmalek Droukdal – NYTimes.com, 1 July 2008. Available at http://www.nytimes.com/2008/07/01/world/africa/01transcript-droukdal.html?pagewanted=all&_r=0. Accessed 22 Jun 2014

Anozie SU (2012) Human rights and terrorism: the Niger Delta Oil War. In: Masaeli M (ed) Morality and terrorism: an interfaith perspective. Nortia Press, Santa Ana

Audu SD (2012) The Almajiri Institution, Boko Haram, and Terrorism in Northern Nigeria. In: Masaeli M (ed) Morality and terrorism: an interfaith perspective. Nortia Press, Santa Ana

Balogun A et al (2012) Many feared dead as bomb explosions rock Kano. Saturday Punch 7107(1597):1, 7

BBC News (2014a) Nigeria Boko Haram crisis 20 women abducted in north. Available at http://www.bbc.com/news/world-africa-27774239. Accessed 20 Jun 2014

BBC News (2014b) Obama West point speech in full with analysis 2014; May 29. Available at http://www.bbc.com/news/world-us-canada-27606537. Accessed 20 Jun 2014

BBC News (2014c) Nigeria's Boko Haram targets village vigilantes. Available at http://www.bbc.com/news/world-africa-27547214. Accessed 20 Jun 2014

BBC News (2014d) Nigeria's Boko Haram 'seizes women' in Borno, http://www.bbc.com/news/world-africa-27998502. Accessed 24 Jun 2014

BBC News Africa (2014) Nigeria Boko Haram crisis: President vows 'total war'. Available at http://www.bbc.com/news/world-africa-27619290. Accessed 20 Jun 2014

Blair D (2011) Does Nigeria's Taliban have the West in its Sights? The Telegraph, London 2011; Dec. 28. Available at http://www.telegraph.co.uk/news/worldnews/africaandindianocean/nigeria/8980000/Does-Nigerias-Taliban-have-the-West-in-its-sights.html. Accessed 21 Jun 2014

Botha A (2013) Practical guide to understanding and preventing suicide operations in Africa. ISS, Pretoria

Cohen HJ (2013) Al Qaeda in Africa: the creeping menace to Sub-Sahara's 500 Million Muslims. Am Foreign Policy Interests 35:63–68

Committee on Foreign Affairs, House of Representatives (2012) Hearing on LRA, Boko Haram, Al-Shabaab, AQIM and other sources of instability in Africa, Apr 25. Available at http://www.gpo.gov/fdsys/pkg/CHRG-112hhrg73998/pdf/CHRG-112hhrg73998.pdf. Accessed 20 Jun 2014

Crowley R, Wilkinson H (2013) Boko Haram: a new threat in West Africa. In: Trémolières M (ed) Conflict over resources and terrorism: two facets of insecurity. OECD (Organisation for Economic Co-operation and Development) Publishing, Paris

Daily Sun (2011) It's Black Christmas, as Catholic Morning Mass Ends in…Mass Murder: 35 Killed as Boko Haram Bombs Church in Madalla, Niger. 6(2267):1, 4, 6–9

Dasuki MS (2014) Nigeria's soft approach to countering terrorism' roll out of Nigeria's soft approach to countering terrorism, Abuja. Available at http://abusidiqu.com/nigerias-soft-approach-countering-terrorism-mohammed-sambo-dasuki/. Accessed 20 Jun 2014

Dinstein Y (2013) The principle of proportionality. In: Larsen KM, Cooper CG, Nystuen G (eds) Searching for a 'principle of humanity' in international humanitarian law. Cambridge University Press, Cambridge

Ehikioya A (2014a) Jonathan offers amnesty to Boko Haram members. The Nation. Available at http://thenationonlineng.net/new/jonathan-offers-amnesty-to-boko-haram-members-2/. Accessed 20 Jun 2014
Ehikioya A (2014b) We'll soon get over insurgency, says Jonathan. The Nation 9(2819):4
Ero C (2014) Nigeria's insurgency has to be tackled at the roots. Financial Times, New York, p 9
Evans M (2012) Algeria: France's undeclared war. OUP, Oxford
Evans M, Phillips J (2007) Algeria: anger of the dispossessed. Yale University Press, Yale
Fisk R (2005) The great war for civilization: the conquest of the Middle East. HarperCollins, New York
Forest JF (2012) Confronting the terrorism of Boko Haram in Nigeria. Joint Special Operations University Press Publications, Macdill Airforce Base, Tampa
Gurr TR (1970) Why men rebel. Princeton University Press, Princeton
Habermas J (1975) Legitimation crisis, Thomas McCarthy English translation. Beacon Press, Boston
Haug H (ed) (1993) Humanity for all: the international red cross and red crescent movement. Henry Dunant Institute, Geneva and Paul Haupt Publishers, Vienna
Heyns C (2003–2004) The African regional human rights system: the African charter. Penn State Law Rev 108:679–689
Hinshaw D (2014) Car bomb at Abuja Mall kills at least 21 people: frustrated Nigerians assemble own armies. Wall Street J A1, A8
Human Rights Watch (2012) Spiralling violence: Boko Haram attacks and security forces abuses in Nigeria 32–34. Available at http://www.hrw.org/sites/default/files/reports/nigeria1012web-wcover_0.pdf. Accessed 20 Jun 2014
Hussey A (2014) French intifida: the long war between France and its Arabs. FSG, New York
Ikhiale E (2014) Convicted Kabiru Sokoto begs Jonathan for pardon. The Nation 2014; May 27. Available at http://thenationonlineng.net/new/convicted-kabiru-sokoto-begs-jonathan-pardon/. Accessed 20 Jun 2014
International Committee of the Red Cross (ICRC) (2008) How is the term "armed conflict" defined in international humanitarian law? Opinion Paper, March. Available at www.icrc.org/web/eng/siteeng0.nsf/htmlall/armed-conflict-article–170308/$file/Opinionpaper-armed-conflict.pdf. Accessed 20 Jun 2014
International Crisis Group (2014) Curbing violence in Nigeria (II): the Boko Haram insurgency. Afr Rep 216:25. Available at http://www.crisisgroup.org/~/media/Files/africa/west-africa/nigeria/216-curbing-violence-in-nigeria-ii-the-boko-haram-insurgency.pdf. Accessed 20 Jun 2014
Iroegbu S (2014) Abuja Emab plaza bombing death toll hits 22. Thisday Live. Available at http://www.thisdaylive.com/articles/abuja-emab-plaza-bombing-death-toll-hits-22/181966/. Accessed 20 Jun 2014
Iroegbu S, Obi P (2011) Victims recall moments before UN bomb attack. Thisday 16(5970):1, 8
Ishaku J (2009) Boko Haram: how religious intolerance threatens Nigeria. Courier Communications, Jos
Jimoh AM et al (2014) 71 feared killed, 124 injured in Abuja terrorist bombing. The Guardian 30(12,892):1–2
Josiah O, Adetayo O (2011) Jonathan declares state of emergency in parts of Borno, Yobe, Niger, plateau: orders border shut. Sunday Punch 18(19,671):1, 11
Lahoud N et al (2012) Letters from Abbottad: Bin Ladin Sidelined? Harmony program: the combating terrorism Center at West Point, U.S. Military Academy; 14. Available at http://www.ctc.usma.edu/wp-content/uploads/2012/05/CTC_LtrsFromAbottabad_WEB_v2.pdf. Accessed 20 Jun 2014; http://www.ctc.usma.edu/posts/letters-from-abbottabad-bin-ladin-sidelined. Accessed 20 Jun 2014
Le Sueur JD (2010) Algeria since 1989: between terror and democracy. Zed Books, London
Maiangwa B et al (2012) Baptism by fire: Boko Haram and the reign of terror in Nigeria. Afr Today 59(2):40–48

Maiese M (2003) Human rights violations. Beyond intractability. In: Burgess G, Burgess H (eds) Conflict information consortium. University of Colorado, Boulder. Available at http://www.beyondintractability.org/essay/human-rights-violations. Accessed 20 June 2014
Miller ZJ (2014) U.S. to send team to Nigeria to help find kidnapped girls. Time 2014; May 6. Available at http://time.com/89665/boko-haram-nigeria-girls/. Accessed 20 Jun 2014
Mohammed A [edited by Mohammed Haruna] (2010) The paradox of Boko Haram. Moving Image Ltd, Kano
Nixon R (2014) Nigeria television becomes front for U.S. in terrorism fight: state department ramps up efforts against Boko Haram. New York Times 2014; Jun 6. Available at http://www.nytimes.com/2014/06/07/world/africa/state-department-ramps-up-efforts-against-boko-haram.html?_r=1. Accessed 20 Jun 2014
Nossiter A (2014) New kidnappings in Nigeria lead U.S. to offer aid. The New York Times 2014; May 7: A1
Nwaubani AT (2014) BBC News Letter from Africa: Nigerian pride and foreign assistance. Available at http://www.bbc.com/news/world-africa-27473428. Accessed 20 Jun 2014
Odebode N et al (2011) FG to spend N11.25bn on foreign trips in 2012. The Punch 17(20,043):1–2
Office of the Spokesperson, U.S. Department of State (2012) Terrorist designations of Boko Haram Commander Abubakar Shekau, Khalid al-Barnawi and Abubakar Adam Kambar. Media Note, Washington, DC. 21 June. Available at http://www.state.gov/r/pa/prs/ps/2012/06/193574.htm. Accessed 20 Jun 2014
Okpi A (2012) Multiple blasts rock Kano: death toll rises to 162. Sunday Punch 18(19,674):3
Oloja M et al (2011) Abuja UN office bombing claims one more worker: EU, Germany condemns attacks on churches. The Guardian 29(12,054):63
Onogu S (2011) We know sponsors of bomb blasts-Jonathan. The Nation 5(1872):1, 3
Onuoha FC (2012a) The audacity of the Boko Haram: background, analysis and emerging trend. Secur J 25(2):136–137
Onuoha FC (2012b) From Ahlulsunna wal'jama'ah hijra to Jama'atu Ahlissunnah lidda'awati wal Jihad: the evolutionary phases of the Boko Haram Sect in Nigeria. Afr Insight 41(4):159–163
Oraá J (1992) Human rights in states of emergency in international law. Clarendon Press, Oxford
OTP Report on Preliminary Examination Activities (2013) 18. Available at http://www.icc-cpi.int/en_menus/icc/press%20and%20media/press%20releases/Documents/OTP%20Preliminary%20Examinations/OTP%20-%20Report%20%20Preliminary%20Examination%20Activities%202013.PDF. Accessed 20 Jun 2014
OTP Report on Preliminary Examinations (2011) 12–13. Available at http://www.icc-cpi.int/NR/rdonlyres/63682F4E-49C8-445D-8C13-F310A4F3AEC2/284116/OTPReportonPreliminaryExaminations13December2011.pdf. Accessed 20 Jun 2014
OTP Report on Preliminary Examinations (2012) 89. Available at http://www.icc-cpi.int/NR/rdonlyres/C433C462-7C4E-4358-8A72-8D99FD00E8CD/285209/OTP2012ReportonPreliminaryExaminations22Nov2012.pdf. Accessed 20 Jun 2014
Paden JN (2012) Postelection conflict management in Nigeria: the challenges of national unity. George Mason University Press, Fairfax
Paulus A, Vashakmadze M (2009) Asymmetrical war and the notion of armed conflict: a tentative conceptualization. Int Rev Red Cross 91(873):95–125
Pham JP (2012) Boko Haram's evolving threat. Afr Secur Brief 20:4. Available at http://africacenter.org/wp-content/uploads/2012/04/AfricaBriefFinal_20.pdf. Accessed 20 Jun 2014
Salihu M (2012) Boko Haram leader, wife killed in 5-hour gunfight. The Punch 17(20,061):8
SAS - NGA - Public version Article 5 Report – 131 (05 August 2013) Available at http://www.icc-cpi.int/iccdocs/PIDS/docs/SAS%20-%20NGA%20-%20Public%20version%20Article%205%20Report%20-%2005%20August%202013.PDF. Accessed 20 Jun 2014
Sassoli M, Bouvier A (1999) How does law protect in war? Cases, documents and teaching materials on contemporary practice in international humanitarian law. ICRC, Geneva
Shelton DR, Carozza PG (2013) Regional protection of human rights. OUP, Oxford

Somorin Z (2014) Liechtenstein to return Abacha's looted fund. Thisday Live. Available at http://www.thisdaylive.com/articles/liechtenstein-to-return-abacha-s-looted-fund/181273/. Accessed 20 Jun 2014

Soniyi T (2014) FG begins process to repatriate Ogwuche, Mastermind of Nyanya Bomb Blasts. Thisday Live. Available at http://www.thisdaylive.com/articles/fg-begins-process-to-repatriate-ogwuche-mastermind-of-nyanya-bomb-blasts/180542/. Accessed 20 Jun 2014

Soniyi T et al (2014) Chibok girls Australia to deploy special forces, IG Overrules Mbu. Thisday Live 2014; Jun 4. Available at http://www.thisdaylive.com/articles/chibok-girls-australia-to-deploy-special-forces-ig-overrules-mbu/180176/. Accessed 20 Jun 2014

Soriwei F, Adetayo O (2014) Emergency rule: FG to decide on extension wednesday. The Punch 19(19,789):2

Soriwei F, Idowu K (2014) Kidnapped schoolgirls: Nigeria extends search to Cameroon, Chad borders. The Punch 19(19,789):2

Soriwei F et al (2014a) Sorrow, tears as Abuja blast kills 89. The Guardian 38(20,640):1–2

Soriwei F et al (2014b) Suicide bomber kills 30 in Maiduguri. The Punch 38(20,576):1–2

The Additional Protocol I (of 8 June 1977) to the Geneva Conventions of 1949

The Additional Protocol II (of 12 August 1949) to the Geneva Conventions of 1949

The Al-Qaida Sanctions Committee. Available at http://www.un.org/sc/committees/1267/NSQE13814E.shtml. Accessed 20 Jun 2014

The American Convention on Human Rights

The European Convention on Human Rights

The Guardian (2014) 'I've lived in Kano for 25 Years, But Today, I am Afraid…So, I've to Move My Family Home'. 29 (12,085): 1–2

The Money Laundering (Prohibition) Act (2011)

The Nation (2014a) 219 Chibok girls' ordeal, by Australian negotiator; Jun 2. Available at http://thenationonlineng.net/new/219-chibok-girls-ordeal-by-australian-negotiator/. Accessed 20 Jun 2014

The Nation (2014b) US drones reveal Boko Haram's movements, new camps; May 17. Available at http://thenationonlineng.net/new/us-drones-reveal-boko-harams-movements-new-camps/. Accessed 20 Jun 2014

The Prosecutor v. Tadic Case No. 160 ICTY (1995) 1. Available at http://www.icty.org/x/cases/tadic/acdec/en/51002.htm. Accessed 20 Jun 2014

The Punch Editorial (2015) Baga massacre: diminishing value of Nigerian lives. The Punch 39(20,838):28

The Rome Statute of the International Criminal Court (1998)

The Terrorism (Prevention) (Proscription Order) Notice (2013) Available at http://www.cenbank.org/Out/2013/FPRD/TERRORISM%20(PREVENTION)%20(PROSCRIPTION%20ORDER)%20NOTICE,%202013.pdf. Accessed 20 Jun 2014

The Terrorism Prevention (Amendment) Act (2013)

U.S. Policy Toward Nigeria: West Africa's Troubled Titan, 10 July 2012. Available at http://www.gpo.gov/fdsys/pkg/CHRG-112hhrg74961/pdf/CHRG-112hhrg74961.pdf. Accessed 20 Jun 2014

Umar MS (2012) The popular discourses of Salafi radicalism and Salafi counter-radicalism in Nigeria: a case study of Boko Haram. J Relig Afr 42:118–144

Usman LM (2008) Assessing the universal basic education primary and Koranic schools synergy for Almajiri street boys in Nigeria. Int J Educ Manag 22(1):67–68

Walker A (2014) Why Nigeria has not defeated Boko Haram. BBC News 2014; May 13. Available at http://www.bbc.com/news/world-africa-27396702. Accessed 20 Jun 2014

Winters CA (1987) Koranic education and militant Islam in Nigeria. Int Rev Educ 33(2):177–178

York G (2014) Boko Haram insurgency exposes Nigeria's extreme economic inequality. The Globe and Mail, Toronto. Available at http://www.theglobeandmail.com/news/world/boko-haram-insurgency-exposes-nigerias-extreme-economic-inequality/article19175409/. Accessed 20 Jun 2014

Chapter 10
Boko Haram's Radical Ideology and Islamic Jurisprudence

Muyiwa Adigun

10.1 Introduction

Terrorism is a relatively recent phenomenon in Nigeria. Nigeria could not be said to have experienced terrorism until the advent of the insurgency of Boko Haram. In 2013, Boko Haram was responsible for 90% of all terrorist acts in Nigeria, and it was responsible for the deaths of about 1587 people.[1] Boko Haram is one of the deadliest terrorist organisations in the world with an average of close to eight deaths per terrorist attack.[2] Between 2009 and 2012, Boko Haram killed over 3500 Nigerians.[3] Around 60% of their attacks are from armed assaults using guns, while a quarter of attacks and fatalities are from bombings.[4] Boko Haram had used not less than 35 bombings.[5] Thus, Nigeria is ranked fourth among countries most hit by terrorist attacks.[6]

Boko Haram is a Sunni Islamic fundamentalist sect.[7] It advocates maximum Sharia[8] and is intolerant of secular institutions. Its killings have been justified by the group in the name of Islam. Because of the magnitude of its killings and its ideological bias against secular institutions, people have regarded its ideology as radical. The word radical has been defined by Merriam-Webster's Dictionary and Thesaurus

[1] Institute for Economics and Peace (2014), p. 19.
[2] Institute for Economics and Peace (2014), p. 19.
[3] Institute for Economics and Peace (2014), p. 53.
[4] Institute for Economics and Peace (2014), p. 53.
[5] Institute for Economics and Peace (2014), p. 53.
[6] Institute for Economics and Peace (2014), p. 19.
[7] Institute for Economics and Peace (2014), p. 53.
[8] Institute for Economics and Peace (2014), p. 19.

M. Adigun (✉)
Department of Public Law, Faculty of Law, University of Ibadan, Ibadan, Nigeria

J.-M. Iyi, H. Strydom (eds.), *Boko Haram and International Law*,
https://doi.org/10.1007/978-3-319-74957-0_10

as something that is 'marked by a considerable departure from the usual or traditional'.

In this study, the alleged radicalism of Boko Haram will be examined. This study is divided into five parts. The first part is the introductory part, which gives a general overview of how vicious Boko Haram is and how it seeks to justify its activities in Islam. The second part discusses Boko Haram and its ideology. Boko Haram's ideology is essentially divided into two. The first is its intolerance of Western/secular institution, while the second one is insurgency. The third part therefore examines the sect's intolerance of Western institution in the light of Islamic jurisprudence, while the fourth part examines the insurgency of the sect in the light of Islamic jurisprudence. The fifth part is the concluding part. Throughout this study, the interpretation of the Qur'an by Yusuf Ali is relied upon.

10.2 Boko Haram and Its Ideology

The term 'Boko Haram' is derived from two sources. The first one is from the Hausa language. The second one is from the Arabic language. 'Boko' is the Hausa expression for book. Book in this context is Western education. Haram is an Arabic word meaning 'forbidden'. Therefore, Boko Haram means Western education is forbidden.[9] Boko also has its own meaning in the Hausa language apart from the corrupt adaptation of the word 'book'. It means deceit, sham, fake or imitation.[10] Thus, the words 'amaryar boko' mean a fake bride in Hausa marriage customs.[11] While Boko Haram is the popular name given to this movement, the movement refers to itself as *Jamā'atu Ahl us-Sunnah Li'd-Da'wah wa'l-Jihād*, meaning the Group of the People of Sunnah for Preaching and Struggle.

Boko Haram emerged around year 2000. At that time, it was a small Islamic sect advocating a strict interpretation and implementation of Sharia law in Nigeria.[12] The group was influenced by the Salafist thought and writings, which consider anything Western/secular as un-Islamic,[13] and by the writings of Ibn Taymiyyah, a medieval Islamic scholar who advocated for the application of Islamic law[14] in its pristine state and sought the end for all forms of innovations.[15] The leader of the group was Mohammed Yusuf, a young charismatic cleric who studied in Saudi Arabia.[16]

[9] Murthadā (2013), p. 4.

[10] Newman (2013).

[11] Pérouse de Montclos (2014), p. 143.

[12] Blanchard (2014), p. 1.

[13] Amy (2014), p. 13.

[14] Amy (2014), p. 13.

[15] Mohammed (2014), p. 15.

[16] Blanchard (2014), p. 2.

The principles of the movement are that democracy is un-Islamic and that politicians who participate in elections are unbelievers. To the movement, ruling by man-made laws is a reflection of unbelief.[17] According to the group:

> Those who formulate evil laws in their parliaments have made themselves partners to Allah, whether or not they feel it, whether or not they agree to this or disagree, whether or not they meant it … Those who follow the legislative [sic] system and agree to take their cases to these courts are in agreement with *taghut* and are idolaters… Parliamentarians and members of assemblies have combined between [sic] them making themselves gods and ascribing partners to Allah. This is because their mace is their object of worship in various ways such as bowing to it, subjecting themselves to it, loving it and using it as a symbol of *shirk* (apostasy), as they do not pass any bill or make decisions without it. [Without the mace] such decisions are unacceptable and has [sic] no legal backing.[18]

The group considers itself the saved sect.[19] Education is forbidden because it only serves to preserve the interest of the colonialists and the missionaries.[20] To the extent that Western education fosters the mixing of the gender and the wearing of revealing attire, it is considered un-Islamic.[21] The group considers Darwin's theory of evolution as un-Islamic.[22] To the group, the earth is not round, and any scientific explanation relating to the solar system is un-Islamic.[23] Similarly, embryology is considered un-Islamic.[24] Mohammed Yusuf says of this body of knowledge as follows:

> I have a book that discusses the knowledge of geography, geology, and sociology. These branches of knowledge are not knowledge but full of unbelief. Even those studying it are aware if they are fair to Allah, except if they haven't studied Islam. If you have read geography, you'll know that in geography there is danger. If you have studied Islam, you'll know, whoever you are, that in sociology there is danger… We are ready to debate any one on this creed. Western education is destructive. We didn't say knowledge is bad but that the unbelief inside it is more than its usefulness. I have English books in my possession which I read regularly. I didn't say English amounts to unbelief but the unbelief contained therein and the polytheism inside. In the process of becoming educated, you become a *mushrik* [idolater]. This is our only fear … Destruction is destruction, whoever it comes from. Because it is the white man that brought it, does it amount to civilisation? Yes, our own is traditional, as you call it, but yours is 'shirkasiation'.[25]

Obtaining employment under a democratic government like that of Nigeria as a police officer, military officer or security agent is an obedience to a disbelieving system and a disobedience to Allah.[26] Thus:

---

[17] See Murthadā (2013), pp. 16–17.
[18] Yusuf (2009), pp. 66–67.
[19] Murthadā (2013), p. 17.
[20] Murthadā (2013), p. 17.
[21] Murthadā (2013), p. 17.
[22] Murthadā (2013), p. 18.
[23] Murthadā (2013), p. 18.
[24] Murthadā (2013), p. 18.
[25] Mohammed (2014), p. 18.
[26] Murthadā (2013), p. 18.

> Our call refuses employment under the government which does not rule by what Allah has revealed such as the French law, the American law, the British law or any other constitution or system that goes against the teachings of Islam and negates the Qur'an and Sunnah.[27]

Initially, the group did not advocate violence, although there were occasional skirmishes between it and the police.[28] It, however, came to a head in July 2009, when about 700 people were killed by the police in a bid to suppress the group. The leader of the group, Mohammed Yusuf, was eventually killed in the process while in police custody.[29] It is, however, worthy of mention that the group's 'Afghanistan' settlement in Nigeria[30] and the failure of the group to observe the new law prohibiting riding motorbikes at night and making the wearing of helmet on motorbikes mandatory[31] attracted the attention of the government with its potential to claim statehood within the Nigerian Federation if not timely checked. With the killing of the leader of the group, the group appeared to have dissipated until its re-emergence under the new leadership in 2010.[32] At this time, it had assumed a completely militant posture signalling it with a large prison break in 2010 where hundreds of prisoners were freed, including its members.[33]

10.2.1 Insurgent Activities of Boko Haram

Boko Haram as a militant group has unleashed mayhem on Nigeria. In 2011, not less than 425 people were killed in bomb attacks and targeted killings by this group in the northern part of Nigeria.[34] Similarly, not less than 24 people died with about 100 injured in suicide bomb attack on the United Nations building in August 2011. In November 2011, the group also killed about 100 people in Damaturu Yobe State of Nigeria with a bomb attack.[35] In January 2012, the group was reported to have killed 180 people in a bomb attack in Kano.[36] In addition, on 29 April 2012, the group was also reported to have killed 16 people with explosives and guns.[37] It was reported that while Christians were worshipping in one of the lecture theatres at Bayero University in Kano, some people believed to be members of the group threw

---

[27] Yusuf (2009), p. 11.

[28] Blanchard (2014), p. 2.

[29] Blanchard (2014), p. 2.

[30] National Consortium for the Study of Terrorism and Responses to Terrorism (Start) (2014), p. 1.

[31] Amy (2014), pp. 12–13.

[32] Blanchard (2014), p. 2.

[33] Blanchard (2014), p. 2.

[34] Human Rights Watch (2012).

[35] Human Rights Watch (2012).

[36] BBC News Africa (2012).

[37] BBC News Africa (2012).

in bomb explosives to cause pandemonium, and as the worshippers tried to flee, they were shot dead.[38]

From July 2014, the group captured and occupied more than 20 towns spanning Adamawa, Borno and Yobe states killing several thousand civilians in those areas under its control and in bomb attacks nationwide.[39] In April 2014, the group abducted 276 girls from Chibok. It is the practice of the group to abduct women and girls and forced them into marriage. The group forcibly recruited men and tortured people under its control who violated its rules. Schools, homes, markets, shops and other civilian facilities were targeted.[40] On 25 February 2014, about 43 people were killed in an attack on a school in Buni Yadi, Yobe State. Most of those killed in the attack were school children.[41] On 14 April 2014, Boko Haram planted bombs in cars at Nyanya, a suburb in Abuja, the Nigerian capital, and not less than 70 people died in the process. On May 1 in the same place, another bomb attack killed 19 people and injured over 60.[42] On 5 May 2014, about 393 people were killed in an attack in Gamborou Ngala, Borno State. Market stalls, shops, homes and vehicles were burnt.[43]

On 1 September 2014, Boko Haram captured Bama town, and about 50 civilians were killed in the process. The group later imprisoned about 300 men, and they were eventually killed as well. Thirty women were forced to marry its members.[44] Between 12 and 14 December 2014, the group killed 24 people and abducted more than 110 children in two attacks on Gumsuri village.[45] On 14 March 2015, the group attacked military barracks in Maiduguri, and several detainees were freed.[46] As of June 2015, the group activities include murder, rape, torture, forced marriages and recruitment of child soldiers.[47] Between June and December 2015, about 1600 civilians were killed, bringing the total death toll to about 3500 civilians in 2015.[48] On 2 July 2015, 120 civilians were killed in Kukawa town, Borno State.[49] People who were unarmed were asked to lie down and were shot dead. Those who tried to escape were also shot.[50] As these Boko Haram assailants were leaving, they burnt houses.[51]

---

[38] BBC News Africa (2012).

[39] Amnesty International (2015a), pp. 274.

[40] Amnesty International (2015a), pp. 274.

[41] Amnesty International (2015a), pp. 274.

[42] Amnesty International (2015a), pp. 274.

[43] Amnesty International (2015a), pp. 275.

[44] Amnesty International (2015a), p. 275.

[45] Amnesty International (2015a), p. 275.

[46] Amnesty International (2015a), p. 275.

[47] Amnesty International (2015b).

[48] Amnesty International (2015c, d).

[49] Amnesty International (2015c, d).

[50] Amnesty International (2015c, d).

[51] Amnesty International (2015c, d).

Between June and December 2015, there were about 14 bomb attacks, and not less than 222 people died.[52] Places targeted include markets, transport hubs, bars, restaurants and places of worship.[53] Young women and girls were recruited as suicide bombers.[54] On June 2, a bomb attack in Maiduguri, Borno State, killed at least 12 people in an abattoir.[55] Bomb attacks killed 16 civilians at Baga road Motor Park, Maiduguri, on 3 and 22 June 2015.[56] About 75 people were killed at a mosque and viewing centre near Ajilari Cross, Maiduguri, on 20 September 2015.[57] In Damaturu, Yobe State, a bomb attack killed at least five worshippers who were celebrating Ramadhan on 17 July 2015.[58] On 5 July 2015, a bomb attack also killed at least eight worshippers inside the Redeemed Church in Potikum, Yobe State.[59]

10.3 Examining Boko Haram's Condemnation of Western/Secular Institution in the Light of Islamic Jurisprudence

Boko Haram's position that democracy is un-Islamic and that politicians who participate in elections are unbelievers is not a position that is sacrosanct and unimpeachable. Democracy has been considered compatible with Islamic jurisprudence through the principle of shūrā (consultation), whereby consensus is achieved in electing an Islamic leader.[60] Shūrā is rooted in Q 3 v 159, where it is stated thus: 'and consult them in affairs (of moment)'.[61] The practice in electing leaders started with the election of the third Caliph by six prominent Meccans in 644. Those prominent Meccans were chosen from different social groups, and they were not limited to religious leaders.[62]

Democracy has also been considered compatible with Islamic jurisprudence through the principle of ijmā (consensus).[63] The prophetic saying that 'my community will never agree upon an error' legitimises the infallibility of the ummah and justifies democracy.[64] Democracy has also been subsumed under the principle of

[52] Amnesty International (2015c).

[53] Amnesty International (2015c).

[54] Amnesty International (2015c).

[55] Amnesty International (2015c).

[56] Amnesty International (2015c).

[57] Amnesty International (2015c).

[58] Amnesty International (2015c).

[59] Amnesty International (2015c).

[60] Malinova (2013).

[61] On Democracy and Shūrā, see Osman (Undated).

[62] Malinova (2013).

[63] Malinova (2013).

[64] Malinova (2013).

vicegerency, which stipulates that Allah has made all humans His vicegerent on earth. In Q 2 v 30, it is stated thus: 'Behold, thy Lord said to the angels; "I will create a vicegerent on earth."' While Q 2 v 30 refers to Adam, Q 6 v 165 refers to humans as the descendants of Adam having stated that 'It is He who hath made you the inheritors of the earth'. Hence, humans in general have inherited the vicegerency of Allah from Adam. Abu al-Ala Mawdudi in *The Islamic Way of Life* states as follows:

> The authority of the caliphate is bestowed on the entire group of people, the community as a whole… .Such a society carries the responsibility of the caliphate as a whole and each one of its individual[s] shares the Divine Caliphate. This is the point where democracy begins in Islam. Every person in an Islamic society enjoys the rights and powers of the caliphate of God and in this respect all individuals are equal.[65]

The position of the sect that ruling by man-made laws is a reflection of unbelief can also not be sustained in Islamic jurisprudence. While Islamic law has elaborate rules on matters of faith and issues like inheritance, there are no elaborate rules on such matters as maritime, aviation and energy. Even on matters of faith, there are instances where a law-making organ still has to intervene. For example, the amount that may be punishable by cutting of hand may have to require a law-making organ having had to fix it since the equivalent monetary value of that era in modern time cannot be ascertained.[66] The implication is that a law-making organ is still not dispensed with. The purpose the Qur'an can serve for a law-making organ is to be a yardstick to determine the compatibility of any law made by the organ with Islam. In fact, a law-making organ has never been dispensed with in any Islamic society from the inception of Islam. The only difference is that a democratic Islamic society will have parliamentarians as opposed to absolute dictators of past eras in Islamic societies.

The argument that parliamentarians worship mace because the mace only confers validity on legislative deliberations is not an indispensable feature of democracy. It is at best a cultural expression peculiar to the West that a democratic Islamic society can dispense with. The Qur'an can be used to replace the mace if the Qur'an itself will not be considered an object of worship. Having stated thus, one point that must be appreciated by this argument on mace is that it strikes at the core of whether democracy, which is considered to have derived its validity from humans rather than from God, is coterminous with an 'Islamic' rule that is essentially theocratic. The view of the former President of Iran, Mohammad Khatami, is most apposite having adequately addressed it:

> the existing democracies do not necessarily follow one formula or aspect. It is possible that a democracy may lead to a liberal system. It is possible that democracy may lead to a socialist system. Or it may be a democracy with the inclusion of religious norms in the government. We have accepted the third option.[67]

---

[65] See Esposito and Voll (2001).

[66] See El-Awa (2000), pp. 3–5.

[67] See Esposito and Voll (2001).

To consider education as forbidden because it only serves the interests of the colonialists and missionaries is pathetically parochial and un-Islamic. The prophetic saying that knowledge should be sought even if it is in China[68] is sufficient to dislodge the position against Western education. In the first place, the Prophet did not specify the kind of knowledge to be sought, invariably implying that all sorts of knowledge, including Western education, are covered. Second, the practices in China at the time could even be considered idolatry from Islamic perspective, which means that even if the knowledge is surrounded by anything un-Islamic, this is not sufficient to prevent Muslims from obtaining it. Third, China was obviously one of the farthest places (if not the farthest) from the Arabian Peninsula at the time, which implies the extent each Muslim must exert himself or herself to obtain knowledge.

With respect to the 'mixing' of the gender, Islam does not forbid the 'mixing' of the gender as there is no Islamic rule prohibiting it. What Islam forbids is the indecent association of male and female (like partying at odd hours) that can lead to immorality.[69]

---

[68] This Hadith is considered weak although it is popular. However, there are other Hadiths which reinforce it as they emphasise the importance of the pursuit of knowledge.The Prophet Muhammad (peace be upon him) said: 'The seeking of knowledge is obligatory for every Muslim.'—Al-Tirmidhi, Hadith 74;The Prophet Muhammad (peace be upon him) said: 'One who treads a path in search of knowledge has his path to Paradise made easy by God…'—Riyadh us-Saleheen, 245; The Prophet Muhammad (peace be upon him) said: 'A servant of God will remain standing on the Day of Judgment until he is questioned about his (time on earth) and how he used it; about his knowledge and how he utilized it; about his wealth and from where he acquired it and in what (activities) he spent it; and about his body and how he used it.'—Al-Tirmidhi, Hadith 148; The Prophet also said: 'Knowledge from which no benefit is derived is like a treasure out of which nothing is spent in the cause of God.'—Al-Tirmidhi, Hadith 108; The Prophet Muhammad (peace be upon him) said: 'God, His angels and all those in Heavens and on Earth, even ants in their hills and fish in the water, call down blessings on those who instruct others in beneficial knowledge.'—Al-Tirmidhi, Hadith 422; The Prophet also said: 'Acquire knowledge and impart it to the people.'—Al-Tirmidhi, Hadith 107; The Prophet Muhammad (peace be upon him) said: 'If anyone travels on a road in search of knowledge, God will cause him to travel on one of the roads of Paradise. The angels will lower their wings in their great pleasure with one who seeks knowledge. The inhabitants of the heavens and the Earth and (even) the fish in the deep waters will ask forgiveness for the learned man. The superiority of the learned over the devout is like that of the moon, on the night when it is full, over the rest of the stars. The learned are the heirs of the Prophets, and the Prophets leave (no monetary inheritance), they leave only knowledge, and he who takes it takes an abundant portion.—Sunan of Abu-Dawud, Hadith 1631. For these Hadiths, see https://www.quora.com/Why-did-Muhammad-say-Seek-knowledge-even-unto-China. Accessed 10 Jan 2016.

[69] Allah says: 'And when ye ask (his ladies) for anything ye want, ask them from before a screen: that makes for greater purity for your hearts and for theirs': Q 33 v 53; The Prophet (peace be upon him) said: 'Never is a man alone with a woman except that Satan is the third party with them.' The Prophet (peace be upon him) also said: 'Do not enter into the company of women.' A man then asked him: 'What about her male in-laws?'; The Prophet (peace be upon him) replied: 'The in-law is the most dangerous'. 'No man should enter into the presence of a woman after this day unless he is accompanied by one or two other men': Sahih Muslim; The Prophet (peace be upon him) never shook hands with an unrelated woman. Umaymah b. Raqiqah said: 'I came to the Prophet (peace be upon him) with a group of the women of Madinah to swear fealty for Islam. The women informed Allah's Messenger (peace be upon him) that they wished to swear fealty to him. The Prophet (peace be upon him) said: 'I do not shake hands with women. The way I accept the pledge from one woman is the same as with one hundred women': al Muwatta', Sunan al-Tirmidhi, Sunan

Where the mixing of the gender will not lead to immorality, gender mixing is not forbidden.[70] There are so many Islamic societies where men and women buy groceries at the market, and it cannot be seriously contended that it is un-Islamic.

---

al-Nasa'i and Sunan Ibn Majah; The Prophet (peace be upon him) also said: 'It is better for one of you to be pierced by a steel pin in his head than to touch the hand of a strange woman.' Allah says: 'Be not too complaisant of speech, lest one in whose heart is a disease should be moved with desire: but speak ye speech (that is) just': Q 33 v 32; The Prophet (peace be upon him) said: 'Any woman who puts on perfume then goes and passes by some men to let them find her scent is a type of adulteress.': Musnad Ahmad, Sunan al-Tirmidhi, Sunan Abu Dawud, and Sunan al-Nasa'i; The Prophet (peace be upon him) said: 'The best of rows in prayer for the man is the first row and the worst for him is the last, and the best of rows for the women is the last row and the worst for her is the first': Sahih Muslim; Ibn 'Abbas relates that he prayed one of the 'Id prayers with the Prophet (peace be upon him). He informs us that the Prophet (peace be upon him) prayed and offered a sermon, then he went to the women and offered to them a separate sermon, admonishing them and encouraging them to give charity: Sahih al-Bukhari; The Prophet (peace be upon him) once saw men and women mixing together after they left mosque and said to the women: 'Hold back a bit. You do not have to walk in the middle of the road. You may keep to the sides': Sunan Abu Dawud; Ibn 'Umar related that the Prophet (peace be upon him) said about one of the mosque's doors: 'We should leave this door exclusively for women to use.' Ibn 'Umar, until he died, never again entered through that door: Sunan Abu Dawud; Al-Albani says: 'Umm Salamah said: 'When the Prophet (peace be upon him) completed the prayer, the women would get up to leave. He would then wait awhile before standing'; Ibn Shahab said: 'I believe that he waited for a while to give the women an opportunity to depart before the men': Sahih al-Bukhari; It was related in Sahih al-Bukhari that women at the time of the Prophet (peace be upon him) did not mix with men while circumbulating the Ka'bah and that a woman once asked Aisha, the wife of the Prophet to go with her to touch the corner of the Ka'bah but Aisha refused; One of Aisha's handmaidens came to her and said: 'O Mother of believers, I went around the Ka' bah seven times and touched the corner twice or trice'. Aisha was reported to have replied: 'May Allah not reward you for pushing your way through men. It would have been sufficient for you to say 'Allahu Akbar' as you passed by': Musnad al-Shafi'i; In Abu Dawud, Hadith No. 4931, it is narrated upon the authority of Aisha as follows: 'I used to play with my friends and whenever the Prophet (peace be upon him) entered they would leave and whenever he (peace be upon him) went out they would come back in'; In Abu Dawud Hadith No.4933, it is narrated that Aisha said as follows: 'The Prophet married me at seven and we had relationship at nine and when I moved to medina some women prepared me for the wedding and they nor I ever mixed with men in a house of women. The women received me and men received the Prophet and then we went to the house.' In Abu Dawud Hadith No. 5273, it is narrated upon the authority of Nafih that the Prophet (peace be upon him) said, 'Do not walk between two men or between two women in the street.'

[70] For the purpose of medical treatment, men and women are allowed to mix. The Sahabiyat used to treat the Sahaba and the Prophet (peace be upon him) consented to it. See http://islamicsystem.blogspot.com.ng/2006/07/shariah-rules-relating-to-mixing.html. Accessed 10 Jan 2016; In Q 24 v 61, Allah says: 'It is no fault in the blind nor in one born lame, nor in one afflicted with illness, nor in yourselves, that ye should eat in your houses, or those of your fathers, or your mothers, or your brothers, or your sisters, or your father's brothers, or your father's sisters, or your mother's brothers, or your mother's sisters, or in houses of which the keys are in your possession, or in the house of a sincere friend of yours: there is no blame on you, whether you eat in company or separately. But if ye enter houses, salute each other:-a greeting of blessing and purity as from Allah. Thus does Allah make clear the Signs to you: that ye may understand.' For the purpose of trading such as buying, selling, hiring, borrowing and lending mixing is allowed. Tirmidhi narrated that the Prophet (peace be upon him) traded with women, and that Abu Bakr saw the Prophet (peace be upon him) trade with a woman. Mixing is also permitted if the nature makes mixing inevitable.

With respect to the wearing of revealing attire, Islam is categorical in its dress code for women: the wearing of revealing attire is forbidden.[71] However, the wearing of revealing attire is not necessarily what Western education stands for. Even if Western education encourages it, all that is required is to take what is beneficial and Islamic and rejects what is un-Islamic. To suggest the impossibility of severance is untenable. As earlier stated, the prophetic injunction that knowledge must be sought embraces all forms of knowledge. It is only what is not in line with the spirit of Islam that must be rejected. To throw the baby out with the water, as contended by Boko Haram sect, cannot be sustained in Islam. If Western education must be rejected in totality, it is indeed contradictory that the sect makes use of sophisticated weapons that are also products of Western education.

There is nothing to suggest that Darwin's theory of evolution[72] is un-Islamic. At best, it is debatable in the light of Islamic jurisprudence.[73] Meanwhile, contending

The Prophet (peace be upon him) permitted Zubayr Ibn Awwam's wife to work. She carried water both to men and women. The Prophet even offered his camel to assist her. See http://islamicsystem.blogspot.com.ng/2006/07/shariah-rules-relating-to-mixing.html. Accessed 10 Jan 2016.

[71] Q 24 v 30-31: 'And say to the believing women that they should lower their gaze and guard their modesty; that they should not display their beauty and ornaments except what (ordinarily) appear thereof; that they should draw their veils over their bosoms and not display their beauty except to their husbands, their fathers, their husbands' fathers, their sons, their husbands' sons, their brothers or their brothers' sons, or their sisters' sons, or their women, or their slaves whom their right hand possess, or male attendants free of sexual desire, or small children who have no carnal knowledge of women, and that they should not strike their feet in order to draw attention to their hidden ornaments'; Q 33 v 59: 'O Prophet! Tell thy wives and daughters, and the believing women, that they should cast their outer garments over their persons (when out of doors), that is most convenient, that they should be known (as such) and not molested'; The Holy Prophet Muhammad (Peace be upon Him) said: 'Those women who seem naked even when dressed and those who walk flirtingly and those who plait their heads like the humps of camels, thus inviting people's attention, will not enter Paradise nor will they smell its fragrance even though its fragrance can be smelt from a very far distance.' (Sahih Muslim Hadith 5310 Narrated by Abu Hurayrah); The Holy Prophet Muhammad (Peace be upon Him) said: 'When a woman reaches puberty no part of her body should remain uncovered except her face and the hand up to the wrist joint.' (Abu Dawud).

[72] On Darwin's theory of evolution, see Darwin (1909).

[73] There are verses suggesting that man was created as man: 'He it is Who has created you from clay' (Q 6 v 2); 'It is He who hath produced you from the earth...' (Q 11 v 61); 'We created you out of dust, then out of sperm, then out of a leech-like clot, then out of a morsel of flesh, partly formed and partly unformed, in order that We may manifest (Our power) to you' (Q 22 v 5); 'He began the creation of man from clay, and made his progeny from the quintessence of despised fluid' (Q 32 v 7-8); 'Verily, when He intends a thing, His command is, "Be"; and it is' (Q 36 v 82). However, there are verses suggesting that the creation of man passed through evolutionary stages. 'Your Guardian Lord is Allah, who created the heavens and the earth in six days' (Q 7 v 54); See also Q 25 v 59, Q 32 v 4 and Q 50 v 38; 'He directs the affairs from the heavens to the earth: then it ascends unto Him, on a Day the measure of which is a thousand years of your reckoning' (Q32 v 5); 'The angels and the Spirit ascend unto Him in a Day the measure whereof is (as) fifty thousand years' (Q70 v 4); 'O thou man! Verily thou art ever toiling on towards thy Lord-painfully toiling,- but thou shalt meet Him... So I do call to witness the ruddy glow of Sunset; the Night and its Homing; and the Moon in her Fullness: Ye shall surely travel from stage to stage' (Q 84 v 6, 16-19). It is pertinent to note that Western scientists have always considered the theory of evolution as belonging to their Muslim counterparts. William Draper, a contemporary of Charles Darwin

that Western education supports Darwin's theory and is un-Islamic bellies the fact that the theory was once outlawed in some parts of the United States (a Western society) before its outlawry was declared unconstitutional.[74] Suppose that Western education lends its weight behind Darwin's theory, it does not remove the fact that an entity that may be called God sets in motion this evolutionary process. There is a world of difference between a programme and a programmer, which the adherents of Boko Haram appear not to have appreciated.

With respect to the condemnation of the solar system and embryology, this argument strikes at the core of the compatibility of science with religion with particular reference to Islam. Interestingly, the solar system and embryology as analysed by science are found to be consistent with the Qur'an.[75] Maurice Bucaille, in his book: *The Bible, the Qur'an and Science*, justifies the Qur'an as a revealed text by stating that the compatibility of the Qur'an with modern scientific discovery is only possible because it was revealed as anyone could not have been able to have such knowledge at the time, most especially when the position in the Qur'an is contrary to the commonly held belief of the time.[76] The condemnation of geography and geology by Muhammed Yusuf similarly strikes at the core of the compatibility of science with religion (Islam) and his failure to appreciate the difference between the programmer and the programme. If science explains the workings of the universe, it does not dispense with the idea that an entity sets these natural principles in motion. Science rather than negates the existence of God tends to confirm it as the order

referred to '...the Muhammadan theory of the evolution of man from lower forms' in his book History of the Conflict between Religion and Science (1874) at page 188. Draper's statement was rooted in the position maintained by Muslim scientists since the ninth century CE that humans evolved from primitive life forms over a long period of time. Al-Jahiz (781-869 CE), a Muslim scholar based in present day Iraq states in The Book of Animals that 'Animals engage in a struggle for existence; for resources, to avoid being eaten and to breed. Environmental factors influence organisms to develop new characteristics to ensure survival, thus transforming into new species. Animals that survive to breed can pass on their successful characteristics to offspring.' Ibn Khaldun also published a book called The Muqadimma' in 1377 CE. In it he states that 'One should then take a look at the world of creation. It started out from the minerals and progressed, in an ingenious, gradual manner, to plants and animals. The last stage of minerals is connected with the first stage of plants, such as herbs and seedless plants. The last stage of plants, such as palms and vines, is connected with the first stage of animals, such as snails and shellfish.' He further states that 'The animal world then widens, its species become numerous, and, in a gradual process of creation, it finally leads to man, who is able to think and reflect. The higher stage of man is reached from the world of monkeys, in which both sagacity and perception are found…' There were other Muslim scholars such as Ibn Miskawahy (932-1030) writing between the ninth and the fourteenth century whose ideas were also similar to those of al-Jahiz and Ibn Khaldun. Ibn Miskawahy (932-1030) probably gave the most detailed account of evolution and sought to reconcile it with the Quranic provisions. See http://www.ascertainthetruth.com/att/index.php/al-islam/al-islam-and-science/871-evolution-was-an-islamic-theory-before-darwin-was-even-born. Accessed 10 Jan 2016.

[74] In Epperson v Arkansas 393 U.S. 97 (1968), the Supreme Court of the United States held that the prohibition of the teaching of human evolution in public schools under the Arkansas statute is unconstitutional and therefore invalid.

[75] See Bucaille (Undated), pp.122–132 and 142–150.

[76] Bucaille (Undated), pp. 122–132, 142–150.

found in the natural world, together with its complexity, could not have happened by chance.

Muhammed Yusuf's condemnation of sociology ostensibly as a discipline invented by the West reflects ignorance of the origin of sociology. Ibn Khaldun, an Islamic scholar, is the father of sociology.[77] Ibn Khaldun preceded Auguste Comte by 400 years through his invention of the 'Science of Culture'.[78] Of course, the very fact that Ibn Khaldun founded sociology does not imply that sociology is Islamic. However, the prophetic injunction that if knowledge is in China it must be sought also justifies sociology. In addition, if discerning patterns of behaviour are found in human societies, which makes human interaction predictable as a scientific enterprise given some parameters, there is nothing to suggest that the principles underlying these patterns are not set in motion by God. It is worthy of emphasis that the conflict between religion and science, which obtained in Western societies in the past and which almost makes science and atheism bedfellows, does not occur in Islamic societies.[79]

As regards the condemnation of taking an employment under a democratic society by a Muslim as a police officer, military officer or security agent and a total rejection of a constitution, the Sunnah of the Prophet attests otherwise. The Sunnah of the Prophet does not prohibit Muslims from cooperating with non-Muslims in jointly establishing a government where necessary. The Constitution of Madina, which is the first constitution in world history authored by Prophet Muhammad, fostered cooperation among the Muslims, the citizens of Madina[80] and the Jews.[81] The Constitution also fostered mutual consultation and honourable dealing among them.[82] Article 54 of the Constitution of Madina stipulates that 'the Muslims and the

[77] Faridah HJ Hassan Ibn Haldun and Jane Adams: The Real Father of Sociology and the Mother of Social Works. http://www2.uned.es/congreso-ibn-khaldun/pdf/04%20Faridah%20Hj%20Hassan.pdf. Accessed 7 Mar 2016.

[78] Faridah HJ Hassan Ibn Haldun and Jane Adams: The Real Father of Sociology and the Mother of Social Works. http://www2.uned.es/congreso-ibn-khaldun/pdf/04%20Faridah%20Hj%20Hassan.pdf. Accessed 7 Mar 2016.

[79] Bucaille (Undated), p. 80.

[80] Article 2 of the Constitution titled 'Constitutional Subject of the State' stipulates that '(This shall be a pact) between the Muslims of Quraysh, the people of Yathrib (the Citizens of Madina) and those who shall follow them and become attached to them (politically) and fight along with them. (All these communities shall be the constitutional subjects of the state.)' Article 3 titled 'Formation of the Constitutional Unity' states that 'The aforementioned communities shall formulate a Constitutional Unity as distinct from (other) people.'

[81] Article 30 titled Guarantee of Freedom of Religion for both the Muslims and non-Muslim minorities (the Jews)' states that 'The Jews of Banu Awf (non-Muslim minorities) shall be considered a community along with the believers. They shall be guaranteed the right of religious freedom along with the Muslims. The right shall be conferred on their associates as well as themselves except those who are guilty of oppression or the violators of treaties. They will bring evil only on themselves and their family.'

[82] Article 46 titled 'Mutual consultation and honourable dealing' provides that 'There shall be mutual consultation and honourable dealing between the allies and there shall be the fulfilment not the violation, of all pledges.'

Jews shall be jointly responsible to defend Madina against any outside attack'. The Constitution also granted equal right of protection to anyone subject to its provision.[83] The necessary implication is that a democratic government can be jointly formed by Muslims and non-Muslims and a Muslim can obtain employment as a police officer, a military officer or a security agent so as to defend that government.

10.4 Examining Boko Haram's Insurgency in the Light of Islamic Jurisprudence

The insurgency of Boko Haram will be examined in the light of Islamic *jus ad bellum* and Islamic *jus in bello*.

10.4.1 Justification in the Use of Force in Islam (Islamic **Jus ad Bellum***)*

The use of force in Islam is essentially defensive. In Q 22 v 39, it is stated that 'to those against whom war is made, permission is given (to fight), because they are wronged'. This was the first time that the Muslims were permitted to use force in the Qur'an.[84] It was after the Prophet migrated to Madina.[85] At that time, Muslims had been persecuted for 13 years.[86] The above verse indicates that Muslims are only permitted to fight when they are wronged. Since it is in the passive, attacks must not be from Muslims as they can only respond to attacks.[87] In Q 42 v 41, it is stated that 'But, indeed, if any do help and defend himself after a wrong (done) to him, against such there is no cause of blame'. Similarly, in Q 2 v 190, it is stated that 'fight in the cause of Allah those who fight you, but do not transgress limits; for Allah loveth not transgressors'. This verse reinforces the earlier verse. It was revealed a year after Prophet Muḥammad migrated from Mecca to Madina.[88] In Q 2 v 191, it is stated further that Muslims can engage anyone in war, be they Christians, Jews or pagans, as long as they fight Muslims. However, Muslims can only engage those who engage them in war, implying that only combatants can be fought while non-combatants

[83] Article 50 of the Constitution provides that 'A person given constitutional shelter shall be granted an equal right of life protection as long as he commits no harm and does not act treacherously.'

[84] Shah (2008), p. 15.

[85] Shah (2008), p. 15.

[86] Shah (2008), p. 15.

[87] Shah (2008), p. 15.

[88] Shah (2008), p. 15.

cannot.[89] In Q 4 v 75, it is stated thus: 'And why should ye not fight in the cause of Allah and of those who, being weak, are ill-treated (and oppressed)?—Men, women and children, whose cry is: "Our Lord! Rescue us from this town, whose people are oppressors; and raise for us from Thee one who will protect; and raise for us from Thee one who will help."' This verse is different from that of Q 22 v 39 for two reasons. The first reason is that this verse allows collective self-defence. The second reason is that it allows intervention on humanitarian ground. The intervention can be to protect not only Muslims but non-Muslims as well provided they believe in God.[90]

In fighting in self-defence, the principle of proportionality is recognised. It is provided that 'The recompense for an injury is an injury equal thereto (in degree): but if a person forgives and makes reconciliation, his reward is due from Allah'.[91] Similarly, it is stated that 'And if ye punish, let your punishment be proportionate to the wrong that has been done: But if ye show patience, that is indeed the best (course) for those who are patient'.[92] It is also stated that 'fight in the cause of Allah those who fight you, but do not transgress limits'.[93] The injunction that limits should not be transgressed implies proportionality.

Fighting in self-defence comes to an end when any of the two conditions recognised in Islam comes to an end. The first one is when there is peace. The second one is where there is no more oppression. In Q 2 v 193, it is stated thus: 'And fight them on until there is no more persecution and the religion becomes Allah's. But if they cease, let there be no hostility except to those who practise oppression.' Similarly, it is stated in Q 8 v 39 that 'fight them on until there is no more persecution and religion becomes Allah's in its entirety; but if they cease, verily Allah doth see all that they do'. While Q 2 v 193 may be considered specific to the event in question, the use of the word 'entirety' in Q 8 v 39 makes the verse general.[94] Since hostility comes to an end only when 'there is no more persecution', the implication is that there must be peace as a condition precedent to bringing hostility to an end. In Q 8 v 61, it is stated that 'But if the enemy incline towards peace, do thou (also) incline towards peace, and trust in Allah'. Also, in Q 4 v 90, it is stated that 'If they withdraw from you but fight you not, and (instead) send you (Guarantees of) peace, then Allah Hath opened no way for you (to war against them)'. In the same vein, since hostility comes to an end except when the practice of oppression continues, the implication is that oppression must have been phased out before hostility can be ceased.

In bringing hostility to an end, the Qur'an recognises two categories of people. The first category is those who keep their covenants, while the second category is those who do not. Muslims are to keep their covenants with those who keep their

[89] Shah (2008), p. 15.

[90] Shah (2008), pp. 15–16.

[91] Q 42 v 40.

[92] Q 16 v 126.

[93] Q 2 v 190.

[94] Shah (2008), p. 17.

covenants with them, while Muslims are not obliged to keep their covenants with those who will not keep theirs with them. In Q 9 v 8, it is stated that 'How (can there be such a covenant), seeing that if they get an advantage over you, they respect not in you the ties either of kinship or of covenant?' Thus, Muslims are not to bring hostility to an end with those who would not war against them only when they do not have an upper hand in hostility. In Q 9 v 7, it is stated that 'those with whom ye made a treaty near the sacred Mosque? As long as these stand true to you, stand ye true to them'.

Where Muslims see insincerity on the part of the enemy, they are to reject their covenants. Thus, in Q 8 v 58, it is stated that 'If thou fearest treachery from any group, throw back (their covenant) to them, (so as to be) on equal terms'. The Qur'an then adds in verse 8 v 60 that 'Against them make ready your strength to the utmost of your power, including steeds of war, to strike terror into (the hearts of) the enemies'.

10.4.2 The Competent Authority to Declare the Use of Force

The competent authority who may declare war in self-defence was Prophet Muhammad in his lifetime and Muslim leaders after his demise, who may be the Imam or the Caliph in the traditional Muslim community. In the Qur'an, it is stated thus: 'O Messenger, rouse the Believers to the fight.'[95] It is also stated in the Qur'an thus: 'O ye who believe! Obey Allah, and obey the Messenger, and those charged with authority among you.'[96] The issue of declaration of war is one of public safety, and it must be referred to the Prophet in his lifetime or those charged with authority after his demise. According to the Qur'an, 'When there comes to them some matter touching (public) safety or fear, they divulge it. If they had only referred it to the Messenger or to those charged with authority among them; the proper investigators would have known it from them (direct).'[97]

Since the Prophet is no longer alive, the necessary implication is that only those who are charged with authority among Muslims can declare war. Thus, in an Islamic state, only those charged with authority can declare war. Where 'those who are charged with authority' fail to act when the situation calls for war and the Muslim community withdraws its trust, then the withdrawal of the trust removes them from the category of 'those charged with authority' as they can be considered lacking in the requisite authority. Since there must not be a vacuum in governance, certain leaders in the Muslim community will almost always act, and once they have the necessary public trust, then they become 'those charged with authority'. Therefore,

[95] Q 8 v 65.
[96] Q 4 v 59.
[97] Q 4 v 83.

'non-state actors' cannot declare war in Islam since the necessary public trust must be present together with the existence of a state.[98]

10.4.3 Aggressive War in Islam

In the light of the preceding analysis, it can be seen that only defensive war is acceptable in Islam. However, some scholars in the exercise of qiyas are of the view that aggressive war as an expression of Jihad is Islamic. The two prominent scholars in modern time who project this view are Sayyid A'la Maududi[99] and Sayyid Qutb.[100] Their position is that Islamic message is meant for mankind and that it is the duty of every Muslim to spread it using force if necessary. The defensive war is only meant to preserve Muslims and consolidate their power, and once the power is consolidated, Muslims can advance to spread Islam.[101] They rely on Q 3 v 110, Q 3 v 104 and Q 22 v 41. Q 3 v 110 states that 'Ye are the best of peoples, evolved for mankind, enjoining what is right, forbidding what is wrong, and believing in Allah'. Q 3 v 104 adds that 'Let there arise out of you a band of people inviting to all that is good, enjoining what is right, and forbidding what is wrong', while Q 22 v 41 states that '(They are) those who, if We establish them in the land, establish regular prayer and give Zakat, enjoin the right and forbid wrong'. Thus, the duty of enjoining what is good and forbidding what is wrong translates to spreading Islam by force.

However, their position is unacceptable on three grounds. The first one is that their interpretation of the above verses is out of context.[102] The second reason is that Islam has its elaborate rules on spreading Islam, which does not include force.[103] The third one is that their interpretation is against Islamic code of armed conflict.[104] The above verses were revealed to the Prophet in comparing Muslims with the People of the Book (Christians and Jews who follow divine scriptures). The People of the Book had failed to enjoin what was good and forbid what was evil, and strife and dissension resulted. Muslims were therefore compared with them. Thus, an ideal Islamic community would not be beset with strife since they are enjoining what is good and forbidding what is wrong.[105] The elaborate rules on spreading Islam are contained in Q 2 v 256, Q 16 v 125 and Q 18 v 29. Q 2 v 256 states thus: 'Let there be no compulsion in religion.' Q 16 v 125 adds that 'Invite all to the way of thy Lord with wisdom and beautiful preaching; and argue with them in ways that

---

[98] Shah (2008), p. 23.

[99] Maududi (1996).

[100] Qutb (2003).

[101] Maududi (1996), pp. 85–149 cited in Shah (2008), p. 24; Qutb (2003), pp. 18–36 cited in Shah (2008), p. 24.

[102] Shah (2008), p. 25.

[103] Shah (2008), p. 25.

[104] Shah (2008), p. 25.

[105] Shah (2008), pp. 25–26.

are best and most gracious', while Q 18 v 29 concludes thus: 'Say, "[t]he truth is from your Lord": Let him who will believe, and let him who will reject (it).' With these, nowhere is the use of force advocated and sanctioned.[106] Lastly, the provisions on defensive war earlier discussed negate the position of Maududi and Qutb.[107]

Sometimes reliance is placed on the injunctions of the Qur'an in verse 3:28 and 8:73 to justify the aggressive use of force in Islam. Q 3 v 28 states as follows:

> Let not the believers take for friends or helpers Unbelievers rather than believers: if any do that, shall have no relation left with Allah except by way of precaution, that ye may Guard yourselves from them. But Allah cautions you (To fear) Himself; for the final goal is to Allah.

In the same vein, Q 8 v 73 states as follows:

> The Unbelievers are protectors, one of another: Unless ye do this, (protect each other), there would be tumult and oppression on earth, and great mischief.

The above-quoted verses were revealed to the Prophet when Muslims were at war with the Christians and Jews. These verses may not necessarily apply in time of peace.[108] In fact, the Qur'an removes the obligation to protect other Muslims who did not join then in war. In Q 8 v 72, it is stated thus:

> Those who believed, and emigrated, and fought for the Faith, with their property and their persons, in the cause of Allah, as well as those who gave (them) asylum and aid,-these are (all) friends and protectors, one of another. As to those who believed but did not emigrate, ye owe no duty of protection to them until they emigrate; but if they seek your aid in religion, it is your duty to help them, except against a people with whom ye have a treaty of mutual alliance. And (remember) Allah seeth all that ye do.

Further, Q 5 v 5 buttresses the position that the above quotations were war-time message. In this verse, it is stated thus:

[106] Shah (2008), pp. 26–27.

[107] In addition, the stipulations of the Quran in 9 v 4, 60 v 8, 9 v 5, 60 v 9, 2 v 191 and 2 v 217 reinforce the preceding discussion. They are as follows: Q 9 v 4: '(But the treaties are) not dissolved with those Pagans with whom ye have entered into alliance and who have not subsequently failed you in aught, nor aided any one against you. So fulfil your engagements with them to the end of their term: for Allah loveth the righteous.' Q 60 v 8: 'Allah forbids you not, with regard to those who fight you not for (your) Faith nor drive you out of your homes, from dealing kindly and justly with them: for Allah loveth those who are just.' Q 9 v 6: 'If one amongst the Pagans asks thee for asylum, grant it to him, so that he may hear the word of Allah. And then escort him to where he can be secure.' Q 60 v 9: 'Allah only forbids you, with regard to those who fight you for (your) Faith, and drive you out of your homes, and support (others) in driving you out, from turning to them (for friendship and protection). It is such as turn to them (in these circumstances), that do wrong.' Q 2 v 191: 'And slay them wherever ye catch them, and turn them out from where they have turned you out; for persecution is worse than slaughter; but fight them not at the Sacred Mosque, unless they (first) fight you there; but if they fight you, slay them.' Q 2 v 217: 'They ask thee concerning fighting in the Prohibited Month. Say: 'Fighting therein is a grave (offence); but graver is it in the sight of Allah to prevent access to the path of Allah, to deny Him, to prevent access to the Sacred Mosque, and drive out its members.' Tumult and oppression are worse than slaughter. Nor will they cease fighting you until they turn you back from your faith if they can.'

[108] Shah (2008), p. 29.

> The food of the People of the Book is lawful unto you and yours is lawful unto them. (Lawful unto you in marriage) are (not only) chaste women who are believers, but chaste women among the People of the Book, revealed before your time.

Therefore, if Allah had wanted non-Muslims to be subdued, it would have been clearly stated and there would not have been any need for the above provisions.

Seeing the incompatibility of the Qur'anic message that only war of self-defence is permitted in contradistinction with that of aggressive war, the advocates of aggressive war seek to justify their position through the doctrine of abrogation.[109] According to them, the verses in support of aggressive war have abrogated those of self-defence. In considering the plausibility of this argument, it is pertinent to consider what the Qur'an itself says about abrogation. According to the Qur'an, 'None of Our revelations do we abrogate or cause to be forgotten, but We substitute something better or similar'.[110] Also, whenever the Qur'an intends to repeal a rule, it is clearly stated.[111] A good example of abrogation is where Muslims face while praying. Initially, Muslims used to face Jerusalem. Later, the Prophet received revelation that Muslims should be facing Qibla, and since then Muslims have been facing Qibla.[112] In the same vein, Qur'an indicated that punishment for lewdness would be made known in future.[113] The said punishment was later made known.[114] In the light of the position of the Qur'an on abrogation, it is difficult to sustain the argument that the aggressive use of force has abrogated the use of force only in self-defence. The verses relied upon do not support the aggressive use of force, nor are they sufficiently clear in support of aggressive use of war.

Similar to the doctrine of abrogation is the suggestion that the Qur'an is self-contradictory. Thus, the Qur'an is speaking from both mouths in allowing the use of force in self-defence only and at the same time in allowing the aggressive use of force.[115] On self-contradiction, the Qur'an absolves itself. The Qur'an says of itself thus: 'Do they not ponder on the Qur'an? Had it been from other than Allah, they would surely have found therein much discrepancy.'[116] Similarly, the Qur'an declares that 'Allah has revealed (from time to time) the most beautiful Message in the form of a Book, consistent with itself, (yet) repeating (its teaching in various aspects)'.[117] In the light of the preceding analysis, it can be seen that the Qur'an allows the use of force only in self-defence and outlaws the aggressive use of force. Therefore, there is no contradiction.

---

[109] Shah (2008), p. 35.

[110] Q 2 v 106.

[111] Q 16 v 89.

[112] Q 2 v 142.

[113] Q 4 v 15.

[114] Q 24 v 2.

[115] Shah (2008), p. 42.

[116] Q 4 v 82.

[117] Q 39 v 23.

10.4.4 *The Conduct of War (Islamic* **Jus in Bello***)*

Once war has been declared, Muslims are enjoined to fight.[118] However, there are rules to be observed in fighting the war so declared. The rules regulating how war is to be fought are founded on the principles of military necessity, distinction, proportionality, humanity and accepting an offer of peace during armed conflict.[119]

War is only permitted to the extent justified by military necessity. In the Qur'an, it is stipulated thus: 'And fight them on until there is no more persecution, and the religion becomes Allah's. But if they cease, let there be no hostility except to those who practise oppression.'[120] Similarly, it is declared that 'And slay them wherever ye catch them, and turn them out from where they have turned you out; for persecution is worse than slaughter; but fight them not at the Sacred Mosque, unless they (first) fight you there; but if they fight you, slay them'.[121] Further, it is stated in the Qur'an that 'if they cease, Allah is Oft-forgiving, Most Merciful'[122] and that 'The prohibited month for the prohibited month,—and so for all things prohibited, –there is the law of equality. If then anyone transgresses the prohibition against you, transgress ye likewise against him…'.[123]

The military necessity is reflected in the use of the clause 'if they fight you' or 'if they cease'. Thus, military necessity comes to the fore if they fight Muslims, and once those who fight them cease, military necessity comes to an end.[124] Also, military necessity is to bring an end to persecution. Limitation is also imposed with respect to place by forbidding Muslims to fight at the Sacred Mosque, while limitation as to time is in forbidding Muslims to fight during the holy month.[125] The Sunnah of the Prophet shows deference for military necessity. At a time, the Prophet sent a military expedition against the tribe of Banu Qazagh camped at the outskirt of Medina so as to attack Medina. These people fled immediately when they saw the Muslim forces. The Muslim forces did not, however, chase them as the objective of

[118] 'Will ye not fight people who violated their oaths, plotted to expel the Messenger, and attacked you first?': Q 9 v 13; 'When ye meet the Unbelievers (in fight), smite at their necks; At length, when ye have thoroughly subdued them, bind (the captives) firmly: therefore (is the time for) either generosity or ransom: Until the war lays down its burdens.'. Q 47 v 4; 'But when the forbidden months are past, then fight and slay the Pagans wherever ye find them, and seize them, beleaguer them, and lie in wait for them in every stratagem (of war); but if they repent, and establish regular prayers and pay Zakat, then open the way for them: for Allah is Oft-forgiving, Most Merciful.': Q 9 v 5; 'But the Messenger, and those who believe with him, strive and fight with their wealth and their persons: for them are (all) good things: and it is they who will prosper.': Q 9 v 88; 'But those who are slain in the Way of Allah—He will never let their deeds be lost.': Q 47 v 4.

[119] Shah (2011), p. 33.

[120] Q 2 v 193.

[121] Q 2 v 191.

[122] Q 2 v 192.

[123] Q 2 v 194.

[124] Shah (2011), pp. 33–34.

[125] Shah (2011), p. 34.

warding off their attack was already achieved.[126] In the same vein, the people of Zeeqard ran away on seeing the Muslim forces. Meanwhile, the Muslim forces had realised that they had run out of water and wanted to pursue them. However, Prophet Muhammad forbade them and told them to show compassion once the enemy is subdued.[127]

Islamic law makes a distinction between combatants and non-combatants. In Q 2 v 190, Muslims are enjoined to 'fight in the cause of Allah those who fight you, but do not transgress limits'. The necessary implication of this verse is that only those who fight against Muslims are Muslims permitted to fight against. Therefore, children, women, the aged and the civilian community who are not engaged in war cannot be fought against. In the days of the Prophet, many tribes used to build forts by using children as shields. When the Prophet was asked about the practice, he responded that the combatants should be targeted by using arrow, while the children being used as forts should be left out.[128] Although collateral damage to non-military targets is acceptable, nonetheless making a distinction between military and non-military target is the rule.[129]

The principle of proportionality can be found in Q 16 v 126, where it is stated that 'And if ye punish, let your punishment be proportionate to the wrong that has been done to you: but if ye show patience, that is indeed the best (course) for those who are patient'.[130] The Sunnah of the Prophet in the battle of Uhud (3 AH) shows deference to this principle. The Prophet's uncle was killed during the battle, and his liver was thereafter chewed by his assailant. The Prophet swore to kill 30 or 70 in retaliation. Fighters who were following the Prophet also swore to cut their enemies into pieces. This verse was then revealed to the Prophet to curb any excess.[131] This Sunnah of the Prophet can also be interpreted as prohibiting mutilation. Q 16 v 126 also lays down the foundation for the principle of humanity. Thus, by forbidding more harm than is necessary, humanity still subsists in war. Similarly, by prohibiting mutilation, humanity is respected.[132]

The Qur'an enjoins Muslims to accept an offer of peace. In Q 8 v 61, it is stated that 'if the enemy incline towards peace, do thou (also) incline towards peace'. It has been suggested that even if the offer of peace is to deceive, it should still be accepted since the intents of the enemy could not be ascertained unless and until a clear, objective and outward show of deceit is manifested.[133] This verse also justifies

---

[126] Shah (2011), p. 34.

[127] Shah (2011), p. 34.

[128] Shah (2011), p. 35.

[129] Shah (2011), p. 35.

[130] See also Q 40 v 40: 'He that works evil will not be requited but by the like thereof.' And Q 42 v 40: 'The recompense for an injury is an injury equal thereto (in degree): but if a person forgives and makes reconciliation, his reward is due from Allah: for (Allah) loveth not those who do wrong.' However, Q 16 v 126 is most apt since it specifically refers to causing harm in conflict.

[131] Shah (2011), pp. 35–36.

[132] See also Q 2 v 213; Q 17 v 70; Q 95 v 4.

[133] Ali (1989), p. 429.

abstaining from the killing of the wounded. Once the wounded surrender after having become incapacitated, their killing is prohibited. It does not matter that they may resume hostility once they are healed. It is sufficient once they make an outward offer of peace.

Apart from the above basic principles, the Qur'an and the Sunnah of the Prophet also have elaborate rules prohibiting genocide or crimes against humanity, war crimes, the maltreatment and killing of war captives, the destruction of the environment, the killing of hostages, obeying unlawful commands and the use of child soldiers. Qur'an prohibits genocide or crimes against humanity by stipulating that 'if any one slew a person—unless it be for murder or for spreading mischief in the land—it would be as if he slew the whole people: and if any one saved a life, it would be as if he saved the life of the whole people'.[134] However, some by their interpretation of the Qur'an have implied the justification of genocide[135] or crimes against humanity. Their argument is that the use of force was first prohibited in Mecca[136] then permitted in self-defence in Medina[137] and then permitted to be used against all non-Muslims at all times.[138] Their argument is that Q 9 v 5 and Q 9 v 29 had repealed Q 22 v 39 and Q 2 v 190.[139] Q 22 v 39 stipulates as follows:

> To those against whom war is made, permission is given (to fight), because they are wronged; – and verily Allah is Most Powerful for their aid.

And Q 2 v 190 stipulates:

> Fight in the cause of Allah those who fight you, but do not transgress limits; for Allah loveth not transgressors.

---

[134] Q 5 v 32.

[135] Shah (2011), p. 38.

[136] They rely on the following verses: 'The blame is only against those who oppress men with wrong-doing and insolently transgress beyond bounds through the land, defying right and justice: for such there will be a Chastisement grievous': Q 42 v 42; 'But indeed if any show patience and forgive, that would truly be an affair of great resolution': Q 42 v 43;'Those who persevere in patience, and put their trust in their Lord and Cherisher': Q 29 v 59; 'Quite a number of the people of the Book wish they could turn you (people) back to infidelity after ye have believed, from selfish envy, after the truth hath become manifest unto them: But forgive and overlook, till Allah brings out His command': Q 2 v 109.

[137] They rely on the following verses: 'To those against whom war is made, permission is given (to fight), because they are wronged-and verily Allah is Most Powerful for their aid': Q 22 v 39; '(They are) those who have been expelled from their homes in defiance of right,-(for no cause) except that they say "Our Lord is Allah". ..Allah will certainly aid those who aid His (cause): Q 22 v 40; 'Fight in the cause of Allah those who fight you, but do not transgress limits; for. Allah loveth not transgressors': Q 2 v 190.

[138] They rely on the following verses: 'But when the forbidden months are past, then fight and slay the Pagans wherever you find them, and seize them, beleaguer them, and lie in wait for them in every stratagem (of war); but if they repent, and establish regular prayers, and pay Zakat, then open the way for them: for Allah is Oft-forgiving, Most Merciful': Q 9 v 5; 'Fight those who believe not in Allah nor the Last Day, nor hold that forbidden which hath been forbidden by Allah and His Messenger, nor acknowledge the Religion of Truth, from among the People of the Book, until they pay the Jizya with willing submission and feel themselves subdued.': Q 9 v 29.

[139] Shah (2011), p. 38.

On the other hand, Q 9 v 5 provides:

> But when the forbidden months are past, then fight and slay the Pagans wherever you find them, and seize them, beleaguer them, and lie in wait for them in every stratagem (of war); but if they repent, and establish regular prayers, and pay Zakat, then open the way for them: for Allah is Oft-forgiving, Most Merciful.

And Q 9 v 29 stipulates:

> Fight those who believe not in Allah nor the Last Day, nor hold that forbidden which hath been forbidden by Allah and His Messenger, nor acknowledge the Religion of Truth, from among the People of the Book, until they pay the Jizya with willing submission and feel themselves subdued.

What is, however, missing in this argument in support of genocide or crimes against humanity is that the Qur'an is quoted out of context. Q 9 v 5 was revealed to the Prophet in dealing with polytheists who broke their peace treaty with the Prophet, specifically the Quraysh, who broke the treaty of Hudaybiyya. The verse does not lay down any new rule for conducting war.[140] A complete reading of chapter 9 from verses 1 to 29 reinforces this argument.[141] With respect to Q 9 v 29, it was revealed when attack from Byzantine was imminent.[142] After the revelation of the verses that some have relied upon to justify genocide or crimes against humanity, the Sunnah of the Prophet also lends credence to the fact that non-Muslims were not killed: the people of Jarba and Adhruh who did not embrace Islam had a peace treaty with the Prophet.[143]

War crimes were also punished during the days of the Prophet. Khalid bin Walid at the earliest period of the attack on Mecca (8 AH) killed a number of people who would not have been killed due to misunderstanding. The Prophet ordered that compensation for their blood should be paid. In fact, compensation was also paid for a dog.[144] It should be noted that murder is treated as a crime and a tort at the same time in Islamic law and that once payment is made, retaliation by way of punishment is

[140] Shah (2011), p. 41.

[141] See some of the most germane verses: 'A (declaration) of immunity from Allah and His Messenger to those of the Pagans with whom ye have contracted mutual alliances': Q 9 v 1; 'Go ye, then for 4 months, (as ye will) throughout the land, but know yet that ye cannot frustrate Allah (by your falsehood) but that Allah will cover with shame those who reject Him': Q 9 v 2; 'And on announcement from Allah and His Messenger, to the people (assembled) on the day of the Great Pilgrimage,-, that Allah and His Messenger dissolve (treaty) obligations with the Pagans. If, then, ye repent, it were best for you; but if ye turn away, know ye that ye cannot frustrate Allah, And proclaim a grievous chastisement to those who reject faith": Q 9 v 3; '(But the treaties are) not dissolved with those Pagans with whom ye have entered into alliance and who have not subsequently failed you in aught, nor aided any one against you. So fulfil your engagements with them to the end of their term': Q 9 v 4; 'How can there be a covenant before Allah and His Messenger, with the Pagans, except those with whom ye made a treaty near the Sacred Mosque? As long as these stand true to you, stand ye true to them': Q 9 v 7.

[142] Shah (2011), p. 41.

[143] Shah (2011), p. 43.

[144] Shah (2011), p. 44.

foreclosed.[145] Also, the dichotomy between a civil wrong and a criminal wrong as it obtains in modern time did not exist at the time. In addition, such legal terms as war crimes and crimes against humanity were not in use generally, nor were they in use specifically in Islamic law.[146]

War captives are not to be killed. According to the Qur'an, 'Therefore, when ye meet the Unbelievers (in fight), smite at their necks; at length when ye have thoroughly subdued them, bind (the captives) firmly: therefore (is the time for) either generosity or ransom; until the war lays down its burdens'.[147] Going by the above stipulation, war captives can only be released as an act of generosity or after ransom has been received. That war captives are not to be killed is further strengthened in the Qur'an where reference is made to those who 'feed, for the love of Allah, the indigent, the orphan, and the captive'.[148] It has, however, been suggested that the above verse has been repealed by verse 8:67.[149] Verse 8:67 states that 'It is not fitting for a Prophet that he should have prisoners of war until he hath thoroughly subdued the land. Ye look for the temporal goods of this world; but Allah looketh to the Hereafter.'

The point is that verse 8:67 was revealed before verse 47:4, which lays down the rule for the treatment of war captives. Verse 8:67 was revealed in 2 AH (after Hijrah), whereas verse 47:4 was revealed 1 AH. Even if there is any repeal, it is verse 47:4 that can be said to have repealed verse 8:67, not the other way round.[150] However, there is no repeal. The correct position is that verse 8:67 was revealed when the Prophet consulted his companions on what to be done to war captives taken during the battle of Badr. Some suggested killing them, while some suggested releasing them on ransom. The Prophet acted on the advice that they should be released on ransom. Verse 8:67 was then revealed to the Prophet warning Muslims about engaging in Jihad for material gains.[151] In fact, verse 8:68 states that 'Had it not been for a previous ordainment from Allah, a severe punishment would have reached you for the (ransom) that ye took', while verse 8:69 states that 'but (now) enjoy what ye took in war, lawful and good'. The purport of these two verses is that verse 8:68 refers to the earlier decree of Allah, which is verse 47:4, permitting taking ransom, while verse 8:69 emphasises its lawfulness. It should, however, be borne in mind that ransom should not be for financial gains but for genuine war reason. This is the essence of the message in Q 8 v 67.[152]

The Sunnah of the Prophet after the revelation of verse 8:67 also does not suggest that war captives were killed except on one occasion.[153] In this instance, there was a

145 El-Awa (2000), pp. 83–85.
146 Shah (2011), p. 44.
147 Q 47 v 4.
148 Q 76 v 8.
149 Shah (2011), p. 45.
150 Shah (2011), p. 45.
151 Shah (2011), p. 45.
152 Shah (2011), p. 45.
153 Shah (2011), p. 45.

peace treaty between Muslims and Banu Qarayza. The tenor of the agreement was that both would not only wage war against the other; they would also not support anyone who waged war against the other. However, Banu Qarayza supported the Quraysh in the battle of Khandaq against the Muslims. After this battle, the Muslims laid siege against Banu Qarayza. Banu Qarayza later surrendered and asked the Prophet to decide their fate. Sad bin Muadh was then appointed to decide their fate, and he decided to kill all adult males and took their property as war booty.[154] It has been suggested that Sad bin Muadh acted according to the applicable Jewish law, which is Deuteronomy 20 v 10–14. Banu Qarayza is a Jewish tribe, and the Qur'an permits the application of Jewish law to the Jews.[155]

Q 33 v 50 states that 'O Prophet! We have made lawful to thee thy wives to whom thou hast paid their dowers; and those whom thy right hand possesses, out of the captives of war'. The above verse allows the Prophet to have sexual intercourse with his wives and war captives. This verse is specific to the Prophet and does not apply to Muslims in general.[156] However, there is no single instance where the Prophet had intercourse with any woman without having first married her.[157] Muslims in general are enjoined to 'guard their modesty',[158] though not from 'those joined to them in the marriage bond, or (the captives) whom their right hands possess,—for (in their case) they are free from blame'.[159] 'But those whose desires exceed those limits are transgressors.'[160] Those whom their right hands possess referred to here are normal slaves and not war captives.[161] The reason is that this verse was revealed in Mecca, which was the time Muslims were not permitted to wage war. Muslims were only permitted to wage war after the Prophet migrated to Medina.[162] Later, Muslims were permitted to marry slave girls who were initially war captives but who were shared as war booty to their owners and became slaves.[163] This verse was revealed in Medina indicating that Muslims cannot have sexual intercourse with war captives. Thus, war captives must not be maltreated.

There is, however, an instance where Muslims had sexual intercourse with war captives.[164] After the battle of Mer Yaseegh, the tribe of Mustalq was defeated, and some Muslims wanted to have sexual intercourse with women who were captured. In order not to have them impregnated, these Muslims practised withdrawal method with them. However, the Prophet was reported to have said that a soul destined to be

[154] Shah (2011), pp. 45–46.
[155] See Q 5 v 48.
[156] Shah (2011), p. 46.
[157] Shah (2011), p. 46.
[158] Q 23 v 5.
[159] Q 23 v 6.
[160] Q 70 v 31; see also Q 23 v 7.
[161] Shah (2011), p. 47.
[162] Shah (2011), p. 47.
[163] Q 4 v 25.
[164] Shah (2011), p. 47.

born would still be born irrespective of the practice.[165] This saying of the Prophet has been considered by some as tacitly legalising having sexual intercourse with female captives.[166] However, it should be borne in mind that the Prophet himself did not do it; it is an isolated event, and the issue of the legality of having sexual intercourse with female captives was not in issue. Rather, what was in issue was the practice of withdrawal method.[167] Perhaps the most important point is that the verse prohibiting having sexual intercourse outside marriage was revealed after this incident.[168]

The environment is protected during war, and no damage to it is allowed unless it is absolutely necessary. Thus, 'Whatever ye cut down (O ye Muslims) of the tender palm-trees, or ye left them standing on their roots, it was by leave of Allah'.[169] There was once a man called Akhan who used to attack Muslims. One day, while he was passing by the farm of a Muslim, he set the farm on fire and killed all the cattle in the farm. Thus, the Qur'an states: 'When he turns his back, his aim everywhere is to spread mischief through the earth and destroy crops and progeny but Allah loveth not mischief.'[170] In the days of the Prophet, poisoning water was used as war strategy. However, the Prophet never practised it, although He had blocked the supply of water to the enemy in certain instances.[171]

It is stated in the Qur'an that no one shall bear the burden of others.[172] Thus, hostages were never killed even where the enemy had killed Muslims hostages.[173] Similarly, even where there is an agreement that hostages could be killed for the guilt of others, Muslims are still precluded from killing hostages.[174] During the prophetic era, hostages could be exchanged as a sign of showing good faith in fulfilling a treaty. An enemy emissary cannot be turned into a hostage, and he or she would be allowed to deliver his or her message and return to the sending authority.[175]

Each person is criminally responsible for his or her conduct. Thus, the Qur'an states that 'Nor can a bearer of burdens bear another's burden'[176] and that 'whoever works evil will be requited accordingly'.[177] The Qur'an also adds that 'whoever works righteousness benefits his own soul; whoever works evil, it is against his own

[165] Shah (2011), p. 47.
[166] Shah (2011), p. 47.
[167] Shah (2011), p. 47.
[168] Q 24 v 1–4.
[169] Q 59 v 5.
[170] Q 2 v 205.
[171] Shah (2011), p. 50.
[172] Q 17 v 15: 'No bearer of burdens can bear the burden of another'; Q 35 v 18: 'Nor can a bearer of burdens bear another's burden. If one heavily laden should call another to (bear) his load, not the least portion of it can be carried (by the other) even though he be nearly related.'
[173] Shah (2011), p. 53.
[174] Shah (2011), p. 53.
[175] Shah (2011), p. 53.
[176] Q 35 v 18.
[177] Q 4 v 123.

soul'.[178] Since each person bears his or her criminal responsibility, it follows that unlawful orders are not to be obeyed.

Using children as soldiers is prohibited in Islam. The minimum age for enlistment is 15 years. A 14-year-old boy called Ibn Omer requested the Prophet to allow him to participate in the battle of Uhud (3 AH), but the Prophet refused him. A year later, when he was 15 years of age, he was permitted to participate in the battle of Khandaq (4 AH).[179]

10.5 Incompatibility of the Insurgent Activities of Boko Haram in the Light of Islamic *Jus ad Bellum* and Islamic *Jus in Bello*

Boko Haram insurgent activities will first be examined in the light of Islamic *jus ad bellum*. Thereafter, its activities will be examined in the light of Islamic *jus in bello*.

10.5.1 Boko Haram and Islamic Jus ad Bellum

Considering the earlier discussion, Islamic *jus ad bellum* can be summarised as follows: the use of force in Islam is solely for defence. Even when it is to be used in defence, it must have been dictated by a situation of extreme urgency. This can be gleaned from the fact that the Prophet did not have recourse to the use of force until after 13 years of persecution. In fact, the Prophet had to leave Mecca and migrated to Medina so as to avoid persecution, which suggests that retreat may be the first rule before resisting attack. While acting in self-defence, Muslims must observe the principle of proportionality. Fighting in self-defence comes to an end whenever there is peace or when there is no more persecution. Where the other party shows the tendency of negotiating peace, then Muslims too should be willing to negotiate. In negotiating peace, Muslims should only keep their covenants with those who will only keep theirs, not with those who will not when they have a military advantage. When there is manifest insincerity on the part of the other party, Muslims should openly reject any treaty arrangement. Non-state actors cannot declare war in Islam.

Boko Haram is a non-state actor and thus cannot declare war. This renders all their actions un-Islamic. Although the killing of Muhammed Yusuf, the then leader of Boko Haram, is deplorable, a retaliatory response by way of military action could only be taken by the Muslim community in Nigeria. Even if Boko Haram can declare war, the killing of Muhammed Yusuf alone cannot be considered sufficient. While the actions of the Nigerian government culminating in the killing of

---

178 Q 41 v 46.

179 Shah (2011), p. 52.

Mohammad Yusuf in 2009 may be somewhat considered underhanded, it does not appear that it had reached the situation of extreme urgency that could justify the use of force by Boko Haram. Of course, actions of Boko Haram before 2009 were also far from being without blame. Truce called by the Federal Government can be considered an offer of peace,[180] and failure of Boko Haram to embrace it is un-Islamic. The Federal Government should have been allowed to openly demonstrate insincerity before rejecting it. Since the Federal Government made an offer of peace at a time, it can be said that hostility on the part of Boko Haram is not justified since peace is a condition that automatically brings hostility to an end. The use of suicide bombers can be said to violate the principle of proportionality. The Nigerian Government, before having recourse to full military action, was initially using the Nigeria Police, which was only making use of guns. Thus, Boko Haram should have waited first for the Nigerian Government to use bombs before it had recourse to its use. Against Islamic *jus ad bellum*, Boko Haram activities fail.

10.5.2 Boko Haram and Islamic Jus in Bello

Going by the preceding discussion, Islamic *jus in bello* can be summarised as follows: once the Muslim community has declared war, there are rules to be observed in fighting the war so declared. The rules regulating how war is to be fought are founded on the principles of military necessity, distinction, proportionality, humanity and accepting an offer of peace during armed conflict. One of the situations that can bring about military necessity is when Muslims are attacked. Muslims cannot fight during the holy month (Ramadan) or near the Sacred Mosque (Ka'ba) except when it is absolutely necessary. Only combatants can be attacked. Thus children, women, the aged and civilians cannot be attacked. The principle of proportionality must be respected. Where the enemy makes an offer of peace, Muslims too must embrace peace. Peace offer must not be rejected unless and until there is manifest insincerity on the part of the other party. The wounded cannot be killed. Forcing people to accept Islam and killing them if they fail to accept Islam is un-Islamic. War captives must not be maltreated or killed. Muslims cannot have sexual intercourse with war captives. Manifestly unlawful orders must not be obeyed. The use of child soldiers is un-Islamic. Minimum age to participate in hostility is 15 years. The environment is protected during war, and no damage to it is allowed unless it is absolutely necessary. The killing of hostages is un-Islamic. Each person is criminally responsible for his or her conduct.

Since non-state actors cannot declare war in Islam, it follows that fighting such war is itself un-Islamic since the legality of the mode of fighting must be rooted in the legality of the fight in the first place. Therefore, even if Boko Haram observes Islamic *jus in bello*, its activities will still be un-Islamic. Suppose that its fighting war is valid, Boko Haram's activities violate the principle of military necessity,

[180] On truce called by the Federal Government, see Pérouse de Montclos (2014), p. 29.

distinction, proportionality, humanity and accepting an offer of peace during armed conflict. As earlier said, at the time Boko Haram had recourse to war; the situation had not made it absolutely necessary. Killing civilians who are unconnected with the war violates the principle of distinction and humanity. In fact, the whole idea of insurgency with civilian targets violates this principle. The use of suicide bombing by the group at a time when the Nigerian Government was only making use of Police Force violates the principle of proportionality. Amnesty suggested by the Federal Government reflects an offer of peace, and failure of the group to take it is un-Islamic without having waited sufficiently for the insincerity of the Federal Government to be openly demonstrated. Killing Christians for their faith is un-Islamic. The use of child bombers is also un-Islamic. Taking women and girls (like the Chibok girls) as hostages by the group violates Islamic *jus in bello*. The marriage of Boko Haram captives to their tormentor is just to justify having sexual intercourse with them, and it is un-Islamic.

10.6 Conclusion

Boko Haram's ideology can be considered radical to the extent that it deviates from what is usual and traditional. What is usual and traditional is what is provided in the Qur'an and what the Prophet said or did as Sunnah. Boko Haram's condemnation of democracy is contrary to the use of Shūrā and ijmā and the Qur'anic injunction making ummah the vicegerent of Allah on earth. The condemnation of man-made law by Boko Haram overlooks the necessity of having had to make law to regulate human affairs in detail since the Qur'an generally lays down the principles except in some few instances where it has detailed provisions. Therefore, the so-called man-made laws are needed, although they must always have to be tested in the light of the Qur'an and the Sunnah. The traditional Muslim societies have always had rulers who were often absolute in their rule by way of decrees in spite of the existence of the Qur'an and Hadith.

To consider Western education as forbidden is contrary to the prophetic injunction that knowledge must be sought even in China, which was known as one of the farthest places from the Arabian Peninsula at the time where idolatry could be said to obtain. Contrary to the prohibition of the mixing of the sexes by Boko Haram, this is not the position in Islam as long as immorality is not occasioned. While Islam condemns the use of revealing attire, this is not what Western education essentially stands for, and there is no basis to reject Western education solely on the use of revealing attire. There is nothing to suggest that Darwin's theory is un-Islamic. At best, it is debatable in Islam. Meanwhile, evolutionary theory is even traditionally a product of Muslim scientists.[181]

The condemnation of the solar system, embryology, geography and sociology by Boko Haram strikes at the core of the conflict between science and Islam as a

[181] See n 73.

religion, and it has been found that both are compatible contrary to what obtains in the West. Similarly, the condemnation of these disciplines reflects the failure of the group to recognise the difference between the programme and the programmer. As regards taking an employment as a security agent, a police officer or a military officer under a democratic government, the Constitution of Madina authored by the Prophet of Islam provides that Muslims and the Jews can jointly protect the government in Madina contrary to the position maintained by Boko Haram suggesting prohibition of a joint cooperation of Muslims and non-Muslims on security issues in a common government.

Boko Haram activities can also be considered radical to the extent that they deviate from what is usual and traditional in Islamic *jus ad bellum* and Islamic *jus in bello* as laid down in the Qur'an and found in the Sunnah. The usual principles in Islamic *jus ad bellum* is that non-state actors cannot have recourse to the use of force, and where Muslim community has recourse to the use of force, it must be in self-defence and the situation must be absolutely necessary. Boko Haram as a non-state entity fails this test, and at the time it even had recourse to war, it was premature.

Islamic *jus in bello* recognises the principle of military necessity, distinction, humanity, proportionality and accepting an offer of peace during armed conflict. The insurgent activities of Boko Haram violate all these principles. Thus, its activities are incompatible with Islamic *jus in bello* and make the group radical for being unusual in what the Qur'an has laid down and in what are found in the Sunnah of the Prophet.

References

Abu-Dawud Sunan. http://islamicsystem.blogspot.com.ng/2006/07/shariah-rules-relating-to-mixing.html. Accessed 10 Jan 2016

Abu-Dawud Sunan. https://www.quora.com/Why-did-Muhammad-say-Seek-knowledge-even-unto-China. Accessed 10 Jan 2016

Ahmad Musnad. http://islamicsystem.blogspot.com.ng/2006/07/shariah-rules-relating-to-mixing.html. Accessed 10 Jan 2016

Al-Bukhari Sahih. http://islamicsystem.blogspot.com.ng/2006/07/shariah-rules-relating-to-mixing.html. Accessed 10 Jan 2016

Ali Y (1989) The meaning of the holy Quran. Amana Corporation, Maryland

Al-Jahiz (781-869 CE). The book of animals. http://www.ascertainthetruth.com/att/index.php/al-islam/al-islam-and-science/871-evolution-was-an-islamic-theory-before-darwin-was-even-born. Last accessed on 10 Jan 2016

Al-Nasa'i Sunan. http://islamicsystem.blogspot.com.ng/2006/07/shariah-rules-relating-to-mixing.html. Accessed 10 Jan 2016

Al-Shafi'I Musnad. http://islamicsystem.blogspot.com.ng/2006/07/shariah-rules-relating-to-mixing.html. Accessed 10 Jan 2016

Al-Tirmidhi Hadith. http://islamicsystem.blogspot.com.ng/2006/07/shariah-rules-relating-to-mixing.html. Accessed 10 Jan 2016

Al-Tirmidhi Hadith. https://www.quora.com/Why-did-Muhammad-say-Seek-knowledge-even-unto-China. Accessed 10 Jan 2016

Amnesty International (2015a) Amnesty international report 2014/15: the state of the world's human rights. Index: POL 10/001/2015. Amnesty International
Amnesty International (2015b) Our job is to shoot, slaughter and kill: Boko Haram's reign of terror in North-East Nigeria. April 2014 Index: AFR 44/1360/2015. Amnesty International
Amnesty International (2015c) Boko Haram: civilians continue to be at risk of human rights abuses by Boko Haram and human rights violations by state security forces. Written statement to the 30th session of the UN Human Rights Council. 14 September-2 October 2015 Index: AFR 44/2428/2015. Amnesty International
Amnesty International (2015d) Boko Haram: bombing campaign sees civilian deaths spiral. 24 September 2015 Index: 44/2490/2015. Amnesty International
Amy P (2014) Boko Haram: an assessment of strengths, vulnerabilities, and policy options. Report to the Strategic Multilayer Assessment Office, Department of Defense, and the Office of University Programs, Department of Homeland Security. National Consortium for the Study of Terrorism and Responses to Terrorism (START), College Park
BBC News Africa (30 April 2012) Deadly attack on Nigeria's Bayero university in Kano. http://www.bbc.co.uk/news/world-africa-17886143. Accessed 2 May 2012
Blanchard LP (2014) Nigeria's Boko Haram: frequently asked questions. Congressional Research Service Jun 10 2014
Bucaille M (Undated) The Bible, the Qur'an and science
Darwin C (1909) The origin of species. PF Collier & Son, New York
Draper W (1874) History of the Conflict between Religion and Science. D Appleton, New York
El-Awa MS (2000) Punishment in Islamic law: a comparative study. American Trust Publications, Plainfield
Epperson v Arkansas 393 U.S. 97 (1968)
Esposito JL, Voll JO (2001) Islam and democracy. Humanities, November/December 2001 vol 22/No 6
Faridah HJ Hassan Ibn Haldun and Jane Adams: the real father of sociology and the mother of social works. http://www2.uned.es/congreso-ibn-khaldun/pdf/04%20Faridah%20Hj%20Hassan.pdf. Accessed 7 Mar 2016
Human Rights Watch (2012) World report 2012: Nigeria. http://www.hrw.org/world-report-2012/world-report-2012-nigeria. Accessed 1 May 2012
Ibn Khaldun (1377 CE) The Muqadimma'. http://www.ascertainthetruth.com/att/index.php/al-islam/al-islam-and-science/871-evolution-was-an-islamic-theory-before-darwin-was-even-born. Accessed 10 Jan 2016
Ibn Majah Sunan. http://islamicsystem.blogspot.com.ng/2006/07/shariah-rules-relating-to-mixing.html. Accessed 10 Jan 2016
Ibn Miskawahy (932-1030). http://www.ascertainthetruth.com/att/index.php/al-islam/al-islam-and-science/871-evolution-was-an-islamic-theory-before-darwin-was-even-born. Accessed 10 Jan 2016
Institute for Economics and Peace (2014) Global terrorism index 2014: measuring and understanding the impact of terrorism. Institute for Economics and Peace
Malinova M (2013) Is Islam compatible with democracy? Center for Studies, Al Jazeera
Maududi SA (1996) Al-jihad fil-islam (Urdu). Lahore, Pakistan
Mohammed K (2014) The message and methods of Boko Haram. In: Pérouse de Montclos M-A (ed) Boko Haram: islamism, politics, security and the state in Nigeria. West African Politics and Society Series, vol 2. African Studies Centre, Leiden, p 15
Murthadā A (2013) Boko Harām in Nigeria: its beginnings, principles and activities in Nigeria. SalafiManhaj
Muslim Sahih. http://islamicsystem.blogspot.com.ng/2006/07/shariah-rules-relating-to-mixing.html. Accessed 10 Jan 2016
National Consortium for the Study of Terrorism and Responses to Terrorism (START) (May 2014) Background report: Boko Haram recent attacks. National Consortium for the Study of Terrorism and Responses to Terrorism (START)

Newman P (2013) The etymology of Hausa boko. Mega-Chad Research Network

Osman F (Undated) Islam in a modern state: democracy and the concept of shura. Occasional Paper Series Center for Muslim-Christian Understanding History and International Affairs. Edmund A Walsh School of Foreign Service Georgetown University Washington DC 20057

Pérouse de Montclos M-A (2014) Boko Haram and politics: from insurgency to terrorism. In: Pérouse de Montclos M-A (ed) Boko Haram: Islamism, politics, security and the state in Nigeria. West African Politics and Society Series, vol. 2. African Studies Centre, Leiden, p 143

Pérouse de Montclos M-A (2014) Nigeria's interminable insurgency? addressing the Boko Haram crisis. Africa Programme Sept 2014. Chatham House

Qutb S (2003) In the shade of the Quran, vol 8 & 9 (trans: M A Salahi). The Islamic Foundation, Leicester

Riyadh us-Saleheen. https://www.quora.com/Why-did-Muhammad-say-Seek-knowledge-even-unto-China. Accessed 10 Jan 2016

Shah NA (2008) Self-Defence in islamic and international law: assessing al-qaeda and the invasion of Iraq. Palgrave Macmillan, New York

Shah NA (2011) Islamic law and the law of armed conflict: the armed conflict in Pakistan. Routledge, Abingdon

The Constitution of Madina

Yusuf M (2009) Hazihi aqeedatun wa minhaju da'awatuna (This is our belief and method of call)

Chapter 11
Government Regulation of Freedom of Religion in a Democratic Society: Islamic Preaching Board Laws and Boko Haram in Nigeria

Ahmed Salisu Garba

11.1 Introduction

In reaction to the intensifying Boko Haram conflict, Borno and Katsina states in northern Nigeria amended and replaced their religious preaching board laws. Niger State's attempt to do a similar thing stopped at the public hearing stage because of protest by religious groups and activists at the venue of the public hearing in the state. Borno and Katsina states' attempts to enforce the laws were resisted by mostly religious groups and human rights activists in and outside the states.

It is not a new thing, however, to regulate religious preaching in northern Nigeria. Beginning from the 1960s, the government of Nigeria's then northern region began the regulation of Islamic religious preaching through a system of licensing of preachers, coupled with prohibitions against preaching without licence, which effort culminated in legislative enactments in 1970 in Kano State and subsequently in Borno,[1] Niger, Sokoto,[2] Bauchi,[3] Plateau,[4] Katsina,[5] Jigawa, Kebbi, Yobe, Zamfara, Gombe and Nassarawa states. Although the right to freedom of religion, including

[1] See The Borno State Admonishing and Interpretation Edict of 1977. It was repealed by the Borno State Islamic Religious Preaching Law in so far as it applied to Islamic religious preaching Law of 1981. It should be noted that Borno has a 2010 law on Islamic Religious Preaching.

[2] See Niger State Islamic Religious Preaching Edict of 1979 which was repealed replaced in 1985. For Sokoto, See The Certain Religious Preaching Edict of 1979. This was amended in 1984; repealed and replaced in 1986.

[3] See Bauchi State Religious Preaching Law of 1984. This Law was suspended by the Bauchi State Religious Preaching (suspension) Law of 1987.

[4] See Plateau State Regulation of Public Preaching Edict of 1986.

[5] See Katsina State Islamic Education and Preaching Law of 2011. This Law consolidated two laws that had been in operation since 1991 in the State. They are the Islamic Education Bureau Law of 1991 and Religious Preaching Regulation of 1991.

A. S. Garba (✉)
Department of Public Law, Faculty of Law, Bauchi State University, Gadau, Nigeria

J.-M. Iyi, H. Strydom (eds.), *Boko Haram and International Law*,
https://doi.org/10.1007/978-3-319-74957-0_11

the right to manifest or exercise such right (individually or collectively, publicly or privately) and even engage in religious propagation in Nigeria, is protected in the Nigerian Constitution,[6] the same Constitution allows states to derogate from these rights through the application of limitation clauses such as 'reasonably justifiable laws in a democratic society', 'public interest', 'public safety', 'health', 'public order or morals' or the 'fundamental rights of others'.[7]

The religious preaching board laws may qualify as valid laws in a democracy having been enacted by the state legislature; questions, however, may still be asked about their reasonability in a democratic Nigeria. This is because in a constitutional democracy, compliance with the rule of law doctrine alone is not sufficient to make a law reasonable; such a law must be substantively positive.[8] It is on this basis that this paper seeks to examine the following questions: how reasonably justifiable the religious preaching board laws are in a democratic Nigeria? What criteria could be applied to determine their reasonability? Lastly, what gave rise to the enactment of these laws in Borno and Niger states in northern Nigeria?

The Nigerian Constitution has not given any clue on the meaning of what constitutes a 'reasonably justifiable' law in a democratic society or the test for ascertaining this. However, European and American courts have generally applied a three-legged standard test to determine the reasonability of laws or restrictions aimed at limiting citizens' freedom of religion in democratic societies. The three-legged standard requires restrictions on freedom of religion to be prescribed by law, be in furtherance of a legitimate state interest and be reasonable.[9]

Gunn has questioned the adequacy of the three-legged standard test, and he observes that constitutions in many democracies have not given any guiding principle for the use of courts when exercising their discretion to resolve conflicts between state regulatory powers and citizens' freedom of religion, especially as regards the kind of evidence to admit or reject, which between the two rights is more important and why and who between the parties (state and the citizen) has the burden of proving what evidence and why.[10] He also criticises the application of the three-legged standard for being 'results-oriented'.[11] He recommended that a tribunal faced with the task of interpreting derogatory clauses with respect to freedom of religion should, first, understand its role; second, understand the burden of proof of each of the parties; third, apply less restrictive alternatives with correct evidentiary obligations placed on both parties; and, fourth, understand the relevant degree of scrutiny to apply.[12]

---

[6] It should be noted that Fundamental Human Right including right to freedom of religion was first introduced in the Constitution of Nigeria 1960 which is called the independence Constitution.

[7] Section 45(1)(a)(b) of the Constitution of the Federal Republic of Nigeria, 1999 (as amended).

[8] See Hasebe and Pinelli (2013), pp. 1–19.

[9] See Section 38 and 45 of the Nigerian Constitution. The word 'necessary' is what can be found in international instruments for the protection of freedom of religion. Example is Article 9 of the European Convention on Human Rights etc.

[10] Gunn (2012), pp. 254–268.

[11] Gunn (2012), pp. 263–264.

[12] Gunn (2012), pp. 264–266.

His first recommendation is the most significant because it will enable the courts to properly appreciate their adjudicatory role and maintain their impartiality without unduly favouring authorities or dominant religious groups over minority religious groups in the adjudication process. However, the main weaknesses in his recommendation are that, firstly, he negated the role of state-religion pattern of countries as a guiding principle in the interpretation of freedom of religion cases. This relationship is relevant when assessing the nature of the protection of freedom of religion in a country, especially considering the fact that religion is indispensable in the maintenance of public order in Nigeria today. Secondly, his fourth recommendation is pregnant; the question is how and by what standard can the relevant degree of scrutiny be determined? Thirdly, he has not considered the notion of substantive due process as a factor necessary for the validity of laws in a democracy. It is already stated that compliance with the rule of law doctrine is not sufficient to make a law reasonable in a democracy.

In addition to Gunn's observation, the application of the three-legged standard is generally based on courts' exercise of discretion. The trajectory of current research, however, demonstrates that the process of exercise of discretion in different legal orders, whether by courts or government officials, is susceptible to bias, especially where it involves groups whose religious ideologies disagrees with that of the majority.[13] This is because such exercise of discretion gives officials too much power, which they easily abuse. Moreover, it allows governments to 'legitimately' silence its critics, which kills open debate that ensures better public enlightenment. Furthermore, it prevents the survival of superior arguments in that it prevents their chances of prevailing over government positions. Finally, it allows few scholars to monopolise the discourse on religion, sometimes leaning towards a particular doctrine in a particular religion. The government's response to this type of conflict in Nigeria has been the use of force to repress dissenters.[14] The dislodgement of Darul Islam and Nibrassiya Huda Islamic groups by the government of Niger State in Nigeria in 2008 and 2014,[15] respectively, without following due process of law and the present case of Boko Haram in Borno, Yobe and Adamawa states of Nigeria starting from 2009 to date illustrate this point. A recent example relating to this is the arrest and subsequent detention of members of a Muslim religious group called *Qur'aniyun* at Kwanar Farakai in Igabi Local Government Area of Kaduna State.[16]

Until Nigeria's legal system provides a viable standard of judicial review for resolving conflicts between state regulatory power and citizens' free exercise rights, a crucial constitutional matter will remain a brainteaser due to legal ambiguity in the determination of reasonability of laws in a democracy, which may probably result in confusion, injustice and extrajudicial killing of innocent citizens in the country. Considering the peculiar nature of Nigeria, this paper applies an argumentative

[13] See Richardson (2004), pp.1–15.

[14] See Adekunle (2009), pp. 329–342.

[15] Leadership Newspaper (2014), p. 62.

[16] Kaduna, *Weekly Trust Newspaper*, Saturday, February 28, 2015, Vol.18, No. 34, pp. 4–5.

approach developed by Jan Smiths[17] to recommend a substantively positive non-liberal standard of judicial review mechanism in Nigeria to resolve this type of conflict. This particular standard is one that considers Nigeria's state-religion configuration, local experience and the notion of substantive due process in constitutional law theory.

11.2 Conceptual Clarification

11.2.1 Islamic Religious Preaching

Islamic religious preaching is called *Da'wah* in Arabic, which means inviting both Muslims and non-Muslims to accept Islam. Scholars have defined it in different ways. For example, Modibbo defines the term in his dissertation as 'an act of inviting people to accept Islam or to observe their religious obligations correctly'.[18] Another scholar, Hafeez, on the other hand, defines it as 'propagating the Religion of Allah by using any lawful means'. Modibbo, however, states that the term 'comprises all acts of disseminating the knowledge of Islam through preaching, sermon and charity with a view of extending the idea of Islam on the one hand and to maintaining the true doctrine of the Oneness of Allah (*Tauhid*) on the other'.[19]

Islamic religious preaching is regarded as obligatory for every individual Muslim.[20] Prophets are believed to be the original Islamic preachers in Islam and are the sources of guidance and knowledge of Islamic law and were ordained by God to transmit the knowledge through preaching to mankind.[21] Al-Qaraḍawi stated that the act of preaching in Islam is an essential duty of all the messengers of God, their successors, the *Ulama* and all genuine believers.[22]

Religious preaching has experienced significant changes as a result of modern developments; it is now done under the umbrella of registered organisations in Nigeria, although we still have individual preachers. Modibbo, however, notes that Islamic preaching under an organisation is contentious among Islamic scholars.[23] For the purpose of this paper, Islamic religious preaching is defined as the act of inviting or propagating the religion of Islam to people by an individual or a group (registered or unregistered) through the open-air medium, sermons in places of worship or electronic media on radio or television or both.

[17] See Smits (2009).

[18] Modibbo (2014), pp. 50–60.

[19] Modibbo (2014), pp. 2–5.

[20] Modibbo (2014), pp. 2–5.

[21] Modibbo (2014), pp. 2–5.

[22] Al-Qaradawi (1985).

[23] Modibbo (2014), pp. 8–9.

11.2.2 Regulation of Islamic Religious Preaching

The Black's Law Dictionary defines regulation as 'the act or process of controlling by rule or restriction'.[24] Mark Findley, on the other hand, defines it

> as the sustained and focused attempt to alter the behaviour of others according to defined standards or purposes with the intention of producing a broadly identified outcome or outcomes, which may involve mechanisms of standard setting, information gathering and behaviour modification.[25]

Grims and Finkes'[26]approach, however, seems to be better and relevant for this paper. Their approach has both governmental and social dimensions. They defined government regulation as 'the restrictions placed on the practice, profession, or selection of religion by the official laws, policies, or administrative actions of the state' and social regulation as 'the restrictions placed on the practice, profession, or selection of religion by other religious groups, associations, or the culture at large'.[27] For purposes of this paper, regulation of religious preaching may be defined as government's attempt at the state level in Nigeria to limit citizens' right to engage in religious preaching, proselytisation or persuasion through legislative enactments irrespective of the motive of such legislation.

11.2.3 Boko Haram

The term 'Boko Haram' is a name used by non-adherents to describe an Islamic organisation that calls itself *Jama'atu AhlisunnahLida'awati Wal-Jihad*.[28] It is a dissident *Sunni* (*Safists-Wahabi*) inclined Muslim group that is convinced of the righteousness of its own cause and the wickedness of all others. It is based in Borno State in the northeastern part of Nigeria but has followership in other parts of Nigeria. Scholars have written a lot about their origin and ideology.[29] It suffices in this paper to say that they are preaching what majority of Muslims believe is unorthodox Islam. They preach against western education, democracy and government employment, and they advocate strict application of Sharia in Nigeria.[30] Although research has shown that the group's early style of religious preaching was peaceful,[31] it, however, became the centre of attention in the world in 2009, when it violently clashed with a combined team of security agents from the Nigerian Army and the

[24] Garner (2014), p. 1398.

[25] Findlay (2013), p. 31.

[26] Grim and Finke (2006), p. 7.

[27] Grim and Finke (2006), p. 7.

[28] Zenn (2014).

[29] See for example Umar (2012), pp. 118–144. See also Adamu (2012).

[30] Adamu (2012).

[31] Adamu (2012).

Nigerian Police, which led to the extrajudicial killing of the group's spiritual leader, Mohammad Yusuf.[32]

Since then, fighting between the group and the Nigerian government ensued and has continued to this day with shootings and bombings in several places in the northeastern part of Nigeria comprising of Borno, Yobe, Bauchi, Gombe and Adamawa states, forcing the government to declare a state of emergency in the three most affected states in 2013. In addition, the Federal Government of Nigeria proscribed the group, along with another Islamic religious group, in 2013.[33] However, crisis degenerated into full insurgency, and the group has captured and taken control of large Nigerian territory in the northeastern part of the country, thereby threatening the corporate existence of Nigeria as a nation.

11.3 Islamic Preaching Board Laws and Boko Haram

11.3.1 Historical Context

The regulation of religious preaching, especially Islamic religious preaching, is an old phenomenon in northern Nigeria.[34] The potential danger of Islamic religious preaching seems to be a major ground that motivated authorities in northern Nigeria and subsequently state governments to adopt this practice. Historically, the attempt by the king of Gobir, Bawa Jan Gwarzo, in the late eighteenth century to control Islamic religious preaching of Usman dan Fodio before the launching of the latter's jihad may probably be the first effort to regulate religious preaching in the region.[35] After the demise of King Bawa, his brother, King Nafata, continued along the same line but with more strictness; he restricted Islamic religious preaching in the land of Gobir,[36] barred people not born to Muslim families from converting to Islam[37] and ordered all proselytes to slip back to their traditional religion.[38] He also proscribed, among other things, the wearing of turbans and veils by men and women respectively.[39] Usman dan Fodio resisted the orders of the king, and this confrontation culminated in the well-known jihad beginning in 1804.[40] The success of the jihad gave rise to a new administration with Usman dan Fodio as the leader. He then

[32] Akanyi (2013).

[33] See Terrorism (prevention) and (proscription) Order 2013. This was yet to be Gazzated at the time of writing this paper.

[34] Gwandu (1986), pp. 10–27.

[35] Larémont (2011), pp. 64–65.

[36] Larémont (2011), pp. 64–65.

[37] Larémont (2011), pp. 64–65.

[38] Larémont (2011), pp. 64–65.

[39] Larémont (2011), pp. 64–65.

[40] Larémont (2011), pp. 64–65.

appointed emirs as his deputies in many parts of today's northern Nigeria, including places such as Sokoto, Zaria, Kano and Nupeland.[41]

The second attempt to regulate Islamic preaching took place under the colonial administration in 1926 as a reaction to incessant disagreements between the dominant Islamic religious groups in the region. These conflicts were essentially between the Qadiriyya and Tijjaniyya Sufi orders, in addition to the friction associated with the emergence of new Islamic religious groups such as the Ahmadiyya and the Wahhabiyya in the region.[42] Moreover, at that time, the region had witnessed a rise in the presence of Christian religious missionaries who were struggling to win more souls for Christianity against the wishes of the northern emirs who were Muslims.[43] As a result, the colonial government issued a circular directing resident governors of Kano, Zaria, Sokoto and Niger to issue proclamations to control religious preaching generally in their areas in order to avoid any possible infringement of law and order.[44] All residents complied with this directive. For example, the proclamation of the Emir of Kano at the time, Abdullahi Bayero, reads as follows (author's translation):

> From Emir of Kano Abdullahi Bayero.
>
> Salutations to the people of the whole land of Kano, District Heads, Village Heads and peasantry, religious scholars and the entire male and female population of the land, as well as to the strangers (inhabiting the jurisdiction). Know that this is a decree from us to you. Let no man amongst you preach, no matter who he may be, in a city, on a road, or in towns, or in wards of towns, or in hamlets or villages. Whosoever wishes to preach, let him go to his mosque to preach there. Or let him preach in his house. Whoever shall disobey this decree and does what we have forbidden, let him blame no one but himself for what will befall on him. Written in friendship on Friday the 3rd of Rajab, 1345 A.H. (7 January, 1927).[45]

This was the situation up to 1950 and then through 1960 when Nigeria became independent and adopted a new constitution. That constitution for the first time provided for full liberal rights, including freedom of religion, expression and association.[46] A third attempt to control religious preaching, however, occurred soon afterwards, and it was probably the consequence of a form of religious

[41] For details of the atrocities committed by Hausa Kings before Jihad, see Mohammed (1957), p. 65.

[42] Wakili (1997), pp. 38–45.

[43] Afolayan (2009), pp. 37–66.

[44] Middleton (1926).

[45] The writer acquired copies of these documents from Dr. Philip Ostien while working as his research assistant on the documentation of sharia project in Northern Nigeria from 2005 to 2007. Dr. Philip Ostien was formerly based at the Faculty of Law, university of Jos and the writer was his student from 1998 to 2004 in the same faculty. Other emirs of the areas have also done the same. The Emir of Zaria issued his circular on the 12th day of January, 1927 while the emir of Katsina issued his own on the 26th day of August, 1927. Also see Lethem J.G., and Memorandum to Resident Province, Preaching in Public Places, 4 January, 1930. Also see Auwal, pp. 88–90.

[46] See Chapter IV of the Constitution of the Federal Republic of Nigeria 1999 as amended.

gerrymandering against minority religious groups in the region by authorities in favour of dominant religious groups. The premier of the Northern Region, Sir Ahmadu Bello (Sardauna of Sokoto), formed what was known as the Council of Ulama on 23 August 1963. This council was mainly composed of members of the dominant Sufi groups (Qadiriyya and Tijaniyya).[47] The council was to advise the northern regional government on Islamic affairs, with emphasis on disagreements among different Islamic religious groups and on grass-roots Islamic preachers in the region.[48]

On 7 January 1964, the youth movement Fityanul Islam, which was linked to the Tijaniyya leadership, wrote a complaint to the Sardauna against some minority Islamic religious group, whom they labelled as *Gardawa* (Hausa term for graduates of Qur'anic schools without further Islamic training), urging him to form a committee of scholars to license the group before they were allowed to preach. They further wrote to the Council of Ulama on 25 July 1964, calling for the banning of *Gardawa* from religious preaching.[49]

In reaction, the Sardauna issued a circular to all the northern provinces, directing them to make the possession of a preaching licence a precondition for Islamic religious preachers before they were allowed to preach in the region, a sort of 'de factor' religious regulation through the indirect influence of the dominant religious groups. That measure forced the *Gardawa* out of the preaching scene for about 2 years and, on the other hand, favoured the dominant religious groups in the religious market square. Although the Sardauna belonged to the Qadiriyya Islamic religious group and his actions impacted negatively on the *Gardawa* group, records indicate that he was fairly liberal and ecumenical in matters of religion until he was killed in the military coup of 1966.[50]

Gardawa resurfaced in 1969 in Kano towards the end of the Nigerian civil war and began to preach without licence.[51] The Ulama in Kano State, which consisted of members of the dominant Sufi order, urged the Emir of Kano to persuade the state government to set up a body to oversee the activities of *Gardawa* preachers in the state.[52] In accordance with this proposal, the emir at that time, Ado Bayero, formed a committee mainly composed of leading scholars from the dominant Sufi order in the state. This committee included Shaykh Nasiru Kabara (d. 1996), Shaykh Tijani Usman (d. 1970), Shehu Maihula (d. 1988) and Shaykh Sani Kafanga (d. 1989). Furthermore, Emir Ado Bayero had also formed the Kano Local Government Area Quranic Interpretation and Admonishing Rules (4 September 1967), which Governor Audu Bako of Kano State subsequently approved on 1 April 1970.[53] This became

[47] Larémont (2011), p. 3. See also Umar (1993), pp. 154–178.

[48] Umar (1993), pp. 154–178.

[49] Umar (1993), pp. 154–178.

[50] Kukah (2011), pp. ix–xiii.

[51] Anwar (1997), p. 84.

[52] Anwar (1997), p. 84.

[53] Kano Local Government Authority (Control of Quranic Interpretation and Admonishing) Rules (1970). This became Kano Local Government Law No. 3, 1970.

the first official legislative enactment on Islamic religious preaching in northern Nigeria and the beginning of de jure religious regulation in northern Nigeria. It is my view that this was the fourth attempt in the regulation of Islamic religious preaching in the region. This committee often denied *Gardawa* a preaching licence to preach in areas under the jurisdiction of Kano State, but *Gardawa* was able to move to Kaduna State to obtain preaching licences from the Jama'atu Nasril Islam, which was then headed by a proponent of Nigerian anti-Sufi reformism Shaykh Abubakar Mahmud Gumi.[54]

It is in this context that Izala, a Wahhabi-oriented Islamic religious group close to Gumi and strongly opposed to Sufi doctrines and practices, emerged on the scene in 1978.[55] The emergence of Izala changed the equation of Muslim intra-religious conflict in northern Nigeria from Qadiriyya vs. Tijaniyya to Tariqa (i.e., Qadiriyya and Tijaniyya collectively) vs. Izala. Izala immediately began a campaign of offensive preaching directed against Sufi doctrines, which it labelled as *bid'a* (heretical innovation) and *shirk* (polytheism). In their preaching, Izala preachers used to mention openly the personal names of the founders of Sufi orders. They engaged in Takfir and even split their mosques from those of the Sufi orders as they did not allow their members to follow an imam affiliated to a Sufi order. This led to a series of skirmishes between the two groups.[56]

While the sectarian confrontation between Izala and Tariqa groups continued, some of the disgruntled members of *Gardawa* re-emerged on the scene under the umbrella of *Yan Tatsine*; these were the followers of Muhammadu Marwa Maitatsine, a peripatetic preacher from northern Cameroon who had settled in Kano, where he had engaged in belligerent public preaching against all the existing Islamic groups in the region.[57] Maitatsine's doctrines were different from those of both Izala and Tariqa. For example, while both Izala and Tariqa accepted the Qur'an and the Hadith as dependable sources of divine revelation and the Sunni jurisprudential tradition (*Fiqh*) as a valid body of interpretation, Maitatsine discarded all except the Qur'an. In 1980, the Maitatsine movement engaged in a militant uprising in Kano State. The ensuing military operation left thousands of dead, and public opinions in the country became increasingly supportive of the need to regulate religious preaching. Although there were Preaching Board laws in most of the states of northern Nigeria, including Kano State, the civilian administration of President Shagari decided to ban open-air preaching instead of applying the existing laws. This decision especially burdened Izala as open-air Islamic religious preaching was its main preaching technique.

Military officers headed by Major General Muhammadu Buhari toppled the civilian administration in 1983. This regime took a cue from the past civilian administration and placed a 'blanket ban on religious activities especially open-air

---

[54] Auwal, p. 4.

[55] Auwal, p. 4.

[56] Auwal, p. 4.

[57] Auwal, p. 4.

preaching'.[58] In addition, it forbade the building of new Friday mosques without the permission of emirate authorities. In order to prevent preachers from circumventing any ban imposed by the Preaching Board of a particular emirate by applying to a neighbouring one, the government also introduced a requirement according to which authorisation for religious preaching must be obtained both in the preacher's emirate of origin as well as in any other emirate where he might wish to preach. As most of the Preaching Boards were constituted by scholars affiliated to the Sufi orders, which at the time represented most of the country's religious scholars, Izala found the new measures to be burdensome. Because of this, the founder of Izala, the late Shaykh Ismaila Idiris, is reported to have said in one of his preaching sessions, after both regimes were out of office, that 'Allah will not forgive the regimes of Shagari and that of Buhari because they blocked the way of Allah'.[59]

Another military junta, led by General Ibrahim Badamasi Babangida, took over power in 1985. Preaching Board laws remained unchanged in the various states. This government, however, became more liberal in its attitude towards religious groups, generally. In 1987, it enacted a law establishing an advisory council on religious affairs to handle issues of religion in the country. It is not clear, however, to what extent this body was actually useful. In the early 1990s, Izala split into two factions, one linked to the group's older leadership based in Jos, with the other linked to the group's new leadership based in Kaduna. This split further changed the nature of the intra-Muslim conflict from Tariqa vs. Izala to 'Jos Izala' vs. 'Kaduna Izala'. Apart from minor skirmishes here and there between members of the two factions of Izala and sometimes Izala (Jos based and Kaduna based) with members of Tariqa, no other major conflict occurred in northern Nigeria as a result of government regulation of religious preaching until 2009 in Borno State between members of the Boko Haram and the government of Nigeria, which event led to the extrajudicial killing of the group's leader, Mohammad Yusuf, and many of his members and other Nigerians.

On a general note, however, the functions of the religious preaching boards are to examine intending Islamic religious preachers and to issue preaching licence to those qualified. The laws of religious preaching boards criminalise preaching without a licence or violating the conditions of a preaching licence. In terms of spread, religious preaching boards are found in thirteen (13) states in northern Nigeria. Eleven (11) of these states have reintroduced the application of some aspects of Islamic laws in their domains. The religious preaching laws are designed to regulate Islamic religious preaching, but in some states like Bauchi, Plateau and Nassarawa, they have elements of general application. The composition of religious preaching boards is determined by the government, and in practice such compositions have mainly favoured dominant religious groups against minority religious groups.

[58] Umar (1993), pp. 154–178.

[59] Umar (1993), pp. 154–178.

11.3.2 Borno State Islamic Preaching Board and Boko Haram

The Boko Haram conflict had ravaged the entire northeast of Nigeria and its neighbouring countries such as Chad, Niger and Chad. It should be noted that Borno State had an Islamic religious preaching board law in place when the Boko Haram conflict started in the state. Borno State was the second state to enact a religious preaching board in northern Nigeria in 1977. The law was amended and replaced by the Islamic Religious Preaching Board Law of 1981. This was also amended and replaced by the Borno State Islamic Religious Preaching Board Law 2010 (as amended) in response to the Boko Haram conflict.

Some key persons in Borno State provided useful information in an interview on the reasons for the enactment of the Borno State Islamic religious preaching board law and its operations. According to Sheikh Goni Mohammed Saad Ngamdu,[60] the religious preaching board law was enacted in Borno State in 1981 to control preachers who were preaching without 'proper knowledge, preaching just anyhow; especially Izala coming to criticise and make trouble'. The board was constituted in the manner below:

- chairman;
- one representative from each Emirate Council, to be so appointed by the Council;
- three representatives of the Islamic religious preachers to be appointed by the governor: these were
  - Sheikh Goni Mohammed Saad Ngamdu for JNI—from Tijaniya;
  - Sheikh Muhammad Abba Aji—from Wahabis/Izala;
  - Goni Sanda—a neutral party;
- three other persons to be appointed by the governor:
  - Sheikh Ibrahim Salih—a popular Tijaniya adherent;
  - Sheikh Abubakar el-Miskin—a popular Tijanija adherent;
  - Goni Kaltumi—a popular Tijani adherent.[61]

These same groups of 'preachers' and 'other persons' have continued on the board to date.[62] The function of the board was to determine the qualifications that preachers must have among other things, depending on what such preacher intend to preach. Licences were then issued to them to preach specific subjects. The board did not discriminate based on sect; it only tried to make sure that a preacher knew whatever subject it was that he wanted to preach. Nevertheless, sometimes there were complaints: people who were disqualified or unqualified and denied licences

---

[60] He is the North East Zonal Coordinator Jama'atu Nasril Islam and Borno State Secretary General of the same organization. He gave this information in 12 day of May, 2012 in an interview he granted with Dr. Philip Ostien; formerly of the Faculty of Law of the University of Jos in Nigeria copy of which is with the author.

[61] Their affiliation to the Tijaniya sufi order is well known in Nigeria.

[62] Referring to the time the interview was granted.

alleged that they had been discriminated against because of their beliefs. There are instances where the board even withdrew licences of preachers. For example, at some point, the board withdrew the preaching licence of Sheikh Muhammad Abba Aji because he was causing 'confusion', calling other Muslims unbelievers. Another example was one Usman Bida, who when asked to give his opinion on the relation between Muslims and non-Muslims replied: 'War!' His licence was suspended for 2 years.

A religious preaching board still exists in Borno State today, and it has so far issued about 500 licences from 1981 to date.[63] However, over the years, many preachers have preached without licences and have never been prosecuted. On Boko Haram, Sheikh Goni Mohammed Saad Ngamdu stated that reports were prepared and sent to the government on people preaching without licences and those preaching hatred on the 'religious unbelief' of others, among other things, and Muhammad Yusuf was one of those people, nevertheless the government has not considered the report in addressing the Boko Haram problem in the state but nothing has come out of those reports. Why was it impossible for the government to apply the preaching law in the state long before the Boko Haram conflict assumed a dangerous dimension? According to Kadi Abubakar Imam,[64] Yusuf was on the board of the Borno State Sharia Implementation Committee in 2003 and had been collecting his allowances from the state government up to the time of his extrajudicial execution. He was also on religious committees in Yobe State and had been collecting salaries from the government while at the same time preaching to people that it was Haram work for a democratic government. It may well be argued that Mohammed Yusuf may have been influenced by the Sharia posture of the State agencies since anything that agrees with Sharia could be acceptable to him.

11.3.3 The Experience in Niger State

Darul Islam was founded in 1993 in Niger State 'by a completely orthodox Sunni malam who only wished to form a pious community that was isolated as much as possible from the rest of the sinful world'.[65] It started gradually and grew in number to about 4000 people. It legally acquired land for its settlement from the government of Niger State.[66] The main occupation of the members was farming generally. They applied Maliki sharia in all civil and criminal matters among themselves with the

[63] As of 2012.

[64] He was a Kadi at the Sharia Court of Appeal, Maiduguri and the secretary of the management committee of the mosque of Al-Amin Daggash Mosque where Yusuf used to preach once a week. He gave the information when he granted an interview with Ostien also on the 12th day of May 2012 copy of which is with the Author.

[65] Philip Ostien, A survey of the Muslims of Nigeria's North Central Geo-Political Zone. In: Nigeria Research Network(NRN), Oxford Department of International Development, Queen Elizabeth House, Oxford University (NRN) Working Paper No. 1.

[66] Ostien (2012).

exception of hard punishments: serious cases were handled by excommunication or by the police.[67] They had their own *qadi* (Islamic judge). They established their own Islamiyya schools where they teach their children, including about western education and hospitals. The government of Niger State knew about them. They have a peaceful disposition in all matters, including their religious preaching style.

The Boko Haram event in July 2009 led the government of Niger State to dislodge them on 15 August 2009 without any cogent reason. The State governor simply sent armed forces that pounced on them, arrested them and subsequently detained them in camps for some time before sending them back to where they all came from.[68] It is important to note that this happened without any recourse to the Islamic religious preaching board in Niger State. In 2008, the same State government also dislodged the Nibrassiya Huda Islamic group from Nigeria, another minority religious group, without following due process of law. The question that arises is, for how long will this impunity continue in a supposedly democratic country? It should, however, be noted that the Niger State attempted to amend its Islamic preaching board law by introducing the Religious Preaching and Place of Worship (amendment) Bill 2013, and though the legislation is still being proposed, it has been resisted by religious groups in the State.[69]

11.3.4 Consequences of Religious Regulation

From the foregoing narrative, it is obvious that the regulation of religious preaching in some northern states of Nigeria has been characterised by violence and state repression of minority religious sect in favour of dominant religious sects, and this has produced and continues to reproduce conflict. This phenomenon has been investigated empirically by Brian J. Grim and Roger Fink, which they published in their work titled *The Price of Freedom Denied.*[70] In the work, they proposed two theses. First is that violent religious persecution and conflict increase when government denies its citizens freedom of religion through the instrumentality of regulation or through legislative and administrative actions. Second is that the same applies when such denial is by social forces, the norms accepted by majority members or religious groups in a society. Another work that supports the theses is the work of Monica Duffy Toft, Daniel Philpot and Timothy Samuel Shah called *God's Century*.[71] This work confronts the secularisation theory that seeks to relegate the role of religion in the public space to the background.

The work proposes ten rules based on the resurgent nature of religion in the public domain, the most relevant of which is that for peace to reign in the world today,

[67] Ostien (2012).

[68] Ostien (2012).

[69] Wakaso (2014), p. 12.

[70] Grim and Finke (2011).

[71] Toft et al. (2011).

we must accept that the 'the more governments try to repress or exclude religion from public life, the more such efforts will be self-defeating'.[72] The history of regulation of religious preaching in northern Nigeria, as discussed above, corroborates these findings.

11.3.5 Changes in the Preaching Board Laws

It is pertinent to point out that the regulation of Islamic religious preaching by means of legislative enactment, as in the case of Kano, brought a new dimension to the scope of the regulation. Before 1970, the scope of the regulation was in the context of what was then the northern region as a whole. After the civil war (1967–1970), however, the three regions that used to constitute the Federal Republic of Nigeria were subdivided into smaller states. Kano became the first state to enact a law for the regulation of Islamic religious preaching. Borno State followed suit in 1977, then Niger and Sokoto states in 1979 and Bauchi State in 1984.

These states subsequently amended their preaching laws with the exception of Bauchi, which suspended its own and instead banned open-air preaching. Plateau and Katsina states enacted their preaching laws in 1986 and 1991 respectively. From 1990 to 1996, the new states of Jigawa, Kebbi, Yobe, Zamfara, Gombe and Nassarawa were carved out from the territory of the former region of northern Nigeria, and all of them inherited the religious preaching laws of their mother states. Most of the preaching board laws were enacted during military regimes.

The only exceptions were, first, Borno State, whose 1981 Islamic Religious Preaching Board Laws was amended under civilian rule in 2010. The second is Kano State's Council for Islamic Affairs Law enacted under civilian rule in 1981 but subsequently repealed and replaced by the Religious Preaching Edict under military rule in 1985. The third is Zamfara State's Religious Preaching and Establishment of Juma'at Mosque and Idi Praying Ground Commission's Law enacted under civilian rule in 2003. The fourth is Kebbi State's Preaching Law enacted under civilian administration in 2004, and finally, the Katsina State's Islamic Education and Preaching Law, which was enacted in 2011 under civilian rule. In fact, most of the preaching board laws were initially the product of military regimes in consultation with local interest groups and were not the product of constitutional democratic processes.

11.3.6 Legal Considerations

The 1999 Constitution of the Federal Republic of Nigeria protects the freedom of religion, speech and assembly in generous terms:

[72] Toft et al. (2011), p. 214.

38. (1) Every person shall be entitled to freedom of thought, conscience and religion, including freedom to change his religion or belief, and freedom (either alone or in community with others, and in public or in private) to manifest and propagate his religion or belief in worship, teaching, practice and observance.

39. (1) Every person shall be entitled to freedom of expression, including freedom to hold opinions and to receive and impart ideas and information without interference.

40. Every person shall be entitled to assemble freely and associate with other persons….

But these freedoms are explicitly made subject to limitation or regulation by the state in the interest of broadly-defined goods:

45. (1) Nothing in sections 37, 38, 39, 40 and 41 of this Constitution shall invalidate any law that is reasonably justifiable in a democratic society—

(a) in the interest of defence, public safety, public order, public morality or public health; or.

(b) for the purpose of protecting the rights and freedoms of other persons.

It is clear that section 45 leaves plenty of room for the more or less standard array of penal and other legislation by which the modern state can function. These provisions agree with the provisions of international freedom of religion norms as contained in Article 18 of the International Covenant on Civil and Political Rights and Article 9 of the European Convention on Human Rights. What is clear from the above constitutional provisions is that the internal forum of religion is beyond the regulatory power of the state.[73] This is called *the forum internum.*[74] In addition, the current trend in the jurisprudence of freedom of speech in the world is based on Baker's autonomy theory of free speech, which advocates that the legitimacy of law in any society should hinge on the need for that law to respect citizens' formal autonomy. In this regard, it is agreed that Boko Haram preaches unorthodox Islamic religious ideology in Nigeria, and its style had been peaceful prior to the event of 2009. But the Constitution of the Federal Republic of Nigeria 1999 (as amended) protects in clear terms the propagation of such unorthodox ideologies provided they are propagated within the confines of the law. The law gives everyone a right to believe whatever he wills and to equally propagate such idea whether alone or in community with others. It is not therefore unconstitutional for Boko Haram as a religious group to espouse and promote its 'unorthodox' beliefs, and no court of law has the competence to punish its members for this. In contrast, however, religious preachers who incite violence or preach hatred or ignore the laws of the land are taken to have violated the law of the land for which they can face the full wrath of the law. What therefore are the preaching boards coming to regulate, the external expression of the religion or the internal one?

---

[73] See Durham (2013), pp. 248–249.

[74] Durham (2013), pp. 248–249.

11.4 Conclusion

This paper has sought to assess the reasonability of the regulation of freedom of religion through preaching boards in selected states in northern Nigeria. The conclusion to be drawn from this analysis is that the function of the preaching boards is to examine aspirant Islamic religious preachers concerning their qualifications and to issue preaching licences to those applicants found to be qualified. Conversely, the laws make it a crime to preach without a licence or to preach in contravention of the terms of the licence. Some of the laws, such as those of Kano, Borno, Jigawa, Zamfara, Sokoto, Niger, Katsina and Kebbi states, are designed specifically to regulate Islamic religious preaching and not preaching by other religious groups like Christians or others. This is in contrast to the laws of Plateau, Nassarawa, Bauchi, Gombe and Yobe states. Why should a law in a supposed democratic society be enacted to target one specific religion? It is indisputable to state that in a constitutional democracy where the rule of law is entrenched, the state must operate by laws of general application.[75]

The power to appoint members of the preaching boards vests in the government of the various states. However, in states where emirate councils exist, these councils are consulted before such appointments are made. One problem that may be envisaged as a result of this arrangement is religious gerrymandering; this is a situation where the law is enacted with the specific aim of burdening specific religious groups, as in the case of Maitatsine and Izala in the late 1970s, in favour of the Sufi orders. A third problem could arise because a state government might determine the composition of the boards in a way that targets some specific religious groups that may not be comfortable with the religious ideology of the majority religious groups—discrimination and favouritism again on the part of government. These discriminatory practices were possible because of lack of proper standard of review in the exercise of discretion by government officials to determine the reasonability or otherwise of the ideas and practices of the minority religious groups.

Another trend that can be inferred from the narrative is that the conduct of state regulation of religious preaching in Nigeria has been characterised by violence and discrimination against minority religious groups, which led to incessant conflicts for years in the region. The factors responsible are religious gerrymandering and the connivance of the government with dominant religious groups. It is the same trend that kick-started the 2009 Boko Haram insurgency in Nigeria and that is still continuing with indiscriminate killings of innocent lives in Nigeria. Nigeria cannot afford to continue with the current extrajudicial means of solving conflicts between two constitutional rights. As it is today, the religious preaching board laws can hardly qualify as reasonable as far as democracy is concerned. Another important conclusion that can be drawn from the narration is the nature of Nigeria's state-religion pattern. Research has shown that Nigeria is a country that identifies with religion in almost everything.[76] Nigeria is a multi-religious country, and so religion

[75] Reitz (2005), p. 180.

[76] Reitz (2005), p. 234.

is a very sensitive matter that the government at all levels identifies with.[77] At the vertical level, Islam and Christianity are the two religions that the government accommodates. At the horizontal level, where Christians are in the majority, the government identifies more with Christianity, and the same thing applies where Muslims are in the majority. I have argued elsewhere in contrast to what scholars have said about Nigeria's state-religion model that Nigeria's state-religion relations is a crossbreed[78] of positive identification regimes at both its vertical and horizontal levels of government. And this is because of the country's history of entanglement with religion, preferred sets of religions pattern at the vertical level and different models of positive identification regimes at the horizontal level.[79]

11.5 Recommendation

This paper recommends a substantively positive non-liberal standard of judicial review for resolving conflict between state regulatory power and citizens' free exercise rights in Nigeria. This balancing mechanism calls for the addition of the principle of substantive due process, state-religion pattern and the local experience of countries to the existing criteria used as standards of review in the resolution of conflicts between the two rival constitutional rights. The reassertive nature of the role of religion in the public square in Nigeria and the world at large indicates that religion is indispensable in the maintenance of public order and security in the world today.[80] Therefore, in the event of conflict between the rights in the modern world today, a substantively positive and non-liberal balancing mechanism is the most appropriate, one that recognises the current role of religion and the need to do justice in the world today.

The changing role of religion in the public domain also underscores the importance of considering the state-religion pattern of a country as a factor for consideration in resolving the kind of conflict in issue. In addition, such a changing role of religion in the public glare, especially from 1970 to date, in Nigeria and the world at large has called into question the capacity of secularism theories to address the present challenges of religious crises facing the world today. Although Cole Durham, Jr.,[81] a well-respected scholar on state-religion relations in the world, has shown that it is doubtful to suggest the existence of correlation between state identification with religion and religious liberty, this paper maintains that such correlation exists when each country is taken alone without any obsession with generalisation. He himself confirmed in his work that such correlation exists in some countries.[82]

[77] Hackett (2011), pp. 853–879.

[78] See Garba (2016), pp. 157–175.

[79] Garba (2016), pp. 157–175.

[80] See Toft et al. (2011), pp. 207–223.

[81] Durham (2012), pp. 360–361.

[82] Durham (2012), pp. 360–361.

Under this thesis, the state can protect its existing relationship with religion through a valid law envisaged by its constitution; this suggests that the actions of a religious group can be subjected to the test to determine its reasonability or otherwise. Conversely, where the practice of a religious group in a country agrees with the country's state-religion pattern, it must be allowed. The United States of America and Germany are countries that have used their state-religion relations in the determination of the reasonability or otherwise of both governmental and individual actions, as shown in the paper.

Part of the local experience of Nigeria for the past 20 years has been managing crises related to religion. Government restriction of the free exercise rights of some religious groups in favour of dominant religious groups in some states of northern Nigeria has contributed to the crises. Neither the government nor any of the victims has approached the court for judicial determination of the conflict. Even if they have approached the courts, only God knows what will happen, considering the mindset of the judges and generally the people of Nigeria on minority religious groups and their ideologies. Another challenge in Nigeria is whether with the present experience the government will allow members of religious groups to determine for the government what religion is.

References

Adamu AU (2012) Insurgency in Nigeria: The Northern Nigerian experience. Paper presented at the eminent persons and expert group meeting on complex insurgencies in Nigeria, held at the Nigeria Institute of Policy and Strategic Studies, Kuru, Jos

Adekunle JO (2009) Government reaction to religious violence. In: Adekunle JO (ed) Religion in politics: Secularism and national integration in modern Nigeria. African World Press, Trenton

Afolayan F (2009) Religion and politics in colonial Nigeria: the life and career of Sir Walter Miller, 1782–1952. In: Adekunle JO (ed) Religion in politics: Secularism and national integration in modern Nigeria. Africa World Press, Trenton

Akanyi T (2013) Insecurity in Nigeria: the Boko Haram dimension. Kas Int Rep 7:86–107

Al-Qaradawi Y (1985) Thaqāfat al-Da'wah. Al-maktab al-Islamiy, Beirut

Anwar A (1997) 'Gardawa', 'Ulama' and the State in Northern Nigeria: The Maitatsine phenomenon, 1962–1985. PhD, unpublished, University of Maiduguri

Durham WC (2012) Patterns of religion state relations. In: Witte J Jr, Green MC (eds) Religion & human rights: an introduction. Oxford University Press, New York

Durham WC Jr, Evans C (2013) Freedom of religion and religion-state relations. In: Tushnet M, Fleiner T, Saunders C (eds) Routledge handbook of constitutional law. Routledge, New York

Findlay M (2013) Contemporary challenges in regulating global crises. Palgrave Macmillan, New York

Garba AS (2016) Nigeria's religion-state relationship and its implication for freedom of religion. In: Coertzen P, Christain Green M, Hansen L (eds) Religious freedom and religious pluralism in Africa: prospects and limitations. Sun Media, Stallenbosch, pp 157–175

Garner BA (2014) Black's law dictionary, 9th edn. West- A Thomson Reuters Business, Eagan

Grim BJ, Finke R (2006) International religion indexes: government regulation, government favoritism, and social regulation of religion. Interdiscip J Res Relig 2:1

Grim BJ, Finke R (2011) The price of freedom denied. Cambridge University Press, New York

Gunn TJ (2012) Permissible limitations on the freedom of religion or belief. In: Witte J Jr, Green MC (eds) Religion & human rights: an introduction. Oxford University Press, New York

Gwandu A (1986) Aspects of the administration of justice in the Sokoto Caliphate and Shaykh Abdullahi ibn Fodio's contribution to it. In: Rashid SK (ed) Islamic law in Nigeria. Islamic Publications Bureau, Kaduna

Hackett RIJ (2011) Regulating religious freedom in Africa. In: Sharia, family and democracy: religious norms and family law in pluralistic democratic states. Emory international law review. Emory University School of Law Atlanta, Georgia

Hasebe Y, Pinelli C (2013) Constitutions. In: Tushnet M, Fleiner T, Saunders C (eds) Routledge handbook of constitutional law. Routledge, New York

Kano Local Government Authority (Control of Quranic Interpretation and Admonishing) Rules (1970)

Kukah MH (2011) Religion, power and politics in Northern Nigeria. Spectrum Books Limited, Ibadan

Larémont RR (2011) Islamic law and politics in Northern Nigeria. Africa World Press, Trenton

Leadership Newspaper July 6th (2014)

Middleton HH (1926) Memorandum to Residents; Kano, Zaria, Sokoto and Niger. Missionary Activities in Muslim Centres, 13 December

Modibbo MS (2014) Proliferation of Islamic Da'wa (propagation) organizations in Plateau State 1948–2008. Unpublished PhD Dissertation University of Jos

Mohammed B (ed) (1957) Infaq al-Mansur CEJ whiting, London

Ostien P (2012) A survey of the Muslims of Nigeria's north central geo-political zone. NRN Working Paper No. 1, Nigeria Research Network (NRN), Oxford Department of International Development, Queen Elizabeth House, Oxford University

Reitz JC (2005) Freedom of religion and its limitations: Judicial standards for deciding particular cases to maintain the state's secular role in protecting society's religious commitments. In: Ostien P et al (eds) Comparative perspectives on Sharia in Nigeria. Spectrum Books, Ibadan

Richardson JT (ed) (2004) Regulating religion: Case studies from around the Globe. Kluwer Academic/Plenum Publishers, New York

Smits JM (2009) Redefining normative legal science: Towards an argumentative discipline. In: Coomans F, Grunfeld F, Kamminga MT (eds) Methods of human rights research. Intersentia, Antwerp

Toft MD, Philpott DA, Shah TS (2011) God's century. WW Norton & Company, London

Umar MS (1993) Changing Islamic identity in Nigeria from the 1960s to the 1980s: From Sufism to anti Sufism. In: Brenner LL (ed) Muslim identity and social change in Sub-Saharan Africa. Indiana University Press, Bloomington

Umar MS (2012) The popular discourses of Salafi radicalism and Salafi counter-radicalism in Nigeria: a case study of Boko Haram. J Relig Afr 42(2):118–144

Aisha Wakaso This Day Newspaper (Tuesday, 1st July, 2014) p 12

Wakili H (1997) The phenomenon of revolts and riots in Kano: 1893–1995. PhD thesis, unpublished, Bayero University Kano

Zenn J (2014) Nigerian Al-Qaedaism. In: Fradkin H et al (eds) Current trends in islamist ideology, vol 16. Hudston Institute, Centre on Islam, Democracy, and the future of Muslim World, Washington, DC

Part IV
Wither International Law? Women, Children and Girls in the Boko Haram Insurgency

Chapter 12
The Weaponisation of Women by Boko Haram and the Prospects of Accountability

John-Mark Iyi

12.1 Introduction

The *Jama'atu Ahlis Sunna Lidda'awati wal-Jihad*,[1] otherwise known as Boko Haram, is notorious for some of the worst atrocities committed by any group anywhere in the world in recent years.[2] According to the 2015 Global Terrorism Index, in 2014, Boko Haram, which recently re-branded itself 'Islamic State West Africa Province' (after pledging allegiance to ISIS in March 2015), is the deadliest terrorist group in the world having killed more people than the Islamic State in Iraq and Syria (ISIS).[3] In less than a year in office and having recorded appreciable gains in the fight against Boko Haram, the Buhari Administration declared that Boko Haram had been 'technically defeated'.[4] Many commentators regard such declaration as premature arguing that although Boko Haram has suffered significant losses both in personnel and territory, it has not really been degraded to the extent of being 'technically defeated' but had merely been pushed back and had now resorted to 'urban

This chapter draws on my presentation entitled "Non International Armed Conflicts: Resilience of Sovereignty and the Search for Accountability: Examining the National and International Response to the Boko Haram Insurgency" (delivered at the 6th Verloren van Themaat Brownbag Lecture Series, College of Law, University of South Africa, Pretoria, 8th October 2014). I am grateful to Prof Babatunde Fagbayibo and participants at the lecture for their questions and comments.

[1] Translated as "The Group of the People of Sunnah for Preaching and Struggle". See Murtada (2013). I do not address the violations committed by members of the Nigerian Security Forces.

[2] In 2014, Boko Haram was responsible for a total of 6644 deaths. See Institute for Economics and Peace (2015), p. 14. As of the time of writing, the Boko Haram conflict has killed over 20,000 deaths. See United Nations, Office of the Coordinator for Humanitarian Affairs (2015).

[3] See Institute for Economics and Peace (2015), p. 22. See generally, Amnesty International (2015b).

[4] BBC News 24 December 2015.

J.-M. Iyi (✉)
Department of Jurisprudence, School of Law, University of Venda,
Thohoyandou, Limpopo, South Africa

J.-M. Iyi, H. Strydom (eds.), *Boko Haram and International Law*,
https://doi.org/10.1007/978-3-319-74957-0_12

terrorist tactics and attacks on soft targets'.[5] Women are one group likely to suffer disproportionately from such premature declaration of victory, which seems to have misled government forces into mistaking tactical gains for overall strategic victory forgetting that in the past, Boko Haram has come under severe pressure from the Nigerian forces but was able to make the necessary tactical and operational adjustments to emerge in a more lethal form.[6] For obvious reasons, women have become the prime targets and instruments in Boko Haram's adjustments and resurgence, and we have seen women being increasingly deployed as suicide bombers by the group.[7] In its present operational and tactical adaptation, Boko Haram has completely weaponised women for a variety of reasons—their feminine nature means women are generally presumed by the public to be gentle and to pose little or no threat, women are less likely to attract suspicion from security forces, and cultural inhibitions also mean that women are less likely to be subjected to invasive body search by security forces.[8]

Whereas Boko Haram is not the first terrorist group to recruit women operatives, increasing pressure by the deployment of the Multinational Joint Task Force (MNJTF) and the loss of territory has made women more critical to Boko Haram's tactics more than ever before in order for the group to continue to infiltrate public spaces, maintain its presence in Maiduguri and sustain its attacks in urban areas generally.[9] Unlike other Salafi groups in Nigeria, Boko Haram is not only opposed to the secular Nigerian state; it also prescribes a gendered role for women, and '[w]omen and girls have become "swords" mobilized and weaponized to carry out attacks while also being used as powerful "symbols" of Boko Haram's ideology'.[10] As of the time of writing this chapter, Boko Haram has stepped up its abduction of women and girls, and the number of women involved with Boko Haram, whether in support roles or as actual suicide bombers, has increased dramatically.[11] When Nigerian security forces captured the notorious Sambisa Forest, they rescued over 600 women and girls in Boko Haram's captivity.[12] The literature on the atrocities against women attributed to Boko Haram will continue to grow as more focus is directed towards the emerging threat of terrorism in Nigeria, the Sahel and the entire sub-Saharan Africa region. The present contribution focuses on Boko Haram's specific targeting and use of women as instruments of warfare.

Part I of the chapter gives a general background of the Boko Haram insurgency, while Part II presents a brief sketch of some of the atrocities against women committed by Boko Haram. Part III examines the international legal framework

[5] Matfess et al. (21 March 2016).

[6] Matfess et al. (21 March 2016), p. 2.

[7] For the latest deployment of females as suicide bombers at the time of writing, see for example, Punch Newspapers (10 Jan 2017); Sahara Reporters (25 Jan 2017a); Vanguard Newspaper (25 Jan 2017b). See Human Rights Watch (29 Nov 2013).

[8] Bloom and Matfess (2016), p. 109.

[9] Bloom and Matfess (2016), p. 111.

[10] Bloom and Matfess (2016), p. 106.

[11] Sahara Reporters (25 Jan 2017a).

[12] Sahara Reporters (14 Dec 2016).

specifically protecting women in situations of armed conflict. Part IV then examines the prospects of holding perpetrators of the atrocities to account and argues that despite being particularly targeted as a group, for a variety of reasons, there is a general lack of interest in prosecuting crimes against women in Nigeria even in peace times because arrests are seldom made and even where arrests are made, charges and prosecution under the 2011 Nigerian anti-terrorism legislation focus mainly on threats to national security, while acts of gender-based violence, rapes, sexual exploitation of women are seldom prosecuted with equal seriousness, thus creating a culture of impunity. Part V concludes the chapter.

12.2 A Brief Sketch of the Evolution of the Weaponisation of Women in Boko Haram's Tactics

The rise of the Boko Haram insurgency has been attributed to everything and anything under the rubric of 'root causes'.[13] These include poverty, socio-economic exclusion and marginalisation, illiteracy, rampant corruption, the brutality of security forces, alienation of the state and its institutions, bad governance, unemployment, lack of accountability and a pervasive culture of impunity.[14] Thus, as a terrorist group, Boko Haram is often presented as a reaction to a general sense of deprivation, repression, frustration and hopelessness or other forms of grievances. Few narratives acknowledge the sometimes central (if often muted) role of entrenched radical ideology or extremism and religious intolerance among some sects in northern Nigeria;[15] the 'role of social capital/resource mobilisation and political opportunity structure in the emergence' and sustenance of different shades of insurgencies in Nigeria, including Boko Haram.[16] This dominant view has obfuscated how Boko Haram's radical ideology feeds into its tactics and strategies and ideological basis of its current use of women as instruments of warfare.[17]

Like other terrorist groups, Boko Haram's tactics has not been static, and its atrocities evolved over a period of more than two decades. Initially, the group was

[13] Alozieuwa (2012), pp. 1–8.

[14] Ogbonnanyan and Ehigiamusoe (Summer 2013), pp. 4–5; Ayandike (2013), pp. 12–23.

[15] See generally, Murtada (2013).

[16] Abdullahi et al. (2014), p. 81. The authors argue that more than any other theory, a combination of economic, social, structural and organisational support, and the incidence of political opportunity structures could better explain the emergence and resilience of the Boko Haram group. See pp. 86–90. See also Thomson (Summer 2012) p. 47, arguing that the rise of Boko Haram can be traced to a combination of factors including the way and manner colonialism unsettled Islam in many parts of Africa including Nigeria.

[17] The Chapter by Ahmed Garba in this volume supports this point in so far as it exposes the fact that State policies and laws (such as the regulation of religious preaching laws) that seek to repress the right to freedom of religion and worship of minority religious groups in favour of dominant religious groups have pushed otherwise moderate members of minority religious groups in some northern states of Nigeria to extremism and radical ideology, and greatly contributed to the rise of Boko Haram.

content to advocate and provoke sectarian violence from where its members progressed to attacking Christians with clubs, machetes and small weapons.[18] From this stage, it progressed to miniature improvised explosive devices (IEDs) constructed by pouring fuel or other combustible elements in empty soft drink cans and throwing them as firebombs from moving motorcycles.[19] Muslim leaders repeatedly warned Nigerian authorities of the danger posed by the growing radical ideology of the group and its intolerance, urging government to act but to no avail.[20] It is reported that

> [m]ore than 50 Muslim leaders repeatedly called Nigeria's police, local authorities and state security to urge them to take action against Boko Haram sect militants but their pleas were ignored, Imam Ibrahim Ahmed Abdullahi said. 'A lot of imams tried to draw the attention of the government' Abdullahi said, drawing nods from other scholars sitting with him in a Maiduguri slum. 'We used to call the government and security agents to say that these people must be stopped from what they are doing because it must bring a lot of trouble.'[21]

This suggests that the group actually existed for a long time before the current wave of killing began when it attacked the towns of Geiam and Kandamma and police stations in Yobe State on 24 December 2003.[22] Between 2008 and 2011, an interplay of inter-communal clashes provided the perfect opportunity for Boko Haram to increase its operations with the concomitant increase in the number of casualties.[23]

Since first launching its current reign of terror in 2009, Boko Haram's tactics have evolved both in viciousness and sophistication. From simple, crude methods like slaughtering their victims, ambushes and sporadic shootings, the group now use suicide bombers with greater frequency and sophistication.[24] The group has also become more careful in its selection of targets, demonstrating a constant and continuing refinement and improvement in its planning and operational capabilities.[25] At the same time, its mastery and use of information technology, particularly social media, and its management of its propaganda apparatus have shown enhanced capability, leading many observers to conclude that the group has established and is receiving training and support from external sources.[26] Within this evolutionary continuum, women and young girls have featured prominently as instruments in

[18] Okpaga et al. (April 2012), p. 83.

[19] Okpaga et al. (April 2012), p. 83.

[20] Associated Press (2 August 2009).

[21] Associated Press (2 August 2009).

[22] Onuoha (2010), p. 55.

[23] Okpaga et al. (April 2012), p. 83.

[24] From 2010 onwards, Boko Haram's use of IEDs became more frequent. See generally, Okpaga et al. (April 2012).

[25] See Weeraratne (2015), p. 10.

[26] Okpaga et al. (April 2012) p. 83. Prior to pledging allegiance to ISIS on 7 March 2015, it was widely suspected that Boko Haram was receiving support from Al Qaeda and Al Shabab. However, this would seem unlikely now since ISIS and Al Qaeda are currently locked in a supremacy battle in Africa. It should be noted that since the fragmentation of Boko Haram, there is the possibility that some factions of Boko Haram could be receiving support from Al Qaeda and Al Shabab.

Boko Haram's strategy and tactics, whether as 'wives', suicide bombers or casualties of attacks. It is imperative to point out that regardless of the role of women in the insurgency, most women in Boko Haram are there against their will.[27] So whether they serve as Boko Haram's facility for building reproductive capacity for self-perpetuation, for launching attacks, as agents of internal cohesion, as marshals in the group's camps or as negotiating tools with the Nigerian authorities,[28] the degree to which women's participation in the insurgency is voluntary should be scrutinised with utmost caution. In the following section, we detail some ways in which women have been instrumentalised by Boko Haram.

12.2.1 Women as Targets of Boko Haram Attacks

Boko Haram has adopted new tactics that specifically target women. Rather than the usual indiscriminate attacks, Boko Haram has resorted to kidnaping young girls and women. In a country like Nigeria where there are challenges of data collection and management it is impossible to give an accurate account of all the attacks carried out against women by Boko Haram since the beginning of the current insurgency.[29] It is even more difficult to determine the casualty figures, age or place of birth of such victims because many victims are often charred beyond recognition. Some observers have attempted to collate data on such attacks over different time frames.[30] Even where statistics are collected, they are hardly gender sensitive and often fail to reflect the gender of casualties and victims of attacks of Boko Haram. This has implications for developing gender-sensitive responses to the conflict and in the negotiations, peace building and post-conflict reconstruction processes.[31] However, few would doubt that women have borne the brunt of Boko Haram's brutality.

In May 2013, Boko Haram abducted a dozen Christian women in Borno State.[32] On 6 May 2014, Boko Haram abducted eight girls aged between 8 and 15 years from a village in Borno.[33] On 10 June 2014, Boko Haram abducted 20 women near Chibok.[34] Again, on 24 June 2014, Boko Haram abducted over 60 women from the village of Kummabza in Damboa, Borno State.[35] On 20 October 2014, Boko Haram again attacked the two villages of Waga Mangoro and Garta in Adamawa State,

---

[27] Bloom and Matfess (2016), p. 109.

[28] Bloom and Matfess (2016), p. 109.

[29] With the exception of the Chibok abductions and other high-profile attacks and abductions, Boko Haram has been and still carries out attacks and abductions that do not receive media attention as a result of the remote and sometimes inaccessibility of some areas in northeast Nigeria. See All Party Parliamentary Group on Nigeria (13 May 2014), p. 4.

[30] Mantzikos (December 2014), pp. 64–80.

[31] United Nations (2009).

[32] Zenn and Pearson (2014), p. 48.

[33] Mark (2014) The Guardian Newspaper.

[34] The Telegraph (10 June 2014).

[35] Aljazeera (America) 24 June 2014.

where it abducted 40 women and girls.[36] On 8 January 2015, Boko Haram abducted an unknown number of women from Karatako village in Gujba Local Government of Yobe State.[37] Depending on the circumstances, Boko Haram's violent attacks on its female victims could vary. The women were generally required to recite verses of the Koran, and in some cases, those who could not do this were killed.[38] In other cases, the abducted women who could not recite the Koran were made to attend Boko Haram's Koranic Schools and to observe the strict version of Sharia'a requiring women to cover themselves. It goes without saying that these women lose everything they have as a result of the attacks, and for several years, most of them are forced to run errands and do chores for Boko Haram, especially those considered to be too old to serve as wives.[39] It is estimated that Boko Haram abducted over 2000 women and girls as of 2015.[40]

Before and after the abductions of school girls in Chibok, Boko Haram had launched series of attacks specifically targeting women, and there have been incidents (sometimes unreported) of the group raiding villages and abducting women and girls, though on a lesser scale than the Chibok abductions.[41] However, it was the 2014 abduction of 276 school girls in the Southern Borno town of Chibok that drew global attention to the plight of women and how Boko Haram had completely instrumentalised women in its tactics. On the night of 14/15 April 2014, Boko Haram attacked Government Secondary School, Chibok, Borno State, northeast Nigeria and abducted about 276 girls.[42] While some of these girls escaped from captivity,[43] others were subsequently released by the group after negotiations with the government.[44] However, a number of them still remain in Boko Haram's captivity 3 years after.

12.2.2 Women as Operatives and Suicide Bombers

Boko Haram has deployed women in different roles as recruiters and to carry out reconnaissance and serve as volunteers or coerced suicide bombers for the organisation.[45] Boko Haram is unsurpassed in its deployment of female suicide bombers in

---

[36] BBC News 23 October 2014a.

For a detailed chronology of abductions of women by Boko Haram, see Mickolus (2016) p. 265.

[37] Matasu (8 Jan 2015).

[38] Matfess (2 August 2016), p. 6.

[39] See Matfess (2 August 2016), p. 4.

[40] Whiting (14 April 2015).

[41] Human Rights Watch (2014), p. 19.

[42] Abubakar (CNN 16 April 2014).

[43] BBC News 27 October 2014c.

[44] Al Jazeera News (13 Oct 2016).

[45] International Crisis Group (5 Dec 2016b), p. 6.

history.[46] The United Nations estimates that Boko Haram has deployed more than 100 abducted women and girls in attacks since 2014.[47] This trend has continued and seems to be increasing. On 11 February 2016, Boko Haram sent three young girls wearing suicide vests into the Dikwa IDP camp, where people displaced by the insurgency had taken refuge. Posing as IDPs, the girls passed the night at the camp only for two of them to detonate their vests the following morning, killing 58 people and wounding 78 others.[48] It is alleged that the third girl and would-be suicide bomber refused to detonate her bomb and chose to surrender to security forces because she saw her parents and siblings among those who had sought refuge at the camp.[49] On 25 January 2017, a female suicide bomber detonated her suicide vest at the home of the Chairman of the Civilian JTF, killing one person and injuring two others.[50] On 17 February 2017, seven suicide bombers attacked Muna Garage in Maiduguri. All seven attackers were female teenagers.[51] According to an analyst, '[n]o other insurgency in history has relied upon women and girls in such an abusive and predatory manner, so systematically', and it will take a long time for their survivors to overcome the trauma and regain normalcy.[52] Abducted women and girls have been forced to join the ranks of Boko Haram and to carry out suicide bombings.[53] In most cases, these female suicide bombers are often too badly burnt to be identified, let alone interrogated about their motivations.[54]

12.2.3 Women as 'Wives' and Sex Slaves

Boko Haram has used rape as a weapon of torture, subjugation of the local communities, humiliation of victims and domination of the local communities and generally as a weapon of war.[55] At another level, it can be argued that it is from the mere fact that these perpetrators are being pricked and convicted by their own consciences about the moral reprehensibility of their conduct that they had quickly turned to the Koran to formulate a logic that regards these innocent young women as war booty in order to assuage their depraved consciences. This partly explains the huge number of female abductees in Boko Haram's captivity. According to someone who once lived in an area controlled by Boko Haram, 60% of the overall Boko Haram

[46] STRATFOR (23 October 2015).

[47] Searcey (11 Feb 2016).

[48] Abubakar et al. (CNN 11 February 2016).

[49] Searcey (11 Feb 2016).

[50] Sahara Reporters (25 Jan 2017b).

[51] Aljazeera (17 February 2017).

[52] Aljazeera (17 February 2017).

[53] Amnesty International (14 April 2015a).

[54] Bloom and Matfess (2016), p. 113.

[55] See generally, Bloom and Matfess (2016). See also, Kishi (25 Feb 2015); Raleigh et al. (2010), pp. 651–660.

Caliphate population is female, and even Boko Haram foot soldiers had several 'wives'. One male survivor of Boko Haram attacks explained how Boko Haram once raided his community, abducting women and '"tossing 5,000 Naira [about $25] on the floor as a bride price" for the kidnapped girls'.[56] It is estimated that Boko Haram has abducted thousands of women and girls, and after such abductions, the exceptionally beautiful ones are selected and groomed to be married to senior members of Boko Haram leadership. According to one 15-year old female victim:

> After we were declared married, I was ordered to live in his cave, but I always managed to avoid him. He soon began to threaten me with a knife to have sex with him, and when 'I still refused he brought out his gun, warning that he would kill me if I shouted. Then he began to rape me every night. He was a huge man in his mid30s, and I had never had sex before. It was very painful, and I cried bitterly because I was bleeding afterwards.'[57]

On 28 April 2015, a total of 293 women and girls were rescued by Nigerian forces from Boko Haram, and according to the spokesman for the UNSG Ban Ki-moon, Stephane Dujaric, '[a] large number of girls and women rescued from Boko Haram have been found to be pregnant', though it was unclear exactly how many as the process continued.[58] According to some local authorities, up to 1000 women and girls were rescued from Boko Haram at Boboshe village, and many claimed to have been used as sex slaves.[59] Other women have been allegedly raped repeatedly by Boko Haram with the intention of impregnating them to bear children who would be future Jihadists for the group.[60] The so-called marriages of abducted girls to Boko Haram commanders and fighters are designed to serve the 'multiple purposes of increasing group cohesion through the provision of women as prizes, cultivating loyalty through the enhanced status following "marriage," and inspiring awe in the local populace'.[61] Abducted women are often dispatched to members of the group to serve as 'wives'.[62]

12.2.4 *Women as Procreators of Boko Haram's Next Generation of Jihadists*

In 2015, the UN Secretary General's Special Representative on Sexual Violence in Conflict observed that by constantly raping and treating female captives as instruments for producing children for its members, Boko Haram was 'waging a war on

[56] Matfess (2 August 2016), p. 5.
[57] Matfess (2 August 2016), p. 5.
[58] UNFPA (6 May 2015).
[59] Searcey (11 Feb 2016).
[60] Searcey (11 Feb 2016).
[61] Bloom et al. (2007).
[62] Bloom et al. (2007).

women's physical, sexual and reproductive autonomy and rights'.[63] According to her, the tactic of Boko Haram and its strategy regarding women should be distinguished from the regular acts of barbarism and violence against women in an armed conflict. Sexual violence in the Boko Haram insurgency was 'not merely incidental, but integral to their [Boko Haram's] strategy of domination and self-perpetuation'.[64] Like the ISIS, Boko Haram's ideology is to abduct women and girls, 'own' and trade them as common chattels, marry them off to fighters and compel them to produce children for fighters who would become the next generation of Jihadists.[65] Thus, Boko Haram's violence against women has been driven not only by the sexual exploitation and pleasures of its members but also by the need to self-perpetuate by turning women into human incubators 'breeding' the next generation of Boko Haram fighters. According to reports, some Boko Haram fighters render prayers before raping their female victims in the hope that the resulting pregnancies would produce children who would become future Boko Haram Jihadists.[66] Alhaji Kashim Shettima, then Governor of Borno State, said that much when he remarked that 'the sect leaders made a conscious effort to impregnate the women … Some … even pray before mating, offering supplications for God to make the products of what they are doing become children that will inherit their ideology.'[67]

Rape, forced marriage, forced pregnancy, sexual slavery, forced labour, forced recruitment and so on are only a few of the atrocities that women have endured under Boko Haram. But more importantly, Boko Haram regards women as having much more value in the group's long-term strategic goal of continuity of the Jihad than just satisfaction of sexual appetites. Women and their reproductive capacity are seen as a critical component of Boko Haram's long-term survival strategies through procreation and self-perpetuation.[68] Boko Haram's weaponisation of women is not only intent on 'destroying existing family and community structures, but it is bent on controlling their future composition …. In order to give rise to a new generation raised in their own image, they are waging war on women's physical and reproductive autonomy and rights.'[69] Women and young girls are deliberately targeted not merely because they are considered soft targets but also because of the short-term goal of sexual satisfaction and the long-term contributions they could make to the cause of Boko Haram by procreating its next generation of foot soldiers.[70]

---

[63] Bangura (27 May 2015).

[64] Bangura (27 May 2015).

[65] Bangura (27 May 2015).

[66] See for example, Nossiter (18 May 2015).

[67] Quoted in Bloom and Matfess (2016), p. 110.

[68] Zenn and Pearson (2014), pp. 46–57.

[69] Bangura (27 May 2015).

[70] Nossiter (18 May 2015).

12.2.5 *Women as Boko Haram's Recruitment Strategy*

The role of sexual appetite in the Boko Haram conflict and the full scale of the resulting atrocities may never be known, but besides serving as wives and sex slaves for Boko Haram fighters, women have also been used as recruitment strategy. As objects of sexual pleasure, when Boko Haram members were forced to abandon their wives in the cities due to intense military presence, they resorted to raiding and capturing women in villages to satisfy their sexual desires. The group deliberately abducts young girls whom it subsequently holds out as rewards or brides for young men who agree to become fighters for the group.[71] As Kyari Mohammed puts it, '[f]or some men in Boko Haram, participation in the insurgency is "mostly about power and access to women … You can take anyone's woman, and she is yours."'[72] In a region where the majority of people are poorer than the poor in other parts of the country, this behaviour is exacerbated by a lack of financial resources, which deprives young men the means to 'court and maintain a wife, [hence] access to women has particularly strong appeal'.[73] Therefore, using young girls to lure young men into its fold and handing women and young girls to its fighters for sexual gratification enables Boko Haram to control and guarantee the allegiance of its fighters and maintain group cohesion.[74]

In its sociocultural context, the heavy reliance on women and the cruelty of the sexual atrocities they have been subjected to by Boko Haram can only be driven by certain lecherousness fighters would otherwise be constrained from expressing by sociocultural inhibitions prevailing in the conservative and predominantly Muslim northeast Nigeria. In communities where the debased desires of deviants had had to be suppressed upon risk of severe sanctions, the outbreak of the Boko Haram conflict suddenly provided an opportunity for the expression of these craving without any form of restraints or inhibitions.

12.2.6 *Women as Boko Haram's Baits and Chips*

In November 2013, Boko Haram abducted a teenage Christian girl, whom they held for several months during which period she was forcefully converted to Islam, served both as a cook and cleaner and was used to bait government security forces to where they could become vulnerable and easy targets.[75] Boko Haram has used

---

[71] Boko Haram has successfully commoditised women not only as a recruitment strategy but also as a way to "reward and retain" fighters. See Bloom and Matfess (2016), p. 120.

[72] Matfess (2 August 2016), p. 4, quoting Kyari Mohammed, Head of the Peace and Security Centre, Modibbo Adama University of Technology, Yola.

[73] Matfess (2 August 2016), p. 4.

[74] International Crisis Group (4 May 2016a), p. 10.

[75] Zenn and Pearson (2014), p. 50.

women as bargaining chips with the Nigerian authorities both to secure family members of Boko Haram operatives in custody of Nigerian government or to secure the release of captured Boko Haram operatives.[76] Women and girls have been used to extract ransom payments, effect prisoner swaps and lure security forces into ambush.[77]

12.3 Weaponising Women in the Boko Haram's Insurgency

Women became part of Boko Haram's insurgency in various ways: some by coercion, others as victims of brainwash and indoctrination and others by choice. In the section below, we take a look at the different circumstances in which women and girls have found themselves as Boko Haram's instruments of warfare.

12.3.1 Women as War Booty in the Jihad Against Infidels

There is a religious dimension to the abduction of women by Boko Haram. There is evidence to show that the majority of women and young girls were abducted by Boko Haram either because they were Christians or because they were students or both.[78] These women were beaten, tortured and threatened with death unless they converted to Islam and stopped attending Western-style schools. A large contingent of those abducted were from Christian-dominated southern Borno State. There are detailed, systematic attacks against Christian women by Boko Haram, who have been subjected to abductions, rape, forced marriages and forced conversion to Islam.[79]

12.3.2 Women as Coerced Members of Boko Haram

According to a recent UNICEF report, Boko Haram abductions and use of young girls in suicide attacks has consistently increased over the last few years.[80] Since 2014, a total of 117 children have been used as suicide bombers by Boko Haram, and over 80% of them are girls.[81] Although not the only terrorist group that deploys

[76] International Crisis Group (5 December 2016b), p. 7.

[77] Human Rights Watch (2014), p. 3.

[78] Human Rights Watch (2014), pp. 16–17.

[79] Barkindo et al. (2013). See also International Crisis Group (4 May 2016a), p. 10; Zenn and Pearson (2014), p. 49.

[80] UNICEF (12 April 2017), p. 6.

[81] UNICEF (12 April 2017), p. 6.

women in its operations, Boko Haram's forced conscription and heavy reliance on girls and women to carry out attacks and as core component of its 'motivations, capabilities and strategies' make it stand out.[82] Boko Haram has successfully mobilised girls as emblems of its ideology and weaponised women as instruments of its Jihad.[83] It has achieved this using a variety of methods, including abductions, indoctrination and ideological persuasions, inducements and so on. For example, a young woman, Tabitha Adamu, was captured with her mother when their village was attacked by Boko Haram, which killed her father and brother. She was forced to convert to Islam, join and marry a Boko Haram fighter, who impregnated her.[84] Fatima Usman was kidnapped in Bama and forced to marry a Boko Haram fighter but preferred this arrangement instead of being single because single girls were raped repeatedly by Boko Haram fighters.[85] Many of the abducted girls are brainwashed and radicalised, then trained to engage in combat and to carry out acts like slitting the throats of victims and suicide bombings.[86]

12.3.3 Women as Cajoled Members of Boko Haram

Boko Haram members have also used duplicity and guile to lure women into its fold, lying about their identity and promising young girls marriage and material gifts.[87] There are some instances where such women and girls inadvertently married Boko Haram fighters, unaware of their identity, only to discover that their husbands are Boko Haram fighters and they too ultimately becoming Boko Haram operatives themselves.[88] This was the case with Hauwa Haruna, who only discovered that her husband was a member of the group when she was already 8 months pregnant and her husband relocated her to a camp.[89] Her husband fled when security forces rescued her, and she admits that though she did not want the marriage on discovering who her husband was, she could not leave. Some girls and women were manipulated into partaking in the atrocities.[90] It has been argued that, in very many cases, the degree of conscious participation of these women is questionable, and some of the girls who are as young as ten are just too young to possess the capacity of making such decisions.[91] According to reports, young girls and women are told that

[82] See Bloom and Matfess (2016), p. 106.

[83] Bloom and Matfess (2016), p. 106.

[84] McLaughlin (2015).

[85] McLaughlin (2015).

[86] Matfess (2016), p. 6.

[87] Oduah (2016).

[88] International Crisis Group (5 Dec 2016b), p. 9.

[89] McLaughlin (2015).

[90] Oduah (2016).

[91] Awford (10 Jan 2015).

suicide bombing is a service to Allah and would take them to paradise. According to a Chadian official:

> [i]n the interview we have conducted with Boko Haram members, they told us that they tell women and girls that they will go to paradise if they commit suicide for Allah. So, they ask girls, 'Who wants to go to paradise?' They tell the girls that they will also wear bombs. So the man straps a bomb to his body and to the girl. They tell the girl, It's [*sic*] do this and well meet again in paradise. So the girl goes forward and detonates herself, expecting the man to do the same. But the man does not. He watches her blow herself up into pieces and then goes to the next girl to lure her to do the same thing.[92]

There is a contradiction between Boko Haram's claim of moral chastity of women and its actual practices such as forced marriages, forced pregnancies, and so on, all of which in reality debase women and betray Boko Haram's claim to moral purity and protection of women.[93]

12.3.4 Women as Objects of Boko Haram Rituals and Cannibalism

There are also reports that as part of its process of administering oath of allegiance to new members, Boko Haram gave these women dates or coconut to eat and tea to drink.[94] The dates were usually 'dipped in blood and sometimes mixed with human flesh'.[95] This sometimes involved some mystical tea and other rituals. According to a former wife of Boko Haram member:

> The first time I came to join Boko Haram, somebody came, the commander who is a mallam, and asked me, 'Do you believe in Allah?' Me, I said yes. 'And the prophet?' I said yes. 'And the Quran?' I said yes. He then gave me a date palm and coconut. I ate it and then I slept for three or four hours. Then I woke up and my heart was changed,' ... 'I loved Boko Haram. I didn't like normal men.[96]

These events were narrated by women who were once married to Boko Haram fighters and lived in Boko Haram camps at different times and places. These stories seem to confirm earlier reports by other sources about Boko Haram's ritual practices.[97]

---

[92] Oduah (2016), quoting a Chadian official.
[93] Bloom and Matfess (2016), p. 108.
[94] Oduah (2016).
[95] Oduah (2016).
[96] Oduah (2016).
[97] See for example, Campbell (2016).

12.3.5 *Women as Volunteer Wives and Members of Boko Haram*

The above cases notwithstanding, there are active women fighters in the ranks of Boko Haram having sworn full allegiance and loyalty to the cause of the insurgency.[98] Young girls and women should not always be cast in the mould of victims of gendered violence in the Boko Haram conflict. In some cases, some are willing active participants.[99] They are involved in different capacities in Boko Haram activities: enforcing camp rules, meting out punishments, giving lessons and so on. Attracted by financial rewards and other financial inducements, some girls and women have voluntarily offered to serve the group at different levels: tactical, strategic, operational, and so on. The Muslim wife of Boko Haram leaders were alleged to have taken part in the beheading of several victims.[100] There are reports that some parents have encouraged and facilitated their children joining Boko Haram.[101] The prevailing view is that women in rich countries are more likely to join terrorist organisations based on ideological convictions than compulsion or necessity, while those in poor countries are more likely to join such organisations more for economic reasons than coercion.[102] Given the increasing number of women and especially young girls in the rank of Boko Haram and the emerging revelations that a significant number of these women actually volunteered to join the group, wished for and preferred their lives with Boko Haram, it becomes quite difficult to determine the extent to which female membership of Boko Haram is voluntary or coerced. Before examining aspects of international law protecting women in situations of armed conflict such as the Boko Haram insurgency, it is imperative to briefly examine Boko Haram's justifications of its weaponisation of women and the motivations for female voluntary participation in Boko Haram insurgency.

12.4 Women's Motivations for Boko Haram Membership

It would be difficult to ascertain who among the females in Boko Haram's rank are volunteers. It most probably is the case that the vast majority of females in Boko Haram were coerced, goaded or brainwashed, especially given the fact that many of them are as young as 7 years.[103] Increasingly, these female operatives, many of whom have been widowed by losing their husbands in the insurgency (whether as a direct result of their husbands being killed in battle or as a consequence of the

[98] Bloom and Matfess (2016), p. 109.
[99] Bloom and Matfess (2016), p. 108.
[100] Zenn and Pearson (2014), p. 50.
[101] BBC News (25 Dec 2014b).
[102] Alfred (28 Feb 2015).
[103] Matfess (2016), p. 8.

excesses of Nigerian security forces), become vulnerable to recruitment at two levels. First, they become prone to indoctrination and radicalisation, and second, vengeance becomes a compelling motivation in the recruitment process. These widows are then indoctrinated and persuaded to avenge the death of their husbands by carrying out suicide attacks.[104] Some commentators observe that whereas the first group of females in the rank of Boko Haram were coerced and made captives of the group, there is a great likelihood that some of those who came later may have been persuaded to volunteer seeing it as 'unique opportunities' to serve in the cause of an otherwise male-dominated Jihad.[105]

Third, it has been suggested that some of the girls and women used might have been ostracised from their communities[106] or could be some of the millions of homeless beggars roaming the streets of northern Nigeria and who would be easy prey for Boko Haram's enticements. For example, in a recent case, a female suicide bomber stated that she was given N200 to go on a suicide mission for Boko Haram.[107] Others who have been victims of various abuses and torture by Boko Haram have been too damaged psychologically to be capable of rational choice, whereas others were completely oblivious to the fact that they had been strapped with suicide vests.[108] Boko Haram has also exploited the psychological 'softness' of young girls, who are alleged to be more gullible and pliant than older women, and this probably explains why we are seeing increasingly younger Boko Haram female suicide bombers.

12.5 How Boko Haram Justifies Its Weaponisation of Women

Whereas many insurgent groups have targeted women for attacks and recruited women into their operations, Boko Haram has weaponised women in a way never before seen in situations of armed conflicts.[109] Zenn argues that in similar conflicts in sub-Saharan Africa, 'women were targeted both for their assets, and as "assets" in themselves' and their value was not only reproductive, but also included their productive ability by contributing their skills and other essential services like cleaning and cooking needed for the success of the war effort.[110] From a tactical point of view, Boko Haram's deliberate targeting of women in many cases could be explained as a 'tactical exploitation of women'.[111] In 2015, a UN report found that ISIL and Boko Haram now adopt sexual violence as a weapon of war.[112]

[104] International Crisis Group (5 Dec 2016b), p. 11.

[105] International Crisis Group (4 May 2016a), p. 11; Zenn and Pearson (2014), p. 49.

[106] Iroegbu (4 Aug 2014).

[107] Vanguard Newspaper (8 Feb 2017a).

[108] Bloom and Matfess (2016), p. 111.

[109] Bloom and Matfess (2016), p. 108.

[110] Zenn and Pearson (2014), p. 50.

[111] Zenn and Pearson (2014), p. 50.

[112] United Nations (25 April 2014).

Generally, Boko Haram's random use of women in suicide bombing and how it rationalises this method underscore how Boko Haram conceptualises women as a disposable piece of artillery in its armoury rather than as an integral part of the organisation.[113]

Boko Haram has also targeted women as punitive measures in retaliation for the harassment, arrests, detention and killing and other perceived injustices meted to women associated with Boko Haram family members by government forces.[114] In many instances, Boko Haram had largely targeted Christian women or the 'women of the infidels'.[115] For example, Barkindo et al. reports that when Boko Haram attacked an educational institution in August of 2013, after killing the men, they separated the Muslim women and went ahead to rape the Christian women.[116] Some have argued that this is a continuation of the pre-existing cultural conditions in which women are discriminated against and exploited in northern Nigeria.[117] Some argue that Boko Haram's ideology does not specifically call for women to be targeted.[118] However, it is beyond doubt that generally, whether Muslim or Christians, women have been targeted by Boko Haram, and in some cases, such attacks have specifically targeted Christian women in an ideological posture that regards them as 'war booty', invoking the Koran to justify this action.[119] Boko Haram's use of women as instruments of war is arguably the worst atrocities against women in situations of armed conflict anywhere in the world in recent years. This once again underscores the vulnerable conditions of women caught in armed conflicts despite series of international instruments affording legal protections to women during armed conflict. In the next section of this contribution, we briefly map out a sketch of these legal protections of women in armed conflict and the extent to which these protections have been afforded women and girls in the Boko Haram conflict.

[113] Zenn and Pearson (2014), pp. 50–51.

[114] International Crisis Group (5 December 2016b), p. 6.

[115] See generally, Barkindo et al. (2013), for a detailed account of some of these attacks.

[116] Barkindo et al. (2013), p. 25.

[117] Barkindo et al. (2013), p. 17.

[118] Barkindo et al. (2013), p. 5.

[119] See United Nations General Assembly, Violations and Abuses Committed by Boko Haram and the Impact on Human Rights in the Countries Affected A/HRC/30/67, 9 December 2015, at para 38, quoting a Boko Haram video. It is pertinent to note that because inhabitants of Southern Borno State are predominantly Christian, any attacks there by Boko Haram might be interpreted as deliberately targeting Christians, but similar attacks have also been carried out in Northern Borno State where the inhabitants are predominantly Muslim. See for example, Faul (30 April 2014). (I am grateful to the anonymous reviewer for pointing out this fact). Whereas generally, Boko Haram launched indiscriminate attacks against civilians, there is evidence to show that the deliberately targeted Christians on several occasions giving them a choice to either convert to Islam or be killed. See Amnesty International (April 2015a), p. 32.

12.6 The Legal Protection of Women in the Boko Haram Armed Conflict

Generally, international law protects individuals in situations of armed conflicts,[120] and in particular, international humanitarian law (IHL), which regulates armed conflicts, whether in international armed conflict (IAC) or non-international armed conflict (NIAC), protects individuals not taking direct part in hostilities or *horse de combat*, in situations amounting to 'armed conflict', regardless of their gender.[121] For a long time, the international community has tried to focus on a legal framework that specifically protects women during armed conflict.[122] Whereas the four Geneva Conventions of 12 August 1949 apply in IAC, it is AP II and Article 3 common to the four Geneva Conventions that apply in situations of NIAC, although there is a growing convergence in the body of law applicable to IAC and NIAC.[123] Interestingly, customary international humanitarian law over the years has developed rules similar to those contained in AP I applicable in IAC and has made them applicable in situations of NIAC.[124] It should be noted that although Nigeria has ratified Additional Protocol II, this treaty is yet to be domesticated into Nigerian law. It is also important to acknowledge from the outset the challenges of applying and securing compliance with rules of IHL in armed conflicts involving non-state armed groups (NSAGs) such as Boko Haram.[125] But to the extent that these rules afford protection

[120] International Humanitarian Law, International Human Rights Law, International Criminal Law, aspects of International Refugee Law protect individuals during and after an armed conflict. It should be noted that Nigeria is a dualist state and a treaty is not enforceable in Nigeria unless it has been domesticated I Nigerian law by an Act of Parliament. See Section 12(1) Constitution of the Federal Republic of Nigeria, 1999. Nigeria became a party to all Four Geneva Conventions by accession on 20 June 1961 and the two Additional Protocols on 10 October 1988. The Four Geneva Conventions were domesticated by the Geneva Conventions Act of 30th September 1960.

[121] See the Geneva Convention for the Amelioration of the Condition of the Wounded and Sick in Armed Forces in the Field of 12 August 1949, 75 U.N.T.S. 31 (hereafter GC 1); Geneva Convention for the Amelioration of the Condition of the Wounded, Sick and Shipwrecked Members of Armed Forces at Sea of 12 August 1949, 75 U.N.T.S. 85, (hereafter GC 2); Geneva Convention relative to the Protection of Prisoners of War of 12 August 1949, 75 U.N.T.S. 135, (hereafter GC 3); Geneva Convention relative to the Protection of Civilian Persons in Time of War of 12 August 1949, 75 U.N.T.S. 287 (hereafter GC 4); Protocol Additional to the Geneva Conventions of 12 August 1949, and relating to the Protection of Victims of International Armed Conflicts, (Protocol I) adopted on 8 June 1977, 1125 U.N.T.S. 3 (hereafter AP I); and Protocol Additional to the Geneva Conventions of 12 August 1949, and relating to the Protection of Victims of Non-International Armed Conflicts, (Protocol II) adopted on 8 June 1977, 1125 U.N.T.S. 609 (hereafter AP II). See Glahn and Taulbe (2010), p. 604.

[122] UN General Assembly, Declaration on the Protection of Women and Children in Emergency and Armed Conflict, UNGA 3318 (XXIX) of 14 December 1974.

[123] Akande (2012), p. 35. See Tadic (Appeal on Jurisdiction) Case, the Appeals Chamber of the ICTY, para 127.

[124] Henckaerts and Doswald-Beck (2004), p. xxii, suggesting that the some of the distinctions may have become blurred by state practice.

[125] See for example, Bassiouni (2008), pp. 712–810.

to women as a group and bind all parties to a conflict, whether state or non-state actors, and even more so for purposes of holding perpetrators of atrocities accountable, we will outline some of the major provisions of these instruments applicable in NIAC such as the Boko Haram conflict.

The International Criminal Court (ICC) has determined that the Boko Haram conflict in Nigeria is a non-international armed conflict, and the ICC is conducting investigations in Nigeria with a view to ensuring that perpetrators of atrocities, particularly against women, are brought to justice should the Nigerian authorities prove themselves unwilling or unable to do so.[126] This is an imperative particularly for women who have borne the brunt of the conflict. Women experience armed conflict differently and in a multitude of ways that require that legal responses to their protection in situations of armed conflict be gender sensitive. We consider some of these provisions below.

12.6.1 *Specific Protection of Women in the Boko Haram Conflict Under International Humanitarian Law*

Generally, all parties to an armed conflict, whether the conflict is an IAC or a NIAC, have obligations under IHL to protect the civilian population.[127] Common Article 3 and AP II, which are the applicable law of IHL to the Boko Haram conflict, offer protection to civilians, including women and girls. Article 13(1) of AP II provides that 'the civilian population and individual civilians shall enjoy general protection against the dangers arising from military operations….'. As we have shown above, Boko Haram leadership has at various times ordered the displacement of the civilian population, particularly women, in violation of this rule. Furthermore, Article 13(2) of AP II provides that '[t]he civilian population as such, as well as individual civilians, shall not be the object of attack. Acts or threats of violence the primary purpose of which is to spread terror among the civilian population are prohibited.'[128] We have seen above that Boko Haram has deployed attacks against civilians, particularly women, with the obvious intention to terrify the civilian population. This is a clear violation of this rule of IHL for which Boko Haram members ought to be held to account. The activities of Boko Haram, such as the abduction and movement of women and girls from various parts of the northeast to Sambisa Forest, violate Article 17 (1) and (2) of AP II prohibiting moving the civilian population or forcing the civilian population to move to a territory different from theirs as a result of the conflict.

[126] See Office of the Prosecutor, ICC, Report on Preliminary Examination Activities 2013, 25 November 2013a at para 218. The ICC has stated that there is basis for concluding that as of 2013, Boko Haram committed crimes against humanity. See The Office of the Prosecutor, the International Criminal Court, Situation in Nigeria: Article 5 Report, 5 August 2013b.

[127] See the contribution by Elijah Okebukola in this volume.

[128] Article 13(2) the 1977 Protocol Additional to the Geneva Convention of 12 August 1949.

The condition of women in armed conflict is particularly precarious because they not only have to look after themselves but also have to see to the needs and survival of other family members, sometimes at great peril to their own physical security in an attempt to cope with the socio-economic dislocations created by the armed conflict.[129] Article 4(1) AP II offers protection to those not taking direct part in hostilities stating that '[a]ll persons who do not take a direct part or who have ceased to take part in hostilities, whether or not their liberty has been restricted, are entitled to respect for their person, honour and convictions and religious practices'. In particular, Article 4(2) AP II provides that '…acts against the persons referred to in paragraph 1 are and shall remain prohibited at any time and in any place whatsoever:

(a) violence to the life, health and physical or mental well-being of persons, in particular, murder as well as cruel treatment such as torture, mutilation or any form of corporal punishment;
(b) collective punishments;
(c) taking of hostages;
(d) acts of terrorism;
(e) outrages upon personal dignity, in particular humiliating and degrading treatment, rape, enforced prostitution and any form of indecent assault;
(f) slavery and the slave trade in all their forms;
(g) pillage;
(h) threats to commit any of the foregoing'.

As we have shown above, for a variety of reasons, Boko Haram has systematically deployed rape as an instrument of warfare in its insurgency. Women and girls have been subjected to the most brutal and horrifying violations with tales of having to endure series of rapes by several Boko Haram fighters a night.[130] In some cases, Boko Haram had sought to break the will and resolve of its female victims who refused to convert to Islam by raping them repeatedly. In other cases, Boko Haram used rape as a weapon of torture and subjugation to beat women and girls into submission and to intimidate the local communities. And in what would appear as perhaps the most bizarre reasons, Boko Haram has raped some victims with the intention of impregnating them in order to produce the next generation of Jihadists who would perpetuate its ideology and insurgency. The rape, forced marriage, forced pregnancy and sexual slavery to which Boko Haram has subjected women and girls in its insurgency violate Article 4(2)(a) and (e) of Additional Protocol II quoted above.

Of all the atrocities committed against women by Boko Haram since the insurgency began, the abductions of women and girls, especially at Chibok, generated the most attention. Women and young girls are frequently taken as hostages by Boko Haram and held under the most deplorable conditions of violence and physical, mental and sexual abuse and exploitation. As we have seen in the cases discussed above, women and girls constitute the largest group of Boko Haram hostages,

[129] International Committee of the Red Cross (6 May 2013).

[130] See generally, Human Rights Watch (October 2014), p. 7.

and more often than not, they have been subjected to various degrees of inhuman and degrading treatment. Young children, especially girls, have not been spared the scourge of Boko Haram's instrumentalisation of women in the conflict.

Article 4(3) (c) AP II provides that 'children who have not attained the age of fifteen years shall neither be recruited in the armed forces or groups nor allowed to take part in hostilities'. In the current conflict, many cases are reported of children who have been orphaned by the conflict being taken by Boko Haram after killing their parents. In and of itself, Boko Haram's use of terrorism in the conflict is prohibited by Article 4(2)(d) AP II, but more grievous is the fact that Boko Haram has resorted to deploying women and young girls in carrying out these terrorist attacks. As we have shown above, in many cases, Boko Haram has turned young girls, some as young as ten, into suicide bombers. Needless to say, Boko Haram routinely violates and has no regard for IHL, and these should ordinarily give rise to the need to hold the perpetrators accountable. Furthermore, Article 3 common to the four Geneva Conventions prohibits wanton killing, acts of sexual violence, torture and inhumane, humiliating, cruel and degrading treatment, all of which have become the hallmarks of the Boko Haram conflict and perpetrated by Boko Haram fighters.[131]

12.6.2 Specific Protection of Women in the Boko Haram Conflict Under International Human Rights Law

International human rights law offers additional protection for girls and women in times of NIAC. Nigeria is a party to several international human rights instruments that seek to protect the right of women to life; freedom from torture, sexual violence, discrimination on the ground of sex; freedom from degrading and inhuman punishment and other ill treatment; freedom from slavery; and freedom from forced prostitution and other common abuses suffered by women in armed conflicts.[132] These international human rights instruments become particularly important in

[131] Common Article 3 of the Four GCs provides "[i]n the case of armed conflict not of an international character occurring in the territory of one of the High Contracting Parties, each party to the conflict shall be bound to apply, as a minimum, the following provisions: (1) Persons taking no active part in the hostilities, including members of armed forces who have laid down their arms and those placed *horse de combat* by sickness, wounds, detention, or any other cause, shall in all circumstances be treated humanely, without any adverse distinction founded on race, colour, religion or faith, sex, birth or wealth, or any other similar criteria. To this end the following acts are and shall remain prohibited at any time and in any place whatsoever with respect to the above-mentioned persons: a) violence to life and person, in particular murder of all kinds, mutilation, cruel treatment and torture; b) taking of hostages; c) outrages upon personal dignity, in particular humiliating and degrading treatment; d) the passing of sentences and the carrying out of executions without previous judgment pronounced by a regularly constituted court affording all the judicial guarantees which are recognized as indispensable by civilized peoples."

[132] See United Nations (2010), p. 36.

situations like the Boko Haram conflict where there was considerable lapse of time (with sexual violence and other abuses of the human rights of women) before the conflict crossed the threshold of NIAC and, more so, in the future post-conflict situation when IHL has ceased to apply or has limited application.[133] These regional and international human rights treaties ratified by Nigeria protect the rights of women and girls and impose obligations on Nigeria to put necessary and adequate measures in place to prevent, prosecute and punish cases of abuses, more so on the scale that we have seen those rights violated by Boko Haram fighters.[134] Article 7 of the International Covenant on Civil and Political Rights (ICCPR) protects against the kind of torture and other cruel and inhuman and degrading treatment and punishment that women and young girls have been subjected to by Boko Haram.[135] Article 10(1) of the International Covenant on Economic, Social and Cultural Rights (ICESCR) protects against forced marriages.[136] The African Charter on Human and People's Rights, which has been domesticated into Nigerian law, contains provisions guaranteeing the rights to life, dignity of the human person, education and so on.[137] Similarly, Articles 11 and 22 of the African Charter on the Rights and Welfare of the Child guarantee the rights of the child to education and the right not to be recruited to take part in hostilities during armed conflicts respectively.[138] Articles 27

[133] United Nations (2010), p. 36.

[134] See for example, Articles 1, 2, 3, 4, 5, 16(2), 18, 26, of the Universal Declaration of Human Rights, which though is not a binding treaty is now customary international law.

[135] International Covenant on Civil and Political Rights adopted on 16 Dec. 1966 and entered into force on 23 March 1976; G.A. Res. 2200 (XXI) U.N. Doc. A/6316 (1966) 999 U.N.T.S. 171. Nigeria acceded to this Convention on 39 July 1993; Convention against Torture and Other Cruel, Inhuman or Degrading Treatment or Punishment adopted 10 Dec. 1984 and entered into force on 26 June 1987, G.A. Res. 39/46, 39 UN G.A.O.R, Supp. (No 51) UN Doc. A/39/51, at 197 (1984); Charter on Human and People's Rights adopted 27 July 1981 and entered into force on 21 October 1986, O.A.U. Doc. CAB/LEG/67/3 Rev. 5; Convention on the Elimination of All Forms of Discrimination Against Women, adopted 18 Dec. 1979 and entered into force on 3 Sept. 1981, G.A. 34/180, 34 UN G.A.O.R., Supp. (No. 46), UN Doc. A/34/46, at 193 (1979), Nigeria ratified this treaty on 13 June, 1985; Convention on the Rights of the Child, adopted on 20 Nov. 1989 and entered into force on 2 Sept. 1990, G.A. Res. 44/25 UN G.A.O.R., Supp. (No. 49), UN Doc. A/44/49 at 166 (1989), Nigeria ratified this treaty on 19 April 1991. In terms of Article 2(3)(a) of the ICCPR, the Nigerian State has an obligation to see to it that these women who have been victims of Boko Haram abuses have remedies.

[136] International Covenant on Economic, Social and Cultural Rights, adopted 16 Dec. 1966 and entered into force on 3 Jan. 1976, G.A. Res. 2200A (XXI), UN. Doc. A/6316 (1966), 993 U.N.T.S. 3. Nigeria acceded to this treaty on 29 July 1993. See also Convention against Torture and Other Cruel, Inhuman or Degrading Treatment or Punishment adopted 10 Dec. 1984 and entered into force on 26 June 1987, G.A. Res. 39/46, 39 UN G.A.O.R, Supp. (No 51) UN Doc. A/39/51, at 197 (1984).

[137] See Articles 4, 5, 6, 8, 12, 17 of African Charter on Human and Peoples' Rights, 27 June 1981, OAU Doc. CAB/LEG/67/3 rev. 5; 1520 U.N.T.S. 217 (hereafter the Banjul Charter). Nigeria ratified the Charter on 22 July 1983.

[138] For other rights and protections enjoyed by the child in terms of this treaty, see for example, see Articles 9, 11, 16 of the African Charter on the Rights and Welfare of the Child. Nigeria ratified this treaty on 23 June 2001.

and 29 guarantee the child's freedom from sexual exploitation and abduction, respectively, both of which have characterised and perhaps represented Boko Haram's worst atrocities against children since the commencement of the armed conflict.[139] Young girls are also protected under the Convention on the Rights of the Child 1989, particularly Article 38, which requires states to respect and make sure that rules of IHL relating to the child are respected in situations of armed conflict, including caring for children affected by armed conflict.[140] The Additional Protocol to the Convention on the Rights of the Child prohibits the use of child soldiers.[141]

Finally, the Convention on the Elimination of Discrimination Against Women and its Additional Protocol would also be of great importance in the post-Boko Haram conflict situation in northeast Nigeria. This is to reduce the abuses and discrimination faced by women and girls who have been affected by the conflict. These women victims of Boko Haram, whether rescued or escapees, face stigmatisation and rejection by their communities notwithstanding the reintegration efforts of government, religious and community leaders and NGOs. This is even more so when sexual abuses and rapes by Boko Haram have resulted in pregnancies and children by these women. The pressures of cultural practices and cleavages subject the women to double jeopardy and victimisation through stigmatisation and ostracism.[142] Some of these women who have been widowed by the insurgency have had their homes looted or burned down by Boko Haram during attacks or, in some cases, by rampaging Nigerian security forces.[143] The women have often been victimised too by their own communities, which stigmatise and discriminate against them because they are considered sympathetic or suspected of being members of Boko Haram.[144] They therefore face all forms of gender discrimination that deprives them access to critical resources such as land to help them rebuild their lives. It is pertinent to note that some of these rights and protections are also enshrined in Chapter IV of the 1999 Nigerian Constitution, including the right to life (s. 33); right to dignity of the human person (s. 34); right to liberty (s. 35); right to private and family life (s. 37); freedom of thought, conscience and religion (s. 38); freedom of movement (s. 41); and freedom from discrimination on grounds of, *inter alia*, sex and religion (s. 42). All of these should provide the necessary domestic and international legal framework for holding perpetrators of abuses against women and girls during the conflict to account.

---

[139] See Articles 27 and 29 of the African Charter on the Rights and Welfare of the Child CAB/LEG/153/Rev. 2, adopted by the Twenty-Sixth Session of the of the Assembly of Heads of State and Government of the OAU, Addis Ababa, Ethiopia, July 1990.

[140] See Convention on the Rights of the Child adopted by the UN General Assembly Resolution 44/25 of 20 November 1989 and entered into force on 2 September 1990.

[141] See Articles 1,2, and 4 of the Optional Protocols to the Convention on the Rights of the Child on the Involvement of Children in Armed Conflict, adopted by the United Nations General Assembly Resolution A/RES/54/263 on 25 May 2000 and entered into force on 12 February 2002.

[142] Bloom and Matfess (2016), p. 117.

[143] See generally, Amnesty International (June 2015c); Human Rights Watch "Spiralling Violence: Boko Haram Attacks and Security Forces Abuses in Nigeria" (2012).

[144] Matfess (2016), pp. 8–10.

12.6.3 Specific Protection of Women in the Boko Haram Armed Conflict Under International Criminal Law

Nigeria is a signatory to the Rome Statute of the ICC (ICC Statute) and has been in the process of domesticating it through legislation for some years now.[145] Article 8(2)(c) of the ICC Statute provides that grave breaches of common Article 3 of the four Geneva Conventions constitute war crimes in the context of a NIAC. Acts directed at civilians not taking active part in the hostilities, including murder, all kinds of violence against the person and cruel treatment and torture, outrages on the dignity of the person particularly 'humiliating and degrading treatment', as well as the taking of hostages, all constitute war crimes. In particular, Article 8(2)(e) of the Rome Statute of the ICC states that serious violations of the laws and customs of war applicable in a NIAC if carried out in a NIAC constitute war crimes, including 'Intentionally directing attacks against the civilian population as such or against individual civilians not taking direct part in hostilities; Intentionally directing attacks against buildings dedicated to religion, education, art, science or charitable purposes, historic monuments, hospitals and places where the sick and wounded are collected, provided they are not military objectives; Pillaging a town or place, even when taken by assault; Committing rape, sexual slavery, enforced prostitution, forced pregnancy, … and any other form of sexual violence also constituting a serious violation of article 3 common to the four Geneva Conventions; Conscripting or enlisting children under the age of fifteen years into armed forces or groups or using them to participate actively in hostilities…'[146] Besides the wilful killing and other atrocities constituting war crimes and crimes against humanity committed by Boko Haram fighters, the use of rape and other sexual violence as instruments of torture and warfare and the weaponisation of women in the armed conflict by Boko Haram fall squarely within the offences defined in the Rome Statute above. In several decisions, both the ICTY and ICTR found that rape was used as and constituted torture during armed conflicts.[147] Thus, the way Boko Haram has deployed sexual violence weaponising women and using rape as instruments of both torture and warfare would constitute war crimes.[148] In *Prosecutor v Delalic and Others*,[149] the ICTY found that the use of rape in an armed conflict constituted torture.

[145] Nigeria ratified the Rome Statute on 27 Sept. 2001.

[146] Article 8(2)(e) of Rome Statute of the ICC.

[147] See for example, *Prosecutor v Furundzija,* Case No IT-95-17/1, Judgement of 10 December 1998; *Prosecutor* v *Nikolic*, First Amended Indictment, Case No IT-94-2; *Prosecutor* v *Jankovic and Others*, Case No IT-96-23, Judgement of 22 February 2001 (appeal decision); *Prosecutor* v *Kvocka and Others*, Case No IT-98-30/1, Judgement of 2 November 2001.

[148] See for example, *Prosecutor v Furundzija,* Case No IT-95-17/1, Judgement of 10 December 1998; *Prosecutor* v *Nikolic*, First Amended Indictment, Case No IT-94-2; *Prosecutor* v *Jankovic and Others*, Case No IT-96-23, Judgement of 22 February 2001 (appeal decision); *Prosecutor* v *Kvocka and Others*, Case No IT-98-30/1, Judgement of 2 November 2001.

[149] See *Prosecutor v Delalic and Others*, Case No. IT-96-21, Judgement of 16 November 1998.

12.7 The Fate of Women in the Aftermath of Boko Haram and the Prospects of Accountability

12.7.1 The Plight of Women

The nature of modern warfare has changed radically as more and more conflicts are now taking place in urban spaces.[150] Urban warfare increases the vulnerability of women and girls regardless of whether they are combatants or civilians, and in the case of Boko Haram, the entrenched system of patriarchy and gender inequality have now been exacerbated by the prevailing conflict, which reproduces and intensifies the suffering of women.[151] Generally, there are more civilian casualty of armed conflict than combatants, and given the traditional roles that women play in taking care of their families, they are open to and suffer disproportionately when conflicts like the Boko Haram insurgency dislocate and displace people and their means of livelihoods and survival such as food, water, fuel, medicines and so on. As the ICRC puts it, '[w]omen in wartime have shown tremendous courage and resilience as survivors and as heads of households – a role for which many of them have had no preparation and which is made more difficult by the social constraints often imposed on them'.[152] This is particularly true in the case of the Boko Haram insurgency in a sociocultural context in northeast Nigeria where patriarchy is entrenched and the role of women is defined by religious practices now legislated by state law. Women and girls have been rendered more vulnerable to Boko Haram attacks by these situations; for example, some have been abducted on their way to fetch firewood for family use.[153]

12.7.2 The Prospects of Accountability

The primary responsibility to investigate, prosecute and punish the perpetrators of the above crimes against humanity and war crimes against women and girls in the insurgency lies with the Nigerian state. From the survey of the above rules of IHL, it is clear that all acts of terrorism are prohibited in a NIAC such as the Boko Haram conflict because terrorist acts are almost always indiscriminate and target civilians and are designed to cause fear, terror and awe among the civilian population. In terms of Article 4(2)(d) of AP II, terrorism violates IHL and should be prosecuted and punished by Nigeria.[154] Prior to the period when the Boko Haram conflict was declared a

[150] International Committee of the Red Cross (6 May 2013).

[151] International Committee of the Red Cross (6 May 2013).

[152] International Committee of the Red Cross (6 May 2013).

[153] See Human Rights Watch (October 2014), p. 21.

[154] See Sections 2, 3, 4 and 5 of the Nigerian Geneva Conventions Act of 30 Sept. 1960, Laws of the Federation of Nigeria (2004). Although this Act only relates to the Four Geneva Conventions (not applicable in NIAC) and not the Additional Protocols of 1977, they nevertheless provide for

NIAC, the penal code, the counterterrorism legislation and other penal legislation would apply to the crimes committed during that period.[155] Boko Haram operatives could be prosecuted under the Terrorism Prevention Act adopted by Nigeria in 2011.[156] Nigeria is a signatory to the Rome Statute of the ICC, and the perpetrators could also be prosecuted for crimes against humanity under Article 7 or for war crimes under Article 8(2)(c) and (e) of the Rome Statute of the ICC.[157] Nevertheless, the international community could invoke its residual obligation to prosecute the perpetrators of these atrocities against women if Nigeria proves unable or unwilling to do so.

In 2000, the UN Security Council adopted Resolution 1325 intended to provide a comprehensive legal framework for the protection of women and girls in situations of armed conflict.[158] In addition, UN Security Council Resolution 1820 requires states to prevent and punish perpetrators of sexual violence against civilians and women and children during an armed conflict.[159] The UN Security Council has a mandate to adopt appropriate measures to hold accountable those who have deployed sexual violence as an instrument of warfare during and after an armed conflict.[160] However, it goes without saying that whereas it has contributed to creating awareness about sexual abuses in armed conflict, these resolutions do not appear to have brought about any meaningful progress in combating sexual violence against women in situations of armed conflict, and it is unlikely that there would be prosecution of perpetrators of atrocities in the Boko Haram conflict with the government only fixated on ending the insurgency, even if that means sacrificing justice on the altar of impunity. Regardless of the existing UN Security Council resolutions on the subject, to the extent that none of them established any monitoring or enforcement systems to ensure compliance, we are unlikely to witness the prosecution of those responsible for the mass atrocities against women in the Boko Haram conflict.[161] It should be mentioned that the Office of the Prosecutor of the ICC has stated that the atrocities committed by Boko Haram would constitute crimes against humanity and war crimes.[162] In terms of Articles 1 and 17 of the Rome Statute, Nigeria as the

---

prosecution and punishment of grave breaches such as "wilful killing, torture or inhuman treatment, including biological experiments, wilfully causing great suffering or serious injury to body or health" as well as taking of hostages. See also Gasser (2002), p. 556.

[155] Akande (2012), pp. 41–41, 46.

[156] See the Terrorism (Prevention) Act No 10, 2011, Laws of the Federal Republic of Nigeria.

[157] Nigeria ratified the Rome Statute of the ICC on 27 September 2001 but is yet to domesticate the treaty and since Nigeria is a dualist country, the Rome Statute will not take effect in the country until domesticated. See Section 12 of the Constitution of the Federal Republic of Nigeria 1999.

[158] See United Nations Security Council Resolutions S/RES/1325 (2000) 31 October 2000; S/RES/1888 (2009) 30 September 2009; S/RES/1889 (2009) 5 October 2009. See United Nations (2010), p. 71.

[159] S/RES/1829 (2008) 19 June 2008, at para 4; S/RES/1888 (2009) 30 September 2009 at para 10.

[160] S/RES/1829 (2008) 19 June 2008.

[161] United Nations (2010), p. 71.

[162] The ICC has stated that it has established eight possible cases of war crimes and crimes against humanity committed by Boko Haram and two cases by Nigerian Security Forces, as of 2015. See Office of the Prosecutor, ICC, Report on Preliminary Examination Activities 2015, at para 195.

territorial state would be preferred to prosecute these crimes, failing which the ICC could step in under the principle of complementarity. However, as stated above, it remains to be seen whether any of these would happen. To date, although there is abundant evidence of prosecution of suspects for acts of terrorism, treason and other crimes related to threats to national security, there is no evidence of prosecution of perpetrators of sexual violence against women whether by Boko Haram or Nigerian security forces.

12.7.3 The Fate of Women Is Sealed in Nigeria's Pervasive Culture of Impunity

The plight of women and girls caught in the complex web of the Boko Haram armed conflict in northeast Nigeria is one of double jeopardy—having endured all manner of sexual violence under Boko Haram, they also have to face further discrimination and perils at the hands of Nigerian forces and their local communities for being associated with Boko Haram. Many of these accusations are unfounded because at the initial stage, the women captured by Boko Haram or by Nigerian security forces in their raids on Boko Haram had no direct involvement in the conflict except that they happened to be family members of Boko Haram operatives.[163] Even the female relatives of Boko Haram operatives arrested by security operatives were not suspected of participation in terrorist activities as of that time, and it was even more doubtful that such family members knew about their husbands' links to Boko Haram.[164] But in a society where impunity is pervasive, arbitrary and vigilante justice would even be more so in the event of an armed conflict, and this is exactly what we are seeing in the plight of women in the Boko Haram conflict in Nigeria, where women now face double jeopardy by the abuses and discrimination they are subjected to, first, by Boko Haram and then by their communities and state security forces.[165] The tragedy of the culture of impunity prevalent in Nigeria is borne out by incidents where some women and girls who had been displaced or either survived or escaped Boko Haram sexual abuses and violence ended up being raped or re-raped in IDP camps by Nigerian officials, including camp leaders, vigilante groups, policemen and soldiers.[166] There are many factors contributing to the culture of impunity in Nigeria that space will not permit us to explore here, but suffice it to say that there are several legislation in Nigerian law that are clear obstacles to accountability for sexual violence and abuses against women. For example, under Section 55 of the Penal Code (which is the primary penal legislation in operation across northern Nigeria), it is apparently legal for a husband to assault his wife.[167] Hence,

[163] Zenn and Pearson (2014), p. 48.

[164] Zenn and Pearson (2014), p. 48.

[165] For a detailed report on this, see for example, Amnesty International (September 2014).

[166] Human Rights Watch (31 October 2016).

[167] Zenn and Pearson (2014), p. 47.

the odds are stacked against women and their quest for justice or redress within the judicial system, and the chances of bringing those who have weaponised women in the Boko Haram insurgency to justice are very slim. This is coupled with the politics of amnesty in Nigeria on the basis of which some argue for granting amnesty to Boko Haram notwithstanding the atrocities committed by the group.[168]

12.8 Conclusion

For a variety of reasons, Boko Haram has successfully weaponised women in the course of its insurgency. Women have been subjected to some of the worst forms of sexual violence and abuses ranging from rape to forced marriage and forced pregnancy to using young girls as suicide bombers. There is evidence to suggest that some of these young girls and women married Boko Haram fighters for love; others joined voluntarily based on ideological convictions and willingly participated in Boko Haram's terrorist atrocities for different motivations. However, the vast majority of these women were abducted and coerced into membership where they have been raped, tortured and subjected to other forms of sexual violence. Women are protected under IHL and IHRL in a non-international armed conflict like the Boko Haram conflict, and where the rights of women victims of Boko Haram under domestic and international laws have been grossly violated, the perpetrators should be brought to justice.

There are different views on how Nigeria can hold Boko Haram perpetrators of mass atrocities accountable, especially for sexual violence against women, without falling into the 'peace versus justice' trap. Some have called for amnesty for Boko Haram members.[169] These proposals have been vehemently opposed by many both within and outside Nigeria.[170] In view of this, it is our proposal that the following steps should be taken in order to hold Boko Haram members accountable for atrocities against women. First, most of the crimes against women such as rape, sexual assault, abductions of school girls, murder of women and girls already constitute crimes under the domestic Penal Code applicable across northern Nigeria. Hence, regardless of whether these offences were committed in a situation of armed conflict, they nonetheless constitute punishable crimes for which perpetrators can be punished if the State has the appetite for prosecution. Second, under the 2011 anti-terrorism act, using terror against civilians is a federal offence, which means that it can be prosecuted in any Federal High Court sitting in any state in Nigeria.[171] Third, the Nigerian government might consider establishing a special court or tribunal to prosecute perpetrators of mass atrocities during the Boko Haram conflict.[172] This

[168] Nwozor (2013), p. 14.

[169] See for example, Ezeamalu (25 July 2016).

[170] See for example, Amnesty International (14 May 2016).

[171] See Section 1(2) (i) & (ii) and section 33(1)(a) of the Terrorism Prevention Act 2011.

[172] See Ewi (24 June 2013).

has the advantage of speedy trial as such court will not be bogged down with case overload, which has characterised the Nigerian justice system. Fourth, given the cross-border nature of Boko Haram's activities, the states of the Lake Chad Basin participating in the MJTF may consider establishing a regional special criminal tribunal with the mandate and jurisdiction to prosecute mass atrocities committed during the Boko Haram conflict. Since the Boko Haram insurgency has assumed transnational character involving Nigeria, Cameroon, Chad and Niger, where Boko Haram has carried out attacks, such tribunal would provide the advantage of having all perpetrators tried on the same platform and being subjected to a common standard of criminal justice. Besides the ease of collection of evidence, this would also have the advantage of ease of access to justice by victims in the Lake Chad Basin and thus facilitate the healing process in local communities that have borne the brunt of Boko Haram's weaponisation of women.

References

Abdullahi AA, Adekeye DS and Balogun OS (2014) A 'Nation' in wilderness: youth and insurgency in Nigeria. S Afr Rev Sociol 45(2):78–96

Abubakar A (2014) As many as 200 girls abducted by Boko Haram, Nigerian officials say. *CNN* 16 April 2014. Available at http://edition.cnn.com/2014/04/15/world/africa/nigeria-girls-abducted/. Accessed 24 Mar 2017

Abubakar A, Melvin D, Busari S (2016) Female suicide bombers kill 58 in a Nigerian camp meant to be a haven. CNN 11 February 2016. Available at http://edition.cnn.com/2016/02/11/africa/nigeria-suicide-bombing-boko-haram/. Accessed 20 Mar 2016

Akande D (2012) Classification of armed conflicts: relevant legal concepts. In: Wilmshurst E (ed) International law and the classification of armed conflicts. Oxford University Press, Oxford, pp 32–79

Alfred C (2015) How Boko Haram uses female suicide bombers to terrorise Nigeria. The Huffington Post, 28 February 2015. Available at http://www.huffingtonpost.com/2015/02/28/boko-haram-femalesuicide-bombers_n_6763386.html. Accessed 24 Mar 2017

Aljazeera (2014) Boko Haram allegedly kidnaps dozens more women, girls in Nigeria's North. 24 June 2014. Available at http://america.aljazeera.com/articles/2014/6/24/kidnapping-boko-haram.html. Accessed 5 Apr 2017

Aljazeera (2016) Nigeria: Boko Haram releases 21 Chibok Girls. Aljazeera News, 13 October 2016. Available at http://www.aljazeera.com/news/2016/10/nigeria-boko-haram-releases-21-chibok-girls-161013102746662.html. Accessed 5 Apr 2017

Aljazeera (2017) Suicide bombers die in failed attacks in Nigeria. 17 February 2017. Available at http://www.aljazeera.com/news/2017/02/boko-haram-bombers-killed-maiduguri-170217114659511.html. Accessed 23 Mar 2017

All Party Parliamentary Group on Nigeria (13 May 2014) Nigeria's Boko Haram crisis: abductions and responses. Meeting Summary

Alozieuwa SHO (2012) Contending theories on Nigeria's security challenges in the era of Boko Haram insurgency. Peace Conflict Rev 7(1):1–8

Amnesty International (September 2014) Welcome to hell-fire: Torture and other ill-treatments in Nigeria. AFR 44/011/2014

Amnesty International (14 April 2015a) Nigeria: Abducted Women and Girls Forced to Join Boko Haram Attacks. Available at https://www.amnesty.org/en/latest/news/2015/04/nigeria-abducted-women-and-girls-forced-to-join-boko-haram-attacks/. Accessed 23 Jan 2017

Amnesty International (2015b) Our job is to shoot, slaughter and kill: Boko Haram's reign of terror in North-East Nigeria. AFR 44/1360/2015

Amnesty International (June 2015c) Stars on their shoulders, blood on their Hands: War crimes committed by the Nigerian Military. AFR 44/1661/2015

Amnesty International (14 May 2016) Boko Haram summit: Human rights must be foundation of regional summit. Available at https://www.amnesty.org/en/latest/news/2016/05/boko-haram-summit-human-rights-must-be-foundation-of-regional-response/. Accessed 15 Mar 2017

Associated Press (2 August 2009) Nigeria accused of ignoring Sect warnings before waive of killing. Available at http://www.guardian.com/world/2009/aug/20/Nigeria-boko-haram-islamist-sect. Accessed 20 Jan 2017

Awford J (10 January 2015) Bomb strapped to a 10-year old girl explodes in a busy market in Nigeria killing 20 and injuring 18. Available at http://www.dailymail.co.uk/news/article-2904497/19-dead-18-injured-Nigeria-market-blastpolice.html. Accessed 24 Mar 2017

Ayandike NO (2013) Boko Haram and national security challenges in Nigeria: causes and solutions. J Econ Sustain Dev 4(5):12–23

Bangura HZ (2015) Condemning use of sexual violence, UN envoy warns Boko Haram aims to destroy family structures. UN News Centre. Available at http://www.un.org/apps/news/story.asp?NewsID=50981#.WICSLVV97Dc. Accessed 17 Jan 2017

Barkindo A, Tyavkase GB, Wesley CK (2013) Our bodies, their battle ground: Boko Haram and gender-based violence against Christian women and children in North-Eastern Nigeria since 1999. Nigeria's Political Violence Research Network Working Paper No. 1

Bassiouni MC (2008) The new wars and the crisis of compliance with the law of armed conflict by non-state actors. J Crim Law Criminol 98(3):712–810

BBC News (23 October 2014a) Nigeria's Boko Haram abducts more women. Available at http://www.bbc.com/news/world-africa-29740204. Accessed 5 Apr 2017

BBC News (25 December 2014b) Nigerian girl says parents volunteered her as suicide bomber. Available at http://www.bbc.com/news/world-africa-30601639. Accessed 24 Mar 2017

BBC News (27 October 2014c) Escaping Boko Haram: How three Nigerian girls found safety. Available at http://www.bbc.com/news/world-africa-29762252. Accessed 5 Apr 2017

BBC News (24 December 2015) Nigeria Boko Haram: Militants technically defeated – Buhari. Available at http://www.bbc.com/news/world-africa-35173618. Accessed 3 Apr 2017

Bloom M, Matfess H (2016) Women as symbols and swords in Boko Haram's terror. Women, peace and inclusive security. PRISM 6(1):104–121

Bloom M, Maftess H, Bastic M, Grimm K, Kunz R (2007) Sexual violence in armed conflict: global overview and implications for the security sector. Geneva Centre for the Democratic Control of Armed Forces Geneva. Available at http://www.essex.ac.uk/armedcon/story_id/sexualviolence_conflict_full%5B1%5D.pdf. Accessed 15 Apr 2016

Campbell LJ (2016) Islamist ritual killing: Al Qaeda, Islamic State, and Boko Haram case studies. In: Bunker RJ (ed) Blood sacrifices: Violent Non-State actors and dark magico-religious activities. Universe, Bloomington

Constitution of the Federal Republic of Nigeria, 1999

Convention against Torture and Other Cruel, Inhuman or Degrading Treatment or Punishment adopted 10 Dec. 1984 and entered into force on 26 June 1987, G.A. Res. 39/46, 39 UN G.A.O.R, Supp. (No 51) UN Doc. A/39/51, at 197 (1984)

Convention on the Elimination of All Forms of Discrimination Against Women, adopted 18 Dec. 1979 and entered into force on 3 Sept. 1981, G.A. 34/180, 34 UN G.A.O.R., Supp. (No. 46), UN Doc. A/34/46, at 193 (1979)

Convention on the Rights of the Child, adopted on 20 Nov. 1989 and entered into force on 2 Sept. 1990, G.A. Res. 44/25 UN G.A.O.R., Supp. (No. 49), UN Doc. A/44/49 at 166 (1989)

Ewi M (24 June 2013) Why Nigeria deeds a criminal tribunal and not amnesty for Boko Haram. Institute for Security Studies. Available at https://issafrica.org/iss-today/why-nigeria-needs-a-criminal-tribunal-and-not-amnesty-for-boko-haram. Accessed 16 Apr 2016

Ezeamalu B (25 July 2016) Lawyer urges Buhari to grant amnesty to Boko Haram members. Premium Times. Available at http://www.premiumtimesng.com/news/top-news/207486-lawyer-urges-buhari-grant-amnesty-boko-haram-members.html. Accessed 15 Mar 2017

Faul M (30 April 2014) Abducted Nigerian school girls sold into marriage with Boko Haram extremists for $12, reports say. The Associated Press. Available at http://www.financialpost.com/m/wp/tag/blog.html?b=news.nationalpost.com/2014/04/30/abducted-nigerian-school-girls-sold-into-marriage-with-boko-haram-extremists-for-12-report-says. Accessed 1 May 2017

Gasser H-P (2002) Acts of terror "Terrorism" and international humanitarian law. IRRC 84(847):547

Geneva Convention for the Amelioration of the Condition of the Wounded and Sick in Armed Forces in the Field of 12 August 1949, 75 U.N.T.S. 31

Geneva Convention for the Amelioration of the Condition of the Wounded, Sick and Shipwrecked Members of Armed Forces at Sea of 12 August 1949, 75 U.N.T.S. 85

Geneva Convention relative to the Protection of Civilian Persons in Time of War of 12 August 1949, 75 U.N.T.S. 287

Geneva Convention relative to the Protection of Prisoners of War of 12 August 1949, 75 U.N.T.S. 135

Geneva Conventions Act of 30 Sept. 1960, Laws of the Federation of Nigeria (2004)

Henckaerts J-M, Doswald-Beck L (2004) Customary international humanitarian law study (2004)

Human Rights Watch (11 October 2012) Spiralling violence: Boko Haram attacks and security forces abuses in Nigeria. Accessed 14 Mar 2016

Human Rights Watch (29 November 2013) Nigeria: Boko Haram abducts women, Recruits children. Available at http://www.hrw.org/fr/node/121029. Accessed 4 Mar 2017

Human Rights Watch (27 October 2014) Those terrible weeks in their camps: Boko Haram violence against women and girls in Northeast Nigeria. Available at https://www.hrw.org/report/2014/10/27/those-terrible-weeks-their-camp/boko-haram-violence-against-women-and-girls. Accessed 2 Mar 2017

Human Rights Watch (31 October 2016) Nigeria: Officials abusing displaced women, girls displaced by Boko Haram twice over. Available at https://www.hrw.org/news/2016/10/31/nigeria-officials-abusing-displaced-women-girls. Accessed 5 Apr 2017

Institute for Economics and Peace (2015) Global terrorism index 2015: Measuring and understanding the impact of terrorism. Available at http://economicsandpeace.org/wp-content/uploads/2015/11/2015-Global-Terrorism-Index-Report.pdf. Accessed 4 Mar 2017

International Committee of the Red Cross (6 May 2013) Protection of women in situations of armed conflicts. Available at https://www.icrc.org/eng/resources/documents/field-newsletter/2013/india-e-newsletter/legal-opinion-05-2013.htm. Accessed 20 Jan 2017

International Committee of the Red Cross. https://www.icrc.org/eng/assets/files/other/what_is_ihl.pdf. Accessed 24 Mar 2017

International Covenant on Civil and Political Rights adopted on 16 Dec. 1966 and entered into force on 23 March 1976; G.A. Res. 2200 (XXI) U.N. Doc. A/6316 (1966) 999 U.N.T.S. 171

International Covenant on Economic, Social and Cultural Rights, adopted 16 Dec. 1966 and entered into force on 3 Jan. 1976, G.A. Res. 2200A (XXI), UN. Doc. A/6316 (1966), 993 U.N.T.S. 3

International Crisis Group (May 2016a) Boko Haram on the Back Foot. Africa Brief No. 120

International Crisis Group (5 December 2016b) "Nigeria" women and the Boko Haram insurgency. Africa Brief No 242

Iroegbu S (4 August 2014) *ThisDay*, Kano bombings traced to female beggars

Kishi R (25 February 2015) Rape as a weapon of political violence, part 2: Where, when, and by whom is this tactic used? ACLED Crisis Blog, http://www.crisis.acleddata.com/rape-as-a-weapon-of-political-violence-part-1-trendsacross-arica/. Accessed 20 Mar 2016

Mantzikos I (December 2014) Boko Haram attacks in Nigeria and neighbouring countries: A chronology of attacks. Perspect Terrorism 8(6):3

Mark M (6 May 2014) Suspected Boko Haram gunmen kidnap eight girls from village in Nigeria. The Guardian. Available at https://www.theguardian.com/world/2014/may/06/suspected-boko-haram-gunmen-kidnap-girls-village-nigeria. Accessed 5 Apr 2017

Matasu HK (8 January 2015) Boko Haram kills 25, abducts others in Yobe. Daily Trust. Available at https://www.dailytrust.com.ng/news/general/b-haram-kills-25-abducts-others-in-yobe/65823.html. Accessed 10 Apr 2017

Matfess H (2 August 2016) Boko Haram is enslaving women, making them join the war Newsweek. Available at http://cco.ndu.edu/Portals/96/Documents/Articles/Matfess%20-%20Boko%20Haram%20Is%20Enslaving%20Women,%20Making%20Them%20Join%20the%20War.pdf. Accessed 20 Mar 2017

Matfess H, Lewis PM, Allen NDF (2016) Unbroken Boko Haram: Buhari prematurely declares victory. Foreign Affairs, 21 March 2016. Available at https://www.foreignaffairs.com/articles/nigeria/20160321/Unbrokenbokoharam. Accessed 12 Jan 2017

McLaughlin E (16 September 2015) Kidnapped Chibok School girls now fighting for Boko Haram, former captive say. Available at http://abcnews.go.com/International/kidnapped-chibok-school-girls-now-fighting-boko-haram/story?id=33776437. Accessed 7 Mar 2017

Mickolus E (2016) Terrorism, 2013–2015: a worldwide chronology. McFarland & Company Inc. Jefferson

Murtada A (2013) Boko Haram in Nigeria: Its beginnings, principles and activities in Nigeria. Available at www.Salafi.Manhaj.com. Accessed 10 Jan 2017

Nossiter A (18 May 2015) Boko Haram militants raped hundreds of female captives in Nigeria. New York Times. Available at http://www.nytimes.com/2015/05/19/world/africa/boko-haram-militantsraped-hundreds-of-female-captives-in-nigeria.html?_r=0. Accessed 17 Jan 2017

Nwozor A (2013) National security, religious anarchism and the politics of amnesty in Nigeria. Covenant Univ J Polit Int Aff 1(1)

Oduah C (22 September 2016) The women who love and loved Boko Haram. Al Jazeera. Available at http://www.aljazeera.com/indepth/features/2016/08/women-love-loved-boko-haram-160823120617834.html. Accessed 7 Mar 2017

Office of the Prosecutor, International Criminal Court (25 November 2013a) Report on preliminary examination activities 2013. Available at https://www.icc-cpi.int/OTP%20Reports/otp-report-2013.aspx. Accessed 20 Mar 2016

Office of the Prosecutor, International Criminal Court (5 August 2013b) Situation in Nigeria: Article 5 Report

Office of the Prosecutor, International Criminal Court (25 November 2015) Report on preliminary examination activities 2015

Ogbonnanyan UM, Ehigiamusoe UK (Summer 2013) Niger Delta militancy and Boko Haram insurgency: National security in Nigeria. Glob Secur Stud 4(3):1–14

Okpaga A, Uwgu SC, Eme OI (April 2012) Activities of Boko Haram and insecurity question in Nigeria. Arab J Bus Manag Rev (OMAN Chapter) 1(9):77–99

Onuoha FC (2010) The Islamist challenge: Nigeria's Boko Haram crisis explained. Afr Secur Rev 9(2):54–67

Optional Protocols to the Convention on the Rights of the Child on the Involvement of Children in Armed Conflict, adopted by the United Nations General Assembly Resolution A/RES/54/263 on A/RES/54/263 and entered into force on 12 February 2002

Organisation of African Unity (1981) African Charter on Human and Peoples' Rights, adopted 27 June 1981, OAU Doc CAB/LEG/67/3 rev. 5, 21 International Legal Material 58 (1982)

Organisation of African Unity (1990) African Charter on the Rights and Welfare of the Child CAB/LEG/153/Rev. 2, adopted by the Twenty-Sixth Session of the of the Assembly of Heads of State and Government of the OAU, Addis Ababa, Ethiopia, July 1990

Prosecutor v Delalic and Others, Case No. IT-96-21, Judgement of 16 November 1998

Prosecutor v Furundzija, Case No IT-95-17/1, Judgement of 10 December 1998

Prosecutor v Jankovic and Others, Case No IT-96-23, Judgement of 22 February 2001 (appeal decision)

Prosecutor v Kvocka and Others, Case No IT-98-30/1, Judgement of 2 November 2001
Prosecutor v Nikolic, First Amended Indictment, Case No IT-94-2
Protocol Additional to the Geneva Conventions of 12 August 1949, and relating to the Protection of Victims of International Armed Conflicts, (Protocol I) adopted on 8 June 1977, 1125 U.N.T.S. 3
Protocol Additional to the Geneva Conventions of 12 August 1949, and relating to the Protection of Victims of Non-International Armed Conflicts, (Protocol II) adopted on 8 June 1977, 1125 U.N.T.S. 609
Punch Newspaper (10 January 2017) Borno bombers kill eight, missing Adamawa cops found dead. Available at http://punchng.com/borno-bombers-kill-eight-missing-adamawa-cops-found-dead/. Accessed 23 Mar 2017
Raleigh C, Linke A, Hegre H, Karlsen J (2010) Introducing ACLED - armed conflict location and event data. J Peace Res 47(5):651–660
S/RES/1829 (2008) 19 June 2008
S/RES/1888 (2009) 30 September 2009
S/RES/1889 (2009) 5 October 2009
Sahara Reporters (14 December 2016) Army rescues 605 women, girls from Sambisa Forest. Available at http://saharareporters.com/2016/12/14/army-rescues-605-women-girls-sambisa-forest. Accessed 20 Jan 2017
Sahara Reporters (25 January 2017a) Boko Haram Suicide Bomber Attack Home of Civilian JTF Commander. Available at http://saharareporters.com/2017/01/25/boko-haram-suicide-bomber-attack-home-civilian-jtf-commander. Accessed 23 Mar 2017
Sahara Reporters (25 January 2017b) Borno Police Commissioner confirms fresh abduction of 7 women, 3 deaths in Askira/Uba. Available at http://saharareporters.com/2017/01/25/borno-police-commissioner-confirms-fresh-abduction-7-women-3-deaths-askirauba. Accessed 17 Feb 2017
Sahara Reporters, Boko Haram Suicide bomber attack home of Civilian JTF Commander 25 January 2017. Available http://saharareporters.com/2017/01/25/boko-haram-suicide-bomber-attack-home-civilian-jtf-commander. Accessed 20 Mar 2017
Searcey D (11 February 2016) Nigeria vexed by Boko Haram's use of women as suicide bombers. New York Times. Available at http://www.nytimes.com/2016/02/12/world/africa/nigeria-vexed-by-boko-harams-use-of-women-as-suicide-bombers.html?_r=0. Accessed 27 Jan 2017
STRATFOR (23 October 2015) An unprecedented use of female suicide bombers. Available at https://www.stratfor.com/analysis/unprecedented-use-female-suicide-bombers. Accessed 5 Apr 2017
Terrorism (Prevention) Act No 10, 2011, Laws of the Federal Republic of Nigeria. Available at https://www.unodc.org/tldb/pdf/Nigeria/NIR_Terror_Prevent_2011.pdf. Accessed 14 Apr 2017
The Telegraph (10 June 2014) Boko Haram gunmen kidnap 20 women near missing school girl village. Available at http://www.telegraph.co.uk/news/worldnews/africaandindianocean/nigeria/10888460/Boko-Haram-gunmen-kidnap-20-women-near-missing-schoolgirl-village-in-Nigeria.html. Accessed 5 April 2017
Thomson V (Summer 2012) Boko Haram and Islamic fundamentalism in Nigeria. Glob Secur Stud 3(3):46–60
UN General Assembly, Declaration on the Protection of Women and Children in Emergency and Armed Conflict, UNGA 3318 (XXIX) of 14 December 1974
UNFPA (6 May 2015) Hundreds freed from Boko Haram require medical care, counselling. Available at http://www.unfpa.org/news/hundreds-freed-boko-haram-require-medical-care-counselling. Accessed 12 Jan 2017
UNICEF (12 April 2017) Silent shame: Bringing out the voices of children caught in the Lake Chad crisis. Available www.unicef.org/wcaro/nigeriaregionalcrisis/UNICEF_Silent_shame.pdf. Accessed 17 Apr 2017

United Nations (2009) Women and armed conflicts: Global commitments. Available at http://www.un.org/womenwatch/daw/beijing/beijingat10/E.%20Women%20and%20armed%20conflict%20(Sep%2009).pdf. Accessed 23 Mar 2017
United Nations (2010) Women, peace and security, Introductory Note by Preeti Kundra Deshmukh. Int Legal Mater 49(1):71–82
United Nations General Assembly (2015) Violations and abuses committed by Boko Haram and the impact on human rights in the countries affected, A/HRC/30/67, 9 December 2015
United Nations, Office of the Coordinator for Humanitarian Affairs (2015) Available at http://www.unocha.org/nigeria/about-ocha-nigeria/about-crisis. Accessed 17 Apr 2017
United Nations, Office of the Special Representative of the Secretary General for Sexual Violence in Conflict (25 April 2014) Sexual violence in conflict, great moral issue of our time, UN Special Representative tells Security Council
United Nations Security Council Resolution S/RES/1325 (2000) 31 October 2000
United Nations Security Council Resolution S/RES/1888 (2009) 30 September 2009
Universal Declaration of Human Rights, United Nations General Assembly Resolution 217A, U.N.G.A. 3rd Session, U.N. Doc. A/RES/3/217A (1948) of 10 December 1948
Vanguard Newspaper (8 February 2017a) Boko Haram gave me N200 to detonate explosive, say suicide bomber. Available at http://www.vanguardngr.com/2017/02/boko-haram-gave-n200-detonate-explosive-says-suicide-bomber/. Accessed 24 Mar 2017
Vanguard Newspaper (25 January 2017b) Suicide bombers' attempts on mosque and security post foiled in Borno. Available at http://www.vanguardngr.com/2017/01/suicide-bombers-attempts-mosque-security-post-foiled/. Accessed 23 Mar 2017
Von Glahn G, Taulbe JL (2010) Law among nations: An introduction to public international law, 9th edn. Longman, New York
Weeraratne S (2015) Theorising the expansion of the Boko Haram insurgency in Nigeria. Terrorism Polit Violence 29:1–25
Whiting A (14 April 2015) Boko Haram has kidnapped 2000 women and girls. Amnesty International. Available at http://www.huffingtonpost.com/2015/04/14/boko-haram-kidnap-girls_n_7061550.html. Accessed 20 Mar 2016
Zenn J, Pearson E (2014) Women, gender and the evolving tactics of Boko Haram. J Terrorism Res 5(1):46–57

Chapter 13
Protecting Conflict-Induced Displacees in Northern Nigeria: Assessing the Compliance of the State with Article 9(2) of the Kampala Convention

Romola Adeola

13.1 Introduction

Globally, the human cost of conflicts has been profound. Over the last seven decades, over 170 million people have died from more than 250 conflicts in the world.[1] In 2014, the global estimate of conflict-induced displacees was in excess of 50 million people for the first time since the Second World War.[2] Of this figure, 16.7 million people were refugees, 1.2 million were asylum seekers, while 33.3 million were internally displaced persons (IDPs).[3] Sub-Saharan Africa, with an estimated 12.5 million internally displaced persons, had the highest number of IDPs, followed by North Africa and the Middle East, which recorded around 9.1 million IDPs.[4] According to the Internal Displacement Monitoring Centre (IDMC), of the 12.5 million African displacees, 3.3 million have been displaced by conflict and generalised violence in Nigeria,[5] an estimated 1.5 million of which have been as a result of the Boko Haram insurgency.[6]

Since the mid-1990s, Africa has recorded a huge proportion of displaced persons in the world. In 1993, an estimated 20 million displaced persons lived in Africa.[7]

This article was originally published by the Comparative and International Law of Southern Africa Journal. A publication of Juta press.

[1] See Derby (2008).

[2] UN High Commissioner for Refugees (2014); Foulkes, BBC News (20 June 2014).

[3] UN High Commissioner for Refugees (2013), p. 2.

[4] Norwegian Refugee Council and Internal Displacement Monitoring Centre (2014), p. 9.

[5] Norwegian Refugee Council and Internal Displacement Monitoring Centre (2014), p. 11.

[6] Internal Displacement Monitoring Centre (2014), p. 1.

[7] This figure is not specific to conflict-induced displacement alone. See Organisation of African Unity (1994).

R. Adeola (✉)
Faculty of Law, Centre for Human Rights, University of Pretoria, Pretoria, South Africa

J.-M. Iyi, H. Strydom (eds.), *Boko Haram and International Law*,
https://doi.org/10.1007/978-3-319-74957-0_13

During a joint symposium by the Organisation of African Union Unity[8] and the UN High Commissioner for Refugees in 1994, the problem of internal displacement in Africa was recognised as 'one of the most tragic humanitarian and human rights crisis in Africa'.[9] But with this recognition, the problem of internal displacement in Africa has persisted. Aside from conflict, other root causes of internal displacement such as climate change, development, natural and human-made disasters have contributed to displacements in Africa. Aside from the 12.5 million conflict-displaced Africans, an estimated 1.8 million people were displaced by disasters in Africa.[10] The rapid wind of development sweeping across many African countries has led to tens of thousands being displaced since the independence of many African countries.

Owing to the prevalence of the problem of internal displacement in Africa,[11] the AU Executive Council in 2004 requested the AU Commission to 'collaborate with relevant cooperating partners and other stakeholders to ensure that [i]nternally [d]isplaced [p]ersons are provided with an appropriate legal framework to ensure their adequate protection and assistance'.[12] Resolving that a legal document was essential to protect IDPs, the AU Executive Council requested that '[t]he specific needs of internally displaced persons (IDPs) such as protection and assistance should be addressed through a separate legal document'.[13] Over a five-year period, the AU Commission, with the involvement of civil society organisations, government officials and legal experts, developed the Kampala Convention.

The Kampala Convention, which was adopted in 2009, came into force on 6 December 2012.[14] Twenty-three countries, the newest of which is the Republic of the Congo,[15] have ratified the Kampala Convention. In April 2012, Nigeria ratified the Kampala Convention, and while it has deposited its instrument of ratification as of 22 May 2012, it is yet to domesticate the Kampala Convention in line with section 12 of the 1999 Nigerian Constitution. As with many African countries, one of the gaps in the protection and assistance of IDPs in Nigeria is the absence of a legal framework—a gap that the Kampala Convention seeks to fill in setting out the obligation of states in the protection of IDPs.

In article 9(2) of the Kampala Convention, specific measures are required of states in protecting and assisting internally displaced persons. Within the framework

---

[8] Now known as African Union (AU).

[9] Organisation of African Unity (1994).

[10] Norwegian Refugee Council and Internal Displacement Monitoring Centre (2014), p. 25.

[11] In 2003, over half of the world's 25 million IDPs were recorded as being in Africa.

[12] African Union Executive Council, fifth ordinary session 25 June–3 July 2004, Addis Ababa, Ethiopia, Decision on the situation of refugees, returnees and displaced persons, Doc EX.CL/108 (V), para 8.

[13] African Union Executive Council, fifth ordinary session 25 June–3 July 2004, Addis Ababa, Ethiopia, *Decision on the meeting of experts on the review of OAU/AU treaties*, Doc EX/CL/95 (V) para 4(i).

[14] African Union (2012).

[15] African Commission on Human and Peoples' Rights (2015).

of this article, this paper assesses the compliance of Nigeria with the obligation to protect conflict-induced displacees in Northern Nigeria.

In advancing the discourse, this paper is divided into four parts. The first part of this paper gives an insight into the insurgency, violence and displacement. The second part of this paper discusses the domestic application of international law treaties in Nigeria in view of the requirement of dualist nature of its domestic legal system. The essence of this discussion relates to the question as to whether there is an obligation on the state to comply with the requirement of the Kampala Convention given the dualist nature of its legal system. In the third part, the compliance of Nigeria with the obligation under article 9(2) of the Kampala Convention is discussed. In the fourth part of this paper, recommendations are advanced on measures that need to be set in place for the protection of conflict-induced displacees in line with the obligation imposed by the Kampala Convention.

13.2 The Insurgency, Violence and Displacement

Although religious violence is not a new phenomenon in Nigeria, the spates of attacks perpetuated by the *Jama'atu Ahlis Sunna Lidda'awati Wal-Jihad* sect (widely known as Boko Haram) are unprecedented. While the existence of the Boko Haram sect has been traced to 1995, the first major attack carried out by the sect in Bauchi state was in 2004.[16] The attack was carried out under the leadership of Yusuf Mohammed, an Islamic fundamentalist of Kanuri origin[17] who upheld the teachings of Ibn Taymiyyah and Ibn Abd al-Wahhab.[18] Both scholars, in the fourteenth and eighteenth centuries respectively, had argued that political and spiritual leadership must follow the laws of Islam. Born in the fourteenth century, Ibn Taymiyyah's teachings were partly influenced by the political clime at the time, which saw the fall of the Abbasid Empire at the hand of the Mongol armies and, consequently, the decline of Islamic thoughts from its pure form.[19] Taymiyyah argued that the practice of Islam and establishment of political authority must be based solely on the Quran and the Sunna of the Prophet.[20] Taymiyyah further argued for the elevation of jihad to the status of the five pillars of Islam and regarded Muslim leaders who did not observe sharia law as apostates who should be rebelled against.[21] Inspired by the teachings of Ibn Taymiyyah, Ibn Wahhab (in the eighteenth century) revived the ideologies of radical jihad. Like Ibn Taymiyyah, Ibn Abd al-Wahhab argued for the establishment of an Islamic caliphate. Followers of the Wahhabi school of thought[22]

[16] Iwuchukwu (2013), p. 112.

[17] Weate (2014).

[18] Walker (2012), pp. 8–9; Bavier (17 January 2012a).

[19] Barkindo (2013), p. 32.

[20] Barkindo (2013), p. 33.

[21] See Simon (2003); Springer et al. (2009), p. 29.

[22] The followers are also known as *Wahhabis* or *Salafis*.

regard non-Wahhabis as *kafirs*,[23] who, in the teachings of Ibn Abd al-Wahhab, must be put to death. This school of thought heavily influences the doctrinal beliefs of terrorist organisations around the world, including the Boko Haram sect, which was originally headquartered in a mosque named after Ibn Taymiyyah.[24]

Through its violent calls for the rejection of western education, the Boko Haram sect furthers the version of Islam that rejects political and social orders built on western education ideals and not on the tenets of sharia.[25] Following the death of Yusuf Mohammed in 2009 and a long lull from violent attacks between 2009 and 2010, the sect commenced a series of sporadic attacks in North and Central Nigeria.[26] On 31 December 2010, a bomb planted by the sect exploded in the Sani Abacha army barracks in Abuja, resulting in the death of four people and injuries to about 13 others.[27] On 27 and 29 May 2011, the sect orchestrated a set of attacks in Borno and Bauchi states killing about 27 people (13 individuals in the attack in Borno on the 27th of May and 14 individuals in the attack in Bauchi on 19 May 2011).[28] On 26 August 2011, the sect claimed responsibility for the bombing of the UN building in Abuja, which resulted in the death of about 25 people.[29] In November 2011, the sect killed over 100 people in attacks in Damaturu in the northeastern state of Yobe.[30] Between December 2011 and December 2014, the sect has killed over 3000 individuals in various states across Northern and Central Nigeria, burnt down places of worship, abducted over 300 individuals (including over 200 girls at Chibok) and perpetuated indiscriminate violence in Nigeria and neighbouring countries such as Cameroon and Chad.[31] In 2013, the Office of the Prosecutor of the International Criminal Court declared the insurgency a non-international armed conflict owing to the intensity of the hostilities and the organisation of the Boko Haram sect.[32] From its small-scale violent attacks in 2010, the sect has morphed into a violent armed group orchestrating large-scale kidnappings and suicide bombings and capturing cities in states across Northern Nigeria.

In recent times, one of the very evident manifestations of the terror of the group has been the displacement of thousands of individuals. The figures on those

[23] Three groups of people may be categorised as kafirs, namely, those 'who are deniers of God, or mushrak … [those who put] gods next to God, or … enervators of religion [Sunni & Shi'a Muslims]'. Frontline (2001).

[24] Iwuchukwu (2013), p. 112.

[25] Chothia (2015).

[26] Bavier (24 January 2012b).

[27] 'Many dead in Nigeria market blast' (2010).

[28] Marama (2011); 'Nigeria attacks claimed by Islamist sect Boko Haram' (2012).

[29] Human Rights Watch (2012).

[30] 'Muslim sect kills more than 100 in attacks on north-east Nigeria' (2011).

[31] 'Boko Haram timeline: from preachers to slave raiders' (2013); 'A year of attacks linked to Nigeria's Boko Haram' (2014); 'Timeline on Boko Haram activities' (2014); Karimi and Abubakar (2015); 'Nigeria's Boko Haram militants attack Chad for first time' (2015); Massalaki (2015).

[32] Office of the Prosecutor, International Criminal Court 'Report on preliminary examination activities 2013' (2013) para 218.

displaced by the Boko Haram crisis have ranged between over 800,000 and 1,500,000 individuals.[33] According to the IOM report, an estimated 917,801 IDPs have been displaced from northeastern Nigeria,[34] and over 120,000 individuals have fled to neighbouring countries such as Chad, Cameroon and Niger.[35] The IDMC reports that about 1.5 million people have been internally displaced, while an estimate of about 150,000 individuals were taking refuge in Chad, Cameroon and Niger.[36] However, the National Emergency Management Agency (NEMA) has disclosed that out of 981,416 IDPs in Nigeria, 868,235 were affected by the Boko Haram insurgency in northeastern Nigeria.[37] In spite of these discrepancies, it is evident that over 800,000 individuals have been displaced by Boko Haram.

With the rise in IDP figures, a relevant concern has been in relation to the treatment of the protection and assistance of the displaced persons. Although Nigeria does not have legislation on IDPs, it has ratified the Kampala Convention. But given the dualist nature of its legal system and the absence of legislation domesticating the Kampala Convention, a significant question that needs to be addressed is whether an obligation exists on the state to comply with the provisions of the Kampala Convention, which has not been domesticated. This issue is addressed in the next section.

13.3 Domestication

Section 12(1) of the Nigerian Constitution provides that '[n]o treaty between the [f]ederation and any other country shall have the force of law except to the extent to which any such treaty has been enacted into law by the National Assembly'.[38] Read in conjunction with sections 1(1) and 1(3), the provision of section 12(1) of the Constitution is imperative for the application of treaties in the Nigerian domestic legal system.

In *the Registered Trustees of National Association of Community Health Practitioners of Nigeria and Ors v Medical and Health Workers Union of Nigeria*, the Nigerian Supreme Court emphasised that international treaties (in this case, the treaties of the International Labour Organisation) can only be applied in the legal

[33] *The Sun* (29 January 2015); International Organization for Migration (2015).

[34] In the north-eastern Nigeria states of Borno and Yobe (where the violence has been intense), an estimate of about 482,286 and 125,991 individuals have been internally displaced. In Adamawa and Taraba, an estimate of about 211,391 individuals have been internally displaced. In Gombe, Bauchi, Plateau, Nassarawa, Kaduna, Kano and Zamfara, an estimate of about 98,133 persons have been internally displaced. In light of these figures an estimate of about 917,801 IDPs exist in north-eastern Nigeria. See International Organization for Migration (2015).

[35] International Organization for Migration (2015).

[36] Internal Displacement Monitoring Centre (2014), p. 1.

[37] National Emergency Management Agency (2014).

[38] The 1999 Nigerian Constitution.

system following compliance with the requirement of section 12(1) of the Constitution.[39] In *Abacha v Fawehinmi*, the Supreme Court had earlier set out this precedence[40]; however, the court equally inferred that although a treaty has not been domesticated, it may 'give rise to a legitimate expectation by citizens that the government, in its acts affecting them, would observe the terms of the treaty'.[41] While the judiciary may not enforce the provisions of an unincorporated treaty, the Supreme Court justices inferred that Nigeria has a responsibility to comply with treaties to which it is party. The African Commission on Human and Peoples' Rights has equally emphasised in its jurisprudence that a state cannot invoke the non-domestication of a treaty as a defence to non-compliance with the treaty obligations.[42]

Although the provision of section 12(1) of the Nigerian Constitution makes treaty obligations non-justiciable in the national courts, it does not excuse Nigeria from the responsibility of complying with international treaty obligations duly ratified. As such, Nigeria has an obligation to ensure that IDPs are protected in line with the Kampala Convention in view of its act of ratification. Against the backdrop of article 9(2) of the Kampala Convention, the next section assesses the compliance of the state with the obligation to protect and assist conflict-induced displacees.

13.4 The Obligation Under Article 9(2) of the Kampala Convention

Article 9(2) of the Kampala Convention places explicit obligation on the states with regard to protecting and assisting internally displaced persons. This section, which is central to the protection of IDPs, sets out basic standards that states are to fulfil in protecting IDPs. Under this article, there are 13 obligations that states are mandated to perform.

In line with the provision of article 9(2) (a) of the Kampala Convention, states are required to '[t]ake necessary measures to ensure that internally displaced persons are received, without discrimination of any kind and live in satisfactory conditions of safety, dignity and security'.[43] Since the rise of the insurgency, the government,

---

[39] *The Registered Trustees of National Association of Community Health Practitioners of Nigeria & ors v Medical and Health Workers Union of Nigeria* (2008) 2 NWLR (Pt. 1072) 575.

[40] *Abacha & Ors v Fawehinmi* (judgement of the Supreme Court, delivered 28 April 2000).

[41] *Abacha & Ors v Fawehinmi* (judgement of the Supreme Court, delivered 28 April 2000). For an elaborate discussion of the application of international in domestic courts see Killander (2010); Akinrinade (2011), p. 448.

[42] *Purohit & another v The Gambia* (2003) AHRLR 96 (ACHPR 2003), para 43; *Legal Resources Foundation v Zambia* (2001) AHRLR 84 (ACHPR 2001), para 60. In line with article 27 of the Vienna Convention on the Law of Treaties, states are prevented from invoking national laws as a ground for non-compliance with the requirement of treaty obligations. See Vienna Convention on the Law of Treaties (1969); See Wachira and Ayinla (2006), p. 465.

[43] The Kampala Convention, above at note 14, art 9(2) (a).

through the National Emergecny Management Agency (NEMA), has set up 22 displacement camps in northeastern Nigeria.[44] While IDPs are received into displacement camps, they do not live in satisfactory conditions. Living conditions in the camps have been described as 'unpleasant',[45] and although facilities (such as rooms, toilets and clinics) exist, these facilities are overstretched.[46] In one of the IDP camps in Borno, 'about 40 IDPs sleep together in one hall, with the entire camp environment looking unkempt'.[47] The unhygienic conditions in some of the IDP camps in Borno and Taraba led to the outbreak of cholera, which resulted in the death of about 27 people in one of the IDP camps in Borno[48] and 48 people in Taraba.[49]

Article 9(2) (b) of the Kampala Convention obligates states to provide IDPs 'with adequate humanitarian assistance, which shall include food, water, shelter, medical care and other health services, sanitation, education, and any other necessary social services'.[50] The provision mandates states to ensure that this is provided 'to the fullest extent possible' and 'with the least possible delay' and emphasises that it should be extended to host communities. As of the time of writing, of the 868,235 IDPs displaced by Boko Haram, only 107,997 individuals are in IDP camps with most IDPs (about 804,732) living with host communities with relations and acquaintances and in makeshift camps.[51] With the rising IDP figures, reports have indicated that most makeshift camps, in addition to being overcrowded, lacked water, hygiene and sanitation and are 'grossly inadequate'.[52] With the increased provisions of humanitarian assistance to IDPs in camps, host communities were most IDPs are situated have been largely forgotten. The resources of these communities, who are 'often poor and disenfranchised' and where 'basic services and infrastructure are limited',[53] have been strained significantly.[54] Psychosocial supports provided to displaced person in camps are not often replicated in host communities.[55] The foreseeable danger in not meeting the needs of IDPs in these communities is that these communities that have been sympathetic to the plight of these persons may become hostile. Hence, factoring the needs of IDPs in these communities to reliefs and other service deliveries are important. But even in displacement camps where there are facilities and relief assistance is being provided,

---

[44] UN Office for the Coordination of Humanitarian Affairs (2015).

[45] Hamza et al. (2014).

[46] Hamza et al. (2014).

[47] Hamza et al. (2014).

[48] Olugbode (2014).

[49] Out of the 70 people who died in IDP camp situated in Bali local government in Taraba, 48 died of cholera, 13 died of the measles epidemic and 9 died of other sicknesses. Ayodele (2014).

[50] The Kampala Convention, above at note 14, art 9(2) (b).

[51] *The Sun* (29 January 2015); Internal Displacement Monitoring Centre (2014), p. 11.

[52] 'Nigeria's forgotten crisis' (2014); Internal Displacement Monitoring Centre (2014), p. 11.

[53] International Organization for Migration (2015).

[54] UN Office for the Coordination of Humanitarian Affairs (October 2014b).

[55] UN Office for the Coordination of Humanitarian Affairs (November 2014a), p. 4.

shortages have been reported. Not only have there been shortages of relief provisions[56]; there have also been shortages of relief staff.[57] These shortages, which have been described as 'a chronic problem in the northeast',[58] have affected the delivery of relief assistance to IDPs.

Aside from these issues, specific groups have not been adequately protected in accordance with the requirement of article 9(2) (c) of the Kampala Convention. Article 9(2) (c) obligates states to provide 'special protection' to IDPs with 'special needs' inclusive among which are 'separated and unaccompanied children, female heads of households, expectant mothers, mothers with young children, the elderly, and persons with disabilities or with communicable diseases'.[59] For the purpose of protecting expectant mothers, the government has taken significant strides in establishing maternal care delivery committees in camps 'to assist women in resolving complicated cases'.[60] Ambulances and health kits have also been provided in cases of emergencies. However, with respect to mothers with young children, the elderly and unaccompanied children, special protection has not been adequately set up. Mothers with young children have engaged in street begging in IDP camps in Maiduguri in order to provide for their children. According to Maina, hundreds of women have expressed that 'their situation in the camps informed their resolve to take to street begging [has] … it is the only way that they can help themselves and their children'.[61] Elderly women in the camps have also expressed the partiality in treatment by government officials, who give more preference to young women, 'while … the older ones are being left out'.[62] According to NEMA, there are about 760 unaccompanied children in IDP camps[63]; however, with the rising insurgency and violent killings of caregivers by the sect, this figure is bound to increase. Many of these unaccompanied children in host communities in Yola have turned to street begging and child labour for sustenance. Ismail notes that those in the IDP camps 'have been forced to live their youthful age without the accommodating parental care that is sought by every growing person'.[64]

With respect to protecting the sexual and reproductive health of women and providing support in situations of abuse in accordance with article 9(2) (d) of the Kampala Convention, effective measures have not been adequately set up. Although the National Agency for Control of Aids and civil society representatives have embarked on free HIV screening in IDP camps,[65] the International Centre for

[56] Internal Displacement Monitoring Centre (2013).

[57] 'Thousands displaced by Boko Haram flood Nigeria city' (2015).

[58] 'Thousands displaced by Boko Haram flood Nigeria city' (2015).

[59] The Kampala Convention, above at note 14, art 9(2) (c).

[60] Marama (2014).

[61] Maina (2014).

[62] Maina (2014).

[63] 'NEMA deploys more personnel, equipment in IDP camps in Adamawa' (2014).

[64] Ismail (2015).

[65] 'Boko Haram: when HIV visited Borno, Yobe IDPs' camps' (2015).

Investigative Reporting (ICIR) has reported sexual abuse and trafficking of children and young girls by government officials in the camps.[66] According to the ICIR, 'many aid workers in the IDP camps allege that there is a conspiracy of silence, which encourages government officials in many of the IDP camps to continue to exploit the displaced persons'.[67] In view of this fact, support mechanisms are difficult to establish. Although the government's investigative panel dismissed the allegations, it concluded that 'two girls might have been raped'.[68] However, traces and evidence of such practices in IDP camps not only makes it difficult for adequate support systems; it also raises concern with regard to the protection of women's health rights.

While the right of IDPs to move freely and seek safety in places of their choice within Nigeria in accordance with article 9(2) (e) and (f) are not hampered, the inadequate security measures existing in the northeast and generally within the country hinders the exercise of the right to movement and free choice of settlement by IDPs. While many of the displaced persons desire to return,[69] the likelihood of fresh attacks in the cities from which they have been displaced constrains their ability to choose even though the conditions in the camps are deplorable.[70]

In accordance with article 9(2) (g) of the Kampala Convention, the state is required to '[r]espect and maintain the civilian and humanitarian character of the places where internally displaced persons are sheltered and safeguard such locations against infiltration by armed groups'.[71] Although security forces are deployed to IDP camps, concerns relating to safety and security of IDPs in camps have also arisen in view of reports on infiltration of camps by suspected members of the Boko Haram sect.[72] For instance, in Yola, security forces arrested a number of individuals suspected to be part of the sect that carried out attacks on communities in the northern part of Adamawa State.[73] According to the head of the National Information Center on Counter-Terrorism, members of the sect have fled into IDP camps as a result of the heavy military bombardments.[74] Such situation not only poses a threat to the security of the camps; it also calls into question the commitment of the state to ensuring that the human rights of IDPs are protected.

In terms of article 9(2) (h) of the Kampala Convention, states are obligated to '[t]ake necessary measures, including the establishment of specialised mechanisms, to trace and reunify families separated during displacement and otherwise facilitate the re-establishment of family ties'.[75] As a result of the insurgency, several IDPs

[66] Dickson (2015).

[67] Dickson (2015).

[68] Idowu (2015).

[69] Ismail (2015).

[70] 'IDPs from north-east Nigeria fear Boko Haram may return' (2015).

[71] The Kampala Convention, above at note 14, art 9(2) (g).

[72] Ibrahim (2015).

[73] 'Adamawa: Boko Haram infiltrate Yola internally displaced persons camp' (2014).

[74] Ajakaye (2015).

[75] African Union (2012), The Kampala Convention, art 9(2) (h).

have been separated from their family members.[76] The implication of this separation for children has been pronounced in view of the fact that they lose parental support and have to survive on their own, sometimes in harsh conditions. Several unaccompanied children from Damboa, Gwoza and Chibok living in camps and host communities in Borno State, who have lost contact with family members for close to a year, have had to fend for themselves, with some turning to begging and child labour.[77] Although some have been reunited with family members, there are still many more children and adults that need to be assisted in tracing family members.[78] However, it is noteworthy to mention that in February 2015, about 158 individuals (52 adults and 96 children) abducted from Katarko town in Gujba local government in Yobe were reunited by government officials with their families.[79]

In line with article 9(2) (i) of the Kampala Convention, states are mandated to '[t]ake necessary measures to protect individual, collective and cultural property left behind by displaced persons as well as in areas where internally displaced persons are located'.[80] Linked to the realisation of this obligation in the context of the Boko Haram crisis is the need for adequate security measures. While the Nigerian military has (over the last five years since the rise of the insurgency) engaged in combat in restoring peace and security, it has faced enormous challenges such as maladministration, corruption and poor military equipment,[81] which has made it difficult to defeat the sect. By extension, protecting the properties of displaced persons has also been difficult. During attacks on towns and villages, members of the Boko Haram sect not only kill people; they also burn down houses, churches and building structures. In an attack in Borno on January 2015, members of the sect destroyed at least 16 towns[82] and damaged an estimate of about 3700 properties.[83] In February 2015, 30 people were killed, and several structures were torched by members of the Boko Haram sect in attacks on two villages close to Chibok.[84] Although the state has taken significant strides in reclaiming cities captured by the Boko Haram sect,[85] livelihood reconstruction and construction of building structures for displaced persons who have lost individual, collective and cultural properties need to form part of the government's central concern in protecting and assisting the displaced persons.

---

[76] Ross (2014).

[77] Ismail (2015).

[78] Ismail (2015); Abdulaziz and Faul (2015); 'Amnesty International: Nigeria massacre deadliest in history of Boko Haram' (2015).

[79] '158 freed Boko Haram abductees reunited with their families' (2015).

[80] The Kampala Convention, above at note 14, art 9(2) (i).

[81] '"Why we could not defeat Boko Haram" – army commander writes a powerful letter to President Jonathan' (2014).

[82] 'Boko Haram destroys 16 towns, villages in Nigeria' (2015).

[83] 'Nigeria: satellite images show horrific scale of Boko Haram attack on Baga' (2015).

[84] 'Deadly Boko Haram raids destroy two Nigerian villages' (2015).

[85] 'Troops reclaim Monguno from Boko Haram' (2015); 'Nigerian army reclaims Baga from Boko Haram' (2015).

Also, the protection of areas where IDPs are located from environmental degradation needs to be part of its central concern in line with the provision of article 9(2)(j) of the Kampala Convention. While this obligation appears to relate more to situations of displacement from development projects such as oil mining and extraction of natural resources, it is equally relevant in the context of conflict-induced displacement (and other forms of internal displacement) in situations where basic amenities are not sufficiently provided in host communities or IDP camps. For instance, issues around environmental cleanliness have been raised in several camps in Adamawa, Borno and Taraba.[86] According to OCHA, 'most IDPs are observed to resort to open defecation in all the camps visited [in Adamawa] and sanitary conditions are deplorable',[87] increasing the likelihood of air and water-borne contaminations and environmental degradation.

Article 9(2) (k) of the Kampala Convention obligates states to 'consult internally displaced persons and allow them to participate in decisions relating to their protection and assistance'.[88] The obligation to consult with IDPs and allow them to participate in the decision-making process is integral to fostering durable solutions as these dual processes are means through which these persons can express concerns and develop initiative with the state on issues around their protection and assistance. Consultation and participation processes are equally important in highlighting challenges experienced by IDPs and addressing them. While the government, through NEMA and with the support of civil society organisations, has been providing humanitarian assistance to IDPs, this assistance is often initiated on the preconceived notion of the basic humanitarian needs of IDPs. While such notions are not wrong, acting solely on them would result in the neglect of other significant issues such as sustainable livelihood reconstruction[89] and the specific needs of different categories of displaced persons, including the elderly, children and persons with disabilities. With regard to health and environmental concerns in the camps, many IDPs lament the poor living conditions that are only addressed in dribs and drags.[90] In Adamawa, the unhygienic toilet conditions were only given priority following the outbreak of cholera.[91] In an IDP camp in Abuja, the sanitary conditions have remained deplorable despite complaints to authorities.[92]

---

[86] 'In Adamawa IDPs camp, it's 300 people to a toilet' (2014); 'Addressing health concerns in IDP camps' (2014); Assessment Capacities Project (2014).

[87] UN Office for the Coordination of Humanitarian Affairs (2014c), p. 3; Internal Displacement Monitoring Centre (2014), p. 11.

[88] African Union (2012), The Kampala Convention, art 9(2) (k).

[89] One of the displaced persons in Daware camp in the Fofure local government area of Adamawa stated that 'I only have one cogent complain to the federal government to help us to our own deserted home as a matter of urgency. This place [IDP camp] is not conducive, and even if we eat all we want to eat, home is home, because there is no place like home.' 'NEMA, UN access IDP camps in Adamawa' (2014).

[90] Hamza et al. (2014), Audu (2015) and Oyoyo (2015).

[91] 'In Adamawa IDPs camp, it's 300 people to a toilet' (2014); 'Addressing health concerns in IDP camps' (2014); Assessment Capacities Project (2014).

[92] 'Pains of war' (2015).

In relation to article 9(2) (l) of the Kampala Convention, which mandates states to '[t]ake necessary measures to ensure that internally displaced persons who are citizens in their country of nationality can enjoy their civic and political rights', the right to vote of IDPs in Nigeria has been a highlight of national discussions in the face of the 2015 General Elections. In December 2014, the Independent National Electoral Commission (INEC) noted that over a million displaced IDPs may not be able to vote due to displacement and security concerns unless the Nigerian Electoral Act is amended.[93] However, the National Assembly of Nigeria, prior to the April/May elections, took a significant step in this regard in amending the Electoral Act and as such empowering INEC to make laws to enable IDPs to vote.[94]

In line with article 9(2) (m) of the Kampala Convention, states are required to '[p]ut in place measures for monitoring and evaluating the effectiveness and impact of the humanitarian assistance delivered to internally displaced persons'. Normatively, the state has taken a significant step in developing a Strategic Response Plan (2014–2016).[95] The plan was developed through the joint effort of NEMA, government institutions, UN agencies and civil society organisations. The objectives of the plan are to '[t]rack and analyse risk and vulnerability',[96] '[s]upport vulnerable populations'[97] and '[d]eliver coordinated and integrated live-saving assistance to people affected by emergencies'.[98] The Strategic Response Plan requires that an 'inter-sector coordination group' be created to 'track and analyse outcome and outputs indicator and measure progress'.[99] If the Strategic Response Plan is properly implemented, humanitarian assistance to conflict-induced displacees in Northern Nigeria will be monitored effectively.

From the discourse on the compliance of Nigeria with the obligation in article 9(2) of the Kampala Convention, it is evident that while the state has taken notable measures in protecting and assisting IDPs, more concrete steps need to be taken in living up to the obligation in the Kampala Convention. These steps are integral to the realisation of the obligation in article 5(6) of the Kampala Convention, which mandates states to 'provide sufficient protection and assistance to internally displaced persons'[100] in view of the fact that—as article 5(1) of the Kampala Convention

[93] In line with article 12 of the Electoral Act, one of the condition upon which a person may be registered to vote is where such person is 'ordinarily resident, works in, originates from the Local Government Area Council or Ward covered by the registration centre'. The Electoral Act further prohibits a person from registering in more than one registration centre at a time. Due to displacement, IDPs stand to be disqualified. The Electoral Act (2010); 'INEC: 1m Boko Haram victims can't vote in 2015' (2014); Ajobe (2015); 'Reps amend electoral act to allow IDPs vote during elections' (2015); Orovwuje (2015).

[94] 'INEC told to uphold voting rights of internally displaced persons' (2014).

[95] 2014–2016 revised strategic response plan: Nigeria (2014), p. 2.

[96] 2014–2016 revised strategic response plan: Nigeria (2014).

[97] 2014–2016 revised strategic response plan: Nigeria (2014).

[98] 2014–2016 revised strategic response plan: Nigeria (2014).

[99] 2014–2016 revised strategic response plan: Nigeria (2014).

[100] African Union (2012), The Kampala Convention, art 5(6).

emphasises—states 'bear the primary duty and responsibility for providing protection of and humanitarian assistance to internally displaced persons'.[101]

13.5 Concluding Remarks

As legislation sets out the normative structure for the protection and assistance of IDPs, this paper argues that the first concrete step that states should take in realising the obligation in the Kampala Convention is the adoption of legislation on IDPs. Although Nigeria has an obligation to comply with the Kampala Convention regardless of an absence of domestic legislation, the adoption of legislation on IDPs is significant for two reasons. First, it fulfils the obligation under article 3(2) (a) of the Kampala Convention, which mandates states to incorporate the provisions of the Kampala Convention into national laws. Second, it sets out clearly the role of different state actors in the prevention of internal displacement and the protection of IDPs. This legislation should incorporate the provisions of article 9(2) of the Kampala Convention, which sets out specifically the modalities for the protection of IDPs in situations of internal displacement.

This paper further argues that Nigeria should set up adequate mechanisms for the protection of vulnerable groups. One underlying concern resonating from the treatment of IDPs is the lack of adequate accountability mechanisms in situations of violation of rights in the camps. As have been indicated in reports, there is 'culture of silence around rape',[102] and '[s]ince the same officials that these cases should be reported to are the perpetrators, many victims just keep quiet for fear of being sent out of the camp'.[103]

This paper further argues that in view of the infiltration of camps by members of the Boko Haram sect, security forces should be better equipped with the state-of-the-art technology significantly with regard to intelligence.

In addition, this paper argues that the state utilises relevant mechanisms of the African Union in view of the pan-Africanist ideology of creating African solutions to African problems. One relevant mechanism in this regard is the Continental Early Warning System (CEWS), which article 4(2) of the Kampala Convention references. Within the context of the displacement in Northern Nigeria, the Continental Early Warning System can assist states in formulating strategies on conflict prevention between displaced persons and host communities significantly in view of the strain on resources in host communities as a result of the influx of IDPs in these communities.

Further, this research argues that states should utilise traditional institutions in Northern Nigeria (significantly, the emirate systems) for the purpose of protecting IDPs under article 9(2) of the Kampala Convention. One of the ways through which

[101] African Union (2012), The Kampala Convention, art 5(6).

[102] 'Nigeria to investigate alleged abuse of refugee camps' (2015).

[103] Dickson (2015).

these institutions can feature is with respect to consultation with IDPs under article 9(2) (k) of the Kampala Convention. Due to the wide respect for these institutions in communities in Northern Nigeria, the state can implore them to foster effective dialogues for the purpose of creating durable solutions to the issue of internal displacement.

References

A year of attacks linked to Nigeria's Boko Haram (2014) http://edition.cnn.com/2014/02/27/world/africa/nigeria-year-of-attacks/. Accessed 22 Feb 2015

Abacha & Ors v Fawehinmi (judgement of the Supreme Court, delivered 28 April 2000)

Abdulaziz I, Faul M (2015) 7 kids reunite with parents lost in Nigeria Islamic uprising. Lubbock Avalanche-J doi: http://lubbockonline.com/filed-online/2015-01-09/7-kids-reunite-parents-lost-nigeria-islamic-uprising#.VO0NgnzLfpU

Adamawa: Boko Haram infiltrate Yola internally displaced persons camp (2014) http://www.today.ng/news/adamawa-boko-haram-infiltrate-yola-internally-displaced-persons-camp/. Accessed 25 Feb 2015

African Commission on Human and Peoples' Rights (2015) Press release on the ratification of the African Union Convention for the Protection and Assistance of Internally Displaced Persons in Africa (Kampala Convention by the Republic of Congo). http://www.achpr.org/press/2015/01/d247/. Accessed 22 Feb 2015

African Union (2012) Entry into force of African Union Convention for the Protection and Assistance of Internally Displaced Persons in Africa (Kampala Convention). http://pa.au.int/en/content/entry-force-african-union-convention-protection-and-assistance-internally-displaced-persons. Accessed 22 Feb 2015

African Union Executive Council, fifth ordinary session 25 June–3 July 2004, Addis Ababa, Ethiopia, Decision on the meeting of experts on the review of OAU/AU treaties, Doc EX/CL/95 (V)

African Union Executive Council, fifth ordinary session 25 June–3 July 2004, Addis Ababa, Ethiopia, Decision on the situation of refugees, returnees and displaced persons, Doc EX.CL/108 (V)

Ajakaye R (2015) Boko Haram infiltrating IDP camps: Nigeria. http://www.aa.com.tr/en/world/467494--boko-haram-infiltrating-idp-camps-nigeria. Accessed 25 Feb 2015

Ajobe AT (2015) We'll ensure IDPs vote in 2015 – Sen Ndume. http://www.dailytrust.com.ng/weekly/index.php/politics/18566-we-ll-ensure-idps-vote-in-2015-sen-ndume. Accessed 25 Feb 2015

Akinrinade B (2011) Nigeria. In: Shelton D (ed) International law and domestic legal systems: incorporation, transformation, and persuasion. Oxford University Press, Oxford, pp 448–467

Amnesty: Nigeria massacre deadliest in history of Boko Haram (2015) http://www.dailymail.co.uk/wires/ap/article-2903305/7-kids-reunite-parents-lost-Nigeria-Islamic-uprising.html. Accessed 25 Feb 2015

Assessment Capacities Project (2014) Nigeria: Borno state cholera outbreak' Briefing note (30 October 2014). http://reliefweb.int/sites/reliefweb.int/files/resources/b-acaps-start-bn-nigeria-borno-state-cholera-30-oct-2014.pdf. Accessed 25 Feb 2015

Audu J (2015) Taraba IDPs lament govt neglect. http://dailyindependentnig.com/2015/02/taraba-idps-lament-govt-neglect/. Accessed 25 Feb 2015

Ayodele W (2014) Taraba: 70 killed in displaced persons' camp. http://www.thisdaylive.com/articles/taraba-70-killed-in-displaced-persons-camp/190296/. Accessed 24 Feb 2015

Barkindo A (2013) Join the caravan: the ideology of political authority in Islam from Ibn Taymiyya to Boko Haram in North-Eastern Nigeria. Perspect Terrorism 7(3):30–43

Bavier J (2012a) Nigeria: Boko Haram 101. http://pulitzercenter.org/reporting/nigeria-boko-haram-terrorist-group-islam-christian-church-targets-youth-military. Accessed 22 Feb 2015
Bavier J (2012b) Who are Boko Haram and why are they terrorizing Nigerian Christians? http://www.theatlantic.com/international/archive/2012/01/who-are-boko-haram-and-why-are-they-terrorizing-nigerian-christians/251729/. Accessed 22 Feb 2015
BBC News (2013) Boko Haram timeline: from preachers to slave raiders. http://www.bbc.com/news/world-africa-22538888. Accessed 22 Feb 2015
BBC News (2015) Nigeria's Boko Haram militants attack Chad for first time (2015). http://www.bbc.com/news/world-africa-31453951. Accessed 22 Feb 2015
Boko Haram destroys 16 towns, villages in Nigeria (2015) http://www.news24.com/Africa/News/Boko-Haram-destroys-16-towns-villages-in-Nigeria-20150108. Accessed 25 Jan 2015
Caring for internally displaced persons (2015) http://sunnewsonline.com/new/?p=102253. Accessed 24 Feb 2015
Chothia F (2015) Who are Nigeria's Boko Haram Islamists? http://www.bbc.com/news/world-africa-13809501. Accessed 22 Feb 2015
Constitution of the Federal Republic of Nigeria, 1999
Daily Trust (2014) Addressing health concerns in IDP camps (2014). http://dailytrust.com.ng/daily/editorial/36467-addressing-health-concerns-in-idp-camps. Accessed 25 Feb 2015
Derby DH (2008) The international prohibition of torture. In: Bassiouni MC (ed) International criminal law: international enforcement, 3rd edn. Koninklijke Brill NV, Leiden, pp 621–658
Dickson C (2015) Grim tales of rape, child trafficking in displaced persons camp. http://icirnigeria.org/grim-tales-of-rape-child-trafficking-in-displaced-persons-camps/. Accessed 24 Feb 2015
Foulkes I (2014) Global refugee figures highest since WW2, UN says. http://www.bbc.com/news/world-27921938. Accessed 21 Feb 2015
Frontline (2001) Interview: Ali Ali-Ahmed. http://www.pbs.org/wgbh/pages/frontline/shows/saudi/interviews/ahmed.html. Accessed 22 Feb 2015
Hamza I, Yahaya I, Sawab I (2014) Tough question from north-east IDP cams: 'how long shall we live in refugee camps? http://www.dailytrust.com.ng/sunday/index.php/feature/18255-tough-question-from-north-east-idp-camps-how-long-shall-we-live-in-refugee-camps. Accessed 24 Feb 2015
Human Rights Watch (2012) Nigeria: Boko Haram widens terror campaign. http://www.hrw.org/news/2012/01/23/nigeria-boko-haram-widens-terror-campaign. Accessed 22 Feb 2015
Ibrahim P (2015) Boko Haram members infiltrate IDP camps – FG reveals. http://www.nigeriatell.com/news/boko-haram-members-infiltrate-idp-camps-fg-reveals. Accessed 25 Feb 2015
Idowu K (2015) Panel dismisses rape in IDP camps, suspects two cases. http://www.punchng.com/news/panel-dismisses-rapes-in-idps-camps-suspects-two-cases/. Accessed 25 Feb 2015
IDPs from north-east Nigeria fear Boko Haram may return (2015) http://www.channelstv.com/2015/02/22/idps-from-north-east-nigeria-fear-boko-haram-may-return/. Accessed 24 Feb 2015
In Adamawa IDPs camp, it's 300 people to a toilet (2014) http://thenigeriatoday.net/in-adamawa-idps-camp-its-300-people-to-a-toilet/. Accessed 25 Feb 2015
INEC told to uphold voting rights of internally displaced persons (2014) http://www.channelstv.com/2014/12/16/inec-told-to-uphold-voting-rights-of-internally-displaced-persons/. Accessed 25 Feb 2015
INEC: 1m Boko Haram victims can't vote in 2015 (2014) http://thenationonlineng.net/new/inec-1m-boko-haram-victims-cant-vote-2015/. Accessed 25 Jan 2015
Internal Displacement Monitoring Centre (2013) Nigeria: fragmented response to internal displacement amid Boko Haram attacks and flood season. http://www.internal-displacement.org/assets/library/Africa/Nigeria/pdf/201307-af-nigeria-overview-en.pdf. Accessed 25 Feb 2015
Internal Displacement Monitoring Centre (2014) Nigeria: multiple displacement crises overshadowed by Boko Haram. http://www.internal-displacement.org/assets/library/Africa/Nigeria/pdf/201412-af-nigeria-overview-en.pdf. Accessed 23 Feb 2015

International Organization for Migration (2015) IOM highlights need for regional response to Boko Haram displacement. http://www.iom.int/cms/en/sites/iom/home/news-and-views/press-briefing-notes/pbn-2015/pbn-listing/iom-highlights-need-for-regional.html. Accessed 23 Feb 2015

Ismail M (2015) The plight of unaccompanied children in Yola IDPs camp. http://leadership.ng/features/399586/plight-unaccompanied-children-yola-idps-camp. Accessed 25 Feb 2015

Iwuchukwu MC (2013) Muslim-Christian dialogue in post-colonial Northern Nigeria: the challenges of inclusive cultural and religious pluralism. Palgrave Macmillan, New York

Karimi F, Abubakar A (2015) Nine days later, bodies still litter bushes from Boko Haram's 'deadliest' massacre. http://edition.cnn.com/2015/01/12/africa/boko-haram-deadliest-attack/. Accessed 22 Feb 2015

Killander M (ed) (2010) International law and domestic human rights litigation in Africa. Pretoria University Law Press, Pretoria

Legal Resources Foundation v Zambia (2001) AHRLR 84 (ACHPR 2001)

Maina M (2014) Boko Haram: women IDPs take to street begging, accuse FG of unfair treatment. http://dailypost.ng/2014/10/25/boko-haram-women-idps-take-street-begging-accuses-fg-unfair-treatment/. Accessed 24 Feb 2015

Many dead in Nigeria market blast (2010) http://www.aljazeera.com/news/africa/2010/12/2010123120182342788.html. Accessed 22 Feb 2015

Marama N (2011) 4 policemen, 9 others killed in fresh Boko Haram attacks. http://www.vanguardngr.com/2011/05/4-policemen-9-others-killed-in-fresh-boko-haram-attacks/. Accessed 22 Feb 2015

Marama N (2014) 30 women give birth in Borno refugee camp. http://www.vanguardngr.com/2014/12/30-women-give-birth-borno-refugee-camp/. Accessed 24 Feb 2015

Massalaki A (2015) Boko Haram attacks island on Niger side of Lake Chad. http://www.reuters.com/article/2015/02/21/us-nigeria-violence-niger-idUSKBN0LP09A20150221. Accessed 22 Feb 2015

Muslim sect kills more than 100 in attacks on north-east Nigeria (2011) http://www.theguardian.com/world/2011/nov/06/nigeria-muslim-sect-attacks-deathtoll. Accessed 22 Feb 2015

National Emergency Management Agency (2014) NEMA deploys more personnel, equipment in IDP camps in Adamawa. http://www.thisdaylive.com/articles/nema-deploys-more-personnel-equipment-in-idp-camps-in-adamawa/195086/. Accessed 25 Feb 2015

NEMA, UN access IDP camps in Adamawa (2014) http://www.thisdaylive.com/articles/nema-un-assess-idp-camps-in-adamawa/194499/. Accessed 25 Feb 2015

Nigeria (August 2014) revised strategic response plan 2014–2016. Available at Nigeria. http://reliefweb.int/sites/reliefweb.int/files/resources/Revision_2014-2016_Nigeria_SRP_August2014.pdf. Accessed 25 Feb 2015

Nigeria attacks claimed by Islamist sect Boko Haram (2012) http://www.bbc.co.uk/news/world-africa-13618775. Accessed 22 Feb 2015

Nigeria to investigate alleged abuse of refugee camps (2015) http://www.bbc.com/news/world-africa-31386340. Accessed 15 Aug 2015

Nigeria: satellite images show horrific scale of Boko Haram attack on Baga (2015) https://www.amnesty.org/en/articles/news/2015/01/nigeria-satellite-images-show-horrific-scale-boko-haram-attack-baga/. Accessed 25 Feb 2015

Nigeria's forgotten crisis (2014) African research bulletin: economic, financial and technical series 20634 51(11)

Nigerian army reclaims Baga from Boko Haram (2015) http://www.channelstv.com/2015/02/21/nigerian-army-reclaims-baga-from-boko-haram/. Accessed 25 Feb 2015

Norwegian Refugee Council, Internal Displacement Monitoring Centre (2014) Global overview 2014: people internally displaced by conflict and violence. http://www.internal-displacement.org/assets/publications/2014/201405-global-overview-2014-en.pdf. Accessed 25 Feb 2015

Office of the Prosecutor, International Criminal Court (2013) Report on preliminary examination activities 2013 (2013) para 218. http://www.icc-cpi.int/en_menus/icc/press%20and%20

media/press%20releases/Documents/OTP%20Preliminary%20Examinations/OTP%20-%20Report%20%20Preliminary%20Examination%20Activities%202013.PDF. Accessed 23 Feb 2015
Olugbode M (2014) Cholera claims 27 lives in Biu refugee camp. http://www.thisdaylive.com/articles/cholera-claims-27-lives-in-biu-refugee-camp/185319/. Accessed 15 Aug 2015
Organisation of African Unity (1994) Addis Ababa Document on Refugees and Forced Population Displacements in Africa. http://www.refworld.org/docid/3ae68f43c.html. Accessed 21 Feb 2015
Orovwuje SA (2015) The 2015 elections: INEC and the rights of IDPs. http://dailyindependentnig.com/2015/02/2015-elections-inec-rights-idps/. Accessed 25 Feb 2015
Oyoyo I (2015) Insecurity: how IDPs cope with threat of displacement. http://leadership.ng/news/413556/insecurity-how-idps-cope-with-threat-of-displacement. Accessed 25 Feb 2015
Pains of war (2015) http://www.thisdaylive.com/articles/pains-of-war/202639/. Accessed 25 Feb 2015
Punch Newspaper (2014) Timeline on Boko Haram activities (2014). http://www.punchng.com/news/timeline-on-boko-haram-activities/. Accessed 22 Feb 2015
Purohit & another v The Gambia (2003) AHRLR 96 (ACHPR 2003)
Reps amend electoral act to allow IDPs vote during elections (2015) http://www.informationng.com/2015/01/reps-amend-electoral-act-to-allow-idps-vote-during-elections.html. Accessed 25 Feb 2015
Ross W (2014) Boko Haram insurgency tearing Nigerian families apart. Available at http://www.bbc.com/news/world-africa-29477760. Accessed 25 Feb 2015
Sahara Reporters "Why we could not defeat Boko Haram" – army commander writes a powerful letter to President Jonathan (2014) http://saharareporters.com/2014/12/15/why-we-could-not-defeat-boko-haram-army-commander-writes-powerful-letter-president. Accessed 25 Feb 2015
Simon S (2003) The new terrorism: securing the nation against a messianic foe. http://www.brookings.edu/research/articles/2003/01/winter-terrorism-simon. Accessed 22 Feb 2015
Springer DR, Regens JL, Edger DN (2009) Islamic radicalism and global jihad. Georgetown University Press, Washington, DC
The Electoral Act (2010) http://www.parliament.am/library/Electoral%20law/nigeria.pdf. Accessed 25 Feb 2015
The Guardian (2015) Deadly Boko Haram raids destroy two Nigerian villages. http://www.theguardian.com/world/2015/feb/20/boko-haram-raids-two-nigerian-villages. Accessed 25 Feb 2015
The Registered Trustees of National Association of Community Health Practitioners of Nigeria & ors v Medical and Health Workers Union of Nigeria (2008) 2 Nigerian Weekly Law Report (Part 1072) p. 575
The Tribune (2015) Boko Haram: when HIV visited Borno, Yobe IDPs' camps (2015). http://www.tribune.com.ng/life-and-living/item/29478-boko-haram-when-hiv-visited-borno-yobe-idps-camps/29478-boko-haram-when-hiv-visited-borno-yobe-idps-camps. Accessed 24 Feb 2015
ThisDay 158 freed Boko Haram abductees reunited with their families (2015) http://www.thisdaylive.com/articles/158-freed-boko-haram-abductees-reunited-with-their-families/202267/. Accessed 25 Feb 2015
Times Live (27 Jan 2015) Thousands displaced by Boko Haram flood Nigeria city. Available at http://www.timeslive.co.za/africa/2015/01/27/thousands-displaced-by-boko-haram-flood-nigeria-city. Accessed 25 Feb 2015
Troops reclaim Monguno from Boko Haram (2015) http://thecitizenng.com/headline-2/troops-reclaim-monguno-from-boko-haram/. Accessed 25 Feb 2015
UN High Commissioner for Refugees (2013) War's human cost. http://www.unhcr.org/5399a14f9.html. Accessed 21 Feb 2015
UN High Commissioner for Refugees (2014) World refugee day: global forced displacement tops 50 million for first time in post-World War II era. http://www.unhcr.org/53a155bc6.html. Accessed 21 Feb 2015

UN Office for the Coordination of Humanitarian Affairs (2014a) Nigeria: update on IDPs in camp and host communities in Adamawa state, situation report No. 2 (as of 4–5 November 2014). http://www.humanitarianresponse.info/sites/www.humanitarianresponse.info/files/assessments/SITREP%20%20Adamawa%20%20-%202014-11-05.pdf. Accessed 25 Feb 2015

UN Office for the Coordination of Humanitarian Affairs (2014b) Nigeria: update on IDPs in camp and host communities in Adamawa state, situation report No. 1 (as of 2 October 2014). http://reliefweb.int/report/nigeria/nigeria-update-idps-camp-and-host-communities-adamawa-state-situation-report-no-1-2. Accessed 25 Feb 2015

UN Office for the Coordination of Humanitarian Affairs (2014c) Nigeria: update on IDPs in camp and host communities in Adamawa state, situation report No. 2 (4–5 November 2014). http://www.humanitarianresponse.info/sites/www.humanitarianresponse.info/files/assessments/SITREP%20%20Adamawa%20%20-%202014-11-05.pdf. Accessed 24 Feb 2015

UN Office for the Coordination of Humanitarian Affairs (2015) Nigeria: northeast crisis, situation report No. 1 (as of 30 January 2015). http://www.humanitarianresponse.info/system/files/documents/files/OCHA%20Nigeria%20SitRep_January%202015.pdf. Accessed 24 Feb 2015

Vienna Convention on the Law of Treaties (1969)

Wachira GM, Ayinla A (2006) Twenty years of elusive enforcement of the recommendations of the African Commission on Human and Peoples' Rights: a possible remedy. AHRLJ 6(2):465–492

Walker A (2012) What is Boko Haram? http://www.usip.org/sites/default/files/SR308.pdf. Accessed 22 Feb 2015

Weate J (2014) Boko Haram's roots in Nigeria long predate Al-Qaeda era. http://america.aljazeera.com/articles/2014/4/23/boko-haram-s-rootsinnigerialongpredatethealqaedaera.html. Accessed 22 Feb 2015

Chapter 14
Boko Haram and the Abduction of Schoolgirls in Nigeria: Reflecting on 'Gender-Based Crimes' as a Legal Misnomer

Avitus Agbor

14.1 Introduction

Boko Haram, a Nigerian-based terrorist organisation, has claimed responsibility for numerous atrocities that have been committed against unarmed civilians. The targets of these atrocities are not limited to any geographical area. However, suffice it to say that Boko Haram operates in Nigeria, as well as neighbouring countries such as Cameroon and Chad. The cross-border nature of its operations has changed the legal character of Boko Haram: they constitute a cross-border terrorist organisation. The atrocities for which Boko Haram have claimed responsibility vary in terms of the scale of victims, the places targeted, as well as the intent underlying these heinous acts. In the perpetration of such atrocities, they make no distinction between men, women and children. From market centres to academic institutions, houses of worship and roadsides, thousands of civilians have either been abducted or murdered in large numbers. In a cross-border attack in January 2015, about 80 hostages were taken by Boko Haram.[1] In early February 2015, about 800 Boko Haram militants attacked the Cameroonian town of Fotokol where churches, mosques and villages were burnt.[2] One hundred people were massacred and about 500 wounded during this attack.[3] These gruesome atrocities were accompanied by looting of foodstuff and livestock.[4] In late February 2015, in the City of Potiskum, Nigeria,

[1] http://www.dailymail.co.uk/news/article-2916648/Cameroon-frees-24-hostages-suspected-Boko-Haram-kidnapping.html. Accessed 9 May 2016.

[2] http://217.218.67.231/Detail/2015/02/05/396273/Boko-Haram-kills-13-Chad-troops. Accessed 9 May 2016.

[3] See note 2.

[4] See note 2.

A. Agbor (✉)
Faculty of Law, North-West University, Mafikeng, South Africa
e-mail: Avitus.Agbor@nwu.ac.za

J.-M. Iyi, H. Strydom (eds.), *Boko Haram and International Law*,
https://doi.org/10.1007/978-3-319-74957-0_14

a suicide bomber detonated explosives that killed 12 people and injured 20 in a bus.[5] Alleged spies have been beheaded in an ISIS-style execution.[6]

Boko Haram's strategies include sporadic and isolated incidents of bombing and burning of communities they attack. Teenage females are used as suicide bombers to detonate explosives in fully packed public places. From commuter buses, markets and shopping centres, mosques and churches, schools and roadsides, civilians have become primary targets of gruesome atrocities. Early June 2015, Boko Haram attacked a busy market in the Nigerian city of Maiduguri killing about 50 people.[7] In mid-June 2015, Boko Haram crossed the Nigerian border and attacked two towns in neighbouring Niger.[8] Homes were set ablaze and about 40 people killed.[9] That same week, two suicide bombings in the Chadian capital that killed 33 people were attributed to Boko Haram.[10] On the evening of 1 July 2015, Wednesday, Boko Haram extremists gunned down about 100 Muslims who were praying in mosques in the Nigerian town of Kukawa.[11] These attacks came a day after the Islamic extremist group attacked a village that is 22 miles away and massacred about 48 men and boys.[12] On 5 July 2015, Sunday, two bombs exploded in a crowded mosque and an elite Muslim restaurant in the Nigerian city of Jos killing 44 people.[13] Sixty-seven people were severely wounded.[14]

These atrocities are grave not only because of the frequency and the number of casualties but more so because they seek to alter the political, religious and cultural balance amongst communities in the affected countries. In addition, the selection of targets is partly motivated by a desire to affect their religious affiliations and beliefs in the hope that they subscribe to the fundamental doctrines and teachings of Islam and ultimately endorse the ideologies of Islamic fundamentalism.

---

[5] http://www.bbc.com/news/world-africa-31604853. Accessed 9 May 2016.

[6] http://www.newsweek.com/report-boko-haram-beheads-two-men-claiming-they-are-spies-310603. Acccssed 9 May 2016.

[7] http://www.nydailynews.com/news/world/nigeria-bombing-kills-50-people-boko-haram-blamed-article-1.2243864. Accessed 9 May 2016.

[8] http://www.nydailynews.com/news/world/boko-haram-kills-40-niger-village-official-article-1.2263151. Accessed 9 May 2016.

[9] See note 7.

[10] See note 7.

[11] http://www.nydailynews.com/news/world/boko-haram-nigeria-kills-97-muslims-ramadan-massacres-article-1.2279505. Accessed 9 May 2016.

[12] See note 11.

[13] http://www.nydailynews.com/news/world/bombs-blamed-boko-haram-kill-44-nigeria-article-1.2282534. Accessed 9 May 2016.

[14] See note 13.

14.2 Boko Haram Abduction of Over 250 Schoolgirls in 2014

In April 2014, Boko Haram abducted about 250 schoolgirls. Unofficial sources disclose that these schoolgirls were targeted because of their gender and religious beliefs (at the time of their abduction, they were all or predominantly Christians). The motive behind these abductions was to disrupt the way of life of the inhabitants of the affected community of Chibok by spreading terror and apprehension, which would ultimately cause them to reject Christianity and its values, principles and practices. As of the time of writing, the abducted schoolgirls have remained in captivity with no clear indication as to whether they are alive and, if so, where they are, what they are doing and who has control over them. This abduction of schoolgirls (most of whom were under the age of 18 at the time of abduction) constitutes a flagrant violation of the rights of women (because of their gender), as well as the rights of children (because of their ages). Beyond the rights that have been violated, when examined from another legal angle, this abduction constitutes gender-based violence and gender-based discrimination, concepts that are worthy of further examination.

14.2.1 The Abduction of Schoolgirls as Gender-Based Discrimination

International human rights instruments detail the substantive content of civil, political, economic, social and cultural rights.[15] The fundamental normative framework of these instruments is the universality of these rights: they are legal entitlements that every human being has. As such, they contain non-discriminatory clauses that prohibit specific forms of discrimination.[16] In addition, there are specific human rights instruments that deal with specific groups. Women constitute one of such groups.

---

[15] At the global level, these instruments include the United Nations' Universal Declaration of Human Rights, United Nations General Assembly Resolution 217A, U.N.G.A. 3rd Session, U.N. Doc. A/RES/3/217A (1948) of 10 December 1948, (hereafter the UDHR); the International Covenant on Civil and Political Rights, 16 December 1966, 999 U.N.T.S. 171, (hereafter the ICCPR) and the International Covenant on Economic, Social and Cultural Rights, 16 December 1966, 993 U.N.T.S. 3 (hereafter the ICESCR). In addition to these, there are regional human rights instruments such as the American Convention on Human Rights, 22 November 1969, O.A.S. Treaty Series No. 36, 1144 U.N.T.S. 123, reprinted in Basic Documents Pertaining to Human Rights in the Inter-American System, OEA/Ser.L.V/II.82 doc.6 rev.1 at 25 (1992) (hereafter the American Convention); the European Convention for the Protection of Human Rights and Fundamental Freedoms, 4 November 1950, 213 U.N.T.S. 222, 312 ETS 5 (as amended by Protocols Nos. 11 and 14) (hereafter the European Convention); and the African Charter on Human and Peoples' Rights, 27 June 1981, OAU Doc. CAB/LEG/67/3 rev. 5; 1520 U.N.T.S. 217 (hereafter the Banjul Charter).

[16] See, for example, Article 2(1) of the ICCPR; Article 2(2) of the ICESCR; Article 1(1) of the American Convention; Article 14 of the European Convention; Article 2 of the Banjul Charter.

Given the inherent inequality that exists between men and women in the world and how it affects the realisation of women's rights, the UN Convention on the Elimination of all Forms of Discrimination Against Women (CEDAW) was adopted.[17] CEDAW urges States Parties to, amongst other things, undertake reforms aimed at addressing the inequality between men and women and also abolish all forms of gender inequality and gender-based discrimination. As used in the CEDAW, gender-based discrimination means

> ...any distinction, exclusion or restriction made on the basis of sex which has the effect or purpose of impairing or nullifying the recognition, enjoyment or exercise by women, irrespective of their marital status, on a basis of equality of men and women, of human rights and fundamental freedoms in the political, economic, social, cultural, civil or any other field.[18]

Based on this definition, it is argued that the abduction of these schoolgirls because of their gender constitutes gender-based discrimination. The abduction of these schoolgirls has had adverse effects on the realisation of their rights (civil, political, economic, social and cultural).

14.2.2 The Abduction of Schoolgirls as Gender-Based Violence

In addition to defining what constitutes gender-based discrimination, the UN adopted another instrument aimed at addressing violence against women: the UN General Assembly Declaration on the Elimination of Violence Against Women.[19] This Declaration addresses the need to uphold, promote and protect the physical and mental integrity of women and prohibits all forms of violence perpetrated against a woman because she is a woman. Violence against women is defined as

> ...any act of gender-based violence that results in, or is likely to result in, physical, sexual or psychological harm or suffering to women, including threats of such acts, coercion or arbitrary deprivation of liberty, whether occurring in public or in private life.[20]

Furthermore, this Declaration stipulates what constitutes violence against women as follows:

(a) Physical, sexual and psychological violence occurring in the family, including battering, sexual abuse of female children in the household, dowry related violence, marital rape, female genital mutilation and other traditional practices harmful to women, non-spousal violence, and violence related to exploitation;

---

[17] CEDAW, 18 December 1976, 1249 U.N.T.S. 13.

[18] Article 1, CEDAW.

[19] United Nations' Declaration on the Elimination of Violence Against Women, U.N. Doc. A/6316 (1966), 999 U.N.T.S. 302.

[20] Article 1, Declaration on the Elimination of Violence Against Women, Resolution adopted by the General Assembly on the Report of the Third Committee (A/48/629) Resolution 48/104.

(b) Physical, sexual and psychological violence occurring within the general community, including rape, sexual abuse, sexual harassment, and intimidation at work, in educational institutions and elsewhere, trafficking in women and forced prostitution;
(c) Physical, sexual and psychological violence perpetuated or condoned by the State, wherever it occurs.

Based on these definitions, it is evident that the act of abducting the schoolgirls itself constitutes gender-based violence.

14.3 Does the Abduction of the Schoolgirls Constitute Gender-Based Crimes in International Criminal Law?

As shown above, the categorisation and definition of what constitutes gender-based discrimination and gender-based violence are spelt out in these two international instruments. However, a problem arises when these are qualified as 'gender-based crimes' in international criminal law. Part of the problem is attributable to the absence of any definition of what gender-based crimes are. Moreover, combing through international instruments, one is left with very little room to think that this categorisation has been endorsed and accepted in international criminal law. Furthermore, the jurisprudence of the international criminal tribunals has not been very helpful as it exudes nothing but a remarkable reticence on the issue of gender-based crimes. Lastly, despite the multitude of scholars who have written on this topic, there is still no definition of what 'gender-based crime' is. To buttress this point, this paper explores the literature on gender-based crimes in international criminal law, the relevant international criminal law instruments and the jurisprudence of international tribunals. In conclusion, it argues that there is yet no instrument that has recognised or defined what gender-based crimes are. Also, even though women are the victims of heinous acts of violence, these do not qualify on their own to be a different category of crime of serious violations of international criminal law. Every atrocity must come within the definition of any of the existing crimes considered to be serious violations of international criminal law: that is, genocide, crimes against humanity and war crimes. Until a category of crimes known as 'gender-based crime' is created and defined, the concept of 'gender-based crimes' remains purely a creation of academics. This paper starts by asking the question whether the abduction of over 250 schoolgirls by Boko Haram constitutes 'gender-based crimes' in international criminal law.

As outlined above, the abduction of over 250 schoolgirls by Boko Haram constitutes gender-based discrimination and gender-based violence. However, the problem that arises is whether every act that constitutes gender-based discrimination and/or gender-based violence amounts to gender-based crimes in international law. To find answers to this question, it is important to evaluate the literature on gender-based crimes in international criminal law.

14.3.1 *Legal Scholars and Their Thoughts on 'Gender-Based Crimes'*

Numerous scholars have written on the topic 'gender-based crimes in international criminal law'. Most of these scholars have addressed what they consider as the substantive crimes perpetrated against women in times of armed conflict. A perusal of these academic writings, however, does not answer the question: what really are 'gender-based crimes' in international criminal law? Rather than cite the avalanche of literature that renders this question more elusive, it is important to limit the focus to a few of the most outstanding authors who have sought to address this issue.

Askin's piece highlights the elusiveness of the concept of 'gender-based crimes' in international criminal law.[21] Even though she scans through the sociological landscape to identify the perpetration of discriminatory acts against women based on the unjustifiably imposed second-class status, her extensive focus on international criminal instruments leaves the task of finding a concise definition of what 'gender-based crimes' are in international criminal law. Even though a litany of gender-based acts is narrated, she looks at these instruments from an end-result perspective: the prosecution of offences in which women were victimised. In my opinion, this approach is narrow and misleading. The prosecution of crimes under the jurisdiction of international criminal tribunals has never been gender biased. The instruments that define the substantive crimes show no bias in favour of or against any gender. Askin presents no persuasive evidence from international instruments that suggests that there is a species of crimes called gender-based crimes in international criminal law.

Cummings-John's contribution to the debate on gender-based crimes is quite remarkable.[22] She looks at the prosecution of gender-based crimes and sexual violence crimes at the International Criminal Tribunal for Rwanda and the Special Court for Sierra Leone. In her view, some themes are central to the discussion. However, she does not offer any definition of what constitute 'gender-based crimes' in international criminal law. The author engages the reader in a topic that is wanting in definition and, therefore, lends no assistance to any scholar in search of definitions.

However, Mouthaan assists in explaining the concept of 'gender-based crimes'.[23] Even though she provides a description rather than a definition, she paints the picture of what ought to be seen as the perpetration of some discriminatory acts against women in terms of general practice and attitudes prior to understanding this conceptualisation of what 'gender-based crimes' are in international criminal law. The specificity of gender-based crimes is that it is directed against persons who, albeit of a specific ethnic or religious origin, are also targeted because of their gender resulting from power imbalances that exploit the distinction between males and females:

[21] Askin (2011), pp. 84–113.

[22] Cummings-John (2015), pp. 379–405.

[23] Mouthaan (2010), p. 17.

> Reference to gender not only reflects developments in recent years at UN level and progress in International Criminal Law gradually to criminalise gender-based crimes, but also because to view these crimes from a gender perspective addresses core issues of inequality and oppression.
>
> Gender refers to social imbalances between men and women legitimised by social institutions and beliefs, including attitudes, values and respective roles and the resulting different needs of men and women. The legitimisation of these social differences are learned and shaped by each person's specific social context and may evolve due to social, political, economic, racial and cultural factors…
>
> To recognise a category of crimes that are directed against persons on the basis of gender resulting from power imbalances that exploit the distinction between males and females is more reflective of the realities and context of these crimes. To link the concept of gender with these crimes goes beyond those strictly committed against women or those solely focussing on the sexual nature of the crime.
>
> Firstly, gender-based crimes, although they affect women and girls disproportionately are also committed against men. In this sense it is important not to limit the debate to women or to equate women and gender, even if generally the focus will be on women's needs. Reference to sex understood as the biological difference between men and women is insufficient, especially if it means that the victim of the crime can only be a woman. Gender should not be perceived as relating to women alone.
>
> Secondly, there is a link between gender-based crimes and sexual violence, but not all gender-based crimes involve sexual violence.
>
> The broader concept of gender-based crimes does not limit the crime to physical or sexual violence, but also addresses the oppressive and discriminatory, even if customary, practices. The root of these types of crime is hatred for gender spurred on by social construction of perceived role differences in which sexual violence may be a means to express the crime.

To Stephens, and as used in this write-up, the concepts of gender violence and sexual violence mean 'violence inflicted primarily, although not exclusively, on women, and involving some form of violent sexual abuse'.[24] Stephens adds that when such violence is inflicted on men, 'such violence usually aims in part to humiliate them by treating them "like women"' (footnote 3).

Stephens does not formulate a definition of what constitutes gender violence. However, she adopts the definition formulated by the Women's Caucus for Gender justices, which distinguishes gender violence from sexual violence as follows:

> By gender violence or violations, the Women's Caucus means violence or violations which have the target or affect women exclusively or disproportionately because they are women. Gender violence also includes violence or violations which are based on or perpetuate socially constructed stereotyped roles based on sex, or the power differential between men and women. Sexual violence, whether directed to women or men, is usually a form of gender violence, since it is an attack on one's gender identity, whether masculine or feminine. That is, women are raped, for example, to control and destroy them as women and to signal male ownership; men are raped to humiliate them through forcing them in the position of women and, thereby, rendering them, according to the prevailing stereotypes, weak and inferior (footnote 3).

[24] Stephens (1999), pp. 1–23.

In my opinion, this definition is more of a sociological perspective that borders on, first, the motive underlying the perpetration of such violence and, second, a distinguishing feature of the victim (that is, the gender). When examined from the view of international criminal law, especially with the absence of any instrument that makes mention of the phrase 'gender-based crimes', I resist following with this kind of definition. Perhaps recourse ought to be made to the different international instruments that contain a substantive definition of what constitutes gender-based discrimination and gender-based violence. These UN instruments, that is, the CEDAW and the Declaration of the Elimination of All Forms of Violence Against Women, become very helpful.

It is beyond dispute that during armed conflicts, heinous crimes are committed against women regardless of whether it is an international or non-international armed conflict. Evidence given by victims during court trials is very disturbing. However, like any other human right, as well as every other human being, international law has prescribed the substantive content of the rights of human beings. When any or some of these rights are violated in a systemic manner, resulting in widespread victimisation, some form of accountability must be ensured. However, to suggest that a particular category of persons, based on their gender, deserve a much higher protection that would constitute another substantive crime discredits the idea of equality of persons, equality of gender and universality of human rights. The substantive content of human rights is available to every human being. The fact that women are victims of heinous crimes during armed conflict should not result in the development of a new genre of crime in international criminal law: an effort by legal scholars to shape and influence the idea that these are crimes that are primarily targeting women. Hence, currently, international criminal law does not expressly recognise any such species of crimes. Rather, the definition of serious violations of international criminal law is so broad that such heinous atrocities may well come within the ambit of any of already existing crimes provided the definitional elements are met. International instruments that have defined what constitute serious violations of international law have never made use of the phrase 'gender-based crimes'.

14.4 The Categorisation of Gender-Based Crimes: The Reticence of International Criminal Law Instruments

Mouthaan's narrative is descriptive of what she perceives as gender-based crimes. However, like other academic writers, she fails to disclose whether there is any such categorisation as 'gender-based crimes' in international criminal law. As mentioned above, the phrase 'gender-based crimes' is a creation of academic writers that has been infused into contemporary international legal discourse to refer to heinous atrocities perpetrated against women, especially during armed conflicts. As academics continue to make use of this phrase, the question to ask is whether such phrase or categorisation as 'gender-based crimes' has ever featured in international criminal law instruments. An examination of some major international criminal law instruments will buttress this argument.

14.4.1 International Criminal Law Instrument(s) Before 1945

Prior to 1945, the relevant international criminal law instrument that would have addressed any concept like gender-based crimes would be the Slavery Convention of 1926.[25] This Convention defined and criminalised slavery, as well as slave-related offences. It defined slavery as 'the status or condition of a person over whom any or all of the powers attaching to the right of ownership are exercised'.[26] In addition, it stipulated what comprises slave trade as follows:

> The slave trade includes all acts involved in the capture, acquisition or disposal of a person with intent to reduce him to slavery; all acts involved in the acquisition of a slave with a view to selling or exchanging him; all acts of disposal by sale or exchange of a slave acquired with a view to being sold or exchanged, and, in general, every act of trade or transport in slaves.[27]

As evidenced by the above definition, there is no mention of the phrase 'gender-based crimes'. The definition stipulated in the Slavery Convention is articulated in a gender-neutral manner: this suggests that any person (irrespective of gender) could be a victim of slavery and slave trade. This Convention is quite helpful as it shows that prior to 1945, the prohibition of slavery, slave trade and other related offences did not have a gender qualification. Rather, it prohibited and criminalised the practice of slavery, slave trade and other related offences that victimise any person.

14.4.2 The Charters of the International Military Tribunal (IMT), Nuremberg, and the International Military Tribunal for the Far East (IMTFE), Tokyo

At the end of the Second World War, the victorious Allied Powers sought to hold those responsible for the atrocities committed in Europe and the Far East to account. To this end, two institutions were established: first, the IMT, Nuremberg, and,

[25] Signed at Geneva on 25 September 1926 Entry into force: 9 March 1927, in accordance with article 12. The Convention was amended by the Protocol done at the Headquarters of the United Nations, New York, on 7 December 1953; the amended Convention entered into force on 7 July 1955, the date on which the amendments, set forth in the annex to the Protocol of 7 December 1953, entered into force in accordance with article III of the Protocol.

[26] Article 1(1) of the Slavery Convention, 1926.

[27] Article 1(2) of the Slavery Convention, 1926.

second, the IMTFE, Tokyo. Worthy of note is the fact that the IMT, Nuremberg, was a joint venture by the Allied Powers, while the IMTFE, Tokyo, was established by the Americans. Despite the fact that these two tribunals were governed by two different instruments,[28] the definitions of the substantive crimes over which the tribunals would have jurisdiction were very similar.[29]

The Charter of the IMT, Nuremberg, provided definitions of what constitute war crimes and crimes against humanity (unlike the Charter of the IMTFE, Tokyo, which made use of the phrase 'Conventional War Crimes' rather than war crimes as used in the Charter of the IMT, Nuremberg). The Charter of the IMT, Nuremberg, defined war crimes as

> violations of the laws or customs of war. Such violations shall include, but not be limited to, murder, ill-treatment or deportation to slave labor or for any other purpose of civilian population of or in occupied territory, murder or ill-treatment of prisoners of war or persons on the seas, killing of hostages, plunder of public or private property, wanton destruction of cities, towns or villages, or devastation not justified by military necessity.

Common to these two charters was a common definition of what constitutes crimes against humanity, both of which defined crimes against humanity to mean

> murder, extermination, enslavement, deportation, and other inhumane acts committed against any civilian population, before or during the war; or persecutions on political, racial or religious grounds in execution of or in connection with any crime within the jurisdiction of the Tribunal, whether or not in violation of the domestic law of the country where perpetrated.

An assessment of the content of these two charters that define the substantive content of the crimes over which the tribunals have jurisdiction reveals that no crimes were sub-categorised into 'gender-based crimes'. The inclusion of offences like ill-treatment or deportation to slave labour in the definition of war crimes or enslavement, deportation and other inhumane acts committed against any civilian population in the definition of crimes against humanity was worded in a gender-neutral way. These instruments neither require nor recognise the gender of any of the victims of these crimes. In other words, enslavement, deportation to slave labour, as well as other inhumane acts, may be committed against any gender, whether male or female. The inescapable conclusion from this analysis is that even at the

[28] See Charter of the International Military Tribunal (IMT), Nuremberg, and the Charter of the International Military Tribunal for the Far East (IMTFE), Tokyo.

[29] See for example the definitions of crimes against peace and crimes against humanity under Articles 6(a) and (c) and 5(a) and (c) of the Charters of the IMT, Nuremberg and Tokyo respectively. However, a major difference between these two Charters was the wording of Article 6(b) and 5(b) respectively: the Charter of the IMT, Nuremberg, made use of 'war crimes' (defined as follows: '…violations of the laws or customs of war. Such violations shall include, but not be limited to, murder, ill-treatment or deportation to slave labor or for any other purpose of civilian population of or in occupied territory, murder or ill-treatment of prisoners of war or persons on the seas, killing of hostages, plunder of public or private property, wanton destruction of cities, towns or villages, or devastation not justified by military necessity'.). On the other hand, Article 5(b) of the IMTFE, Tokyo, created the offence of 'conventional war crimes' which was defined as 'violations of the laws or customs of war'.

conclusion of the Nuremberg and Tokyo trials, there was no such thing as gender-based crimes in international criminal law. Even if specific acts under the different rubrics could have a larger scale of victimisation of a specific gender, it still does not warrant such a classification or categorisation given the fact that the instruments were written in a gender-neutral language. This same line of reasoning would apply to the Allied Control Council Law No. 10 given the language with which it was written in describing the offences over which the Control Council Courts would have jurisdiction.[30]

14.4.3 Post-1945 Developments in International Criminal Law

After the Nuremberg and Tokyo trials, significant developments occurred in international criminal law: these include the adoption of international instruments that created some international crimes and the development of institutional mechanisms to hold perpetrators of serious violations of international law accountable (such as the UN *ad hoc* tribunals and hybrid courts). A close look at these international instruments will show that some conspicuously recognised women as a protected group, while others made use of phrases that could be construed as not excluding women as a protected group. Specifically, these developments are, firstly, the United Nations' Convention on the Prevention and Punishment of the Crime of Genocide (the Genocide Convention)[31]; secondly, the Supplementary Convention on the Abolition of Slavery, the Slave Trade, and Institutions and Practices Similar to Slavery[32]; thirdly, the Convention Against Torture and Other Cruel, Inhuman or Degrading Treatment or Punishment (hereafter referred to as the Convention Against Torture)[33]; fourthly, the statutes of the United Nations Security Council's *ad hoc* tribunals[34]; fifthly, the Rome Statute of the International Criminal

---

[30] See, for example, the definition of crimes against humanity:

> Atrocities and offences, including but not limited to murder, extermination, enslavement, deportation, imprisonment, torture, rape, or other inhumane acts committed against any civilian population….
>
> Article II(c) of Control Council Law No. 10.

[31] United Nations General Assembly Resolution 260(III), U.N. GAOR, 3rd Session, 179th meeting, U.N. Doc. A/RES/260A (1948).

[32] Adopted by a Conference of Plenipotentiaries convened by Economic and Social Council resolution 608(XXI) of 30 April 1956 and done at Geneva on 7 September 1956.

[33] UN General Assembly, *Convention Against Torture and Other Cruel, Inhuman or Degrading Treatment or Punishment*, 10 December 1984, 1465 U.N.T.S. 85; U.N.G.A. Res. 39/46, 39 U.N. GAOR Supp. (No. 51) at 197; U.N. Doc. A/39/51 (1984), entered into force on 26 June 1987.

[34] Statute of the International Criminal Tribunal for Rwanda (hereinafter referred to as the ICTR), annexed to United Nations Security Council Resolution 955, U.N. SCOR, 3453rd meeting, U.N. Doc. S/RES/955 (1994); Statute of the International Criminal Tribunal for the former Yugoslavia (hereinafter referred to as the ICTY), annexed to United Nations Security Council Resolution 827, U.N. SCOR, 3217th meeting, U.N. Doc. S/RES/827 (1993).

Court[35]; and, sixthly, developments that have taken place since the adoption of the Rome Statute of the International Criminal Court such as the Statute of the Special Court for Sierra Leone.[36] Specific aspects of these instruments would be looked into.

14.4.3.1 The Genocide Convention

The Genocide Convention defines the crime of genocide as

> …any of the following acts committed with intent to destroy, in whole or in part, a national, ethnical, racial or religious group, as such:
> (a) Killing members of the group;
> (b) Causing serious bodily or mental harm to members of the group;
> (c) Deliberately inflicting on the group conditions of life calculated to bring about its physical destruction in whole or in part;
> (d) Imposing measures intended to prevent births within the group;
> (e) Forcibly transferring children of the group to another group.[37]

In addition to defining the crime of genocide, the Genocide Convention stipulates the different punishable acts.[38] In part, the Genocide Convention stipulates the *dolis specialis* for the crime of genocide, which is the intent to destroy, in whole or in part, any of the protected groups of people. In addition to this, the Genocide Convention makes mention of what is considered genocide for the purpose of the Genocide Convention. A range of acts are captured in this definition and include killing members of the group,[39] causing serious bodily or mental harm to members of the group,[40] deliberately inflicting on the group conditions of life calculated to bring about its physical destruction in whole or in part,[41] imposing measures intended to prevent births within the group[42] and forcibly transferring children of the group to another group.[43] It must be noted, however, that the Genocide Convention expressly stipulates the protected groups: national, race, religious or

[35] Rome Statute of the International Criminal Court, U.N. Doc. A/CONF.183/9 (1998), reprinted in 37 I.L.M. 999 (1998) (hereinafter referred to as the Rome Statute of the ICC).

[36] Statute of the Special Court for Sierra Leone (hereinafter referred to as the SCSL), annexed to the Agreement between the United Nations and the Government of Sierra Leone on the Establishment of a Special Court for Sierra Leone pursuant to United Nations Security Council Resolution 1315, U.N. SCOR, 4186th meeting, U.N. Doc. S/RES/1315 (2000).

[37] See Article II(a)–(e) of the Genocide Convention.

[38] See Article III(a)–(e) of the Genocide Convention which makes punishable the following acts: genocide, conspiracy to commit genocide, direct and public incitement to commit genocide, attempt to commit genocide and complicity in genocide.

[39] See Article II(a) of the Genocide Convention.

[40] See Article II(b) of the Genocide Convention.

[41] See Article II(c) of the Genocide Convention.

[42] See Article II(d) of the Genocide Convention.

[43] See Article II(e) of the Genocide Convention.

ethnic.[44] In other words, the commission of any of these acts must be directed against any member of any of these groups, and it must be accompanied by the intention to destroy such a group, whether in part or in whole.[45]

Numerous inferences can be made from the wording of the Genocide Convention: first, that specific groups are protected: racial, ethnic, national or religious. There is no mention of gender or sexual grouping. Even though the Trial Chamber of the ICTR was bold to construe the meaning of the phrase 'as such' to mean the exclusion of mobile or unstable groups, it was, however, unwilling to bring within the purview of the Genocide Convention any group that is based on gender.[46] Clearly, therefore, the perpetration of any of these crimes may be genocidal if, and only if, it is accompanied by the requisite intention and directed against any protected group. In cases where such atrocities are perpetrated against women, they do not qualify to be termed genocide unless the requisite *mens rea* is proved and it is established that the women fit within any of the protected groups. Consequently, it becomes difficult to accept that there is an element of gender-based crimes when committed within the framework of the definition of genocide if these words are read literally. This, however, does not mean that women are not targeted for the perpetration of such atrocities. The argument here is that the Genocide Convention does not specifically protect women as a group.

[44] See Article II of the Genocide Convention.

[45] See note 44.

[46] *The Prosecutor v Jean-Paul Akayesu*, Judgment, Case No. ICTR-96-4. T. Ch. I, 2 September 1998. The Trial Chamber held as follows:

> On reading through the *travaux préparatoires* of the Genocide Convention, it appears that the crime of genocide was allegedly perceived as targeting only 'stable' groups, constituted in a permanent fashion and membership of which is determined by birth, with the exclusion of the more 'mobile' groups which one joins through individual voluntary commitment, such as political and economic groups. Therefore, a common criterion in the four types of groups protected by the Genocide Convention is that membership in such groups would seem to be normally not challengeable by its members, who belong to it automatically, by birth, in a continuous and often irremediable manner. (Para 511)

Moreover, the Chamber considered whether the groups protected by the Genocide Convention, echoed in Article 2 of the Statute, should be limited to only the four groups expressly mentioned and whether they should not also include any group which is stable and permanent like the said four groups. In other words, the question that arises is whether it would be impossible to punish the physical destruction of a group as such under the Genocide Convention, if the said group, although stable and membership is by birth, does not meet the definition of any one of the four groups expressly protected by the Genocide Convention. In the opinion of the Chamber, it is particularly important to respect the intention of the drafters of the Genocide Convention, which according to the *travaux préparatoires*, was patently to ensure the protection of any stable and permanent group. (Para 516, emphasis added).

14.4.3.2 Supplementary Convention on the Abolition of Slavery, the Slave Trade, and Institutions and Practices Similar to Slavery (Hereafter Supplementary Convention)[47]

In 1956, the Slavery Convention of 1926 was supplemented for purposes of completely abolishing the institutions of slavery and slave trade. In addition, it stipulated some institutions and practices that were not contained in, and addressed by, the Slavery Convention of 1926. Of specific importance to the current theme, the 1956 Supplementary Convention addressed some practices that affect women:

> Section I. – Institutions and practices similar to slavery
>
> Article 1
>
> Each of the States Parties to this Convention shall take all practicable and necessary legislative and other measures to bring about progressively and as soon as possible the complete abolition or abandonment of the following institutions and practices, where they still exist and whether or not they are covered by the definition of slavery contained in article 1 of the Slavery Convention signed at Geneva on 25 September 1926:
>
> … (c) Any institution or practice whereby:
>
> (i) A woman, without the right to refuse, is promised or given in marriage on payment of a consideration in money or in kind to her parents, guardian, family or any other person or group; or
>
> (ii) The husband of a woman, his family, or his clan, has the right to transfer her to another person for value received or otherwise; or
>
> (iii) A woman on the death of her husband is liable to be inherited by another person;
>
> (d) Any institution or practice whereby a child or young person under the age of 18 years, is delivered by either or both of his natural parents or by his guardian to another person, whether for reward or not, with a view to the exploitation of the child or young person or of his labour.

The Supplementary Convention further requires States Parties to

> undertake to prescribe, where appropriate, suitable minimum ages of marriage, to encourage the use of facilities whereby the consent of both parties to a marriage may be freely expressed in the presence of a competent civil or religious authority, and to encourage the registration of marriages.[48]

As seen from the above, this Supplementary Convention was the first instrument to define the substantive content of an international crime with a gender provision—the identification and stipulation of specific practices that affect a gender: women. Unfortunately, these stipulations were non-exhaustive as they were limited to these practices occurring only within the context of slavery, slave trade and other related offences.

---

[47] Adopted by a Conference of Plenipotentiaries convened by Economic and Social Council Resolution 608(XXI) of 30 April 1956 and done at Geneva on 7 September 1956. It entered into force on 30 April 1957 in accordance with Article 13.

[48] Article 2 of the Supplementary Convention on the Abolition of Slavery, the Slave Trade, and Institutions and Practices Similar to Slavery.

14.4.3.3 The Work of the International Law Commission (ILC)[49]

Over the years and with specific reference to international crimes, the ILC produced two draft codes: these two draft codes reflect the current international law at the time. However, if there was ever any such thing as gender-based crimes in international criminal law, the ILC would have formulated or recognised this new categorisation of crimes in international criminal law. The substantive content of these two draft codes are stated below:

The 1954 Draft Code of Offences Against the Peace and Security of Mankind (the 1954 Draft Code of Offences)[50]

As stated in the 1954 Draft Code of Offences, the following were classified as serious offences against the peace and security of mankind:

> Article 1
>
> Offences against the peace and security of mankind, as defined in this Code, are crimes under international law, for which the responsible individuals shall be punished.
>
> Article 2
>
> The following acts are offences against the peace and security of mankind...
>
> (10) Acts by the authorities of a State or by private individuals committed with intent to destroy, in whole or in part, a national, ethnic, racial or religious group as such, including:
>
> (i) Killing members of the group;
>
> (ii) Causing serious bodily or mental harm to members of the group;
>
> (iii) Deliberately inflicting on the group conditions of life calculated to bring about its physical destruction in whole or in part;
>
> (iv) Imposing measures intended to prevent births within the group;
>
> (v) Forcibly transferring children of the group to another group.
>
> (11) Inhuman acts such as murder, extermination, enslavement, deportation or persecutions, committed against any civilian population on social, political, racial, religious or cultural grounds by the authorities of a State or by private individuals acting at the instigation or with the toleration of such authorities.
>
> (12) Acts in violation of the laws or customs of war.

---

[49] The International Law Commission was created by the United Nations for the purpose of promoting 'the progressive development of international law and its codification'. See the United Nations General Assembly Resolution 174(II), U.N. GAOR, 2nd Session, 123rd meeting, U.N. Doc. A/RES/174(II) of 21 November 1947. United Nations General Assembly Resolution 177(II) mandated the International Law Commission to formulate 'the principles of international law recognised' in the Charter of the IMT, Nuremberg, and 'in the judgment of the Tribunal': see the United Nations General Assembly.

[50] The Draft Code of Offences against the Peace and Security of Mankind, 1954, was adopted by the International Law Commission, 6th Session, 1954, was submitted to the United Nations General Assembly as part of the ILC's Report covering the work of that session (at para 54). The report, which also contains commentaries on the draft articles, appears in the *Yearbook of the International Law Commission, 1954,* Vol. II.

The 1996 Draft Code of Crimes Against the Peace and Security of Mankind (Hereafter the 1996 Draft Code of Crimes)[51]

The 1996 Draft Code of Crimes expressly defined what the content of crimes against the peace and security of mankind is. These crimes were defined as follows:

Article 17: Crime of genocide

A crime of genocide means any of the following acts committed with intent to destroy, in whole or in part, a national, ethnic, racial or religious group, as such:

(a) Killing members of the group;

(b) Causing serious bodily or mental harm to members of the group;

(c) Deliberately inflicting on the group conditions of life calculated to bring about its physical destruction in whole or in part;

(d) Imposing measures intended to prevent births within the group;

(e) Forcibly transferring children of the group to another group.

Article 18: Crimes against humanity

A crime against humanity means any of the following acts, when committed in a systematic manner or on a large scale and instigated or directed by a Government or by any organization or group:

(a) Murder;

(b) Extermination;

(c) Torture;

(d) Enslavement;

(e) Persecution on political, racial, religious or ethnic grounds;

(f) Institutionalized discrimination on racial, ethnic or religious grounds involving the violation of fundamental human rights and freedoms and resulting in seriously disadvantaging a part of the population;

(g) Arbitrary deportation or forcible transfer of population;

(h) Arbitrary imprisonment;

(i) Forced disappearance of persons;

(j) Rape, enforced prostitution and other forms of sexual abuse;

(k) Other inhumane acts which severely damage physical or mental integrity, health or human dignity, such as mutilation and severe bodily harm….

Article 20: War crimes

Any of the following war crimes constitutes a crime against the peace and security of mankind when committed in a systematic manner or on a large scale:

(a) Any of the following acts committed in violation of international humanitarian law:

(i) Wilful killing;

(ii) Torture or inhuman treatment, including biological experiments;

(iii) Wilfully causing great suffering or serious injury to body or health;

(iv) Extensive destruction and appropriation of property, not justified by military necessity and carried out unlawfully and wantonly;

(v) Compelling a prisoner of war or other protected person to serve in the forces of a hostile Power;

(vi) Wilfully depriving a prisoner of war or other protected person of the rights of fair and regular trial;

---

[51] This Draft Code of Crimes against the Peace and Security of Mankind, 1996, was adopted by the International Law Commission at its 48th session in 1996. It was submitted to the United Nations General Assembly as part of the ILC's Report covering the work of the session (at para 50). The report, which also contains commentaries on the draft articles, appears in *Yearbook of the International Law Commission, 1996,* Vol. II (Part Two).

> (vii) Unlawful deportation or transfer of unlawful confinement of protected persons;
> (viii) Taking of hostages;
> (b) Any of the following acts committed wilfully in violation of international humanitarian law and causing death or serious injury to body or health:
> (i) Making the civilian population or individual civilians the object of attack;
> (ii) Launching an indiscriminate attack affecting the civilian population or civilian objects in the knowledge that such attack will cause excessive loss of life, injury to civilians or damage to civilian objects....
> (d) Outrages upon personal dignity in violation of international humanitarian law, in particular humiliating and degrading treatment, rape, enforced prostitution and any form of indecent assault....
> (f) Any of the following acts committed in violation of international humanitarian law applicable in armed conflict not of an international character:
> (i) Violence to the life, health and physical or mental well-being of persons, in particular murder as well as cruel treatment such as torture, mutilation or any form of corporal punishment;
> (ii) Collective punishments;
> (iii) Taking of hostages;
> (iv) Acts of terrorism;
> (v) Outrages upon personal dignity, in particular humiliating and degrading treatment, rape, enforced prostitution and any form of indecent assault;
> (vi) Pillage;
> (vii) The passing of sentences and the carrying out of executions without previous judgement pronounced by a regularly constituted court, affording all the judicial guarantees which are generally recognized as indispensable....

The 1954 Draft Code of Offences and the 1996 Draft Code of Crimes share some common features: first, they both define all these serious crimes against the peace and security of mankind in a gender-neutral context. Second, these instruments neither created nor recognised the categorisation of 'gender-based crimes'. Some of the listed acts, such as enslavement, rape, enforced prostitution and other forms of sexual abuse, and 'other inhumane acts which severely damage physical or mental integrity, health or human dignity, such as mutilation and severe bodily harm', which may be primarily directed against women, would require that they come under any of the rubrics of the crimes stipulated in these draft codes: that is, genocide, war crimes or crimes against humanity. The commission of crimes like enslavement, rape, enforced pregnancy and other forms of sexual violence, even if directed against women on massive scale, must be subsumed in a more specific category of any of the crimes considered serious offences against the peace and security of mankind. In conclusion, it is argued that the 1954 and 1996 Draft Codes of Offences and Crimes neither created nor recognised anything as 'gender-based crimes' in international criminal law.

14.4.3.4 The Convention Against Torture

The Convention Against Torture defines torture as follows:

> ...any act by which severe pain or suffering, whether physical or mental, is intentionally inflicted on a person for such purposes as obtaining from him or a third person information or a confession, punishing him for an act he or a third person has committed or is suspected

of having committed, or intimidating or coercing him or a third person, or for any reason based on discrimination of any kind, when such pain or suffering is inflicted by or at the instigation of or with the consent or acquiescence of a public official or other person acting in an official capacity.[52]

Like the Genocide Convention, this definition of torture is prescribed in gender-neutral words. However, as discussed below, different acts that would result in severe physical or mental pain would not only be qualified as torture but did qualify as genocide, crimes against humanity, war crimes, violations of Article 3 common to the four Geneva Conventions and Additional Protocol II.

14.4.3.5 The Statutes of the United Nations' *ad Hoc* Tribunals

Two *ad hoc* tribunals were created by the UN Security Council as mechanisms to hold accountable persons bearing responsibility for grave breaches of international law occurring in the former Yugoslavia and Rwanda respectively. These are the International Criminal Tribunal for the Former Yugoslavia (ICTY) and the International Criminal Tribunal for Rwanda (ICTR). The statutes of these tribunals spelt out the categories of crimes over which the tribunals would have jurisdiction. As would be noted, the crime of genocide, as well as its punishable acts, as defined in the Genocide Convention, was featured in both statutes of the tribunals. Some variations occurred in the definitional elements of crimes against humanity. In order to identify whether there was any gender element in the definition of these crimes, it is important to look at the crimes stipulated in the statutes of the tribunals.

The Statute of the ICTY

The Statute of the ICTY gave the ICTY jurisdiction over four crimes: grave breaches of the Geneva Conventions of 1949,[53] violations of the laws or customs of war,[54] genocide[55] and crimes against humanity.[56] The definitions of what these crimes constitute are as follows:

Article 2: Grave breaches of the Geneva Conventions of 1949

The International Tribunal shall have the power to prosecute persons committing or ordering to be committed grave breaches of the Geneva Conventions of 12 August 1949, namely the following acts against persons or property protected under the provisions of the relevant Geneva Convention:

(a) wilful killing;

(b) torture or inhuman treatment, including biological experiments;

[52] Article 1, Convention against Torture.

[53] Article 2, Statute of the ICTY.

[54] Article 3, Statute of the ICTY.

[55] Article 4, Statute of the ICTY.

[56] Article 5, Statute of the ICTY.

(c) wilfully causing great suffering or serious injury to body or health;
(d) extensive destruction and appropriation of property, not justified by military necessity and carried out unlawfully and wantonly;
(e) compelling a prisoner of war or a civilian to serve in the forces of a hostile power;
(f) wilfully depriving a prisoner of war or a civilian of the rights of fair and regular trial;
(g) unlawful deportation or transfer or unlawful confinement of a civilian;
(h) taking civilians as hostages.

Article 3: Violations of the laws or customs of war

The International Tribunal shall have the power to prosecute persons violating the laws or customs of war. Such violations shall include, but not be limited to:
(a) employment of poisonous weapons or other weapons calculated to cause unnecessary suffering;
(b) wanton destruction of cities, towns or villages, or devastation not justified by military necessity;
(c) attack, or bombardment, by whatever means, of undefended towns, villages, dwellings, or buildings;
(d) seizure of, destruction or wilful damage done to institutions dedicated to religion, charity and education, the arts and sciences, historic monuments and works of art and science;
(e) plunder of public or private property.

Article 4: Genocide

1. The International Tribunal shall have the power to prosecute persons committing genocide as defined in paragraph 2 of this article or of committing any of the other acts enumerated in paragraph 3 of this article.
2. Genocide means any of the following acts committed with intent to destroy, in whole or in part, a national, ethnical, racial or religious group, as such:
(a) killing members of the group;
(b) causing serious bodily or mental harm to members of the group;
(c) deliberately inflicting on the group conditions of life calculated to bring about its physical destruction in whole or in part;
(d) imposing measures intended to prevent births within the group;
(e) forcibly transferring children of the group to another group.
3. The following acts shall be punishable:
(a) genocide;
(b) conspiracy to commit genocide;
(c) direct and public incitement to commit genocide;
(d) attempt to commit genocide;
(e) complicity in genocide.

Article 5: Crimes against humanity

The International Tribunal shall have the power to prosecute persons responsible for the following crimes when committed in armed conflict, whether international or internal in character, and directed against any civilian population:
(a) murder;
(b) extermination;
(c) enslavement;
(d) deportation;
(e) imprisonment;
(f) torture;
(g) rape;
(h) persecutions on political, racial and religious grounds;
(i) other inhumane acts.

The Statute of the ICTR

The Statute of the ICTR gave the ICTR jurisdiction over three crimes: genocide,[57] crimes against humanity[58] and violations of Article 3 common to the Geneva Conventions and of Additional Protocol II.[59] With regard to the crime of genocide, the Statute of the ICTR maintained the definition contained in previous international instruments such as the Genocide Convention and the Statute of the ICTY.[60] For crimes against humanity, the Statute retained the core crimes but introduced some novel elements in the definition.[61] It required any of the enlisted crimes to be committed within the framework of a widespread or systematic attack, and such attack must be directed against any civilian population based on any of the discriminatory grounds (national, racial, ethnical, religious or political).[62] Jurisdiction over violations of Article 3 common to the Geneva Conventions and of Additional Protocol II was defined as follows:

> The International Tribunal for Rwanda shall have the power to prosecute persons committing or ordering to be committed serious violations of Article 3 common to the Geneva Conventions of 12 August 1949 for the Protection of War Victims, and of Additional Protocol II thereto of 8 June 1977. These violations shall include, but shall not be limited to:
>
> a. Violence to life, health and physical or mental well-being of persons, in particular murder as well as cruel treatment such as torture, mutilation or any form of corporal punishment;
> b. Collective punishments;
> c. Taking of hostages;
> d. Acts of terrorism;
> e. Outrages upon personal dignity, in particular humiliating and degrading treatment, rape, enforced prostitution and any form of indecent assault;
> f. Pillage;
> g. The passing of sentences and the carrying out of executions without previous judgement pronounced by a regularly constituted court, affording all the judicial guarantees which are recognized as indispensable by civilised peoples;
> h. Threats to commit any of the foregoing acts.

It is clear that both the statutes of the ICTY and ICTR did not give definitions of the different particular crimes such as murder, extermination, rape, enslavement and so on. As observed earlier, practice may indicate that the commission of offences like rape, enforced prostitution, indecent assault and other forms of sexual violence may be directed primarily against women. However, clarity is needed from international criminal law instruments on their silence in creating and recognizing a specific category of crimes in international law called 'gender-based crimes'. Similar to

[57] Article 2, Statute of the ICTR.

[58] Article 3, Statute of the ICTR.

[59] Article 4, Statute of the ICTR.

[60] See Article 2 of the Genocide Convention; Article 4 of the Statute of the ICTY and Article 2 of the Statute of the ICTR.

[61] See Article 5 of the Statute of the ICTY and Article 3 of the Statute of the ICTR.

[62] See Article 3 of the Statute of the ICTR.

the previous international instruments discussed above, these offences are spelt out in a gender-neutral language. This means two things: firstly, the crimes in question could be committed against any gender and, secondly, gender alone does not suffice as the basis for the prosecution of these crimes: they must be committed and situated within the definitional elements of the crimes over which the tribunals have jurisdiction. For example, to be prosecutable, the commission of rape, murder, torture and so on must satisfy the definitional elements of genocide, crimes against humanity, grave breaches of the Geneva Conventions, etc.

Also worthy of note is Article 4 of the Statute of the ICTR with a crime captioned 'Violations of Article 3 common to the Geneva Conventions and of Additional Protocol II'. As indicated, the list of crimes under this rubric is non-exhaustive. However, sub-paragraphs (a) and (e) indicate clearly the criminalisation of specific acts when committed within the framework of 'serious violations of Article 3 common to the Geneva Conventions of 12 August 1949 for the Protection of War Victims, and of Additional Protocol II thereto of 8 June 1977'. Sub-paragraph (a) deals with 'violence to life, health and physical or mental well-being of persons, in particular murder as well as cruel treatment such as torture, mutilation or any form of corporal punishment'. In addition, sub-paragraph (e) penalises 'outrages upon personal dignity, in particular humiliating and degrading treatment, rape, enforced prostitution and any form of indecent assault'.

Under the Statute of the ICTR, three categories of crimes (genocide, crimes against humanity and violations of Article 3 common of the Geneva Convention and of Additional Protocols II) are brought under the jurisdiction of the ICTR. These forms of violence would be genocidal when committed with the intention to destroy any of the protected groups of people as contained in the Genocide Convention and the Statute of the Tribunal.[63] Moreover, such violence would qualify as a crime against humanity if it constituted torture, enslavement, rape or other inhumane act. It will also qualify as a violation of Article 3 common to the Geneva Conventions and of Additional Protocols II if such violence against a person (that is, men and women) constituted violence to physical life, health, physical or mental well-being; torture; cruel, degrading or inhumane treatment or punishment, an outrage on the personal dignity, in particular humiliating and degrading treatment, rape, enforced prostitution and any form of indecent assault.

Based on the inclusion of such acts within the statutes of the *ad hoc* tribunals, it is plausible to argue that significant progress has been made in recognizing the commission of unacceptable forms of violence against the human person without any reference or limitation to gender. These instruments protect every human being irrespective of his or her gender. It is therefore arguable that very little help is obtained from the statutes of the ICTY and ICTR, respectively, when one seeks to find out if there has been any classification or categorisation of 'gender-based crimes' in international criminal law.

---

[63] See Article II of the Genocide Convention and Article 2(2) of the Statute of the ICTR.

14.4.3.6 The Rome Statute of the International Criminal Court (ICC)

A major development in international criminal justice is the establishment of a permanent International Criminal Court to try persons who bear responsibility for serious crimes in international law.[64] These crimes are war crimes,[65] the crime of aggression,[66] genocide[67] and crimes against humanity.[68] Except for the crime of aggression, the Rome Statute of the ICC defines the crimes over which it has jurisdiction. With reference to the crime of genocide, the Rome Statute of the ICC replicates the definition contained in the Genocide Convention, as well as the statutes of the UN *ad hoc* tribunals.[69] However, with reference to crimes against humanity, the Rome Statute of the ICC regurgitated most of the definitional elements of crimes against humanity, as stipulated in the Statute of the ICTR, but removed the different categories of targeted civilian population. The Rome Statute of the ICC defines crimes against humanity as follows:

> Article 7(1):
>
> For the purpose of this Statute [the Rome Statute of the International Criminal Court], 'crime against humanity' means any of the following acts when committed as part of a widespread or systematic attack[70] directed against any civilian population, with knowledge of the attack:
>
> a) Murder;
>
> b) Extermination;
>
> c) Enslavement;
>
> d) Deportation or forcible transfer of population;
>
> e) Imprisonment or other severe deprivation of physical liberty in violation of fundamental rules of international law;
>
> f) Torture;
>
> g) Rape, sexual slavery, enforced prostitution, forced pregnancy, enforced sterilization, or any other form of sexual violence of comparable gravity;
>
> h) Persecution against any identifiable group or collectivity on political, racial, national, ethnic, cultural, religious, gender as defined in paragraph 3, or other grounds that are universally recognized as impermissible under international law, in connection with any act referred to in this paragraph or any crime within the jurisdiction of the Court;
>
> (i) Enforced disappearance of persons;
>
> (j) The crime of apartheid;
>
> (k) Other inhumane acts of a similar character intentionally causing great suffering, or serious injury to body or to mental or physical health.

---

[64] Article 1 of the Rome Statute of the ICC.

[65] Article 8 of the Rome Statute of the ICC.

[66] Article 5(1)(d) as read in conjunction with Article 5(2) of the Rome Statute of the ICC.

[67] Article 6 of the Rome Statute of the ICC.

[68] Article 7 of the Rome Statute of the ICC.

[69] For a comparative analysis of the definitions as expressed in international instruments, see for example Article II of the Genocide Convention; Article 4 of the Statute of the ICTY; Article 2 of the Statute of the ICTR and Article 6 of the Rome Statute of the ICC.

[70] Article 7(2)(a) of the Rome Statute of the ICC defines an attack to mean

> …a course of conduct involving the multiple commission of acts referred to in paragraph 1 against any civilian population, pursuant to or in furtherance of a State or organizational policy to commit such attack.

A significant novelty introduced by the Rome Statute of the ICC is the elaboration it gives to the constituent crimes under crimes against humanity. These crimes were further defined.[71] In this regard, some of the listed acts under the definition of crimes against humanity indicate what they are, for example, the crime of enslavement. Enslavement as a crime against humanity means

> the exercise of any or all of the powers attaching to the right of ownership over a person and includes the exercise of such power in the course of trafficking in persons, in particular women and children.[72]

Other series of acts that fall under the definition of crimes against humanity are rape, sexual slavery, enforced prostitution, forced pregnancy, enforced sterilization or any other form of sexual violence of comparable gravity. Of all these, the Rome Statute of the ICC defines only the offence of forced pregnancy as follows:

> the unlawful confinement of a woman forcibly made pregnant, with the intent of affecting the ethnic composition of any population or carrying out other grave violations of international law. This definition shall not in any way be interpreted as affecting national laws relating to pregnancy.[73]

The Rome Statute of the ICC neither creates nor recognises anything like gender-based crimes. Rather, like other international criminal law instruments, it simply defines what constitutes serious crimes in international law that comes under the jurisdiction of the ICC. The crime of enslavement, even elaborated in Article 7(2) of the Rome Statute of the ICC, does not limit it to women but rather emphasises the fact that such practices may be primarily against women and children. Forced pregnancy, obviously, is limited to women who are 'forcibly made pregnant'. This qualification, however, should not be construed to mean that, as used in the context, there is a creation or recognition of a category of crimes called 'gender-based crimes' in international criminal law.

The post-Rome Statute of the ICC era has been marked by significant developments in international criminal law, especially with the establishment of hybrid courts like the Special Court for Sierra Leone (SCSL). Even though the Statute of the SCSL gave the Special Court jurisdiction over crimes in international law and domestic law, there was no creation or categorisation of crimes as 'gender-based crimes'. In terms of the definition of substantive crimes over which the SCSL would have jurisdiction, the Statute of the SCSL was not so different.[74]

In sum, it can be argued that even though occasional references to crimes committed against women have been made in some of these international instruments,

---

[71] See Article 7(2) of the Rome Statute of the ICC for the definitions of some of these acts under crimes against humanity.

[72] See Article 7(2)(c) of the Rome Statute of the ICC.

[73] See Article 7(2)(f) of the Rome Statute of the ICC.

[74] See for example Article 3 of the Statute of the SCSL which criminalised numerous acts including

> outrages upon personal dignity, in particular humiliating and degrading treatment, rape, enforced prostitution and any form of indecent assault.

the unequivocal message that is communicated by the substantive provisions of these instruments is that there is no categorisation of any crime(s) as 'gender-based crimes' in international criminal law. Inasmuch as no one disputes the fact that some crimes are primarily aimed at women, the substantive definitions of what constitute these crimes are written in a gender-neutral language. Moreover, even if this abstract academic conceptualisation could crystallise in the future, what has been perceived as being gender-based crimes would still have to fit into any or all of the definitions of serious crimes in international criminal law, which, as used in this context, are genocide, crimes against humanity and war crimes.

Having examined these instruments, it is clear that they do not provide answers to the question of what gender-based crimes are in international criminal law. These instruments neither create nor recognise any such category of crimes in international criminal law. Nevertheless, it is important to examine the jurisprudence of international criminal tribunals to see if any such category of crimes does exist.

14.5 Have There Been Prosecutions for 'Gender-Based Crimes' at the International Criminal Tribunals?

Over time, international criminal tribunals became tools for the achievement of international criminal justice: holding to account persons responsible for serious violations of international law. The organic document establishing these tribunals would define the crimes over which they have jurisdiction. As has been noted above, since 1945, different tribunals have had jurisdiction over different crimes. In 1945, serious crimes brought under the jurisdiction of the Nuremberg and Tokyo tribunals, respectively, were crimes against peace, war crimes and crimes against humanity. The UN ad hoc tribunals were given jurisdiction over genocide, crimes against humanity, war crimes and other violations of the Geneva Conventions and their Additional Protocols. The Rome Statute of the ICC has jurisdiction over the crimes of genocide, crimes against humanity, war crimes and aggression.

All these instruments (charters and statutes included) recognised and criminalised acts such as enslavement, forced pregnancies, rape and other forms of sexual violence. However, they were defined in a gender-neutral language, which makes it possible for these crimes to be committed against any gender (except, at least, for the crime of forced pregnancy). In the following discussion, this paper examines some of the landmark judgments that were delivered by these tribunals. The relevant portions of these judgments are discussed to show how the tribunal construed the crime in question, especially as to whether their commission was seen as 'gender-based' for them to be described as gender-based crimes.

14.5.1 The Nuremberg Trials

As indicated above, the Charter of the IMT, Nuremberg, 1945, gave the first definition of crimes against humanity.[75] As stipulated in the Charter of the IMT, Nuremberg, the Tribunal

> [...] shall have the power to try and punish persons who [...] committed any of the following crimes: The following acts, or any of them, are crimes coming within the jurisdiction of the Tribunal for which there shall be individual responsibility: (a) Crimes against Peace [...]: (b) War Crimes: namely, violations of the laws or customs of war. Such violations shall include, but not be limited to, [...] deportation to slave labor [...]: (c) Crimes against Humanity: namely, murder, extermination, enslavement, deportation and other inhumane acts committed against any civilian population [...].[76]

Like the other crimes contained in the Charter, the crime of enslavement was never defined. However, the Nuremberg indictment included charges such as deportation to slave labour and enslavement.[77] Unfortunately, like the Charter of the IMT, Nuremberg, the judgment of the Tribunal did not define these crimes. Neither did it try to highlight any distinction between them. However, as would have been observed, in the section of the Tribunal's judgment that dealt with legal findings in relation to each individual defendant, reference was made to the involvement, in one way or another, in the slave labour programme of 13 defendants. Another major observation is the conspicuous lack of clarity as to whether the conduct indicated counted for conviction for war crimes or crimes against humanity. The exception to this was the case of Van Schirach, the only defendant convicted of a crime against humanity in relation to his involvement in forced labour.[78]

The conclusion to be drawn from Von Schirach's conviction is that the Tribunal construed forced labour to constitute both a war crime and a crime against humanity. Other logical inferences need to be made: regarding the voluntary recruitment of forced labourers, the Tribunal, in relation to Sauckel, a defendant appointed by Hitler as Plenipotentiary General for the Utilisation of Labour, said that he

> [...] described so-called 'voluntary' recruiting by 'a whole batch of male and female agents just as was done in the olden times for shanghaiing. [...]'.[79] Speer, another defendant, was convicted for participating in the slave labour programme even though he 'insisted that the slave labourers be given adequate food and working conditions so that they could work efficiently'.[80] Thirdly, reference was made by the Tribunal to 'female domestic workers'.

---

[75] Annexed to the Agreement for the Prosecution and Punishment of the Major War Criminals of the European Axis (London Agreement), 8 Aug 1945 (signed by Britain, France, the USA and the USSR, and acceded to by 19 other states (Australia, Belgium, Czechoslovakia, Denmark, Ethiopia, Greece, Haiti, Honduras, India, Luxembourg, the Netherlands, New Zealand, Norway, Panama, Paraguay, Poland, Uruguay, Venezuela and Yugoslavia)).

[76] Article 6, Charter of the IMT, Nuremberg.

[77] Reprinted in *Trial of Major War Criminals Before the International Military Tribunal*, Nuremberg, 14 November 1945–1 October 1946, Vol 1 (1947), pp. 27–92.

[78] See note 77, pp. 565–566.

[79] See note 77, p. 567.

[80] See note 77, p. 579.

Within the context of the slave labour programme, it specifically referred to the transfer of almost half a million female domestic workers from the eastern-occupied territories to Germany. Defendants Sauckel, Himmler and Bormann had control over these female domestic workers.[81] The Tribunal's trial transcripts reveal that these female domestic workers were procured to relieve German housewives and the wives of German farmers.[82] These female domestic workers were never at liberty to claim free time, even though as a reward for good work they could be given a leave to stay outside the assigned home for three hours, once a week.[83]

14.5.2 Allied Control Council Law No. 10 of 1945

Allied Control Council Law No. 10 codified crimes against humanity, which included enslavement in terms akin to the Charter of the IMT, Nuremberg. Some of the judgments of Control Council Law No. 10 failed to, first, define the crime of enslavement and related concepts and, second, distinguish war crimes from crimes against humanity. However, these judgments reveal some important factors to be considered when deciding whether enslavement was committed. In the *Pohl* case, the United States Military Tribunal, in considering war crimes and crimes against humanity charges, held that

> [s]lavery may exist even without torture. Slaves may be well fed, well clothed, and comfortably housed, but they are still slaves if without lawful process they are deprived of their freedom by forceful restraint. We might eliminate all proof of ill-treatment, overlook the starvation, beatings, and other barbarous acts, but the admitted fact of slavery – compulsory uncompensated labour – would still remain. There is no such thing as benevolent slavery. Involuntary servitude, even if tempered by humane treatment, is still slavery.[84]

A year later, in the *Milch* case before the United States Military Tribunal, the accused was charged with slave labour and deportation to slave labour of German nationals and nationals of other countries as a crime against humanity.[85] The Tribunal held as follows:

> Does anyone believe that the vast hordes of Slavic Jews who laboured in Germany's war industries were accorded the rights of contracting parties? They were slaves, nothing

---

[81] See note 77, p. 586.

[82] See note 77, p. 451.

[83] See note 77, p. 452.

[84] *US v Oswald Pohl and Others*, Judgement, 3 November 1947, reprinted in *Trials of War Criminals Before the Nuremberg Military Tribunals under Control Council Law No 10*, Vol V (1997), p. 958 at p. 970. Other CCL 10 cases in which enslavement and related aspects were considered, include IG Farben (*US v Carl Krauch and Others*), summarised *in Law Reports of Trials of War Criminals*, The UN War Crimes Commission, Vol X (1997), pp. 1–68 at 53; and Flick (*US v Friedrich Flick and Others*), reprinted in *Trials of War Criminals Before the Nuremberg Military Tribunals under Control Council Law No 10*, Vol VI (1997).

[85] *US v Milch*, Judgement, 31 July 1948, reprinted in *Trials of War Criminals Before the Nuremberg Military Tribunals under Control Council Law No. 10*, Vol II (1997), p. 773.

less – kidnapped, regimented, herded under armed guards, and worked until they died from disease, hunger, exhaustion. [...]. As to non-Jewish foreign labour, with few exceptions they were deprived of the basic civil rights of free men; they were deprived of the right to move freely or to choose their place of residence; to live in a household with their families; to rear and educate their children; to marry; to visit public places of their own choosing; to negotiate, either individually or through representatives of their own choice, the conditions of their own employment; to organize in trade unions; to exercise free speech or other free expression of opinion; to gather in peaceful assembly; and they were frequently deprived of their right to worship according to their own conscience. All these are the sign-marks of slavery, not free employment under contract.[86]

14.5.3 The IMTFE, Tokyo[87]

The Charter of the IMTFE, Tokyo, like the Charter of the IMT, Nuremberg, stipulated the jurisdiction of the Tribunal over crimes against peace,[88] conventional war crimes[89] and crimes against humanity.[90] The Tokyo indictment[91] (in the portion of the indictment dealing with conventional war crimes and crimes against humanity[92]) made references to war labour, forced labour and enslavement without distinguishing

[86] See note 85, p. 789. Milch was found guilty of war crimes charged in Count one of the indictment in that he was responsible for the 'slave labor and deportation to slave labor of the civilian populations of countries and territories occupied by the German armed forces, and in the enslavement, deportation, ill-treatment and terrorization of such persons. [...]' (see note 85, p. 790). Milch was also found guilty of crimes against humanity (count three) for the same war crimes insofar as they related to foreign nations (see note 85, pp. 790–791). With reference to the definition of the crimes in CCL 10, Judge Fitzroy D Phillips in his concurring opinion stated that CCL 10 treats as separate crimes and different types of crime deportation to slave labour (as a war crime) and enslavement (as a crime against humanity) (see note 85, Concurring Opinion, p. 860 at p. 866). In the *Krupp Case* (*US v Krupp and Others*, Judgement of 31 July 1948, reprinted in *Trials of War Criminals Before the Nuremberg Military Tribunals under Control Council Law No 10*, Vol IX, Part 2 (1997), p. 1327), the US Military Tribunal adopted the statement of the law applicable to the deportation to slave labour and enslavement of the *Milch Case* made by Judge Phillips (see note 85, pp. 1432–1433). In that case, the Tribunal also held that the employment of concentration camp inmates under the circumstances disclosed was a crime (see note 85, pp. 1433–1435).

[87] 'Special Proclamation: Establishment of an International Military Tribunal for the Far East', Order of the Supreme Commander for the Allied Powers, Tokyo, 19 January 1946, as amended on 26 April 1946.

[88] Article 5(a), Charter of the IMTFE, Tokyo.

[89] Article 5(b), Charter of the IMTFE, Tokyo.

[90] Article 5(c), Charter of the IMTFE, Tokyo.

[91] Reprinted in Pritchard, *The Tokyo Major War Crimes Trial, The Records of the International Military Tribunal for the Far East With an Authoritative Commentary and Comprehensive Guide*, Vol 2 (1998).

[92] 'Group Three: Conventional War Crimes and Crimes against Humanity' (Counts 53–55): see note 91, pp. 12–14 of the indictment.

war crimes from crimes against humanity.[93] Like the Nuremberg Tribunal, the judgment[94] of the Tokyo Tribunal failed to develop a systematic distinction between deportation and slave labour, slave labour and enslavement.[95] More conspicuous was the failure of the Tribunal to adjudicate these as gender-based crimes. In addition, it did not attempt to define any of these crimes in any detail. However, regarding the use of labour by civilians from occupied territories, the Tokyo Tribunal held as follows:

> Having decided upon a policy of employing prisoners of war and civilian internees on work directly contributing to the prosecution of the war, and having established a system to carry that policy into execution, the Japanese went further and supplemented this source of manpower by recruiting labourers from the native population of the occupied territories. This recruiting of labourers was accomplished by false promises, and by force. After being recruited, the labourers were transported to and confined in camps. Little or no distinction appears to have been made between these conscripted labourers on the one hand and prisoners of war and civilian internees on the other hand. They were all regarded as slave labourers to be used to the limit of their endurance. For this reason, we have included these conscripted labourers in the term 'civilian internees' whenever that term is used in this chapter.[96]

[93] Count 53 obliquely contained a conspiracy charge, also referring to 'persons in charge of each of the camps and labour units for prisoners of war and civilian internees [...]' (see note 92, p. 13 of the indictment). Appendix D to the indictment was incorporated under Group Three of the charges in the indictment. Section Two of Appendix D referred to 'Illegal employment of prisoner of war labour [...]' (see note 92, p. iii). Section Twelve of Appendix D referred to 'Failure to respect family honour and rights, individual life, [...], and deportation and enslavement of the inhabitants [...], contrary to [Article 46 of Annex III ('Military Authority over the Territory of the Hostile State') of the 1907 Hague Convention] the Laws and Customs of War: Large numbers of the inhabitants of [occupied] territories were murdered, tortured, raped and otherwise ill-treated, arrested and interned without justification, sent to forced labour, and their property destroyed or confiscated' (at p. vi).

[94] Röling and Rüter (1977), pp. 1–466.

[95] References to forced labour and slave labour in the Tokyo judgement include, in Chapter VIII ('Conventional War Crimes (Atrocities)'): see note 94, p. 388 ('Many of the captured Chinese were [...] placed in labour units to work for the Japanese Army [...]. Some of these captives [...] were transported to Japan to relieve the labor shortage in the munitions industries.'); see note 94, pp. 403–406 (use of forced labour to construct Burma-Siam railway, including use of conscripted 'native labourers'); see note 94, pp. 413–414 (labour of prisoners of war and civilian internees); see note 94, p. 416 (use of prisoners of war and internees to work on war-related projects); see note 94, pp. 416–417 (use of forced 'native' labour). References to forced labour and slave labour in relation to individual defendants include: Kimura (see note 94, p. 452, use of prisoners of war in forced labour, including work on the Burma-Siam railway); and Tojo (see note 94, pp. 462–463, ill-treatment of prisoners of war and internees, including use of prisoners of war in construction of Burma-Siam railway).

[96] See note 94, pp. 416–417 (the Chapter referred to is Chapter VIII ('Conventional War Crimes (Atrocities)') of the judgement.

14.5.4 The UN ad Hoc Tribunals

The two UN ad hoc tribunals had jurisdiction over specific crimes, which, amongst other things, include genocide, crimes against humanity, war crimes and violations of the Geneva Conventions. As discussed earlier, the definitions of these crimes were stipulated in a gender-neutral language. It must be admitted, however, that certain crimes could only be committed against women: for example, the crime of forced pregnancy. Furthermore, the statutes of the ad hoc tribunals, like the charters of the Nuremberg and Tokyo tribunals, do not define the listed crimes over which they have jurisdiction; rather, they set the framework within which such acts would amount to a crime over which the Tribunal would have jurisdiction. It is therefore important to examine the ways that the different tribunals have construed these definitional elements, as well as the content of the crimes.

14.5.4.1 Gender-Based Violence as Genocide

Genocide is a crime under the jurisdiction of the ICTY and ICTR with their statutes repeating the definition contained in the Genocide Convention. The crime of genocide protects specific groups of people, which could be national, racial, religious or ethnic. It requires the commission of specifically listed acts with the intent to destroy, in part or in whole, any of these groups of people.[97] It must be noted that the categorisation of the different protected groups is followed by a comma and then the phrase 'as such'. A reading of this definition gives rise to the following questions: first, are these the only protected groups? Second, does the phrase 'as such' suggest that there is a possibility of expanding or adding another group to the list? The first judgment rendered by the Trial Chamber of the ICTR in the *Akayesu* case sought to answer these questions.[98]

In *Akayesu*, the Trial Chamber was of the opinion that, with the required intent, the accused's genocidal act must target a specifically protected group. The concept of protected groups, however, enjoys no generally or internationally accepted definition. As emphasised in the case of *The Prosecutor v Jean de Dieu Kamuhanda*,[99] rather, each group 'must be assessed in the light of a particular political, social, historical and cultural context'.[100] Citing the *Akayesu* judgment, the Trial Chamber

---

[97] Article II of the Genocide Convention; Article 4(2) of the Statute of the ICTY; and Article 2 of the Statute of the ICTR.

[98] *Akayesu* note 46, paras. 516–517.

[99] Judgment, Case No. ICTR-95-54A-T, T. Ch. II, 22 January 2004.

[100] *Kamuhanda* note 99, para. 630. See also the cases of *The Prosecutor v Ignace Bagilishema*, Judgement, Case No. ICTR-95-1-A, T. Ch. I, 7 June 2001, para. 65; *The Prosecutor v Alfred Musema*, Judgment, Case No. ICTR-96-13-T, T. Ch. I, 27 January 2003, para. 161; *The Prosecutor v Juvénal Kajelijeli*, Judgment, Case No. ICTR-96-44-T, T. Ch. II, 1 December 2003, para. 811. As discussed above, in *Akayesu* (note 46), the Trial Chamber was unwilling to interpret the words 'any such group', and preferred to flow with the intention of the drafters of the Genocide Convention.

in the *Kamuhanda* case held that 'for the purposes of applying the Genocide Convention, membership of a group is, in essence, a subjective rather than an objective concept [where] the victim is perceived by the perpetrator of genocide as belonging to a group slated for destruction'.[101] In different cases, the trial chambers have emphasised that determination of the categorised groups should be made on a case-by-case basis, with reference to both subjective and objective criteria.[102]

The definition of genocide stipulates the *actus reus* of the crime, which may comprise any of the listed acts: killing members of the group, causing serious bodily or mental harm to members of the group, deliberately inflicting on the group conditions of life calculated to bring about its physical destruction in whole or in part, imposing measures intended to prevent births within the group and forcibly transferring children of the group to another group. In the case of *The Prosecutor v Mikaeli Muhimana*,[103] the Trial Chamber construed causing serious bodily or mental harm to members of the group to mean 'serious physical injury to the victim, such as torture and sexual violence'.[104] Such serious bodily or mental harm should be determined on a case-by-case basis.[105] In addition, such injury need not be permanent or irremediable,[106] and it includes non-fatal acts of sexual violence, rape, mutilations and interrogations that are combined with beatings and/or threats of death.[107] Serious mental harm could be construed as some type of impairment of mental faculties or harm that causes serious injury to the mental state of the victim.[108] The Trial Chamber held that the rape of Tutsi women at the Mugonero

[101] *Kamuhanda* note 99, para. 630; *The Prosecutor v Georges Rutaganda*, Judgment, Case No. ICTR-96-3-T, T. Ch. I, 6 December 1999, para. 56; *Musema* note 100, para. 161; *The Prosecution v Laurent Semanza*, Judgment, Case No. ICTR-97-20, T. Ch. II, 15 May 2003, para. 317; *Kajelijeli* note 100, para. 811.

[102] *Kamuhanda* note 99, para. 630; *Semanza* note 101, para. 317; *Kajelijeli* note 100, para. 811. See the case of *The Prosecutor v Sylvestre Gacumbitsi*, Judgment, Case No. ICTR-01-64, T. Ch. III, 17 June 2004, para. 254, where the Trial Chamber held that '[M]embership of a group is a subjective rather than an objective concept.... Indeed, in a given situation, the perpetrator, just like the victim, may believe that there is any objective criterion for determining membership of an ethnic group on the basis of an administrative mechanism for the identification of an individual's ethnic group.'

[103] Judgment, Case No. ICTR-95-1B-T, T. Ch. III, 28 April 2005.

[104] *Muhimana* note 103, para. 502.

[105] *Kajelijeli* note 100, para. 815.

[106] *Akayesu* note 46, para. 502; *The Prosecutor v Clément Kayishema and Obed Ruzindana*, Judgment, Case No. ICTR-95-1-T, T. Ch. I, 21 May 1999, para. 108; *Semanza* note 101, para. 320.

[107] *Akayesu* note 46, para. 502; *Kayishema and Ruzindana* note 106, para. 108; *Kajelijeli* note 100, para. 815; *Semanza* note 101, para. 320.

[108] *Muhimana* note 103, para. 502; *Gacumbitsi* note 102, para. 291. See also the ILC Report (1996) para. 14, under Article 17 of the Draft Code of Crimes. Bodily harm is defined therein as 'some type of physical injury', while mental harm is defined as 'some type of impairment of mental faculties'. See *Muhimana* note 103, footnote 463. In *Kayishema and Ruzindana* (note 106, para. 110), the Trial Chamber construed 'serious mental harm' to include more than 'minor or temporary impairment of mental faculties such as the infliction of strong fear or terror, intimidation or threat'. See also *Semanza* note 101, para. 321. The state of the law on this issue is well captured by the Trial Chamber in *Semanza* (note 101, para. 322) after a review of the case law: 'The Chamber

complex, as well as the shooting of Tutsi refugees who died or were injured in the attack, amounted to serious bodily or mental harm to members of a protected group (the Tutsis) and definitely qualified as genocide.[109] The rape of these Tutsi women also qualified as a crime against humanity for which the accused was found guilty.[110]

The unanswered question is whether women should comprise a protected group in international criminal law. As observed by the Trial Chambers of the ICTR, there is no generally and internationally accepted definition of these protected groups, and plenty of liberty is given to judicial institutions to assess, both subjectively and objectively, whether a victim should be perceived as belonging to a group that deserves protection. That requires an assessment of the social, political, historical and cultural context. As cautioned by the Trial Chamber in *Akayesu*, groups that are mobile and not stable, and which are voluntarily joined, such as economic and political groupings, should be excluded from consideration as a protected group.[111]

It must therefore be noted that even though these acts of sexual violence were aimed at women, the Trial Chamber came short of labelling them 'gender-based crimes'. Rather, in its opinion, such acts, when committed with the requisite genocidal intent, would qualify as genocidal acts as contemplated in the definition of genocide. This position clarifies two things: first, the ICTR never gave legal recognition to, or classified these crimes as, gender-based crimes. Rather, in developing the elements of the crime of genocide, the Trial Chamber construed the mental element of the crime, as well as the actus reus. These genocidal acts could be perpetrated against any gender (as the definitions are gender-neutral). It is therefore illogical and incorrect to infuse such characterisations into the jurisprudence of the tribunals, as well as inject a new genus of crime that has the tendency of suggesting that it exists in international criminal law. The perpetration of these atrocities against women, for it to be genocidal, must not only be accompanied by genocidal intent but must also fit within the defined punishable acts. Committing 'gender-based crimes' is insufficient for the prosecution of genocide as this is not contemplated in the relevant international instruments.

14.5.4.2 Violence Against Women as a Crime Against Humanity

Even though some nuances exist between the definition of crimes against humanity as stipulated in the statutes of the ICTY and ICTR, subsequent practices of the trial and appeal chambers of these ad hoc tribunals have been to accept the definition contained in the Statute of the ICTR as it represents the 'common-law of crimes

---

adopts the foregoing standards pronounced in *Akayesu* and *Kayishema and Ruzindana* as to the determination of serious bodily or mental harm. In addition, the Chamber finds that serious mental harm need not be permanent or irremediable' (cited in *Kajelijeli* note 100, para. 815, emphasis added).

[109] *Muhimana* note 103, paras. 513, 519.

[110] *Muhimana* note 103, paras. 552–553, 562–563.

[111] *Akayesu* note 46, para. 516.

against humanity'.[112] The listed acts that qualify as crimes against humanity if the definitional elements are met are not so different in the two statutes. Some of these acts include murder, extermination, torture, rape, enslavement, forced pregnancy and deportation. In numerous cases that have been decided by the trial chambers of the tribunals, different individuals were indicted for some form of sexual violence, more specifically for the offence of rape as a crime against humanity. In *Akayesu*,[113] the Trial Chamber was of the opinion that the traditional mechanical definition of rape did not adequately capture its true meaning. The Trial Chamber formulated the following definition of rape:

> [a] physical invasion of a sexual nature, committed on a person under circumstances which are coercive. Sexual violence which includes rape is considered to be any act of a sexual nature which is committed on a person under circumstances which are coercive.[114]

In the case of *Musema*, the Trial Chamber approved this conceptual definition wherein it highlighted the distinction between a 'physical invasion of a sexual nature' and 'any act of a sexual nature' as being the difference between rape and sexual assault.[115] However, the Trial Chamber in the case of the *Prosecutor v Anto Furundžija* modified earlier definitions contained in previous judgments (rendered by both the ICTR and ICTY).[116] In this case, the Trial Chamber chose a more detailed definition that relates to objects and body parts and proceeded to define rape as the forcible sexual penetration of the human body by the penis or the forcible insertion of any other object into either the vagina or the anus.[117] In the *Prosecutor v Dragoljub Kunarac, Radomir Kovač and Zoran Vuković*,[118] substantial modification was made to this definition by Trial Chamber II and later endorsed by the Appeals Chamber. The definition of rape was formulated as follows:

> The actus reus of the crime of rape in international law is constituted by: the sexual penetration, however slight:
>
> (a) of the vagina or anus of the victim by the penis of the perpetrator or any other object used by the perpetrator; or
>
> (b) of the mouth of the victim by the penis of the perpetrator; where such sexual penetration occurs without the consent of the victim. Consent for this purpose must be consent given voluntarily, as a result of the victim's free will, assessed in the context of the surrounding circumstances.[119]

In *Kamuhanda*, the Trial Chamber of the ICTR opined that the *Kunarac* definition was of a more persuasive authority.[120] In *Gacumbitsi*, the Trial Chamber held

[112] Luban (2004), p. 93.

[113] *Akayesu* note 46, para. 596.

[114] *Akayesu* note 46, para. 598. See also *Kamuhanda* note 99, para. 705.

[115] *Musema* note 100, para. 965.

[116] Judgment, Case No. IT-95-17/1-T, para 176.

[117] *Furundžija* note 116, paras. 176–186.

[118] Judgment, Case No. IT-96-23-T, IT-96-23/1-T, 22 February 2001.

[119] *Kamuhanda* note 99, para. 707.

[120] *Kamuhanda* note 99, para. 709.

that any penetration of the victim's vagina by the rapist with his genitals or with any object constitutes rape even though rape under Article 3(g) of the Statute of the ICTR is not limited to such acts alone.[121] The Trial Chamber was of the view that the penile penetration or insertion of sticks into the vaginas of the victim (witnesses TAQ, TAS and TAP alongside seven other Tutsi women and girls) amounted to rape.[122] Rape is just a form of sexual violence. The trial chambers have highlighted that sexual violence is of a broader category in which rape is classified. In addition to rape and other forms of sexual violence, that same act would qualify as torture if it met the definition of torture in international criminal law.

It must, however, be cautioned here that the definition of all forms of sexual violence is gender-neutral. The construction of the elements of rape based on the practices of different legal systems across the world evidenced, to a greater extent, the gender-neutrality adopted in defining the offence of rape. The definition of crimes against humanity contains chapeau requirements and does not refer to any category of 'gender-based crimes'. Even though numerous cases that were prosecuted involved the women victims, it is argued that scholars ought to resist the temptation to develop this new category of crimes that have no place in these international instruments.

14.5.4.3 Violations of Article 3 Common to the Geneva Conventions and of Additional Protocol II

The definition of what constitutes violations of Article 3 common to the Geneva Conventions and of Additional Protocol II is contained in the Statute of the ICTR. In essence, it is much similar to the substantive content of war crimes.

Of specific importance is the prohibition of 'violence to life, health and physical or mental well-being of persons, in particular, murder as well as cruel treatment such as torture, mutilation or any form of corporal punishment' and 'outrages upon personal dignity, in particular, humiliating and degrading treatment, rape, enforced prostitution and any form of indecent assault'. These crimes, when committed within an armed conflict, international or internal in character, would amount to war crimes.

14.5.5 The Overlapping Provisions of the Different Crimes

As discussed earlier, except for the Rome Statute of the ICC, the constituent elements of serious crimes in international law were never defined. The Nuremberg and Tokyo tribunals and Control Council Law No. 10 began construing the meaning

[121] *Gacumbitsi* note 102, para. 321. See also *Akayesu* note 46, paras. 597–598; *Dragoljub Kunarac, Radomir Kovač and Zoran Vuković v Prosecutor*, Judgment, Case No. IT-96-23 & IT-96-23/1-A, Appeal Chamber, 22 February 2001, paras. 127–133.

[122] *Gacumbitsi* note 102, para. 321.

of words such as 'enslavement' and 'forced labour' as both crimes against humanity and war crimes. The jurisprudence of the ad hoc tribunals shows a continuation of this practice. With the statutes of the ad hoc tribunals, the trial and appeal chambers of the ICTY and ICTR have construed the definitional elements of serious crimes in international law (which are the crimes over which they have jurisdiction). In addition, they have examined the *actus reus* of these crimes by interpreting and distinguishing them from one another.

It is obvious from a strict construction of the relevant portions of these statutes and the jurisprudence of the ad hoc tribunals that some of these crimes overlap. For example, acts of sexual violence perpetrated on Tutsi (an ethnic group) women such as rape and genital mutilation. Depending on the intention of the perpetrator, such acts would qualify as genocide (causing serious bodily or mental harm to members of a protected group—Tutsi—and deliberately inflicting on the group—Tutsi—conditions of life calculated to bring about its physical destruction in whole or in part). In *Akayesu*, the Trial Chamber gave a glimpse of how 'imposing measures intended to prevent births within the group', as stipulated in the Genocide Convention, could be committed:

> For purposes of interpreting Article 2(2)(d) of the Statute ['imposing measures intended to prevent births within the group], the Chamber holds that the measures intended to prevent births within the group, should be construed as sexual mutilation, the practice of sterilization, forced birth control, separation of the sexes and prohibition of marriages. In patriarchal societies, where membership of a group is determined by the identity of the father, an example of a measure intended to prevent births within a group is the case where, during rape, a woman of the said group is deliberately impregnated by a man of another group, with the intent to have her give birth to a child who will consequently not belong to its mother's group.
>
> Furthermore, the Chamber notes that measures intended to prevent births within the group may be physical, but can also be mental. For instance, rape can be a measure intended to prevent births when the person raped refuses subsequently to procreate, in the same way that members of a group can be led, through threats or trauma, not to procreate.[123]

The perpetration of rape, genital mutilation and other forms of sexual violence against Tutsi women would also qualify as crimes against humanity if such acts were committed within the framework of a widespread or systematic attack directed against any civilian population based on any of the discriminatory grounds: Tutsi women qualify as a civilian population. In addition, ethnicity is considered a discriminatory ground.

Lastly, the same acts of rape, genital mutilation and other forms of sexual violence would qualify as war crimes because they constitute 'violence to life, health and physical or mental well-being of persons, in particular murder as well as cruel treatment such as torture, mutilation or any form of corporal punishment' and 'outrages upon personal dignity, in particular humiliating and degrading treatment, rape, enforced prostitution and any form of indecent assault'.[124]

[123] *Akayesu* note 46, paras. 507–508.

[124] Article 4 of the Statute of the ICTR.

14.6 Conclusion

The *ad hoc* tribunals and special courts played an invaluable role in, first, recognising the existence of specific crimes against women; second, in construing the constituent elements of these crimes, at times, giving meaning to lose phraseology; and, third, affirming the recognition of women as a vulnerable and specific group in international law against whom heinous crimes of unspeakable gravity can be committed. In addition, as reflected in, and required by, these international instruments, different rules for the imposition of criminal responsibility were developed, and even though the statutes of these tribunals recognised these modes of participation, responsibility has been imposed on perpetrators who participated in any way and time in these crimes. Crimes against any human being are particularly odious in that they constitute a serious attack on humanity, human dignity or grave humiliation or degradation. They could be isolated or sporadic. However, when framed as part of a group (formal or informal) policy, and such atrocities that target women are endorsed, co-signed or tolerated by such a group, then international criminal justice ought to bring such perpetrators to justice.

However, as has been shown in the foregoing analysis, international criminal law instruments protect all human beings. No crime is defined based on the intent to discriminate against any gender as these instruments, in addition to international human rights instruments, protect all human beings. Without denying the sensitivity aroused by the perpetration of grave abuses of women, it must be acknowledged that this should not translate into the creation and infusion of a new category of crimes called 'gender-based crimes'. The conspicuous silence of international criminal law instruments on this issue suggests and lends weight to the view that 'gender-based crimes' is a phrase that is purely an academic creation that has neither been recognised nor endorsed in the jurisprudence of international criminal tribunals.

The foregoing analysis has examined the progressive evolution of international criminal law instruments and jurisprudence that seek to protect women as a vulnerable group in the event of mass atrocities. Unfortunately, violence against women in international law is not a serious crime in international law unless such violence fulfils specific circumstances that would qualify it to be classified under any of the rubrics: it must be perpetrated with the intent to destroy a people, in part or in whole, for it to qualify as genocide. For such violence to be classified under the crimes listed in the definition of crimes against humanity, it must be shown that such violence was committed as part of a widespread or systematic attack directed against a civilian population with knowledge of such an attack. Lastly, for it to qualify as a war crime or a violation of the laws and customs of war, it must be proved that there was an armed conflict at the time of the commission of the violence.

As pointed out in the Trial Chamber's decision in the *Akayesu* case, there was no willingness to take the protected groups in the Genocide Convention further, a decision that was reaffirmed by subsequent trial chambers of the ICTR. Of greater interest is the fact that some criteria were articulated for a group to qualify as a protected group. Groups that are mobile, or not stable, and to which membership is obtained voluntarily are excluded. In other words, groups into which someone is born may qualify as a group that requires protection. In addition to the application of some objective criteria and based on the sum of factors, the possession of some immutable characteristic should qualify as a group. Gender, assessed objectively, is an immutable characteristic, and there is apparently no logical reason why women cannot be qualified as a protected group. Gender is obtained at birth and could be used as a determining criterion for the establishment of a stable group. Probably international criminal law should, firstly, take the great step of recognising women as a group, given the fact that gender is immutable, and, secondly, ensure that it is a protected group in international law.

Evidently, these technical considerations are needed for international criminal law to step in. Unfortunately, the commission of violence against women occurs in every corner of the world, especially in rural communities wherein traditional practices and cultural beliefs still have a stronghold on the lives and ways of living of those dwelling therein. The efforts of international criminal justice must be supported by national mechanisms to combat and reduce such injustices perpetrated against women. National domestic legal systems must take steps in ending violence against women. Laws must be enacted that criminalise every form of violence against women. In addition, technical rules of procedure must be eliminated, and interested third parties must be given standing to ensure that socio-economic and cultural factors do not impede a victim's access and accessibility to justice. Judicial institutions must summon the courage to apply the principles and norms of international human rights and criminal laws. Law enforcement should ensure zero tolerance towards gender-based violence at all times, in all forms, irrespective of who the perpetrator is.

References

Adopted by a Conference of Plenipotentiaries convened by Economic and Social Council resolution 608(XXI) of 30 April 1956 and done at Geneva on 7 September 1956

Adopted by a Conference of Plenipotentiaries convened by Economic and Social Council Resolution 608(XXI) of 30 April 1956 and done at Geneva on 7 September 1956. It entered into force on 30 April 1957 in accordance with Article 13

African Charter on Human and Peoples' Rights, 27 June 1981, OAU Doc. CAB/LEG/67/3 rev. 5; 1520 U.N.T.S. 217

American Convention on Human Rights, 22 November 1969, O.A.S. Treaty Series No. 36, 1144 U.N.T.S. reprinted in Basic Documents Pertaining to Human Rights in the Inter-American System, OEA/Ser.L.V/II.82 doc.6 rev.1, p. 25 (1992)

Annexed to the Agreement for the Prosecution and Punishment of the Major War Criminals of the European Axis (London Agreement), 8 Aug 1945

Article 2 of the Supplementary Convention on the Abolition of Slavery, the Slave Trade, and Institutions and Practices Similar to Slavery

Article 5(c), Charter of the IMTFE, Tokyo

Askin KD (2011) Crimes against women under international criminal law. In: Brown BS (ed) Research handbook on international criminal law. Edward Edgar, pp 84–113

CEDAW, 18 December 1976, 1249 U.N.T.S. 13

Charter of the IMT, Nuremberg Reprinted in *Trial of Major War Criminals Before the International Military Tribunal*, Nuremberg, 14 November 1945–1 October 1946, Vol 1 (1947), pp. 27–92

Charter of the International Military Tribunal (IMT), Nuremberg, and the Charter of the International Military Tribunal for the Far East (IMTFE), Tokyo

Cummings-John T (2015) Justice and gender: prosecuting gender-based and sexual violence crimes at the International Criminal Tribunal for Rwanda and the Special Court for Sierra Leone. In: Jalloh CC, Olufemi E (eds) Shielding humanity: essays in international law in honour of Judge Abdul G. Koroma. Martinus Nijhoff, Leiden, pp 379–405

Declaration on the Elimination of Violence Against Women, Resolution adopted by the General Assembly on the Report of the Third Committee (A/48/629) Resolution 48/104

Draft Code of Crimes against the Peace and Security of Mankind, 1996, adopted by the International Law Commission at its 48th session in 1996 and submitted to the United Nations General Assembly as part of the ILC's Report, *Yearbook of the International Law Commission, 1996,* Vol. II (Part Two)

Dragoljub Kunarac, Radomir Kovač and Zoran Vuković v Prosecutor, Judgment, Case No. IT-96-23 & IT-96-23/1-A, Appeal Chamber, 22 February 2001

European Convention for the Protection of Human Rights and Fundamental Freedoms, 4 November 1950, 213 U.N.T.S. 222, 312 ETS 5

Flick (*US v Friedrich Flick and Others*), reprinted in *Trials of War Criminals Before the Nuremberg Military Tribunals under Control Council Law No 10,* Vol VI (1997)

http://217.218.67.231/Detail/2015/02/05/396273/Boko-Haram-kills-13-Chad-troops. Accessed 9 May 2016

http://www.bbc.com/news/world-africa-31604853. Accessed 9 May 2016

http://www.dailymail.co.uk/news/article-2916648/Cameroon-frees-24-hostages-suspected-Boko-Haram-kidnapping.html. Accessed 9 May 2016

http://www.newsweek.com/report-boko-haram-beheads-two-men-claiming-they-are-spies-310603. Accessed 9 May 2016

http://www.nydailynews.com/news/world/boko-haram-kills-40-niger-village-official-article-1.2263151. Accessed 9 May 2016

http://www.nydailynews.com/news/world/boko-haram-nigeria-kills-97-muslims-ramadan-massacres-article-1.2279505. Accessed 9 May 2016

http://www.nydailynews.com/news/world/bombs-blamed-boko-haram-kill-44-nigeria-article-1.2282534. Accessed 9 May 2016

http://www.nydailynews.com/news/world/nigeria-bombing-kills-50-people-boko-haram-blamed-article-1.2243864. Accessed 9 May 2016

IG Farben (*US v Carl Krauch and Others*), summarised *in Law Reports of Trials of War Criminals,* The UN War Crimes Commission, Vol X (1997), pp. 1–68

International Covenant on Civil and Political Rights, 16 December 1966, 999 U.N.T.S. 171

International Covenant on Economic, Social and Cultural Rights, 16 December 1966, 993 U.N.T.S. 3

Judgment, Case No. ICTR-95-1B-T, T. Ch. III, 28 April 2005

Judgment, Case No. ICTR-95-54A-T, T. Ch. II, 22 January 2004

Judgment, Case No. IT-95-17/1-T, Para 176

Judgment, Case No. IT-96-23-T, IT-96-23/1-T, 22 February 2001

Krupp Case (*US v Krupp and Others,* Judgement of 31 July 1948, reprinted in *Trials of War Criminals Before the Nuremberg Military Tribunals under Control Council Law No 10,* Vol IX, Part 2 (1997), p. 1327)

Luban D (2004) A theory of crimes against humanity. Yale J Int Law 29:85–167

Mouthaan S (2010) The prosecution of gender crimes at the ICC: challenges and opportunities. University of Warwick School of Law Legal Studies Research Paper No 17

Pritchard J (1998) The Tokyo major war crimes trial, the records of the International Military Tribunal for the Far East with an authoritative commentary and comprehensive guide, Vol 2. E. Mellen Press

Reprinted in Pritchard, *The Tokyo Major War Crimes Trial, The Records of the International Military Tribunal for the Far East With an Authoritative Commentary and Comprehensive Guide*, Vol 2 (1998)

Röling BVA, Rüter CF (1977) The Tokyo judgment: the International Military Tribunal for the Far East (I.M.T.F.E.) 29 April 1946–12 November 1948. APA-Univ. Press, Amsterdam

Rome Statute of the International Criminal Court, U.N. Doc. A/CONF.183/9 (1998), reprinted in 37 I.L.M. 999 (1998)

Signed at Geneva on 25 September 1926 Entry into force: 9 March 1927

Slavery Convention, 1926

'Special Proclamation: Establishment of an International Military Tribunal for the Far East', Order of the Supreme Commander for the Allied Powers, Tokyo, 19 January 1946, as amended on 26 April 1946

Statute of the International Criminal Tribunal for Rwanda (hereinafter referred to as the ICTR), annexed to United Nations Security Council Resolution 955, U.N. SCOR, 3453rd meeting, U.N. Doc. S/RES/955 (1994)

Statute of the International Criminal Tribunal for the former Yugoslavia annexed to United Nations Security Council Resolution 827, U.N. SCOR, 3217th meeting, U.N. Doc. S/RES/827 (1993)

Statute of the Special Court for Sierra Leone (hereinafter referred to as the SCSL) annexed to the Agreement between the United Nations and the Government of Sierra Leone on the Establishment of a Special Court for Sierra Leone pursuant to United Nations Security Council Resolution 1315, U.N. SCOR, 4186th meeting, U.N. Doc. S/RES/1315 (2000)

Stephens B (1999) Humanitarian law and gender violence: an end to centuries of neglect? Hofstra Law Policy Symp 3:87

The Draft Code of Offences against the Peace and Security of Mankind, 1954, adopted by the International Law Commission, 6th Session, 1954 and submitted to the United Nations General Assembly as part of the ILC's Report covering the work of that session (at para 54), *Yearbook of the International Law Commission, 1954,* Vol. II.

The Prosecution v Laurent Semanza, Judgment, Case No. ICTR-97-20, T. Ch. II, 15 May 2003, para. 317

The Prosecutor v Alfred Musema, Judgment, Case No. ICTR-96-13-T, T. Ch. I, 27 January 2003, para. 161

The Prosecutor v Clément Kayishema and Obed Ruzindana, Judgment, Case No. ICTR-95-1-T, T. Ch. I, 21 May 1999, para. 108; *Semanza* note 101 para. 320

The Prosecutor v Georges Rutaganda, Judgment, Case No. ICTR-96-3-T, T. Ch. I, 6 December 1999, para. 56

The Prosecutor v Ignace Bagilishema, Judgement, Case No. ICTR-95-1-A, T. Ch. I, 7 June 2001, para. 65

The Prosecutor v Jean-Paul Akayesu, Judgment, Case No. ICTR-96-4. T. Ch. I, 2 September 1998. The Trial Chamber held as follows:

The Prosecutor v Juvénal Kajelijeli, Judgment, Case No. ICTR-96-44-T, T. Ch. II, 1 December 2003, para. 811

The Prosecutor v Sylvestre Gacumbitsi, Judgment, Case No. ICTR-01-64, T. Ch. III, 17 June 2004

The United Nations War Crimes Commission (1949) Law reports of trials of war criminals, Vol X

Trial of Major War Criminals Before the International Military Tribunal, Nuremberg, 14 November 1945–1 October 1946, Vol 1 (1947)

Trials of War Criminals Before the Nuremberg Military Tribunals under Control Council Law No 10, Vol IX, Part 2 (1997)

Trials of War Criminals Before the Nuremberg Military Tribunals under Control Council Law No 10, Vol V (1997)

Trials of War Criminals Before the Nuremberg Military Tribunals under Control Council Law No 10, Vol VI (1997)

Trials of War Criminals Before the Nuremberg Military Tribunals under Control Council Law No. 10, Vol II (1997)

U.N. Doc. A/39/51 (1984), entered into force on 26 June 1987
UN General Assembly, *Convention Against Torture and Other Cruel, Inhuman or Degrading Treatment or Punishment*, 10 December 1984, 1465 U.N.T.S. 85; U.N.G.A. Res. 39/46, 39 U.N. GAOR Supp. (No. 51) at 197
United Nations General Assembly Resolution 174(II), U.N. GAOR, 2nd Session, 123rd meeting, U.N. Doc. A/RES/174(II) of 21 November 1947. United Nations General Assembly Resolution 177(II)
United Nations General Assembly Resolution 260(III), U.N. GAOR, 3rd Session, 179th meeting, U.N. Doc. A/RES/260A (1948)
United Nations' Declaration on the Elimination of Violence Against Women, U.N. Doc. A/6316 (1966), 999 U.N.T.S. 302
United Nations' Universal Declaration of Human Rights, United Nations General Assembly Resolution 217A, U.N.G.A. 3rd Session, U.N. Doc. A/RES/3/217A (1948) of 10 December 1948
US v Milch, Judgement, 31 July 1948, reprinted in *Trials of War Criminals Before the Nuremberg Military Tribunals under Control Council Law No. 10*, Vol II (1997), p. 773
US v Oswald Pohl and Others, Judgement, 3 November 1947, reprinted in *Trials of War Criminals Before the Nuremberg Military Tribunals under Control Council Law No 10*, Vol V (1997), p. 958

Part V
Responding to Insurgency: Boko Haram and the (In)Adequate Reach of International Law

Chapter 15
Eradicating Extremism: A Ten Cs Approach

Dan Kuwali

15.1 Prologue

The massacre of innocent university students in Kenya following a siege by operatives of the extremist group al-Shabaab in 2015 and the kidnapping of over 200 girls in Nigeria's Borno State in 2014 on the African continent have raised concerns whether eradicating extremism is possible. Extremism and radicalisation have fuelled the violence and terrorism that afflict communities around the world today.[1] These scourges are borderless in their effects, and countering them is in the interest of all States. An extremist is emblematic of a person who advocates or resorts to measures beyond the accepted norm, especially in politics, religion or culture. A related term, radicalism, denotes political principles focused on altering social structures through revolutionary means and changing value systems in fundamental ways. Extremism and radicalisation have fuelled violence and terrorism, which are some of the burning issues that affect communities around the world. On the African continent, from Somalia, al-Shabaab terrorists have launched attacks across East Africa. In Nigeria and neighbouring countries, Boko Haram kills and kidnaps innocent men, women and children, especially girls. Today, the greatest terrorist threat in the world is not a meticulously plotted spectacular attack like that of 11 September 2001 in the United States (US) but rather homegrown citizens who become radicalised on their own or by a foreign terrorist organisation.[2]

Since the September 11 attacks, the international community has stepped up efforts on how to deal with radicalisation, violent extremism and terrorism. Countering these

---

[1] United Nations, "First Report of the Working Group on Radicalisation and Extremism that Lead to Terrorism: Inventory of State Programmes, CounterTerrorism Implementation Task Force," para. 1, http://www.un.org/en/terrorism/pdfs/radicalisation.pdf, accessed January 5, 2015. See also Chimimba (2013), pp. 51–94.

[2] See Yoroms (2007), pp. 3–14.

D. Kuwali (✉)
Centre for Human Rights, University of Pretoria, Pretoria, South Africa

J.-M. Iyi, H. Strydom (eds.), *Boko Haram and International Law*,
https://doi.org/10.1007/978-3-319-74957-0_15

scourges is in the interest of all States, considering the borderless effects of such criminal acts. The proliferation of violent extremism in Africa has presented the continent with a geopolitical situation that calls for a rethinking of security paradigms beyond the sole military- or police-based approach to rather re-examine human security issues that span political and religious spaces, the clash of cultures and other socio-economic factors that lead to grievances and exclusion of some segments of the society.

The extent of the violence and the transnational and multifaceted nature of the actors have raised questions about the ability of States to counter extremist messages, which has a reach and agility on social media that far outstrips that of most governments. The relative ease with which extremists recruit and carry out their attacks seems to suggest that governments are being outdone both in terms of amplification strategies and capability to lead in the battle of ideas. It is generally accepted that military might is only one dimension in tackling extremism and terrorism. Although military force can hypothetically annihilate the entire safe haven for extremists, the ideology and the threat of extremism cannot be eliminated given the massive propaganda they disseminate over social media.

The creation of the Working Group on 'Addressing Radicalisation and Extremism that Lead to Terrorism' by the United Nations (UN) was a response to Member States' demand for help in furthering their understanding of what makes a terrorist to be a terrorist and in identifying effective policies and practices to prevent this from happening.[3] The UN Working Group has highlighted the importance of preventive and long-term measures in fighting terrorism, separate from, and in addition to, suppressive and coercive action that may involve the use of force.[4] The main focus of the UN Working Group is on non-coercive approaches to violent extremism that rely on engagement with, and winning the hearts and minds of, the segments of society that are normally targeted by extremist and radical groups for recruitment, support and funding.[5] Building on the strategies outlined by the UN Working Group, this paper seeks to interrogate the rationale behind radicalisation and examine how extremism can be eradicated on the African continent. The paper does so by assessing how an anthropological dimension can be integrated into the prevention of radicalisation in order to eradicate extremism by taking advantage of African cultural, religious and political diversity to embrace dialogue, address grievances, prevent exclusion and promote tolerance.

15.2 The Causes of Extremism in Africa

To eradicate extremism, it is key to find out the causes of extremism. Without addressing the causes, any strategy purporting to eradicate extremism may only combat or alleviate the symptoms and not the causes. There are various forms of

[3] First Report of the Working Group on Radicalisation and Extremism that Lead to Terrorism: Inventory of State Programmes, CounterTerrorism Implementation Task Force, (UN Report), para. 1.

[4] See also UN Working Group Report, para 2.

[5] See UN Working Group Report, para. 2. See also Schillinger (2007), pp. 3–14.

extremism, especially political, religious or cultural, with variety of causes ranging from political, religious or cultural marginalisation, a vacuum in governance and security, as well as colonial influences. The diverging ideological influences from the colonial era (Arabic, English and French) in Africa and the clashes between religious models on the continent have resulted in socio-economic and religious imbalances in several countries. The issue of an ideological confrontation resonated following the appearance of radical ideological groups, terrorist activities and hostage-taking in the Maghreb societies and the Horn of Africa. Given the porous borders on the continent, it was inevitable for the phenomenon of extremists to extend to the south of the Sahara. The instability on the continent has been exacerbated by the diverging interests and rivalries between both foreign powers and neighbouring countries on a strategic and economic level, the scramble for the abundant oil, cocoa, and other minerals and energy resources on the continent.[6]

Political instability, which creates power vacuum and security lapses; discrimination; political marginalisation; discrimination on the basis of religious or such other status; economic crisis, including social penury; and the proliferation of small arms and light weapons are some of the key factors that have contributed to the breeding of extremist groups such as al-Shabaab, Boko Haram and Ansaru Dine, al-Qaeda in the Islamic Maghreb (AQIM), the Movement for the Oneness and Jihad in West Africa (MOJWA) in North and West Africa, the Lord's Resistance Army (LRA) and the *Movement pour l'Unification et le Jihad en Afrique de l'Quest* (MUJAO) on the continent. The infiltration of the terrorist organisation Islamic State of Iraq and al-Sham (ISIS) in North Africa has caused panic and brought to the fore the search for effective strategies to countering terrorism. Extremist groups are generally amorphous groups or, figuratively speaking, 'combatants without borders' who recruit terrorists willing to conduct attacks in their home countries and to travel abroad for this atrocious purpose. With steady funding from drug trafficking and hostage taking, the transnational nature of the actors and the porosity of borders, together with the shrinking of global space through modern means of communication, tend to favour the propagation of the extremism on the continent.[7]

Article 4(o) of the Constitutive Act of the African Union (AU) calls for 'respect for the sanctity of human life, condemnation and rejection of impunity and political assassination, acts of terrorism and subversive activities', which is underscored in the preamble as the need to promote peace, security and stability as a prerequisite for the implementation of Africa's development agenda.[8] The ninth recital of the preamble of the AU Convention on the Prevention and Combating Terrorism notes that 'terrorism constitutes a serious violation of human rights and, in particular, the rights to physical integrity, life, freedom and security, and impedes socio-economic

[6] See Makinda (2007), pp. 15–21.

[7] See generally, Botha (2007), pp. 23–41.

[8] African Union (2001).

development through destabilization of States'.[9] Further, the first recital of the preamble of the Protocol to the AU Convention on the Prevention and Combating Terrorism highlights 'the growing risks of linkages between terrorism and mercenarism, weapons of mass destruction, drug trafficking, corruption, transnational organized crimes, money laundering, and the illicit proliferation of small arms'.[10] While the AU has established an impressive legal framework to address radicalisation and extremism and combat terrorism, what is needed is not only the political will to implement and enforce the law but also, as this chapter outlines below, a strategy to eradicate the causes of extremism.

15.3 How to Eradicate Extremism in Africa

In an effort to facilitate information sharing among Member States, the UN Working Group embarked on a mapping exercise with the objective of creating an inventory of counterradicalisation and deradicalisation measures implemented by its Member States. The Working Group identified eleven key strategic issues (or types of programmes) involving counterradicalisation and deradicalisation measures implemented by some States. These are (1) engaging and working with civil society, (2) prison programmes, (3) education, (4) promoting alliance of civilisations and intercultural dialogue, (5) tackling economic and social inequalities, (6) global programmes to counter radicalisation, (7) the Internet, (8) legislation reforms, (9) rehabilitation programmes, (10) developing and disseminating information and (11) training and qualifying agencies involved in implementing counter-radicalisation policies.[11] Therefore, to address radicalisation and extremism that lead to terrorism on the continent, African States need to build on these strategies and integrate an anthropological dimension that capitalises on the diverse cultural, religious and political resources, including dialogue, mediation and socialisation on the continent, to which I now turn.

15.3.1 Conflict Prevention Through Broad-Based Socio-Economic Development

There is an implicit recognition among many States that economic and social inequalities (real or perceived) fuel discontent and encourage grievances that create conditions conducive to the spread of terrorism.[12] Although not all individuals who share the same fate of deprivation turn to terrorism, terrorism is always the action of a few within the

[9] See African Union, African Union (AU) Convention on the Prevention and Combating Terrorism, adopted at the 35th Ordinary Session of the OAU Ordinary Summit held in Algiers, Algeria, in July 1999.

[10] African Union, Protocol to the AU Convention on the Prevention and Combating of Terrorism.

[11] UN Working Group Report, note 1, para. 9.

[12] UN Working Group Report, note 1, para. 20.

larger group or community. When people—especially young people—feel completely trapped in impoverished communities where there is no order and no path for advancement, no educational opportunities and means to support families, no escape from injustice and the humiliations of corruption, these conditions feed instability and disorder and make those communities ripe for extremist recruitment. Therefore, to counter violent extremism, States should confront these socio-economic grievances. Hence, governments should formulate policies that help young people to forge new collaborations in entrepreneurship and science and technology. In doing so, States should ensure broad-based development that creates growth, jobs and opportunities not just for the few at the top but for the majority. Governments should ensure to promote economic growth and development, fight corruption and encourage other countries to devote more resources to education, including education for girls and women.[13]

There is a need to break the cycles of conflict that have become magnets for violent extremism by addressing underlying inequalities that fuel terrorist activity. Causal factors need to be delineated and measures implemented that allow equal access to resources and sustainability for all people. Such policies empower citizens and ensure 'freedom from fear' and 'freedom from want'.[14] For example, The Netherlands authorities have undertaken several policies to address discrimination, including in the labour market, as well as to equip youth with the skills they require to find work. They have also provided financial resources for language training and to encourage young people to complete their schooling and have increased support for parents to help them equip their children to participate in Dutch society.[15] To promote broad-based growth, the AU has encouraged its Member States to ensure the successful implementation of their economic development and poverty alleviation policies and programmes. In this respect, the AU Commission seeks to work with the African Development Bank and the United Nations Economic Commission for Africa to provide the necessary support to Member States.[16]

15.3.2 Countering Extremism with Respect for Human Rights and Humanitarian Law

Oftentimes, counterterrorism programmes trample on human rights. Strategies such as gathering intelligence, using military force and law enforcement cannot by themselves solve—and, when misused, can exacerbate—the problem of violent

[13] Kuwali (2014).

[14] This can take many forms including the provision of clean drinking water, education, vaccination programs, provision of food and shelter and protection from violence, military or otherwise. Successful human security campaigns have been characterized by the participation of a diverse group of actors including governments, non-government organisations (NGOs), and citizens.

[15] UN Working Group Report, para. 21.

[16] See African Union, Statement Delivered by the African Union Commissioner for Peace and Security, Ambassador Smäil Chergui, at the Ministerial Component of the White House Summit to Counter Terrorism (2015).

extremism. Such measures should, therefore, be developed and implemented in full compliance with international law norms and standards, particularly, international human rights and humanitarian law, as well as with the principles and purposes of the UN Charter.[17] At the same time, States should be seen to be protecting the rights, as well as the safety and security, of individuals rather than just monitoring their religious and political expressions.[18]

At the same time, when governments oppress their people, deny them human rights, stifle dissent or marginalise ethnic and religious groups or favour certain religious groups over others, they create an environment ripe for terrorists to exploit. When peaceful, democratic change is impossible, it feeds into the terrorist propaganda that violence is the only answer available. Such violations make those communities more vulnerable to recruitment.[19] As violent extremists might seek to destabilise governments and sow internal friction within societies, it is important that governments uphold and preserve democratic principles and promote the rule of law to address these challenges. States should behave in a way that assures victims of hate crimes and violent extremism that government agencies are there to protect their rights, safety and security and not just to monitor their religious and political expressions.[20]

15.3.3 Capability of Security Agents to Protect Populations at Risk

Firstly, there is need for security agents to train and attain capacity in countering radicalisation. Such training is crucial to improving the cultural competence of counter-radicalisation agencies, qualify them to do their jobs and equip them with essential knowledge and capability to protect populations at risk. Secondly, security and law enforcement agents should have a deterrent capability, including show of decisive force to deter attacks against civilians. This is because deterrence is the best way to stop violent extremism at lowest cost and risk. As such, the presence of troops (show of force) in areas infested by extremists can have a significant deterrent effect. The show of force should be accompanied by credible political statements. Thirdly, troops and law enforcement officers should have the capacity to execute arrest of armed extremists. This view arises from the fact that the failure to arrest and punish extremists compromises the protection of civilians and promotes the proliferation of violent extremism. Although the International Criminal Court (ICC) has the jurisdiction to prosecute perpetrators of such atrocities, the Hague-based court does not have its own police force to arrest suspects for purposes of

---

[17] See also Kegoro (2007), pp. 51–57.

[18] White House Office of the Press Secretary, "Statement from the Press Secretary on the White House Summit on Countering Violent Extremism," 11 January 2015.

[19] In Syria for example, Assad's war against his own people and deliberate stoking of sectarian tensions helped to fuel the rise of *Islamic State of Iraq and the Levant* (ISIL).

[20] See also Kollapen (2007), pp. 131–134.

bringing them to justice.[21] Therefore, the troops and law enforcement agents of the relevant State should have the capability to arrest armed extremists and bring them to justice.[22]

15.3.4 Community Empowerment to Deter Extremist Groups and Control Borders

Extremists groups may sometimes promise services and food supplies to communities in areas they control in order to win the support of the locals. Thus, to prevent people from being susceptible to the false promises of extremists, the international community should offer better opportunities and access to social services. To this end, Article 3(1)(a) of the Protocol to the AU Convention on the Prevention and Combating of Terrorism requires States to 'take all necessary measures to protect the fundamental human rights of their populations against all acts of terrorism'.[23] Countering violent extremism (CVE) efforts are effective where there are well-informed and resilient local communities. Investing in contacts with local communities not only facilitates and accelerates the process of information gathering but can also act as an early observation or recognition system of any violent extremist tendencies, hence permitting an early and effective counterstrategy.[24] For this reason, States should empower communities to protect themselves from violent ideologies and recruitment through public awareness and provision of policing services. In the United States, for example, several States have embarked on building CVE frameworks integrating a range of social service providers, including education administrators, mental health professionals and religious leaders, with law enforcement agencies to address violent extremism as part of the broader mandate of community safety and crime prevention.[25]

There is need to explore how development and other relevant foreign assistance could contribute to addressing populations at risk of recruitment by violent extremists and the conditions conducive to radicalisation to violence. More advanced and richer countries should help less advanced and poorer countries to build up their security forces so that they can secure ungoverned spaces where terrorists find safe haven and deter them from committing their atrocious acts. For its part, the UN Working Group Report has recommended the creation of Global Programmes to Counter Radicalisation

---

[21] The International Criminal Court (ICC) depends upon the cooperation of States to arrest and surrender those indicted by the Court. Where such support or cooperation is not forthcoming, the perpetrators may go scot-free, thereby defeating the purpose of the establishment of the ICC.

[22] Kuwali (2011), pp. 166–179.

[23] African Union, Protocol to the AU Convention on the Prevention and Combating of Terrorism.

[24] UN Working Group Report, para 10.

[25] See generally, Mayson (2007), pp. 77–80. See also White House Press Statement on Countering Violent Extremism (2015).

and Build Capacity in Third Countries.[26] More importantly, governments must take robust measures to monitor and regulate their borders to keep away terrorists and their weapons while welcoming all legitimate travellers and commerce.

15.3.5 Choking Off Extremists' Financing

Securing and sustaining funding is at the heart of any extremist or insurgent organisation's success, but it is also its Achilles' heel. It has been observed that skilful financial management is at the heart of the success of any extremist or insurgent organisation. Securing and sustaining funding is the key to moving from fringe radical group to a more planned and organised terrorist organisation. Funding is clearly the lifeblood of such organisations, but it is also their Achilles' heels.[27] Generally, terrorist groups can draw on financing in two primary ways: internally, through illegal taxation and trade, as well as proceeds from kidnap and ransom, and, externally, from donors sympathetic to their causes.[28]

As observed across northern Syria and Iraq, however, starving extremists of financing is no easy task once they evolve from external reliance to internal self-sufficiency. This is why there is need for concerted efforts by countries and individuals to suffocate extremists from funding through legislative frameworks such as anti-money laundering and other anti-corruption strategies.

Reports that the US Central Intelligence Agency (CIA) paid al-Qaeda ransom to free an Afghan diplomat are disturbing.[29] To suffocate terrorist groups, the AU Assembly has strongly condemned the payment of ransom to terrorist groups in exchange for the release of hostages and suggested that the payment of ransom to terrorist groups be considered a crime.[30] Following the AU's suggestion, the UN Security Council adopted Resolution 2133 (2014), which reaffirms earlier Security Council decisions requesting Member States to prevent and suppress the financing of terrorist

[26] See also Anton du Plessis (2007), pp. 85–92. See UN Working Group Report, para. 22.

[27] This explains why the United States (US)-led coalition against ISIS has directed a considerable portion of its air strike effort against the oil refineries and smuggling routes believed to be the mainstay of the group's financial survival in the belief that disrupting funding sources to precipitate its demise.

[28] Often from Gulf state countries, sometimes referred to as the "Golden Chain". But not all groups control territory containing populations ripe for taxation and extortion. Based in the vast, sparsely inhabited regions across the Sahara and Sahel, AQIM raises its funding from two main sources: abduction of foreign tourists and workers for ransom in a trade which is believed to have earned the group close to $100m over 5 years; and control over smuggling routes for drugs which are flown in from Latin America along "Highway 10"—referring to the 10th parallel—as the most direct route across the Atlantic en route to Europe.

[29] Korte (2015), p. 2A.

[30] African Union, "Report of the Chairperson of the Commission on Terrorism and Violent Extremism in Africa at the Peace and Security Council 455th Meeting at the Level of Heads of State and Government, Nairobi, Kenya", para. 44.

acts and refrain from providing any form of support to entities or persons involved in terrorist acts, as well as to prohibit their nationals or any persons or entities within their territories from making any funds, financial assets or economic resources available for persons and entities involved in the commission of terrorist acts. Resolution 2133 calls upon UN Member States to prevent terrorists from benefiting directly or indirectly from ransom payments or from political concessions and to secure the safe release of hostages.[31] Hence, States and individuals need to make concerted efforts to cut extremists off from funding by legislative means such as prohibiting money laundering and the use of other anti-corruption strategies, such as condemning the payment of ransom to terrorist groups in exchange for the release of hostages.[32]

15.3.6 Combating Corruption and Promoting the Rule of Law and Good Governance

Lasting stability and real security require democracy. Countries that are emerging and developing should create structures of governance and transparency so that any assistance provided actually works and reaches people. This entails free and periodic elections where people can choose their own future, independent judiciaries that uphold the rule of law, police and security forces that respect human rights, and free speech and freedom for civil society groups. These implicate freedom of religion—because when people are free to practice their faith as they choose, it strengthens diversity and cohesion in societies. Governments should step up efforts against corruption so that people can go about their day and an entrepreneur can start a business without having to pay a bribe. Governments should expand education, including for girls. There is also need to expand opportunities, including for women, since there cannot be sustainable development without the contributions of women.

For its part, the UN has a central role to play in efforts to address violent extremism and the comprehensive framework that the UN Global Counter-Terrorism Strategy offers for addressing the conditions conducive to the spread of terrorism. In line with the Strategy, the Working Group aims to help identify programmes and initiatives directed at furthering, inter alia, the dialogue, respect, tolerance and understanding among civilisations, cultures, peoples and religions; social inclusion of the marginalised; countering incitement to commit terrorist acts; and human rights and the rule of law.[33] In line with Article 2(b) of the AU Convention on Prevention and Combating of Terrorism, States should, as a matter of priority, sign or ratify or accede to international instruments condemning terrorism and other forms of extremist violence.

---

[31] UN Doc. UNSC/RES/2133(2014) adopted on 27 January 2014.

[32] African Union, "Report of the Chairperson of the Commission on Terrorism and Violent Extremism in Africa at the Peace and Security Council 455th Meeting at the Level of Heads of State and Government, Nairobi, Kenya," para. 44.

[33] UN Working Group Report, para. 3.

15.3.7 Curbing Terrorist Propaganda and Recruitment Through the Internet

With nearly 70% of its population under the age of 30, Africa is the world's youngest continent. As the youth in Africa are becoming more tech-savvy, extremist groups are taking advantage of the poverty and high rate of unemployment among the youth by manipulating them with promises of quick gains. Violent extremists have also used social media as a virtual training camp by establishing various forms of online, private, persontoperson or group communication platforms to exchange experience and knowledge. Violent extremists have successfully turned the brighter side of the Internet—low cost, ease of access, lack of regulation, vast potential audience and fast communication and flow of information—to its darker side by using it as a means of propaganda and to attract recruits.[34] Governments have toiled on the question of how to limit terrorist abuse of social media. The debate centres on whether governments should intervene through censorship, monitoring and counterpropaganda programmes or allow the free flow of online traffic to avoid undermining democratic values such as freedom of expression.[35] As a way forward, mechanisms should be established in collaboration with Internet service providers to monitor websites that facilitate and encourage violent extremism and recruitment. In this way, Internet sites that incite hatred and violent extremism can either be shut down or systematically monitored and investigated in order to initiate counter-radicalisation and curb brainwashing and indoctrination.[36]

For example, Nigeria has organised several seminars on combating terrorism through the Internet, including the organisation of capacity building and training/workshops on law enforcement and digital technologies for all agencies involved in countering radicalisation, as well as the initiation of online projects aimed at undermining the capacity of violent extremists to propagate violent ideologies through the Internet.[37] Another example is in the United Kingdom, where the government has been using the Internet as an instrument to support mainstream voices to articulate a moderate understanding of various religions in the country.[38] On the same vein, the European-Commissionsponsored 'Check the Web' project, proposes a common European approach to Internet monitoring based on strengthened cooperation and coordinated monitoring and evaluation of open Internet sources.[39]

[34] See Wilson (2007), pp. 103–105. See also UN Working Group Report, para. 24.

[35] UN Working Group Report, para. 25.

[36] UN Working Group Report, para. 26. See also Lone (2007), pp. 123–126.

[37] UN Working Group Report, para. 24. See also Kollapen (2007), pp. 131–134.

[38] UN Working Group Report, para. 24.

[39] See Lone (2007), pp. 123–126. UN Working Group Report, para. 27.

15.3.8 Counter-radicalisation and De-radicalisation Programmes

Extremists are made, not born and are therefore receptive to de-radicalisation.[40] Deradicalisation involves programmes directed at radicalised individuals to dissuade them from violence and reintegrate them into society through, for example, psychological counselling, vocational education and employment and by preventing incarceration facilities from becoming breeding grounds for extremists. Counter-radicalisation, on the other hand, aims to protect people from extremism by addressing conditions that may propel individuals to become extremists. It involves undermining leadership, challenging ideology, exposing hypocrisy and providing incentives to withdraw from extremist groups.[41]

The political exclusion, religious alienation, social isolation in a community can play a role in how someone becomes radicalised. Usually, extremists tend to brainwash their audiences that some countries, religions, policies or cultures are hostile to others. When people spew hatred towards others because of their faith, race, ethnicity, culture or such other status, it feeds into extremist narratives. If entire communities feel that they can never become a full part of the society in which they reside, it breeds a cycle of fear and resentment and a sense of injustice upon which extremists prey. In this way, what propels individuals to join radical groups is the quest for personal significance. For example, when people feel alienated from society or they see the opportunity in gaining significant personal gain such as becoming a hero or martyr, then they become attuned to those narratives that provide a means to achieve that very goal.

On the one hand, the term counterradicalisation refers to policies and programmes aimed at addressing conditions that may propel individuals down the path of terrorism. In this sense, the term counterradicalisation is used broadly to refer to a package of social, political, legal, educational and economic programmes, specifically designed to deter disaffected (and possibly already radicalised) individuals from crossing the line and becoming terrorists, in other words, preventing and protecting people from radicalisation. Counterradicalisation includes a range of strategies such as undermining leadership, challenging ideology, exposing hypocrisy and incentivising withdrawal from terrorist groups.[42] The term deradicalisation, on the other hand, is used to refer to programmes that are generally directed at individuals who have become radical with the aim of reintegrating them into society or at least dissuading them from violence,[43] that is to say, reintegration and resettlement of ex-extremist, which is akin to demobilisation, disarmament and reintegration (DDR) processes in post-conflict settings. Such initiatives seek to rehabilitate disengaged

[40] Africa Defense Forum (ADF) (n.d.), p. 45.

[41] See Statement by the AU Commissioner for Peace and Security, Ambassador Smäil Chergui at the White House Summit to Counter Terrorism (2015).

[42] ADF, "Exiting Terror: How Government Can Draw Defectors", p. 45.

[43] UN Working Group Report, para. 8.

extremists and support their reintegration into their communities. Such initiatives are already underway in Somalia and will soon be expanded to other AU Member States.[44] Another way to de-radicalise people is to provide psychological counselling and vocational education. Countries such as Germany and Denmark have implemented such programmes to fulfil the quest for personal significance in a positive way.[45] The programmes aim, for example, at ensuring that ex-extremists have employment and education in order to reintegrate them into society.

Reforms in correctional facilities in several countries have developed special programmes aimed at preventing incarceration facilities from becoming breeding grounds for extremists and a pool for recruitment.[46] Initiatives that promote an alliance of civilisations and foster intercultural understanding to counter radicalisation have been launched in New Zealand through the cosponsorship of the 'AsiaPacific Interfaith Dialogue', which brings together 15 representatives of the major faith and community groups in the Southeast Asian and South Pacific regions.[47] The Swiss Federal Department of Foreign Affairs has made 'religiopolitical conflicts' a special priority and launched the 'Montreux Initiative' in cooperation with Islamic charities and the Graduate Institute of International and Development Studies in Geneva to improve trust and understanding between the Swiss federal authorities and charitable organisations.[48]

15.3.9 Condemning Violence and Correcting Misinterpretations

Usually desperate for legitimacy, extremists manipulate ideologies to justify their violence and recruitment. Categorically condemning all acts of violent extremism and correcting misinterpreted ideologies espoused by extremists are thus imperative. Since extremists brainwash young impressionable individuals, leaders and clerics at all levels should provide clear and correct understanding of cultural, religious and political diversity, including the principle of unity in diversity, and promote tolerance and cooperation among youths.[49]

It is generally accepted that no political ideology, religion or culture is responsible for violence and terrorism. This is where leaders and clerics at all levels have the duty to counter extremist ideologies by correcting misinterpreted and distorted notions espoused by extremists to incite people to violence. It is the responsibility of religious and community leaders to exclude from the community and report to the authorities those extremists who pose a danger to the community. As pointed out

---

[44] See Statement by the AU Commissioner for Peace and Security, Ambassador Smäil Chergui at the White House Summit to Counter Terrorism (2015).

[45] UN Working Group Report, para. 8.

[46] UN Working Group Report, 1, para. 13.

[47] UN Working Group Report, para. 18. See also Mayson (2007), pp. 77–80.

[48] UN Working Group Report, para. 19. See also Mayson (2007).

[49] UN Working Group Report, para. 19. See also Mayson (2007).

above, extremists use brainwashing of young minds as a recruitment strategy. It is therefore imperative to provide a correct and proper understanding of cultural and religious diversity and promote tolerance, cooperation and unity in diversity among the youths of all groups across the globe.[50]

For example, where groups such as Boko Haram (a Kanuri dialect in Nigeria meaning 'Western education is forbidden') and al-Shabaab are deliberately targeting their propaganda to Muslim communities, particularly Muslim youth, Imams, clerics and scholars should correct twisted interpretations of Islam and debunk theories of a 'clash of civilizations'.[51] Likewise, Christian clerics should clearly and explicitly reject narratives that Christianity is at war with Islam or that it seeks to suppress Muslims. On a positive note, it is encouraging to see that Muslim clerics have been working for peace with Christian pastors and priests in Nigeria and the Central African Republic (CAR) to put an end to the cycle of hate in those countries. The AU is also engaging the media through the AU-created Network of African Journalists for Peace (NetPeace) for it to be an active partner in countering terrorist narratives and delegitimising violent ideologies.[52]

15.3.10 Communication Through Cross- and Intra-cultural, Faith and Political Dialogue

Promoting an alliance of civilisations and encouraging intercultural dialogue are important for cultivating a culture of peace and unity in diversity, as well as for bringing about understanding, respect and tolerance among religious and cultural communities and combating stereotypes and dismantling prejudices on all sides. There is need for a concerted effort to counter extremism to cultivate a culture of peace, tolerance, inclusion and acceptance of unity in diversity using various means that amplify positive African values, especially online. To achieve the alliance of civilisations for the promotion of intercultural dialogue, it is necessary to build and bolster bridges of communication and trust in order to eradicate extremism through dialogue. However, initiating and sustaining dialogue may not be easy because extremists are not part of a centralised organisation but rather comprise factions that subscribe to varying degrees of extremism. In the words of King Abdallah:

> [Dialogue] stems the flow of blood and rejects sectarianism, ignorance and extremism; it allows peace to prevail around our world … [Teachers] must prepare their students for living in a way that accepts the 'other,' to debate with them in the best way possible. The educational curriculum is a suitable environment for making the student familiar with dialogue, and that any disagreement can be solved with dialogue and debate.[53]

---

[50] See also Mayson (2007).

[51] See generally, Huntington (1993).

[52] See Statement by the AU Commissioner for Peace and Security, Ambassador Smäil Chergui at the White House Summit to Counter Terrorism (2015).

[53] Asharq Al-Awsat, (6 Oct 2014).

Thus, schools and other educational establishments can play a crucial role in the development of a resilient community that upholds values of non-violence, peaceful coexistence and tolerance.

This is why education features highly in the counterradicalisation programmes developed by most States.[54] To combat extremism, there is need to find solutions to the issue of the duality of education systems, which carry the seed of protest, marginalisation and frustration of the disciples of radicalism that can be exploited by extremists. For instance, efforts to use education as a means to counter violent extremist ideology in the United States have included programmes designed specifically to reach out to the youths, as well as to marginalised groups and racial and religious minorities.[55] For its part, the AU has facilitated open discussions and engagement between State authorities and civil society, including religious authorities and women organisations. The AU seeks to use the Nouakchott Process to engage in outreach campaigns, open fora and consultations to allow communities air their grievances and contribute actively to efforts to counter extremist ideologies.[56] As such, African States should build and bolster bridges of communication and trust to eradicate extremism through dialogue and amplify positive values, especially online.

15.4 Epilogue

When governments oppress the people and deny their human rights, particularly along sectarian lines or ethnic lines, they sow the seeds of extremism and violence. The horrendous events in the CAR, Egypt, Kenya, Libya, Nigeria and Somalia have brought to the fore the plight of innocent civilians as a result of the proliferation of extremism and terrorism on the continent. These cycles of extremism should not be allowed to tear the fabric of African cultural, political and religious diversity. Leaders at all levels should encourage dialogues across and within faiths, cultures and political groupings and across countries. To this end, religious and community leaders should play their role in tackling the root causes of extremism and terrorism by providing young people with the best examples of how to engage in dialogue with other people and cultures and how to treat them well. Ex-extremists also have the responsibility in debunking terrorist ideologies. Education is one of the most effective tools that can eradicate extremist attitudes.

Governments should formulate targeted policies that promote undistorted political and religious ideologies to ensure that they are widely heard and thereby remedy the clear lack of alternatives to the radical discourse that is fuelled by social injustice and the lack of socialisation frameworks. By working with civil society

[54] UN Working Group Report, para. 15.

[55] UN Working Group Report, note 1, para. 16.

[56] See Statement by the AU Commissioner for Peace and Security, Ambassador Smäil Chergui at the White House Summit to Counter Terrorism (2015).

and local communities, governments can help counter extremist ideologies and promote peaceful dialogue. As such, there is need for a concerted effort to counter extremism to cultivate a culture of peace, tolerance, inclusion and acceptance of unity in diversity using diverse methods by amplifying positive African values, especially online.

Violent extremism and terrorism should not be associated with any religion, nationality, civilisation or ethnic group. Some people become extremists, but it is not because of the religion—it is because of themselves as individuals. Instead of being entangled in terminology, dealing with extremism is, in fact, dealing with criminality. Obviously, military might cannot eradicate extremist ideology. At best, military force can temporarily limit the ability of extremists to perpetrate mindless acts of terror.[57] Using strategies such as intelligence gathering, military force and law enforcement alone to curb extremism can exacerbate extremism when misused. What is required is a holistic and multi-pronged counterterrorism policy, which includes soft power mechanisms to win hearts and minds and addresses the core issues that result in the breeding, enablement and enactment of extremism.[58]

There is need for a multi-pronged approach to understanding the end-to-end process of extremism, that is to say, the underlying ideology, the agents and locations of radicalisation, the people who are radicalised, the logistics of radicalisation, the people who fight radicals and the capability of State institutions to handle extremism.[59] Most extremists are the youth who find themselves unemployed and face social and political exclusion, and it is no wonder that they resort to extremist violence. Hence, governments should formulate policies that ensure broad-based social and economic growth and development, including creating decent jobs, especially for the youth, without discrimination; fighting corruption; and providing equal opportunities and access to social services such as education, especially for girls and women.

Countries and individuals have a responsibility to cut off funding that fuel hatred and corrupt young minds and endanger communities. Poverty, illiteracy and high rate of unemployment among the youth and the general population render them vulnerable to the manipulative messages of terrorist groups and their promises of quick gain.[60] As such, States should also focus more on human security, including the prevention of conflict and political instability, as well as combating drug traf-

---

[57] Military action will come to an end—war cannot be perpetual—and when it does, those who ceased to operate will return with their ideology intact, those who were killed will leave behind loved ones ripe for recruiting, and those already in the pipeline being brainwashed will be cited the death and destruction caused by this military action in order to further ingrain them with extremist ideology.

[58] See generally White House Summit Statement on Countering Violent Extremism (2015).

[59] Bokhari (2014).

[60] African Union, Report of the Chairperson of the Commission on Terrorism and Violent Extremism in Africa.

ficking and other organised crime, which tend to finance terrorists and other extremist organisations.[61]

The 'ten Cs' approach advanced in this chapter provides a roadmap for tackling these tasks and eradicating extremism in Africa by way of (1) conflict prevention through broad-based socio-economic development, (2) countering extremism with respect for human rights and humanitarian law, (3) capability of security agents to protect populations at risk, (4) community empowerment to deter extremist groups and control borders, (5) choking off extremists' financing, (6) combating corruption and promoting the rule of law and good governance, (7) curbing terrorist propaganda and recruitment through the Internet; (8) counter-radicalisation and deradicalisation programmes; (9) condemning violence and correcting misinterpretations and (10) communication through cross- and intra-cultural, faith and political dialogue.

References

Africa Defense Forum (n.d.) Extremists are made, not born. Countering Terrorist Recruitment 5(2):45

Africa Defense Forum. Exiting Terror: How government can draw defectors

African Union, African Union (AU) Convention on the Prevention and Combating Terrorism, adopted at the 35th Ordinary Session of the OAU Ordinary Summit held in Algiers, Algeria, in July 1999. Available at: http://www.au.int/en/sites/default/files/OAU_CONVENTION_PREVENTION_COMBATING_TERRORISM.pdf. Accessed 10 Mar 2015

African Union, Protocol to the AU Convention on the Prevention and Combating of Terrorism. Available at: http://www.au.int/en/sites/default/files/PROTOCOL_OAU_CONVENTION_ON_THE_PREVENTION_COMBATING_TERRORISM.pdf. Accessed 20 Feb 2015

African Union, Protocol to the AU Convention on the Prevention and Combating of Terrorism. Available at: http://www.au.int/en/sites/default/files/PROTOCOL_OAU_CONVENTION_ON_THE_PREVENTION_COMBATING_TERRORISM.pdf. Accessed 14 June 2015

African Union, Report of the Chairperson of the Commission on Terrorism and Violent Extremism in Africa at the Peace and Security Council 455th Meeting at the Level of Heads of State and Government, Nairobi, Kenya. Available at: http://cpauc.au.int/en/content/report-chairperson-commission-terrorism-and-violent-extremism-africa-peace-and-security-co-0. Accessed 10 Mar 2015

African Union, Statement Delivered by the African Union Commissioner for Peace and Security, Ambassador Smäil Chergui, at the Ministerial Component of the White House Summit

[61] On 8 September 2006, the General Assembly unanimously adopted the United Nations Global CounterTerrorism Strategy. Member States embarked upon a new phase in their counterterrorism efforts by agreeing on a global strategy to counter terrorism. The Strategy marks the first time that all Member States of the United Nations have agreed to a common strategic and operational framework to fight terrorism. The Strategy forms a basis for a concrete plan of action: to address the conditions conducive to the spread of terrorism; to prevent and combat terrorism; to take measures to build state capacity to fight terrorism; to strengthen the role of the United Nations in combating terrorism; and to ensure the respect of human rights while countering terrorism. The Strategy builds on the unique consensus achieved by world leaders at their 2005 September Summit to condemn terrorism in all its forms and manifestations.

to Counter Terrorism. Available at: http://www.peaceau.org/uploads/auc.cps.statement.wh.summit.violent.extremism.19.02.2015.pdf. Accessed 10 Mar 2015

African Union, The Constitutive Act of the African Union, adopted in 2000 at the Lomé Summit (Togo), entered into force in 2001. Available at: http://www.au.int/en/about/constitutive_act. Accessed 20 Feb 2015

Asharq Al-Awsat, "King Abdullah: we will eradicate terrorism, religious extremism", 6 October 2014. Available at: http://www.aawsat.net/2014/10/article55337252/king-abdullah-we-will-eradicate-terrorism-religious-extremism. Accessed 20 Dec 2014

Bokhari H (2014) Eradicating extremist ideology. Available at: http://pakteahouse.net/2014/12/30/eradicating-extremist-ideology/. Accessed 9 Jan 2015

Botha A (2007) Africa's vulnerability to terrorism and its ability to combat it. In: Okumu W, Botha A (eds) Domestic terrorism in Africa: defining, addressing and understanding its impact on human security. Institute for Security Studies, Pretoria, pp 23–41

Chimimba TP (2013), Defining terrorism under the United Nations system. Zanzibar Yearb Law 51–94

Du Plessis A (2007) The role of the United Nations in providing technical assistance in Africa. In: Okumu W, Botha A (eds) Domestic terrorism in Africa: defining, addressing and understanding its impact on human security. Institute for Security Studies, Pretoria, pp 85–92

First Report of the Working Group on Radicalisation and Extremism that Lead to Terrorism.: Inventory of State Programmes, CounterTerrorism Implementation Task Force. Available at http://www.un.org/en/terrorism/pdfs/radicalisation.pdf. Accessed 5 Jan 2015

Huntington SP (1993) Clash of civilizations? Foreign Aff 72(3):22–49

Kegoro G (2007) The effects of counter-terrorism measures on human rights: the experiences of East African countries. In: Okumu W, Botha A (eds) Domestic terrorism in Africa: defining, addressing and understanding its impact on human security. Institute for Security Studies, Pretoria, pp 51–57

Kollapen J (2007) Human rights, terrorism and the interests of a secure society. In: Okumu W, Botha A (eds) Domestic terrorism in Africa: defining, addressing and understanding its impact on human security. Institute for Security Studies, Pretoria, pp 131–134

Korte G "Report: CIA Paid Al-Qaeda Ransom to Free Official", USA Today, Monday March 16, 2015, p 2A

Kuwali D (2011) Humanitarian rights: enforcement of international humanitarian law by the African Court of Human Rights. Afr Yearb Int Humanitarian Law 166–179

Kuwali D (2014) Just peace: achieving peace, justice, and development in post conflict African countries. Policy paper, Africa Peacebuilding Network, New York, Social Science Research Council, 2014. Available at: http://webarchive.ssrc.org/workingpapers/APN_WorkingPapers02_Kuwali.pdf. Accessed 10 May 2015

Lone S (2007) Terrorism, media and the search for an African voice. In: Okumu W, Botha A (eds) Domestic terrorism in Africa: defining, addressing and understanding its impact on human security. Institute for Security Studies, Pretoria, pp 123–126

Makinda SM (2007) The history and root causes of terrorism in Africa. In: Okumu W, Botha A (eds) Domestic terrorism in Africa. Defining, addressing and understanding its impact on human security. Institute for Security Studies, Pretoria, pp 15–21

Mayson C (2007) Engaging religious communities and building partnerships. In: Okumu W, Botha A (eds) Domestic terrorism in Africa: defining, addressing and understanding its impact on human security. Institute for Security Studies, Pretoria, pp 77–80

Schillinger K (2007) The role of the international community. In: Okumu W, Botha A (eds) Domestic terrorism in Africa: defining, addressing and understanding its impact on human security. Institute for Security Studies, Pretoria, pp 3–14

Statement by the AU Commissioner for Peace and Security, Ambassador Smäil Chergui at the White House Summit to Counter Terrorism (2015)

UN Doc. UNSC/RES/2133(2014) adopted on 27 January 2014

United Nations., First Report of the Working Group on Radicalisation and Extremism that Lead to Terrorism: Inventory of State Programmes, CounterTerrorism Implementation Task Force. Available at http://www.un.org/en/terrorism/pdfs/radicalisation.pdf. Accessed 5 Jan 2015

White House Office of the Press Secretary. Statement from the Press Secretary on the White House Summit on Countering Violent Extremism. 11 January 2015. Available at: http://www.white-house.gov/the-press-office/2015/01/11/statement-press-secretary-white-house-summit-countering-violent-extremis. Accessed 9 Mar 2015

Wilson B (2007) Detection and prevention of terrorist threats. In: Okumu W, Botha A (eds) Domestic terrorism in Africa: defining, addressing and understanding its impact on human security. Institute for Security Studies, Pretoria, pp 103–105

Yoroms G (2007) Defining and mapping threats of terrorism in Africa. In: Okumu W, Botha A (eds) Domestic terrorism in Africa: defining, addressing and understanding its impact on human security. Institute for Security Studies, Pretoria, pp 3–14

Chapter 16
Beyond the Law to Socio-Legal Intervention: The Boko Haram Insurgency and the Nigerian Child

Azubike Onuora-Oguno and Mariam Adepeju Abdulraheem-Mustapha

16.1 Introduction

With the development of international law, the status of a child has transformed the parameters of what counts as violence against children. A child is generally agreed to be a person below the age of 18 years.[1] The notion is grounded in the fact that everyone has the right to be respected and be safe,[2] regardless of his/her race, ethnicity, religion, gender, disability or age.[3] Violence, harassment and bullying are violations of human rights.[4] As a contribution to the debate on ways of promoting and securing children's fundamental rights, respect for their human dignity and physical and psychological integrity through the prevention of all forms of violence, this paper adopts a social-legal perspective in proffering solutions to the *Boko Haram* menace in Nigeria as it affects children.

The aspirations of nations in the Millennium Development Goals (MDGs) among several objectives include the recognition of certain rights aimed at protect-

[1] Article 1 Child Rights Convention 1989.

[2] Article 5, Universal Declaration of Human Rights (UDHR), 1948, Article 7, International Covenant on Economic Civil and Political Rights (ICESCR) and Article 19, Convention on the Rights of the Child (CRC), 1989.

[3] Article 2, Universal Declaration of Human Rights (UDHR), 1948, Article 2, International Covenant on Civil and Political Rights (ICCPR), 1966 and Article 2, International Covenant on Economic Civil and Political Rights (ICESCR), 1966.

[4] Article 19 CRC.

A. Onuora-Oguno (✉)
Jurisprudence and International Law Department, Faculty of Law, University of Ilorin, Ilorin, Nigeria

M. A. Abdulraheem-Mustapha
Public Law Department, Faculty of Law, University of Ilorin, Ilorin, Nigeria

J.-M. Iyi, H. Strydom (eds.), *Boko Haram and International Law*,
https://doi.org/10.1007/978-3-319-74957-0_16

ing the child. Rights such as the right to universal primary education,[5] promotion of gender equality[6] and the reduction of child mortality[7] are directly related to the child. Aside from the MDGs, Nigeria is a signatory to several international law instruments that aim to protect the child. National laws exist that are primed to aid the realisation of the goals of the MDGs with the Constitution of the Federal Republic of Nigeria (CFRN) being the major legal protective instrument.[8]

However, despite the existence of these laws, the condition of the Nigerian child remains abysmal. Nigeria is estimated to have the largest number of out-of school children in the world.[9] The safety of the Nigerian child in the school space became more worrisome with the abduction of over 200 schoolgirls in Chibok in northeastern Nigeria.[10] Prior to the abduction, attacks on children, specifically the girl child, were heightened.[11] The activities of *Boko Haram* present new challenges to the issues of law and security in all aspects of national life.[12] *Boko Haram* is presently classified as a terrorist organisation.[13] The primary meaning of the word 'Boko Haram' when translated into English is 'Western education is a crime'. It should be noted that besides the problem of Boko Haram, the emergence of several similar militia groups has continued to trouble the peace of Nigerians across Nigeria, for instance the *Bakassi Boys* in eastern Nigeria, the Niger Delta militants in southern Nigeria and *Oodua* People's Congress (OPC) in western Nigeria. Others are *Egbesu* Boys, *Obtase*, among several others.[14]

It is on the basis of the seeming ineffective role of the law to stem the operations of such groups that this paper examines the possibility of a socio-legal approach to restoring peace in the northeast of Nigeria, which is the area most affected by the security challenges arising from the *Boko Haram* insurgency. To achieve this, this paper not only highlights and examines the general and specific legislative, institutional, policy and administrative measures in addressing various forms of violence against children; it also examines the short- and long-term strategies to provide care, security, rehabilitation and reintegration of child victims into their communities. To achieve this, the authors draw on the historical context of the north and south of

[5] Millennium Development Goals 2.

[6] Millennium Development Goals 3.

[7] Millennium Development Goals 4.

[8] The Nigerian Child Rights Act; the Criminal and Penal Codes all contains provisions aimed at protecting the rights of the child.

[9] See generally the UNESCO statistics on out of school children (2015).

[10] Zenn (2014).

[11] There are gory images of Boko Haram's attacks on school children. See for example.

[12] This assertion does not foreclose the fact that the Nigerian state have been plagued with numerous challenges that makes it not fulfil its treaty obligations. In the past the long years of military rule; Islamic law in the northern states and cultural bias are certainly other factors that have affected respect for treaty obligations. In this paper, however, the menace of Boko Haram is focused on.

[13] A list of foreign terrorist organisations can be found at US Government website.

[14] Egbewole Onuora-Oguno (2014), pp. 63–77.

Nigeria and the emergence of militia groups and interrogate the efficacy of the law in resolving the challenges posed by *Boko Haram*. Utilising a socio-legal approach, this concludes with proposals that could guide policy formulation and interventions for the advancement of child rights and the prevention and mitigation of the effects of violence against the Nigerian child.

16.2 The Historical Background of Northern and Southern Nigeria

The entity known as Nigeria today was created by virtue of the amalgamation of the northern and southern protectorates in the British colony in 1914.[15] Described as a marriage of convenience in several quarters, the amalgamation represents the sole choice of the British to facilitate the administration of what is today agreed to be the most populous black nation in the world. Nigeria as it is today is a complex web of politically divergent ethnic nationalities and a deeply divided nation.[16] The major divisive coordinates of the Nigerian state have been religious and ethnic. Religion and ethnic nepotism have informed a deepened inability of Nigeria to attain democracy and stem continuous violence that is often religiously or ethnically motivated.[17] The high point of the crisis seems to have been the civil war between 1967 and 1970.[18] Since then, conflicts have become more or less pervasive and intense in the post-civil war period, and disintegration continues to be contemplated by aggrieved sections of the country as one of the possible ways of resolving the 'National Question'.[19] This means that the consequences of Nigeria's diversity in an unstable political context remain as dire as ever.[20]

The genesis of the above conflicts has been informed by suspicion by northern Muslims of what could be termed a Christian missionary agenda to erode the Islamic belief systems that was already a well-entrenched system before the advent of the colonialists. According to authors like Fafunwa,[21] Hansungule and Onuora-Oguno,[22] this suspicion negatively impacted the way Western education is perceived in the North and perhaps explains why *Boko Haram's* philosophy describes Western education as being evil.

[15] Nwaoga et al. (2014).

[16] See, generally, Nmoma (1995).

[17] Dudley (1973). See also, Maier (2000).

[18] The Civil war was as a result of ethnic insecurity and the desire of the Eastern part of Nigeria desiring to secede from Nigeria. In many quarters it is basically seen as an Hausa v Igbo war.

[19] Diamond (1987), pp. 117–128.

[20] Egbewole Onuora-Oguno (2013).

[21] Fafunwa (1975).

[22] Hansungule and Onuora-Oguno (2013).

Nigeria today is represented in sharp divisions between a largely Muslim North[23] and a predominantly Christian South with ethnic, religious and social ties that have been responsible for holding the country together through many episodes of turbulence. Nigeria has experienced recurrent violent conflicts[24] as a result of several complex and interlocking factors, including a volatile mix of historical grievances, political manipulation and ethnic and religious rivalries.[25] It is important to point out that both religious and ethnic factors are present in the majority of social conflicts witnessed in Nigeria,[26] and since independence, Nigeria has remained a multi-ethnic country with over 400 ethnic groups.[27] Nigeria has been grappling and trying to cope with the problems of ethnicity on the one hand and the problem of ethno-religious conflicts on the other hand.[28]

Over the years, these problems have led to recurrent social crises that have given birth to many militias like the *Bakassi* Boys, *Oodua* People Congress (OPC), the *Ijaw* Youth Congress (IYC), the *Egbesu* Boys, the Igbo People Congress (IPC), the *Arewa* People Congress (APC), the Movement for the Actualization of the Sovereign State of Biafra (MASSOB) and the infamous *Boko Haram* terrorist group.[29] The major causes of ethno-religious conflicts in Nigeria are connected with marginalisation, accusations of neglect, nepotism, oppression, domination, exploitation, victimisation, discrimination and bigotry.[30] The listed challenges, therefore, in the opinion of the authors, speak more to a socio imbalance and not necessarily legal causal factors, thus necessitating a socio-legal approach in the search for a solution to the current conflict.

It is important to note here that the failure of Nigerian leaders[31] to establish good governance, forge national integration and promote what can be called real economic

---

[23] The Hausa, Fulani and Kanuri are the largest groups in northern Nigeria and are predominantly Muslim. The Muslim population is concentrated in the far northern states but significant numbers of Christians also reside in these states. There are about 160 smaller ethnic groups across northern Nigeria that are mainly Christian along with a considerable percentage that follow traditional religious practices. Most of the northern population, about 70%, lives in rural agrarian communities but historically significant urban centres such as Kaduna, Kano, Maiduguri, Sokoto and Zaria have attracted diverse people from all over the country.

[24] Conflict usually occurs when deprived groups and individuals attempt to increase their share of power and wealth or to modify the dominant values, norms, beliefs or ideology.

[25] Scc generally, Pinkney (2003).

[26] Salawu (2010), p. 345. See Daily Trust (2002-08-20), p. 16.

[27] Imobighe (2003), pp. 14–15.

[28] Jega (2002), pp. 35–39.

[29] Salawu (2010), p. 345; Egbewole and Onuora-Oguno (2014), pp. 63–77.

[30] Ikelegbe (2001), p. 145.

[31] The worsening challenges with poverty, youth unemployment, poor infrastructure, illiteracy and insecurity are inherently systemic, and a consequence of the collective failure of leaders at all tiers of government to properly deliver public goods and services or to accountably manage public funds. For instance in 2010, nine of the 19 Northern states had the highest levels of unemployment in Nigeria as some as high as 40%, like Zamfara state in the Northwest recorded the highest rate of unemployment at 42.6%. Overall unemployment in Nigeria was 23.9% as at 2010, showing a 10% jump since 2006. See National Bureau of Statistics, Annual Abstract of Statistics, 2011.

progress, through deliberate and articulated policies, has led to mass poverty and unemployment.[32] This has resulted in communal, ethnic, religious and class conflicts that have now characterised the Nigerian nation, and this explains why all ethno-religious crises that ever occurred in Nigeria have recorded large turnout of people, including the underaged.[33] The Nigerian child in recent times has become vendors for suicide bombing in various public locations. The situation brings to the fore the inability of the law to protect the rights of the Nigerian child. As noted by an observer, '[s]imilarly, the long military intervention in politics tends to encourage and legitimize the use of force and violence as instruments of social change and attainment of set goals and demands'.[34] From this, it is easy to see that as a hangover from the military era, the resort to force in settling conflicts has become a tradition in Nigerian politics.[35] Closely related to this is the uncontrolled supply of arms, which has also contributed to the outbreak of conflicts and encouraged belligerents to continue fighting rather than seeking and accepting peaceful dispute resolution options.[36] Another important cause of ethno-religious conflicts in Nigeria is the breakdown of vehicles of social control that characterised traditional African societies—the family, education, law, religion and political system that cared for the well-being of all citizens.[37]

Indeed, the malfunctioning of all these important institutions has increased ethnic and communal conflicts in Nigeria.[38] According to Madu and Goni[39]:

> ...the inability of many homes to make ends meet with the family income tends to increase immorality, broken fatherless/motherless homes, divorces and drunkenness, leading again to a large reserve of youths who could be employed for execution of ethno-religious conflicts.

The above scenario depicts the poor quality of education that is the present state of education of the Nigerian child. The poor state of education in Nigeria further supports the view that the school system in Nigeria today is in shambles and of poor quality. As further asserted by Madu and Goni, the inability of religious bodies to help educate people has not helped in curbing the violence that has affected the

[32] Northern Nigeria continues to display some of the worst human development indicators in the world. For instance, in the northeast Nigeria, 71.5% of the population lives in absolute poverty and more than half are malnourished, making it the poorest part of the country. 40% of Nigerian children aged 6–11 do not attend any primary school in the North, and it is Northern Nigeria that has the worst school attendance rates, especially for its girls. Like in Kano State, it is 49%, in Borno State, the epicentre of the Boko Haram insurgency, it is under 15%. But in the South, particularly in Lagos, the literacy rate is 92%. See British Council Nigeria (2012). Gender in Nigeria Report. See also, High-Level International Round Table on Literacy, UNESCO, Paris, 6–7 September 2012, 'National Literacy Action Plan for 2012–2015, Nigeria'.

[33] High-Level International Round Table on Literacy, UNESCO, Paris, 6–7 September 2012, 'National Literacy Action Plan for 2012–2015, Nigeria'.

[34] Alanamu et al. (2006), p. 291.

[35] Alanamu et al. (2006), p. 291.

[36] Omorogbe and Omohan (2005), p. 557.

[37] Salawu (2010), p. 345.

[38] Albert (1999), p. 85.

[39] Madu and Ibrahim (2013), p. 149.

Nigerian child.[40] This general decadence has also permeated law enforcement agents who are heavily drowned in corruption.[41] The failure to ensure the rule of law in as a fundamental principle of good governance in Nigeria is demonstrated by the growing failure of various national institutions.[42] This state of affairs partly explains why *Boko Haram* has thrived on a self-preservation philosophy of protecting Islamic tenets and principles. Consequently, it is arguable that the law has failed in building a harmonious society in Nigeria. However, to justify this conclusion, it is imperative to examine some of the legal instruments that should have been relied upon to ensure the protection of people from the menace of groups like *Boko Haram*.

16.3 Emergence of the Boko Haram and Militia Groups

The responsibility of a state is to ensure a peaceful existence of persons within its territory, provide infrastructure and maintain law and order. According to Heyns, when a state fails in these core obligations, the resort to a struggle approach becomes the means of self-help and demand for rights and obligations.[43] Where the laid-down structures are not performing optimally, then violence is inevitable.[44] This argument is advanced on the premise of the strong link between governance and viable institutional structures.[45]

Closely linked to the question of the struggle approach is the self-determination paradigm. The self-determination concept is concerned with individual awareness and desire to realise common social goals and objectives.[46] It is usually hinged on personal striving and agitation.[47] The quest for self-determination therefore is in most circumstances linked to situations where a group of people feels marginalised and deprived of social amenities, as well as political involvement and good governance.[48] According to the African Commission on Human and Peoples' Right in the *Katangese* case[49]:

> The Commission believes that self-determination may be exercised in any of the following ways - independence, self-government, local government, federalism, confederalism, unitarism or any other form of relations that accords with the wishes of the people, but is fully cognisant of other recognised principles such as sovereignty and territorial integrity.

---

[40] Carefronting. Muslim/Christian cooperation for conflict management and prevention.

[41] Madu and Ibrahim (2013), p. 149.

[42] This assumption is made on the basis of the failure of the security agencies to curb the menace of the *Boko Haram* sect; increasing corruption among executive and legislative arms of government among several other examples of weak institutions in Nigeria.

[43] See generally, Heyns (2006).

[44] See generally, Rahim (2002), p. 26.

[45] Werlin (2003), p. 329.

[46] Kleven (2014), p. 20.

[47] Deci and Ryan (2002), pp. 3–33.

[48] See generally Thornberry (1989), pp. 867–889; McCorquodale (1994), pp. 857–885.

[49] ***Katangese Peoples' Congress v Zaire*** 2000 AHRLR 72 (ACHPR 1995).

Premised on the above view, it is our opinion that the question of self-determination would not avail the various faces of militia insurgents in Nigeria.[50] The continued failure of the Nigerian state to perform its good governance functions has led to the emergence of ethnic militias and has exacerbated existing crises.[51] Some of these militia groups initially started as security outfits with the sole purpose of protecting lives and property. However, over time, this objective changed into groups making economic demands on the Nigerian state and presently constitutes social nuisance and has degenerated into outright terrorist activities.[52] Analyses of the activities of the various militia groups show a violation of fundamental human rights with particular respect to the right to life. For instance, the *Bakassi* Boys engaged in several extrajudicial killings in the eastern part of Nigeria; the Niger Delta militants have violated the liberty and right to life and freedom of movement of a number of their victims.[53]

The emergence of the *Boko Haram* sect, however, presents a sharp contrast to other groups that have existed in Nigeria. While the other groups engaged in violation of the rights of persons, they could be argued to have been based on economic demands, demand for better economic policies for the groups and an enhancement of access to social amenities. But *Boko Haram* has propagated a deadly religious extremist agenda exhibited in suicide bombings and abductions of school children.

16.4 Nigeria's Responsibilities Under National and International Laws: Is a Legal Regime Sufficient?

The starting point for municipal protection of the rights of the Nigerian child is the CFRN 1999. Chapter 4 of the CFRN enshrines several fundamental human rights that accrue to all Nigerians. Section 18 of the CFRN restates the importance of everyone to have compulsory and free basic education. Aside from the CFRN, other pieces of legislation also exist that aim at the protection of the rights of the child. Two major enactments that are of interest here are the Compulsory, Free Universal Basic Education Act[54] and the Child Rights Act[55] (CRA). The provisions of these bodies of legislation are 'based on certain fundamental principles relating to the promotion and sustenance of child dignity and enhancement of child development'.[56]

[50] This assumption however does not foreclose the fact that agitations from several groups already mentioned continue to defy the numerous laws in place in Nigeria aimed at protecting the rights of the child and the society at large.

[51] Adesola (2007).

[52] Egbewole and Onuora-Oguno (2014), pp. 63–77.

[53] Egbewole and Onuora-Oguno (2014), pp. 63–77.

[54] Compulsory, Free Universal Basic Education Act Cap C52, Laws of the Federation of Nigeria, 2011.

[55] Child Rights Act Cap C50, Laws of the Federation of Nigeria, 2011.

[56] A bill proposed by Amadi Gary Kelechi & Okpara Nnenna Joy.

Education is conceived to have great potential for enhancing the dignity of an individual and enabling the child to contribute meaningfully to the community.

As a state party to many human rights treaties, Nigeria has specific obligations under international law to further ensure the protection of the Nigerian child. Nigeria has ratified the United Nations Convention on the Rights of the Child (UNCRC)[57] and the African Charter on the Rights and the Welfare of the Child (ACRWC)[58] as a demonstration of its commitment to the protection of the rights of the child. With the domestication of the Child Rights Act in 2003, Nigeria showed her great resolve to protect the Nigerian child from all forms of rights violations. Consisting of 278 sections and 11 schedules, the Act promises a uniform standard for the concerns of the rights of children. However, in reality, the situation is not encouraging. Currently, the Child Rights Act 2003 has been promulgated into law in 23 states out of the 36 states in the federation.[59] The failure to have all 36 states of the federation domesticate the CRA has created a lack of uniformity in the application of the provisions of the Act with particular reference to the right of the Nigerian child to education.

Significantly, section 3 of the Child Rights Act provides for all the fundamental human rights enshrined in the Constitution of the Federal Republic of Nigeria 1999 (as amended), in addition to the specific rights specifically intended to protect the rights of a child. Section 10 of the Child Rights Act 2003 specifically provides for the right of the child to freedom from discrimination merely by reason of his or her belonging to a particular community or ethnic group or by reason of his or her place of origin, sex, religion or political opinion. In section 15 of the Act, a child is entitled to free, compulsory and universal primary education. This particular provision even goes to the extent of giving a female child who becomes pregnant before completing her education the opportunity to continue her education after delivery.[60] A parent or guardian of a child who fails to comply with this provision shall, in terms of section 15 (6), be liable on a first conviction to a reprimand and community service. Upon a second conviction, such a person shall be liable to a fine of 2000 naira or imprisonment for a term not exceeding 1 month or both and on any subsequent conviction to a fine not exceeding 5000 naira or imprisonment for a term not exceeding 2 months or both.

Section 34 of the Act prohibits the recruitment of any child into any branches of the armed forces of the Federal Republic of Nigeria, and no child should be directly involved in any military operation or hostilities. The recent recruitment of children in the activities of *Boko Haram* consequently suggests some lapses in the fulfilment of government's obligations. The challenge is that despite the adoption of the Act in

[57] Nigeria ratified the United Nations Convention on the Rights of the Child in 1991.

[58] Nigeria signed the African Charter on the Rights and Welfare of the Child in 1999 and ratified it in 2001.

[59] Child Rights Act has been promulgated into Law in only twenty-three States which are Abia, Anambra, Bayelsa, Eboniyi, Ekiti, Imo, Jigawa, Kwara, Lagos, Nassarawa, Ogun, Ondo, Plateau, Rivers, Taraba, Kogi, Oyo, Benue, Osun, Edo, Delta, Cross River, Akwa Ibom.

[60] Section 15 (4) Child Rights Act, 2003.

some states in Nigeria, the provisions of the Act are unable to protect the Nigerian child from the activities of the *Boko Haram* insurgents.

It is submitted that the inability of the federal government to ensure that all states in Nigeria domesticate the CRA in their respective jurisdictions continues to undermine uniformity in the protection of the rights of the child, and this, according to Ladan, hinges on socio-religious grounds and not a question of the law.[61] This position is supported by several investigations by non-governmental organisations that the reluctance by most of the states in northern Nigeria is founded on religious and cultural tenets.[62] It is, however, argued here that having ratified the CRC and domesticated it in Nigeria, Nigeria cannot abdicate her treaty obligations under the CRC by the mere refusal of some states not to give legislative backing to the CRA within their respective states. This argument is further strengthened by the supremacy of the CFRN 1999.[63] Thus, a state is bound to act only in line with the commitment of the government at the federal level and also to respect government obligations under international law.

Moreover, the Compulsory, Free Universal Basic Education Act (CFUBE Act) contains the obligation of the Nigerian government to ensure that every child has access to quality basic education. The Act places obligations on parents and guardians to ensure that their children or wards attain free and compulsory education as provided by the government.[64] The intent of the CFUBE Act is in consonance with the provisions of the CRA discussed above. However, poor access to basic education, especially in the northeast of Nigeria, has contributed to the activities of *Boko Haram*. Aside from its duties under its national laws and legislation, Nigeria has other relevant obligations in international law. The following section gives a brief analysis of Nigeria's obligations under the African regional human rights architecture.

The ACRWC places responsibilities on states parties to protect the child. In article 1, it provides as follows[65]:

> Member States of the Organization of African Unity Parties to the present Charter shall recognize the rights, freedoms and duties enshrined in this Charter and shall undertake to the necessary steps, in accordance with their Constitutional processes and with the provisions of the present Charter, to adopt such legislative or *other measures* as may be necessary to give effect to the provisions of this Charter.

The reliance on 'other measures' is of special interest here, as will be shown in the following section, and according to the proposition of the authors, it suggests a reliance on socio-legal measures. The pathetic situation of the law calls for a socio-legal

---

[61] Ladan (2007).

[62] Wellbeing Foundation, State of the CRC Ratification Process in Nigeria: Are the Children Protected Yet? Available at http://www.wbfafrica.org/press-releases/archive/112-an-article-state-of-the-crc-ratification-process-in-nigeria-are-the-children-protected-yet.html (accessed 8 March 2015).

[63] See section 1(1) of the Constitution of the Federal Republic of Nigeria, 1999.

[64] See sections 2(2) and 4(1) of the Compulsory, Free Universal Basic Education Act, Cap C52, Laws of the Federation of Nigeria, 2011.

[65] Emphasis supplied.

approach to ensuring the protection of the Nigerian child. The ACRWC projects education forward as a premise on which the potentials of a child can be identified and enhanced. It places obligations on the child to effectively contribute to the peaceful existence of the state.[66] However, where the government fails in its responsibility to provide access to quality education, the child will be unable to carry out the obligations required by the Charter.[67]

The obligation of Nigeria to further ensure access to basic education was examined before the ECOWAS Community Court of Justice in the case of *SERAP v Nigeria.*[68] The Court found that Nigeria was in violation of its responsibility to ensure that the right of access to education was fulfilled and also ensure the efficient management of available resources. This has further reinforced Nigeria's obligations under relevant regional human rights law.

16.4.1 The Response of the Law to the Emergence of Militia Groups

The Nigerian Police Force (NPF) has the responsibility of maintaining law and order in the country. However, given the pervasive corruption within the Police Force, the credibility of the NPF has been seriously eroded. According to an Amnesty International Report, the Nigerian Police Force and the military have continuously engaged in acts of impunity and extrajudicial killings.[69] The Nigerians Supreme Council of Islamic Affairs (NSCIA) and similar groups have criticised the NPF and other security agencies for their failures and penchant for impunity.[70] With particular respect to the Nigeria Police and recently the military, the NSCIA has condemned the 'brutality used by the forces to attempt to quash the *Boko Haram* rebellion in the North East of Nigeria, where unarmed Nigerians, some of them cripples were lined up, ordered to lie down and were shot to death in cold blood'.[71] It is claimed in some quarters that the *Boko Haram* insurgents became deadlier after the extrajudicial murder of Mohammed Yusuf, the leader of *Boko Haram*, by the Nigerian Police Force.[72] Generally, Nigerian forces have been criticised for not adhering to human rights standards in their campaign against Boko Haram.

---

[66] ACRWC article 11 (b).

[67] ACRWC article 31.

[68] ECW/CCJ/APP/12/07.

[69] Nigeria: 'Pragmatic policing through extra-judicial executions and torture' An Amnesty International Report (2008-05-16). AI Index AFR 44/006/2008.

[70] The statement was made by the secretary general of the body in an interview with Daily Sun (2010-02-15) cited in Egbewole and Onuora-Oguno (2014), pp. 63–77.

[71] Egbewole and Onuora-Oguno (2014), pp. 63–77.

[72] Olamilekan (2014); Olaposi (2014), p. 8.

Aside from the failures of security forces, the judiciary has not been able to decide some of the cases brought against alleged members of the sect.[73] This could be as a result of the inability of prosecutors to build solid cases against the suspects. For instance, as of the time of writing, the prosecution of the alleged mastermind of the Nyanya bombing arrested in Sudan and extradited to Nigeria continues to drag on due to lack of evidence.[74] The case of Senator Ndume, who was alleged to be a sponsor of *Boko Haram*, is yet to be decided as the prosecutors are struggling to build a formidable case against him.[75]

16.4.2 Nigerian Law and Emerging Acts of Terror-Specific Response to Boko Haram

With the labelling of the *Boko Haram* sect as a terrorist group, the need to have a specific law that will be relied on to crush the menace became paramount. To this end, the Terrorism (Prevention) (Amendment) Act 2013[76] has become the main legislation relied upon to fight the insurgency and other related activities described therein as constituting terrorist activities.

Divided into 40 sections, the Act provides for the punishment attached to offences described therein and also confers jurisdiction on the Federal High Court to try cases of terrorism. The Office of the Attorney General of the Federation is saddled with the responsibility of prosecution, while the Office of the National Security Adviser (ONSA) is the coordinator of all security activities to combat all

[73] For various factors and circumstance that has frustrated judicial efforts in deciding cases of Boko Haram suspects see generally the following, Judge threatens to discharge 24 Boko Haram suspects See The Nigerian available at http://www.gistmania.com/talk/topic,114736.0.html (accessed 18 May 2015); 'Absence of Prosecution Witness Stalls Trial of Suspected Killers of Boko Haram Leader' available at http://www.thenigerianvoice.com/news/140160/1/absence-of-prosecution-witness-stalls-trial-of-sus.html (accessed 18 May 2015); 'Escape of Boko Haram Suspects: Prosecutor, Defense Counsel Close Cases' available at http://www.nigerianbestforum.com/blog/escape-of-boko-haram-suspects-prosecutor-defense-counsel-close-cases/ (accessed 18 May 2015).

[74] 'The case against Aminu Sadiq Ogwuche was struck out for lack of diligent prosecution.' See generally Court Strikes Out Charges Against Nyanya Bomb Blast Mastermind available at http://www.thisdaylive.com/articles/court-strikes-out-charges-against-nyanya-bomb-blast-mastermind/194955/ (accessed 19 May 2015); 'Nyanya Bomb Blast Mastemind Demands N100M Compensation from FG' available at http://www.nigerianmonitor.com/2014/12/05/nyanya-bomb-blast-mastermind-demands-n100m-compensation-from-fg/ (accessed 19 May 2015).

[75] 'Judge threatened to dismiss terrorism case against Ndume.' Available at http://www.punchng.com/news/judge-threatens-to-dismiss-terrorism-case-against-ndume/ (accessed 19 May 2015); 'Ex-Gov Sheriff, accused of sponsoring *Boko Haram*, ready to face justice.' Available at http://www.premiumtimesng.com/news/headlines/167706-ex-gov-sheriff-accused-of-sponsoring-boko-haram-ready-to-face-justice.html (accessed 19 May 2015).

[76] Terrorism Prevention Amendment Act (2013).

forms of terrorist activities. The responsibilities placed on the ONSA include the following[77]:

(a) provide support to all relevant security, intelligence, law enforcement agencies and military services to prevent and combat acts of terrorism in Nigeria;
(b) ensure the effective formulation and implementation of a comprehensive counterterrorism strategy for Nigeria;
(c) build capacity for the effective discharge of the functions of all relevant security, intelligence, law enforcement and military services under this Act or any other law on terrorism in Nigeria; and
(d) do such other acts or things that are necessary for the effective performance of the functions of the relevant security and enforcement agencies under this Act.

A perusal of the core functions mentioned above reveals several shortcomings if the activities of *Boko Haram* is to be contained.[78] However, in our view, section 1A (d) of the Act could assist Nigeria in curbing the menace, especially as it relates to the Nigerian child. The proposition for reliance on non-legal approach does not remove the fact that atrocities committed by insurgents are violations of fundamental human rights and constitute heinous crimes but rather brings to the fore the inadequacy of the law to protect the rights of Nigerians and particularly the Nigerian child.[79] To this end, the clause 'such other acts or things that are necessary for effective performance' may be given a broad interpretation to include the proposed socio-legal perspective. We now turn to the proposed socio-legal approach.

16.5 Socio-Legal Approach to Curbing the Boko Haram Menace

Like most conflicts, the first assumption is that poor governance is the genesis of the conflict. The absence of good governance, which includes but is not limited to the absence of the rule of law, development, equality and improved standard of living, is sufficient to stir a struggle or quest for self-determination. With particular reference to the *Boko Haram* crisis in Nigeria, it is assumed that the lack of adequate quality education in northern Nigeria has contributed to the crisis. Given the already huge disparity between the North and the South in the number of children able to access basic education, it is clear that the outbreak of the present *Boko Haram* crisis was inevitable. This assumption is based on the fact that a large number of youths who were unable to access education were motivated to fight against the state.[80]

[77] Section 1A of the Terrorism Prevention Act 2013.

[78] See generally David (2013).

[79] For detailed discuss on the insurgency. Its violation of human rights and inability of the law see generally Ladan (2012).

[80] Olaposi (2014), p. 8.

Gbadamosi opines that the activities of *Boko Haram* are traceable to the neglect of the majority of northern youths who were unable to access education.[81] This situation further reinforces the effect of lack of good governance.

According to Ciakudia, the outbreak of violence is always tied to the absence of good governance.[82] The absence of good governance in most circumstances plays out when a minority group (whether religious, ethnic or otherwise) feels neglected and marginalised.[83] Consequently, the need to ensure a reorientation of the perceived victims of non-violent injustices is an important means of attempting to drive a positive resolution of the *Boko Haram* menace.

Another measure that could be effective in curbing the crisis is a clarification of conflict situations. The question would then be to examine the basis and philosophies that inform *Boko Haram's* activities and distinguish them from other militia groups that have existed in Nigeria prior. Rummel advances this important socio-legal approach by arguing that there is a need to, among other approaches, endeavour to (i) 'uncover the underlying or hidden goals and beliefs' and (ii) 'uncover the hidden, perhaps even unconscious, beliefs and values'.[84]

In relying on the above proposition, it is important that the socio-religious and ideological undercurrents of the insurgency be examined and defined and a conscious effort made to advance a possible overriding interest geared towards resolving the challenges. For instance, according to Tomasveski, education among other options would be acceptable and adaptable strategies.[85] In that respect, it would be important to examine the extent to which western values, including the curriculum of western education, is at variance with the predominant Islamic beliefs of the peoples of northern Nigeria.

Aside from the position of Rummel, Kelven suggests that an equitable sharing approach will aid the stability of society. Kelven stresses the need to ensure that in the equitable sharing of in any society, each group or individual should as of necessity benefit from the good or bad that the society presents.[86] This position is all important as it will ensure that the state understands the basic demands of every group in a country and thus ensure an equitable satisfaction of their wants and needs.

The views echoed by Gbadamosi bring to the fore the poor dialectical materialistic approach in ensuring a cohesive society in the education sector in Nigeria. The dialectical approach seeks to ensure that societal goods are evenly spread to benefit everyone. It is the perception of the class disparity between individuals who accessed education and the ones who failed to access education that generates a violent response. According to Friedman, dialectics bring to the fore 'contradictions within a structure; for example, between classes, or more generally, between systematically

[81] Olaposi (2014), p. 10.

[82] Ciakudia (2010).

[83] See generally, Yamamoto (1997), p. 495.

[84] Rummel (1975).

[85] Tomasevski (2005), p. 30.

[86] See generally Kleven (2014).

self-contradictory aspects of a social relation'.[87] Consequently, the dialectical approach will enhance the bridging of the gap in access and quality of education. This is advanced because quality education of a child will ensure effective and positive contribution towards the building of state institutions.

It is therefore viewed that for the dialectical materialistic approach to be adopted, there is the need to ensure full participation of the society in every process. If this is achieved, education policies will be adaptable and acceptable in eliminating all forms of suspicions and rejection, as presently done by the *Boko Haram* sect.[88] It is therefore paramount that a high level of consultation be embarked upon to try and align curriculum with the religious beliefs of the progenitors of the dreadful *Boko Haram* insurgents. Analysing the neglect of the material dialectic aspect of the activities of *Boko Haram*, Alafuro and Uranta, opined:

> the state's indifference to the contradictions of social materialism is generating constant centrifugal forces against its autonomy. It anchors on a very basic fundamental hypothesis that Boko Haram is symptomatic of not only a weak state, but also a desperate and marginalized class whose only source of drawing the state's attention is through organized violence.[89]

The above, therefore, reiterates the need for the government to stand firm in its resolve to ensure that education as a 'material' is effectively disseminated to all regions of Nigeria. This is premised on the ground that if the aspirations as contained in the CRA and UBE Act are effectively implemented, it will contribute to the reduction of violent agitations. Embracing this approach will also ensure the structural efficiency and effectiveness[90] of various institutions saddled with the responsibility of ensuring efficiency in all spheres of the Nigerian state.

As highlighted before now, the lack of good governance and delivery of social amenities like education, health and the eradication of poverty contributes immensely to the activities that lead to violence. It is also noted that a state is comprised of several structures and institutions that are put in place to ensure the delivery of social goods and, in the present case, the achievement of the right to education for the Nigerian child as espoused in the various national and international legal and policy frameworks, including the Millennium Development Goals (MDGs). However, for structural functionalism approach to be effective in eradicating the *Boko Haram* insurgency, all the structures in Nigeria will need to function optimally.[91] A combination of the material dialectics and the structural functionalist approach will ensure that each ethnic nationality in Nigeria plays a substantive role

---

[87] Friedman (1974), p. 447.

[88] Fafunwa (1975).

[89] Alafuro and Uranta (2014), p. 528.

[90] For a detailed discuss of the structural functionalist approach, see Achu et al. (2012).

[91] The proposition here is that all government ministries and departments must delivered effective to help increase the standard of living of individuals especially in the health, education and security sectors.

in all structures of the Nigerian nation. This will require equal development opportunities and exposure to education.[92]

Another important socio-legal paradigm that could be useful in curbing the activities of *Boko Haram* is the hospitality theory.[93] The term 'hospitality' is used in this regard to highlight the friendly nature of all major religions in Nigeria. It is accepted that the two major religions in Nigeria—Islam and Christianity—as well as traditional religions, have embedded in them basic principles of love, peace and harmonious coexistence. With the proper education of the child and ultimately the society, it is likely that the values of hospitality of the different religions could be used to engineer sustainable peace more than what military might could achieve. The reliance on sociolegal approach, as proposed in this paper, premised on the fact that conflicts are generally a clash of values, interests, perspectives, perceptions and expectations. To effectively resolve a conflict, it is only proper that the actual players are heard and the interests and expectations that are represented are considered. The efficacy of the legal approach is debatable as it has been argued that[94]

> No stand-alone strategy, tactic or technique is equally sufficient to combat and outwit the constantly improving manoeuvres of terrorists. In order to record more success in the fight against terrorism, a combination of anti-terrorism, counter-terrorism and other measures are required.

The advantage that a sociolegal response has over a legal approach in the quest to curb *Boko Haram* is further hinged on the fact that the sociological approach views conflicts beyond being just social menaces; it sees conflicts as interactions between individual players (persons) in the society who are both part and essential to the community's progress. Thus, based on this, the position of Rummel and Kleven and other social approaches discussed above remain important theories in resolving the *Boko Haram* challenge in Nigeria. Aside from the positions already canvassed above, other viable sociological approaches that could be relied upon in curbing the *Boko Haram* challenge include but are not limited to restorative justice theory[95] and peacemaking theory.[96] A clash such as the one between *Boko Haram*

---

[92] The inference made here is to the effect that if access to education is enhance in all regions of Nigeria, the functioning of all institutions will be optimal devoid of any suspicions by any ethnic group. In addition, it will greatly reduce the issue of marginalisation that continues to rear its head in various social conflicts in Nigeria.

[93] This is described as a hospitality approach that is existent in all religions and can actually be engaged in resolving religious conflicts. See generally, Akanji (2011).

[94] Ekundayo (2012).

[95] This involves rehabilitating terrorist offenders, after they have been convicted and reconciling them with the community and country which they once sought to destroy. This may also demand the establishment of a body of trained experts who shall handle this process. This reconciliation process may also demand that these rehabilitated offenders are trained as activists of peace and non-violence (apologising also to the victims of their offence). See generally Ted (2003).

[96] This demands taking positive steps to resolve an already existing dispute. This would involve such steps such as appointing an agreed arbiter, narrowing the areas of dispute, agreeing on the areas of agreement, focus on compromise, consider the propriety of each party's interest, and maintain equality of power and influence, resisting aggression and intimidation. See, generally, Rummel (1981).

and the Nigerian government could be resolved through the application of one of the sociological conflict resolution theories, consecutively or as hybrids.

16.6 Conclusions

From the foregoing, it is concluded that there is sufficient legal regime to protect the interest of the Nigerian child. Notwithstanding Nigeria's history of ethno-religious conflicts, the rise of *Boko Haram* is particularly worrisome. It is important that the Nigerian political class embrace good governance and ensure that all indices of good governance are followed in Nigeria. We have argued that it is imperative to bridge the poverty gap by ensuring that the dividends of good governance trickle down to the masses. Hopefully, this will initiate an equitable distribution of wealth and drive a more harmonious coexistence in society. To achieve this, it is necessary to ensure adequate access to education and equal opportunities for all.

Furthermore, the law as it stands is not sufficient in resolving the *Boko Haram* conflict, especially as it affects the Nigerian child. To this end, the need to explore other socio-legal paradigms becomes paramount. In this paper, we have identified two major socio-legal approaches as possible premises for reappraising the situation. The structural functionalism and material dialectic offer a socio-legal approach to the overreliance on the law in ensuring that the activities of *Boko Haram* are curbed. This is possible, for instance, if education is treated as material dialectic with the expected impact on the structures of governance in Nigeria bringing about good governance. It is our belief that these two options, alongside the hospitality approach and equitable sharing, would aid the resolution of the current security crisis in the northeast of Nigeria. In addition, there is a need to address the seeming religious suspicion and advance an all-inclusive approach in enhancing the protection of the rights of the Nigerian child in the face of the *Boko Haram* insurgence.

16.7 Recommendations

With the foregoing propositions, this paper suggests that the reliance on the use of force may only provide a temporary palliative, but a cure is needful by identifying the root causes and addressing the same objectively. To achieve this, therefore, it is recommended that the government at both federal and state levels must show political will in implementing the laws and policies formulated to curb the activities of *Boko Haram* and other militia groups; this should be done by adopting a socio-legal post-mortem of the present crisis. In addition, there is the need to set up a think-tank to examine the grievances of various militia groups and, in this respect, the *Boko Haram* sect with a view to finding the best means possible to averting similar crises in Nigeria in the future.

Finally, there is the need for government to ensure that education programmes are revamped at all levels in order to bring sound, quality and functional education to the Nigerian child.

References

A bill proposed by Amadi Gary Kelechi & Okpara Nnenna Joy. Available at http://nials-nigeria.org/proposed-bill/ENFORCEMENTOFEDUCATIONOFCHILDRENANDYOUNGPERSONS BILL.pdf. Accessed 20 Feb 2015

Achu AA et al (2012) Curbing multi-dimension violence in Nigeria society: causes, solutions and methods of solving this trend. http://reference.sabinet.co.za/webx/access/electronic_journals/sl_jeteraps/sl_jeteraps_v3_n5_a3.pdf. Accessed 8 Mar 2015

Adesola F (2007) National security, democratization and the menace of ethnic militias in Nigeria. West Afr Rev 11. http://www.westafricareview.com/issue11/adesola.html. Accessed 23 Feb 2015

Akanji AI (2011) Towards a theology of conflict transformation: a study of religious conflict in contemporary Nigerian society. https://www.era.lib.ed.ac.uk/bitstream/handle/1842/5464/Akanji2011.pdf;jsessionid=8D22445033CDDB6DD74C02B96EEB6F18?sequence=1. Accessed 24 Feb 2015

Alafuro E, Uranta IB (2014) Political economy of violence: interpreting the Nigerian *Boko Haram*. Mediterr J Soc Sci 5(10):528

Alanamu AS, Muhammed AY, Adeoye MN (2006) Education: a panacea for religious violence in Nigeria. In: Oyekanmi FAD, Nwabueze N (eds) Education and regeneration of traditional values in Nigeria. Available at https://www.unilorin.edu.ng/publications/muhammeday/Edu%20&%20Religion.pdf. Accessed 23 Feb 2015

Albert IO (1999) Community conflict in Nigeria: management, resolution and transformation. Spectrum, Ibadan

Amnesty International (2008) Nigeria: pragmatic policing through extra-judicial executions and torture. Amnesty International Report (2008-05-16). AI Index AFR 44/006/2008

British Council Nigeria (2012) Gender in Nigeria report: improving the lives of girls and women in Nigeria, actions issues policies, 2nd edn. British Council, Nigeria. Available at http://www.unicef.org/nigeria/children_1937.html. Accessed 20 Jan 2015

Child Rights Act Cap C50, Laws of the Federation of Nigeria, 2011

Child Rights Convention 1989

Ciakudia J (2010) Socio-legal international judicial responses to conflict: the case of the International Criminal Court and the Democratic Republic of Congo. Available at http://julienciakudia.over-blog.org/article-socio-legal-international-judicial-responses-to-conflict-62753442.html. Accessed 22 Feb 2015

Compulsory, Free Universal Basic Education Act, Cap C52, Laws of the Federation of Nigeria, 2011

Constitution of the Federal Republic of Nigeria, 1999

Convention on the Rights of the Child (CRC), 1989

Daily Trust (2002-08-20) 16

David JO (2013) The root causes of terrorism: an appraisal of the socio-economic determinants of *Boko Haram* terrorism in Nigeria. Unpublished MA dissertation, School of Social Sciences, University of KwaZulu-Natal. Available at http://researchspace.ukzn.ac.za/xmlui/bitstream/handle/10413/10628/David_James_Ojochenemi_2013.pdf?sequence=1. Accessed 23 Feb 2015

Deci EL, Ryan RM (2002) Overview of self-determination theory: an organismic dialectical perspective. In: Handbook of self-determination research, pp 3–33

Diamond L (1987) Ethnicity and ethnic conflict. J Mod Afr Stud 25(2):117–128

Dudley B (1973) Instability and political order. Ibadan University Press, Ibadan
ECW/CCJ/APP/12/07
Egbewole WO, Onuora-Oguno AC (2013) Social conflicts in Nigeria: non justiciability of economic and social cultural rights as a catalyst? Delivered at the international conference of Society for Peace Studies and Practice, Ado-Ekiti, 25–27 March 2013
Egbewole WO, Onuora-Oguno AC (2014) Impunity and justice in Nigeria: weeping for the innocent, extra judicial killings on the rise? Univ Benin Law J 15(1):63–77
Ekundayo V (2012) Nigerian terrorism act: a right step forward. Available at http://www.punchng.com/opinion/nigerian-terrorism-act-a-right-step-forward/. Accessed 15 Mar 2015
Fafunwa AB (1975) History of education in Nigeria. Unwin, London
Friedman J (1974) Marxism, structuralism and vulgar materialism. Cambridge University Press, Cambridge
Hansungule M, Onuora-Oguno AC (2013) African perspective of education: a catalyst for the desired Africa of tomorrow? Delivered at conference on 'Finding solutions to Africa's Development', Thabo Mbeki Advanced Leadership Institute, South Africa, 22–23 August 2013
Heyns CH (2006) A struggle approach to human rights. In: Heyns C, Stefiszyn K (eds) Human rights, peace and justice in Africa: a reader
High-Level International Round Table on Literacy, UNESCO, Paris, 6–7 September 2012, "National Literacy Action Plan for 2012–2015, Nigeria"
Ikelegbe A (2001) The perverse manifestation of civil society: evidence from Nigeria. J Mod Afr Stud 39(1):145
Imobighe TA (2003) Ethnicity and ethnic conflicts in Nigeria: an overview. In: Imobighe TA (ed) Civil society and ethnic conflicts management in Nigeria. Spectrum, Ibadan, pp 14–15
International Covenant on Civil and Political Rights (ICCPR), 1966
International Covenant on Economic Social and Cultural Rights (ICESCR), 1966
Jega AM (2002) Tackling ethno-religious conflicts in Nigeria. Niger Soc Sci 35–39
Judge threatens to discharge 24 Boko Haram suspects. Available at http://www.gistmania.com/talk/topic,114736.0.html. Accessed 18 May 2015
Katangese Peoples' Congress v Zaire 2000 AHRLR 72 (ACHPR 1995)
Kleven T (2014) Equitable sharing, distributing the benefits and detriments of democratic society. Lexington Books
Ladan MT (2007) The Child Rights Act, 2003 and the challenges of its adoption by state governments in the 19 northern states. Available at http://gysd-ng.org/pdf/Child_right_act_and_the_challenges_of_its_adoption_in_19_northern_states.doc. Accessed 6 Mar 2015
Ladan MT (2012) Diagnostic review of insurgency in Nigeria: the legal dimension. https://doi.org/10.2139/ssrn.2336171. Accessed 22 Feb 2015
Madu AY, Ibrahim G (2013) Ethno-religious conflict in Taraba State and its implications on socio-economic, political and educational development of youths. Int J Soc Sci Humanit Rev 4(3):149–155
Maier K (2000) This house has fallen: Nigeria in crisis. Penguin Books, London
McCorquodale R (1994) Self-determination: a human rights approach. Int Comp Law Q 43(04):857–885
Muslim/Christian cooperation for conflict management and prevention. Available at http://carefronting.org/48-2/. Accessed 23 Feb 2015
National Bureau of Statistics, Annual Abstract of Statistics, 2011
Nigerian Monitor (2014) Nyanya bomb blast mastermind demands N100M compensation from FG. Available at http://www.nigerianmonitor.com/2014/12/05/nyanya-bomb-blast-mastermind-demands-n100m-compensation-from-fg/. Accessed 19 May 2015
Nmoma V (1995) Ethnic conflict, constitutional engineering and democracy in Nigeria. In: Glickman H (ed) Ethnic conflict and democratization in Africa. The African Studies Association Press, Atlanta
Nwaoga C, Nche G, Olihe A (2014) The national conference, ethno-religious pluralism and the challenge of national unity in Nigeria. Glob J Arts Humanit Soc Sci 2(3):44

Olamilekan AA (2014) A perusal analyses on Boko Haram crisis in Northern Nigeria and its implication on educational psychology of school children and teachers. J Educ Hum Dev 3(2):361–380
Olaposi GM (2014) Understanding Boko Haram crisis in Nigeria. Int Aff Global Strat 27:8–15
Omorogbe SK, Omohan ME (2005) Causes and management of ethno-religious conflicts: the Nigeria experience. In: Yakubu AM et al (eds) Crisis and conflict management in Nigeria since 1980, vol 2. Baraka Press and Publishers Ltd, Kaduna, p 557
Pinkney R (2003) Democracy in the third world, 2nd edn
Premium Times (2014) Ex-Gov Sheriff, accused of sponsoring *Boko Haram*, ready to face justice. Available at http://www.premiumtimesng.com/news/headlines/167706-ex-gov-sheriff-accused-of-sponsoring-boko-haram-ready-to-face-justice.html. Accessed 19 May 2015
Punch Newspaper. Judge threatens to dismiss terrorism case against Ndume. Available at http://www.punchng.com/news/judge-threatens-to-dismiss-terrorism-case-against-ndume/. Accessed 19 May 2015
Rahim MA (2002) Toward a theory of managing organizational conflict. Int J Conflict Manag 26
Rummel RJ (1975) Understanding conflict and war: the just peace. Available at https://www.hawaii.edu/powerkills/TJP.CHAP10.HTM. Accessed 22 Feb 2015
Rummel RJ (1981) Understanding war. Vol 5. The just peace. Chapter 10: principles of conflict resolution. Available at https://www.hawaii.edu/powerkills/TJP.CHAP10.HTM. Accessed 3 June 2015
Salawu B (2010) Ethno-religious conflicts in Nigeria: causal analysis and proposals for new management strategies. Eur J Soc Sci 13(3):345
Ted W (2003) In pursuit of paradigm: a theory of restorative justice. Available at http://www.iirp.edu/article_detail.php?article_id=NDI0. Accessed 3 June 2015
The Nigerian Voice (2014) Absence of prosecution witness stalls trial of suspected killers of Boko Haram leader. Available at http://www.thenigerianvoice.com/news/140160/1/absence-of-prosecution-witness-stalls-trial-of-sus.html. Accessed 18 May 2015; 'Escape of Boko Haram Suspects: Prosecutor, Defense Counsel Close Cases'. Available at http://www.nigerianbest-forum.com/blog/escape-of-boko-haram-suspects-prosecutor-defense-counsel-close-cases/. Accessed 18 May 2015
ThisDay (2014) Court strikes out charges against Nyanya bomb blast mastermind. Available at http://www.thisdaylive.com/articles/court-strikes-out-charges-against-nyanya-bomb-blast-mastermind/194955/. Accessed 19 May 2015
Thornberry P (1989) Self-determination, minorities, human rights: a review of international instruments. Int Comp Law Q 38(04):867–889
Tomasevski K (2005) Globalizing what: education as a human right or as a traded service? Indiana J Global Leg Stud 12(1):30
UNESCO statistics on out of school children. Available at http://www.uis.unesco.org/Education/Pages/out-of-school-children.aspx. Accessed 25 Feb 2015; http://www.unicef.org/nigeria/children_1937.html. Accessed 25 Feb 2015
UNICEF, Child Rights Act promulgated into law in twenty-three states. Available at www.unicef.org/wcaro/WCARO_Nigeria_Factsheets_CRA.pdf. Accessed 18 Nov 2014
Universal Declaration of Human Rights, United Nations General Assembly Resolution 217A, U.N.G.A. 3rd Session, U.N. Doc. A/RES/3/217A (1948) of 10 December 1948
Wellbeing Foundation, State of the CRC Ratification Process in Nigeria: Are the Children Protected Yet?. Available at http://www.wbfafrica.org/press-releases/archive/112-an-article-state-of-the-crc-ratification-process-in-nigeria-are-the-children-protected-yet.html. Accessed 8 Mar 2015
Werlin HH (2003) Poor nations, rich nations: a theory of governance. Publ Admin Rev 63:329
Yamamoto EK (1997) Conflict and complicity: justice among communities of color. Harv Latino Law Rev 2:495
Zenn J (2014) Boko Haram and the kidnapping of Chibok school girls. Available at https://www.ctc.usma.edu/posts/boko-haram-and-the-kidnapping-of-the-chibok-schoolgirls. Accessed 23 Feb 2015

Chapter 17
After Dusk They Came: International Responsibility of States in Relation to Human Rights Violations Committed by Rebel Groups

Marek Jan Wasiński

17.1 Introduction

It was around midnight, 14 April 2014, when the students of Government Secondary School in Chibok, Borno State, Nigeria, heard gunshots some kilometres away. Soon after, a group of men entered the compound. An anonymous witness has described the subsequent events in the following way:

> Two men told us we should not worry, we should not run. They said they had come to save us from what is happening inside the town, that they are policemen. We did not know that they were from Boko Haram. The rest of the men came and started shouting 'Allahu Akbar' and at that moment we realized, they were Boko Haram. We were told to be quiet. One of them told us that the horrible things we heard happening elsewhere, like burning houses, killing people, killing students, kidnapping people, would happen to us now. We all started crying and he told us to shut up.[1]

On the next morning, press agencies worldwide announced that approximately 270 girls had been abducted by members of an organisation, which soon after—on 22 May 2014—was to be listed by the United Nations Security Council (UN SC) as a terrorist and military group associated with Al-Qaida.[2] At the time of writing this chapter, 9 months since the above-mentioned incident, some girls have been reunited with their families. Most of them, however, still remain in captivity.

[1] Human Rights Watch (2014).

[2] Listed as Jama'atu Ahlis Sunna Lidda'Awati Wal-Jihad (Boko Haram) (QE.B.138.14). The list has been established and is maintained by the Al-Qaida Sanctions Committee with respect to individuals, groups, undertakings and other entities associated with Al-Qaida. UN. 2015. Security Council Committee pursuant to resolutions1267 (1999) and 1989 (2011) concerning Al-Qaida and associated individuals and entities. http://www.un.org/sc/committees/1267/aq_sanctions_list.shtml. Accessed 11 June 2015.

M. J. Wasiński (✉)
Department of Public International Law and International Relations, University of Łódź, Łódź, Poland

J.-M. Iyi, H. Strydom (eds.), *Boko Haram and International Law*,
https://doi.org/10.1007/978-3-319-74957-0_17

Only 3 months since the dramatic events that took place in Nigeria, in the morning of 17 July 2014, Malaysia Airlines Boeing 777-2H6ER operating as flight MH17 departed from Amsterdam Schiphol Airport on a scheduled passenger flight to Kuala Lumpur International Airport in Malaysia. The plane, which was carrying 283 passengers and 15 crew members, crashed near Hrabove, Eastern Ukraine. There were no survivors. Preliminary report published by the Dutch Safety Board pointed out that

> [t]he damage observed in the forward section of the aircraft appears to indicate that the aircraft was penetrated by a large number of high-energy objects from outside the aircraft. It is likely that this damage resulted in a loss of structural integrity of the aircraft, leading to an in-flight brake up.[3]

The aircraft was downed as a result of an act of violence against the safety of international aviation,[4] but it still remains unclear who launched those 'high energy objects'. Thus, it may be argued that the ambiguity makes the legal analysis of the case premature. However, considering the overwhelming difficulties in revealing the truth, some tentative versions of events are necessary if the situation is to be discussed at all. In particular, unconfirmed opinions commonly articulated in the aftermath of the incident suggested that the aircraft had probably been brought down by a missile fired by pro-Russian separatists operating on Ukrainian territory near Donetsk.[5] Adopting this version of events, one can observe some striking analogies between the events in Chibok and Donetsk (discussed below), which justifies the decision to employ them as anchoring points for a comparative analysis. Therefore, without prejudice to any further possible fact-finding and decisions of international bodies concerning the Ukrainian case, it is *assumed* in the following study that the above-mentioned allegation is sound and verified. At the same time, the resulting conclusions cover only the one version of events.

17.2 Nigerian Abduction and Ukrainian Plane Downing: Is There Anything to Compare?

To all appearances, the above-mentioned cases do not seem to be comparable in many aspects as they are rooted in different socio-political contexts and ostensibly engage diverse primary rules of public international law. Abduction by a terrorist group is, at best, a very distant cousin of a plane downing perpetrated by insurgents. Nonetheless, they do have a lot in common.

First of all, various human rights obligations remain relevant to both cases. In particular, the first one may be prima facie analysed through the prism of duties encapsulated in at least six provisions of the African Charter of Human and Peoples'

---

[3] Dutch Safety Board (2014), pp. 11, 30.

[4] UN SC Resolution of 21 July 2014. S/RES/2166 (2014).

[5] Gude and Schmid (2014), Rushe and Walker (2014) and Tharoor (2014).

Rights (African Charter)[6]: Article 1 (General Obligation to Give Effect to Human Rights), Article 5 (Prohibition of Torture and Cruel, Inhuman and Degrading Treatment), Article 6 (Right to Personal Liberty and Protection from Arbitrary Arrest), Article 8 (Right to Freedom of Conscience), Article 18 (Protection of Family and Vulnerable Groups), Article 19 (Right of All Peoples to Equality and Rights).The second case principally involves the provisions of Article 2 (Right to Life) of the European Convention for the Protection of Human Rights and Fundamental Freedoms (European Convention).[7]

The above-mentioned conclusion in itself, quite evidently, barely justifies making both cases amenable to a joint study. However, there is yet another commonality to be found in the circumstances concerning each of those acts of private entities. Its existence can be determined by the five following factors: (a) the acts of violence were committed on the territories of sovereign states (Nigeria and Ukraine respectively); (b) the acts of violence were allegedly committed by private actors, namely by members of insurgent movements (Boko Haram and pro-Russian separatists), herein understood as organised factions aimed at the overthrowing of a constituted government through the use of subversion and armed conflict; (c) there is no proof indicating that both acts of violence were instructed, directed or controlled by either Nigeria or Ukraine; (d) there is no confirmed evidence that any form of military, financial, logistic or technical support was provided by respective states to relevant insurgent movements[8]; (e) effective governmental control exercised by the respective states over the relevant parts of their territories, where the incidents took place, was either significantly weakened (Nigeria) or repealed by insurgent groups (Ukraine). In particular, Boko Haram seized the town of Gwoza, Borno State (about two-hour drive from Chibok), only in August 2014—it was the first time it has taken control of a substantial urban area. In October 2014, Boko Haram, being in control of that major town and of more than 50,000 people, declared the creation of a 'caliphate'.[9] In fact, *before* July 2014 and the subsequent capture of Damboa city, there was no official report proclaiming Boko Haram as exercising control over a defined territory by resorting to, for example, setting up roadblocks and checkpoints.[10] However, the volume, scale and widespread character of persecution[11] in the first half of 2014 (with an appalling toll of more than 2000 Nigerians killed in

---

[6] Banjul. 27 June 1981.

[7] Rome, 4 November 1950.

[8] Putting aside unverified claims concerning alleged assistance provided by the Russian Federation for the pro-Russian separatists, see Letter dated 7 November 2014 from the Permanent Representative of Ukraine to the UN addressed to the President of the SC, S/2014/798.

[9] Letter dated 27 October 2014 from the Chair of the SC Committee pursuant to resolutions 1267 (1999) and 1989 (2011) concerning Al-Qaida and associated individuals and entities addressed to the President of the SC, S/2014/770, paras. 5, 25.

[10] European Parliament (Directorate General for External Policies), Insecurity in Context. The Rise of Boko Haram in Nigeria, July 2014, DG EXPO/B/PolDep/Note/2014_13, PE 536.393, p. 9.

[11] Human Rights Council, Written statement submitted by Jubilee Campaign, a nongovernmental organization in special consultative status, 7 March 2014, A/HRC/25/NGO/184.

the campaign and 650,000 displaced[12]) cast serious doubts on the ability of the Nigerian government to execute full effective control over Borno State in April 2014, when the abductions took place. In the second case, the crash site was under the control of the pro-Russian separatist groups that obstructed the international investigation into the crash of the Malaysia Airlines flight MH17 despite an order issued by the President of Ukraine to implement a 40-kilometre ceasefire zone.[13]

The common features shared by those two tragic events reveal a more general problem that seems underestimated in the present context. Namely, while both states involved appear to be suffering from the insurgents' actions, it is still perfectly possible to ask a tricky question of a kind. Is Nigeria and Ukraine not responsible under international law on account of what happened to the girls from Chibok Secondary School and the passengers of MH17 respectively? The following analysis constitutes an attempt to tackle this issue. It is aimed at sketching the limits of international responsibility of states for breaches of selected human rights treaties with respect to acts of insurgent groups in circumstances delineated by the five above-mentioned parameters.

The said task is going to be accomplished in three stages. Firstly, the article briefly recapitulates the basic tenets of general international law on the responsibility of states in relation to acts of private entities. Secondly, the survey of international human rights treaties systems is undertaken to uncover any possible deviations from the 'standard' approach. Finally, the problem is going to be tackled from its bottom-line perspective to explain the possible consequences for both the victims and the states involved.

17.3 When Pilate Tries to Wash His Hands: Responsibility of States in Relation to Acts of Private Entities Under General International Law

17.3.1 Insurgents Are Not State Organs

In a nutshell, the concept of responsibility of states for internationally wrongful acts is quite obvious. A breach of international law results in certain consequences for the state that had committed the violation. Namely, it brings about the obligation of cessation when the breach is extended in time[14] and the obligation of

[12] See note 9, para. 25.

[13] Office of the UN High Commissioner for Human Rights, Report on the human rights situation in Ukraine 17 August 2014, para. 8.

[14] France-New Zealand Arbitration Tribunal, Case concerning the difference between New Zealand and France as for the interpretation or application of two agreements concluded on 9 July 1986 between the two States and which related to the problems arising from the Rainbow Warrior affair, Award of 30 April 1990, United Nations Reports of International Arbitral Awards (UNRIAA), Vol. XX, p. 270.

non-repetition[15]—to mention only two fundamental duties involved. The state that is in breach should be determined as a result of an intellectual process of attribution. Within this process, a fundamental question whether a given conduct causing the infringement may be regarded as a conduct of the state must be answered. The problems with attribution are understandably caused by the obvious fact that states are abstract entities of a kind. Formed as special amalgamation of territory, population, government and independence, they can act only through human beings. On the other hand, every human being is as a rule a private actor and as such is not bound by most international law norms. Therefore, private conduct may constitute a breach of the state's obligation primarily if a private person acts *qua* state, i.e. in the capacity of state organs.[16] Basically, two situations are relevant here: (a) where a private person possesses that status in accordance with the internal law of the state (*de iure* organ)[17] or (b) cases in which a private person does not have the legal status of a state organ but exercises elements of sovereign authority or remains under such strict control of the state that it must be treated as state body for the purposes of attribution (de facto organ).[18] The latter issue, especially relevant in the discussed context of international responsibility of the state for acts of insurgents, was elaborated by the International Court of Justice (ICJ) in the *Military and Paramilitary Activities in and Against Nicaragua Case*.[19] Its famous conclusion was that because of the lack of clear evidence of total dependence of the *contras* on United States aid, the acts of the rebels could not be treated as the acts of the United States. Thus,

[15] International Court of Justice (ICJ), La Grand (Germany v. United States of America), Judgment of 27 June 2001, ICJ Reports 2001, p. 485, para. 48.

[16] Articles on the Responsibility of States for Internationally Wrongful Acts (ARS), International Law Commission Report, A/56/10, Yearbook of the International Law Commission, 2001, vol. II, Part Two. Pursuant to Article 4 ARS: 'The conduct of any State organ shall be considered an act of that State under international law, whether the organ exercises legislative, executive, judicial or any other functions, whatever position it holds in the organization of the State, and whatever its character as an organ of the central Government or of a territorial unit of the State'. Customary character of this norm was confirmed by the ICJ in Application of the Convention on the Prevention and Punishment of the Crime of Genocide Case (Genocide Convention Case, Bosnia and Herzegovina v. Serbia and Montenegro), Judgment of 26 February 2007, ICJ Reports 2007, para. 385.

[17] See Salvador-USA Arbitration Tribunal, Claim of the Salvador Commercial Company ('El Triunfo Company'), Award of 8 May 1902, RIAA, Vol. XV, p. 477.

[18] ICJ, Armed Activities on the Territory of the Congo (Democratic Republic of the Congo v Uganda), Judgment of 19 December 2005, ICJ Reports 2005, para.160; Genocide Convention Case, see note 16, paras. 385–395. For antecedents see USA-Mexico Arbitration Tribunal, Charles S. Stephens and Bowman Stephens (U.S.A.) v. United Mexican States, Award of 15 July 1927, RIAA, Volume IV, pp. 265–268—on responsibility of state for auxiliary forces acts. See also Articles 5–8 ARS. While some provisions of ARS are widely perceived as codification of responsibility of states under international law, the ICJ in the abovementioned Genocide Convention Case refrained from deciding whether Articles 5–7 ARS reflect customary international law or not, para. 414.

[19] ICJ, Military and Paramilitary Activities in and against Nicaragua (Nicaragua v. United States of America), Merits, Judgment of 27 June 1986, ICJ Reports 1986, paras. 109–115; see also similar pronouncements by ICJ in the Genocide Convention Case, note 16, para. 399, Armed Activities Case, note 18, para. 160.

taking into consideration that in both cases, which have been chosen as the anchor point for the present examination, there is nothing to suggest either any form of effective and direct control or support or cooperation between the territorial states and the insurgent groups (needless to say, which are not state organs at all), the attribution attempts are definitely unsound and fail. It means that one cannot say that either Ukraine downed the plane or that Nigeria abducted the girls from Chibok School. Consequently, the above-mentioned states are not responsible *for* the respective acts of the rebels.

17.3.2 But Their Acts May Still Involve State Responsibility

Nevertheless, even if a private conduct does not qualify for attribution under the aforementioned rules, there is still the possibility of state responsibility being involved *in relation* to the acts of private entities. That is to say, there is a rich variety of primary norms of international law (as opposed to secondary norms governing results of non-compliance therewith) establishing a state's obligation to prevent certain results irrespective of whether such results appear as consequences of a state's act or a private entity's behaviour. For example, the ICJ, in its very first decision in the contentious *Corfu Channel* case, confirmed that every state is obliged under a 'general and well recognized [principle] [...] not to allow knowingly its territory to be used for acts contrary to the rights of other States'.[20] More specifically, the Vienna Convention on Diplomatic Relations[21] establishes a series of obligations for a receiving state to protect the envoys and premises of a sending state against violations regardless of their source.[22] Another example is Article 194.2 of the UN Convention on the Law of the Sea of 1982,[23] providing that 'States shall take all measures necessary to ensure that activities under their jurisdiction or control are so conducted as not to cause damage by pollution to other States and their environment [...]'.The Convention on International Liability for Damage Caused by Space Objects goes even further and objectifies a state's responsibility. As provided in Article II, read in conjunction with Article I(c)(ii), a launching state from whose territory or facility a space object is launched shall be absolutely liable to

[20] ICJ, Corfu Channel Case, Judgment of 9 April 1949, ICJ Reports 1949, p. 22. The existence of the general obligation of States to ensure that activities within their jurisdiction and control respect the environment of other States or of areas beyond national control is now part of the corpus of international law relating to the environment; see also ICJ, Legality of the Threat or Use of Nuclear Weapons, Advisory Opinion of 8 July 1996, ICJ Reports 1996, para. 29.

[21] Vienna, 18 April 1961.

[22] E.g. Article 22(2): 'The receiving State is under a special duty to take all appropriate steps to protect the premises of the mission against *any* intrusion or damage and to prevent any disturbance of the peace of the mission or impairment of its dignity'; see also ICJ, United States Diplomatic and Consular Staff in Tehran (United States of America v. Iran), Judgment of 24 May 1980, ICJ Reports 1980, para. 67.

[23] Montego Bay, 10 December 1982.

pay compensation for damage caused by its space object on the surface of the Earth or to aircraft in flight.[24]

In such circumstances, the act of a private entity, even though not attributable to a given state, may result in the latter being held responsible for its own failure (which is attributable to its organs) to take necessary diligent steps toward a specified aim or to prevent certain results. Evidently, the application of such primary norms raises questions concerning (a) the scope of positive obligation to prevent an illegal outcome and the required diligence to this effect and (b) rules of attribution for proscribed omissions. While the former is to be answered in reference to the content of the primary norm involved[25] and the circumstances of the case,[26] the latter remains within the scope of the standard set of attribution rules provided by general international law and partly codified by the Draft Articles on Responsibility of States for Internationally Wrongful Acts (DARSIWA)—unless *lex specialis* is applicable.[27] Both issues are to be discussed below under special regimes established by the relevant regional instruments of human rights protection and against the backdrop of related Nigerian and Ukrainian cases.

17.4 States as Guardian Angels: Is It Not Too Much to Expect?

17.4.1 Positive Obligations Under Relevant Human Rights Treaties

At the outset, it is to be emphasised that states' obligation to protect human rights indubitably embraces what is sometimes called 'a positive component'. Therefore, states are expected not only to refrain from violating rights and freedoms of individuals (what stands for negative obligation) but also to 'positively' secure them

---

[24] Moscow, London, Washington, 29 March 1972.

[25] ICJ, Pulp Mills on the River Uruguay (Argentina v. Uruguay), Judgment of 4 May 2006, ICJ Reports 2010, found that 'the principle of prevention, as a customary rule, has its origins in the due diligence that is required of a State in its territory […] A State is thus obliged to use all the means at its disposal in order to avoid activities which take place in its territory, or in any area under its jurisdiction, causing significant damage to the environment of another State', para. 101; see also: Legality of the Threat or Use of Nuclear Weapons, note 20 para. 29.

[26] Iran-U.S. Claims Tribunal, Gould Marketing, Inc. v. Ministry of National Defence, Award of 27 July 1983, No. ITL 24-49-2: 'By December 1978; strikes, riots and other civil strife in the course of the Islamic Revolution had created classic force majeure conditions at least in Iran's major cities. By "force majeure" we mean social and economic forces beyond the power of the state to control through the exercise of due diligence. Injuries caused by the operation at such forces are therefore not attributable to the state for purposes of its responding for damages' pp. 152–153.

[27] Article 55 ARS: 'These articles do not apply where and to the extent that the conditions for the existence of an internationally wrongful act or the content or implementation of the international responsibility of a State are governed by special rules of international law.'

against possible breaches by other private entities, for example by members of insurgent militias.

The European Convention puts it clearly in Article 1, which provides that 'The High Contracting Parties shall secure to everyone within their jurisdiction the rights and freedoms defined in Section I of this Convention'. While the scope of positive obligation varies depending on the particular human right involved, it is, nonetheless, established in the jurisprudence of the European Court of Human Rights (the European Court) on the ground of the right to life that states should not only refrain from the intentional and unlawful taking of life but also take appropriate steps to safeguard the lives of those within their jurisdiction, in particular by putting in place effective criminal law provisions backed up by law-enforcement machinery.[28] Simultaneously, it seems axiomatic that positive obligations should be interpreted in a way that does not impose an impossible or disproportionate burden on authorities. In particular, taking into account

> difficulties involved in policing modern societies, the unpredictability of human conduct and the operational choices which must be made in terms of priorities and resources, the positive obligation must be interpreted in a way which does not impose an impossible or disproportionate burden on the authorities.[29]

Accordingly, not every alleged risk to life can entail that the state authorities shall be required to take operational measures to prevent that risk from materialising.

The African Charter uses different wording and in its Article 1 stipulates that '[t]he [...] parties to the present Charter shall recognise the rights, duties and freedoms enshrined in the Charter and shall undertake to adopt legislative or other measures to give effect to them'. While the provision is silent on securing the rights and freedoms, the African Commission on Human and Peoples' Rights (African Commission) interpreted this provision in a similar vein to its European counterpart, finding as follows:

> The respect for the rights imposes on the State the negative obligation of doing nothing to violate the said rights. The protection targets [also-MW] the positive obligation of the State to guarantee that private individuals do not violate these rights [...] [T]he negligence of a State to guarantee the protection of the rights of the Charter having given rise to a violation of the said rights constitutes a violation of the rights of the Charter which would be attributable to this State, even where it is established that the State itself or its officials are not directly responsible for such violations but have been perpetrated by private.[30]

---

[28] The European Court of Human Rights (ECHR), L.C.B. v. the United Kingdom, No. 23413/94, Judgment of 9 June 1998, para. 36; Osman v. the United Kingdom, No. 23452/94, Judgment of 28 October 1998, para. 115. For a more detailed analysis see Mowbray (2004).

[29] ECHR, Osman Case, note 28, para. 116.

[30] African Commission, Association of Victims of Post Electoral Violence & INTERIGHTS v. Cameroon, No. 272/03, Decision of 25 November 2009, para. 88; Commission nationale des droits de l'Homme et des libertés v. Chad, No. 74/92, Decision of 11 October 1995, para. 18; Social and Economic Rights Action Center (SERAC) and Center for Economic and Social Rights (CESR) v. Nigeria, No. 155/96, Decision of 27 October 2001, para. 46.

Thus, when exploring the dramatic events that took place in Chibok and near Donetsk from the point of view of possible violations of the states' respective human rights obligations, a question arises whether Nigeria and Ukraine breached their positive duty *to give effect to* or *to secure* the rights of the abducted girls and the MH17 passengers and their families against the acts of private individuals respectively. To be effectively tackled, the problem, however, requires raising another and even more fundamental issue: whether the scope of this positive obligation or the scope of the accompanying international responsibility was affected—and to what extent—by the fact that pertinent events took part in territories controlled by insurgent groups (as in the case of Ukraine) or at least with a significant presence of insurgent groups (as in the case of Nigeria).

17.4.2 Within or Without? Much Ado About States' Jurisdiction

One must start with *jurisdiction* understood as a precondition for state's obligations to arise under international human rights treaties. Apparently, jurisdiction in this very particular context stands for sovereign *authority* and directly has nothing to do with either personal or subject-matter scope of sovereign's *obligation* under human rights treaties or responsibility for violations thereof. However, in practice, the former may significantly influence and condition the latter.

17.4.2.1 European Court's Position: Jurisdiction as the Actual Power to Secure Human Rights and Freedoms: Thus It May Be Tailored

Basically, the European Convention in its very first provision declares that the states parties have obligation to secure the rights and freedoms to all entities *within* their respective jurisdictions.[31] Therefore, the jurisdiction here reaches the rank of the threshold criterion,[32] namely, it determines a fundamental parameter for individuals who qualify for protection against violations of their rights guaranteed by the European Convention. Only individuals *within the jurisdiction* of the state party remain shielded by this treaty against every possible infringement of their rights and are entitled to lodge a petition to the European Court. Hence, it also means that the existence of jurisdiction constitutes a constant intrinsic factor in the hypothesis part of all diverse subject-matter norms derived from the European Convention. Thence,

[31] See also slightly different wording of e.g. Article 2.1 of the International Covenant on Civil and Political Rights, New York, 16 December 1966. See also Human Rights Committee, General Comment 31, CCPR/C/21/Rev.1/Add.13, paras. 10–11.

[32] ECHR, Al-Skeini and Others v. the United Kingdom, No. 55721/07, Judgment of 7 July 2011, para. 130.

if a given individual remains *outside the state's jurisdiction* when an alleged violation occurs, in the light of the provisions of the European Convention, that fact precludes the responsibility of this very state for the violation against that particular individual, even if the alleged breach turns out to be attributable to the state's organs. For example, in 2005, the Danish authorities permitted the publication of what could be considered as offensive and blasphemous caricatures of the prophet Muhammad, thus allegedly violating Article 9 in conjunction with Article 14 of the European Convention. However, the applicants—a Moroccan national residing in Morocco and two Moroccan associations that were Morocco based and operating there—were found to be outside the Danish jurisdiction, in this way preventing the European Court from deciding on the merits.[33] The impact of jurisdiction on the personal scope of a sovereign's *obligation* under this human rights treaty is thus evident. So far, so good. But what is the meaning of *being within jurisdiction* under the European Convention? And how may this factor also influence the subject-matter scope of the sovereign's obligation?

State jurisdiction in general international law refers to the state's *authority* and the accompanying *power* to act by means of its legislative, executive or judicial powers in order to shape the legal and factual position of individuals and objects. While this competence remains primarily territorial,[34] it may sometimes be exercised over individuals or an area outside the national territory.[35] This perception is roughly adhered to by the European Court[36] emphasising that the *actual power* of a state is to shape the legal and factual position of individuals and objects. Consequently, the Court in Strasbourg developed three modes of exercising jurisdiction[37]: (a) through

[33] ECHR, Ben el Mahi and Others v. Danmark, No. 5853/06, Decision of 11 December 2006.

[34] Netherlands-USA Arbitration Tribunal, Island of Palmas Case, Award of 4 April 1928, RIAA, Vol. II, p. 838.

[35] ICJ, *Advisory* Opinion on the Legal Consequences of the Construction of a Wall in the Occupied Palestinian Territory, Advisory Opinion of 9 July 2004, ICJ Reports 2004, para. 109; Armed Activities Case, note 18, paras. 179–180.

[36] ECHR, Banković and Others v. Belgium and Others, No. 52207/99, Decision of 12 December 2001, paras. 55–63.

[37] As a matter of fact, one might wonder if this nuanced approach has been adopted as solely reflecting particular character of the human rights treaty regime or just arisen exaggerated as a result of the lack of solid international legal background demonstrated by some of the European Court's judges. It is an open secret that there had been judges selected on the basis of friendly relations of the candidate with some influential political personalities and with neither the training in human rights nor the adequate proficiency at the official working languages of the Court; see Loucaides (2010). Consequently, ECHR's jurisprudence on state jurisdiction appears as a patchwork created without a plan with subsequent patches basted as necessitated by facts of new cases and even underlying political considerations. When political underpinnings of judicial decisions are searched within ECHR's jurisprudence the Banković Case is usually evoked, wherein ECHR found that victims of NATO aerial bombardment in Belgrade had been outside the jurisdiction of NATO member states involved, thus barring potential influx of similar claims connected with the war on terror waged beyond the European soil. For more on the issue, see e.g.: da Costa (2013), p. 155; Gondek (2005), Lawson (2004), Milanovic (2008), pp. 422–425; Milanovic (2011), Milanovic (2012), pp. 121–139; Miller (2009), pp. 1223–1246.

a state's own territory,[38] (b) extraterritorially on the basis of *effective control over area*,[39] (c) extraterritorially on the basis of *state agent authority and control over person*.[40] As only the first mode is directly relevant from the perspective of Ukraine's responsibility, the two remaining perplexing extraterritorial modes will not be examined here.

It is assumed that the state has jurisdiction over all individuals present within its territory and remains obliged to ensure that they enjoy *free and full* exercise of the rights guaranteed in both negative and positive aspects. Still, one must not overlook a quite obvious fact (illustrated by the mere wording of both extraterritorial modes) that execution of power over a territory may be precluded or impaired by circumstances seemingly far beyond the control of the territorial state as, for example, a foreign military intervention or rebellion. In particular, the question arises, again, whether the MH17 passengers and their families remained within or stayed outside the scope of Ukrainian jurisdiction while being subjected to alleged ill-treatment with relation to the acts of insurgents. It must be taken into account that now (at the time of writing) and then (at the time of downing the plane) the insurgents have controlled a part of the Eastern Ukraine or at least effectively prevented the exercise of effective control by the Ukrainian Government over that area.

Unsurprisingly, the European Court is ready to rebut the aforementioned natural presumption of territorial jurisdiction in certain situations. This, in turn, unveils (as shown below) the impact that the *actual authority* has upon the subject-matter scope of sovereign's *obligation*. It is to be noted from the outset, however, that this limitation affecting jurisdiction applies only in exceptional circumstances. In particular, when the state is prevented from exercising its entire authority in parts of its territory as a result of, for example, (a) military occupation by the armed forces of another state, which effectively controls the territory[41]; (b) acts of another state supporting the installation of a separatist regime within the territory of the state

[38] ECHR, Assanidze v. Georgia, No. 71503/01, Judgment of 8 April 2004, para. 139.

[39] European Commission of Human Rights (European Commission), X. v. the Federal Republic of Germany, No. 1611/62, Decision of 25 September 1965; X and Y v. Switzerland, No. 7289/75, decision of 14 July 1977; *X.* v. the United Kingdom, No. 7547/76, Decision of 15 December 1977; M. v. Danmark, No. 17392/90, Decision of 14 October 1992; Ramirez Sanchez v. France, No. 28780/95, Decision of 24 June 1996. ECHR, Öcalan v. Turkey, No. 46221/99, Judgment of 12 May 2005; Medvedev and Others v. France, No. 3394/03, Judgment of 29 March 2010; Hirsi Jamaa and Others v. Italy, No. 27765/09, Judgment of 23 February 2012; Jaloud v. The Netherlands, No. 47708/08, Judgment of 20 November 2014.

[40] ECHR, Al-Skeini and Others v. the United Kingdom, No. 55721/07, Judgment of 7 July 2011, paras. 130–140.

[41] ECHR, Loizidou v Turkey(Preliminary Objections), No. 15318/89, Judgment of 23 March 1995, paras. 60–64.

concerned[42]; or (c) acts of war or rebellion without any direct foreign intervention.[43] Needless to say, the last situation seems to be applicable to MH17 case.

In order to rebut the presumption of territorial jurisdiction in the aforementioned circumstances, one must take into account two main factors: (a) all the objective facts capable of limiting the effective exercise of a state's authority over its territory on the one hand and (b) the state's own conduct on the other. As a matter of fact, jurisdiction is not perceived by the European Court as 'zero-one' situation. Being understood as the actual power, not only may it be totally replaced by another state or annihilated as a result of insurgency, but also it is amenable to be *partly* diminished as a consequence of civil war, rebellion, foreign intervention, etc. The European Court dealing with cases concerning the loss of effective control by the Republic of Moldova over the Transdnistrian region stressed that the positive obligation remains even in cases where the exercise of the state's authority is *limited* in certain part of its territory. Therefore, Moldova had a duty to take all the appropriate measures that *were still remaining* within its power in order to protect the rights of individuals.

Accordingly, such 'residual jurisdiction' of the territorial state persisting in spite of effective control being exercised over the area by, for example, separatist groups implies the obligation of such state to secure the rights and freedoms to everyone within its limited jurisdiction. Nonetheless, this obligation is *tailored* to a somewhat elusive sphere of positive obligation to take the diplomatic, economic, judicial or other measures that might be remaining in the state's power and could be exercised in accordance with international law.[44]

17.4.2.2 African Commission's Position: Territorial Jurisdiction: A Competence That Is Not to Be Tailored

The term *jurisdiction* is not used by the African Charter in the general clause of its Article 1, and it is scarcely present in the African Commission's reasoning. Hence, seemingly an attempt at presenting its precise meaning may resemble a painstaking reconstruction of a frozen mammoth's genetic sequence. Some basic assumptions are easily discernible though.

---

[42] ECHR, Ilaşcu and Others v. Moldova and Russia, No. 48787/99, Judgment of 7 May 2004, para 312.

[43] ECHR, Sargsyan v. Azerbaijan, No. 40167/06, Decision of 14 December 2011, citing Ilaşcu Case in para. 73. See also:Tagayeva and Others v. Russia, 26562/07 which is still pending before ECHR but seems particularly relevant in the context of the Nigerian abduction as it concerns the terrorist attack on a school in Beslan, North Ossetia (Russia), in September 2004, and the ensuing hostage-taking, siege and storming of the school, which resulted in the deaths of over 330 civilians including over 180 children.

[44] ECHR, Ivanţoc and Others v Moldova and Russia, No. 23687/05, Judgment of 15 November 2011, para 105; Catan and Others v. Moldova and Russia, No. 43370/04, Judgment of 19 October 2012, para. 109.

At the outset, it must be noted that while the African Commission acting under Article 60 of the African Charter used to rely heavily on the jurisprudence of other international human rights bodies and sometimes emulated concepts that had been forged in Strasburg, the European decisions on the pertinent matter were not invoked. Consequently, the complex *Strasburg acqui* on the issue of jurisdiction is not followed under the African Charter. Nonetheless, *jurisdiction* still appears as the threshold criterion within the meaning described above. Notably, it was stressed that 'human rights law imposes obligations on States to protect citizens or individuals *under their jurisdiction*[MW] from harmful acts of others'.[45] Hence, the citizens and individuals outside the state's jurisdiction are not protected by the African Charter. As a matter of principle, in this instance, again, the scope of jurisdiction indubitably possesses a chiefly territorial dimension,[46] although it may as well exceptionally appear extraterritorially (in particular, when foreign territory is effectively controlled by another state party in the course or in the aftermath of a military intervention[47]). Therefore, every state party to the African Charter 'is presumed to be sufficiently aware of the situation prevailing on its own territory and holds the ultimate responsibility for harnessing the situation and correcting the wrongs complained of [within its boundaries]'.[48] Unfortunately, there were only a few African Commission decisions in cases involving rebel movements diminishing a state's actual control over its territory. In one of them, the Government of Chad, which acted as a respondent state, claimed that none of the alleged violations were committed by its agents and that it had no control over the violations committed by other parties because Chad had been in a state of civil war. The African Commission rejected this argument noting the following:

> In the present case, Chad has failed to provide security and stability in the country, thereby allowing serious and massive violations of human rights. The national armed forces are participants in the civil war and there have been several instances in which the Government has failed to intervene to prevent the assassination and killing of specific individuals. Even where it cannot be proved that violations were committed by government agents, the government had a responsibility to secure the safety and the liberty of its citizens, and to conduct investigations into murders. Chad therefore is responsible for the violations of the African Charter.[49]

---

[45] African Commission, Zimbabwe Human Rights NGO Forum v. Zimbabwe, No. 245/02, Decision of 15 May 2006, paras. 143, 154, 171.

[46] African Commission, Luke Munyandu Tembani and Benjamin John Freeth (represented by Norman Tjombe) v. Angola and Thirteen Others, No. 409/12, Decision of 30 April 2014, para. 90.

[47] African Commission, Democratic Republic of Congo v. Burundi, Rwanda, Uganda, No. 227/99, Decision of 29 May 2003.

[48] African Commission, Malawi African Association, Amnesty International, Ms. Sarr Diop, UIADH and RADDHO, Collectif des veuves et ayants droit, AMDH v. Mauritania, No. 54/91, 61/91, 98/93, 164/97 & 196/97, 210/98, Decision of 11 May 2000 paras. 143, 154, 171. See also: Amnesty International, Comité Loosli Bachelard, Lawyers Committee for Human Rights, Association of Members of the Episcopal Conference of East Africa v. Sudan, No. 48/90, 50/91, 52/91, 89/93, Decision of 15 November 1999; Zimbabwe Human Rights NGO Forum Case, note 45, para. 70.

[49] African Commission, Commission nationale des droits de l'Homme et des libertés Case, note 30, para. 22. See also: Malawi African Association Case, note 48, para. 140.

Such an unconditional pronouncement may suggest that under the African Charter, the presumption of territorial jurisdiction is not to be rebutted. In consequence, the African Commission seemingly refrains from accepting the European concept of truncated territorial jurisdiction that affects the scope of positive obligations. In another case, it has been noted that even if a state

> is going through a civil war, civilians in areas of strife are especially vulnerable and the State must take all possible[MW] measures that they are treated in accordance with international humanitarian law.[50]

It means then that the sovereign jurisdiction over a territory implies the state's ability to give effect to human rights obligations through the prevention of events that might result in impairing rights and freedoms of individuals. Consequently, the issue of jurisdiction ceases to be a viable defence option for respondent states before the African Commission if alleged violations had occurred within their boundaries. Civil wars or rebellions leading to ill-treatment of an individual may only be invoked as the circumstances precluding wrongfulness of possible violations of the African Charter on the basis of *force majeure*.[51]

Considering the aforementioned remarks, it is to be concluded that, in spite of the ongoing insurgencies, Nigeria and Ukraine retained jurisdiction over individuals present on their respective territories plagued by rebellion. Hence, both states were obliged to take appropriate measures still available to them in order to protect the rights of the abducted girls and of the passengers of the fatal flight respectively. The question remains, however, whether any such measures were in fact available under the circumstances of the relevant cases.

17.4.3 Was There Anything to Be Done to Avoid Casualties?

Both the African Charter and the European Convention envisage two aspects of positive obligation to guarantee human rights and freedoms: (a) substantive and (b) procedural. When the right to life is at stake, the European Court emphasises that states must

> take appropriate steps to safeguard the lives of those within its jurisdiction. This involves a primary duty on the State to secure the right to life by putting in place effective criminal-law provisions to deter the commission of offences against the person, backed up by law enforcement machinery for the prevention, suppression and punishment of breaches of such provisions [procedural aspect-MW]. It also extends, in appropriate circumstances, to a positive obligation on the authorities to take preventive operational measures to protect

[50] African Commission, Amnesty International Case, note 48, para. 50.

[51] Association of Victims Case, note 30, paras. 98, 118. From the standpoint of general international law it is accepted that e.g. the unforeseeability of rebel attacks precludes the responsibility of the territorial State for resulting damage suffered by foreigners. See e.g.: American-British Claims Commission, Saint Albans Raid Case, United States-Venezuela Claims Commission, Wipperman Case, Moore (1898) IV, p. 4042; III, p. 3039.

> an individual or individuals whose lives are at risk from the criminal acts of another individual [substantive aspect-MW].[52]

In the same manner, the African Commission, dealing with the alleged violations of the right to security and the right not to be subjected to cruel, inhuman or degrading treatment, has found that governments

> have a duty to protect their citizens, not only through appropriate legislation and effective enforcement [procedural aspect] but also by protecting them from damaging acts that may be perpetrated by private parties [substantive aspect].[53]

These two aspects will be examined in turn.

17.4.3.1 Positive Obligation in Substantive Aspect

The substantive aspect may be described as a general duty of states to prevent the violation of human rights with its borders delimited by (a) the existence of a causal nexus between the breach of such obligation and the resulting infringement of protected rights and freedoms, (b) the foreseeability of future violation (if the state knew or should have known that violation is going to materialise),[54] (c) the controllability of the events leading to future violation.[55] Considering the unpredictability and the uncontrolled nature of the abduction and downing of the plane by rebel forces, it is tempting to abort further examination of this issue with a common sense conclusion that the prevention of the resulting infringements was far beyond the scope of the relevant subject-matter treaty commitments of Nigeria and Ukraine respectively. However, a more scrupulous, zoom-in approach reveals possible weaknesses of such reasoning and may lead to somewhat unexpected outcomes.

---

[52] ECHR, Gongadze v. Ukraine, No. 34056/02, Judgment of 8 November 2005, para. 164.

[53] African Commission, Social and Economic Rights Action Center Case, note 30, para. 57; J.E. Zitha& PJ.L. Zitha v Mozambique, No 361/08, Decision, paras. 81, 94.

[54] ECHR, Kılıç v. Turkey, No. 22077/10, Judgment of 5 March 2013: 'For a positive obligation to arise, it must be established that the authorities knew or ought to have known at the time of the existence of a real and immediate risk to the life of an identified individual or individuals from the criminal acts of a third party and that they failed to take measures within the scope of their powers which, judged reasonably, might have been expected to avoid that risk', para. 63. See also Berü v. Turkey, No. 47304/07, Judgment of 11 January 2011, the case concerned the death of a child in an attack by dangerous dogs. ECHR was of the opinion that the series of incidents that had already taken place before the attack were not sufficient to find that the authorities had had a positive obligation to take preventive measures. In particular, there was no evidence that the authorities had known or should have known that there was an immediate risk to the victim. African Commission put it in similar terms in the Association of Victims Case, note 30: 'For the post electoral events which gave rise to serious violations against the lives and property of the citizens would not have taken place if the State which, through its investigations knew or should have known about the planning of the said events, had taken the necessary measures to prevent their happening', para. 115.

[55] ECHR, Osman Case, note 28; African Commission, Amnesty International Case, note 48. See also: Stubberfield (2012), p. 117.

The states' obligation to secure human rights guaranteed by the relevant international treaties against possible violations by non-state actors in a particular context of insurgency is a complex one. At least two fundamental elements are discernible thereof. Let us note in the first instance that, as a rule, states facing insurgent activities retain their sovereign status. For this reason, they remain in a position to maintain or regain effective control over *their* territories (if already lost)—as to both: the actual power and the legal title (needless to say that this presumption clearly appears in the concept of *residual jurisdiction*, as described above). Consequently, it is to be examined whether the state used appropriate means to re-establish or to maintain control over the area affected by rebel activities,[56] thus *generally* preventing rebel-committed violations of human rights from materialising. Failing to do so may result in breaching the substantive aspect of positive obligation. Yet the analysis does not end here. Even if the state fulfils its obligation in the aforementioned respect, in the second leg of our examination, a more specific question arises, namely, whether the state duly prevented a *particular* violation from materialising.

This two-tier character of the positive obligation involved is clearly visible in the European case. Ukraine, when confronted with separatist movement taking control over a part of its territory before the downing of the plane happened, had impeccably carried out several positive steps to regain control over Donetsk area. In particular, Ukraine (a) expressed its firm protests at the international level against the illegal separatist movement[57]; (b) continued to take all accessible and legally acceptable measures to regain full control over its territory[58]; (c) kept seeking support, bilaterally and internationally, in particular through the UN[59]; and (d) refrained

[56] ECHR, Ilascu Case, note 42, paras. 339–340 and partly dissenting opinion of Judge Ress, para. 4; African Commission, Zimbabwe Human Rights NGO Forum Case, note 45, para. 160: '[A] State can be held complicit where it fails systematically to provide protection of violations from private actors who deprive any person of his/her human rights. However, unlike for direct State action, the standard for establishing State responsibility in violations committed by private actors is more relative. Responsibility must be demonstrated by establishing that the State condones a pattern of abuse through pervasive non-action. Where States do not actively engage in acts of violence or routinely disregard evidence of murder, rape or assault, States generally fail to take the minimum steps necessary to protect their citizens' rights to physical integrity and, in extreme cases, to life. This sends a message that such attacks are justified and will not be punished. To avoid such complicity, States must demonstrate due diligence by taking active measures to protect, prosecute and punish private actors who commit abuses'.

[57] See, e.g.: the speech by representative of Ukraine before UN SC during its 7185th meeting of 28 May 2014, S/PV.7185, p. 15 *et seq.*

[58] Four days before the incident, heavy fighting, which involved the use of artillery, was reported in Donetsk area, Organization for Security and Co-operation in Europe, see Latest from the Special Monitoring Mission (SMM) in Ukraine based on information received until 13 July 2014, http://www.osce.org/ukraine-smm/121255. Accessed 11 June 2015. See also: Letter dated 1 July 2014 from the Permanent Representative of Ukraine to the UN addressed to the President of the SC and annexing Address of President of Ukraine Petro Poroshenko, S/2014/460. The President stressed Government's determination to '[…] attack [the separatists] and liberate [the] land'.

[59] E.g., the speech by representative of Ukraine before UN SC during its 7154th meeting of 13 April 2014, S/PV.7154, p. 14: 'We consider it to be the SC's duty to find a proper and peaceful solution to this crisis'.

from lending any support to the rebel regime. Nonetheless, the positive obligation still might have been violated as a result of failure to use all available legal measures to prohibit foreign aircraft from entering certain parts of Ukrainian air space, which eventually led to the *particular* incident involving the alleged human rights violation. As a matter of fact, MH17 appeared within the Ukrainian airspace on the basis of Article 1 of the International Air Services Transit Agreement.[60] The aircraft was transiting at Flight Level 330 (approximately 10,000 metres/33,000 feet) when it disappeared from the radar. This route had been closed by the Ukrainian authorities[61] from ground to flight level 320 but was open at the level at which the aircraft was flying.[62] Indubitably, the incident would not have taken place had Ukraine closed relevant flight information region (FIR) entirely. On the other hand, however, it must be noted that the European Aviation Safety Agency (EASA) drew the attention of the aviation community to the possible existence of serious risks to the safety of international civil flights within the FIR only *after* the tragic event,[63] although the information on heavy artillery usage had been widely circulated before. The silence of this specialised agency may thus serve as an evidence of unpredictability considering the plane's downing. The European Court has been seized of the matter as a mother of a German woman killed during the incident sued the Ukrainian authorities for failure to close the airspace.[64] If the case reaches its merit stage, the Court's reasoning will constitute a significant contribution to the discussion on the limits of the substantive aspects of positive obligations.

The abduction case reveals similar complexity but not at the point of Nigeria's failure to maintain control over Borno State (as it was to be partially lost only *after* the events of April 2014) and to suppress Boko Haram's activities[65] but regarding rather its inability to prevent the particular violation.

Testimonies gathered by Amnesty International revealed that Nigerian security forces had allegedly failed to act on multiple advance warnings about Boko Haram's armed raid while being informed that the Government Secondary School would be the target of the armed men present in the area. Amnesty International claims that Nigeria's military headquarters in Damboa (36 km. from Chibok) and Maiduguri (130 km. from Chibok) had been warned about the impending attack close to 4 h

[60] Chicago, 7 December 1944. Article 1 reads: 'Each contracting State grants to the other contracting States the following freedoms of the air in respect of scheduled international air services: (1) The privilege to fly across its territory without landing'.

[61] Article 9 of the Convention on International Civil Aviation, Chicago, 7 December 1944, reads: 'Each contracting State may, for reasons of military necessity or public safety, restrict or prohibit uniformly the aircraft of other States from flying over certain areas of its territory'.

[62] See http://www.eurocontrol.int/news/mh-17-ukraine. Accessed 11 June 2015.

[63] EASA Safety Bulletin of 18 July 2014. http://ad.easa.europa.eu/ad/2014-21. Accessed 11 June 2015.

[64] Hudson (2014).

[65] In January 2014, actions taken against Boko Haram were assessed as 'robust' by the UN Secretary General. See Report of the Secretary-General of 9 January 2014 on the work of the UN to help States and sub-regional and regional entities in Africa in fighting terrorism, S/2014/9, para. 9.

before Boko Haram began its assault on the town. Only a small contingent of security forces based in the town—army personnel of 17 men, along with the local police—had attempted to repel the Boko Haram's assault but was finally overpowered and forced to retreat. Notably, no reinforcements were sent to the area.[66]

While Nigeria's authorities replied casting doubts on the veracity of the report,[67] it is still to be proven whether such early warnings had been made. But *assuming*, for the sake of the present analysis, the accuracy of the aforementioned enunciation, it might have far-reaching consequences under Article 1 of the African Charter. Considering the particular circumstances, the analysis is being shifted here, in comparison to the Ukrainian case, from the foreseeability issue to the controllability of events.

Although violations of Article 1 of the African Charter inherently result from infringements of other stipulations of this treaty,[68] the norm in itself provides autonomous subject-matter content amenable to being breached. The African Commission maintains that the provision imposes upon all states parties thereto the obligation to use the necessary diligence to achieve a particular result, namely, to implement the provisions prescribed by the Charter and thus to protect individuals against violations of their rights by non-state actors.[69] The due diligence appears here as the threshold criterion determining required efforts to be taken by the state to accomplish the obligation to protect. As the said diligence has to evolve in relation to time, space and circumstances, its scope is to be established on a case-by-case basis, bearing in mind, though, that the minimum standard of due diligence—that is, a basic set of necessary measures at a state's disposal required to prevent violations—is higher in respect of non-derogable rights as relevant here.[70] Consequently, Nigeria had the obligation to guarantee the protection of rights and freedoms endorsed by the African Charter by adopting all the relevant measures of its choice to prevent illegal outcomes. Failing to do so, the state would be able to extricate itself from responsibility for the act of others only if *force majeure* situation could be proven with its extremely high standard of irresistibility and uncontrollability (assuming that 'unpredictability' is inapplicable in this case against the backdrop of the above-mentioned claims of prior warnings given to Nigerian security forces).[71] However, considering the presence of Nigerian troops in close vicinity and the alleged failure of the local administration to reinforce the town in spite of multiple warnings, the advancement of irresistibility prima facie does not seem a viable option of argumentation.

[66] Amnesty International (2014).

[67] BBC (2014).

[68] African Commission, Sir Dawda K. Jawara v. Gambia (The), No. 147/95-149/96, Decision of 11 May 2000, para. 46; Abdel Hadi, Ali Radi& Others v. Republic of Sudan, No. 368/09, Decision of 4 June 2014, paras. 91–92.

[69] Association of Victims Case, note 30, para. 110.

[70] Zimbabwe Human Rights NGO Forum Case, note 45, paras. 155, 158.

[71] African Commission, Association of Victims Case, note 30, paras. 111–113. See also: Kevin Mgwanga Gunme et al. v. Cameroon, No. 266/03, Decision of 27 May 2009, para. 96 *in fine*.

Regardless of the aforementioned remarks, considering the fact that the abducted girls are still missing (at the time of writing), another corresponding issue arises. Specifically, the prolonged failure of the Nigerian government to establish the whereabouts and to free the Chibok women may constitute lack of effective enforcement, thus amounting to a *separate* violation of their rights and freedoms. The rising insecurity in north-eastern Nigeria and Boko Haram activities spilling across the borders into Cameroon, Niger and Chad[72] do not absolve Nigeria of the positive obligation in this respect, although they may potentially constitute mitigating circumstance supporting arguments based on the uncontrollability of the situation.

17.4.3.2 Positive Obligation in Procedural Aspect

As advanced earlier, both the European Convention and the African Charter envisage not only substantive but also procedural aspects of human rights protection. While the former is of preventive nature, the latter has remedial character and should be considered from the perspective of the specific states' behaviour in the wake of the abduction and the downing of the plane. In particular, independent, impartial, prompt and open-to-public-scrutiny inquiries should be put in place to establish the facts of the cases in order to secure the effective implementation of the domestic laws that protect human rights and to ensure the accountability of those responsible for the ill-treatment.[73] Whereas the fulfilment of this obligation should be examined considering prolonged impediments to effective control over the territory and volatile security situation in the Eastern Ukraine[74] and north-eastern Nigeria,[75] the limited control over territory and the involvement of foreign states in the investigation of the MH17 incident[76] do not relieve the territorial states from undertaking accessible and pertinent measures in order to complete effective inquiry. Possible deficiencies in this respect have been heralded by a wave of protests of civil society and the victims' families, both in Nigeria and the Netherlands, angered at the alleged

---

[72] Report of the Secretary-General of 8 January 2015 on the activities of the UN Office for West Africa, S/2014/945.

[73] ECHR, Anguelova v. Bulgaria, No. 38361/97, Judgment of 13 June 2002, para. 137, Jasinskisv. *Latvia*, No. 45744/08, Judgment of 21 December 2010, para. 72. African Commission, Association of Members Case, note 48, para. 51; Egyptian Initiative for Personal Rights & INTERIGHTS v. Egypt, No. 323/06, Decision of 12 October 2013, citing jurisprudence of ECHR in para 228.

[74] Letter dated 16 December 2014 from the Permanent Representative of the Netherlands to the UN addressed to the President of the SC, S/2014/903.

[75] Note 73, paras. 18 *et seq.*

[76] A joint investigation team comprising of Australia, Belgium, the Netherlands and Ukraine was set up on 7 August 2014 to establish culpability, see: https://www.om.nl/algemeen/english/@86120/joint-investigation/. Accessed 11 June 2015.On 23 July 2014 The National Bureau of Air Accidents and Incidents Investigation with Civil Aviation of Ukraine and the Dutch Safety Board concluded an Agreement on Investigation in Respect of Aircraft Accident Involving MH17 flight for the purpose of the prevention of accidents and incidents, see http://www.onderzoeksraad.nl/uploads/fm/MH17/Agreement_NBAAI_and_DSB_website.pdf. Accessed 11 June 2015.

failures to effectively investigate the relevant cases. In both situations, the protesters appealed for UN involvement in handling the inquiries concerning the downing of the plane and rescuing the abducted girls.[77]

17.4.4 *Attribution: Everybody Knows*

As explained earlier, the issue of attribution appears in every single case involving legal responsibility, be it international or domestic. The case law of the European Court and the African Commission is no exception in this regard, although a definite majority of decisions assume attribution *sub silentio* and without prolonged disquisition.[78] As a matter of fact, this issue is rarely advanced by the parties or both international bodies acting *motu proprio*, even if the circumstances of a given case suggest to do so,[79] not to speak of the cases concerning violations of positive obligations wherein the state allegedly failed to act as required. The state fails to act *as a whole*, thus making it unnecessary to establish which *particular* branch of government should have reacted.

In both instances discussed herein, the problem does not require any further examination as the cases involve violations of positive states' obligations committed within their territories. That is to say, non-compliance therewith *implies* omissions attributable to the state regarded as a governing entity, which is, as a whole, both legally authorised and practically equipped with governmental apparatus enabling it to secure human rights. Therefore, it is not necessary to establish which particular organ of the state of Nigeria or Ukraine refrained from acting. Certainly, the issue of attribution in cases concerning violations of positive obligations may involve significant legal problems, in particular, when so-called *failed* or *fragile* states are involved as the lack of effective governmental structures may cast serious doubts as to the possibility of attribution. This dilemma, however, remains outside the scope of the present paper.

17.5 Conclusion

The analysis presented in this article inevitably explores only a very narrow aspect of a complex, multidisciplinary dilemma concerning the activities of rebel groups and suggests that the responsibility of Nigeria and Ukraine in connection with the relevant acts of rebels cannot be a priori excluded. While approaching this quandary from the perspective of the states involved and the international community as a

[77] Payne (2015) and Deutsh (2014).

[78] There are, however, interesting exceptions as: ECHR, Behrami and Behrami v. France, Saramati v. France, Germany and Norway, No. 71412/01, No. 78166/01, Decision of 2 May 2007.

[79] African Commission, Luke Munyandu Tembani Case, note 46.

whole, one may come to a false conclusion that this is the marginal issue. Allegedly, proclamation by the European Court, the African Commission or possibly the Court of Justice of Economic Community of West African States (ECOWAS)[80] that Ukraine or Nigeria, respectively, violated their international obligations will be of limited value at best. Such decisions neither restore the infringed values from the grassroots perspective nor contribute to efforts undertaken in order to definitely remove terrorist or separatist threat to both international security and territorial integrity of the affected states. In particular, the legal struggles of exquisite lawyers—lazily leafing through the files while sipping coffee from Starbucks cups—would not bring any immediate relief to those who are still abandoned deep in the interior of Nigeria, Central African Republic or Republic of Sudan, afraid of Boko Haram, Seleka or SPLM-N rebels to come when the night comes.

Nonetheless, one must not neglect the fact that international monitoring bodies equipped with the competence to decide individual applications are also guardians of the interstate contractual order. Certainly, human rights treaties principally serve as instruments protecting individual freedoms. But they, nonetheless, still remain, to a significant extent, the custodians of interests of all states parties concerned.[81] It must not be disregarded that the effective protection of human rights constitutes one of the pillars of international peace and security, as evidenced by the UN Charter proclaiming in Article 1 that 'promoting and encouraging respect for human rights and fundamental freedoms' is one of the purposes of the organisation. In the particular context of the Chibok abduction, it is to be noted that kidnapping and hostage-taking committed by terrorist groups constitute one of the most serious threats to international peace and security. Consequently, it should be combated by all means in accordance with, for example, applicable human rights treaties.[82] Positive obligations of states, as enshrined in the African Charter, do not cease to exist in violent times of rebellion, insurgency or terrorist threat. States do stay obliged to protect individuals against violations of their rights and freedoms by non-state actors, even if the scope of this obligation remains restricted to some extent considering the occurrence of uncontrollable and irresistible events. The obligation to prevent violations of human rights and freedoms appears then as an

[80] The Revised Treaty of ECOWAS, Cotonou, 24 July 1993, declares in Art 4(g) that the high contracting parties adheres to the principle on 'recognition promotion and protection of human and peoples' rights in accordance with the provisions of African Charter. Originally individuals lacked access to the ECOWAS Court under ECOWAS treaties, see ECOWAS Court, Afolabi Oladjide v Nigeria, No.ECW/CCJ/JUD/01/04, Decision of 27 April 2004. It was only Supplementary Protocol A/SP1/01/05 Amending the Protocol Relating to the Community Court of Justice, Accra, 19 January 2005, that equipped the Court with human rights jurisdiction. Pursuant to Art 9(3) of the amended Protocol: 'The Court has jurisdiction to determine case of violation of human rights that occur in any Member State'. Art 10(d) thereof provides that: 'Access to the Court is open to (…) Individuals on application for relief for violation of their human rights (…)'.

[81] ICJ, Barcelona Traction, Light and Power Company, Limited (Belgium v. Spain), Judgment of 5 February 1970, ICJ Reports 1970, p. 3, para. 33.

[82] SC Resolution of 27 January 2014, S/RES/2133 (2014)—Preamble. See also Resolution of 19 December 2014, S/RES/2195 (2014)—Preamble.

indispensable part of the international legal framework protecting international peace and security. In this vein, the pronouncement by the African Commission that the state is responsible for omissions that gave rise to human rights violations aims at calibrating state apparatus and thus definitely will help (if complied with[83]) to establish a desired pattern of its actions for the future.

References

Amnesty International (2014) Nigerian authorities failed to act on warnings about Boko Haram raid on school. https://www.amnesty.org/en/articles/news/2014/05/nigerian-authorities-failed-act-warnings-about-boko-haram-raid-school/. Accessed 11 June 2015

BBC (2014) Nigeria abductions: Chibok raid warnings 'ignored'. http://www.bbc.com/news/world-africa-27344863. Accessed 11 June 2015

da Costa K (2013) The extraterritorial application of selected human rights treaties. Martinus Nijhoff

Deutsh A (2014) Angry families of MH17 crash victims seek U.N. investigation. Reuters, December 5

Dutch Safety Board (2014) Preliminary Report. Crash involving Malaysia Airlines Boeing 777–200, Flight MH17, pp 11, 30. http://www.onderzoeksraad.nl/uploads/phase-docs/701/b3923acad0ceprem-rapport-mh-17-en-interactief.pdf. Accessed 11 June 2015

Gondek M (2005) Extraterritorial application of the European Convention on human rights: territorial focus in the age of globalization? Neth Int Law Rev 52(3):349–387

Gude H, Schmid F (2014) Deadly Ukraine Crash: German Intelligence Claims Pro-Russian Separatists Downed MH17. Spiegel Online International. October 19

Hudson A (2014) Mother of MH17 plane crash victim sues Ukraine in European Court. Reuters, November 30

Human Rights Watch (2014) Those Terrible Weeks in their Camp - Boko Haram Violence against Women and Girls in Northeast Nigeria. http://features.hrw.org/features/HRW_2014_report/Those_Terrible_Weeks_in_Their_Camp/index.html. Accessed 11 June 2015

Lawson R (2004) Life after *Bankovic*: on the extraterritorial application of the European Convention on human rights. In: Coomans F, Kamminga MT (eds) Extraterritorial application of human rights treaties. Intersentia, p 84 *et seq*

Loucaides LG (2010) Reflections of a former European Court of Human Rights Judge on his experiences as a Judge. Roma Rights Q 1:61–69

Milanovic M (2008) From compromise to principle: clarifying the concept of state jurisdiction in human rights treaties. Hum Rights Law Rev 8(3):411–448

Milanovic M (2011) Extraterritorial application of human rights treaties. Law, principles, and policy. OUP, Oxford

Milanovic M (2012) Al-Skeini and Al-Jedda in Strasbourg. Eur J Int Law 23(1):121–139

Miller S (2009) Revisiting extraterritorial jurisdiction: a territorial justification for extraterritorial jurisdiction under the European Convention. Eur J Int Law 20(4):1223–1246

Moore JB (1898) History and digest of the international arbitrations to which the United States has been a party. U.S. Government Printing Office

Mowbray AR (2004) The development of positive obligations under the European Convention on Human Rights by the European Court of Human Rights. Hart, Oxford

Payne J (2015) Desperate parents of abducted Nigerian girls turn to UN for help. The Toronto Sun January 2

[83] See Viljoen and Louw (2007).

Rushe D, Walker S (2014) MH17 Crash: Kerry Lays out Evidence of Pro-Russia Separatists' Responsibility. The Guardian. July 20

Stubberfield C (2012) Lifting the organisational veil: positive obligations of the European Union following accession to the European Convention on Human Rights. Aust Int Law J 19:117–142

Tharoor I (2014) The evidence that may prove pro-Russian separatists shot down MH17. The Washington Post, July 20

Viljoen F, Louw L (2007) State compliance with the recommendations of the African commission on human and peoples' rights, 1994–2004. Am J Int Law 101(1):1–34

Chapter 18
Boko Haram and the Ambivalence of International Legal Response

John-Mark Iyi

18.1 Terrorism, Boko Haram and International Law

Traditionally, nation states have enjoyed the monopoly of use of force through the establishment of the army, police force and other institutions of organised violence, and they have consistently tried to maintain this monopoly. However, other groups operating in the 'shadows' of the state continue to challenge this monopoly and themselves demonstrate organised violence to attain different goals, including political, economic or religious objectives. These legal, quasi-legal or outright illegal entities manifest in different forms answering to different names and descriptions, including 'insurgents, militias and radical ideological organisations, tribes and kinship networks, political parties and diasporas, criminal gangs and private contractors such as mercenaries, privateers, pirates and business firms'.[1] Of these groups, terrorists have presented perhaps the most formidable challenge to contemporary international law and international peace and security.

It would be observed that while focusing on Boko Haram as a terrorist group, contributors to this volume did not attempt to distinguish between 'domestic terrorism' and 'international terrorism'. However, while such distinction might seem helpful for purposes of describing the objectives, the operational scope, as well as the appropriate legal framework for responding to Boko Haram as a largely localised terrorist group, subsequent developments did in fact make such differentiation irrelevant and perhaps misleading in the case of Boko Haram. Firstly, in an era of 'terror brand franchising', such distinction might suggest that Boko Haram is a terrorist group confined to Nigeria and without links to foreign terrorist networks, however remote such connections or organisational links might be. This is clearly

[1] See Grassiani and Ben-Ari (2011), p. 7.

J.-M. Iyi (✉)
Department of Jurisprudence, School of Law, University of Venda, Thohoyandou, South Africa

J.-M. Iyi, H. Strydom (eds.), *Boko Haram and International Law*,
https://doi.org/10.1007/978-3-319-74957-0_18

not the case. Boko Haram subsequently underscored this point when it pledged allegiance to ISIS and re-branded itself as the West African Province of ISIS.[2]

Secondly, such distinction would have been based on the assumption that Boko Haram only has domestic objectives limited to Nigeria. But it is well known that Boko Haram has now extended its activities and objectives to include other countries such as Cameroon, Chad and Niger. Thirdly, and perhaps more importantly, such distinction would have discountenanced the trans-boundary activities and the international elements of Boko Haram as a terrorist organisation. This international element is important because, as Cassese points out: all types of international terrorism must contain an international element, and the act must demonstrate a connection with an international armed conflict or a non-international armed conflict; be of such magnitude as to show signs of a crime against humanity; involve state authorities or exhibit a *transnational character in the sense that the acts are not limited to the territory of one state but spill over into and threaten the security of other states.*[3]

The Boko Haram conflict possesses all of these characteristics. From a legal perspective, these international characteristics are decisive because, first, the territorial state bears the primary responsibility for the prosecution and punishment of all manifestations of domestic terrorism through the adoption of either a counter-insurgency approach or law-enforcement approach or a combination of both.[4] As already noted in this volume, another importance of the distinction between domestic and international terrorism lies in the fact that, generally, international treaties do not apply to domestic terrorism because international law can only be invoked where the activities of the terrorist group have a trans-boundary element.[5] Since the prosecution and punishment of the domestic manifestation of terrorism is the responsibility of the territorial state, and international law is primarily invoked only when the activities of the terrorist has trans-border character as Boko Haram's activities do, the appropriate legal reponse would require the application of both municipal and international law as well as the cooperation of the territorial states and the international community.Thus, although Nigeria remains the central focus of the group, a description of Boko Haram as a 'domestic terrorist group' as against an 'international terrorist group' would perhaps be misleading and of no conceptual or practical utility beyond merely indicating the group's initial operational capabilities.

18.2 Reconstructing Nigeria's Many Fault Lines and Responding to Insurgencies

In Chaps. 1, 2 and 3 of this book, Iyi, Olowu and Akintayo examined the socio-economic and political anatomy of the Nigerian state in order to better appreciate the context in which Boko Haram was birthed. Nigeria's estimated 180 million

[2] See Laccino (28 April 2015).

[3] See Cassese (2006), p. 749 (emphasis mine).

[4] See Flory (1997), p. 31.

[5] See Flory (1997), p. 31; Cassese (2006), p. 749.

people are roughly divided equally between the largely Muslim North and Christian South. The Middle Belt region where the Christian South meets the Muslim North has been the hotbed of ethno-religious conflicts for decades resulting in thousands of deaths, torture, rapes and other forms of atrocities perpetrated by one ethnic group against another.[6] Even at the time of completing this manuscript, there are incessant clashes between farmers and herders in the competition for resources such as grazing land and farm land. There are identity contestations between the so-called indigenes and those considered to be 'settlers' in communities. Given the geography and demographics of these areas, clashes quickly assume ethnic and religious dimensions and spread to other parts. Despite the number of past atrocities committed, perpetrators are hardly ever prosecuted. Thus, as Olowu and Akintayo point out, the inability or unwillingness of the Nigerian state to fulfil the primary *raison d'etre* for its existence: provide basic services such as security, ensure the rule of law and maintain law and order while respecting the rights of citizens—or as Iyi notes, its outright complicity in these violence—has created a culture of impunity, lawlessness and violence, first, by state officials and institutions and, second, by citizens. The failures of the Nigerian state combined with a culture of state violence and impunity have alienated the Nigerian state from its citizens, and it is perhaps the single most potent threat to social cohesion and stability in Nigeria. It partly explains why Nigeria is perpetually on the radar of the *Weak-Fragile State* country index and has been unable to respond to the Boko Haram insurgency.

The effect of this is the emergence of militia groups that now challenge the legitimacy of the state and its claim to monopoly of organised violence. This theme of violence and its contagious characteristics discussed in-depth by Akintayo using Frantz Fanon's theory that *violence begets violence* and the genesis of group violence in Nigeria cannot be resolved by the palliatives that the Nigerian state has offered so far because, as Akintayo notes, and rightly so too, like all other previous conflicts in Nigeria, the Boko Haram crisis is nothing but an offspring of the violent historical origins of Nigeria and the exploitation of group differences for material and political gains in elite political continuity. As already mentioned above, Nigeria is a very diverse country with a predominantly Muslim North and a predominantly Christian South. It is not surprising therefore that when Boko Haram began its insurgency by targeting Christian worshippers and their churches in the early phase of the insurgency, many observers in the South and the Middle Belt saw the insurgency as a continuation of the pre-existing sectional and religious tensions. Needless to say that this impacted how well the authorities could respond to the insurgency without reigniting those tensions. However, Boko Haram has since gone ahead to attack mosques and killed Muslims. These subsequent developments show how misplaced the initial assumption was, and any response built on it could only have reproduced further violence. A collective response to Boko Haram is therefore impossible in the absence of a shared understanding by the diverse communities and groups about the threat posed by Boko Haram and how and what the state response should be.

[6] See the contribution of Akinola Akintayo in this volume.

18.3 Forging a Coherent Response to Insurgencies Amidst Ethnic and Religious Diversity

The above also holds true for many other insurgencies in Africa with ethno-religious dimensions; whether it is the LRA in Uganda, Seleka Rebels in the Central African Republic or M23 in the DRC, responding to insurgencies has proved particularly challenging for African states. Africa is still very much a continent torn apart because of the resurgence of armed groups, and these armed groups continue to pose threats to regional peace, security and stability. Like the Boko Haram conflict in Nigeria, which has become a cross-border insurgency affecting Chad, Niger and Cameroun, it is shown in Chap. 4 by Jose Ngoto on 'Mapping Foreign Insurgencies in the East Democratic Republic of the Congo' how easily localised conflicts in Africa quickly become regional conflicts because of a combination of domestic, regional and (in some cases) international factors. This has been the experience of not only the DRC but also countries like Sudan and Uganda for several decades. However, as earlier noted in Chapter 1, there are few marked differences in the nature of the insurgency in the DRC and the Boko Haram conflict in Nigeria. First, until the rise of Boko Haram, previous conflicts in Nigeria have largely been localised.[7] Second, whereas insurgencies in the DRC are primarily driven by ethnic, economic and political motives, and sometimes sheer criminality, Boko Haram is primarily driven by religious extremism.[8] Yet the insurgencies in the DRC share some characteristics with the Boko Haram insurgency in terms of the scale of atrocities committed particularly against women and the civilian population, the ability to cross national borders and the insurgents' penchant for cross-border attacks in neighbouring countries.

The arbitrary and porous colonial borders of most African States have exacerbated the cross-border nature of most African insurgencies, including that of Boko Haram. This theme that Godwin Anyalemechi examines using a functionalist approach to the causes, operational modalities and responses to the Boko Haram conflict links up with *uti possidetis*, which is today at the heart of many of Africa's insurgencies. Thus, it is no surprise that many conflicts in Africa become intractable because, as Anyalemchi notes in Chap. 6, the design of responses ignore local factors, and in this case, the lack of understanding of the modus operandi of cross-border insurgencies such as Boko Haram undermined Nigeria's and the international community's initial response to the conflict. For example, Boko Haram's pool of recruitment is the Kanuri ethnic group that is scattered across countries in the Lake Chad Basin, including Nigeria, Chad and Niger. This does not only enhance recruitment but also proves useful in times of tactical withdrawal whenever the group comes under attack from security forces. The decision of the AU to facilitate the establishment of the MJTF comprising units from the affected countries stemmed from the understanding that given Africa's colonial legacy or arbitrary borders,

[7] See the chapter by Akintayo in this volume.

[8] See the chapter by Adigun in this volume.

designing strategies for state response to a cross-border insurgency like Boko Haram must be based on an appreciation of its cross-border character. This also explains the significant progress recorded in combating Boko Haram since the establishment of the MJTF.

Notwithstanding the cross-border element of the insurgency, another factor that has undermined the effective response to terrorism, particularly by Boko Haram, is the lack of a generally accepted definition of terrorism. As mentioned above, Udoka addresses this question and how it impacts the response to the Boko Haram (see Chap. 5). However, it is pertinent to underscore here how this lacuna in international law was exploited by competing domestic political, religious and sectional forces within Nigeria to try and influence the international response to Boko Haram, as well as to win local sympathy (for or against the group), and thereby shape government's response. Once again, the North–South/Christian–Muslim divides in Nigeria and the inability of the state and state institutions to insulate themselves from parochialism were exploited and perhaps sent the wrong signals to the international community about the proper characterisation of Boko Haram. This partly explains the belated US designation of Boko Haram as a foreign terrorist organisation under the (FTO Act) as different groups from different parts of Nigeria lobbied Washington to designate or not designate Boko Haram as an FTO.[9] Not everyone thought Boko Haram was a terrorist group, and some in Northern Nigeria viewed soliciting bilateral cooperation with states such as Israel to combat terrorism in Nigeria with suspicion.[10] Similarly, some in Southern Nigeria are suspicious of Nigeria joining the recent Saudi-led initiative for an international coalition of Muslim countries to combat terrorism.[11] Thus, the socio-economic, political and even legal responses of the Nigerian state to Boko Haram mirror the complexity of the internal fault lines of the Nigerian state. Perhaps, more than anything else, the age-old international law debate of who is a 'terrorist', combined with internal factors in Nigeria, greatly undermined the collective resolve to tackle Boko Haram and hampered the initial response of the Nigerian state and its ability to mobilise its citizens and its resources for this task.

18.4 The Legal Regulation of Use of Force Against Boko Haram

The question of how to respond to Boko Haram again turns on the classification of Boko Haram, and this in turn underscores the significance of defining 'terrorism', which is analysed in this context by Michael Ibanga and James Achibong. They underscore the legal implications of designating Boko Haram as a terrorist group in

[9] See generally, Connell (Summer 2012), pp. 87–93.

[10] See Thomson (2012), p. 51.

[11] See Adibe (2017), pp. 135–136.

municipal and international laws. We have already highlighted how the definition (or lack thereof) of terrorism and the designation of a group as a 'terrorist organisation' could have serious domestic and international ramifications for the response to the threats from terrorism and terrorist groups at home. Notwithstanding the initial uncertainty surrounding the proper legal characterisation of Boko Haram, Ibanga and Achibong clearly map the law of armed conflict and its application to the Boko Haram conflict and conclude that the conflict crossed the legal threshold and now constitutes a non-international armed conflict (NIAC) to which the relevant principles of IHL and IHRL are applicable. However, solving the classification problem does not answer other pertinent questions raised by the nature of the conflict. For example, so far in the conflict, there are cases of what Okebukola (see Chap. 8 in this volume) calls 'state-recognised civilian groups' such as the Civilian Joint-Task Force (CJTF) directly participating in hostilities. Are the CJTF operatives combatants? Where does command responsibility for actions of CJTF operatives lie? Would non-military law enforcement agents qualify as civilians taking direct part in hostilities when they carry out law enforcement duties that may disrupt the military activities or objectives of Boko Haram who is a party to the NIAC? How do we characterise the Boko Haram conflict seeing that it initially involved only Nigerian troops and Boko Haram within the territory of Nigeria but later spilled over and drew in other neighbouring countries such as Chad, Cameroon and Niger? Furthermore, at the time of writing, there is no available Status of Forces Agreement between Nigeria and these other countries whose forces are on Nigerian soil and when they may be said to be in Nigeria legally or otherwise, thus raising issues of a possible violation of Nigeria's sovereignty and territorial integrity. Some of these questions form part of the perplexing questions posed to IHL by the changing nature of contemporary armed conflict and would require further interrogation.

For now, Okebukola rightly points out that Boko Haram's deliberate attacks on non-military targets take the conflict outside conventional warfare. The use of these tactics should not come as a surprise but underscores Boko Haram as a terrorist group that has managed to transform its acts of sporadic violent attacks into a full-blown insurgency and a NIAC with the Nigerian state. It is therefore to be expected that in its choice of means and methods of warfare, Boko Haram would conduct hostilities by using terror in clear violation of the law of armed conflict, for which Boko Haram arguably has little or no knowledge and could not care less as the weaker party in an asymmetric war.[12] Okebukola's nuanced approach amplifies an often missed but significant issue: the need to distinguish the identity of Boko Haram as a terrorist organisation from any classification of the legal nature of the Boko Haram conflict and its choice of conduct of hostilities in that conflict.[13] Okebukola agrees with Ibanga and Achibong on the fact that at all material time before the conflict reached the threshold of NIAC, Nigeria's municipal laws and human rights standards were binding on all parties. (Marek Wasinski takes this issue

[12] For a discussion of why terrorist often prefer to act in violation of the *jus in bello*, see French (2003), pp. 32–34.

[13] For an explanation of this distinction, see Haines (2012), p. 27.

further in Chap. 17). The implication of this is that it is irrelevant that the Nigerian state did not recognise the existence of a belligerency; for purposes of accountability, Nigeria has a legal obligation to enforce municipal laws and international human rights standards recognised under domestic law by arresting, prosecuting and punishing violators, whether Boko Haram members or state security operatives.

18.5 The Spread of Radical Ideology and the Groundswell of Terrorism in West Africa: Preparing for the Dangers Ahead

There is an upsurge in terrorism in West Africa. In Chap. 9, Ogunfolu et al. draw an analogy between the emergence of Al-Qaeda in the Islamic Maghreb (AQIM) and the descent of Algeria into armed conflict on the one hand and the rise of Boko Haram in Nigeria and the possible links between the two groups on the other hand. The authors support the view that, besides other causal factors, competition for political power is more central to the rise of Boko Haram than poverty, corruption and poor governance, which is the dominant narrative in mainstream literature. The authors place reliance on the anonymous author of an article in the African Journal of Religion. Many observers share the view that the political inclination of Boko Haram made the group amenable to political alignment with some political forces pursuing mainly political objectives in the broader Nigerian political space,[14] so much so that even without a clear alignment of strategic goals in terms of politics (the political elites do not appear to really desire a Sharia State or Caliphate in Nigeria where they would lose political authority to an imam or other theocratic leader), but they nevertheless ostensibly seek to be seen to be pursuing this objective if only to secure the support of groups like Boko Haram and its followers in order to achieve their own desired immediate political objectives.

Thus, for Boko Haram, having the support of such political forces strengthens its cause and increases the prospects of an Islamic Caliphate in Northern Nigeria, if not in the short term through legislation, then in the long term through jihad.[15] More importantly, Ogunfolu et al. note how the overthrow of the Gaddafi regime in Libya has contributed to the rise of jihadists in sub-Sharan Africa. The burgeoning terrorism and the competition for space and influence between dominant global terrorist networks (notably, IS and Al-Qaeda) in sub-Saharan Africa make this observation pertinent. Although there is as yet no clear indication that the different groups operating in North Africa and those in the immediate countries of the sub-Saharan region are expanding downwards, the series of terrorist attacks in the region in recent years should serve to warn that the future possibility of such expansion should be a cause for concern to the African Union and the Regional Economic Communities.

[14] See Onuoha and George (2016), pp. 208–214.

[15] Some argue that the adoption of Sharia law in some northern states contributed to the spread of radicalisation of youths in Northern Nigeria and by extension the rise of Boko Haram.

In Chap. 10 titled 'Boko Haram's Radical Ideology and Islamic Jurisprudence', Muyiwa Adigun unpacks Boko Haram's ideology, interpretation and application of Islamic principles in relation to various concepts and conduct. He examines the group's propositions and practices and situates them in their proper Islamic jurisprudential context, thus bringing a much-needed insight. For example, according to Adigun, in Islam, there is a basis for humanitarian intervention to protect (only those who believe in God, whether Muslims or not) and collective self-defence. The rule of proportionality must be obeyed, and the vulnerable—women, children, the sick and the wounded—are to be spared. Only those in authority can declare war in Islam, and 'non-state actors' such as Boko Haram cannot declare war in Islam since it lacks the necessary elements of public trust and the existence of a state. Adigun argues that Islamic *jus in bello* is consistent with principles of IHL and shows that the crimes against humanity committed by Boko Haram are illegal even in Islamic law. Adigun challenges the claim by Boko Haram that the Qur'an permits the treatment of women and girls captured in the conflict as 'wives' with whom members of Boko Haram could have sexual intercourse. He contends that the relevant verse in the Qur'an was specific and only applicable to the Prophet. Not only are Muslims forbidden from having sexual intercourse with war captives; they are also prohibited from killing hostages. However, Adigun concedes that there are areas in which Islam appears to permit some of the practices of Boko Haram. For example, the minimum recruitment age for military service in Islam is 15, whereas this would qualify as child soldier in international law.[16] Nevertheless, there are less clear areas. For example, the Qur'an records certain practices (though not by the Prophet himself) that would constitute war crimes and crimes against humanity under IHL, such as water poisoning or sleeping with war captives. The Prophet did not indulge in these practices, but are Muslims allowed to? Are Muslims allowed to take hostages as distinct from war captives or prisoners of war? Adigun argues that Muslims are only permitted to use force when they are wronged. By whom and how is 'wrong' to be determined and what are the criteria? Be that as it may, it is clear from Adigun's contribution that stripped of their distortions by terrorist groups like Boko Haram, one comes to the inevitable conclusion that notwithstanding minor variations, there are shared fundamental values of humanness underpinning international law and Islamic jurisprudence. There is a tendency to describe Northern Nigeria as the 'Muslim North'. Whereas this description is broadly correct, it often obscures the existing sectarian tensions within the so-called 'Muslim North'.

In Chap. 11, titled 'Government Regulation of Freedom of Religion in a Democratic Society: Islamic Preaching Board Laws and Boko Haram in Nigeria', Ahmed Garba amplifies this subtle sectarian divide that is hardly noticeable but always bubbling under the surface with occasional spills into the open. Thus, in his contribution, while Garba may not be seen as justifying Boko Haram's extremist views, he is, however, at pains to point out how this otherwise innocuous sectarian divide between Muslim groups in Northern Nigeria may become volatile in the hands of politicians and state officials. Garba rightly notes that whereas there is nothing wrong with spreading unorthodox views in a predominantly Muslim

[16] See Akanji (2007), p. 60.

Northern Nigeria, it is the government's repression of the religious freedom of minority Muslim sects in Northern Nigeria through the regulation of preaching board laws that ultimately drove groups like Boko Haram to extremism and the pursuit of an Islamic Caliphate. The practice whereby the government and government institutions restrict the right to freedom of religion and worship of some Muslim sects while protecting the dominant Muslim group in some states in Northern Nigeria has contributed to the rise of Boko Haram. As Garba notes, there is no record of any judicial pronouncement on this issue, and even if the matter were to come before the courts, there is widespread perception that there is no independence of the judiciary, and the individual religious prejudices and mindset of presiding judicial officers would most likely work against religious minorities in Nigeria and nail the coffins of minority Muslim sects in Northern Nigeria.

This fact is often missed by many commentators because of a tendency to overemphasise the North–South/Christian–Muslim divide in Nigeria. However, as Garba's contribution shows, there is sectarian divide between the Shiaa and the Sunnis amongst the Muslims in Northern Nigeria, and the inability of the state and state officials and institutions to insulate themselves from parochialism means that citizens have lost faith and confidence in the ability of the state to protect their rights. This is particularly so when religious minority groups in Northern Nigeria feel that their freedom to practice their religion has come under threat, and in many cases, they have come under attacks from the dominant religious group. This is not limited to non-Muslims, but as Garba has demonstrated in his contribution, the marginalisation and lack of equal protection by the law, if not outright discrimination by state institutions, extend to minority Muslim sects as well. In fact, it is believed in some quarters that the adoption of Sharia law in 12 states in Northern Nigeria provided the right climate for radicalisation and gave the impetus for radical ideology and the ultimate rise of Boko Haram. As pointed out by Garba, the preferential treatment of one religious group over another is an affront on the Nigerian Constitution, which proclaims Nigeria as a secular state and therefore puts a knife in the chord that had bound Muslims (of different sects), Christians and other religious groups together in a harmonious and peaceful coexistence for centuries. The Boko Haram conflict is a manifestation of this broken chord. Add to the above the deep socio-economic poverty in Northeast Nigeria and one would find that all the recipes for disaster had been present in the region for a long time.

18.6 Differing to Sovereignty: International Protection of Women and Girls During the Boko Haram Insurgency

The territorial state has the primary responsibility to protect those within its borders from massive violations of human rights, but where does this difference to sovereignty end and at what cost? The mass atrocities committed by Boko Haram against women and girls and the lack of serious prosecution by the Nigerian state or the international community again underscore the resilience of sovereignty. In this volume, John-Mark Iyi examines Boko Haram's weaponisation of women and argues that the fate of women is sealed in Nigeria's pervasive culture of impunity. He outlines several international and domestic legal instruments that protect women from sexual violence and contends that it is unlikely that those responsible for the mass atrocities committed against women by Boko Haram would ever be brought to justice in Nigeria. He examines how women have been instrumentalised by Boko Haram in different ways and contends that all of these would ordinarily fall to be prosecuted under domestic or international law. He suggests three ways to hold perpetrators accountable. Firstly, crimes against women such as rape, sexual assault, abductions of school girls and murder of women and girls already constitute crimes under the domestic Penal Code applicable across Northern Nigeria. Hence, regardless of whether these offences were committed in a situation of armed conflict, they nonetheless constitute punishable crimes for which perpetrators should be punished, if the state has the appetite for prosecution. Secondly, under the 2011 anti-terrorism Act, using terror against civilians is an offence punishable under the Act, and Boko Haram operatives can be prosecuted under the Act. Thirdly, given the cross-border nature of Boko Haram's activities, the states of the Lake Chad Basin participating in the MJTF may consider establishing a Regional Special Criminal Tribunal with the mandate and jurisdiction to prosecute mass atrocities committed during the Boko Haram conflict. Since the Boko Haram insurgency has assumed cross-border character and the group has carried out attacks in Nigeria, Cameroon, Chad and Niger, such tribunal would provide the advantage of having all perpetrators being tried on a common platform and being subjected to a common standard of criminal justice system. Besides the ease of collection of evidence, this would also bring justice closer to the victims of Boko Haram in the Lake Chad Basin. Finally, such tribunal and prosecution would contribute to facilitating the healing process in local communities that have borne the brunt of Boko Haram's weaponisation of women.

For her part, Romola Adeola takes a somewhat moderate view of Nigeria's failure to protect the rights of internally displaced persons (IDPs) in Northeast Nigeria under Article 9(2) of the Kampala Convention (see Chap. 13). She argues that Nigeria has positive obligations to protect people displaced in the Northeast by the Boko Haram conflict but has repeatedly failed to fulfil these obligations. Besides its failures to protect IDPs, it is disturbing, as Adeola notes, that some Nigerian security officials have actually sexually abused some of the IDPs they were employed to protect in IDP camps.[17]

In his contribution on gender-based crimes (see Chap. 14), Avitus Agbor argues that nowhere in international instruments or the jurisprudence of international criminal tribunals is the word 'gender-based crime' recognised or used. Thus, to the extent that any of the crimes committed against women must first come within a broader category of crimes such as genocide, war crime, crimes against humanity, the terminology 'gender-based crimes' is a legal misnomer created by legal

[17] See the contribution by Romola Adeola in this volume.

academics and should be approached cautiously. Until such a time that women become a protected group and this recognition is accorded to crimes specifically targeting women as a protected group, the term 'gender-based crimes' remains a misnomer that must be used with caution.

Kuwali's proposal of a '10 Cs' approach to preventing radicalisation and eradicating extremism is the theme of Chap. 15. States should strike a balance between emphasis on military/counter-insurgency and counterterrorism capabilities to protect populations at risk on the one hand and the adoption of a broad-based socio-economic developmental approach to conflict prevention, coupled with respect for human rights, good governance and the rule of law on the other hand.

Kuwali's approach to combating Boko Haram is based on developing appropriate responses to the underlying causes that makes it easy for Boko Haram to recruit and radicalise impressionable youths who are most susceptible to indoctrination. However, not all members of Boko Haram were recruited from a common pool. If that is so, the *causa rationae* would also be different or mixed. For the marginalised, exploited and deprived, the reason or root cause would be poverty, and the response could be to provide opportunities for socio-economic development. For the illiterate, ignorant and uneducated, expansion of access to educational opportunities would be an appropriate response. However, for the intimidated or coerced, these responses would be inappropriate, and authorities would need a different approach. For the refined, educated and affluent member, the appropriate response would be some other motive than such ideology. In this case, the proper response would be some broader form of counter-narrative (of tolerance and coexistence) to the terrorist's hate and religious intolerance. But there are no guarantees that this would work. The source, circumstances, conditions favouring radicalisation might be rooted in the social background, family, school, and peer group of the member.

18.7 The International Law Obligations of State to Respond to the Boko Haram Insurgency and Prevent Violations

In Chap. 16 on 'Beyond the Law to Socio-Legal Intervention: The Boko Haram Insurgence and the Nigerian Child', Onuora-Oguno Azubike and Abdulraheem-Mustapha argue that despite the fact that Nigeria has ratified and domesticated the UN Convention on the Rights of the Child and the African Charter on the Rights and the Welfare of the Child, many states in Nigeria are yet to enact appropriate legislation to give effect to the provisions of the Child Rights Act 2003, and this has created discrepancies and variations in how child rights issues are addressed from one state to another. Section 34 of the Act prohibits the recruitment of a child into the armed forces of Nigeria. The mere fact that some northern states whose sociopolitical foundations are entrenched in religious and cultural practices have refused to enact legislation to back the domestication of the Convention on the Rights of the Child does not excuse Nigeria from discharging its treaty obligations under the

Convention on the Rights of the Child. Although the authors highlight the fate of child victims of the Boko Haram conflict, a more detailed assessment of the current socio-economic impact and future implications of the conflict on the Nigerian child certainly merits a study of its own in the future.

Marek argues that in terms of the applicable legal principles in the law of state responsibility, the activities or conduct of private actors cannot be attributed to a state, except when there is a relationship that can be established as a matter of fact between the territorial state and members of the insurgent groups (see Chap. 17). Using the abduction of the 276 schoolgirls in Chibok and the shooting down of the MH17 plane in Ukraine as references, Marek examines the jurisprudence of the African Commission on Human and People's Rights and the European Court of Human Rights and the response to the thorny legal issues arising from these circumstances. He contends that regardless of the nature of the armed conflict, a territorial state is not relieved of its positive obligations to protect individuals and communities not taking part in the armed conflict from violations of human rights by insurgent movements. And this obligation extends to and continues in force even within territories under the effective control of insurgent groups like Boko Haram in Northeast Nigeria notwithstanding that it receives no support whatsoever from the Nigerian state.

As noted above, some commentators hold the view that Boko Haram was created by northern politicians as a bargaining chip to wrestle political power from the Jonathan administration for breaking the North-South and Christian-Muslim rotational presidency arrangement. For example, governors of Kano, Borno and Bauchi states who needed the group to win elections and bargain at the national level were at some point known to have put the group on payroll in their respective states.[18] Unfortunately, the group grew beyond what was anticipated and what it was designed for and spiralled out of control. This claim may be right or wrong. However, it is not uncommon, for the sake of being politically correct, that politicians would condemn, ignore or even deny the nexus between religion and terrorism or the religious motivations of particular terrorist attacks. Even though records show these phenomena as traditional allies, religion as the motivation for terrorism is sometimes seen as an exception rather than the rule (statistically, this might even be correct; after all, only very few adherents of a particular faith resort to terrorism to promote their creed or reject other faiths). Thus, it is described as the characteristic of a minority religious extremist in contrast to the tolerant pluralistic majority. This rather simplistic view ignores the fact that religion has been as much a force for good as for evil.[19] Whereas 'secular terrorists' could be motivated by a variety of reasons, religious terrorists are largely driven by religious motives. This is not to say

[18] See Amaliya and Nwankpa (2014), p. 81. Senator Ndume was once arrested and charged with financing the group; recently, a local council boss was also arrested for links with the group. Several security personnel within the armed forces and the police, sometimes at very senior levels have been implicated for either being members, funders, or supporters or sympathisers of the group.

[19] See Onuoha and George (2016), p. 209.

that religious terrorists are not 'driven by day-to-day practical political considerations within their context-specific environment'[20]; rather, it does underscore that this blended motivations make it difficult to differentiate the political motivations from the religious considerations of terrorist groups like Boko Haram. Boko Haram's radical ideology is blended with its long-term political objectives: the establishment of an Islamic Caliphate in Northern Nigeria. Thus, in their view, attacks resulting in Muslim casualties are short-term pragmatic sacrifices for a long-term ideological goal: the establishment of an Islamic Caliphate where both political and religious authority of the State would be unified in one body and would have a common source of authority and legitimacy: the Koran.

18.8 Conclusion and Future Research

Our understanding and explanation of organised violence has always been shaped by our Westphalian nation-state paradigms. For a long time, we have ignored the emergence or existence of 'multiple centres of power in and around' the nation state. These centres of power, so long as they exist and regardless of whether we acknowledge them or not, present certain problems as they continue to challenge the idea of state sovereignty and its monopoly of organised violence.[21] At its height, apart from engaging the Nigerian state in armed conflict, Boko Haram actually controlled its own territory and managed to establish an administrative system, however rudimentary. Throughout, it is unclear how the Nigerian government treats members of the group, besides the 'terrorist' label. For example, when Boko Haram fighters were first arrested in active combat, what legal status were they accorded by the Nigerian government? Since the insurgency began as mere violent disturbance, how did the Nigerian government treat Boko Haram members apprehended at that stage since this has implications for their rights under international law? And from the stage where the conflict was declared to have reached the threshold of NIAC, how did the Nigerian government treat Boko Haram fighters? Evidence suggests that members of Boko Haram who have been apprehended and prosecuted have largely been tried under the anti-terrorism legislation of Nigeria, as opposed to treason (taking up arms against the state). Not enough research has been done in this area as of yet, and it would therefore merit further research.

Amongst other things, the declared objectives of Boko Haram are to overthrow the secular Nigerian state and replace it with an Islamic State under strict Sharia political and legal order.[22] The group adopts different strategies in recruiting members, including through jailbreaks, inducements by promising financial rewards,

[20] Onuoha and George (2016), p. 210.

[21] See Grassiani and Ben-Ari (2011), p. 7.

[22] See Onuoha and George (2016), p. 209.

abductions, family networks, voluntary membership and coerced membership.[23] As Onuoha and George put it, 'those recruited are subsequently radicalised and persuaded through ideological psychic conversion, indoctrination, hypnosis and brainwashing, and/or intimidation to fight for its cause or provide other supportive services. Once integrated into the group, members are denied the option of wilful disengagement.'[24] We have seen Boko emerge as one of the leading terrorist organisations in the deployment of child soldiers and child suicide bombers. However, beyond the fact that there is a teeming population of out-of-school children in Northern Nigeria, little is still known about Boko Haram's recruitment strategies and the group's tactics in the deployment of female suicide bombers. It is generally believed that Boko Haram gets its funding from various sources: membership dues, donations from politicians and foreign terror groups, bank robbery, cattle rustling, drug trafficking, ransom from hostages, extortion, collection of levies and engaging in 'front' business. All of these aspects of the insurgency merit further investigation beyond the scope of our modest contribution in this volume.

It is also noteworthy that, throughout, the regional response to Boko Haram was almost non-existent until the members of the Lake Chad Basin Commission worked with the African Union to transform the MNJTF into a regional multinational force. However, it is worthy of note that the ECOWAS has played no significant role in the conflict. This also raises some disturbing questions not only about the capacity of ECOWAS but also about the preparedness of member states to deal with the growing threat of terrorism in West Africa, both at national and sub-regional levels. This would merit further interrogation.

References

Adibe J (2017) On the purported merger of Christian and Islamic studies in schools. In: Debating Nigeria: a collection of essays. Adonis-Abbey, London, pp 135–136

Akanji OO (2007) The politics of combating domestic terrorism in Nigeria. In Okumu W, Botha A (eds) Domestic terrorism in Africa: defining, addressing and understanding its impact on human security. Institute for Security Studies, Pretoria, pp 55–64

Amaliya M, Nwankpa M (2014) Assessing Boko Haram: a conversation. J Terroirsm Res 5(1):81–87

Cassese A (2006) International criminal law. In: Evans MD (ed) International law. Oxford University Press, Oxford, pp 719–52

Connell S (Summer 2012) To be or not to be: is Boko Haram a foreign terrorist organisation. Glob Secur Stud 3(3):87–93

Flory M (1997) International law: an instrument to combat terrorism. In: Higgins R, Flory M (eds) Terrorism and international law. Routledge, London, pp 30–39

French SE (2003) Murderers not warriors: the moral distinction between terrorists and legitimate fighters in asymmetric conflicts. In: Sterba JP (ed) Terrorism and international justice. Oxford University Press, New York, pp 31–46

[23] See Onuoha and George (2016), p. 209.

[24] Onuoha and George (2016), p. 209.

Grassiani E, Ben-Ari E (2011) Violence operators: between state and non-state actors. Stichting Etnofoor 23(2):7–15 (*State/Violence*)

Haines S (2012) The nature of war and the character of contemporary armed conflict. In Wilmshurst E (ed) International law and the classification of conflicts, 1st edn. Oxford University Press, pp 9–31

Onuoha FC, George TA (2016) The Abuja bombings: Boko Haram's reaction to President Buhari's actions. Afr Secur Rev 25(2):208–214

Thomson V (Summer 2012) Boko Haram and Islamic fundamentalism in Nigeria. Glob Secur Stud 3(3):46

The manufacturer's authorised representative in the EU is Springer Nature Customer Service Centre GmbH, Europaplatz 3, 69115 Heidelberg, Germany. If you have any concerns regarding our products, please contact ProductSafety@springernature.com

Printed and bound by CPI Group (UK) Ltd, Croydon, CR0 4YY
22/09/2026
02220988-0005